WOLVES OF WATER

A STUDY CONSTRUCTED FROM ATOMIC RADIATION, MORALITY, EPIDEMIOLOGY, SCIENCE, BIAS, PHILOSOPHY AND DEATH

BY
CHRIS BUSBY

Green Audit ❖ 2006

Wolves of Water
A Study Constructed from Atomic Radiation, Morality, Epidemiology, Science, Bias, Philosophy and Death
Chris Busby

Green Audit Books, October 2006
Green Audit
Aberystwyth SY23 1DZ, Wales, UK

Typeset in Times New Roman 11
Cataloguing Information: Busby Chris: Wolves of Water. A Study Constructed from Atomic Radiation, Morality, Epidemiology, Science, Bias, Philosophy and Death.
A catalogue for this book is available from the British Library.

ISBN 1-897761-26-0

The author would like to acknowledge the assistance of the
Joseph Rowntree Charitable Trust

Printed in Wales by Cambrian Printers Ltd.

Also available on this issue from Green Audit
Wings of Death , 1995
ECRR 2003: The health effects of low doses of Radiation, 2003
Chernobyl-20 Years On: Health effects of the Chernobyl Accident

(Cover photo : The first and last School photo of Gemma D'Arcy who lived near Sellafield and died of leukaemia. Used with permission of Suzanne D'Arcy)

Contents

Page

Preface 1
Acknowledgements 6

Part I Introduction 9

1 **Background: The Environment and Cancer** 11
1.1 Background 11
1.2 Cancer and the environment: waters, airs and places 21
1.3 Cancer risk is localised 24
1.4 What is the genetic proportion of cancer risk? 27
1.5 Changes of incidence over time 30
1.6 Cancer trends in England and Wales: strange happenings 33
1.7 Identification of specific causal agents 35

2 **How Cancer is Caused** 40
2.1 A genetic disease 41
2.2 Single cell origin 45
2.3 Mutation and repair 45
2.4 Chromosome damage 49
2.5 Internal and external radiation 50
2.6 The control of cell proliferation and the repair of DNA 55
2.7 The consequences for radiation and health 59
2.8 Retinoblastoma 71

3 **Sellafield and the Irish Sea** 73
3.1 Radioactive discharges from Sellafield into the Irish Sea 74
3.2 Routes of contamination and levels of exposure 80
3.3 Circulation in the Irish Sea 82
3.4 Inter-tidal sediments in Wales 88
3.5 Sea-to-land transfer of radioisotopes 89
3.6 Exposure routes 99
3.7 Summary 100

Part II Discoveries 103

4 Epidemiology 107
4.1 Bradford Hill's canons 109
4.2 Types of study and general problem 113
4.3 The play of chance, and its evaluation 122
4.4 Adjusting for disadvantagement 125
4.5 Evaluating trends 130
4.6 Computer methods 134
4.7 Why epidemiology? 135

5 The Irish Sea Part 1. Cancer in Wales 1974-89 137
5.1 Wales 137
5.2 The data and the exercise 139
5.3 Results 148

6 The Irish Sea Part 2 Childhood Cancer in Wales and Other Relevant Studies 179
6.1 Introduction 179
6.2 All cancers in children ages 0-4 and 0-14 181
6.3 Leukaemia 184
6.4 Brain tumours, lymphomas and cancer of the eye. 186
6.5 Trawsfynydd and Wylfa study (Welsh Office, 1994b) 188
6.6 Other possible reasons for the effects found in the Wales data 190
6.7 Conclusions from the Welsh studies 202

7 Ireland 205
7.1 Background 205
7.2 Cancer in Carlingford and Greenore 208
7.3 A Cancer Questionnaire 210
7.4 Irish National Cancer Registry small area study 1994-6 219
7.5 Lancashire and Galloway 224

8 Studies Near Coasts and Estuaries 227
8.1 Mortality studies 227
8.2 Cancer near Hinkley Point in Somerset 228
8.3 Results of the Hinkley Point studies 229
8.4 Oldbury and the Welsh leukaemias 233

8.5 Bradwell 235
8.6 Cardiff and the Amersham isotope factory 238
8.7 The small area mortality studies: conclusions 242

9 The Way to Dusty Death 243
9.1 Gathering it together 243
9.2 Dust 244

Part III Denials 251

10 Post War Developments 255
10.1 After the Bomb 255
10.2 The control groups for the A-Bomb study 256
10.3 Genetic effects at Hiroshima/Nagasaki and the sex ratio test 258
10.4 The winds over Windscale 264
10.5 Cancer in England and Wales after Chernobyl 272

11 The Nuclear Mafia 279
11.1 ICRP, NRPB, COMARE and SAHSU 279
11.2 COMARE's Sellafield calculations 283

12 Cover-up in Wales 287
12.1 A long and complicated story begins 287
12.2 Ireland pays to study the data 289
12.3 First meeting with the new Wales Cancer Intelligence and Surveillance Unit WCISU 291
12.4 Two sets of data: a Sea of Troubles 293
12.5 COMARE discusses the issue 294
12.6 Steward's report: a tale of two studies 296
12.7 Raising the dead: Byd ar Bedwar 300
12.8 Decide on your own scenario 303

13 More Cover-ups in England 305
13.1 Nordic leukaemia study revisited 305
13.2 Hakulinen sees: fallout brings disease 307
13.3 The data magically appears 310
13.4 Johannes Clemmesen and Otto Carlsen 311
13.5 Was there an increase in childhood and infant leukaemia after the weapons fallout? 313

13.6 Darby, Doll and the Atomic Test Veterans 317
13.7 SAHSU, random clusters and Bayesian smoothing 322
13.8 The UKCCCS study, Ray Cartwright and childhood leukaemia 328
13.9 The Section 7 Data Protection Act requests 332

Part IV Explanations and Resolutions 337

14 The Litmus Test 341
14.1 Political activism and recent developments 341
14.2 Greens in the European Parliament 344
14.3 The Euratom Directive 346
14.4 Michael Meacher 351
14.5 The European Committee on Radiation Risk 353
14.6 Making it happen 355
14.7 Litmus tests 359
14.8 Minisatellite DNA mutations 365

15 Science and Society 369
15.1 Rapportage 369
15.2 Atomic Lies 374
15.3 I don't know much about science 379

16 The Oppositional Science System Experiment: CERRIE 397
16.1 New mechanisms for arriving at the truth 397
16.2 CERRIE: a first attempt at an oppositional advice committee 406
16.3 The Minority Report at the child leukaemia conference 426
16.4 Some good news 428
16.5 Conclusions 430

17 Lessons 431
17.1 Apology 431
17.2 Ray Fox and the Leukaemia Triangle 434
17.3 Depleted Uranium 444
17.4 Wolves of Water 463

References, Appendices, CV 467

Wolves

I do not want to be reflective anymore
Envying and despising unreflective things
Finding pathos in dogs and undeveloped handwriting
And young girls doing their hair and all the castles of sand
Flushed by the children's bedtime, level with the shore

The tide comes in and goes out again, I do not want
To be always stressing either its flux or its permanence
I do not want to be a tragic or philosophic chorus
But to keep my eye only on the nearer future
And after that let the sea flow over us

Come then all of you, come closer, form a circle
Join hands and make believe that joined
Hands will keep away the wolves of water
Who howl along our coast. And it be assumed
That no one hears them among the talk and laughter

Louis Macneice

I am angry to the depths of my soul that the earth has been so injured while we were all bemused by supposed monuments of value and intellect, vaults of bogus cultural riches. I feel the worth of my own life diminished by the tedious years I have spent acquiring competence in the arcana of mediocre invention, for all the world like one of those people who knows all there is to know about some defunct comic-book hero or television series. The grief borne home to others while I and my kind have been thus occupied lies on my conscience like a crime. This book is written in a state of mind and spirit I could not have imagined before Sellafield presented itself to me, so grossly anomalous that I had to jettison almost every assumption I had before I could begin to make sense of it. My writing has perhaps taken too much of the stain of my anger and disappointment. I must ask the reader to pardon and assist me by always keeping Sellafield in mind- Sellafield, which pours waste plutonium into the world's natural environment, and bomb grade plutonium into the world's political environment. For money.

Marilynne Robinson
Mother Country 1989

Preface

Galileo: Your Highness, would you care to observe those impossible and unnecessary stars through the telescope?
Mathematician: One might be tempted to reply that if your tube shows something that cannot exist, it must be a rather unreliable tube.

Berthold Brecht: Life of Galileo

In *Star Trek*, when the hull of the Starship Enterprise is punctured or the support systems are damaged, a klaxon begins to scream. No one can miss this sound or fail to interpret its message. *Star Trek* was one of the first Science Fiction series on television that introduced the public to ironic metaphors about the human predicament. The aliens of course were us, from all the different angles and perspectives of sociology. The message was that we needed to take care or we would perish. Those who are alive now, on this spaceship Earth, are living at the most important time in all the history of the human race. The decisions we make now, to allow this specific technological development or to ban the releases of that substance, will decide whether we survive: perhaps whether life itself survives. I am, by nature, an optimist, but I am horrified at the cavalier use that is being made of science for making money, making reputations and just having fun. The children are inside the armoury and are playing with loaded guns. Soon it is almost inevitable that one of the guns goes off. When the SARS epidemic began I thought this might be it. Didn't you? Now we are holding our breath about 'bird flu' and looking nervously at sea levels and global warming.

This book is a consequence of my desperation to ensure that the public - ordinary people with a minimum of scientific knowledge - take control of the direction we are taking as a species. And the very first thing that we must do is to set up and continuously monitor indicators of status for human health. Unfortunately it seems we must do this as individuals, because the structures of society that are in place to do this elementary job are no longer functioning to save us. We are flying blind. There are no instruments that we can see on the panel of our own starship. The Priesthood collect the data that might inform us of danger with reverence. They place it in deep locked vaults. No one is allowed to look at it or, if they are, they must do so through distorting lenses that prevent them from seeing what it means. Children can die of leukaemia near the largest emitter of radiation in the world. Everyone can know that radiation is the major known cause of childhood leukaemia. The distorting lenses of the Priests dismiss causality. They are the mathematician in Brecht's Galileo. They know that low level radiation cannot cause cancer. So why look?

You will find some alarming assertions here. Cancer risk is associated with living near the sea and tidal rivers. Plutonium discharged into the Irish Sea by the nuclear reprocessing plant at Sellafield, on the Irish Sea, is now absorbed within the teeth of children living in South East England. Ordinary dust collected in filters near Basingstoke in Hampshire has 100 times the radioactivity that defines it as nuclear waste under the present legislation. As hundreds of tons of cancer-producing Uranium particles float about the world from the battlegrounds and military test ranges, the Health Authorities continue to avoid protecting the health of those they are paid to look after. Cancer Registries are desperately keeping secret - and retrospectively altering - the data that will reveal details of a public health scandal: the systematic poisoning of the human race. You will find in here evidence that demonstrates cover-up and skulduggery, chapter and verse. I hope what I report will blow a whistle, on behalf of our children, to call for help. Who will come?

This book will review the results of the researches into the origin of the present cancer epidemic that I have undertaken since the publication in 1995 of *Wings of Death: Nuclear Pollution and Human Health.* There, I drew attention to the development of a cancer epidemic and asked about its environmental cause, something which few cancer researchers seemed to be doing. At the time that I wrote *Wings of Death,* the existence of this epidemic was being routinely denied, although today this at least has changed: few now would be brave enough to take the position that the cancer epidemic does not exist. My thesis was that the cause of contemporary cancer increases was exposure to novel radioactive elements produced by nuclear fission of Uranium and dispersed throughout the environment in the last 50 years as a result of global atmospheric tests, nuclear power station releases, and accidents and other activities associated with the Atom. At the time this was allowed because it was believed that the exposure doses to the fallout material were too small to cause any health effect since these doses were very low, similar to natural background radiation. I argued that there were a number of mechanisms of radiation action that distinguished these natural background doses from the fallout doses. Because of this, the models used to assess harm were based on external radiation whereas it was internal radiation exposure to a whole range of novel isotopes which we were dealing with, and scientific method demanded that these be examined separately.

Since 1995 there have been two significant developments. The first has been the increasing realisation, partly due to new scientific research, partly due to pressure brought by the Low Level Radiation Campaign, that the risk model used to predict or explain the effects of radiation exposure is indeed valueless when applied to internal irradiation. By the end of 2001 this was so clear that the British government set up the new Committee Examining Radiation Risk from Internal Emitters (CERRIE) to investigate the validity and application of the conventional radiation risk model. This committee developed within it and around it, as you might imagine, several layers of deceit and bias but, thanks to the Environment Minister Michael Meacher, we were at least inside the tent where we could see what was going on. The extraordinary outcome of this attempt to get to the truth in this area is reported in this book.

The second development was more generally important. It was the increasing realisation, following Mad Cow Disease (BSE) and the cover-ups that occurred after Chernobyl, that the scientific hierarchy could not be trusted; particularly scientists who work for large organizations who have a project they wish to pursue. This realization extends to trust in the government scientific advisory and research bodies.

The present book uses Sellafield as its base for argument. The releases of radioactive material into the environment from this nuclear plant and the effects that these substances have on human health are a scandal. Although the discoveries I report have general consequences, which move beyond Sellafield and take us to the distribution and cause of cancer, even this is only a symptom of a larger problem: the misuse of science by politicians and by scientists themselves to achieve power, glory and money. It is this larger problem which is the real issue here. I have spent the last thirteen years investigating the way in which radioactive releases have harmed human health, figuring out the complex systems of belief and power which sustain organisations and structures of belief in the face of clear evidence that their projects and processes are killing people. I have spent a great deal of time discussing and debating strategy for effecting change and devising ways in which independent scientists can influence policy. I have spoken with the regulators, the politicians, the scientists and the victims. I have stood at the bedside of a little girl in Baghdad, dying of cancer as a result of exposure to Depleted Uranium from US weaponry in the first Gulf War. I have talked with young women in this country, living near nuclear pollution, who have since died of breast cancer. I have been with young children in Kosovo, whilst they played in an area where radioactive Uranium dust swirled about in the air; I have collected the dust and measured Uranium in it. I have stood in court and argued as expert witness in trials where grandmothers have cut their way into atomic sites, nuclear bases, spray painted the House of Commons, done anything they can to draw attention to the deadly effects of nuclear radiation. I have sat on government committees on radiation effects and listened to the sly weasel words, specious arguments arising from a system of institutional chicanery. I have watched the Royal Society committee on Depleted Uranium twist and turn about trying to escape the inevitable conclusion about low dose radiation exposures (and succeeding).

I have analysed thousands of cancer prevalence questionnaires and datasets, sitting in front of a computer screen reading and calculating cancer risks in wards with bizarre names paging down numbers of deaths until I have become dizzy and sick. I have learned to drive a printing press and have swayed with fatigue in front of it as it clicked and thundered all night making tens of thousands of leaflets drawing attention to the effects of radiation. I have chained myself to the gates of nuclear power stations with a banner in one hand and a loudspeaker in the other. I have given countless TV and radio interviews, been involved in many documentaries and spoken in several European cities and to many European State parliament meetings. I have been attacked in the Press by the nuclear industry, politicians, civil servants and official government bodies. I have been called a bogus scientist, a loony, a fascist, a sadist and a professional scaremonger. Indeed, I have been accused of making a living out of my scaremongering: I should warn anyone who sees a possible lucrative profession in this that they will be very poor if they rely on independent environmental research for a living! I have organised research epidemiology and environmental radioactivity measurements with students and drop-outs, young men and women living on the edge. They have given up their time and energy for small amounts of money donated by a few charities, small anti-nuclear groups and pensioners' ten-pound notes posted to us in envelopes.

But what I have learned in all this is that it is possible to change the world if you want to and the cause is just. And what I would like to try and do in this book is to pass on what we all have learned so that others can take heart, and perhaps use some of our experiences, mistakes and successes to try and change the system themselves. If together we succeed, then we can make a world where we can use the best of Science to create justice and happiness. I think we all know now and can see clearly, that if we do not succeed, and Science is taken away and used to make money or provide power for the few, or for the multinational companies, the outlook is bleak.

The story rehearsed through radiation and cancer, and the interpenetration of scientific argument and evidence through political control and secrecy, is being repeated all over again in the area of genetics and in all the other areas where knowledge can generate profit in a moral vacuum. If we do not devise ways in which these complex scientific issues can be addressed in such a way as to reveal the real consequences of new technological procedures, we will be doomed to repeat the mistakes that led to the opening of the Pandora's Box of radioactive isotopes in 1945, with the consequences which I shall show in this book.

Like *Wings of Death*, the present book will look at some complex areas but, in the same way, I will try to prevent it becoming too dry. I will talk in this book about the lighter things also, and describe what it is to be a scientist, or my kind of scientist anyway, an amateur, a natural philosopher. Science is in danger of becoming a religion and its methodology and systems are in danger of preventing any assault on a black boxed and dogma-controlled structure of belief and, consequently, blocking any new developments. I hope that what I have to report is so important, energetic and new that the light rays carrying the words will leap from the paper and impress themselves on your retinas. I feel that anyone who has worked for the nuclear industry or supported their project should, after reading this book, consider wearing sackcloth and checking into a monastery to spend the rest of their life in penitential prayer. And, finally, I hope that the results presented here will influence the policy-makers of national governments, first, to abandon the nuclear project and, second, to set up true freedom of information structures and better systems of science advice, so that we have no more technology-assisted collisions with reality.

Love
Chris Busby

Acknowledgements

In the last twelve years I have been encouraged, helped and supported in my research work, the political activism that grew out of it, and the general political and philosophical thinking that grew out of that, by a very large number of people. Once we see that one part of the world is askew, and that the beliefs that support this part are constructed out of the desires and contrivances of what in *Star Wars* they term the Dark Side, it is a short step to discovering that much of the system which we live in is founded on greed, power and lies. Ironically it also increasingly rests on a kind of Marxist false consciousness predicated on a belief in the ability of scientific rationalism, as practiced by the high priests of science, to provide objective truths. This has been said before, and throughout history. But seldom has it been so contingent a message with regard to the entire survival of the human race. The discovery in modern times that this is so usually leads people to the Green Party, where the survivors of such epic shipwrecking of belief systems come ashore in small boats to try to find a way forward for all who live together on this small planet. So I will start by acknowledging the debt I have to the Green Party and its clever members. It was there I learned to think politically and to see the world in terms of Power and Influence, rather than as Truth and Structure. For Science, as the philosopher Bruno Latour shows us, is constructed by people and is not (nowadays anyway) as we somehow feel, an account of Natures Secrets, wrested from her by experiment. And anyway, as Pontius Pilate (anticipating the French philosophers) asked long ago, 'What is Truth?'

First among the green philosophers I should place Molly Scott Cato, Green Economist and Radical Thinker, whom, until we split up two years ago, I slept with every night, and who turned my life into an opera presented in colours which lie outside the physical spectrum. She has acted as a source of many of the ideas I have and together (as Bill and Ted might have said) we were *Green Audit.* Molly says that women never get justice in the acknowledgement of their influence and ideas and I feel that this has been and is still true.

Second I acknowledge an enormous debt to my friend and colleague Richard Bramhall, ex-Buddhist and ex-double Bass player for the London Symphony Orchestra, another escapee that fell through the looking glass into the Welsh wonderland. Richard was our co-founder in the Low Level Radiation Campaign, set up in 1996 to bypass the media and peer-review publication block on evidence of the harmful health effects of radiation. He has endlessly and tirelessly worked for this project on minimal funding, organising conferences and petitions, writing leaflets and letters, chaining himself to conference stages and nuclear power stations, and speaking on platforms and to the media in England, Wales and various countries in Europe.

There are many who worked for me on these issues, usually for free or for miserable sums. They include Molly, Helen Rowe, Saoirse Morgan, Mireille de

Messieres, Mark Carter, Rachel Kaleta, Alasdair Stocking, Bruce Kocjian, Laura Lewis, Evelyn Mannion, my son Joe Busby and my daughter Rosa Cato.

I want to acknowledge all the Irish people at STAD in Dundalk, Ireland, James Mac Guill, Grattan Healy, Ollan Herr and Mark Deary. I have worked with and been helped by Roger Coghill, Alasdair Philips, Vyvyan Howard, Hugh Richards, Alex Begg, Jim Duffy, David Taylor, Paul Dorfman and Ernest Sternglass. I have been helped by Paul Lannoye, Caroline Lucas, Jean Lambert and the Irish MEPs Nuala Aherne, Patricia McKenna, by Michael Meacher, Richard Livsey and Cynog Dafis. I have also been helped by the Green Group in the European Parliament, by the late Professor Alice Stewart, by Rosalie Bertell, Sam Epstein, Otto Carlsen, Eva Fidjestol, Hans and Edel Beukes, by Alexey Yablokov, Inge Schmitz Feuerhake, VT Padmanabhan, Hugo Charlton, Spencer FitzGibbon and Wendy and Mick Gilford. I have been encouraged and supported by Zac and Teddy Goldsmith, the late Sir James Goldsmith, by the late David Gillett and by Jo Englekamp and, most of all, by the Trustees of the Joseph Rowntree Charitable Trust. My thanks go to all the brave: the brave women nuclear fence cutters, the spray painters and the direct action squads, bashing military aircraft with hammers. My special thanks to Bill Gates and Microsoft whose software and systems have levelled the playing field immeasurably.

I'm sure I must have left more people out than I have named. If Newton said 'I see further because I stand on the shoulders of the ancients', I might say that I function in this area because I have the enthusiasm and support of hundreds of people who help me, who encourage me, who give me small sums of money they can often ill afford and who give me love. Without you I wouldn't be able to do any of this. I also want to name my children and some friends and loves here because they have also helped me and argued with me and kept me (relatively) sane: Lorraine Busby, Helen Rowe, Saoirse Morgan, Mireille de Messieres, Daren Messenger, Sarah Rachel, Cecilia Busby, Araceli Busby, Frances Busby, Joe Busby and my littlest daughter Rosa Cato aged 12. My 7 children and 8 grandchildren connect me with the future and are the reason I want that future to be safe for them. I will finally of course, and again, acknowledge the enormous debt of gratitude I have for the Joseph Rowntree Charitable Trust and their Trustees and Secretaries who have endlessly put up with the shifts in fortune that this project and its author have suffered. This book is three years overdue.

Finally, I have to admit that I have been inspired most to do all this work by a ghost. I have, on my wall, the picture on the cover, of Gemma D'Arcy, a little girl who lived near Sellafield and died of leukaemia. Whenever things get too much and I feel like giving up, I see her lovely little smile and the reflection of her spirit and soldier on. I hope that, wherever she is, she can feel that I will not let her, and all the other darlings, down.

I wrote a poem about her. It is on the next page.

At Sellafield, along that coast
Out of the corner of your eye
You'll maybe see a little ghost
A girl who didn't have to die
If you're lucky you may see her dance
Sadly along that altered shore
They say she only died by chance
That's what I heard
I can't say more.

Part 1
Introduction

Those that hold that all things are governed by
fortune had not erred, had they not persisted there
Sir Thomas Browne

In Part One, I will give an account of how it was chance that determined that I came to be sitting at this desk writing this account of the effects of radiation on living creatures and the institutional cover up of these effects. Because it is part of my thesis, I want also to explain how cancer is an environmental disease and to review the evidence that this is so. I will also briefly explain what is presently known about the cause of cancer at the cellular or organism level and offer some very recent evidence that touches on this, which shows that living systems are extremely sensitive to radioactive exposures. I think that this information will make it easier to understand what follows later. I shall complete Part One with a description of the nuclear reprocessing operation at Sellafield and its releases into the Irish Sea and I will review some of the arguments that have developed surrounding the health effects of these releases.

1
Background: The Environment and Cancer

Because that Elements can not be spi'd
by human eyes; behold what bodies now
in things thou canst not see, yet must allow.

Lucretius

1. 1 Background

I have been engaged in research on the health effects of ionising radiation since 1987, when I was living in North Wales with my wife and three daughters. We had moved to Wales at the end of a long period of escape and adventure. Prior to Wales we had been living on various yachts, big boats and sailing barges in Rochester and cruising about the East Coast and the continental waterways (Plate 26). This is a physically difficult life, involving some hardship, low status and little income, but it had a quality of immediacy, brightness and contact with a reality which was entirely absent from the alternatives which I had rejected: of a life working for the Wellcome Research Laboratories as a physical chemist, or later at the University of Kent as a Raman spectroscopist. I tell young people now to get out of it all by the age of thirty and to become tramps or whatever the modern equivalent is (Plate 27). My friend Ernest Sternglass, Emeritus Professor of Physics at the University of Pittsburgh, and the man who started all this low level radiation research off in the 60s, told me that when he was a young man he had a long interview with Albert Einstein, who told him to give up academic science and become a cobbler. Einstein told him that his physics would improve but, if he stayed in the university, he would stultify and become trapped like a fly in the amber of the belief system.

Anyway, I had come to this conclusion independently. For me, in the late 1960s, I decided that, although tinkering with the Universe to tease out its secrets can be good fun and has its moments, the prospect of a lifetime of this in a laboratory was more than I could take. And so, at the age of twenty nine, I ran away to sea from my well-paid job with the Wellcome Foundation. After playing on boats for some years, I rejoined the scientific community but, after three years of research, I again ran away: this time to Wales, dragging my poor family with me. We came (Lorraine and the three girls) in a narrow boat, one of those long ones that you see on the canals, (appropriately) illuminated with escapist paintings of castles and roses. We spent a year travelling along these strange shallow waterways to try and find the rainbow's end, eventually running aground in Wales, where we bought a small derelict cottage by a stream in Merioneth. This was an idyllic setting for a wild frontier existence, living in caravans, sawing down trees and building up the house, stone by stone. The river, which flowed past the cottage, roared over its weir in the winter rains and in the summer a fine mist over the pools scattered the sunlight in a thousand colours.

This part of Wales, at the head of the Dyfi Valley, is very, very wet. All the moisture from the Atlantic is funnelled up the valley and squeezes into the mountains at Mallwyd, where we lived; with the result that much of the time it is like living under water. Part of the reason for all this escapism was the belief (which was partly responsible for the boat period) that the world was likely to disappear in a nuclear flash at any moment, following the antics of the Soviet and American generals (a feeling that was quite common then), although it now seems to have been forgotten. Recently I learned that, at this exact time, the world almost did vanish in a nuclear flash. On 26 Sept 1983, as I was digging in the Welsh mountains, Col. Stanislav Petrov, duty officer at the Serpukhov 15 surveillance facility near Moscow personally overrode the data from the Oko satellite, which had suddenly reported US missile launches from the North Dakota bases. Petrov saved the human race by refusing to believe erroneous satellite data. Of course, they sent him to gaol for disobeying orders. However, we knew nothing of all this then. We read all the books on nuclear effects and, on occasion, had stocked up with food, candles, fuel and so forth. I suppose it made us feel safer because we were doing something, rather than just sitting and worrying about our children. This was the period informed by *A Canticle for Liebowitz* or the CND cinema film *The War Game* and similar bright views of the future. There were many such survivalists in Wales (and still are). Mallwyd was so surrounded by mountains that the Soviets would have had to accurately target our house to blow us up, and we thought that it would be unlikely that they would take the trouble.

It was therefore extremely vexing when I heard on the radio, in April 1986, that the nuclear reactor at Chernobyl had exploded, and that the radioactivity had been falling in Wales with the rain, rushing down our river and projecting a fine radioactive mist through the valley. I heard this on the 6 o'clock news on a day that I had been fishing in the same rain for trout near Machynlleth, some ten miles to the south, and had become quite wet. We were informed that NRPB (the National Radiological Protection Board) had said that the radiation levels were safe and that there would be no health consequence. I had some knowledge of the effects of atmospheric nuclear test fallout since I had read various reports in our earlier apocalypse survival phase and thought that this was probably unlikely to be true, so we rushed off and bought boxes of tinned milk. In those days, it was very difficult to get hold of a Geiger counter, even assuming we had been able to afford to buy one, and so we had this feeling of being surrounded by invisible death rays - a feeling that I now perceive to have been quite an accurate response to the situation. Thus began my radiation research phase, which led to the publication of *Wings of Death* in 1995.

I have always considered the search for truth in any area a personal matter: that is to say, I want to know answers to questions for myself, rather than to impress others or even to let anyone else know what I might have discovered. It is a kind of arrogance, I guess; maybe it is a feeling also of insecurity about not being able to understand something. I had had similar feelings long ago about the Theory of Relativity, and also the Theory of Probability, Quantum Theory and Thermodynamics and had spent a great deal of time (many years) trying to understand what was beneath all of these. I found that very few people try to see what is beneath any of the complex and seemingly bizarre explanations that science has developed about the nature of the physical world. The 'understanding' is actually more an acceptance of how a theory operates, not at all a true understanding of what it is and its internal logic. Science is often more about taxonomy, reducing complex systems to simple ones and then naming the parts and passing on. Radiation effects seemed to be in the same category. Something was missing. I felt upset that I could not understand the physics and biology of radiation and health and it seemed to me that there was something very odd in the descriptions which I read in the books that were available at the time. In all these areas, I now realise that what is missing is a set of assumptions that is taken as a 'given', but which somehow passed me by. In the case of radiation, the reason why it passed me by is that I couldn't believe that anyone would make such a crazy set of assumptions. Of course, I now know that, just as the equations of Economics merely mirror the desires of Capitalism, the models of radiation and health are reductionisms which are there to allow the nuclear military complex to continue to function in its manufacture of bombs, power and dead children. This is how Science works nowadays in all areas. But, in those far off days, I was trying to examine the propositions of radiation science like some naïve native from a book by Voltaire or some noble Victorian gentleman scientist; Cavendish perhaps, or Lord Kelvin, people whom I always admired. What a laugh!

By 1992 I had developed a basic understanding of the science behind the risk models, and had discovered that it was extraordinarily simplistic, physics-based and reductionist. Biology was absent. Cell behaviour was absent. Repair was absent. Immune surveillance was absent. The models entirely failed to address point source irradiation from internal radioisotopes or particles. They did not deal (except crudely) with the biochemical affinities of substances like Strontium-90 or Plutonium-239, which, following the releases from weapons fallout, reprocessing plants and accidents were now in the living cells of all life forms from Baffin Bay to Borneo, from Kut to Kandahar. In passing, we have now seen the contamination by the United States bombers of both Kut, in Iraq and Kandahar in Afghanistan. There you go.

In order to see if there were effects from these substances it was no good looking at the Hiroshima A-bomb data, which was from very big external acute flash doses. What was needed was a comparison of two similar populations that had been differentially contaminated with these substances. One comparative system was afforded by those exposed to the global weapons-testing fallout from the period 1959-63. This had become distributed all over the world and there were published measurements of contamination that showed the presence of fallout isotopes (e.g. Sr-90) in most populations on earth. I believed that I might exploit the wetness of Wales and look at differences in cancer rates between Wales and England, which was drier, and where there was less contamination. It seemed to me that this was a more scientific and inductive process than making deductions from the completely different exposures of Hiroshima. I had to enter the realm of epidemiology, the study of the relationship between disease and cause in populations.

The published cancer incidence data in Wales (from Wales Cancer Registry) and England (from OPCS, the Office for Populations Census and Surveys) showed that there was indeed more cancer in Wales than England and that the rates had begun to diverge from the England rates in the mid 1970s, about twenty years after the exposures from weapons fallout began to fall with the rain and contaminate the milk. The mathematical analysis revealed a very high degree of correlation with earlier published cumulative doses from Strontium-90, and the levels of cancer could be compared with these doses. This comparison gave a factor of 300 for the difference between the external radiation Hiroshima-based risk model (used by the governments of the world to sanction their nuclear discharges) and the number of cancers caused by the equivalent doses of internal radioisotopes.

Remember that this was the time of the nuclear site leukaemia clusters. A great deal of argument and heat had been generated following the discovery of the Sellafield child leukaemia cluster at Seascale and by 1993, when two of the victims took BNFL to court for compensation, the battle was well and truly under way. All the authorities held that the doses from Sellafield were too small to have caused the child leukaemias and something else must be the cause. The judge, Mr Justice French, decided that the case turned on:

Whether there exists a plausible, or reasonably plausible biological pathway or mechanism whereby radiation emitted by the Sellafield plant could have caused or materially contributed to one or both of the two diseases.

Reay and Hope vs. BNFL; Judgement 1993

(What extraordinary jokes we are handed by the demons: consider the two litigant leukaemia victims names in this trial about radiation: Reay and Hope! Perhaps it was all the isotopes with their deadly rays that emerged from Pandora's Box followed by Fairy Hope).

It turns out, when one looks at the admitted releases, that the factor required to 'explain' the Sellafield leukaemias is 300, exactly the factor I found for the Wales cancer excess. By then, apart from the epidemiology (which showed the effect), I had also discovered a number of mechanisms (such as those required by Mr Justice French) that could be used to show that internal irradiation from certain isotopes could be far more harmful than the equivalent dose from external irradiation. I had tried to get a paper published on one of these ideas (the 'Second Event Theory') but it had been soundly and rudely rejected by the referees of the journal I sent it to, although a few eminent radiation biologists that I had tried it out on were supportive. About this time, I began to see that what was keeping the radiation risk modelling system in place was not scientific plausibility or 'facts', but a political structure, and I decided that, to effect change in this area, we had to think politically as well as scientifically. Failing to obtain space in the scientific literature or news media, with my friends in the Green Party, we began to use non-violent direct action to draw the attention of the media to our discoveries and theories. We began by chaining ourselves to power stations. Plates 17 and 21 show us attached firmly to the electric gate of the Magnox Nuclear station at Trawsfynnydd in North Wales in 1992. The station was subsequently closed, and this confirmed for us that it was possible to mobilise public opinion and win. As part of this strategy, in 1992 I obtained, for £80 from a printer in Caernarfon, a small offset litho printing press that needed attention, and I taught myself to operate it and produce small A5 books and A4 leaflets.

The Chernobyl radiation had been taking its toll. Despite early reassurances from NRPB that the radio-Caesium (Cs-137 was the main isotope contamination from Chernobyl) would dissipate in six weeks, large areas of north Wales were (and are *still* in 2006) under sheep sale restrictions set at body activity of 1000Bq/kg. This means 1000 disintegration per second in a kilogram of sheep meat! My lovely dog, Rosie, had died young in Wales of cancer in 1990. Two white rats, that my daughter Frances had as pets, died of cancer whilst young animals at about the same time. Data from Wales Cancer Registry showed that cancer rates in Wales had increased in the year after Chernobyl by 30%, inspiring Richard Bramhall to write a song about it (see Appendix A). It was time to get away from the high rainfall radioactive sheep area. I decided that I must try to get my findings to a larger audience. I set up Green Audit with a fellow Green Party member, Patrick Adams, and in 1992 printed and published *Low Level Radiation from the Nuclear Industry* (also translated into Welsh) and *Radiation and Cancer in Wales* in 1994. I approached the Joseph Rowntree Charitable Trust in late 1994 to ask for six months funding to write a larger book on the issue. The Trust agreed and I produced *Wings of Death* in 1995.

At this time the anti-nuclear movement seemed to have become emasculated. The belief then was that the pro-nuclear lobby somehow had Science on their side. The arguments, played over again and again in the media, suggested a position where the scientific (i.e. correct) world view was being opposed by emotional arguments from scientifically illiterate environmentalists, usually women. I was told by senior figures in Greenpeace and Friends of the Earth, and by some members of the Green Party, that we couldn't compete with the scientists employed by Nuclear Electric or BNFL over some point relating to health risks and we would just be made to look silly if we tried. I was warned off on the basis that this silliness would somehow rub off on the NGOs. There is some truth in this. The media would not believe that what we were saying was right: the belief that the arguments came down to science versus emotion (the old intellectual split set up by the Vienna Circle philosophers) was deeply embedded in the culture. This Science versus Emotion argument is in itself interesting and I will return to it at the end of the book.

The anti-nuclear groups had given up after the defeat they received at the Reay and Hope trial. This left them in a state of schizophrenia about nuclear power (which they haven't quite recovered from today). Because if the trial was correct in finding for BNFL, then it followed that low level radiation is safe and the ten-fold excess of child leukaemia at Sellafield must be caused by something other than radiation. If this was the case, why oppose nuclear at all? I had this argument with Bruce Kent, Chair of the Campaign for Nuclear Disarmament (CND) when we spoke in a public meeting in Oxford in 1997. Bruce believed that nuclear weapons were wrong, but nuclear power was OK. This has been the position of CND (whose policies have been affected by the Trade Unions) until recently. The NGO groups switched to economic arguments. It was a waste of taxpayers' money, they argued, to support nuclear power. The alternative argument was that there might be a catastrophic accident. But even the accident arguments were now being de-fused by the nuclear scientists. Following Chernobyl, it was being suggested that no one was dying of cancer and that all the fuss was hysterical over-reaction. We were given a new concept: radiophobia. Well, I was certainly suffering from radiophobia. Richard Bramhall, Molly Scott Cato and I put in some deep thought to an analysis of the problem. It was clear that what the Green movement needed was to develop a belief in its own theories and prescriptions. What, we asked, (and this went far beyond radiation risk) gave one group the right to be automatically believed, even when the belief was manifest nonsense, whilst another group was excluded or marginalized for pointing out an obvious truth? The answer seemed to be some quality of 'credibility'. It was an 'Emperors New Clothes' affair. Remember the story by Hans Andersen? The Emperor has new clothes that can only be seen by the intelligent. No one wished to be thought of as unintelligent. So it is a little boy in the crowd, who sings out that the Emperor is naked.

What gave you credibility? Well, at a simple level, it was merely a circular argument, you obtained credibility by donning some kind of metaphorical uniform or golden crown and saying loudly that you were credible to as many people that you could address. We had used this idea already when we set up the 'Wales Green Party Research Department' in 1990, an entirely paper exercise involving Letraset and photocopiers and we developed it with our small Vickers printing press. What we came quickly to realise is what should have appeared obvious to anyone. Such a process is behind all credibility, even that of government departments or scientific advice committees. I remember writing a paper for a scientific journal in 1981 and sending it to a professor in America. The address on my covering letter was 'Ivy Cottage'. The reply came back addressed to 'Ivy College' and the paper was published.

The year following this, and after discussion along these lines over the problems that there were in changing beliefs, the three of us set up the Low Level Radiation Campaign and began to produce and distribute a new journal, *Radioactive Times*. The Goldsmiths helped us financially and (the late) Sir James Goldsmith gave us some money to buy a first class offset litho printing press, which I bought from Ceredigion District Council and stored and ran from a huge warehouse. This was the year before Sir James died of cancer of the pancreas, a very sad affair for us. Molly had brought a PC computer with her when she ran away from her husband and came to Aberystwyth and this made an enormous difference to the operation. Prior to this we were so poor that everything was done, including all the epidemiological calculations, on a BBC 64K micro, which I had been given and which I beefed up with software and hardware additions. We used a statistical teaching package developed at the University of Reading called 'INSTAT', a tremendous (and free) little system. I thank Joan Knock who helped write the programs I needed and who let me have the software for nothing. When I was in Mallwyd, the BBC computer lived in a prefabricated concrete garage, heated with a wood stove, and on cold mornings I would have to open up the computer and dry the processor chip out with an electric hairdryer before it would operate.

The analysis seemed to be correct. Our publications and press releases began to be taken seriously by the media. Although the nuclear industry sneered at our creations, because we were employing accurate analysis and commenting on official data, the sneering was reported in the media along with fair coverage of our reports.

By 1995 we had created sufficient pressure in the media, among members of the public and in county councils that it began to be accepted that cancer increases in Wales were related to low level radiation exposure from internal, ingested or inhaled radioisotopes from fallout, Sellafield or the nuclear sites. The pressure from the Welsh Association of County Councils produced a meeting with the directors of Wales Cancer Registry and the Medical Officer for Health at the Welsh Office, Dr Deirdre Hine, to discuss the arguments and see what data could be released that might help resolve the issue. At this meeting in February 1995, we argued that to examine the relation between nuclear pollution and health we had to have small area cancer data, i.e. the numbers of people who contracted cancer in an area near a nuclear site or near contaminated parts of the coast. This was data that WCR was refusing to give us on the grounds that it was confidential. Dr Hine asked the WCR directors to release this data to us. They refused again. Eventually they agreed to give us data to the County District level. This is an area with a population of about 30,000 or above and in north and mid Wales, where there are low population densities, these units cover an area of about 40km by 40km.

This was an improvement on the published data we had been using, which was for the larger County level. However, either someone slipped up, or else someone decided to leak the data; when the disc arrived in May 1995 it contained the entire Wales Cancer Registry database for 1974-1989 aggregated to 'Areas of Residence'. These AORs were much smaller units, the population size of towns, a goldmine of information for anyone attempting to look at cancer risk by distance from the sea, or from a nuclear site. The trouble was, the files were too big for Molly's early PC, which just locked up trying to load up the data even into a word-processing program. There were 194 AORs, two sexes, 16 years, 68 different types of cancer and 14 five-year age groups giving a total of just under six million pieces of data. These had been supplied as compressed files on disc as continuous text downloaded from the Welsh Office VAX mainframe system. After a few attempts, I put the data to one side. But clearly someone in the Welsh office had registered that the cat was out of the bag. Shortly after the disc was posted to us, Wales Cancer Registry was closed down completely, everyone was sacked and the cancer data file wiped from the VAX computer. The serious management of cancer incidence data had begun. I will return to this story in Part II.

By 1996 the Low Level Radiation Campaign had been publishing Radioactive Times for a year and had organised a successful debate on the issue at an international symposium in the House of Commons [Bramhall 1996]. The idea that low dose internal radiation exposure was very harmful was gaining ground in the media. I was asked to speak at various meetings in the UK and abroad. One of these was a meeting in January 1996 in Drogheda, on the east coast of Ireland, organised by Fergus O'Dowd (related to Boy George) now a member of the Daill, but at that time the Mayor of Drogheda. This was to discuss the health effects of Sellafield on the Irish population. At this meeting I met the Irish Minister Avril Doyle. It was here that I learned that Ireland did not have any national cancer registry operating continuously over the period of peak releases from Sellafield. I suggested that the Irish government buy us a decent computer and pay for the analysis of the Welsh cancer data. Over the following year I corresponded with Mr Emmett Stagg, the Minister responsible in the Irish government, but his feeling was that there was no evidence of harm and nothing need be done. However, by 1997, further political pressure to do something about Sellafield had been put on the Irish State by the people of County Louth, and eventually there was an agreement to help fund research in connection with the court case against Sellafield being taken by four individuals who lived in Dundalk, County Louth. These were Ollan Herr, Mark Deary, Mary Kavanagh and Constance Short. Their solicitor, James MacGuill, contacted us and asked if we were able to undertake the research on cancer risk by distance from the Irish Sea. We provided a research protocol, which was eventually agreed and we began the job of analysing the Wales Cancer

Registry data in January 1998. In the course of the research we were able to extend the original study to Ireland and also obtained radiation-measuring equipment and made some measurements there.

The work took three years, but the results were astonishing. What we found was that the risk of cancer rose sharply near the sea in those people living near estuaries or contaminated offshore mud banks. These results, and the extension of this work to other parts of the UK, form the basic data which I will report and discuss in the present book.

But this book is not only about the Irish Sea and Sellafield. The Irish Sea study and its extension to other areas (described later) is a case study both about the cause of cancer and responses to evidence about that cause. The research reported in *Wings of Death* led to the identification of the major specific cause of the present cancer epidemic. This is ionising radiation exposure to material in what we eat, drink and breathe: radioactive substances released to the environment through atmospheric weapons testing, from nuclear power stations, fuel reprocessing plants and nuclear accidents like Chernobyl. What the Irish Sea study showed is an extension of this work. On a grand scale it is easy to suggest that the whole population of Wales, or England, or any country is suffering cancer excess as a result of radioactive fallout exposure. It is much more startling to see this translated into cancer risk by small area, at a very small grain size and by proximity to geographical features or industrial sources of pollution. The notion that cancer is an environmental disease becomes startlingly crystallized when we begin to look at cancer risk in small areas, less than a kilometre in diameter. And, at this stage, the vague generalisations put out by the cancer charities about lifestyle and eating habits become worthless and infuriating to those who have watched the victims or their friends and family desperately try to explain the disease, looking inward guiltily for something they should have done, or not done. One young woman at a conference tearfully asked me if I thought her cancer had been caused by her having begun using a new brand of tampons.

Of course, the mapping of cancer risk is not new: Large scale maps of cancer risk have been produced in the last twenty years, but these maps show very little that is helpful. The indication of a cancer risk difference between two counties like Somerset and Dorset tell us very little about any environmental cause, since it is the extremely local effect which is likely to be significant. Whether you live in Somerset or Dorset is much less likely to result in internal contamination than whether you live near a source of contamination in either county, like a waste tip, incinerator or nuclear power station. But, of course, everyone knows where the nuclear power stations are, or the waste tips. The wealthy can avoid them and can live somewhere clean (by the sea, perhaps, read on . . .). It is only the poor who have to live near landfill sites or industrial areas. But what we have discovered is that no-one is safe from nuclear pollution. It is invisible. It does not smell. And because rain carries everything to the sea via rivers, it is to be found near the sea and near rivers: just the places that are most picturesque, and where children laugh and play and swim and splash each other.

The idea that variation in the concentration of cancer producing substances should be high in the vicinity of landfill sites, polluting factories or point sources of release of radioactivity or toxic chemicals is so intuitively obvious that we should rather ask why no-one seems to be looking at small area cancer risk. Because cancer now represents one third of all causes of death and this fraction is increasing. And cancer is killing children and younger people, women and men in the prime of life. But the enormous amount of money spent on cancer research is swallowed up by whatever cutting edge science holds out the possibility of cure. Why is no one interested in cause? There are two possible explanations. One is that no one is looking because they don't believe that there will be anything useful to find. This is a 'cultural blindness' argument. The other is that the cancer research establishment is encouraged or controlled by government. They are only too aware of the cause, but they don't want the public to know, since this will make people very angry. It will result in large legal claims against the government and private companies; it will wreck house prices and tourism in certain areas. It will affect 'economic growth', that new yardstick to measure wellbeing. Look! Here is a bright future of shopping centres where everything will be available to buy and everyone will have money in their pockets. But half of them will be on chemotherapy and dying. They can buy fashion wigs! The true appreciation of the problem will also certainly shut down the nuclear industry and wipe billions off the shares of those who have invested in the mining companies, like Rio Tinto Zinc. I favour this second reason.

There is a strong argument for looking for the cause of cancer in environmental agents, rather than intrinsic factors like genetic susceptibility. It is that we, as a society, can stop producing the substances we identify. Although this will not help the existing victims, it will ensure that the problem will not get worse. And when I say 'we' can stop releasing these substances I do not mean you or I, since actually we don't make and release this stuff. I mean large industrial organisations which make money by processes that produce these substances as by-products. But first, since the cancer charities give the impression that cancer is caused by a combination of bad genes, lack of exercise, insufficient green vegetables in the diet, eating chips, boozing and smoking, let me review the evidence that if you contract cancer (and more than one in three of you will, if you have not already) it is probably not your fault. The odds are that it is the fault of the warmongers and cold war warriors from the US, Britain, France and the Soviet Union, who released radioactive material into the world from nuclear testing, nuclear reprocessing and nuclear accidents.

Cancer is a modern disease and a disease of groups living in complex modern polluted environments. It was very rare among members of traditional pre-industrial societies and since this is an important starting point for my thesis, I will briefly review some of the proof that this is so (see also Nikolopolou-Stamati et al (2004).

Albert Schweitzer, the Nobel laureate wrote,' on my arrival in Gabon in 1913, I was astonished to encounter no case of cancer. I can not of course say positively there was no cancer at all, but, like other frontier doctors, I can only say that if any cases existed, they must have been quite rare' (Schweitzer 1957). Stefansson (1960) cites various authors on this topic of cancer in primitive peoples. In 1908 Powell (The Pathology of Cancer) stated, 'There can be little doubt that the various influences grouped under the title of *civilisation* play a part in producing the tendency to cancer'. Bainbridge, in 1914, wrote that cancer susceptibility becomes more marked as civilisation develops, in other words, the environment changes. Tanchou (1843) in addressing the French Academy of Sciences quoted a Dr Bac, surgeon in Chief of the 2nd African Regiment, who in 6-years of practice in Senegal had not seen a single case of cancer. He also spoke of Dr M Baudens, surgeon in Chief at Val de Grace, who in eight years practice in Algeria had only seen two cases of cancer. There was also a Dr Puzin, who, of the 10,000 people he had examined, discovered only one case of cancer, that of the female breast. Similar observations have been made by Bulkley (1927) about the Inuit. Reporting that in 12 years work among the Alaskan Tribes he did not see a single case of cancer. Preston Price (1937) reported an interview with a Dr Romig who said that in 36 years work among the Inuit he had never seen a case of malignant disease (Price 1939). In 1915 F.L.Hoffman, for the American Society for the Control of Cancer, analysed all the available data on cancer throughout the world and concluded that, '...the rarity of cancer among native man suggests that the disease is primarily induced by the conditions and methods of living which typify modern civilisation...cancer is exceptionally rare among primitive peoples'. Let us begin by trying to find out why.

1.2 Cancer and the environment: waters, airs and places

In September 2001 I was asked by an organisation of scientists called ASPIS (an acronym which refers to the health effects of industrial pollution) to come to Kos Island (the Greek island of Hippocrates) to talk about the discoveries I had made in the period 1997-1999 whilst researching the effects of Sellafield (the results are shown later in this book). ASPIS is a group of eminent scientists and doctors who are principally concerned with the effects of industrial pollutants on human health. The title of the conference on Kos was, 'Is cancer an environmental disease?' Also due to appear was the eminent epidemiologist, the late Sir Richard Doll, who was billed to argue that cancer was not an environmental disease. This was intriguing, since Doll himself had written in 1981 that the majority of cancers were caused by extrinsic factors, either environmental or determined partly by human behaviour, and that the majority were therefore avoidable. In the event Doll pulled out. This was a shame as I would have been interested to see his reaction to our map of lung cancer mortality risk by census ward in Somerset (Plate 1).

Doll, some may recall, became famous for his work in the 1950s associating lung cancer and cigarette smoking (Doll, 1964). What is less well known is that he squandered the credibility he achieved in this area, denying the association between low level radiation and cancer. These denials became routine, and he was routinely asked to make them. Together with Richard Wakeford, Sellafield's chief radiation risk scientist, he spent a considerable time denying that the celebrated child leukaemia cluster there was anything to do with the radiation from the plant (e.g. Doll, 1999). They argued that it was caused by population mixing increasing the chance of being infected by a hypothetical leukaemia virus which was yet to be discovered and still has not been. By 1997, as introductory keynote speaker at the British Nuclear Energy Society (BNES) conference at Stratford on Avon, he was denying the association between low level radiation and cancer. I attended this conference myself, together with my friend Richard Bramhall who, claiming to be Dr Alice Todd, dressed up as 'Death' (copying the grim reaper from Bergman's *Seventh Seal*) and chained himself to the stage beside Doll, whilst Green Party activists handed out copies of *Wings of Death* and leaflets pointing out that 'Death is present at all your conferences' (Plate 17). The police were called and we were thrown out. Later, in September 2002, I was invited by the same people, BNES, to be a plenary speaker at their international conference in Keble College, Oxford. I gave my talk, dressed in black and carrying the skull of a child. So you see that the landscape of belief is slowly changing.

However, back to Hippocrates, who lived, taught and worked on Kos, and who is called 'the father of medicine'. He would have had no trouble accepting what the Somerset maps I showed there indicated (e.g. Plate 1). Hippocrates wrote (*Waters, Airs, Places*) that illness was connected with where you lived and what you ate and drank. Who is surprised? The map of lung cancer in Somerset shows, astonishingly but quite clearly, that lung cancer is associated with living near the tidal sections and estuary of the river. After adjustment for Social Class, it was clear that people living in the flood plain of the tidal river Parratt, which flows out near the nuclear power station Hinkley Point, had two to four times the chance of dying of lung cancer than those living on the high land. Clearly this is not because smokers tend to live near the river so that there is a convenient water source in case they set the house on fire accidentally or alternatively that they have somewhere to chuck their dog-ends. No. There is some other factor that causes lung cancer and is present near tidal rivers.

Also present at the Kos conference was Dr Annie Sasco, head of cancer prevention with the International Agency for Research on Cancer (IARC) in Lyon, a suspect organization that seems to turn up at the centre of any investigation into the radiation—cancer link. IARC have been busy running huge and expensive studies to show that Chernobyl has had no effect on childhood leukaemia in Europe and I shall return to this issue later in this book. Annie Sasco's section is (she says) underfunded and understaffed because no one there seems interested in the cause of cancer (where there is no money), only in finding cures. She was astonished by the suggestion, implicit in our small area studies, that lung cancer mortality risk is affected by living near the sea or near rivers. 'I cannot believe this' she said.

The reason that no one knows about these environmental causes of cancer, even the epidemiologists, is that there has been no way of examining them because the small area cancer incidence data is kept secret. This is true in every country I have visited or region I have examined, and everyone I meet who is trying to link the environment with ill health has run up against this problem. The cancer registries, which hold the data in the UK, recently refused point-blank to give it to the Minister of the Environment, Michael Meacher, MP. Why is this?

Epidemiology is the study of the causes of disease by examination of the patterns of illness in space and time. It is like a detective process. Its methods are those of the detective in a *roman policier*, and they are very necessary today. Very, very necessary. As global capitalism drives forward in its march for power, markets and money, its industrial processes are expanding at levels that border on madness. Vast engines create huge amounts of pollution, new plastics, solvents, chemicals, radionuclides, gases, genes, creatures, diseases, foods, information, all spew forth from the market driven Cornucopia. People walk about like zombies buying things that are impossible, things that no one could need, things that they already own. The engine is driven by energy that is destroying the planet and is producing substances that are destroying the planet. No one seems to notice, to care or to act. Big Brother is not watching you: Orwell was mistaken. Big Brother is Entertaining You. Big Brother is poisoning you. The complexity of stress that this produces is too great for analysis and seems unstoppable. In most people it creates a kind of mental fog. All we can do is look at the instrument panel of spaceship earth and attempt to steer through the fog produced by lies, half-truths and spin, on the basis of the movements of the needles on the dials. We use epidemiology. But where are these dials? Where is the health compass? Where is the cancer danger direction finder? The carcinogen radar? The detectors do not appear to exist: no one is constructing them. It is an amazing fact that no one is making any direct attempt to examine the relationship between industrial pollution and the general health of the population. The data are there, certainly, but they are kept secret. Annie Sasco, like everyone, assumes that lung cancer is caused by smoking, and perhaps exposure to air pollution in cities. That is enough. How can it be caused by living near a river in a quiet and peaceful county in western England? The more critical epidemiology becomes to our survival and that of our children, the more difficult it seems to be to get hold of the basic health data, and the greater the level of complexity that is introduced into the epidemiological exercise by those whose job it is to protect the public. This they do not even attempt to do: it is, in fact, no one's job. And it is worse than this, because when anyone does accidentally discover that there is some link between disease and an environmental risk, they are immediately attacked, marginalized and, if possible, sacked from their job. We have seen this in the case of Mad Cow Disease (BSE) and we are seeing it in the case of research into Genetically Modified (GM) Foods and organisms. This is a general problem: the institutional cover-up. I have enough evidence now of an institutional cover-up of the environmental cause of cancer and this I will present later on in Part II.

Returning to the cause of cancer, I should say that there is no real argument about this now. In 1981, when the cancer epidemic began, Richard Doll himself was commissioned by the US Congress to comment on the suggestion that there was a significant increase in cancer rates and to reassure the public. His report, published with Richard Peto, as *The Causes of Cancer* (Doll and Peto, 1981) did two things. First, as required, it said that there was no increase in cancer rates in real terms: only the population was ageing. This was manifestly untrue even at the time. Second, it pointed out that cancer was largely environmental and avoidable. They brought forward all the arguments and, because I shall be examining the environmental cause of cancer in relation to small areas and local effects, I will, in this book, cover what they said and add some more. I now review the main evidence that cancer is largely environmental, though not, sadly, courtesy of the nuclear-military project, avoidable.

1.3 Cancer risk is localised

Over the seventy or so years that reliable cancer incidence data have been collected and published, it has become clear that incidence rates for different cancer types found in people of the same age living in different communities in different parts of the world vary by as much as 100-fold. For most of the major types of cancer, every type that is common in one community in an area is very rare in another community in a different area. Here are three examples. The highest rate of lung cancer was in England where the cumulative rate in 1976 was 11%. The rate of this disease in Nigeria was 35 times lower than this. In 1976, the highest rate of breast cancer was in Canada, in British Columbia with a cumulative incidence of 7% (although this disease is increasing rapidly in most western countries). In Israel, the non-Jewish population had seven times less breast cancer (IARC, 1976). For stomach cancer, it is Japan that has the highest incidence where the cumulative incidence is 11%. This is 25 times higher than the incidence in Uganda. So the first thing we can say is that these large variations in cancer incidence must reflect either some external stress, which varies with the area, or some community sensitivity to particular types of cancer. If the community were fairly isolated, this could be a genetic predisposition, but there is persuasive evidence that the cause is environmental.

Ethnic groups from one country acquired the cancer rates and types of cancer that prevailed in the country they moved to. For example, compare the cancer rates in Japanese migrants to Hawaii with those in Japan. I show some of these in Table 1.3.1. You can easily see that the spectrum of cancer sites and rates relate to where the Japanese live and presumably what they drink and breathe. In Japan there are high rates of stomach cancer and low rates of breast cancer. This reverses in the Japanese migrants and the reason is that in Hawaii they are exposed to different cancer producing agents.

There are many similar examples of changes of incidence on migration, for example, Indians who went to Fiji and South Africa (and lost their high risk of cancer of the mouth) and the British who went to Fiji (and acquired high levels of skin cancer). References to studies of this sort are many: some examples are IARC, 1976, Petrakis, 1971, Haenszel, 1970, Kmet 1970, King and Locke 1980a, 1980b Locke and King, 1980 and Lanier 1980.

Another example of evidence that cancer is caused by environmental factors, rather than genetic factors, is the cancer rate in black Americans compared with Africans. The former experience the rates and cancer types of the white Americans, rather than those of the black people living in West Africa, a group from which they were originally descended. Table 1.3.2 shows some of this data. These changes are not the result of genetic dilution through interbreeding, since, for most types of cancer, the differences between black and white American rates in certain specific areas are independent of the degree of mixing in of white genes in the black population. (Petrakis 1971)

Table 1.3. 1 Comparable cancer incidence rates per 100,000 in Japan, in Japanese residents and Caucasians in Hawaii based on ages 35-64yrs in 1968-72 (*Source: Doll and Peto, 1981)*

Site of cancer	**Patients sex**	**Rate in Japan Miyagi/ Osaka**	**Rate in Hawaii**	**Caucasian rate in Hawaii**
Oesophagus	Male	15/ 11.2	4.6	7.5
Stomach	Male	133/129	39.7	21.7
Colon	Male	7.8/8.7	37.1	36.8
Rectum	Male	9.5/9.0	29.7	20.4
Lung	Male	23.7/29.9	37.9	96.2
Prostate	Male	1.4/1.3	15.4	34.3
Breast	Female	33.5/29.5	122.1	186.9
Cervix	Female	322.9/39.8	14.9	24.3
Uterus	Female	3.2/2.0	40.7	71.4
Ovary	Female	5.1/5.5	16	27.4

Table 1.3.2 Comparison of cancer incidence rates for Ibadan, Nigeria and San Francisco, USA for black and white men and women for selected cancer sites. (*Source; Doll and Peto, 1981)*

Primary site	Sex	Rate Ibadan Nigeria 1960-69	Rate USA black 1969-73	Rate USA white 1969-73
Colon	Male	3.4	35.9	29.4
Rectum	Male	3.4	15.9	21.7
Liver	Male	27.2	6.7	3.9
Lung	Male	2.7	154.5	98.3
Breast	Female	33.7	126.8	182.8
Uterus	Female	4.2	23.5	69.5

1.4 What is the genetic proportion of cancer risk?

In the last ten years medical research has increasingly concentrated on human genetics. The cancer research establishment, a huge machine that is funded by the desperation and despair of sufferers and their families, has switched its focus onto the genetic basis of cancer. It has not done this in order to point out that the risk of acquiring the genetic mutations which give rise to cancer may be reduced by cleaning up the environment, but to concentrate on the development of gene-based cancer therapies, which can be sold to sufferers and make large amounts of money for the pharmaceutical operators. This new vision follows the failure of the cancer chemotherapy hype that raised so many billions of dollars in the period of research to 1980. Then, the rich and fearful, the poor and desperate, were told to hand over their cash because the cure for cancer was round the corner. Just another push and the magic bullet would be found. Maybe it was in the Amazon rain forest; some rare plant, nature's bounty and gift to mankind? It was not found. Some dreadful toxic substances were developed (some from plants, like vincristine) that killed cells, and therefore killed cancer cells, were injected or perfused into patients so that their lives became a misery and they lived in agony for a while. Some of these substances caused remission. They were hailed as great successes, but always the begging bowl came out: just give us more money and we will find the cure. And there was always radiation, the good old standby for killing tumours (and creating others). The real Marie Curie Cancer Care, after Marie Curie who helped start it all.

The cancer chemotherapy gravy-train has been shunted into a siding. All that money resulted in very little. We are losing the war against cancer that President Nixon declared and which has raised money for the cancer research industry ever since: the New Growth Industry. The age-standardised rates continue to climb. Following the chemotherapy failure, a new train was constructed: the gene therapy train. Now we are told that the genetic basis of cancer will soon be elucidated and therapies based on this knowledge, the sequence of the human genome, will enable cures to be found. Well, let us hope this is true, and cross our fingers as we sign our wills, leave our bequests and die. But what does it mean? That research into human genetics will enable us to understand the cause of cancer? And does it follow that even if we knew the genes that caused cancer, we would be able to do anything about it? We cannot reverse complex changes cell by altered cell. All the Kings Horses and all the King's Men, even with the assistance of gene therapy, cannot put Humpty together again.

As it happens, we now know the proportion of cancers that are influenced by genetic predisposition. The knowledge comes from a very large study by a team led by epidemiologist Dr Paul Lichtenstein of the Karolinska Institute in Stockholm. Lichtenstein et al. looked at risk of cancer in identical and non-identical twins whose cancer details are held by the Swedish, Danish and Finnish cancer registries. The work was a population-based analysis that had complete data on outcomes and a sample size at least four times larger than any other study that had been done. The results, reported in July 2000, in the *New England Journal of Medicine* should have made more of an impact on cancer research than they apparently did. (Lichtenstein et al, 2000). The team combined data on 44,788 pairs of twins in the combined cancer registries to assess the risks of cancer at 28 anatomical sites for the twins of persons with cancer. Because the proportion of genetic effect is larger in identical twins (monozygotic), who share all genes, than non-identical (dizygotic) twins, who only share 50% of their genes, it was possible to use a statistical method to estimate the relative importance of heritable and environmental factors at 11 of the cancer sites studied. Results are given in Table 1.4.1.

Among the 44,788 pairs of twins included in the analysis, there were 10,803 (among 9512 pairs) in whom at least one cancer had been diagnosed. Of course, overall, the twin of a person with cancer had an increased risk of having the same cancer and this was most clear for stomach, colorectal, lung, breast and prostate cancer. The twin of a male identical twin who had stomach cancer was 9.9 times more likely to have stomach cancer than the twin of a person without stomach cancer. The 'concordance' for stomach cancer in male identical twins was 0.08, which means that there is an 8% probability that the identical twin of a man with stomach cancer will also develop the disease, all other factors being the same. The concordance was usually less than 0.1 and no concordant pairs were observed for cancers at nine sites, non-Hodgkin's lymphoma, Hodgkin’s disease, cancer of the lip, mouth, pharynx, kidney, thyroid, bone and soft tissue.

What do these results mean? They mean that unequivocal proof now exists that environmental factors are the predominant cause of cancer. Even though Lichtenstein *et al* found familial (hereditary and non-hereditary) effects for cancers at many sites, the rate of concordance in twins was generally below 0.1. Their result indicates that, for nearly all sites, the twin of a person with cancer has only a moderate (20%) risk of developing cancer at the same site.

Their statistical models, which analysed the identical-and non-identical twins, enabled them to estimate the contribution of shared and non-shared environmental factors, which included any unique environmental cause of cancer that is not inherited, and not shared between twins. For different cancers, this contribution ranged from 58 to 82%.

Table 1.4.1 Proportions of cause of cancer at various sites by heritable, shared environmental and non-shared environmental factors from Nordic twins study of Lichtenstein et al., 2000

Cancer	**% heritable**	**% shared environment**	**% non-shared environment**	**p-value for finding**
Stomach	28	10	62	0.001
Colorectal	35	5	60	0.07
Pancreas	36	0	64	0.08
Lung	26	12	62	0.12
Cervix uteri	0	20	80	0.04
Corpus uteri	0	17	82	0.01
Ovary	22	0	78	0.001
Prostate	42	0	58	0.91
Bladder	31	0	69	0.36
Leukaemia	21	12	66	0.01
Breast	27	6	67	0.07

So environmental factors are the overwhelming cause of cancer (and remember, this is not a new idea, but one that has been indicated by many pieces of evidence). Surely, it must be reasonable to expect cancer researchers, or Public Health officials, to look for variation in risk according to where people live. This is screamingly obvious. But even in the case of nuclear sites, which spew forth cancer-producing substances every day, no sensible attempt to examine risk of the disease in adults living nearby has ever been carried out. And the almost accidental observation of ten-fold childhood cancer increases near the largest source of radioactive pollution in Europe, Sellafield, was brought to the attention of the public by Yorkshire Television, and not by the local public health officials. And instead of welcoming the discovery of what was, by any measure, and important piece of potentially life saving information, the authorities immediately attacked the television company and ridiculed their primitive statistical procedures. Given that the World Health Organisation (WHO) drew attention to the environmental basis of cancer as early as 1964 it seems strange that no-one has looked at the possibility that people living near to such a place, breathing, drinking and eating radioactive pollutants, might suffer excess risk.

So Lichtenstein et al. have conclusively shown that for most cancer, genetic predisposition represents less than 1/5th of the cause. What can we now say about the remaining 4/5ths? What other evidence is there that might help?

1.5. Changes of incidence over time

The human race is functionally much the same as it has been for at least a million years. The biology and physiology of people, the body as a machine has not changed; therefore, changes in cancer rates for specific cancer types over time, for the same population groups, living in the same areas, indicate change in some external factor as probable cause. We have seen that a group of people can move from one part of the world to another and change their cancer rates and spectrum of disease. But there is also evidence showing that groups living in the same area can experience changes in cancer rates over time. This is because their environment changes. An example given by Doll and Peto is change in rates for stomach cancer and lung cancer mortality between 1952 and 1975. Table 1.5.1 shows changes in some of the countries.

Table 1.5.1 Percent changes in mortality from stomach and lung cancer between 1951 and 1975. Average male and female rates from IARC 1976 according to Doll and Peto, 1981.

Country	Stomach	Lung
Australia	-53	+146
Austria	-53	-8
Chile	-56	+38
Denmark	-62	+87
England and Wales	-49	+33
West Germany	-50	+36
Ireland	-54	+177
Israel	-49	+58
Japan	-37	+408
Norway	-59	+118
Scotland	-46	+44
Switzerland	-64	+72
United States	-61	+148

The increased risk of lung cancer shown in Table 1.5.1 has been associated with the increased cigarette smoking behaviour which occurred some twenty years previous to the cancer expression, although some have suggested an association with radioactivity in the tobacco. The reason for the decrease in stomach cancer, which has been fairly uniform across countries, has not been identified, but may have to do with the improvements in the food quality and clean water which also resulted in dramatic reduction in infant mortality over the same period. Since stomach cancer had been associated with some specific bacterial infections, the increased routine use of antibiotics may also be partly responsible.

More recent and dramatic evidence of change is what some have called the 'cancer epidemic' that began in the UK and US in the late 1970s and early 1980s. It was the early public perception of the increases that caused the US government to call in that environmental scare fireman, Richard Doll to examine the issue. I will briefly look at this increase, in order to introduce here a major piece of evidence for the general thesis that is the subject of this book. Fig 1.5.1 shows a graph of standardised incidence for all cancer combined in England and Wales and, also, separately in Wales. The increases are occurring all over the world. The rapid increases in breast cancer, which are a significant component responsible for the effects in England and Wales shown in Fig 1.5.1, are also found globally.

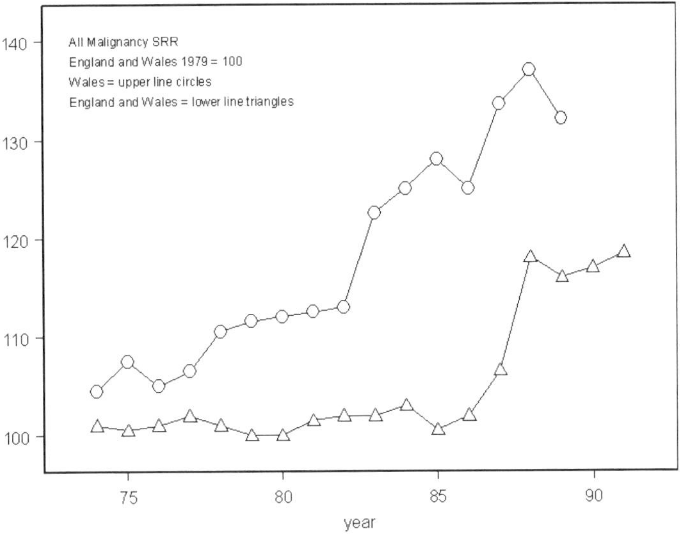

Fig 1.5.1 Increases in all malignancy-standardised registration ratios in Wales (upper, circles) and lower (triangles) England and Wales combined. (*Calculated from data in publications of Wales Cancer Registry and Office of National Statistics).*

I argued in *Wings of Death* in 1995 that the cause was exposure to radioactive pollution from atmospheric nuclear weapons tests. The peculiar step change in the cancer trend in Fig 1.5.1 and its earlier onset in Wales argue for a sudden exposure, peaking around the 1960s, to a universal carcinogenic substance with a higher dose in Wales than in England. There is only one possibility that fits these two requirements. The fallout occurred twenty years before the changes shown. The cumulative dose from Strontium-90 is lagged by 20 years and plotted against the Wales SRR in Fig 1.5.2. This is broad brush stuff, of course, and individual components can be examined, but the correlation is extraordinary. And although in epidemiology correlation doesn't mean causation, no one has been able to find a persuasive alternative explanation. I first suggested this possibility for the cancer epidemic in the *British Medical Journal* in 1994 (Busby 1994). At that time the cancer epidemic was being denied (Coggon and Inskip, 1994). Of course, no one would now deny it and, as this book will show, there is now other evidence.

When we look more closely at the way in which cancer is initiated at the molecular level in the cell, it will be clear that changes like these follow genetic mutations or the initiation of genome changes, which may have begun up to twenty years or more before the cancer developed and was diagnosed. Yet this may not always be the case. Cancer can also develop very quickly following the exposure to the mutation, and this kind of effect is seen in Wales and England after Chernobyl, although there seems to have been an attempt to cover it up, as I will show later.

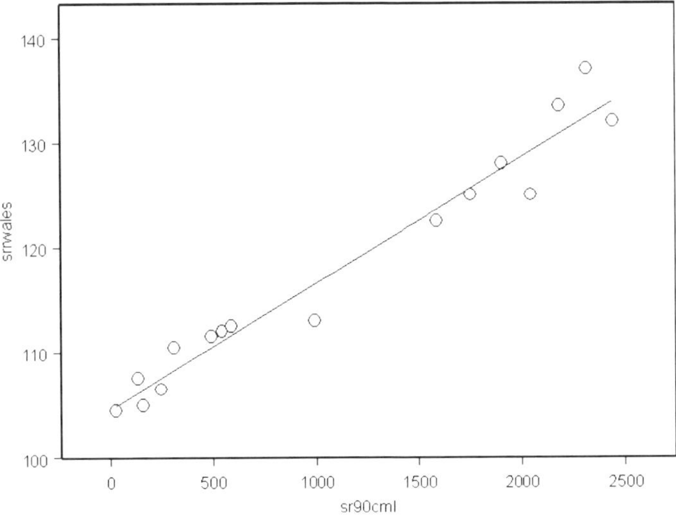

Fig 1.5.2 Cumulative dose in Wales from Strontium-90 in weapons fallout (μSv, microSieverts) 1954-1974 lagged by 20 years and plotted against Standardised Registration Ratios for all cancer 1974-1994 averaged over both sexes.

1.6 Cancer trends in England and Wales: strange happenings

There is an interesting aspect of the cancer epidemic graph for England and Wales, which I will introduce now and consider further in Part II. The Standardised Registration Ratio (SRR), plotted in Fig 1.5.1 is an index that represents the level of cancer incidence in a country relative to a standard year and population. The SRR in the standard year is given the value of 100. A value of 150 would mean that there was an increase in cancer incidence in real (age standardised) terms of 50%, i.e. if there were 100 cases in the base year there was now 150 cases in a similar population. And, of course, from what we have just seen, this means that something has happened in the victim's environment that caused the increase.

There is a straightforward method of calculating the value of the SRR and, until recently, for every year since 1971 the Office for Population Census and Surveys (OPCS) and, more recently, the Office of National Statistics (ONS) - which is largely the same organisation translated into an agency - have calculated these values of the SRR for all cancers combined and for each cancer site separately for the nine years prior to the data year of each Annual Reference Volume (ARV) of cancer incidence [Ref ONS; MB1 No 1, 1971]. The volume for a data year is published some five years (see below) after the data year of the year for which the figures are given. Thus each ARV gives ten years of trend in cancer incidence up to and including its own year. This is so that changes in age adjusted cancer incidence rates can also be adjusted for changes in the population so that they can be examined to see if any trend might suggest the cause of the increase or any sudden increase may be detected in time to do something about the cause. For data from 1962 until 1979 the base year was 1968. From 1979 on, the base year was 1979; however, these two series can be seamlessly joined together by simply adjusting the first series to fit the base of the second so that an uninterrupted series of cancer incidence trends can be shown from 1962 to the latest year for which data is available. This kind of process, after all, is largely why the cancer registries were set up. In addition, standardised rates in different Health Authority areas are similarly tabulated and referenced to England and Wales = 100, so that, in principle, trends in the various areas can be assessed to see if anything strange is happening in one of them, Wales, for example. Using this published data, I drew attention in the early 1990s to an anomalous increase in bone cancer in Wales over the period 1974-86 and showed also that both this and the prostate cancer increases in Wales over the same period could be explained by earlier exposure to the isotope Strontium-90 in fallout. [Busby, 1993, 1994a, 1995].

I draw attention to these trend series here because something odd happened to the data given for SRR over the period which related to the Chernobyl accident, suggesting that the data began being managed in such a way as to cover up the cancer increases. This is a serious accusation, and it is intended as such. Every year, the ARV tabulates the cancer trend for the prior ten years. Therefore, if we look at these trends by year, each ARV shows (or should show) the same SRRs for the ten years of overlap between the volumes. For example, in 1984, each SRR for the ten years 1974-1984 was tabulated. In 1985, the years 1976-85 were listed; in 1986, the years 1977-86 and so forth. So there are always eight years that are common to each ARV and clearly these numbers cannot change retrospectively unless some error is discovered.

I repeat, these ARVs are always published well after the data year they represent. The volume for the first data year, 1971, was published in July 1979, a delay between the person developing cancer and tabulation of about 8 years. Over the period 1979-84, the approximate lag between data and diagnosis was 3.5 years. It then increased in 1985 and 1986 to 5 years. The 1987 ARV was published in 1993, a gap of seven years, which remained in the 1988 ARV (1994) but reduced in the 1989 ARV (1994). The 1990 ARV was published in 1997 and this seven-year gap remained until the latest publication in 2001 of the combined data for 1995-1997. Following the 1997 publication, the ARVs began to be put onto the ONS website and can now be downloaded from www.statistics.gov.uk.

All the recent ARVs no longer contain the table of SRR trends. This table was the first in each blue book and arguably the most important. It was the dial on the instrument panel of our spaceship, the 'cancer risk' meter. As soon as it began to register something, the authorities taped it over so no one could read it. The last year it was included was 1989. It was clear in that year that the cancer rates were beginning to rise startlingly in real terms, in age standardised SRR terms, and this followed Chernobyl, which the government had assured everyone was not a health risk and so the Table that showed this was quietly dropped. From 1990 onward Table 1 became a table of registration numbers for the different cancer sites and a new trend was devised. The table contents were changed. Skin cancer, which was a component of the previous 'all malignancy' SRR was no longer reported, so no one could make up a continuous trend from 1974.

There is more. There was some curious retrospective data alteration. It is clear that the organisation that collects and publishes the data, ONS, has plenty of time to assess the data before it is published- between five and seven years. Up to 1987, although cancer incidence had been increasing in real terms in Wales for about eight years (for reasons which I gave above, and are explored in Part II and in *Wings of Death*), the trend line in England and Wales combined had been comparatively flat over the period from 1971, rising slightly in 1986-87 from 99 to 103 for men and 105 to 110 for women. However, in the 1988 ARV (which you will recall, was produced five years late) the trend was suddenly retrospectively altered without any explanation. The airbrushing was repeated the following year in the 1989 volume where the new figures were repeated. In the 1990 volume, as I state above, the trend tables were discontinued altogether. I return to this matter in Chapter 10 where I look at why this may have been done, and calculate the correct numbers for the SRRs over the Chernobyl fallout period, when the reporting became embarrassing and was stopped.

1.6 Identification of specific causal agents

There is now enough evidence that exposure to specific agents causes cancer. The list of such agents is immensely long but some examples are given in Table 1.6.1. What they generally all have in common is an ability to effect increases in the chance of acquiring a fixed genetic mutation in somatic cells. This is because, as I shall outline below, cancer is essentially a genetic disease that is expressed at the cellular level. The increased risk of genetic damage might be through exposure to some chemical substance which reacted with the DNA that makes up the genetic information that tells the cell how it functions. Genetic mutation might also follow exposure to some agent that increases the normal rate at which cells become damaged, by altering the normal repair mechanisms. Thus exposure of the cells in the body to chemical substances which either interact with the DNA to change it, or interact with the DNA repair systems to prevent the change being dealt with, may result in an increased probability of acquiring a fixed mutation. Most recently, it seems that exposure to such substances also increases the general rate of acquisition of random mutations, a process called 'genomic instability', and that this is a built-in feature of living systems which may be there to improve the chances of a cell or a species surviving an evolutionary stress (by diversification). However acquired, fixed mutation may then result in cancer through various mechanisms, which are discussed briefly in the section on mechanism.

Substances that cause mutations are called mutagens. Substances that cause cancer are known as carcinogens, and it has been argued that all mutagens are potential carcinogens. Indeed in the USA for a long time, new and existing chemicals have been subjected to tests for the ability to cause mutations in simple bacterial systems or in mice and graded as mutagens by the authorities in order to restrict their release to the environment. There is also a class of cancer causing agents that are believed to act as 'promoters' of the initial lesion or event, which ultimately leads to cancer, and some chemicals can effect increased risk of cancer through this mechanism.

Of course, apart from chemical mutagens, there are other physical agents that increase the risk of mutation and cancer; and the most universal and powerful mutagenic agent is ionising radiation. Ionising radiation causes its effect at the level of the DNA by producing a track of ionised particles, mainly water molecule fragments, that have been torn apart by the high energy of the radiation fields or primary ionised high-energy particle. This track can be thought of as a stripe of sparks, like the tail of a rocket, and each spark, or ionised fragment, is capable of destroying a chemical bond in a DNA helix. Whilst the chemical mutagen acts in a quite specific way, reacting with some chemical grouping or reactive site on the DNA, the radiation effect is more like a shotgun or scattergun in its ability to attack the whole helical structure at the place that it happens to pass across it. The density of ionisation varies with the type or quality of the radiation. For alpha particles there is a very high density of ions along the track. The absorbed dose in a single cell from an alpha track can be as high as 500 milliGray, an energy density which can be compared with the annual whole body dose of about 2 milliGray. Thus the alpha track (and similar high density ionisations from internal radiation due to ingested radioisotopes from Sellafield releases) has a sufficient density of ionised particles to cut both strands of DNA and thus prevent accurate repair of the genetic code. This is called a 'double strand break' and is thought to be the main way in which radiation causes fixed mutation. But I am getting ahead of myself here. The main point is that the argument about whether cancer is caused by environmental exposures is also informed by observation of cancer in people who have been exposed to specific agents, and, where the evidence is sufficiently good, to induce causal explanation.

One of the first instances where this happened was the observation of cancer of the scrotum in the boys who used to sweep chimneys and who were exposed to the carcinogenic hydrocarbons and other residues of coal tar. It is, of course, never possible with cancer to blame a particular agent beyond doubt. No one is allowed to experiment with a small child, to subject this child to radiation or some mutagenic chemical and (presto!) demonstrate leukaemia, as a chemist might add a blue liquid to a clear one and obtain a red colour.

This is partly due to the lag period between exposure and expression. Cancer is usually expressed well after the exposure that caused it, or rather that began the process that led to it. Therefore there is a big problem for anyone who is trying to sue a company or the government for compensation or to prove liability. In a case of murder, Mrs A sticks a knife in Mr B and someone sees her, or the blood-stained knife is found in Mrs A's house and the jury have to decide. But with cancer it is not at all that simple, even in the case of exposures to known carcinogens. The whole development of cancer from the initial lesion is a long sequence of low probability decisions, and only the person who is unlucky enough to pass through each binomial filter gate (yes or no) gets the prize. But in practice, the jury, whether scientific or lay, decides on the basis of overall probability. In most cases where there is no political, cultural or financial bias, it is not too difficult to decide, especially when the exposures and the practices were in the past (as in scrotal cancer and boy chimney sweeps). As we shall see, this book deals with the situation in which there *is* both political and financial bias, and when this is the case, we are drawn into an Alice in Wonderland world of logic based on a fairly simple system of cover-up, alteration and deceit.

However, since it has been possible to find that occupational exposures to certain agents that cause cancer of certain types in those exposed at a much higher rate than in the general population, we can feel more secure in our belief that cancer is caused by these agents, although other events are probably needed, since not all those who are exposed develop cancer. So this is further evidence that cancer is primarily an environmental disease. What we do not know is the quantitative relationship. For example, a person working with high levels of carcinogenic material may suffer a high risk of some cancer. Thus it was with the boy chimney sweeps. But what of those (usually poor people) living near a source of the same materials, people living near a gas coking works, for example, where the continuous slight smell signals the presence in the air that they breathe of low concentrations of the same materials that are associated with scrotal cancer in the chimney sweeps? What about farmers and their families or workers who live in parts of the country where there is a great deal of bracken, a plant that contains substances linked to liver cancer.

Table 1.6.1 Some specific and identified associations for cancer.

Agent	Main exposure	Cancer site
Aflatoxin	Food and bracken	Liver
Alkylating agents	Chemotherapy	Bladder and other sites
Aromatic amines e.g. beta napthylamine	Food and some occupations	Bladder
Arsenic	Occupational+	Lung
Asbestos	Occupational+	Pleura, peritoneum
Benzene	Occupational+	Leukaemia
Cadmium	Occupational+	Prostate
Tobacco	Chewing	Mouth
Tobacco	Smoking	Lung
Ionizing radiation	Occupational+ environmental	All cancer sites
Mustard gas	Occupational	Lung, larynx, other cancer sites
Nickel	Occupational+	Nasophaynx, larynx, lung
Polycyclic aromatic hydrocarbon	Environmental	Skin, scrotum, lung
Dioxins	Environmental	All sites
Late age at first pregnancy	Social choice + environmental	Breast
Parasites	Environmental	e.g. Schistosomiasis and bladder cancer
Sexual promiscuity	Social choice + environmental	Cervix uteri
Ultraviolet light	Occupational, social choice, environmental	Skin, lip
Virus	Social	Hepatitis B and liver cancer
Heavy metals, zinc, mercury	Occupational, environmental	All sites

It would be reasonable to believe that the cancer producing effects of cancer-producing materials do not depend on being present in large concentrations in the body, but, instead, that it is the probability of receiving the specific mutation leading to cancer that increases with their concentration. That is to say, at the higher concentration found in occupational exposures there are more carcinogen molecules in more cells. On this basis, we should expect a reasonably continuous reduction in hazard with reduction in dose. Thus everyone who is exposed, no matter what the concentration of the substance, has some chance of developing cancer. On a strictly linear relation between dose and effect, if we reduce the concentration in the air by 100-fold, the risk falls by the same factor. This is the Linear No Threshold dose-response relationship used by the nuclear industry to regulate its releases. It says that if 1 in 10 workers who are occupationally exposed to carcinogen X develop cancer early (and the rate in the general population for this cancer is 1 in 1000) then, if the people who live near the plant are exposed to 1/100th the concentration of substance X (due to leakages from the plant), then the rate in this population will be 1/100th of 1 in 10, which is 1 in 1000. This pollution will, therefore, cause the rate in the local population to double to 2 in 1000, and if anyone found a doubling of this cancer in the local population they might reasonably blame it on the plant. To do so with certainty we would need also to ensure that the increase could not reasonably have occurred by chance alone, and this is the job of epidemiology, covered later in this book.

In reality, in 2006, it is much more difficult. First, the cancer data in the small area near such a plant is usually kept secret by the authorities. Second, no one is paying anyone to look at such a possibility (and the local public health officials do not look) and third, for the first two reasons, and because the plant employs workers who want to keep their jobs, and local people don't want their house prices blighted, anyone who does stumble on cancer increases close to industrial plants or other sources of carcinogens is swiftly attacked and marginalized.

But it is rare that the dose response is either simple or linear. There are many examples where low dose has a proportionately greater effect (passive smoking and lung cancer is one). There is evidence that radiation exposure is like this. Then there is also the area of interaction between two or more agents, a nightmare for scientific research. There is certainly some initial evidence that two different agents can cause illness at rates that are greater than the sum of the effects of each agent separately. For example, there is evidence from uranium miners who are also smokers that the risk factors for smoking and exposure to radiation in the mines multiply with one another rather than add, as they should if they were acting on the same biological system. Rather, for this to occur, it seems that they must be operating as component events of a compound event, i.e there must be two separate events A and B, both of which are necessary for the outcome. I will review what seems to be known about the process that leads to cancer briefly, and then give a short account of ionising radiation, how it is measured, how its health effects have been assessed, and how the models that have been developed from this are far from secure.

2
How Cancer is Caused

A useful way about thinking about how a disease might occur is in terms of:
1. a susceptible population, which is
2. exposed to the causative factor of a disease and
3. receives a dose of the causal agent sufficient to produce the disease

LH Roht, BJ Selwyn, AH Holguin, BL Christiansen
Principles of Epidemiology (1982)

But what is the mechanism of cancer causation? No one knows exactly but there are some useful pointers in terms of how we deal with the issue. From what we have seen so far, it has become clear that cancer is caused by exposure to environmental agents, substances that are able to alter or increase the rate of alteration of cellular genes in such a way that some cells acquire a set of mutations that cause them to replicate continuously and uncontrollably. This is what the environmental evidence indicates. It is therefore clear that if we wish to reduce the rates of cancer in human populations the place to begin would be to reduce the general levels of exposure to the carcinogens. So far, so good. However, when we need to decide how we might reduce our own risk or exposure, it becomes more difficult to decide what to do. For example, what should we avoid eating? Which industries should we lobby to reduce emissions? What processes should we ask our politicians to refuse permission for? All that we are told by the cancer research charities and the UK Department of Health is to keep out of the sun, eat lots of vegetables, avoid excess alcohol and avoid smoking cigarettes. In passing, I should point out that in Wales we were able to analyse the answers to a very large health survey, the Welsh Health Survey, involving almost 30,000 questionnaires and it was not clear that this healthy lifestyle approach had any effect on cancer incidence risk. Where you lived was considerably more important.

Even once it is coyly conceded that environmental agents are the cause of cancer, none of the industries responsible for releasing these agents want to admit that their particular process is to blame. It is not us, they say, but the other industries. The nuclear industry tries, for example, to divert attention to some chemical that it uses for the cause of measured increases in prostate cancer in its workforces. The mobile phone companies, accused of manufacturing and selling phones which are linked with lymphomas, fund flawed studies to show that there is no such link [see e.g. Scott Cato *et al*, 2000]. Business must go on making items, making money. Even the tobacco industry has been funding research that shows that smoking is not the cause of lung cancer. Everyone is innocent but the cancer rates inexorably increase.

In order to follow the arguments relating to the discoveries and cover-ups, some basic knowledge of the biology is needed in addition to the epidemiology. I will briefly give an outline of how cancer seems to be caused at the cellular level and how the final expression of the disease can be seen as the consequence of lots of very improbable events stacking up over a lifetime. An account of the cellular basis of cancer can be found in many textbooks and I refer you also to Chapter 2 of *Wings of Death* where I have condensed much of what is known about the cause of the disease.

2.1 A genetic disease

Much of the early evidence that cancer is essentially a genetic disease comes from the environmental observations already reviewed, together with studies of family (i.e. genetic) susceptibilities. These, taken together with the linking of specific cancers with specific exposures to certain chemicals, indicate that it is genetic mutations in certain cells that are the origin of cancer in the organs made up of these cells. Although this is not the whole picture, since something controls the development of the initial genetically damaged cells into cancer, it is a major part of the chain of causation.

The normal operation of a cell requires access to a set of instructions coded on the DNA in the chromosomes of that cell. Human cells contain 46 chromosomes, 23 derived from the mother and 23 from the father. The 46 chromosomes contain about 6×10^9 (6 billion) base pairs of DNA. The total number of genes is in the range of 50-100,000 per set of chromosomes. These genes, or a set of them in each cell, need to provide, essentially, the same information to the cell throughout its life for its continued normal functioning. Damage to, or alteration of, this genetic information can result in a number of outcomes. First, the damage may be fatal and the cell will die. This would occur if some large or critical section of the code were altered beyond repair or to a level where no useful information were maintained. Such damage would not cause cancer since the cell would not have any descendants that carried one of the genes required for uncontrolled replication. Second, the cell might acquire a fixed mutation that was not one of the set needed for the complement which produced cancerous transformation. Such a mutation might merely reduce the effectiveness of the cell. Finally, the cell might acquire one of the fixed mutations needed to make up the full complement associated with cancerous behaviour. (Note that the rate of acquisition of such mutation might also be altered following exposure to some stress through the induction genomic instability.) Therefore, however the mutations are acquired, if the cell survives the mutagenic process, the acquisition of certain specific mutation will increase the risk of cancer. Even if a cell acquires all these necessary mutations, clearly there is also a level of functional surveillance to overcome before the cancer will reach the stage of clinical detection. Screening of populations for cancer has been increasing in the last twenty years and it seems, from the results of such expensive exercises, that pre-cancerous conditions routinely form and regress 'spontaneously'. [personal commun. Muir Gray]. Screening followed by surgery is therefore not necessarily as valuable as it may seem.

Thus the clinical expression of cancer is essentially a consequence of a probabilistic sequence of binomial (yes/no) events at the cellular level followed by or paralleled with a different set of binomial events occurring at different layers in the levels of the function of the whole organism. A cell may acquire a mutation which is one of the set needed to cause cancer or it may not. If it does pick up the mutation, it passes through this binomial gate and is now at the second stage. This second stage cell or any of its identical descendants may now acquire a second one of the necessary set of mutations; or none of them may. This represents a second binomial gate. At every stage in this sequence the probability of passing through the gate is very small. The normal mutation rate per cell division is about one in 10^5. But there are a great deal of cells (10^{13}) and a great deal of cell divisions in the lifespan of an individual, so it is obvious that the risk of cancer will increase with the age of the individual. Since each cell divides to give two daughter cells with (usually) identical genetic makeup, and these daughter cells themselves divide, resulting in four cells descended from the original cell, and so forth, there is a geometrical increase in the daughter cells of any mutated cell which will all carry the mutation. So although the probability of acquiring such a mutation is very small indeed, involving the sequential probabilistic steps outlined (and shown in Table 2.1.1), the number of cells available to acquire a second critical mutation will be increasing as an exponential function of age.

There have been a number of more or less successful mathematical descriptions of the cancer process which mainly depend upon modelling the kind of sequences given in Table 2.1.1 The most simple model is that of Armitage and Doll who developed a two-stage theory of carcinogenesis in 1957 and showed that for many cancers the theory explained the exponential increase in cancer incidence with age. In essence, and if there were no change in the exposure to mutation agents, the rate of acquisition of mutations in the lifetime of the individual is the same as the rate of ageing. Indeed, ageing is caused by the same process, the continuous and cumulative acquisition of genetic mutation leading to decreasing cellular efficiency and ultimately functional efficiency also. This is probably why the radiation resistance of different mammals is closely proportional to their lifespan, an observation which is discussed in *Wings of Death*.

So it is fairly easy to see how the cancer process develops and to get some idea of how the components of the cancer lottery interact over the lifespan of the individual. The end result is a consequence of the movement of a cell clone (all the descendants of a single cell) through multiple stages of increasing genetic damage together with failures of checks and blocks to progression. The most recent developments of the original two-stage description concede between 5- and 6-stages necessary for the development of the main cancer types. The mathematical description is, however, largely the same in form, with an exponential (increasingly increasing) increased risk with age.

Of course, the development also involves genetic lesions that have been inherited; set down for each of us at birth. These include pre-existing genetic mutations which of themselves may not inexorably lead to cancer but which merely add to the overall risk. They include inherited variations in DNA repair efficiency also: we know about some rare inherited diseases which result from DNA repair efficiency errors and which provide direct evidence that genetic mutation is a prerequisite for cancer. Some of these conditions are given in Table 2.1.2

Table 2.1.1 The sequential steps necessary for the development of cancer in the case of a three-mutation process.

Event	Progression affected by
Initial mutation	• Concentration of environmental mutagens • DNA Repair efficiency/genomic instability • Inherited components
Increase in number of cells carrying mutation (1)	• Viability of (1) cells • Rate of replication • Replication rate promoters/ inhibitors
2nd Mutation	• Concentration of environmental mutagens • DNA Repair efficiency/genomic instability • Number of mutation (1) cells
Increase in number of cells carrying mutations (1) and (2)	• Viability of cells carrying mutation (1) and (2) • Rate of replication • Replication rate promoters/ inhibitors
3rd Mutation	• Concentration of environmental mutagens • DNA Repair efficiency/genomic instability • Number of cells with mutation (1) and (2)
Clinical expression	• Inhibition by local cell fields • Destruction by immune system • Other processes

These inherited syndromes are, fortunately, very rare. However the connection between the specific genes, their role in the cell and the relation to increased risk of cancer represents irrefutable evidence of the central role of genetic damage at the cellular level in the development of cancer. In the case of the ATM gene (which is associated with the rare disease *ataxia telangiectasia*) it has recently been suggested that about 6% of the population are heterozygous for this (recessive) gene and that this confers increased risk of cancer on these individuals [Hall, 2002]. That is to say that they are carriers of the gene, but that it does not confer the condition because it is a recessive gene, i.e. one in which both parents must pass it to their child for it to become expressed. If this is so, then this invalidates the radiation risk models that are presently used as a basis for environmental legislation on human exposure, which implicitly assumes that everyone has the same response to radiation.

Table 2.1. 2 Some genetic disorders that give rise to a predisposition to cancer. (Source: Little 2002)

Condition	Gene	Function	Major cellular abnormality	Cancer Type
Ataxia Telangiectasia	ATM	DNA damage surveillance	Chromosome instability/ radiosensitivity	Leukaemia and lymphoma + some solid tumours
Nijmegen Break syndrome	NBS1	Re-combinational DNA repair	Chromosome instability/ radiosensitivity	Lymphoma and leukaemia
Fanconi's anemia	Six FA genes	DNA damage repair	Chromosome instability/ Sensitivity to DNA cross-linking agents	Leukaemia and solid tumours
Familial breast cancer	BRCA1 BRCA2	Re-combinational DNA repair	Chromosome instability/ radiosensitivity	Breast and ovarian cancer
Hereditary colon cancer	MMR	Mismatch DNA repair	Microsatellite DNA instability/ Mutational instability	Colon and some other solid tumours
Li-Fraumeni syndrome	p53	Loss of cell cycle control checks	Chromosome instability/ apoptosis loss	Multiple malignancies

2.2 Single cell origin

The evidence for the single cell origin of cancer in certain tissues is very important in the understanding of the cause of the disease. In the last thirty years methods have been developed in biology to enable a study to be made of the development of cells in relation to their origin in the embryo. It turns out that the sex of animals is determined by a particular pair of chromosomes. In mammals these are the X chromosome and the Y chromosome: females are XX having inherited an X from each parent; male are XY having inherited one of their mother's X and one of their father's, Y chromosomes. Now the sex chromosomes are odd: the Y is much smaller than the X and so the X, in males, has to operate alone. To maintain the balance, in the female, the spare X chromosome is tightly packaged and set apart. The choice of which of the X chromosomes is inactivated, the mother's or the father's is decided early on in the development of the embryo (Nesbitt, 1971; Takagi, 1974). Also, the choice is random and irreversible. Thus every female is made up of two kinds of cell, those descended from the twenty or so that became inactivated, and those that are descended from the twenty that were not inactivated. The resulting adult is a `mosaic' of the two types of cell, which have different genetic codes, derived from their mother's and their father's codes respectively for the X chromosome.

This mosaic character can be demonstrated in cases where there is some genetic marker; for example a gene that codes for a particular response, perhaps to an enzyme. There are women, for example, who can be studied for mosaic difference between cells to the enzyme glucose 6-phosphate dehydrogenase (G6PD); it has been shown that the individual organs of such women are invariably mosaic and therefore must have descended from the different types of cell that were present at the embryonic inactivation of the spare X chromosome (Gartler *et al.*, 1971). It turns out that the tumours in such individuals are unlike the surrounding tissue in that they are found almost invariably to contain only one type of G6PD. This is true whether the tumours are benign or malignant, implying that each tumour has arisen from a single cell (Fialkow, 1974, 1976). Thus the growth of cancers is not like an infection being spread from cell to cell: it is the unchecked development of a single family of cells, derived originally from only one. There is one caveat here. We assume in this argument that the genetic identity of a cell cannot be changed. It may be biological heresy to suggest otherwise, but no-one has yet proven this assumption.

2.3 Mutation and repair

Molecules of a substance called DNA, deoxyribonucleic acid, carry the data that constitute the genetic memory of a cell or an individual. The mechanism by which such data are copied to successive generations of cells was discovered by J. B. Watson, F. Crick, M. Wilkins, and R. Franklin in 1953. The copying of the data turned out to be something that was made possible by the physical structure of the DNA molecule, which was discovered by the process of X-ray crystallography, a kind of photographic procedure that uses X-rays to determine the positions of atoms in a crystal. DNA consists of a double helix, where two chains of complementary or conjugate sub-units, called bases, twine around one another. You have all seen the pictures. The individual units, or bases, consist of four different molecular building-blocks called nucleotides. It is clear that anyone who knew the sequence of bases in one chain could write down the sequence in the other (Albert *et al* 1994).

Since proteins in cells consist of long chains of different building-blocks called amino acids and since there are only about twenty different amino acids used, it is obvious that the four base nucleotides can be used by life to construct an alphabet, enabling data on the synthesis of proteins to be coded into the genetic memory which they constitute in the double helix. And, of course, the double structure of this DNA molecule makes possible the replication of the molecule by the unwinding of the double helix.

The foundation of the complementarity of the DNA bases is a specific physical interaction between the shapes and chemical nature of the four bases in DNA. These are called adenine (A), thymine (T), guanine (G), and cytosine (C). Adenine is always opposite thymine and guanine is always opposite cytosine: they fit together like jigsaw pieces. In order to duplicate such a molecule it is only necessary to separate the two chains alongside each of them. Evidence that showed that this is what occurred came in two parts. First, an enzyme was discovered which separated the chains, and would assemble complementary chains from a given solution of DNA *in vitro* (i.e. in a glass test-tube). Secondly, it was demonstrated, by the use of labelled markers, that the two chains of DNA do indeed come apart and go their separate ways when the molecule is duplicated. The pathway by which the exact sequence of bases in a stretch of DNA is translated into the sequence of amino acids in a protein is now understood in fine detail: the genetic code for proteins has been deciphered and the various enzymes involved have been discovered and purified.

The primary function of DNA is to dictate the sequence of amino acids in proteins and thus to ensure the synthesis of the correct proteins in the correct quantities. Using four different bases, the cell must be able to code for the twenty different amino acids plus punctuation. In fact its `vocabulary' (the genetic code) consists of the 64 possible three-letter words that can be made from a four-letter alphabet. Of the 64 words, three are punctuation signals (equivalent to the use of a stop in a telegram). The remaining 61 words, one of which is a start punctuation, are distributed among the twenty amino acids, some being coded for by more than one word. No spaces are used, so in order to get the message right the sequence has to be read in the correct frame. Between adjacent regions coding for different proteins, i.e. adjacent genes, there is always a stretch of DNA, bounded by stop and start signs: these regions are not translated but are used for control purposes. These regions have sequences that are the same for all forms of life - warthogs, slugs, sunflowers, bacteria, or wasps - suggesting that it may have evolved very early.

In replication, both chains of DNA are faithfully copied: any changes that might have occurred in the sequence of bases, in the message, will also be handed down from one generation to the next. These heritable changes are the mutations. In the extent to which their effects are restricted to the cell, or the creature, they are somatic mutations.

Mutation is caused by chemical and physical agents, by some viruses and also by random (thermal) errors in transcription. The chemical agents that are known to cause mutation often have a high chemical reactivity. One example, used in cancer chemotherapy, is the group of chemicals called methylating agents. These add alkyl or (CH_2) groups to anything they come up against. This includes DNA bases that thus change, upon reaction, their chemical and genetic identity. Reactive free radicals associated with oxidative metabolism in the cell also can attack the DNA and cause mutation. Ionizing radiation causes damage to DNA in this way, since it is the energy of the radiation that causes the breakage of chemical bonds in molecules in the cell and leads to the formation of free radicals and other 'hot species', which then react with the DNA. Radiation is one of the most powerful mutagens known, particularly for the induction of fixed mutations through simultaneously attacking both strands. Table 2.3.1 compares the mutagenic efficiency of the most powerful known chemical mutagens with ionising radiation and shows some of the mechanisms of damage. The reason that radiation is such a powerful and dangerous mutagen is that the radiation produces its damage mediated through the tracks of charged particles, mainly either electrons or alpha particles. These tracks can actually be seen in experiment. They can be seen in detection devices like the cloud chamber where they cause a kind of vapour trail like those of high altitude aircraft. The track is a trail of ionised reactive chemical fragments, mostly free radicals and ions resulting from the splitting of the H-O-H bond of water molecules in the cell. Ward *et al* (1988) have shown that the quantity of damage produced by ionising radiation is orders of magnitude lower than for most other agents for equal cell killing efficiency.

It is now known that cells have both small scale and large scale mechanisms for repair of DNA damage. Repair enzymes are constantly and continuously checking one strand against the other and when a mismatch between the complementary bases is detected, various different processes occur to repair the damage. These procedures differ in their complexity depending on the type of damage detected. Some damage is easy to repair. A single base on one strand may have been changed by a chemical reaction e.g. the alkylation of guanine caused by exposure to methyl nitroisourea. This may result in a point mutation: one gene is altered. The defective base is cut out and replaced by enzymes. Small-scale damage on one DNA strand is not considered biologically significant since it can be repaired using the complementary template. The more likely origin of death and mutation is LMDS or local multiply damaged sites. These are not usually produced by chemical mutagens, except at enormously high concentrations. They result from radiation exposure and from the high local energy deposition that results from tracks of free radicals that trail the fast electron and alpha particles and are associated with radiation interaction with water in the cell.

If high enough energy density occurs in a track that traverses the two DNA strands, a double strand break can occur. This is a most effective mutagenic process since, if both strands are broken in the same region of the DNA, it is not possible for repair to occur accurately since there is no template available. Such breaks can lead to breakages of the entire chromosome and incorrect recombination of the two ends of the break lead to chromosome aberrations.

Table 2.3.1 DNA damage from different mutagens compared with gamma radiation. Yields of DNA damage necessary to kill 2/3rds of cells exposed. *(Source: Ward et al, 1988; BEIR V 1990)*

Agent	**DNA lesion**	***Number of lesions per cell per D_{37}**
Ionizing (gamma) radiation	Single strand break (ssB)	1000
	Double strand break (dsB)	40
	Local multiple damage sites	440
	DNA protein cross links	150
UV light	Thymine dimerisation	400,000
Hydrogen peroxide	Single strand break	2,600,000
Benzo[a]pyrene	DNA strand intercalation	100,000
Aflatoxin	Chemical adduct	10,000
1-nitropyrene	Chemical adduct	400,000
Methylnitrosourea	7-methylguanine	800,000
	3-methylguanine	30,000
	O^6-methylguanine	130,000

* *D_{37} is the dose of the agent required to reduce the survival of cells to 37% of those exposed*

It is therefore clear by now that the most important aspect of a mutation process is that it can somehow bypass the ability of a cell to detect that there is DNA damage and repair that damage. This can be effected by making the damage essentially unrepairable, as in the case of the double strand break, or by damaging the repair process itself. The first of these occurs with ionising radiation because of the way in which the radiation tracks consist of ionised fragments, which can attack localised regions of DNA and cause local multiple damaged sites. The extent of the local damage is very important. If the track consists of sparse ionisation, as in the case of secondary electrons produced by the absorption of X-rays and Gamma rays, there is generally too low a concentration of free radicals to cause sufficient damage in a local region of DNA to break both strands. The probability of this is very low. However, highly ionising particles like alpha particles produce an enormous number of free radicals along their much shorter tracks and here the probability is much higher. In both cases we can usefully think of the tracks as if they were the blast of a shotgun. In the case of the gamma and X-rays, there are only a few pellets in the cartridge, but the alpha particle contains a large number of particles that can blow away the DNA in one region totally.

2.4 Chromosome damage

Most mammalian cells have a diploid complement of more than 40 chromosomes that can be seen clearly using a light microscope (scored) at mitosis. Some have fewer chromosomes: the Chinese hamster has 22 and the rat kangaroo 12. If cells are irradiated by X-rays, breaks are produced in the chromosomes and the ends appear to be sticky and can rejoin with other sticky ends. The various fragments can rejoin in a number of ways. They can:

- Rejoin to give back the original structure.
- Not rejoin at all and leave an aberration which can be scored at the next mitosis
- Rejoin other broken ends to give grossly distorted new chromosomes that can be scored at the following mitosis.

Many types of aberration are possible in principle but there are two types of aberration that can be used to infer that a cell has been irradiated and to obtain some idea of the dose involved. These are dicentrics and centric rings and they can be easily seen and counted as a proportion of normal cell chromosomes using a light microscope. Their preponderance in human lymphocytes can be used to assess historic radiation doses received by an individual, although they decline with time after the irradiation (Hoffman and Schmitz Feuerhake 1999). On the other hand, there are stable chromosome aberrations like translocations, which are passed on unchanged and may persist for many years. A translocation involves a break in two pre-replication (G1 phase) chromosomes with the broken ends being exchanged between the two chromosomes symmetrically. Such aberrations cannot normally be 'seen' but new fluorescence chromosome painting techniques enable sections to be 'painted' with a dye and then the pieces can be tracked by observation under ultraviolet light. The yield of chromosome aberrations is a linear quadratic function of dose for external radiation. That is to say that the dose is related to the yield by the equation:

$$\text{Yield} = A(\text{Dose}) + B(\text{Dose})^2$$

The yield of radiation induced leukaemia and many other cancers also follow such a relationship in the case of external irradiation at intermediate and high dose, though in the low dose region, there are a number of relationships that occur.

2.5 Internal and external radiation

The reason I have described these mechanisms of genetic damage is that we need to understand how a serious error has been incorporated into the science at the core of radiation risk assessment. First we need to realise that the process we label 'radiation' is a heading and not a complete description of the phenomena. Strictly speaking, radiation is an electromagnetic phenomenon. Visible light is one aspect of it; radio and TV signals are also radiation. These are but two regions of the total electromagnetic spectrum, a description of a range of processes of energy transfer through vacuum and at the speed of light. These phenomena, which are fundamental in the physical universe, are not really understood at the metaphysical level even now. Other regions of the electromagnetic spectrum, the infra red, the ultra violet, the microwave are all now well known and can be generated by machines. Any particular type of radiation is defined by its wavelength λ (the Greek letter lambda). The wavelength of (green) visible light is about 500 nanometres, which is 500×10^{-9} metres, or half a micron, roughly one twentieth the size of most human cells. As the wavelength gets smaller, the energy packed by the electromagnetic radiation gets larger. Blue light ($\lambda = 460$nm) can knock electrons out of the surface of certain sensitive metals (e.g. Caesium) and this is utilised in photoelectric light meters. But red light ($\lambda = 650$nm) is too weak to do this, and so these photocells become useless in the far red. As the wavelength gets smaller the energy goes up. Ultraviolet light (λ= 250-320nm) is energetic enough to knock electrons out of most metals and also break bonds in DNA in skin cells and it causes mutation by making two Thymine molecules in the DNA bond together to cause a dimer. A dimer is a new molecule made where two molecules of a certain compound stick together with a chemical bond. Such a process will destroy the function of the original molecule; in this case a component of the genes. The result can be skin cancer. The lower wavelengths transmitted by the sun to earth are screened out by the ozone layer but we are in deep trouble if this breaks down.

Even more energetic electromagnetic radiation is the X-radiations of different wavelengths that originate in electronic rearrangements in atoms of different elements and more energetic still than these are the gamma (γ) -rays which are caused by internal atomic nuclear rearrangements. X-rays and γ rays pass through but also interact with matter. The shadow pictures of broken bones on the X-ray plate mean that the bones have absorbed some of the X-rays leaving a white shadow on the photographic film. The bones absorb more X-ray energy because they contain Calcium which has a higher atomic number than the Hydrogen, Oxygen, Carbon, Nitrogen and Phosphorus that make up most tissue. Absorption of gamma and X-rays is proportional to the fourth power of the atomic number of an element and this has some interesting implications for heavy metal poisoning, particularly for Uranium poisoning as I shall outline later.

The most important biological consequence of this process is that where the rays are absorbed, electron tracks are produced and, in living tissue, along these tracks there is a trail of ionised and reactive fragments, capable of damaging cell components, including DNA.

X-rays are produced by high voltage machines; X-rays and γ-rays are both produced by atom bombs, γ-rays are emitted by natural radioactive materials like Radium and man-made radioactive materials like Caesium-137, a significant component of the Chernobyl fallout. If someone stands near a source of such radiation, and the radiation is absorbed in their bodies, they are said to be 'exposed' and the amount of energy absorbed is called the absorbed dose. It is defined as energy absorbed per unit mass, Joules per Kilogram, and the units are Grays. Although X-rays and γ-rays are very penetrating (γ-rays will pass though six inches of concrete) such an exposure is said to be external. It starts outside the body, and the absorption of energy is uniform over the whole of the body. Under these circumstances, the number of ionisation tracks formed in the tissue is approximately the same in all parts of the body. This is an important distinction between external and internal exposure, as I shall show.

At this stage, to examine internal radiation exposure, I now have to introduce a different category of ionising radiation, which is not essentially electromagnetic, but instead is comprised of fast charged particles. As I described, fast electrons are produced in materials subjected to γ-rays and these whiz along trailing sparks of ionised fragments. But rearrangements within certain unstable nuclei of certain materials that exhibit radioactivity (e.g. Uranium-235, Caesium-137) generate such fast particles spontaneously. These unstable radioactive isotopes are in the process of spontaneously changing into different isotopes of different elements and, as they do so, the energy changes occurring within the atoms produce various different high-energy charged particles that shoot out of the atom like bullets from a gun.

It is easy to see from Table 2.5.1 and 2.5.2, that the chance of hitting the same cell twice (let alone the same section of DNA) is very small. There are a number of different charged particles produced by radioactive decay, but the most important ones are α (alpha-) and β (beta-) particles. The α– particles are relatively massive, doubly charged nuclei of the element Helium. They have very low penetrating power, and can be stopped by a sheet of paper (or by human skin). Their range in air is a few centimetres and in tissue their ionisation track traverses about 30 cells. β- particles are fast electrons which emerge from the decaying isotope and, so long as the decay energy of the isotope producing them is high, are not any different from the electrons produced in tissue following absorption of a γ–ray of similar energy. However, very low energy β- particles are produced by some isotopes e.g. Tritium and by some rearrangements in certain isotopes called Auger emitters. These weak β- particles have very short tracks and cause very dense ionisation in a small tissue volume. Table 2.5.1 describes these radiation types and gives their biological effectiveness at producing genetic damage.

Table 2.5.1 Radiation types of biological significance with Linear Energy Transfer LET classification and Relative Biological Effectiveness RBE values employed by the ICRP and other historical risk models

Type	Sources	*Range in tissue	Note
X-rays (low LET)	Medical (High voltage tube)	Fully penetrating	Produces the same ionisation effects in the whole body irradiated externally. RBE = 1
γ– low LET)	Isotopic decay, fission	Fully penetrating	Produces the same biological effects in the whole body irradiated externally. RBE=1
α high LET)	Isotopic decay, fission	40 cells	No external hazard. Very high local dose to cells in region of internal decay. RBE=20
β– low LET)	Isotopic decay, fission	400 cells	Little external hazard. Internal effect same as electrons produced by external γ but some man-made internal β–emitters carry enhanced hazard due to Second Event effects (see text). RBE = 1
Auger and weak β– medium LET)	Isotopic decay	1/10th of a cell or less	Produce very high local dose to parts of the cell where the decay occurs. If on or near DNA then serious hazard exists. RBE = 5-20

* Depends of decay energy. The column shows mean values for decay energy 0.5-2 MeV

The historic physics-based radiation models that have been used to assess risk distinguish between the different types of radiation (X-rays and γ-rays, α- and β-particles) on the basis of the ionisation density they produce in tissue. This model is generally associated with the International Commission on Radiological Protection (ICRP). It employs two concepts. The first is a measure of the ionisation density in a track produced by the radiation type called Linear Energy Transfer or LET. It distinguishes between low-LET which includes X-rays and γ-rays and β-particles, and high LET which mainly comprises α-particles. The Relative Biological Effectiveness or RBE is then defined as a measure of the comparative mutagenic or cell-killing consequence of equal dose exposure based on 1.00 being the baseline. In this scheme the value of 1.00 refers to X-rays, γ-rays and β-particles and a value of 20 is used to multiply doses from high LET exposures from α-particles. The fundamental unit of absorbed dose, the Gray (Gy) becomes, upon multiplication by a weighting factor based upon relative biological effectiveness, a new quantity called *dose equivalent.* After this multiplication or weighting has been done, the new units are now called Sieverts (Sv).

This process results in some quite significant changes in the relative doses from different sources of exposure insofar as they are assessed for human protection. For example, the pie chart of radiation exposure of human populations shown in most textbooks, or referred to by Risk Agencies like the National Radiological Protection Board (NRPB) in the UK, uses this weighting for α-particles to inflate the apparent exposure to the natural radioactive gas Radon, which is a decay product of Uranium. This method of weighting, or artificially enhancing the doses of harmful exposure types has been extended recently by the European Committee on Radiation Risk (ECRR) in its report [ECRR2003] which I was involved in developing. The ECRR, addressing some of the concerns I make in this book, has distinguished between the internal and external exposures and its scheme deals with specific exposures from a range of isotopes and isotopic forms which epidemiological evidence and mechanistic arguments show to carry excess risk. This will be addressed in Part III.

I can now collect together the properties of these radiation types and sources to compare their ability to cause mutation, and thus cancer. Clearly a key quality is the ability to cause dense ionisation in the region of the DNA double helix, so that both strands are broken and cannot be repaired. An alternative way of effecting the same process is to produce less dense ionisation in the region of the DNA but do so twice or three times within the normal time period involved in repair of the damage and replication - about twelve hours. Fig 2.5.1 illustrates the effects of high density and low density ionisation density tracks on the DNA.

The first thing we discover is that external radiation cannot cause double strand breaks, except at very high doses. It is easily possible to show this by simple calculation. Both Professor Dudley Goodhead of the UK Medical Research Council, and Professor John Gofman of the US Committee for Nuclear

Responsibility pointed out as early as the mid 1980s that the key quality in radiation risk assessment is not the average absorbed dose (in Gy), but the number of tracks per cell delivered over the period involved in DNA repair. At the normal dose levels involved in exposure to external natural background radiation, cells are 'hit' by a low ionisation density track only once in a year. Such hits, involving sparse ionisation density from low-LET radiations (remember, high LET radiation cannot penetrate the skin) are unlikely to even damage a single strand of the DNA and in the unlikely event of a direct hit, will merely cause a single strand break which is easily repaired (so long as there is no pre-existing or later induced problem with the repair system). Table 2.5.2 shows the mean number of hits per cell per annum following some external radiation exposures.

So we have established that only high ionisation density tracks are likely to cause mutation at low dose through double strand breaks because the single strand breaks from low LET radiation tracks can be repaired. At low doses around the external natural background levels of 1mSv, there is vanishingly small likelihood of two tracks of low LET radiation traversing the DNA. But there are other ways in which low LET radiation can cause mutation at low dose. This is through hitting the DNA twice sequentially at low dose or by damaging the repair process. To understand this we have to now briefly review the way in which cells respond to radiation damage and how they repair it and replicate.

Table 2.5.2 Typical annual whole body external doses in mGy and mean number of radiation tracks per cell produced.

Condition	**Radiation LET**	**Annual absorbed dose (mGy or mSv)**	**Mean number of tracks per cell per year**
Average public	Low	1	1
Public in high background region	Low	2-4	2-4
Nuclear workers	Low	50	<50

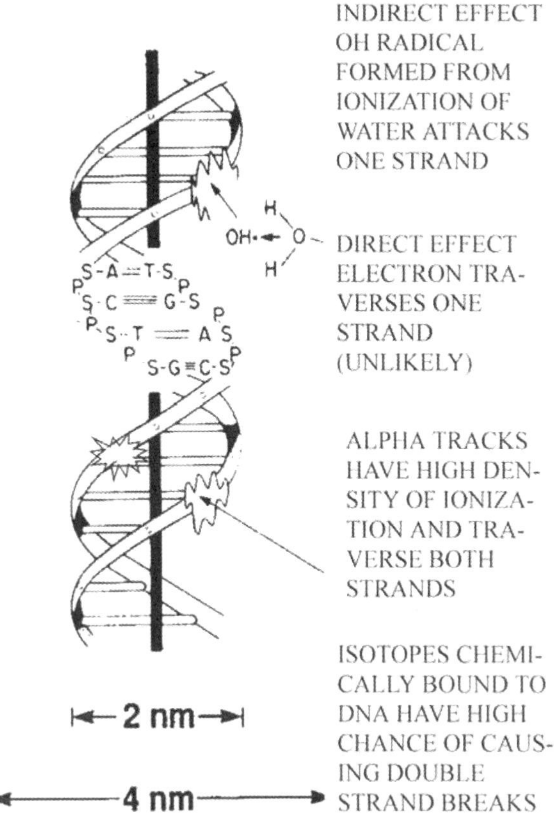

Fig 2.5.1 The direct and indirect effects of low and high ionisation density (LET) on complementary DNA strands showing the greater likelihood of the high LET radiation causing unrepairable double strand breaks.

2.6 The control of cell proliferation and the repair of DNA

There is only space in this book to provide an overview of this subject and pick out what we need to proceed with our arguments about radiation and health. I refer those who wish to dig deeper to Hall 2002 and to Sonnenschein and Soto (1999) and also to recent texts on cell biology, which is a rapidly moving field.

Cells in growing organisms replicate rapidly. In the foetus, which grows fastest of all, as soon as a cell has replicated it begins another sequence of replication. It is a continuous cycle of cell division. In infants and children the rate slows, but cell replication for most cell types (nerve and brain cells are an exception) is still rapid. In general, the more rapid the cell replication rate for any particular type of cell, the more radiosensitive the cell is. This fact is used in radiotherapy for cancer where rapidly dividing cancer cells are preferentially killed by the high radiation doses applied to the tumours and the hope is that the therapy has less effect on the surrounding normal non-replicating cells.

In the adult, most cells are preferentially in a non-replication state called 'quiescence'. Much of the knowledge we have about cell behaviour has come from studies of certain cell lines that can be grown in culture, in a glass dish. These *in vitro* studies have established cells are engaged in a continuous cycle. This ‘Cell Cycle’ was described by Howard and Pelc in 1953, shortly after the discovery of the DNA structure. These two discoveries together generated a wave of research into the cell cycle behaviour in normal and cancer tissue cells in culture. The cell cycle was defined as two measurable events. These are DNA synthesis (S-phase) and mitosis (M-phase) There are also two 'silent' intervals called G1 (or Gap 1) and G2 (Gap 2). These are shown in Fig 2.6.1. For mammalian cells the cell cycle period is about 12 hours. In the body, however, (or *in vivo*) the continuous cycling that takes place in culture does not occur. Most of the time cells are in a resting state that is indistinguishable from the G1 phase and this state was called G0. There is some argument about whether the 'quiescent' cells in living tissue are in a separate phase G0 or in a prolonged version of G1. For my purposes this distinction is not important. Whatever label is given to the 'quiescent' state of cells, it is the nature of this state that it responds to signals to force it out of the state to enter the repair replication sequence defined by the 12-hour progression G1-S-G2-M.

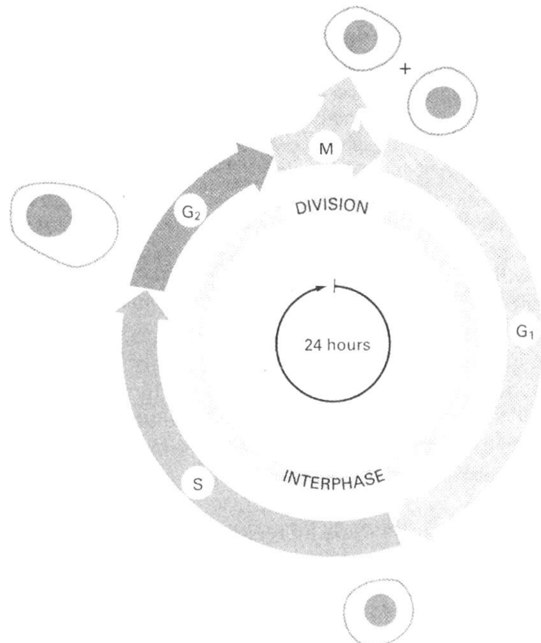

Fig 2.6.1 The cell cycle. For eukaryotic cells cycling continuously in culture. In the tissue of a live animal, the G1 phase may or may not contain the quiescent phase G0. On the other hand, cells may leave the cycle immediately at post M and may be considered to be outside the cycle in a true separate G0 or quiescent phase. The sequence G1 to M takes about 12 hours in most mammalian cells

There are a number of signals that cause this to happen. The quiescent cell monitors its status and responds to a number of stimuli. These include:

- Awareness of senescence at some point in the cell age.
- Awareness of need to make up tissue volume due to death of proximal cells.
- Awareness of sub-lethal damage from external stress e.g. DNA damage, heat shock, disruption of cellular organelles, etc.
- Signals from local cells for other purposes.

In other words, regulation of cell proliferation is exerted by means of signals that switch cells in and out of the cycle. It may be that these signals are positive or negative and it is not assumed that quiescence is the default state in *metazoa* (organisms made of many cells).

It was shown in the earliest studies that radiation exerted a profound effect, delaying the cell cycle progression not in S or M but in either G1 or G2. It was also recognised that these arrests were related to the process of cancer development because normal cells would arrest in both G1 and G2, but tumour cells only arrested in G2. Thus in the tumour cells, radiation did not affect the progression from G1 to S, the start of the cycle. The regulation of the passage through the cycle is a consequence of passage through a series of checkpoints at the boundaries between each phase. Once extracellular or stress signals commit the 'quiescent ' cell (G0) to enter the repair replication cycle at G1, molecular events in G1 prepare the cell for DNA synthesis. In the cells *in vitro* there is a stage in G1, called the G1 restriction point, which may correspond to the G0-G1 boundary. The process is controlled by the activity of enzymes known as cyclin dependent kinins (cdk).

Either way, after cells are committed to move into the cycle from G0 or a quiescent extended G1, they enter S-phase and no longer respond to external growth signals. Once the cell has entered S-phase it must begin the difficult task of accurately copying over 300 billion bases of the genome. This is accomplished by enzymes called DNA polymerases and happens in about three hours. The process is aided by DNA repair genes and involves the removal and repair of mismatched sections. After the cell has copied its entire genome, the next task is to segregate the two copies of the genome into the progeny cells. There is a gap in G2, however, between the end of DNA synthesis and the beginning of cell division during which the process of segregating and condensing the chromosomes occurs. After this, and after the integrity of the system has been established, the cell passes another checkpoint (regulated also by cdk activity) and enters mitosis. Once mitosis has been accomplished, the two daughter cells enter G1 (or *in vivo* G0).

Each event in the cell cycle depends on an earlier event having taken place and so there are check points throughout the cycle and junctions between the phases so as to ensure that the initiation of later events follows the completion of earlier events. Checkpoints function at:

1. The G0/G1 boundary *in vivo*
2. The G1/S boundary *in vitro* (possible the same)
3. The S-phase
4. The G2/M boundary.

If DNA is damaged, cells are arrested at one of these checkpoints depending on their positions in the cell cycle. Cells with damaged DNA in G1 (in vitro) avoid replicating that damage by arresting at G1/S, causing a delay at that point until the damage is repaired. If they have passed that boundary they may arrest for a while in S. This leads to an avoidance of replicating DNA damage by allowing longer time for the repair. The tumour suppressor gene p53 is critical to the mechanism of G1 arrest. The G2/M checkpoint prevents cells with damaged chromosomes from attempting mitosis. They are arrested in G2 to allow DNA repair to be completed. Cells lacking the G2/M checkpoint are radiosensitive because they try to divide although their chromosomes are damaged. There is a window of opportunity in late G2/M that is extremely sensitive to radiation, presumably because any damage that occurs here cannot be repaired and is passed on to the daughter cells. The controlling genes for this checkpoint include the ATM gene.

So that is how cells have evolved to survive in an environment that is naturally radioactive and also contains other natural processes that damage the genes. They have evolved complex systems of repair and replication that are intended to enable the genes to survive as long as possible. This repair system is clearly of greatest importance in species with long life spans such as humans, and indeed may define an important difference between humans and experimental mammals like mice and hamsters, which have often been employed to examine radiation induced cancer and other effects. Although they are cheap and the experiment can be completed in a year or so, the results may be useless in an extrapolation to humans, where the longevity is so dependent on DNA repair. This is as far as we know at present, except for some new frills to do with cell communication, which I shall present shortly. How is all this important for radiation and cancer?

2.7 The consequences for radiation and health

The Second Event Theory

The reason why I have reviewed this area of the control of cell proliferation is that no-one in radiation risk modelling has considered the effects of irradiation at this level of complexity or in terms of the different targets that cells present at different stages in their life history. The concept 'absorbed dose' merely dilutes energy into a bag of water. But cancer is caused by very specific alterations of genes in cellular systems that are altering themselves throughout the life of the individual cell and is therefore not one target but many. First, it is intuitively clear from this description of the behaviour of cells *in vitro*, that there is likely to be a variation in sensitivity to cell killing and also variation in fixed mutation sensitivity over the cell cycle. This is because of the complexity of what is necessary in the cell for accurate templates of the gene to be handed between phases of the cycle and to the daughter cells. For tracks traversing cells in G0 or G1, it is as if a cannon were to be set up outside a building site and discharged at a period when all the bricks and pieces of wood, sacks of cement fastenings, scaffolding and so forth were laying around in corners waiting to be used to build a small house. Some of the materials would be damaged but enough undamaged material would still be there after the cannon shell had hit the yard to build a house. Extending the analogy to G2 and the G2M border, imagine that the house was in the process of being built in the centre of the yard, or almost finished. The scaffolding is erected; the walls are up. All the pieces of the arrangement are in place and supporting each other. A cannon shell discharged into such a structure would destroy the whole edifice. If the detection end point were a new perfect house, then this stage would represent a sensitive stage. Similar sensitive stages in the cell cycle have been proposed, theoretically, and later discovered experimentally.

The variation in sensitivity of various cells over the cell cycle has been measured and described. For cell killing, Sinclair and Morton found a 25-fold difference between the G1 and S phase in Chinese Hamster Ovary cells at 7Gy [1966]. In this system the peak sensitivity for cell death appeared at the G1/S border. However, for cancerous transformation and at lower doses, in a human hybrid cell line, Redpath and Sun [1990], using 1Gy of γ-radiation from Cs-137 showed a 20-fold variation in sensitivity to cancerous transformation for cells in M and G2 phase than those in mid G1. The evidence was that this enhancement of effect increased as the dose decreased. These are large external doses that involve significant cell killing. The idea of a sensitive window for mutagenesis or cell death (not always the same window) has been proposed also by Elkind [1991], Brenner and Hall [10] and Hall *et al* [1991] and modelled by Rossi and Kellerer [1986]. It follows that if cells can be moved out of quiescence G0 into the 12 hour repair replication cycle G1-S-G2-M, the result is to suddenly provide a sensitive window for mutation. This is the basis of the 'Second Event Theory' which I proposed in 1987 and which was described in various forms since then (Busby 1995, 2001 etc.)

What I proposed is that the normal state for 99.9% of cells in tissue is quiescence, which I identify with G0. The period between cell divisions for most cells is between months and years, as so these cells will normally be in a low radiation sensitivity phase of their life. If such cells are hit by a radiation track and become damaged, they can do a number of things. They can die, or they can move into the cycle at G1 and try to repair the damage and replicate. If they do repair the damage and pass the G1/S checkpoint, they enter a sequence of processes from which there is no escape, and which contains events where further radiation damage cannot be repaired. If they do not repair the damage and die, then proximal cells will detect this fact and will move out of quiescence into repair replication, in order to maintain tissue integrity. Thus either way, cells are induced to move from an insensitive to a sensitive phase. Therefore, two separate doses to a cell and its neighbourhood, separated by about twelve hours, represent an enhancement of hazard over a single dose of double the size. This is the essence of the idea. It distinguishes fundamentally between the health consequences of exposures from man-made internal isotopes or particles and external exposure and for this reason has been attacked by the nuclear industry and their supporters in NRPB (Cox and Edwards.2000, CERRIE 2004a, 2004b).

There are three kinds of exposure that theoretically lead to Second Event Exposures. The first is from internal sequentially decaying isotopes, particularly $\beta-$ and $\alpha-$ emitters. The main isotopes of radiological interest here are Strontium-90, which decays to the radioactive daughter Yttrium-90 and Barium-140, which decays to radioactive Lanthanum-140. Both Strontium and Barium are of the same chemical family as Calcium and therefore bind to chromosomes. Both daughter isotopes, Y-90 and La-140 have reasonable short half-lives of 64 and 40 hours respectively so that a second decay into the twelve-hour repair replication period defined by G1-S-G2-M is likely. There is a great deal of evidence from both animal studies and human epidemiology that suggests Sr-90 exposure causes heritable genetic damage and leukaemia [Busby 1995].

It should be pointed out that the sequential beta decays do not have to be directed along the same geometrical path or track. All that is required is that the second decay causes ionisation in the DNA after the first one also has. This is a criticism that has been levelled against the Second Event idea. It occurs from an isotope attached to the DNA and has to do with the geometry of the two decays. It was argued by Dudley Goodhead and others that the two decays will have to direct tracks along the same path for the hits to be registered by the DNA. This is not true. All that is required is for the two tracks to cause sufficient damage to the DNA; the damage does not have to be in the same place. The chromatin, the coiled coils of genetic material, have a diameter of about 700nm. Any Strontium-90 (for example) bound to the Phosphate backbone will generally be inside this structure. Sr++ ions have an ionic radius of 0.132 nm, so almost all the possible decay track directions will be into the chromosome structure. In addition, the higher atomic number of the Calcium and Phosphorus atoms than the effective atomic number of the cellular water will increase the ionisation density along the track in the region of the decay. This effect becomes especially important for elements of high atomic number that bind to the DNA, like Uranium.

The second important type of Second Event exposure is from internal immobilised micron-sized alpha emitting particles. Here we have mainly the Plutonium Oxide particles from Sellafield and weapons fallout and the Uranium Oxide particles, which result from the burning of Depleted Uranium shells in battlefield conditions. These particles are small enough to be resuspended into the air from dust or from sea spray and following inhalation pass across the lung into the lymphatic system. Once immobilised in the body, they produce a continuous bombardment of local tissue with highly ionising alpha particles and in the case of sub-micron sized particles, the track frequency in cells local to the particle is sufficient to produce Second Events at a high level of probability.

The third source of Second Event processes is from exposure to low doses of radiation from the very weak beta- emitter Tritium, a form of hydrogen. Because the emission particle energy of a Tritium decay is very small, about 0.018MeV, there are many more decays per unit dose from Tritium than for most isotopes of radiological significance. The decay energy of the natural background internal isotope Potassium-40, (K-40, which only decays once) is 1.35MeV and so, for the dose produced by a single decay of K-40, Tritium produces 75 tiny tracks. These tracks are all the more dangerous for the cell since Tritium freely exchanges with hydrogen atoms on DNA and therefore the energy is deposited at the most sensitive part of the cell. In this case, as with the particles, different atoms will deliver the two events.

I will return to the evidence that exposures from these substances cause high levels of illness and look at attempts to cover this evidence up in Part III. But first there is one more way that two or more hits can produce a larger probability of mutations than one hit of two or more times the unit size.

The quadratic response at low dose

In experimental results from external exposure studies of cell cultures, animals and human populations (primarily Hiroshima) over the full range of effect from medium dose to high dose that the response is best described by a linear quadratic relationship. The effect has been observed in many systems (e.g. leukaemia induction in the Hiroshima group and the production of chromosome aberrations following high dose exposures).

This linear quadratic relation is written:

$$\text{Effect} = \text{a (dose)} + \text{b (dose)}^2$$

Where 'a' and 'b' are constants.

This is an equation that describes a linear increase in the low dose range (certainly up to about 5mSv) and as the dose increases the response, leukaemia rate or chromosome aberration frequency increases much more rapidly. In the linear region, moving from 1mSv to 10mSv should increase the effect ten-fold. But if a quadratic relationship existed, moving from 1 mSv to 10 mSv would produce 100-times the effect. There are sound theoretical reasons for interpreting this as being due to independent track action in the linear range but with a much increased effect when the dose is so great that two tracks impinge on a cell at the same time, a 'double hit'. These two tracks (or correlated tracks) are thought by most to have a high probability of inducing a mutation because they can cause damage to both DNA strands in such a way that there is a 'double strand break', an event which is difficult for the cell to repair (see above). This may not be the true reason for the increased mutation efficiency but the observation that two hits have a very much larger chance of causing mutation is now well accepted. Recent work with alpha particles and cell cultures has confirmed this empirically [Miller *et al*, 1999].

Clearly, if the dose-squared region of the accepted risk model, as defined above is due to correlated double hits, then it follows that for these high ionisation density exposures the response should be proportional to the square of the dose. It also follows that internal exposures like this cannot be subsumed within the external risk model without a weighting for this effect. Indeed, it may be that the true dose response is a polynomial, in which case, triple correlated events carry a cubed hazard weighting and so on.

So how likely are these two-hit processes to occur following external irradiation? For a dose of 1mSv of 0.6 MeV external irradiation, the probability of producing two hits in a specified cell within the period of 12 hours, which associated with cell repair and replication, has been calculated to be between 1x10-4 per year - assuming a mathematical model for close packing of 1μ diameter cells and 5 x 10-6 per year if an experimentally determined i.e 'real' packing fraction (based upon Leblond, 1981) is used. In other words, the two hit process is very rare at normal background levels i.e. in the low dose range. However, the same is not true for the situations involving internal irradiation already described. The same three types of internal exposure that may lead to a high probability of Second Event processes also represent enhanced hazard due to two hit processes occurring within the period of the cell's ability to repair a single strand break.

The chemical affinity of isotopes for DNA

Different chemical elements have preferential affinity for different organs of the body and also different parts of the cell. The concentration of certain radioisotopes in organs through biochemical affinity is incorporated into the conventional risk model only through the organ weightings. Thus it is accepted that Iodine concentrates in the thyroid and that this represents a hazard in terms of thyroid cancer and other thyroid conditions. However, arguments from physico-chemical considerations of the interactions of internalised radioactive elements and biological tissue should also be applied to all isotopes, and extended to concentration effects at the molecular level, as well as the organ level. For example, Strontium has a particular affinity for the DNA phosphate backbone: indeed, Strontium Phosphate co-precipitation is a method of choice in genetic research for removing DNA from solution. Thus exposure to the isotopes Strontium-90 and Strontium-89 should result in decays within the DNA itself. This effect should also extend to isotopes of Barium, like the isotope Ba-140, which is a common environmental contaminant from nuclear processes and indeed to Uranium since the Uranate ion UO_2^{++} has tremendous affinity for DNA. From earlier considerations it is clear that a radioactive atom bound to DNA should produce a far larger dose to the DNA when it decays than an atom bound to some other protein constituent of the cell. Strontium and Barium isotopes, on this basis, should represent particular hazards, quite apart from any effect to do with multiple decays.

It turns out that we can assess the relative enhancement due to DNA binding of a radioactive atom through examination of some Auger emitters, which either bind themselves to DNA or can be incorporated into the DNA by cunning experimentation. The enhancement of mutagenic risk from localisation of the DNA seems to be quite significant, of the order of between 10 and 50-fold.

Auger emitters

There is a type of radioactive decay that follows electronic rearrangements inside the electron shells of certain atoms that involve the release of a fast electron or a shower of such electrons all of relatively low energy. The effect is called the Auger effect and the electrons are Auger electrons. They cause much denser ionisation than the tracks of β- particles and for this reason are highly mutagenic or cytotoxic (cell killing) if the atoms that are decaying are close to or bound to DNA. There was a certain amount of interest in these substances in the 1990s since it was thought that they might be used for cancer radiotherapy and the most promising isotope was Iodine 125. At the time of this interest it was also noted that Auger emitters included some fairly widespread nuclear industry contaminants and concern was expressed that their enhanced hazard for mutation was not being conceded and modelled by the ICRP risk model. However, there were two sets of experiment that were of interest for the purposes of examining the effect of distribution of ionization tracks in the cell following exposure to radiation. The first type compared the Auger emitter Iodine-125 bound chemically to the DNA incorporation molecule Iodo-Deoxy Uridine (125-IUdR) with the β-emitter I-131 bound to the same molecule (131IUdR). Clonogenic survival was measured in Chinese Hamster V79 fibroblast cells in culture after being exposed to either of these substances at different concentrations. Results showed that the Auger emitter I-125UdR behaved like an α-emitter producing much greater cell killing at much smaller doses. At the lowest concentrations approaching 5mBq/cell, the enhancement of effect approached 100-fold or more. This showed that Auger emitters are very hazardous if they are bound to DNA. However, the DNA-bound β-emitter I-131 also had a significant effect, causing death in 50% of the cells at a cell concentration of 40mBq

Very small concentrations of Auger emitters consisting of metals which bound to DNA, e.g. Chromium-51, were shown to have a profound effect on the cell cycle. At 20mBq per cell, Cr-521 caused a doubling of the cell cycle time and reduction in the cell replication rate due to division delay. The Auger emitters seemed to have an RBE of from 5-7 for cell killing compared with X-rays (Baverstock and Charlton 1988).

The other type of experiment was one that compared the effects of decay of I-125 bound to the DNA through I-125UdR with I-125 bound to a protein that was fluorescent and could be seen to distribute the isotope throughout the cell, i.e. remote from the DNA. In these experiments, the dose for 37% survival was 1.25mBq per cell (DNA bound) versus 109mBq/cell (protein bound). The relative enhancement of the effect of localisation on the DNA was thus 87-fold (Kassis *et al* 1988).

These Auger experiments show conclusively that it is the location of the radioisotope in the cell, specifically its proximity or binding to the DNA or chromosome material that decides its radiological effect. New radioactive elements that bind to DNA, like Strontium or Barium are therefore likely to be orders of magnitude more mutagenic, and this is what is found, as I have written in *Wings of Death*.

I shall now summarise this account of the factors that affect the progression of a cell from initial radiation damage to cancer. This summary is laid out in Table 2.7.1

Table 2.7.1 The progression of radiation damage to cancer

Contributions	Factors
Increasing density of ionization	1. Radiation quality; α,β,γ 2. Auger emitters, weak decays e.g. Tritium 3. Electromagnetic field interactions.
Increasing track density in space	1. Increasing dose 2. Internal exposure from point source 3. Internal exposure from hot particle 4. Internal exposure from immobilised sequential decay 5. Concentration of ionic radionuclides at interfacial layers by adsorption 6. Concentration of radionuclides in organelles by biochemical affinity
Increasing track density in time	1. Internal exposure from point source 2. Internal exposure from hot particle 3. Internal exposure from immobilised sequential decay 4. Concentration of ionic radionuclides at interfacial layers by adsorption 5. Concentration of radionuclides in organelles by biochemical affinity
Increased replication rate of cell	1. Cell type 2. Prior exposure/prior damage 3. Electromagnetic field 4. Growth rate of individual (e.g. children) 5. Concentration of replication promoters including radiation
Position in cell cycle	1. Prior exposure/prior damage 2. Electromagnetic field
Decreased repair efficiency	1. Genetic identity 2. Prior exposure/prior damage 3. Antioxidant status/repair enzyme status 4. Concentration of repair system poisons
Decreased immune surveillance	Various, including prior exposure
Decreased replication inhibitory field	1. High local doses 2. Hot particles

First, it is clear from all the research that it is not *organ dose*, but the level of *ionisation density* on or close to the cell DNA that defines the risk of mutation up to the point where the ionisation density is so great that the cell is just killed. So the risk of mutation, and hence cancer cannot, from this consideration alone, be linear with even ionisation density, let alone dose. Thus internal radionuclides which bind to DNA must be more hazardous than ones that do not. Second, there are various ways in which internal radioactive decays can provide multiple tracks to the same nuclear genetic material, both at the same time, or sequentially in time. Hot particles, warm particles, immobilised sequential (second event) emitters, interfacial adsorption, biochemical affinity for DNA, all are overlooked by the conventional model, even though calculations and measurements suggest very large enhancements of ionisation density of the DNA are involved. Then there are considerations of cell type and the point in the cell cycle that the cell is at the time of exposure: this also, as we have seen, is critical to the efficiency of mutagenesis. The replication rate of the cell can be affected by external stimuli, including both prior non-radiation exposures and prior radiation exposures. A look at Table 2.6.1 should demonstrate to any biologist that the physics based approximations used to protect the public are totally unreal. They were developed by people who believed they could model living systems as if they were stretched wires upon which weights were hung. The force causes the stretching of the wire, until the elastic limit is reached; stress is proportional to strain and so forth. What were these people thinking of? Any self respecting biologist, biochemist or physical chemist should be able to think of other ways in which the ionisation density at the DNA might be altered.

Then of course, there are various ways in which radiation action subsequent to early exposures may be affected by the earlier exposures. This is not always intuitive. For example, the most recent data from the Chernobyl exclusion zone looking at small mammals shows that 22 generations after the initial exposure these animals are more, not less radiosensitive than controls.

The ECRR have made a preliminary assessment of the enhancement factors needed to multiply the conventional doses by in the cases where internal radionuclides are in any of the categories listed in Table 2.7.1 and this work is continuing.

Finally, before completing this account with some very new research findings and their significance, I will briefly address some other classes of phenomena that have been overlooked by the radiation risk establishment.

Transmutation

A mechanism that is entirely absent from the risk model of the ICRP, results from the effect of the radioactive decay process changing one atom into another. There are three common radioisotopic pollutants where this effect is likely to have serious consequences: Carbon-14, Tritium and Sulphur-35. All three are major components of enzyme systems and critical to the processes which are fundamental to living systems. The macromolecules, which are the operators of living systems—proteins, enzymes, DNA and RNA— depend upon their tertiary structure, or overall three dimensional shape, for their activity and biological integrity. Alteration of this shape results in inactivity of the macromolecule. This inactivation could in principle be effected by the sudden transmutation or alteration of one atom in the macromolecule. Since the molecular weight of these macromolecules is usually greater than 100,000 it is clear that incorporation of one atom (of e.g. C-14 which decays to Nitrogen) may result in an enhancement of effect of many thousand-fold. The isotope Tritium is a form of hydrogen and the biochemical processes in living systems depend on the weak bonds called Hydrogen Bonds which bridge and support all enzyme systems and hold together the DNA helix. The sudden decay of such a Tritium atom to Helium (which is inert and does not support chemical bonds) may have a catastrophic effect on the activity and normal processing of such macromolecules. Hydrogen bonded in these systems is easily exchangeable and will exchange under equilibrium conditions with Tritium Oxide, or tritiated water, the normal form of this isotope in the environment. There is also some evidence that Tritium may be preferentially taken up in some systems. This needs to be confirmed by further research. Sulphur is also an important component in macromolecular proteins, forming disulphide bridges, which support tertiary structures.

Genomic instability and cell communication fields

Although the evidence that ties cancer to genetic mutation has been overwhelming, there has always been a problem with quantities. As we have seen, cancer is a consequence of the acquisition of a number of specific mutations in genes, all of which are necessary before clinical expression occurs. If there are three to six specific mutations needed to result in cancer, it is possible to get some idea of the level of probability required for this to happen. A number of the specific events have been identified in the case of colon cancer and in this case they have been identified with increasing levels of malignant change [Vogelstein and Kinzler 1993]. The puzzle is, how a single cell line can accumulate this number of specific mutations within the lifetime of the individual if each of these mutations arise at the normal background rate of 1×10^{-5}.

However, in the last ten years, a new phenomenon has been discovered which may explain how the necessary number of mutations can be acquired. It turns out that if a cell is damaged by radiation even if such damage does not show, there is some factor induced in the cell and its descendants that predispose them to general mutation increases, which may be manifested as chromosome aberrations or other more invisible damage. The process is termed 'genomic instability'. And this is not all. It also turns out that it is not only the primary cell that is hit that manifests the genomic instability, but also about one third of all the cells within a vicinity of a radius of about 400 cell diameters which also exhibit this phenomenon. This is called the 'bystander effect'.

Thus radiation induces a process of genomic instability in individual cells that is transmitted to their progeny and this leads to a persistent enhancement of the rate at which genetic changes arise in the descendants of the irradiated cells, that is cells that, themselves, have had no direct exposure. Radiation therefore increases the frequency at which genetic changes arise spontaneously in the cell population arising from the irradiated cell and also cells which are nearby and have not themselves received any direct hit. The instability appears to occur in about 30% of the irradiated population and 30% of the cells nearby. Thus the original genetic theory of cancer stages, which involved specific cell lines acquiring initial, second and third specific mutations (and which was difficult to square with the known spontaneous mutation rate) has to be modified. The original model and its modification are shown in Table 2.7.2. In this table I have included a second speculative consideration of the progression to cancer. This follows an interesting argument by Sonnenschein and Soto relating to cell proliferation fields.

Their theories of cancer expression [Sonnenschein and Soto, 1999] address the finding that transplanted cancer cells do not grow in non-cancerous tissue whilst normal cells transplanted into cancerous tissue become cancerous. These researchers propose the existence of a cell communication field effect that requires a certain threshold number of genetically damaged cells to occur before cancer can develop. The arguments are based on the theory that the default state for cells in metazoa is, like metaphyta, proliferation: it follows that there has to be a permanent inhibitory signal. Sonnenschein and Soto assume that this involves various components of cell-cell communication collectively termed a 'field'. If this is found to be generally so, then the effects of high local doses, as occur in the region near hot particles, may be particularly effective in causing cancer, since the damaged cells are all close to one another. The discovery of the bystander effect is almost evidence that such fields do exist. In the bystander effect, genomic instability is found to occur in cells which are close to the cell which is traversed by a radiation track but which do not themselves receive any direct track traversals. It would seem therefore that the final stage in cancer expression involves the breakdown of such an inhibitory process. In turn, this has very important implications for the effects of high local dose from internal particles since such exposures, carrying on in time in the same place in the tissue, would persistently cause genomic instability in a large volume of cells surrounding the cell that acquires the cancerous transformation genome.

Photoelectron amplification of natural background

This is a speculative idea that I have been working on since I began writing this book. If it is a real effect then it is an important consideration for radiation and health. I presented the idea to a conference in Oxford in 2004 and published two papers presenting the theory in 2005 (see Busby 2005): so it is quite new. For completeness, I will just outline it here, and will return to the issue in Chapter 17 where I examine the effects of exposure to Uranium in this context.

Everyone is bathed in natural background gamma rays: the dose is about 1mSv a year, or roughly 100nSv/hour. We know that all matter absorbs gamma radiation in proportion to the fourth power of the atomic number of the elements in the material concerned. The atomic number, Z, is the number of electrons in the element. Hydrogen has 1, Helium 2, Lithium 3 and so on. So gamma rays are absorbed by pure Helium 264 times more than Hydrogen. By the time that the atomic number gets large, e.g. for heavy elements like lead (Z = 82) and uranium (Z = 92), the absorption is very great. That is why lead is used to shield against X-rays in hospitals. Nowadays, uranium is also used and walls are made of uranium impregnated concrete.

When the gamma ray is absorbed, the energy is turned into a number of processes, but finally these all amount to the production of energetic fast electrons called photoelectrons. These are identical to beta particles and Auger electrons. They cause ionisation in exactly the same way. So if elements of high atomic number are located inside the tissue they will absorb gamma rays and turn them into photoelectrons much more efficiently that the elements of low atomic number that make up all living systems. The highest atomic number element that is used in a living system is Calcium (Z = 20) This is a major component of DNA. If it is replaced by Uranium (Z=92) the resulting increase in absorption of gamma rays due to the 4th power law is about 500 times. And Uranium binds strongly to DNA. So we would expect Uranium to have an anomalously high radiation mutation effect. And it does. We would expect similar genotoxic effects if we bound any high Z element to DNA. And we do find this. The platinum anticancer drugs were designed to bind to DNA. Platinum has a high Z (= 78). The general effect will also be important for micron sized particles like those produced by Uranium weapons..

Table 2.7.2 Modification of a 2-mutation genetic theory of radiation carcinogenesis by new discoveries in genomic instability and bystander regulation effects.

Stage	Genetic mutation theory	Genomic instability modification
1	Single cell is hit and acquires initial specific mutation and replicates: daughters carry the cancer mutation. $P = 10^{-6}$	Single cell is hit and it and a proportion of local cells acquire genomic instability and replicate. All daughters have genomic instability.
2	One of the line with the cancer (1) mutation acquires the cancer (2) mutation. $P = 10^{-12}$ x N where there are N cells in the daughter line with cancer (1) mutation.	One of the large number of genomically unstable progeny randomly acquires the cancer (1) mutation and replicates: daughter carries the cancer (1) mutation
3		One of the cancer (1) cell line acquires the cancer (2) mutation. $P = 10^{-6}$ x N where there are N cells in the daughter line with (1) mutation
4	Cell field surveillance breakdown. Unlikely if all local cells are untransformed.	Cell field surveillance breakdown likely since vicinity of transformed cell has other cells with scrambled genome.
5	Cancer	Cancer

All these considerations arise from research which has occurred very recently and which is ongoing. They show that the process of cancer induction is essentially genetic, that radiation is the largest class of carcinogen and that cancer can follow the lowest dose. They also show that there is a fundamental difference between external and internal exposure, a matter that we return to in later discussions. They show that the dose response relationship cannot be linear, except over a small range. The close examination of the biological effects of radiation make it clear that the use of absorbed dose, energy per unit mass, as a quantitative estimator of radiation damage is only possible over a narrow range of external irradiation exposure. For internal exposure to novel isotopes that bind to DNA, like Strontium-90 or Uranium, to immobilised particles of Plutonium Oxide or Uranium Oxide, the use of 'absorbed dose' is meaningless, and is likely to underestimate the mutation and cancer effects by a large amount. This is why we have to turn to epidemiology to provide the answer to the questions about whether living near a nuclear site, or drinking contaminated water and milk, can result in death. Before leaving this area, I will briefly make a direct connection between these arcane considerations of the microscopic, molecular and genetic with a specific and rare cancer and also with the main example of my thesis, Sellafield.

2.8 Retinoblastoma

Although the disease is very rare, Retinoblastoma (RB) is the most common eye tumour in children. It is a disease that causes the growth of malignant tumours in the retinal cell layer of the eye and is the third most common cancer overall in children below the age of 5. The frequency of RB has increased in the last 50 years, in line with the increase in nuclear pollution, and now has a base rate of about 3 per 100,000 in infants in England and Wales. Untreated, the disease is fatal. The child's eye has to be removed before the tumour invades adjoining tissue. This disease has been studied intensively and much is known about its genetic basis. It is present in the human population in sporadic and familial forms. The sporadic form is rare and occurs in about 1 in 20,000 children. Cancer results from the lack of a functional copy of the retinoblastoma (Rb) gene. This suppressor gene inhibits formation of cancer. In familial retinoblastoma one normal and one mutated Rb gene are inherited. Subsequent mutation in any retinal cell inactivates the remaining normal Rb gene leading to loss of growth control and a tumour clone. In sporadic retinoblastoma, two normal Rb genes are inherited. First a mutation inactivates one copy and then a second mutation inactivates the other copy, leading to the cancer. These processes were proposed by Knudsen as early as 1971 [Knudsen AG, 1971) and by the early 1980s the gene was located on chromosome 13 and has now been cloned and sequenced. The Rb gene has now been implicated in several other cancers indicating that it plays a generalised role in growth suppression in a variety of tissues. Children who are cured of retinoblastoma are at increased risk of bone cancer, lung cancer and breast cancer in later life.

So here we have an identification of a specific gene that in mutation or loss causes a specific cancer and increases risk of other cancers. Now let us look at radiation and the Sellafield connection. The village of Seascale near the Sellafield reprocessing plant is famous for its long standing childhood leukaemia cluster, the starting point for much of my research, and the contents of this book. What is less well known is that the risk of all cancers in children is also elevated. The increased risk is persisting and the cancers are mainly leukaemia and non-Hodgkin lymphoma. No cases of retinoblastoma have been found in Seascale itself but at least five cases have occurred in children whose mothers had lived there at some time from 1950 onwards [Morris.1993]. The maternal grandmothers of three of these children had worked at Sellafield. Three further cases have occurred among children born in Copeland, the county district that contains both Seascale and Sellafield, but whose mothers had never lived in Seascale; the father of one and the paternal grandfather of the other had worked at Sellafield. The observed incidence in children of mothers who lived in Seascale is about twenty times that which is expected. As I will relate, there is also apparently a high level of retinoblastoma in North Wales, where the radioactivity from Sellafield adds to the fallout from Chernobyl. This epidemiological evidence completes the circle of causality. The origin of the disease is identified in a genetic mutation, either inherited or acquired. The genetic mutation is known and identified: it can be caused by radiation. The rate of the disease in the vicinity of the largest source of radiation exposure in the UK is twenty times the value expected by chance alone. As in the case of the leukaemia, the retinoblastomas were caused by radiation exposure to internal radioisotopes from the Sellafield plant. It is now time to take a closer look at this factory of death.

3
Sellafield and the Irish Sea

The sea has always been regarded by coastal and seafaring peoples as the ideal place for dumping their waste and this is, of course, a very reasonable and proper attitude. Almost everything that is put into the sea is either diluted to insignificant concentrations or broken down by physical and biological action or stored harmlessly on the sea bed. Most of the objects that do ultimately find their way to the shore are harmless and are a considerable source of pleasure to children.

Mr H.J Dunster, United Kingdom Atomic Energy Authority,
(Proceedings of the International Conference
on the Peaceful Uses of Atomic Energy, Geneva 1958)

It is hard to imagine how the phenomenon of Sellafield came to be an accepted part of life on Earth. In my mind's eye, I see some alien sociologists, studying our history and trying to piece together the origins of the place, and the mind-states of those who developed the technology, studied the effects of the materials being used and then permitted the operation. They would probably fail, as I have, and as Marylyn Robinson, the American novelist has, in her work *Mother Country*, which I strongly recommend. She has come close in that book to an understanding of part of the reason how it has been countenanced. She sees Sellafield, and its cavalier daily release of poison to the Irish Sea, to the people who live nearby and to the planet and its unsuspecting inhabitants, as an extension of the male-dominated class culture of England. To her, the separation of the poor from the human race by the rich, which occurs in England's vertical class structure, is a separation of humanity and rights, similar, perhaps, to the separation in Germany during the Third Reich of the Jews, Slavs and other *untermenschen*. Therefore it is a simple matter, when you need atom bombs to secure your power and wealth, to place the poison factory as far away as possible from where you live so that the harm is only to the poor people, fisherfolk, farmers and their families, who were unfortunate enough to live in such a marginal area. Of course, I now learn that this is exactly what happened. The original death factory was just south of Oxford at Harwell: this is where the research into the radiation and bombs began in the war years. At that time, the radioactive waste went into the Thames at Sutton Courtenay (as some still does: see Plate 32). But when the quantities of radioactivity began to rise in London drinking water, the public health officials began to complain. Although they were fobbed off or diverted (evidence released under the 30 year rule) the great and the good began to feel uneasy at the prospect of having to drink the Tritium and eat Plutonium with their dinner.

The first suggestion was for building a (very long) pipe to send the waste to the Bristol Channel, but the physical pressures in the pipe would have to be very high to pump it over the hills: it might explode and spray radioactivity over the stockbrokers. Can't have that. Then someone at the Club suggested Trawsfynydd Lake in Wales. Build the factory there and tip the poison in the lake: why not? Only sheep and Welsh people live there. However, luckily for the Welsh (although the plan was not forgotten: a nuclear power station was sited there later in 1966), the quantities of material involved were very large and at the time of the decision, the British Nylon Spinners plant at Windscale (a jolly remote place) became available. This began the nightmare for the people of Cumbria, and the coastal populations of Wales, Ireland, Lancashire, the Solway Firth and eventually everyone in the UK, even the inhabitants of the East coast of England, facing the North Sea, and the people living in Scandinavia.

As we shall see later, the material released by Sellafield since the start of operations in 1952, has caused the deaths of countless numbers of people. Instead of remaining politely in the Irish Sea, it has been thrown back on the land, as the soldiers of the sea might throw back a smoking grenade. Plutonium from Sellafield has drifted over the British Isles and Ireland in the sea-spray, an evil invisible mist carrying illness and death, penetrating all living creatures, to be found in the dust from Barmouth in Gwynedd to Bexleyheath in Kent. I will outline the evidence for this and the mechanisms, but first let us take a look at the place.

3.1 Radioactive discharges from Sellafield into the Irish Sea

The nuclear reprocessing facility at Sellafield, formerly Windscale, in West Cumbria has operated since 1952, extracting plutonium from spent nuclear fuel and discharging radioactive waste. In the period 1952-95, 1.35PBq of alpha and 115 PBq of beta-emitting man-made radioisotopes have been reportedly discharged into the Irish Sea. A peta-Bequerel (PBq) is a very large number. It is a one followed by 15 noughts or a thousand thousand thousand million. How about that? That is disintegrations per second. The trend in releases over the period relevant to this study is given in Figure 3.1.1

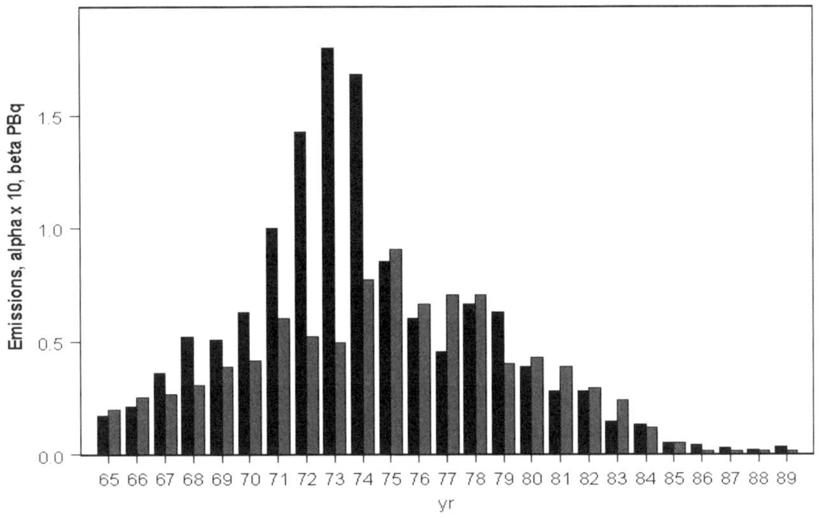

Figure 3.1.1 Trend in releases of alpha and beta emitting radioisotopes to the Irish Sea from Sellafield (PBq).
(Data source: MAFF, CEGB, FoE 1993)

In the early days of its operation the issue of pollution from the Windscale plant was raised as a cause of concern. Most of the poison ends up in the sea, either directly from the pipeline, or following washout from the atmosphere and runoff into rivers and streams. Most finds its way to the sea eventually. The justification for releasing liquid radioactive waste into the Irish Sea was that the sea would provide an infinite dilution and dispersion route for radioactive waste, as Dunster argued in 1958. Since that time, a huge body of evidence has accumulated that clearly demonstrates that a considerable quantity of long-lived man-made radioisotopes has come ashore and is contaminating beaches, estuaries, sea, air and water. The stuff is picked up from the contaminated mud by wave action and pitched into the air. Particles of various sizes, mostly too small to be visible, but seriously radioactive, are dispersed over enormous distances. The most studied of these isotopes is Plutonium-239, an alpha emitter with a half-life of 24,000 years, but many other fission products and reprocessing isotopes contaminate the Irish Sea and the littoral. The plutonium contamination exists as micron and sub-micron-diameter oxide particles, PuO_2. This material is glassy, virtually insoluble, and as a speck of dust, a mote in a sunbeam, is both microscopic, invisible and infinitely mobile. In addition, huge quantities of Uranium isotopes have been thrown into the Irish Sea. Uranium is not measured or, if it is, it is rarely reported. It is considered to be 'natural' though the concentration and type of particle is far from natural. Other poisons like the alpha emitter Americium-241 and the beta emitters, Caesium-137 and Strontium-90 float about and are washed up. The list of horrible substances is very large and each isotope has their own biophysical or biochemical characteristic, concentrating in particular tissue or dispersing in the environment through different specific mechanisms.

Radioisotopes from Sellafield may be distinguished from radioisotopes from other sources by measuring isotopic ratios using various sophisticated techniques. The technology for these measurements is now so awesome that we are able to measure vanishingly small amounts. For example, I am a member of the UK Ministry of Defence Depleted Uranium Board where we are engaged in arranging measurements of Uranium Isotopes in the urine of Persian Gulf War veterans at concentrations of a few nanograms (one thousand millionth of a gram) per litre.

Measurements of Plutonium 239 and Caesium-137 made in Wales after the Chernobyl contamination of the Welsh uplands showed that most of the radiation in silt in estuaries and along the coast had the characteristic fingerprint of Sellafield. It was only at the inland head of estuaries that the situation reversed and Chernobyl isotope ratios were observed (Assinder *et al.,* 1994). After the material was released from the outfall pipe at Sellafield it moved away and became dispersed through the Irish Sea and further afield by various mechanisms depending on the reactivity, chemical identity or physical form of the specific substance. The material in the silt in Cumbria has been moving slowly across the Irish Sea to Ireland. The finer particles of silt pick up the plutonium and other isotopes and swirl around the Irish Sea by tidal action to be precipitated in areas where the tidal energy is low, like bays and river estuaries and tidal slacks. Contamination resulting from releases from Sellafield could be found on the coast of North Wales, at the MAFF measuring point of Cemlyn Bay on the Isle of Anglesey about one year after their releases (see Figure 3.1.2)

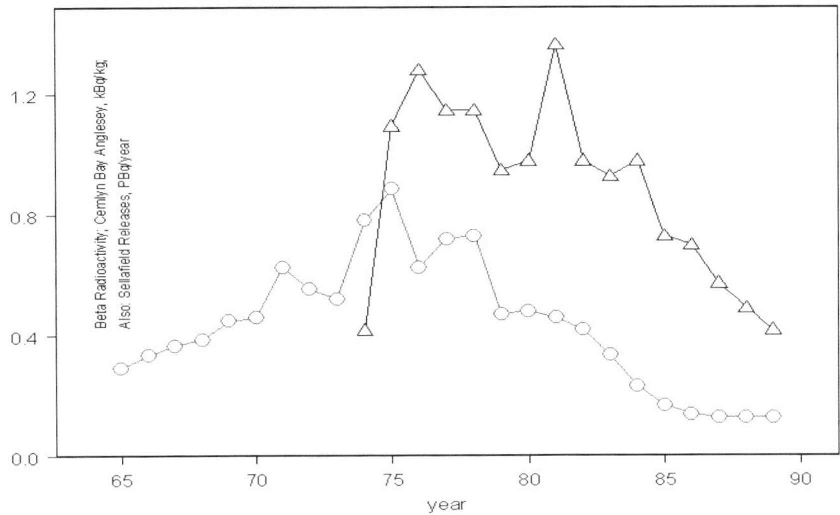

Figure 3.1.2. Trend in Caesium-137 in silt in Cemlyn Bay, North Wales (circles) and trend in total beta emissions to Irish Sea (mainly Cs-137) from Sellafield (squares) (*Source: MAFF).*

By the mid 1980s Plutonium from Sellafield was being mapped by scientists from Harwell to parts of England and Wales more than 150 miles from the Irish Sea as I show in Fig 3.1.3. (Cawse and Horrill, 1986). Since this first grassland survey of plutonium, a number of other researchers have discovered that the concentrations in soil and grass in middle England have been mysteriously increasing. For example, in the late 1990s, there were public concerns about increases in child leukaemia rates in the districts of Newbury and Reading in Berkshire and South Oxfordshire. These are the County Districts containing the Atomic Energy Research Establishment site at Harwell and the Atomic Weapons Establishment sites at Aldermaston and Burghfield. All these sites release radioisotopes, including plutonium, to the environment. In addition, there was concern about an atomic bomb fire, which had apparently occurred at the USAF Greenham Common airbase in 1959. I discovered that County Districts containing these nuclear sites had the highest leukaemia mortality rates for children and, with Molly, had written this up in a research note for the *British Medical Journal* in 1997. (Busby and Scott Cato, 1997). Newbury Council responded by funding a £300,000 study of Uranium and Plutonium in the vicinity of the Greenham Airbase, and this was undertaken jointly by the Scottish Universities Research Reactor Centre (SURRC) and the

Southampton Oceanographic Centre. The measurements showed a significantly large increase in the concentrations of Plutonium from those given by the 1986 Cawse and Horrill report from Harwell. Whilst the latter showed levels of about 0.02-0.07 Bequerels per kilogram, Dr Ian Croudace at Southampton was finding more than 100-times this, between 0.5 and 10 Bq/kg in samples some considerable distance from Aldermaston. Croudace has been unable to square his high readings with the earlier Cawse and Horrill readings, although he has tried hard in his reports to imply that the plutonium he found is from weapons fallout, the other possible source.

The Atomic Weapons Establishment at Aldermaston measures radioactivity and its annual reports list unusually high levels in dust collected on filters placed as far away as Basingstoke and Reading. Routine measurements of dust in filters near to and remote from the Aldermaston site in West Berkshire show that alpha activity in some dusts is as high as 2500Bq/kg and beta activity as high as 60,000 Bq/ kg. (AWE, 1992, 1993, 1994, 1995). These levels exceed the threshold level of 400Bq/kg defining low-level radioactive waste under the Radioactive Substances Act 1993.

By the mid 1990s, Plutonium was being found in children's teeth over the whole of the United Kingdom (Figure 3.1.4) (Priest *et al.*, 1997). I came across this research when, in 1998, I had begun the research in support of an Irish court case against British Nuclear Fuels begun by four people living in Dundalk, County Louth. We were attempting to discover what effect, if any, Irish Sea contamination might be having on health. To look at correlations with cancer effects in Ireland or Wales we needed to examine relative concentrations of radioisotopes on the coast, look at routes of exposure and ask certain questions. Having read the paper by Nick Priest et al., one question was, how did plutonium from Sellafield become incorporated into children's teeth from parts of England and Wales over 200 miles distant from the plant and in a pattern that appears to vary monotonically with distance? This led to other questions. Where in the Irish Sea were the highest levels found? Was there any evidence that might cast light on the route from Sellafield to the children's teeth? It turned out that answers to all of these questions existed and had been ignored or actively suppressed by the UK radiation risk establishment. Indeed, in the course of the Irish Sea research, I accidentally learned that the UK Department of Health were themselves worried and had jointly, with BNFL, funded the scientist, Nick Priest, who discovered the trend in plutonium in children's teeth, to carry out a larger and more searching enquiry into the source of the plutonium. This was to be a confidential study to establish for certain that the plutonium isotope ratios pointed unequivocally to Sellafield as the source. But I will now turn to the question of how the plutonium came to be in the teeth.

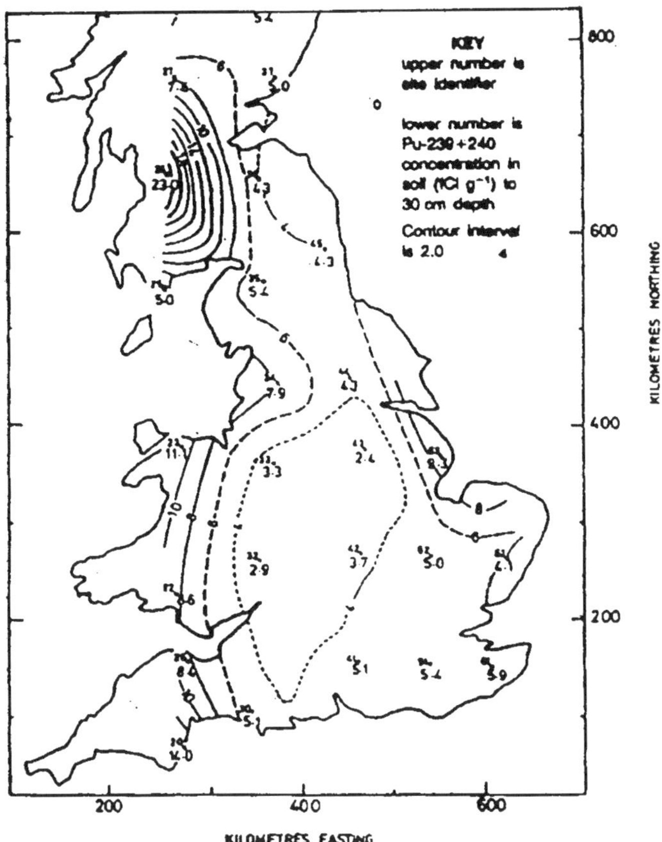

Figure 3.1.3. Plutonium in grassland and soil over England and Wales, 1977 (*Source:* Cawse and Horrill, 1986)

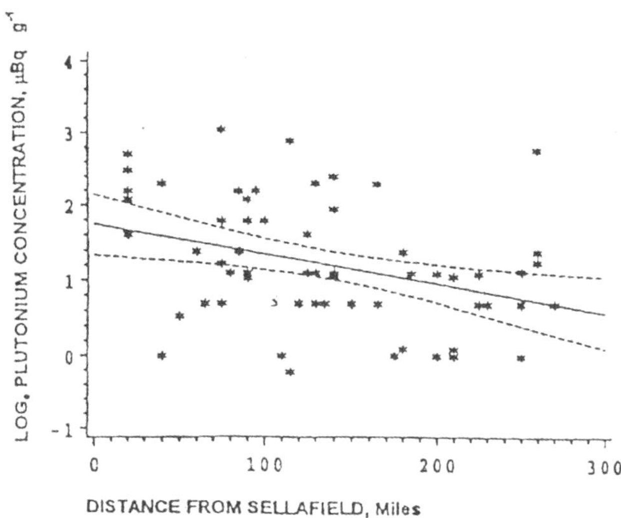

Figure 3.1.4. Concentration of Plutonium in children's teeth by distance from Sellafield in the whole of the United Kingdom (*Source*: Priest *et al.*, 1997)

3.2 Routes of contamination and levels of exposure

First it is worth getting the amounts of radioactivity released by Sellafield in perspective. There is an enormous amount of radiation involved. For example, the largest injection of radioactive pollution into the global environment has been from atmospheric weapons tests which occurred in the post war period and which culminated in massive megaton bomb tests in the period 1959-1963 when Kennedy and Kruschev signed the Test Ban Treaty. If we are looking for radiation effects in cancer and other diseases then this was the primary source prior to 1970 and it is this that represents the main cause of the present cancer epidemic, as I argued in *Wings of Death.* Despite the overall large quantities of the bomb test fallout, in terms of concentration in the Irish Sea they were dwarfed by the releases from Sellafield. In Table 3.2.1 I compare the alpha emitters Plutonium and Americium-241 from bomb fallout deposition per unit area with the releases of the same isotopes from Sellafield, which I have diluted uniformly into the Irish Sea. As far as the people living near the Irish Sea are concerned, the reprocessing waste is more than 50 times greater. In terms of all the plutonium released to the world, Sellafield is in a class of its own. All the weapons fallout plutonium to the entire planet Earth has been about 11 PBq (11×10^{15} Bq). Sellafield has released about one eighth of all this Plutonium to what is effectively a small shallow pond, surrounded by people living in coastal towns and villages.

Table 3.2.1 Plutonium 239+240 and Americium-241 (alpha emitters) released into the Irish sea from Sellafield up to 1990 and 1999 compared with total weapons fallout deposition in the UK

Area (sq.m x 10^{-9}); source	**Total deposited up to 1990 (TBq)**
UK (244); fallout	20.2
Irish Sea (57); Sellafield	1350-2250

*Based on 83Bq/m² Pu239+240 plus Am-241 given in UNSCEAR 1993 and *estimates from Green et al 1993 and Kershaw et al. 1999*

The highest concentrations of pollution are, of course, found very near Sellafield itself. However, the fall-off in concentration with distance by sea does not follow the inverse-square-law pattern expected, or any pattern that might have been predicted. Although there are many complexities, in general, it turns out that the radioisotopes attach themselves to fine silt particles by a process known as adsorption, and it is the movement and re-distribution of these fine silt particles by the water circulation in the Irish Sea that determines the coastal distribution of radiation in mud, silt and sand. (Assinder, 1983, Assinder *et al.,* 1994, 1997; Hamilton, 1998).

Professor Murdo Baxter directed the 1989 Department of the Environment and Scottish Universities joint study of the redistribution of Sellafield radioactivity in the Irish Sea (Baxter, 1989). This report to the DoE concludes:

On the Irish Sea bed, artificial nuclide concentrations are variable primarily as a function only of sediment type or grain size rather than distance from source. This may explain the common finding that levels of radioactivity in inter-tidal regions are highest in areas of low tidal flow or water movement, so-called low-energy zones. These include harbours, tidal inlets and estuaries. The reason is that slack water conditions permit the fine particles to precipitate, and these fine particles are brought up river estuaries where their concentrations are highest at the inland end of the estuary (Assinder *et al.,* 1994, 1997). In addition to this, hot spots, small areas of inter-tidal mud where radiation detectors begin to chatter, have been found on the coast of Ireland, north Wales and in the Cumbria, Lancashire and Solway regions (FoE, 1993). Janine Allis Smith, who operates the Cumbrians Opposed to a Radioactive Environment, CORE tells me of a Japanese scientist who had been to the Chernobyl exclusion zone to study radiation effects and had visited her. It seems he went for a walk along the coast with a Geiger counter and was astonished at the levels of radioactivity, which he said were comparable to the Chernobyl areas he had visited.

Concentrations of isotopes in sediment and marine biological samples from fish and crustacean to seaweeds have been measured since the 1970s by the Ministry of Agriculture, Fisheries and Food (MAFF), now CEFAS. In Ireland, the Radiological Protection Institute (RPII) measure radionuclide concentrations from time to time and make reports. In Wales, there are results available that suggest that the concentrations of Sellafield isotopes in silt are about twice as high on the north coast as on the west coast, although concentrations in the river estuaries are comparable (Garland *et al.*, 1989). All the studies and data support Murdo Baxter's conclusions about particle size and also suggest that on the East coast of Ireland, river estuaries like the Boyne at Drogheda, and the muddy inlets at Dundalk Bay and Carlingford Lough where there are slack tide or low energy conditions are similarly contaminated. Measurements are also made by MAFF in Northern Ireland showing that in Carlingford Lough and Oldmill Bay levels of plutonium 239+240 are comparable with those in North Wales, and for the same reason. The reason for this distribution is, as Murdo Baxter stated, due to the tidal energy conditions at the places where the isotopes accumulate. Therefore; it is of some interest to examine the general circulation of the Irish Sea, and in particular its tides.

3.3 Circulation in the Irish Sea

Measurement of the concentration of Caesium-137 in filtered water in the Irish Sea has enabled MAFF to draw maps that show the relative levels of this isotope. Such a map for the year 1989 confirms that there was appreciable transfer of material to the coast of north Wales and Ireland (Figure 3.3.1). It should be borne in mind that this map does not indicate the relative concentration of nuclides in silt, but merely acts as an indication of the general circulation involved. Although there are limited numbers of measurements available that indicate the levels of isotopes in silt on the coast of Wales and Ireland, MAFF have measured Caesium-137 and Plutonium 239 + 240 in Carlingford Lough in Northern Ireland and also Cemlyn Bay on the northern tip of the Isle of Anglesey in North Wales since 1988. Cemlyn Bay sediments are almost exclusively from Sellafield and readings of Caesium-137 at Cemlyn Bay were made back to 1970. The trends in Caesium and Plutonium isotopes roughly correlate and so it may be reasonable, to a first approximation, to use Caesium in silt as an indicator for all isotopes, including Plutonium-239 + 240 in silt.

Table 3.3.1 shows the trends in silt concentrations in Carlingford Lough, Ireland after 1988 and in Cemlyn Bay, north Wales, over most of the period of the major releases. Also shown is the concentration for some years of the isotope Americium-241, which acts as a marker for the isotope Plutonium-241 and may indicate the approximate amount of Plutonium 239 in those years when no measurements were made.

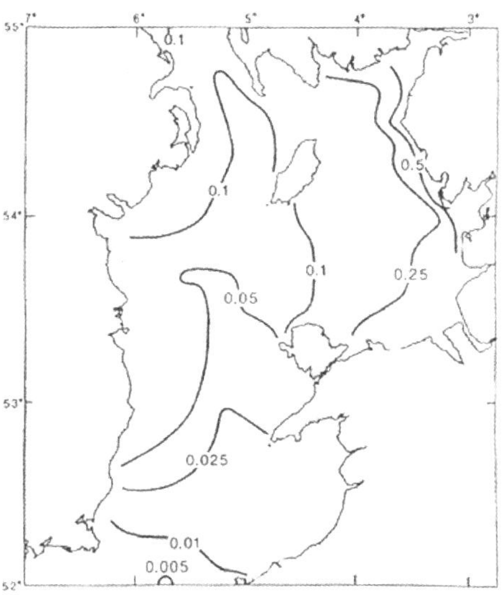

Figure 3.3.1 Caesium-137 in filtered seawater in the Irish Sea, 1989 (Source: MAFF).

Examination of results of these surveys indicates that the distribution of Sellafield isotopes on the coasts of the Irish Sea lag the discharge by about a year and depend upon particle size and upon the tidal flow rates or energy of the sea conditions at the point of interest. The tidal circulation is of great importance for the coast of the Irish Republic, since it turns out that there is a very large and continually maintained area of slack water off the north-eastern coast, from Dundalk Bay to Carlingford. This is the place where the south-going, anti-clockwise tidal stream meets the north-going, clockwise stream and this results in a very large area where fine silt and mud precipitates out. It is where fine silt particles containing large quantities of radionuclides can precipitate, and measurements made by The Radiological Protection Institute of Ireland (RPII) show that this process does indeed occur. These muddy, silty areas extend into Dundalk Bay where there are large offshore drying mud-flats (see Plate3) and silty mud comes up the river Boyne and Carlingford Lough with the tide (Plate 10). Admiralty tidal stream maps show that there is always slack water, with no tidal flow off the north-eastern coast of the Irish Republic (Admiralty Hydrographic Office, 1992) and I show such a map in Fig 3.3.2

Table 3.3.1 Trends in concentration of Sellafield isotopes in mud: North Wales (Cemlyn) and Carlingford Lough, Ireland, (Bq/kg)

Year	Carlingford Cs-137	Carlingford Pu-239+240	Cemlyn Bay Cs-137	Cemlyn Bay Pu 239 +240	Cemlyn Bay Am-241
1970					
1971	-	-	207	Not listed	-
1972-3	-	-	362	Not listed	-
1974	-	-	344	Not listed	-
1975	-	-	1150	Not listed	-
1976	-	-	1400	Not listed	-
1977	-	-	1200	42	-
1978	-	-	1200	44	-
1979	-	-	950	44	-
1980	-	-	1000	56	-
1981	-	-	1500	Not listed	92
1982	-	-	1000	Not listed	54
1983	-	-	930	78	88
1984	-	-	1000	84	88
1985	-	-	700	58	76
1986	-	-	670	47	58
1988	224	15	430	41	53
1989	240	15	350	39	52
1990	160	13	320	48	71
1991	170	16	250	39	54
1992	-	-	-	-	-
1993	180	14	270	39	55
1994	Not listed	13	220	30	46
1995	120	13	180	23	33
1996	110	14	150	22	31
1997	100	13	170	23	32

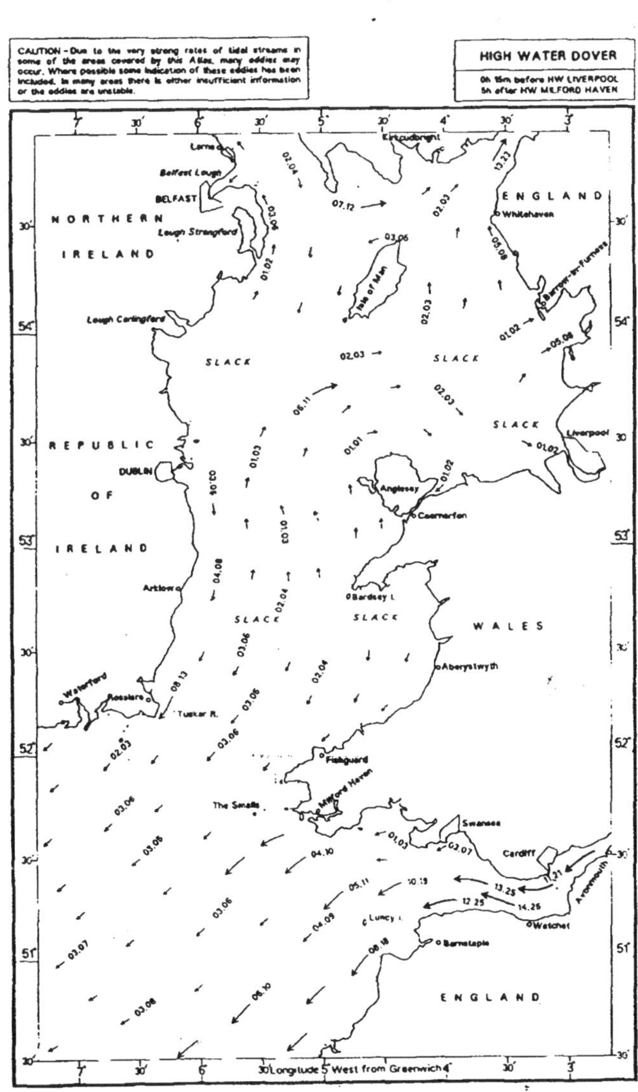

Fig 3.3.2. Admiralty tidal stream atlas picture of tidal flows at High Water Carlingford. There is slack water in Dundalk Bay (NE Ireland) at every state of the tide.

The behaviour of plutonium in silt in the Irish Sea over the last 20 years has recently been re-examined by Kershaw *et al.* (1999) and the results are unnerving. Fig.3.3.3 and 3.3.4 shows the slow movement of Plutonium 239 away from Sellafield and towards the shores of Ireland and Wales over the period 1978 to 1995. A wave of Plutonium-239, a fearfully toxic element with a half-life of 24,000 years, is moving slowly towards Ireland and Wales. By 1983 the 1kBq/m^2 isoline had reached the Welsh coast at Llandudno and the Irish coast at Warren Point. A dense band of Plutonium contamination released into the sea at Sellafield is creeping towards the shores of Wales and Ireland.

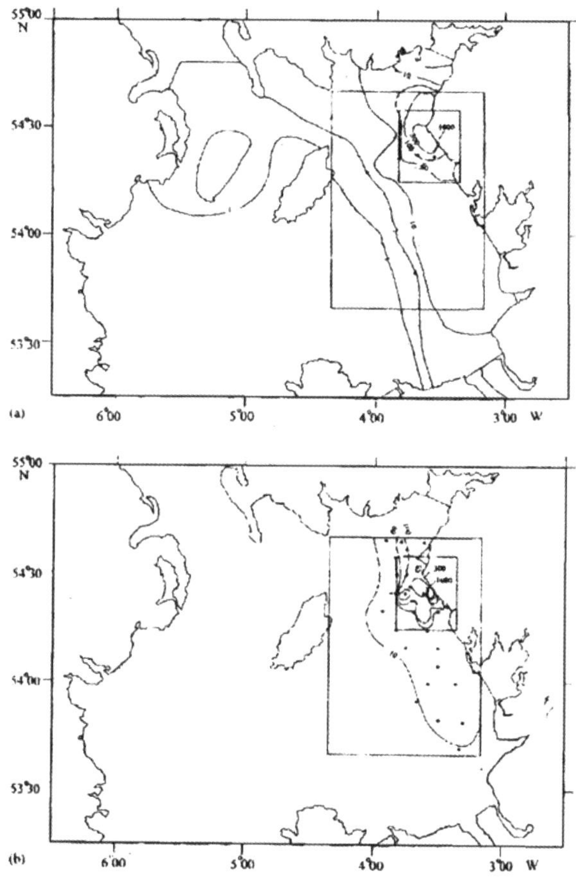

Fig 3.3.3 Movement of plutonium in sediment in the Irish Sea. (kBq/m^2 Upper, 1983 and lower 1978. (*Source:* Kershaw *et al.* 1999)

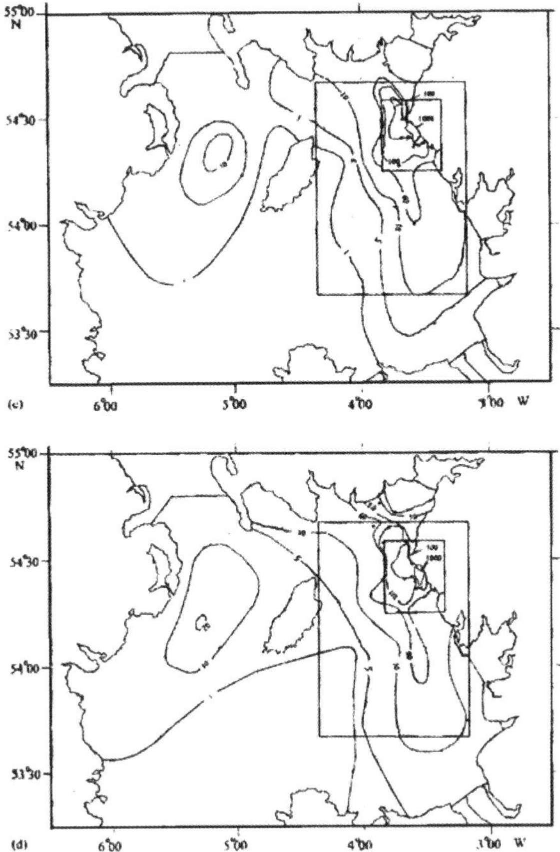

Fig 3.3.4 Movement of plutonium in sediment in the Irish sea. (kBq/m^2 Upper, 1988 and lower 1995. (*Source:* Kershaw *et al.* 1999)

In addition to the slow movement of Plutonium away from Sellafield, Kershaw *et al.* (1999) noticed something even more curious. The total inventory of Plutonium in the Irish Sea did not correspond to the amount released from Sellafield. In the words of Kershaw *et al.*:

A budget of Plutonium-alpha and 241-Americium has been estimated based on published observations in three main compartments: water column, sub-tidal and intertidal sediments. This amounts to . . . . 60-61% of the decay corrected reported discharge.

In other words, about 40% of the Plutonium and Americium had disappeared. Where had it gone? Perhaps we should look on the shore, inside people and their teeth. This seems to me to be the source of the increases in grassland plutonium in the Home Counties found by the Ian Croudace survey I referred to. But before we do this, because later I will describe the effects on cancer rates in Wales, we must look more closely at the shores of Wales.

3.4 Inter-tidal sediments in Wales

In Wales, measurements of radioisotopes in inter-tidal sediment were made by the Harwell team of Garland *et al.* in 1989. This report measured artificial radioactivity in coastal seawater, in sea spray, in beach sand and sediment. In the abstract the authors state:

The results show low but measurable concentrations of plutonium isotopes, Am-241 and Cs-137 in samples from the north coast. Concentrations were even lower in samples from the west and south coasts and many samples were below the detection limit. Sea-to-land transfer was seen in measurements of plutonium isotopes and Am-241 in sea spray, air, and in material deposited from the air close to the north coast. The results show that the radiation dose to the population due to the actinides and Cs-137 in the coastal environment is a small fraction of the recognised limit.

The report is an extensive one. For our purposes, its findings may be briefly summarised:

- Levels of plutonium-239+240 were greatest in intertidal sediment in the north of Wales.
- On the north coast of Wales, 80 per cent of the plutonium and other isotopes were in the coastal strip between the northern entrance to the Menai Strait and the town of Bangor, and Great Orme's Head and the town of Llandudno. The largest deposit was in the offshore drying bank known as the Lavan Sands, lying between the north-eastern entrance to the Menai Strait and the western entrance to the River Conway estuary.
- A moderate concentration of plutonium, about one fifth of the Lavan Sands concentration, existed over the whole of the northern coastal intertidal region from the north of Anglesey to the mouth of the Dee, taking in the towns and areas of Amlwch and Beaumaris on Anglesey and Colwyn Bay, Abergele, Rhyl and Prestatyn. The levels in the River Dee estuary (Mostyn Bank) were comparable with those on the Lavan Sands. The main area affected here is Flint and Holywell.

- South of Anglesey levels were lower and in Cardigan Bay levels were about one tenth of those on the north coast, except for estuaries of rivers like the Teifi and Dyfi, where the low tidal energy increases the levels in the silt.
- Sea-to-land transfer of plutonium occurred and the isotopes were measured in air, sea spray and on the ground in a pattern showing rapid fall-off in the first kilometre and at concentrations that correlated with the levels in the intertidal sediment.

Very large amounts were involved. For example, the quantity present in the Lavan Sands mud-bank represents about 100 times the inventory of the cooling water lake at Trawsfynydd nuclear power station, also in Wales. This lake was recently the subject of a study by the National Radiological Protection Board (Carey *et al.* 1996) in which they explicitly stated that to minimise health risks to the (small) local population the water levels should not be allowed to fall and expose the radioactive isotopes in the sediment. These isotopes are largely the same ones that exist in the Lavan Sands but at one hundredth the concentration and quantity. Yet the Lavan Sands, and indeed, the entire coast of north Wales, is uncovered on every tide and subject to the energy and power of the wind and waves. Living close by are large populations of moderate sized coastal towns and holiday resorts. Table 3.4.1 below gives levels of Plutonium and Americium-241 in samples measured by Garland *et al.* (1989), confirming that the plutonium does not fall off with distance from the source, but according to some other process. As far as coastal populations are concerned, however, there is a major source of risk. The material does not stay in the sediment: it comes ashore.

3.5 Sea-to-land transfer of radioisotopes

It has become apparent that the radioisotopes in silt and sand are associated with particles. This is particularly true of the alpha emitters. Thus exposure from inhalation of dust is not a molecular transfer, as eating a Caesium-contaminated fish might be, but involves the total transfer of what is effectively a tiny radioactive hot particle from the environment to the inside of the person exposed. As I pointed out in an earlier section, such a particle may deliver a very high dose to adjacent tissue. Alpha emitters are notoriously difficult to measure. This is because the range in air of an alpha particle is a few centimetres. A Geiger counter is therefore useless because the particles do not penetrate the window glass even if the detector is placed next to the source. We have to use scintillation counters, devices that rely on the energy of the alpha emission causing a special chemical in solution or embedded in very thin plastic foil to emit a spark of light which is subsequently amplified and measured. Such devices are horribly expensive. Thanks to the Irish State on the one hand and the Goldsmith Foundation on the other, we have two of these machines, which we have used to measure alpha and beta activity in silts around the Irish Sea.

But there is another and much cheaper way. Eric Hamilton (1998) used to work at NRPB. In the 1980s he began to use a novel method for measuring alpha activity, which involved the discovery of an alpha-particle-detecting plastic, allyl diglycol carbonate, called CR-39.

I have also used this magic material. What we do is to place a piece of the plastic next to the source for a measured period, take it away and develop it using concentrated hot potassium hydroxide solution. This etches out tiny track holes in the plastic, which we count under a microscope (see Fig 3.5.1). The numbers of tracks per unit area give a measure of the activity. It is even possible to perturb the tracks in a magnetic field, or examine their shape or structure, and obtain the energy and thus identity of the isotope.

Table 3.4.1 Plutonium in inter-tidal sediment in Wales, 1989 (Garland *et al.* 1989)

Sample area	Distance from Sellafield	Pu-239+240 (Bq/m2)
Lleyn peninsula SE	227	120
Lleyn peninsula SW	189	300
Lleyn peninsula NW	181	260
Caernarfon Bay	177	160
Foryd Bay	156	720
Traeth malynog	154	800
Llanddwyn bay	169	2100
Malltreath sands	165	1160
Aberffraw bay	154	1520
Rhosneigr	147	570
Cymryan bay	144	500
Anglesey NW	141	200
Dulas/Lligwy bay	125	350
Red Wharf bay W	131	2270
RedWharf bay E	130	770
Beaumaris	134	520
Menai Strait	148	1570
Lavan sands W	136	780
Lavan sands E	135	12400
Conwy sands S	128	770
Conwy sands N	125	4200
Ormes bay	123	1840
Rhos on sea	123	4700
Colwyn Bay	125	2300
Abergele	123	3200
Kinmel Bay	122	2700
Prestatyn	119	1800
Point of Air	118	1700
Dee estuary	130	14500

Hamilton used this CR39 technique and also normal X-ray film to examine `hot particles' in silt in Cumbria which have an average diameter of 70 μm and a mass of 2 μg. He found the average specific activity of such particles to be 706,000 Bq/kg and each particle had average activity of 0.0014 Bq. This represents a decay every 12 minutes into a volume of tissue defined by the alpha particle range of about 0.1mm. If such a particle is immobilised within tissue for any length of time the resultant dose to the adjacent cells is enormously high. Hamilton's method (and one we have also used for samples from Wales and Ireland (Plate 3) involves cutting a mud core by hammering a piece of plastic drainpipe into the inter-tidal sediment to a depth of about 18 inches in an 'accretion zone', a place where the mud has been undisturbed, close to the high water mark. The surrounding mud is then dug out and the core removed. It is then frozen at -18 degrees and cut longitudinally with a saw to give two half-cylinders. These are then dried under vacuum and placed alongside a piece of CR39 which we purchase from Prof. Denis Henshaw's TASL company in Bristol. This is then developed and examined under a metallurgical microscope. After retirement from NRPB, Hamilton argued at some length that the sediment contamination represents a serious source of risk and in 1999 published a frightening autoradiograph of a half-core taken from the estuary of the Esk near Ravenglass, showing the presence of hot particles in the sediment (Fig3.5.2).

Hamilton's core shows the presence of large hot particles and though these are serious hazards, they are relatively stationary. In addition, even of they were to be re-suspended and inhaled, they would not pass through the lung into the lymphatic system. I am much more concerned with the effects of micron and sub micron sized material which are much more mobile, more widely dispersed and of lower activity. According to a recent NRPB report, plutonium in the environment is in the form of particles whose size ranges from sub-micron to 5 microns in diameter, but with the mean size being about 0.5-1micron. Such particles are extremely resistant to natural destruction and are virtually insoluble, only being dissolved with difficulty in strong acid (Wilkins *et al*., 1996). Post-mortem analysis of children from the Chernobyl-affected territories of the former Soviet Union found these plutonium particles in lymph nodes, and such particles have also been found in the lymphatic system of animals grazing near the Nevada test site in the USA (Wilkins *et al*., 1996). Eakins *et al*. (1984) measured plutonium in sheep faeces from St Bees in Cumbria, near Sellafield, across the whole of northern England to Whitby on the eastern coast. They showed that the levels fell off rapidly with distance up to about 20 km and then stabilised. A typical result is shown in Figure 3.5.3. This pattern is most easily explained by models involving the dispersion of larger precipitating particles and smaller, continuously airborne aerosol particles. The hot particles get into the marine life and can therefore be transferred to anything that eats such creatures. Fig 3.5.1 shows a CR39 track developed from a cross section of an edible mussel. If you had eaten that mussel then that stuff would be inside you!

Fig 3.5.1 Hot particle from Sellafield detected in the intestine of an edible mussel from Ravenglass using CR39 (Source: Hamilton and Clifton 1980)

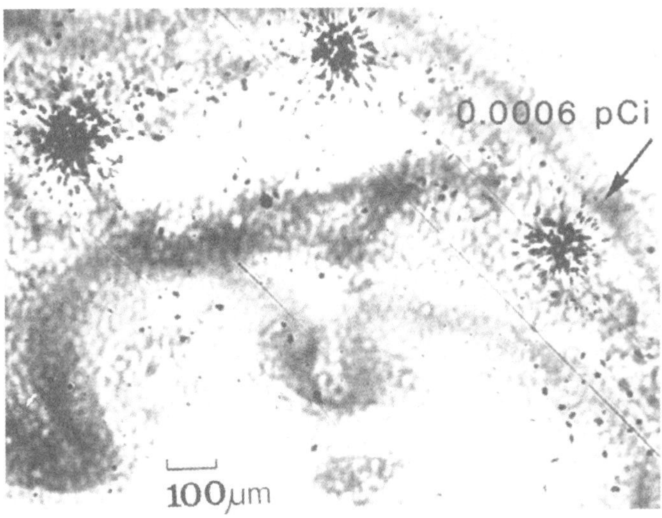

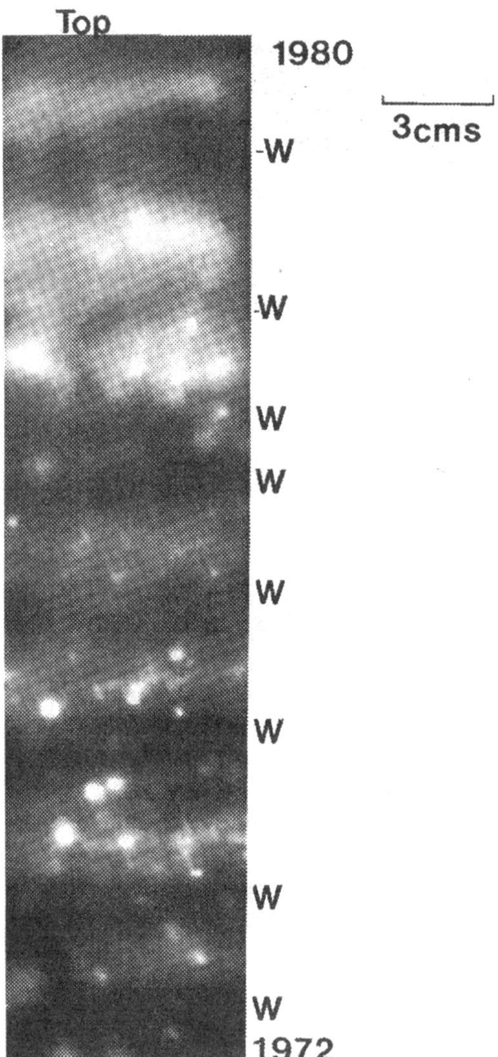

Fig 3.5.2 Beta gamma autoradiograph of a sandy Esk estuarine core sampled in September 1980 using Kodak Industrex C No Screen X-ray film. The white zones show that deposition of the radioisotopes occurs during the summer, the black zones indicate that, in the winter, where the mud is stirred up by gales, the material does not sediment. (Hamilton, 1998)

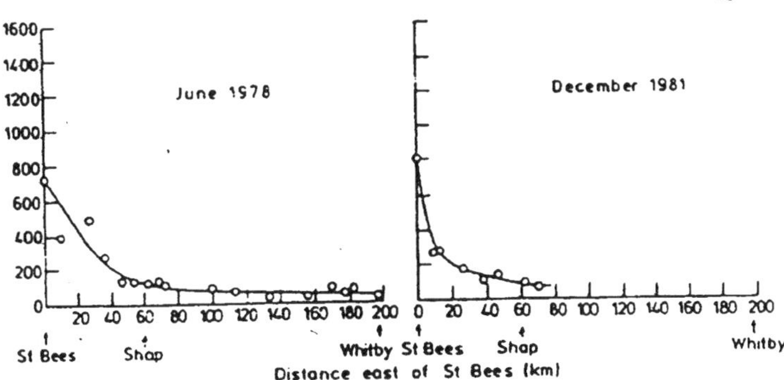

Figure 3.5.3 Concentration of Plutonium-239 in sheep faeces by distance from St Bees in Cumbria.
Source: redrawn from Eakins *et al.*, 1984.

The Welsh Office commissioned a radiological survey of Wales in 1984, and results showed Plutonium contamination of sheep droppings up to 10 km from the Irish Sea coast (Cawse *et al.,* 1988). The isotopic signatures confirmed the origin of the Plutonium as the Sellafield plant. The study by Garland *et al.* (1989) also detected Plutonium sea-to-land transfer. If particles can contaminate sheep then clearly people must also be at risk. Supporting evidence that this is the case comes from measurements made on cadavers in the UK. Plutonium levels in post-mortem tissue seem to be highest in the tracheo-bronchial lymph nodes and highest in Cumbrian residents and occupationally exposed workers in Cumbria, relative to other UK citizens. Some results from a report by Popplewell of the NRPB are given in Table 3.5.1

Table 3.5.1. Plutonium in various organs at post-mortem, from members of the public and from occupationally exposed workers living in Cumbria. (mBq/kg; numbers of cases are in brackets)

Tissue	Occupationally exposed (Cumbria)	Members of public (Cumbria)	Members of public (elsewhere UK)
Rib	130, 360, 94	9 (10)	6 (43)
Femur	132, 250, 100	5.4 (11)	3.6 (35)
Liver	91, 400, 83	49 (10)	26 (47)
Lung	940, 1140, 120	6.8 (11)	1.9 (47)
Tracheo-bronchial lymph nodes	450, 73300, 1600	35 (12)	10 (37)

Source: Popplewell, 1986.

The parameters of sea-to-land transfer were investigated by Harwell scientists in the early 1980s (Eakins and Lally, 1984). They were able to show that 95 per cent of the plutonium precipitated inside about one kilometre from the sea and thereafter the trend in plutonium in air was flatter. Thus there was always a residual level of plutonium which remained across the whole of their sampling transect, up to 10km inland. This result is shown in Fig.3.5.4 In addition; in 1993 a Harwell team investigated the physical mechanism of sea spray enrichment (McKay *et al.* 1993). They showed that enrichment occurred by the scavenging of silt particles by rising bubbles, which produce particulate rich droplets on bursting at the surface.

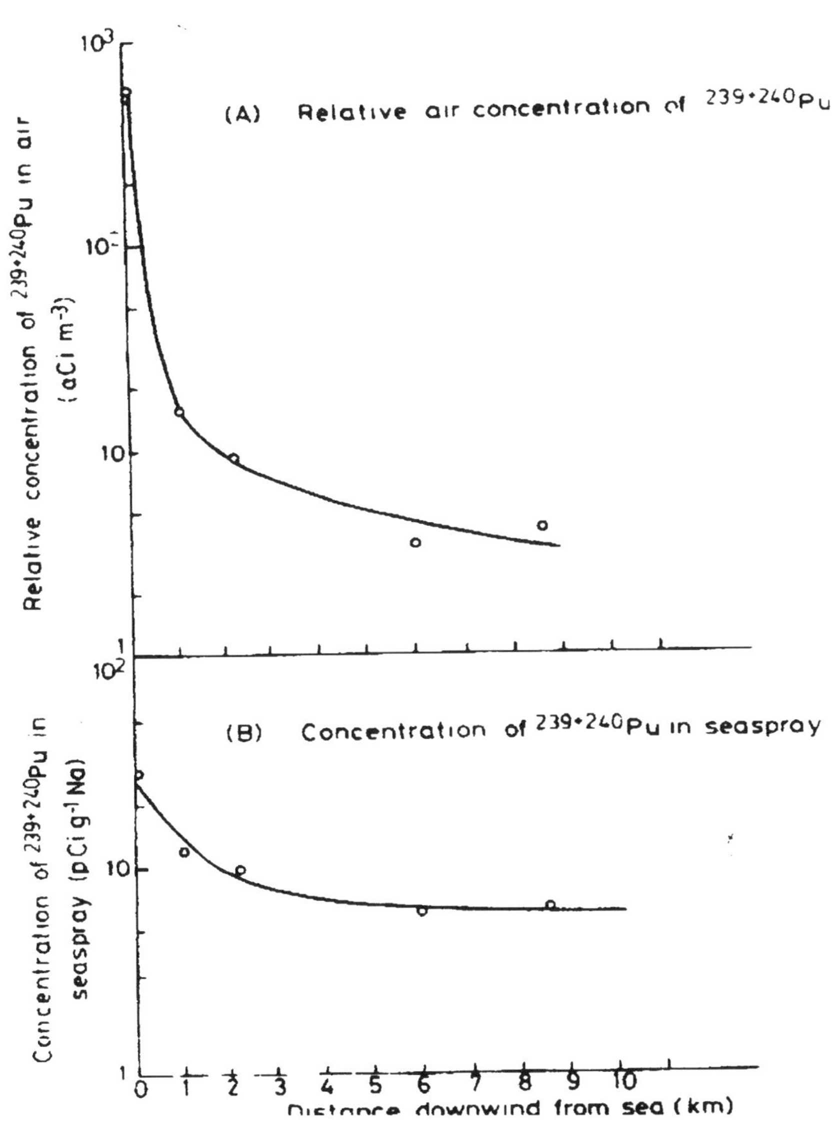

Fig 3.5.4 Penetration of plutonium and sea spray inland. (*Source:* Eakins and Lally, 1984)

It is clear from comparing the two graphs in Fig 3.5.4 that it is the sea spray that carries the plutonium inland. A recent report from the UK government's Airborne Particle Research Group (APEG, 1999) relates that up to 30 per cent of PM10 particles in the UK originate from the sea. This is probably the answer to the question of the concentration of plutonium in children's teeth and also the origin of the radioactive dust in middle England (of course, it is not only plutonium that is transferred; all the isotopes are re-supended). The penetration inland of material from the sea has been known for some time prior to the period of main discharges to the sea from the Sellafield plant. The map shown in Fig 3.5.5 shows penetration of sea spray in the United States. Compare it with that of Fig 3.1.3., showing plutonium in grassland in the UK.

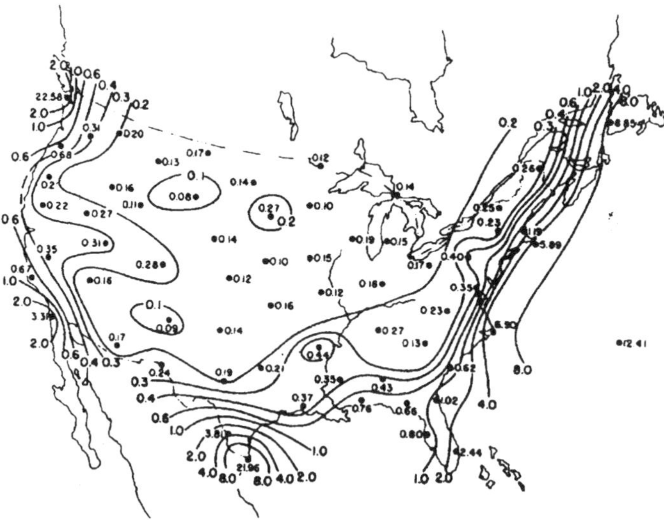

Fig 3.5.5 Sea spray penetration inland in the US (*Source:* Junge, 1963)

Although the prevailing wind over the Irish Sea is south-westerly, easterly winds do occur, and the sea-to-land transfer of radioactive particulates would also occur on the Irish eastern coast under these conditions. The Irish Radiological Protection Institute measure radioactivity in air at a number of stations on the east and west coasts of Ireland; In their 1993 report there are tables of gross beta activity in airborne dust measured monthly. I have reduced the tables to give annual mean values for 1990-3 for two locations chosen to represent the west coast, namely Galway, and the east coast nearest to the mud flats, namely Clonskeagh. These results are given in Table 3.5.2. It is clear that levels of radioactivity are twice as high in dust on the east coast as on the west. We would expect the higher value to be on the west coast because of higher rainfall: this is what occurs in England and Wales. In fact, as I shall show, both cancer rates and radioactivity in dust in Ireland are higher in the east.

The questions we need to ask are: what is the speciation of the dust in the Clonskeagh filters? What size are the particles and what is the specific activity, what isotopes are present and where do they originate? These questions remain open.

Table 3.5.2 Gross beta activity in airborne dust in Galway and Clonskeagh, Dublin (annual mean value: mBq/cu:metre)

Year	Galway (SD)	Clonskeagh (SD)
1990	0.40 (0.27)	0.76 (0.26)
1991	0.17 (0.06)	0.50 (0.15)
1992	0.22 (0.13)	0.51 (0.46)
1993	0.39 (0.19)	0.42 (0.22)
1990-3 av.	0.26 (0.2)	0.56 (0.3)

Mean differences are statistically significant at the p = .04 level; 95% Confidence Interval = .022<x<.483mBq/cu:m (Source: RPII, 1993).

3.6. Exposure routes

How has all this been permitted by the authorities? First we must realise that the risk model for internal exposure is wrong, as I outlined in the previous chapter. But second, because it is the absorbed dose that is calculated, the main exposures of interest, and on which the limits are set, are believed to be from standing on the seashore or handling fishing equipment. Internal doses are mean doses from eating fish or shellfish. These doses are estimated by the radiological protection agencies and they use their method to protect members of the public. This method, we now see, depends upon *ab initio* modelling of exposure doses. They choose a 'critical group' of people who, they believe, are those most likely to be exposed according to their theoretical model. This method is utilised by both the RPII and the NRPB. These models rely heavily on averaging dose to tissues and the main exposure groups chosen as critical in the case of exposure to Irish Sea contamination were, in 1974:

- Fishermen exposed to beta/gamma radiation from fish flesh
- Fishermen exposed to beta/gamma dose to whole body from estuarine sediment.
- Porphyra laverbread eaters, because of the high beta dose to Gastric tract from the isotopes (mainly the beta emitter Ruthenium-106) in the seaweed used to make the laverbread.

Ireland has a significant inshore fishing industry with small boats operating in inshore waters, including the Irish Sea. By 1993, in Ireland, internal dose had become of greater concern than external dose, because of the far greater number of people eating contaminated seafood and critical groups had been extended to eaters of shellfish, fish and prawns. The calculation of exposure dose follows the crude averaging methods of ICRP 60 (ICRP, 1990), which I have criticised for not taking account of anisotropies of dose either temporally or microscopically. Thus the radioactivity in the fish or shellfish is assumed to transfer to the whole body or organ in the human body that is being considered. Because of this, the ingestion of hot particles, either by inhalation or ingestion does not carry any risk, since decay energy is diluted out into the mass of tissue of the body. In reality, of course, the multiple decays of a particle trapped in tissue will give a massive dose to the adjacent tissue. In fact, many shellfish contain hot particles, which may be transferred to the human gut, as we see in the autoradiograph of a mussel from the Irish Sea shown in Fig 3.5.1. What happens when a shellfish like this is eaten? Can the particles get across the intestine of the person eating the shellfish? What if the particle is trapped in the colon?

3.7 Summary

In this chapter I have looked at the operation at Sellafield purely from the point of view of its releases to the Irish Sea. This is because it is here that I made the first discovery of the immediate effects of internal radiation exposure from man-made fission-products, effects that I will later be describing. The ethical basis of the operation at Sellafield is that of cost-benefit analysis. The benefit in this exchange accrues to the rich and powerful, the cost to those who live near the plant or near the coast. In the case of Ireland, there is no benefit whatever, only cost. I will return to the matter of the ethical underpinning of the nuclear project later, but here I merely want to finish this account by summarising what we need to know about Sellafield in order to understand what follows. Sellafield is a huge nuclear fuel reprocessing plant that takes in spent radioactive fuel from nuclear power stations in the UK and elsewhere in the world. By chemical processes the plant extracts the Plutonium from these fuels for manufacturing atom bombs, and more recently as a feedstock for a new and largely untested and dangerous nuclear fuel called MOX.

Part of this process involves the production of large quantities of radioactive waste. Significantly large quantities of this waste, including the alpha emitters Plutonium 239, Plutonium-240 and Americium-241 and the beta emitters Caesium-137 and Strontium-90 are discharged to the Irish Sea through a pipe. Releases are also made to the atmosphere by chimney, but a large proportion of these aerial emissions also end up in the sea. In terms of the alpha emitters, the quantities are very large and comparable with all the fallout from weapons testing.

In terms of density or concentration, the material represents a much larger risk to people living near the Irish Sea than weapons fallout. The dispersion of the material is affected by tidal energy: specifically, radioactive material is concentrated on the shores of the Irish Sea in areas of low tidal energy and particle size. These highlight areas like estuaries, coastal inlets and coastal mudflats that dry at low tide. There is sufficient evidence to show that the contaminated sediment in such areas becomes resuspended by wave action and is driven inland. Radioactive particles of plutonium and other isotopes can be found in the air near the coast, and although the smallest particles have been crossing the entire country, the highest levels of aerosol concentration are in a narrow coastal strip, maybe 1km deep. These levels of exposure are very low, when assessed as absorbed dose, but there are plausible biological and mechanistic arguments to suggest that such an averaging approach is unsafe. If this is so, and these particulate internal exposures carried enhanced hazard for cell mutation and cancer, then looking at the trend in cancer with distance from the sea, might be expected to show a cancer trend effect. In Part II, which follows, I pursue this line of enquiry.

Part II
Discoveries

I argued in Part One that cancer was a genetic disease and people developed cancer because they had been exposed to some environmental agent or carcinogen that caused the cancer. This is not really an area of dispute. We cannot walk down any high street in the country now without noticing the huge expansion in the numbers of cancer charity shops. To use Molly's black joke, this is a new growth industry. Everywhere people are sporting ribbons, usually with flowers: pink, white, or yellow flowers. How nice. Look at the exciting pink shop display in Plate 28. In Wales, St David's Day has become transmuted into Marie Curie Cancer Care, an irony in the context of the real cause of cancer, since Marie Curie's discoveries are largely behind the increases. Here everyone sports artificial daffodils to display both their Welshness and the evidence of their decision to defeat cancer, a curious marriage of identities. This is because now few remain untouched by the disease (especially in Wales). Aunts, husbands, mothers, children, pet dogs, canaries: all have been kissed by death and carried off. Everywhere these tragedies are the reality behind the pink balloons and shrill requests for money, more money and yet more money to defeat the new plague. There has been some mistake about the Age of Aquarius, the water carrier: this is the age of the Crab.

The massive increase in the incidence of the disease in the last thirty years has been ascribed by the establishment of epidemiologists working for the cancer research foundations and the government epidemiologists -desperately trying to reassure- to increasing life span. I have just such an epidemiologist as Chairman of my Ministry of Defence Depleted Uranium Committee. Professor David Coggon took over as head of the Medical Research Council Epidemiology Unit in Southampton University where the previous Director was Martin Gardner, the man who confirmed the Sellafield leukaemia cluster. Gardner died at the age of 50, of cancer, oddly and conveniently before the Reay and Hope Sellafield Court Case came to trial. The trial failed because the chief witness for the prosecution was dead. Coggon, his successor, closed down the research into Sellafield. In 1994 Coggon and a colleague, Hazel Inskip, wrote a paper in the *British Medical Journal* denying the cancer epidemic, displaying graphs with a logarithmic axis so that increases in the disease are straightened out.

The philosopher Mary Midgley sees Science becoming the new religion (Midgley 1985, 2002). This is especially true in the area of belief and truth with regard to evidence that the human race is slowly being polished off by toxins, which it produces itself in order to get rich. This is the hole we have dug for ourselves and we are now falling into it. As we do so, these people, the epidemiologists, show us figures that prove that nothing is wrong. Suddenly your friend disappears. A neighbour's daughter vanishes. Look! There's a child with no hair. Never mind: this is all anecdotal evidence. It can be ignored. The numbers, the statistical significance, show that there is no problem. It is a random cluster. No one need weep.

It was the beginning of the century when numbers and their analysis began to replace religion as the ultimate revelation of truth. The Victorians had been increasingly realising that their 'givens', their world structures of certainty, based on a combination of God and the Empire, the rich man in his castle and the poor man at his gate, had no substance in rational analysis. Empirical measurement had done for belief. Everyone was descended from apes, even the heroes and queens. It was worse. Our actions were not even decided by us, but by the strange (and embarrassing) invisible antics of our subconscious. Remember Matthew Arnold's complaints in *Dover Beach*?

The sea of faith
Was once too, at the full, and round earth's shore
Lay like the folds of a bright girdle furled
But now I only hear
Its melancholy, long withdrawing roar

Poor chap. What was left?

Confused alarm of struggle and flight,
Where ignorant armies clash by night?

Well actually no, all was not lost and not everyone's army was ignorant. Numbers could be used to fortify the establishment. Hurrah! Even if the poor could now justifiably argue that everyone was equal, the rich still had mathematics. They could continue to say, Ho Varlet! The data shows this and that objectively! We are objectively better than you: that is why we are rich! That is why we own the castles and you remain at the gate. It is because you can't do statistics. You don't understand economics, the technique which objectively places us at the top and you at the bottom. The philosophical movement associated with this latest development in the science of keeping the mob in its place was that of the Vienna School: logical positivism. If it couldn't be tested it was meaningless. If it could be tested (mathematically, statistically) it must be true. If everything was up for grabs, and everything was relative, then all that was left was the objectivism of mathematics. Numbers are neutral and the only truths were in numbers!

Nowadays, of course, all this has collapsed. There are two main reasons; the first has developed from the assaults on the concept of objectivity associated largely with the French philosophers, Foucault *et al.* (and I will return to this matter of science and objectivity), the second, which is the basis of this book, is more mundane. In the last ten years only, the tremendous advances in technology have enabled the poor (in which category I include myself) to get access to awesome computing power in the form of the PC. This enables us to undertake tasks, which, before 1990, would have needed a mainframe University Computer and a whole department of programmers. I can use free software available on the Internet, and cheap commercial software to analyse a database containing 20 million cells. I can present my results in a report that looks as good as (often better than) those produced by an entire government department. I can send this report by email to hundreds of people by pressing a button. Or I can put the report on the Internet as a free resource. Thank You, Bill Gates!

Back to the question I asked earlier. As the biosphere fills up with the poisonous by-products of progress, to what extent are human beings suffering? Or put another way; is it worth being rich if our children die? Well, of course, the people who are getting rich, and the governments who are afraid of being poor don't want any messages of doom from the public health sector. To pursue business-as-usual we have to believe that there are no cancer increases; hence Coggon, a safe pair of hands, is put in charge. In this battlefield, the weapons are the guns of epidemiology and these need to be loaded with data. And that is why we have now to look at both these items. First we need to examine the tools and methods of cancer epidemiology, and mainly small area cancer epidemiology, to enable us to follow the evidence and counter arguments that follow. This is the last bit of difficult stuff that you will need to read, and actually, you could probably skip much of it. But because it is so important, I want to provide in this book a basic template for small area epidemiology, so that anyone can examine the data on health effects in a small area near some putative source of risk and blow the whistle if there is a problem. Too often, activists near some nuclear plant, incinerator or landfill call attention to what seems to them a clear excess of illness, only to be fobbed off (and the newspapers also) by a statistician from the establishment, defending the status quo. A whole arsenal of bogus statistical methods has been developed for this purpose. It is time we drew attention to this development and fought back; and so, at the end of this section, I present some simple methods for analysing data and determining whether it shows important indicators of harm, or effects that are just a consequence of the natural play of chance.

4
Epidemiology

Was it bad luck that caused both my aunts to die of cancer, one of them in her 40s? How could I tell? This is the question of the probabilistic basis of causality. It can be seen as a long chain of gates through which various necessary preceding events have to pass for the final event (we are interested in) to happen. These gates are called 'binomial' gates since they define two possibilities: Yes and No, pass or remain behind. The Victorian statistician Francis Galton devised a simple machine which he called the 'quincunx' to illustrate how such binomial decisions result in what is called a Normal Distribution, the well known bell-shaped curve. I show this in Fig 4.1.1

Three years ago, Frances, one of my daughters was knocked over on a zebra crossing and badly injured. This must be quite a rare event. For it to have happened there were many gates through which antecedent events had to pass. The van that hit her was driven by an old man with poor response and bad eyesight: two gates, not passed by a young man with good eyesight. It was dusk: another gate. The crossing was sited near a crossroads and a panel truck pulled out from the side street to move across the main road, shielding the accident van from my daughter, and she from it: more gates. If we were to devise a quincunx for such series of antecedents, her accident would be well out to the right of the centre of the distribution in Fig 4.1. Similar gates were no doubt involved in the cancer deaths of my aunts. There was some bad luck, and maybe some genetic damage. Maybe the genetic damage was a result of bad luck in my grandparents' lifetime. If we are looking to blame something, or someone, we have to try and dissect out the gates responsible and we have to be certain that the event we are trying to understand was not one that could have occurred as a consequence of the play of chance alone. And in this regard, it is more than just understanding. It is about being able to change things so that the same thing does not happen to someone else.

One way we can do this is to study people and see how their levels of cancer relate to their exposures, their genetic makeup and their lifestyles. For this we use the science of epidemiology. Epidemiology is the study of the distribution and determinants of disease in human populations. A key aspect is that it is observational rather than experimental and therefore has to operate in an area where bias or confounding of the inferences drawn from the data may occur. In chemistry, a blue liquid may be mixed with a green liquid to give a red precipitate: this will always happen so long as the experiment is exactly repeated and the results can be used to draw inferences about the nature of the processes involved. But it is rare that an epidemiological study has the specificity of design and sufficient exclusion of uncontrolled variables between the study and control groups to enable unequivocal conclusions to be drawn. Therefore, this is an area where studies may be electively biased or directed to find either a result or no result. (Actually, most of science suffers from the same problem). In addition, all epidemiological studies may be subject to considerable criticism by groups who hold opposite views for reasons that may include culture, employment or political pressure. I will provide evidence of all three of these mechanisms of bias in published papers and review articles later in this book. What we learn is that in drawing inferences from all the epidemiological studies of radiation and health, we have to consider very carefully the provenance of the study and in particular the likely directional bias of the studies' funding bodies and researchers. I make this point in the report of the Policy Information Network for Child Health and Environment (van den Hazel et al 2006) which I helped produce.

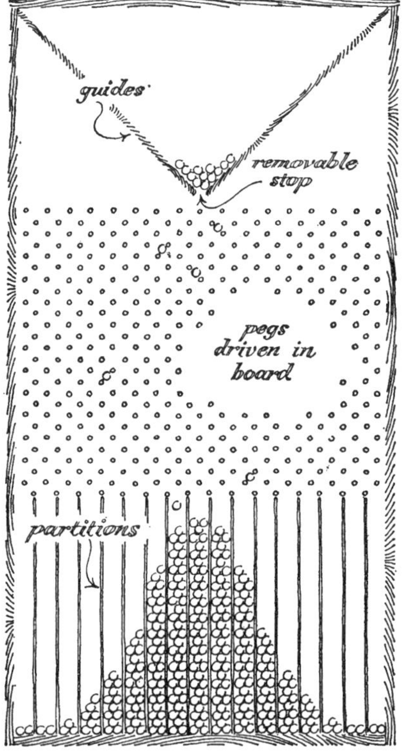

Fig 4.1.1 Galton's Quincunx illustrating the binomial (yes/no) gates that have to precede filtration of events into categories of likelihood in the normal distribution.

All epidemiological studies compare a study group or groups, in this case those exposed to a known quantity of radiation, or some surrogate for it, with a control group, who should be matched in every way except that they are not exposed. Before examining real studies that attempt to translate this ideal study into practice and quantify the risks, I must introduce some aspects of the analytical procedure. The first thing we have to look at is *inference*. The most valuable list of procedures that should be followed in order to draw safe inferences from evidence in epidemiological studies was devised by Sir Austin Bradford Hill in the 1950s and is termed Bradford Hill's Canons. They are sufficiently valuable in assessing the case of radiation and health to give a short account of them so that they may be applied to the radiation studies presented later.

4.1 Bradford Hill's canons

4.1.1. Statistical significance

A secure foundation for argument in any comparison of an exposed study group with an unexposed control group is that the difference in health deficit, (cancer mortality for example) is statistically significant and is unlikely to have occurred by chance. Significance testing is an area of statistics and a number of basic mathematical tests may be applied to see if a result is statistically significant.

The word 'significant' is one that within the scientific community has a specific technical meaning, but can also be interpreted generally by those without a scientific background. When a research finding is said to be 'significant' this means that it may be considered to be meaningful, in the sense of not being a chance finding. Since statistics is a methodology based on probability, it accepts a certain level of error as inevitable, meaning that some scientific findings that have passed the 'significance' test are still bound to be wrong.

The level of 'significance', which, of course, is directly related to the level of error, is chosen by the researcher, and should be set higher if the findings have more potentially dangerous implications. The level of significance generally adopted in scientific research is 5 per cent. This means that researchers are accepting a 5 per cent level of error, or that they will be wrong 1 in 20 times.

The procedure of testing whether results are 'significant' is known as 'hypothesis testing'. The scientist tests the 'null' hypothesis, which is the proposition that there is nothing unusual going on, or that the distribution of results found does not differ from what would be expected by chance.

The reason we have to be on guard when we feel a study shows the existence of some effect is that our conclusion might be wrong: we may be in error. Statistics defines two types of error that can be made when undertaking research. The first, known as a Type I error, is the one of most concern to most scientists. It involves making a claim to have a research finding when in fact the results were generated by chance. An example might be a medical trial that indicated that a certain drug was effective in slowing the progress of AIDS; follow-up research might fail to find a similar result, suggesting that the original findings fell into the 5 per cent error area. For professional and credibility reasons, this is the kind of error most feared by a researcher: the error of claiming a significant result when in fact the finding resulted from chance. It is the terror of professional epidemiologists, as a career can be destroyed through making a claim that was subsequently shown to be false. This may be why modern epidemiologists seem so loathe to commit themselves to any positive statement about anything.

But there is another type of error, which is equally important, particularly in terms of potentially harmful consequences of radiation exposure. This is the Type II error, defined as the failure to find a significant result when the hypothesis is in fact correct. It represents the risk of carrying out a study and, for reasons that may relate to technical issues such as the size of the sample, failing to find a statistically significant result. It may not necessarily mean that the hypothesis is wrong, only that significance was not found this time. However, it may allow conclusions to be drawn to justify use of a technology. Or because of extreme caution it may result in a conclusion that processes are not causing any ill effects when in fact they are.

Radiation risk studies in the low dose range very often involve small numbers of people in the exposed study group, those living near a point source such as a nuclear power station for example. Studies with large populations may have small numbers of cancer cases due to very low natural rates from the disease in question: an example is childhood leukaemia. In each of these types of situation, statistical methods have been developed to deal with the mathematical problem, yet finally there may not be sufficient evidence in each study to draw an inference from measured excess risk from the radiation exposure because chance could not be ruled out, i.e. the result was not significant at the 5% level. This is usually a consequence of the small numbers involved. When a material difference is apparent between two groups, but, with the numbers involved, is insufficient to pass the significance test, Bradford Hill argues that it is better to take ‘statistically not significant’ as the ‘non-proven’ of Scottish law rather than the ‘not guilty’ of English law. It is nevertheless true that policy decisions in the area of radiation and health have fallen into the trap of assuming that 'there is no evidence that low level radiation exposure is hazardous' means 'low level radiation exposure is not hazardous.'

In giving weight to such evidence, we need to make decisions about the possible outcome of accepting or not accepting a certain hypothesis and its supporting evidence. First we should take a precautionary approach and avoid making a Type II error in areas of low probability high impact risk, for if the evidence showing excess risk from the exposure were in fact a chance finding, the mistaken inclusion of it as evidence of radiation-induced effects would not harm the human race. If, on the other hand, we were to take the opposite view and exclude it as evidence when it was, in fact, a true measure of a real effect but merely formally non-significant, then much harm would follow its dismissal. In addition, there is the matter of what we do with non-significant results from different studies. How should we deal with these? It may be that several different studies each suggest that radiation is a cause of cancer but in each study the formal statistical significance falls short of the magic 5% needed to state that the finding was not due to chance. It turns out that we can combine these studies in such a way as to obtain a very high degree of certainty using a statistical theorem due to a Victorian mathematician the Rev. Thomas Bayes. Bayesian statistics is in vogue at the moment as it can be used to teach robots (and computer programs) to learn. Microsoft 'Word' learns as a result of Bayesian analysis of previous inputs made by the person using the program. On this basis we might use a Bayesian approach to the refinement of belief in the area of risk assessment and allow each non-significant observation (including unpublished results) to weight and modify the overall probability of belief in the area of radiation risk according to their degree of significance. Thus the discovery of a child leukaemia cluster in the 1980s near the nuclear reprocessing plant at Sellafield in Cumbria, UK has been criticised on the basis that the statistical significance of the result for the ward ($p = .002$) enabled no inference to be drawn since there are more wards in the UK than the 500 wards needed for such a result to be a chance occurrence. However, since this discovery, child leukaemia excesses have been discovered near two other reprocessing plants and a number of nuclear installations in Europe. The Bayesian modification of the probability of the causal relation by each new example gives us a firmer basis of belief in the association and enables more robust conclusions to be drawn about the levels of risk from exposure under these circumstances.

4.1.2 Strength of association

There should be evidence of a strong association between the risk factor and the disease: in other words, it is necessary to consider the relative incidence of the condition under study in the populations contrasted.

4.1.3 Consistency

The association should have been repeatedly observed by different persons in different places, different circumstances and times. With much research work in progress many environmental associations may be thrown up. On the customary tests of statistical significance, some of them will appear unlikely to be due to chance. Nevertheless, whether chance is an explanation or whether a true hazard has been revealed may sometimes only be answered by a repetition of the circumstances and the observations. Broadly the same answer should be given by studies using a wide variety of techniques and in different situations.

4.1.4 Specificity and reversibility

The association should be specific. The disease association should be limited, ideally, to exposure to the putative cause and those exposed should not suffer an excess risk from other kinds of illness or causes of death. In the area of radiation risk, where the plausible biological model involves genetic and somatic damage, disease specificity may be hard to define. One condition that has become considered as a specific consequence of radiation exposure is leukaemia, particularly in children. However, the specificity should be defined accurately in terms both of cause and effect. In the case of low-level radiation exposure, the lack of distinction between external and internal exposure has led to conclusions being drawn that are incorrect. Associated with *specificity* is *reversibility*. Thus removal of the cause should ideally reduce the incidence of the disease, although this is a consideration that is difficult to apply in the case of cancer, where genetic damage is not removed by removing the cause of the damage.

4.1.5 Relationship in time.

There should clearly be evidence that the risk factor preceded the onset of the disease.

4.1.6 Biological gradient

There should be evidence of a dose-response effect. This is usually taken to mean that as the dose increases, the illness rate should also increase in some proportion. However, some thought will reveal that this may not be true for certain end-points. Take, for example, birth malformations due to an exposure; increasing the stress from zero will cause increasing damage to embryos which may eventually present as increasing risk of malformation. At some point, the weight of damage will prove too great and the embryos will die: at this dose, there will be no further congenital malformation, merely a reduction in the birth rate. Since there are many possible reasons for reduction in the birth rate, including social ones, the fact that exposure to a large dose of some putative mutagen has not caused any increase in birth defects ought not be taken as evidence of no effect unless lower doses are also considered and the dose-response relation adequately considered. This exact misunderstanding appears to have led to the belief that exposure to radiation from Chernobyl caused no harmful effect on birth defect, stillbirth and infant mortality rates in European populations. A number of papers asserted this on the basis of the data without drawing attention to the sharp fall in the birth rate that occurred some nine to twelve months after the exposure. A similar type of error also applies to ecological studies where some groups of individuals may have greater susceptibility to radiation. The existence of a dual sensitivity to radiation as a consequence of normal cell division also results in a dose-response relation that is biphasic, i.e. has two areas where increased effect follows increased dose, with an intervening area where increased dose results in reduced effect. The existence of

inducible cell-damage repair results in a similar biphasic relationship between cause and effect.
The statistical method called 'regression' is widely used today to examine health effects following exposure. If the dose response is not linear, the method is unsound.

4.1.7 Biological plausibility: mechanism
A key question in the area of radiation risk is: what is the mechanism of radiation induced cancer? Mechanisms advanced in the early years of radiation research, based on direct hits to genes and induction of specific mutations underpinned the use of a linear relationship between dose and final cancer expression. But we now see that this was too simplistic a reduction of what happens, and that the response to exposure is extremely complex. Bradford Hill was aware of this problem of lack of knowledge. He stated,
It will be helpful if the causation we suspect is biologically plausible, though this is a feature we cannot demand. What is biologically plausible depends upon the biological knowledge of the day. It was lack of biological knowledge in the 19th century that led a prize essayist writing on the value and fallacy of statistics to conclude that among other 'absurd associations . . . it could be no more ridiculous for the stranger who passed the night in the steerage of an emigrant ship to ascribe the typhus, which he there contracted, to the vermin with which the bodies of the sick might be infected.
For this reason we should be anxious to avoid dismissing evidence of health detriment following low level radiation exposure on the grounds of lack of a plausible biological mechanism. In particular, the ICRP's assumptions about cell dose at low level exposures provide a good example of how mechanistic arguments have been used to argue for a linear relation between dose and response, a thesis which is only valid for external random irradiation of large tissue volumes and which, in any case, is being overtaken by recent research on genomic instability and bystander effects.

4.1.8 Alternative explanation
There should be no convincing alternative explanation or confounding for the observed association. This is often described by the sentence: Correlation is not Causation.

4. 2 Types of study and general problem

There are two questions we need to ask. The first is: how much ill health, specifically how much cancer, will be caused as a result of some unit dose of radiation exposure of a specific kind? The second is: Have the discharges from nuclear site X caused increases in cancer or ill-health in people living nearby? In order to answer these questions we must devise epidemiological studies of various sorts. I am going to outline some simple methods that we have used and which will help understand the results I present and discuss later. For those who want to look further into the interesting field of epidemiological methods I suggest the excellent book by Woodward (1999).

As far as the nuclear industries and governments of the world are concerned, the question of how much ill health is caused by radiation has been answered by the study of the survivors of Hiroshima and Nagasaki. I describe these studies in some detail in *Wings of Death*. A group of Japanese people who were out in the open at the time of the A-bombs and groups of which were situated at different distances from the explosion in 1945 have been followed up from about 1952 to the present day. They have been compared on the basis of their various distances (and presumed) doses and also have been compared with groups who were not in the city at the time of the bomb or groups who came into the city much later. The study recorded the cancer rates over their whole lifespan (the study is still going on), and this enabled the calculation of relative risk of cancer following various external exposure doses from gamma rays. In this simple formulation, relative risk RR is simply the age-standardised rate in the irradiated population divided by the age standardised rate in the un-irradiated or control population.

Why do we need to examine age-standardised rates and what does this mean? Cancer incidence increases exponentially with age, for reasons I have outlined earlier. Therefore cancer mostly occurs in older people. So if we are comparing two groups of people there has to be a way of allowing for this since, even if there were identical environments and stresses, in two equal sized groups, the one with the oldest people in it would have the highest numbers of cancer cases. Age standardisation is fairly straightforward and I explain how to do this later on in this chapter.

The Hiroshima studies are the main basis for radiation risk factors used to predict or explain the cancer yield from any exposure, but there have been some other studies of people who were irradiated for various medical conditions (at the time when this was believed to be harmless and the results of these have been generally supportive of the Hiroshima risk factors). Our argument is, of course, that the Hiroshima risk factors (and those of the other supportive studies) were all of external acute radiation exposures and can't be used to assess internal exposure. The Hiroshima studies are an example of a cohort study, one where a group of people who have been identified as experiencing a particular risk are followed over a period of time to see what diseases they suffer compared with a similar group who have not been exposed to the risk. The other main type of epidemiological study is the case-control study, where cases who are identified as having some disease are compared with controls who are matched with the cases in as many ways as possible so that differences in aspects of the environment or behaviour between the two groups might point to a cause for the disease in the cases. I don't have space here to deal with all the problems of epidemiology. And you won't have the patience. In the last ten years, as the pollution effects begin to bite and human health begins to suffer, the science of epidemiology has become infested with philosophical complication and mathematical fog. The reason for the obfuscation is partly psychological denial by the public health and cancer epidemiologists in the face of the evidence that we are all being poisoned. But for our purposes in this book we can bypass all this. We just need sufficient arithmetical machinery to ask some simple questions about risk near sources of pollution and to see how we can obtain answers to the questions we need to examine. This approach might perhaps be called barefoot epidemiology. I shall describe now how we can learn fairly simply what is going on the world.

4.2.1 The necessary data

Before we find out if the risk of cancer near the nuclear plant is high, we need to know three things:

1. The numbers of cases of cancer of interest in some defined area near the plant, the area where the most exposure is likely.
2. The numbers of men and women living in this area in each 5-year age group.
3. The rates for the cancer of interest in each 5-year age and sex group in the national population which we use as a control or basis for estimation.

In addition, if we wish to look at the trends in cancer near the plant, or further afield, we need the numbers of cases of cancer and the populations for defined areas, which are more distant from the plant. There is one other refinement. Some cancers are naturally more prevalent (incidence and deaths) in poor people or disadvantaged people. The effect is large for lung cancer, the most common cancer in men, and is believed to be due to cigarette smoking behaviour. Some people think it is because poverty and disadvantage may have effects through immune system suppression. But for some other cancers, notably breast cancer and leukaemia, there is a weaker effect in the opposite direction. Thus there is more breast cancer in less disadvantaged or richer women. This could be because of differences in nutrition (more dairy) or behaviour (having fewer children later in age), or a combination. But these effects should be controlled for, or adjusted for mathematically, and this can be accomplished in various ways, using indices of disadvantage. The easiest way to control is to adjust the expected numbers by multiplying by a weighting factor calculated from the relationship between Social Class and cancer rates in the national population. Social Class makeup of an area is obtained directly from the census. Many other indices, Carstairs, Townsend, which include unemployment, multiple occupancy of houses, car ownership etc. can be calculated from data in the census.

There are basically two sources for these kinds of data, national databases and questionnaires. The problem with national databases, as far as our examination of point sources of risk are concerned, is that, generally speaking, the establishment will not give out the data, so no one can find out anything. This seems to be true for the USA and Europe as well as the UK and it is getting worse. I will discuss the problem further elsewhere but there is one tremendously useful exception. Although the rules for releasing such data are held to refer to both incidence (developing the disease) and mortality (dying of it) [M Quinn, 1992], since about 1999, ward level cancer mortality (deaths) for all malignancy, lung cancer, breast, stomach and prostate cancer annually in England and Wales from 1995 has been sold by the UK Office for National Statistics (ONS). This oversight, which was regretted by 2001 because of the use we have put to the data, came about probably because, when ONS was split off from government by Mrs Thatcher, they were told they had to be self sufficient, and so they began to sell off the data to make ends meet. Anyone could buy this data. So for about £500 we were able to obtain seven years of cancer mortality data for the main cancer types by ward, 1995 to 2001. In 2002, the ONS cottoned on to our use of the data and refused to give us any more. In a letter from the appropriately named Alison Holding of ONS I was told the data were confidential and I should never have been given them. In 2004 I began to use the Data Protection Act to get this data and then in 2005, the Freedom of Information Act. Following this pressure, ONS changed their mind in 2006 and I again began to get the data. We now have all the ward level cancer mortality data for the main cancer types from 1995-2004 and have written a huge computer program that will determine the cancer risk in any ward in England and Wales for this 10 year period.

In England and Wales the smallest areas that can be reasonably studied from official data are the administrative units called wards. Wards are the smallest sizes of area for which the population makeup can be obtained: they have populations of roughly between 1000 and 10,000 individuals and various areas, in country or mountainous regions some have quite large areas. The census in 1981, 1991 and 2001 gives numbers of men and women in each 5-year age group for all the wards in the UK, and these data are also available from the ONS for a fee. Before I turn to an explanation of how to proceed from here, I will briefly examine two other sources of data: questionnaires and local doctor's records.

If we wish to examine cancer risk in a smaller area than a ward, or if locals can take the matter into their own hands they can bypass the cancer registries and knock on doors. *Green Audit* developed this local area cancer questionnaire technique originally because it seemed that we were going to be refused small area data for Ireland. In the event we did get some numbers from the new National Cancer Registry in Cork, but by then we had gone ahead in the small area around Carlingford and Greenore in County Louth. Later, we used the method in Burnham on Sea, near the nuclear power station at Hinkley Point in Somerset and recently near Trawsfynydd in Wales. Briefly, the method consists of defining an area and visiting all the houses in the area with a questionnaire. This questionnaire asks the head of the household, or some responsible person to record the ages and sex of each person living in the house, together with any case of cancer diagnosed in the last ten years, the type of cancer and the age at diagnosis. This information allows the calculation of risk on the basis of the population living in all the houses.

The other possibility is to approach local GP surgeries and ask if anonymised totals of cancer incidence can be made available for research. For a meaningful result, we also need the total age breakdown of the surgery population. It may seem unlikely that these data will be forthcoming, but we were able to use this approach in Ireland and the results were very valuable. I will now turn to the basic method used to convert the data into meaningful patterns of risk.

4.2.2 Calculating Risk from the data

1. Ward level data

The method is essentially the same whatever the source of data. We have to calculate the *expected numbers* of cancer deaths or diagnosed cases in the area of interest for the period we are studying. We then must compare these with the *observed* or recorded numbers. It is best to look at as long a period as possible in order to get the largest number of cases into the study. This is because the larger the number of cases, the less likelihood there is of any effect we find being a consequence of chance. The procedure is simple but quite tedious if many wards are involved. We start with the population of each ward making up the area close to our proposed source of risk. The source of risk may be a nuclear site, or it may be a coastal strip where radioactive materials are known, by measurement, to accumulate. To give an example, I will show how the sums are done for an area we have been interested in, the ward of Burnham-on-Sea North in Somerset. The 1991 census population of females in this ward is shown in Table 4.2.2.1 below together with the England and Wales death rates from breast cancer and calculated annual expected numbers of deaths. These populations can be obtained from ONS as computer text files; and this is the best way, since they can be imported directly into a spreadsheet program and the calculations done from within it. There are, therefore, no transcription errors.

The rates for the cancer in question are calculated from national figures published by ONS. Table 2 of the publication Series DH2, *Mortality by Cause* gives the numbers of deaths in each 5-year age group, and also the population. So that it is easy to follow this, I also calculate the rate for one year in Table 4.2.2.1

These calculations, and the others that follow, are very tedious, but are made straightforward and can be done in blocks of as many wards as you like, using the computer. The most widely used software that will deal with these calculations quickly and efficiently is Microsoft EXCEL, but other spreadsheet programs will do just as well e.g. LOTUS 123. Whole columns containing hundreds of populations of wards can be multiplied by rates to give new columns of expected cases. These can then be added for all the age groups and the result put into a new column with a few clicks of a computer mouse. For those who are able to do these procedures by batch programming, the whole process can be automated, and indeed we have now developed a system (SACRIS) here that will enable us to obtain cancer mortality risks in any ward in Britain.

Let us look at how we do this in Table 4.2.2.1. The 1991 female population of the ward of Burnham on Sea North is given by 5-year age group. In the table we are calculating the expected annual numbers of breast cancer deaths, based on the rates in England and Wales. (These rates themselves are calculated from the England and Wales data by a straightforward process shown in Table 4.2.2.2.) Then each 5-year age group population is next multiplied by the appropriate rate, given in column (C) to give the expected numbers in column (D). All ages are then added up to give the total expected number of deaths, 2.178. What this tells us is that if Burnham-on-Sea North has exactly the same risk as the population of England and Wales, and the population had not changed from 1991, there would be 2.178 deaths from breast cancer every year. What we found, in the first of these studies we did in 2000, was that there were 17 recorded deaths from breast cancer in the four years 1995 to 1998. The expected number would be 2.178 x 4 years = 8.7 deaths. Thus we can calculate the age standardised mortality risk or Standardised Mortality Ratio as:

$$SMR = 17/8.7 = 1.95$$

This is a valuable discovery. We have found that there is almost twice the probability of dying of breast cancer here than the mean for England and Wales. And yet Burnham-on-Sea is not in the middle of some industrial slum area surrounded by chemical factories: It is a pretty little seaside town, where people go on holiday and children play in the sand. But it is also directly opposite and downwind of the Hinkley Point nuclear power station complex just across the bay. I will return to this.

The same calculation can be done for any cancer type and for men and women combined. All that we need is the appropriate rates, the ward population by sex and 5-year groups and the observed numbers.

Table 4.2.2.1 1991 female census population of Burnham North ward with expected numbers of deaths from breast cancer (D) calculated by multiplying each age group population (B) by the average England and Wales mortality rate (D).

(A) Age group (females tabulated)	**(B) Ward population at census**	***(C) Annual cancer rate in England and Wales for 1995-2000 per 100,000**	**(D) Expected numbers of cases per year (D) =(B) x (C)**
0-4	101	0	0
5-9	113	0	0
10-14	131	0	0
15-19	127	0	0
20-24	83	1.27E-6	0.00001
25-29	106	1.26E-5	0.0013
30-34	117	5.0E-5	0.0058
35-39	122	0.000123	0.0149
40-44	163	0.000234	0.038
45-49	136	0.000395	0.054
50-54	122	0.000603	0.073
55-59	145	0.000719	0.104
60-64	175	0.000872	0.152
65-69	237	0.00103	0.244
70-74	237	0.00126	0.299
75-79	176	0.00150	0.264
80-84	181	0.00188	0.34
85-89	137	0.00246	0.337
90+	81	0.0031	0.251
All ages			2.178

** calculated from annual figures of deaths tabulated by cause published by ONS (series DH2) for England and Wales*

Note: the E-notation means 'multiply by 10 to the power of-' so E-6 is 1 x 10^{-6}

Table 4.2.2 Calculating the England and Wales breast cancer mortality rates for 1995

(A) Age group	(B) 1995 Female population (thousands)	(C) 1995 Breast cancer deaths	(D) 1995 Rate D = C/B
0-4	1651.9	0	0
5-9	1656.4	0	0
10-14	1563	0	0
15-19	1469	0	0
20-24	1703	2	1.17E-6
25-29	2002.9	28	1.4E-5
30-34	2074.6	114	5.5E-5
35-39	1810.6	218	0.00012
40-44	1669.1	404	0.000242
45-49	1828.2	795	0.000435
50-54	1478.8	979	0.000662
55-59	1339	1042	0.000778
60-64	1254	1132	0.000903
65-69	1245.8	1397	0.00112
70-74	1231	1591	0.00129
75-79	933.5	1412	0.00151
80-84	768.8	1517	0.00197
85-89	468	1151	0.00246
90+	240	761	0.0032

2. Questionnaire and GP studies.

The approach in both of these types of study is exactly the same. The questionnaire responses give the numbers of cancers diagnosed in each household, the type of cancer, the sex, age and year at diagnosis and the sex, age and number of everyone living in the house. When all these data are added together we have a sample population, drawn randomly from the total population of the area being canvassed. We know the sex and age breakdown of this population at the time of the questionnaire and can calculate the annual expected numbers of cases of all cancers or any specific cancer from the national database. We then compare this expected number with the reported numbers over any period we choose, to see if there is an excess. There are some particular problems with this approach for questionnaires. The main one is that as we go back in time from the date of the questionnaire, there will be leakage of people with cancer from the sample due to deaths and of course, the population itself will have changed slightly from the 'snapshot' population at the time of the study. We always find that the number of annual cases reported falls off for earlier years and the effect is greatest for the fatal cancers like lung cancer. This is shown in Table 4.2.2.3. below for the 2001 Burnham-on-Sea North questionnaire undertaken by 'Parents Concerned about Hinkley' (PCAH). This survey was a response to denials by the Somerset Health Authority that there was any increase in breast cancer in the ward following the first mortality study we carried out in 2000 [Busby, Dorfman, Rowe 2000]. The survey obtained answers from addresses that added up to about one third of the census population of the ward.

Table 4.2.2.3 All cancer cases by year of diagnosis reported in 2002 in Burnham-on-Sea North according to PCAH questionnaire. Numbers fall off in earlier years because many have died and their families have moved away.

Year diagnosed	Number of cases
2001	17
2000	12
1999	8
1998	8
1997	10
1996	9
1995	6
1994	4
1993	2

Now, on the basis of the population defined by the response, the expected number of all types of cancer was 11 per year, so if we choose to look at 2000 and 2001 together, this will define a risk of 29/22 or 1.32. For year 2000 alone, the risk is 17/11 = 1.55. The risk we calculate for all cancers falls off rapidly with time. This is because the numbers will be dominated by lung cancer, which is usually fatal, and for all cancers together, lung and certain other cancers which have poor survival, the questionnaire method is of little use. But for looking at types of cancer that are treatable, or are less immediately fatal, like breast cancer, prostate and leukaemia, the method is valuable. It also has some great advantages. The first is that you can believe the results. If there is a significant excess of cancer shown by a survey like this, then you have immediate connection with the people who are reporting this. You know where they live and can relate this to the source of pollution by dividing your area up into bands of distance from the source, as we were able to do in Carlingford in Ireland, which I will discuss later. Best of all, you know that no one in the establishment has altered the data or re-evaluated the numbers and retrospectively removed cases that might indicate a problem. I will show later that all these things happen. The PCAH questionnaire showed that the Somerset Health Authority was covering up a real effect. It showed a doubling of the breast cancer incidence rate in the ward, confirming what we found in the mortality study. And in reality the true risk will always be higher than the calculated risk because of the leakage of population, so if the questionnaire shows a problem, there is one. In addition to locating sufferers on a map so that their distance from the source of pollution can be assessed, we can also ask questions about lifestyle e.g. smoking, eating habits etc., which may be valuable indicators of exposure routes or other stresses. In the Trawsfynydd study, which we designed and analysed in 2006 for the Welsh S4C company we asked if people ate (radioactive) trout from the nuclear power station lake. It turned out that those who did were twice as likely to have developed cancer.

GP studies involve exactly the same calculations as those we carried out for the mortality studies. The only difference is that the age breakdown of the study population is that of the surgery patient list. You have to be able to persuade the doctor to get the data out; often a very difficult exercise.

Part of my purpose here is to show that anyone can do such calculations and that people who are concerned about illness near any source of pollution, nuclear plants, landfill sites, incinerators, can check out what is going on for themselves. But we can't get too carried away at this stage; there is one more question we must address before we are secure in our belief that there is a problem at Burnham-on-Sea North, or anywhere where we find an apparent increased risk. We have to establish, as Bradford Hill's Canon asks: could this doubling of the risk of death occurred by chance? Here we have to deal with some statistical methods that enable us to answer this question.

4.3 The play of chance, and its evaluation.

I think I am going to upset the epidemiologists here. As I mentioned, in the last fifteen years, the discipline has collapsed under the intellectual weight of statistical methods developed to answer the simple question about whether an event might be a real indicator of an underlying causal relation (e.g. radiation and leukaemia) or merely an example of the random play of chance. Part of the problem we have to deal with is that the levels of risk we will find for adult cancers are usually modest. In Burnham-on-Sea, downwind from the Hinkley Point nuclear power station, in 2001 we found that there was a 2-fold excess of breast cancer based on 17 deaths over the four years 1995-98. In public health epidemiology the diseases that are being tracked are usually more immediate and graphic than the development of cancer some ten to twenty years after the initial causal exposure. Public Health departments deal with more mundane questions. Some people eat at a restaurant and suffer food poisoning: why? Twenty out of thirty who attended a picnic are in hospital vomiting with a high fever: what was the cause? It is unlikely to be chance, in these cases. But, with the cancer risk situation, it may be chance and we have to establish whether it is. I am going to avoid the complexity of modern statistical methods and offer a few simple tests that will let us know whether our discoveries are statistically significant or not. When we discover some increased risk level and report it, the health authorities will usually respond immediately with the cry: this is a random cluster of cases! In order to see if this is so, for small numbers of cases up to 40, the most important weapon in our armoury is the Cumulative Poisson Probability Table. This is a table which is published in most compilations of statistical tables and which enables us to see at a glance what the probability of observing some number of events is, given that the expectation is some other number of events. The tables are constructed from the Poisson Equation, which is an approximation to the Normal Distribution (or Bell-Shaped Curve) for rare events in the wings of the distribution. If this means nothing, don't worry, just use the tables and assume they tell you what you wish to know. I refer you to *Statistical Tables* by J Murdoch and JA Barnes (Macmillan 1998), but all these tables are the same. In the case of Burnham-on-Sea and breast cancer deaths from 1995-1998 we expect 8.7 and find 17. In the Cumulative Poisson Tables we look along the columns of expected numbers to 8.7 and then look down the rows to observed numbers 17. The Table gives the value 0.008. This value means that for an expectation of 8.7 deaths, you could expect to find 17 or any number fewer deaths with a probability of 0.008. That is 1 chance in 1 divided by 0.008 or 125. It tells us that if we looked at about 125 wards of the same size as Burnham-on-Sea, we would expect to find one ward with this apparent increase in breast cancer by chance alone.

The level of statistical significance conventionally accepted by statisticians as showing that a finding is 'significant' is taken to be below 0.05 (1 chance in 20) so in this case we certainly achieve this level. The numbers of cases involved in the calculation is very critical to this question of significance. Between 1995 and 1998 there were 17 breast cancer deaths. By 2001, another three years, the number of deaths was 14 more taking the total to 31. In the seven years the expectation is (assuming the same population) increased to 2.178 x 7 = 15.3. We now have a new risk 31/15.3 = 2.03. In the Poisson Tables this gives us a probability of 0.0002 or one chance in 5000 of these events being due to chance. There is not much difference between SMR's of 1.95 and 2.03, but the significance has hugely increased because the numbers are greater. This shows the importance of getting as many people into a study as possible.

For larger numbers than 40, we use a different method, which is much easier and quicker. It is called Chi-squared and is written χ^2. All we have to do is calculate the number from the following equation:

$$\chi^2 = (\text{Observed-Expected})^2/\text{Expected}$$

Thus for the previous case, we would have:

$$\begin{aligned}\chi^2 &= (31-15.3)^2/15.3 \\ &= 246.49/15.3 \\ &= 16.1\end{aligned}$$

There are values for χ^2 in all compilations of statistical tables. For these simple cases we have to use the value for 1-degree of freedom and the critical points for various levels of significance (0.05, 0.01, 0.005 and 0.001) are all we need to know. These are given in Table 4.3.1

Table 4.3.1 critical values for the Chi-squared (χ^2) distribution on 1-degree of freedom.*

p-value less than:	**χ^2 more than:**	**One chance in:**
0.05	3.84	20
0.01	6.64	100
0.005	7.88	200
0.001	10.8	1000

**Note: these values are for 2-tailed hypothesis tests where we are asking if the result is significantly greater than or smaller than the expected result. This is now the conventional test, although usually we are asking if the cancer is greater than expected, and in these circumstances a one-tailed test is correct, and this lets in more results as being significant*

Our calculation gives 16.1 and since this is greater than 10.82, the statistical significance is lower than 0.001, which we found in the Poisson Tables also. Some researchers demand that we also give the 95% confidence limits, and there is some reason for this. These are rather harder to work out than the p-values we have just calculated but can be obtained easily enough using a computer program. There are a number of excellent statistical computer programs which can be used to deal with these issues, and I will say a bit more about these below. Before I do this I need to briefly address the small numbers problem, since this is usually referred to by health officials trying to dismiss the significance of a finding.

We saw that the p-value from breast cancer mortality in Burnham-on-Sea North over the 5-year period was 0.008 and the RR was 1.95. This means that if we are looking for some effect near a nuclear site, or other putative source of risk where we are studying a number of wards, we should be aware that for every 125 wards there would be an excess of 1.95 by chance alone. In our first study we looked at about 109 wards, so finding the effect in one of them was not unexpected. On the other hand we already had a hypothesis suggesting the pattern of risk, close to the contaminated mud where Burnham-on-Sea was. This suggested the problem was a real one. So we have to look at more than just the value in one particular ward: we have to look for a pattern in several wards which share some attribute that can act as a surrogate for the exposure. In our case, it was proximity to the inter-tidal sediment. As it happened, increasing the period to 2001 increased the risk slightly but hugely increased the statistical significance to 0.0002. For this to have been a chance finding we would have to study about 5000 wards.

But there is yet another pitfall for the amateur epidemiologist. This is referred to (by the epidemiological community) as the 'Texas Sharpshooter' problem. In this (the argument goes), the student examines all the different cancers in all the different wards near a point source of pollution. This gives a large number of results and, by chance, one of these will show a high risk (merely because there are lot of numbers). At this point, the student decides that this particular cancer is being caused by the releases. This apparently is not allowed. It is like the 'Texas Sharpshooter' firing his pistol at the wall of a barn and then after he has hit the wall, drawing a bull's-eye around his bullet hole. Whilst I have sympathy with this argument, I get extremely irritated at the way it is mindlessly trotted out by establishment or government to deny real problems. I will return to a specific example of this later, but at this stage I want to point out that such an argument would make it impossible to discover anything on first notice. What if we lived near a factory that produced a seriously carcinogenic substance that caused throat cancer? We do not know this for sure, but we may have some (plausible) general belief that pollution is a bad thing and causes disease. So we do a cancer study of the area using 100 wards (to get a control) and look at all cancer types and find that the ward near the plant has a 4-fold excess of throat cancer. We are not allowed to conclude anything from this because of the Texas Sharpshooter argument. In this case it is nonsense.

4.4 Adjusting for disadvantagement.

It is quite commonly stated, when attention is drawn to high levels of cancer incidence in an area where there is a source of some environmental pollution, that the high rates are a consequence of socioeconomic factors. The (unstated) argument generally follows the following reasoning. People who are poor or unemployed smoke or drink too much alcohol and eat too many chips and not enough fresh fruit and vegetables. These behaviour patterns, it is argued, are associated with elevated cancer risk. It is also said that the genetic constitution of people in the lowest socio-economic groups is, in some un-elaborated way, 'poor' and this also adds to the cancer risk. Furthermore, these people get ill more often owing to their damp houses and overcrowded conditions with higher levels of infective illness or virus infection. No doubt they do too much sex also (cervical cancer), have too many babies and are generally a bad lot. Otherwise, if they were industrious, they would not be poor.

The study of deprivation and health is associated with a large body of literature. Deprivation indices using data easily extracted from the Census (such as that first suggested by Townsend) include such indicators as multiple dwelling occupancy, car ownership, home ownership, unemployment rates and so forth. The report by Carstairs and Morris (1991) discussed the development and use of the now widely utilised 'Carstairs Index' of deprivation. However, even if it is subsequently shown that the area in question has a higher index of socioeconomic deprivation, great care must be exercised in attributing the cancer to the deprivation. A common method to examine trend in cancer incidence near a putative source of pollution is to use least-squares multiple regression to examine trend with distance. This is a method that has become much in vogue since the development of computers. It can be used for looking at data where there are multiple possible causal factors for some measurement of interest and in principle enables us to see what the most important contributors are. I will discuss it further below. In its approach to effects near a point source, distance may be entered as one of the independent variables as a surrogate for pollution level and we can also include some measure of socio-economic deprivation. Implication of causation by the pollutant is flagged up by high statistical significance for the slope coefficient of the regression line or curve. Implication of socioeconomic deprivation may also be confirmed in this way. This, however, may be entirely spurious since it is only generally poor areas where sources of pollution exist. Either the polluting factories are built in poor areas because there is insufficient political power in such areas to oppose the project or else, following the identification of such a source, people rich enough to move away, do so. Furthermore, it is an extraordinary fact that in the UK there is in force a statutory planning instrument encouraging the siting of environmentally polluting sites in areas of high unemployment.

Examination of the relationship between cancer incidence and the Carstairs index of deprivation in Scotland reveals that, except for lung cancer in males and cervical cancer in females, the differences between the most deprived and least deprived are not very great. (Carstairs and Morris, 1991). Similar data for England has been obtained from the OPCS longitudinal study and uses Social Class as a measure of disadvantage (Leon, 1988). The direction of the trend in cancer with increasing levels of deprivation may be positive as well as negative. In our work we follow Leon (1988) in defining a 'positive' effect as being an increase in cancer risk in going up the socioeconomic scale and a 'negative' effect as an increase in cancer in going down the socioeconomic scale. A large number of studies have investigated such effects both in the UK and elsewhere in the world and, in general, the results indicate that lung cancer in males and cervical cancer in females suffer negative effects. Positive effects exist for colon cancer, female breast cancer and leukaemia. A Table of Carstairs deprivation index and cancer incidence in Scotland is shown in Table 4.4.1 below. The relationship is also shown graphically in Fig 4.4.1. Note that there is an inverse association between both breast cancer and leukaemia and social deprivation, an interesting observation which I have elsewhere explained as being due to the higher dairy intake of richer people in the period after the Second World War when the dairy was rich in Strontium-90 from weapons test fallout.

We used both Carstairs and a Welsh Office index of deprivation for regression analysis in the Wales small area study, but in our cancer mortality studies we carry out an adjustment of the expected numbers of cases in a ward using the relation between mortality and Social Class in England and Wales discovered by Leon in 1988. Since this is a straightforward calculation, I show how it is done. The relationship is given in Table 4.4.2 for the main cancers of interest. The trends with Social Class are similar to the trends shown by Carstairs indices. In practice, the adjustment is made to the expected numbers of cases. To use our example of breast cancer mortality in Burnham on Sea, first we have to obtain from the Census the numbers of each household in the ward in each of the Social Class categories as a proportion of all the households.

Table 4.4.1 Standardised Incidence Ratio of cancer sites by Carstairs deprivation score in Scotland 1979-82. (*Source:* Carstairs and Morris, 1991) The ranges of status in the rural areas we have examined are given in bold.

Cancer site	-12	-8	**-4**	**0**	**+4**	+8	+12
All malignancy	95	96	**94**	**100**	**101**	107	122
Oesophagus	78	86	**101**	**92**	**104**	118	148
Stomach	79	80	**86**	**103**	**109**	128	138
Colon	104	106	**99**	**99**	**98**	97	96
Lung	69	77	**80**	**100**	**110**	128	183
F.breast	114	109	**99**	**100**	**96**	95	89
Leukaemia	107	107	**96**	**102**	**89**	104	100
Prostate	115	106	**99**	**103**	**96**	90	92
Cervix	67	72	**91**	**94**	**120**	124	166

Table 4.4.2 Standardised Mortality Ratio (0-64yrs) by Social Class for some common cancers (1971-72)

Social Class	**All cancers**	**Lung**	**Breast**	**Prostate**	**Leukaemia**
1 Male *Female	75 99	53 73	117	91	113 88
II Male *Female	80 97	68 82	 112	89	100 108
IIIn Male *Female	91 99	84 89	 110	99	107 98
IIIm Male *Female	113 113	118 118	 109	115	101 105
IV Male *Female	116 116	123 125	 103	106	104 110
V Male *Female	131 116	143 134	 92	115	95 127

*Females based on married women classified by husband's occupation

Next, we obtain a single number that represents the adjustment factor, which we must use to multiply the expected numbers of deaths from breast cancer before adjustment for Social Class. From Table 4.4.2. we see that if all the women in Burnham on Sea were in Class I, then if there was no causative stress at all, we should have to increase the expected number of cases based on the age breakdown (which we have already calculated) by 117/100 or 1.17. The unadjusted expected number of 8.7 deaths now becomes 10.18 and the SMR falls to 17/10.18 = 1.67. To adjust for the actual number of women recorded as being in each Social Class group, we use a weighted average. If there are A women in group I and B in group 2 and C in group IIIn and so on, the factor F (SMR) is first obtained:

F(SMR) = (A*117) + (B*112) + (C*110) + (D*109) +(E *103) + (F*92)/(A+B+C+D+E+F)

Table 4.4.3 gives the numbers of households and persons in the 10% Census sample of Burnham North in the different Social Class categories, taken from Table 90 of the 1991 Census dataset.

Table 4.4.3 Numbers of households in different Social Class categories in the 10% sample of the 1991 Census for Burnham North with Social Class SMR for breast cancer mortality from Leon 1988, showing calculation of adjustment factor for expected numbers of deaths.

Social Class	(B) Households	(C) Social Class SMR	(D) = B * C
I	6	117	702
II	32	112	3584
IIIn	15	110	1650
IIIm	17	109	1853
IV	11	103	1133
V	2	92	184
Total	83		9106
Factor SMR	9106/83 = 109.7		
Factor	1.097		

So to obtain the correction factor for the expected numbers of breast cancer deaths we just use the data in this table. The result is that we must multiply the expected number by 1.097.

$$F(SMR) = (6*117)+(32*112)+(15*110)+(17*109)+(11*103)+(2*92)/83$$
$$F(SMR) = 109.7$$
$$F = 1.097$$

The result, 109.7 is an SMR; that is, it is based on England and Wales being considered to have the value 100. The expected numbers of deaths calculated on the basis of age alone therefore has to be increased by the ratio 109.7/100 or merely multiplied by 1.097.

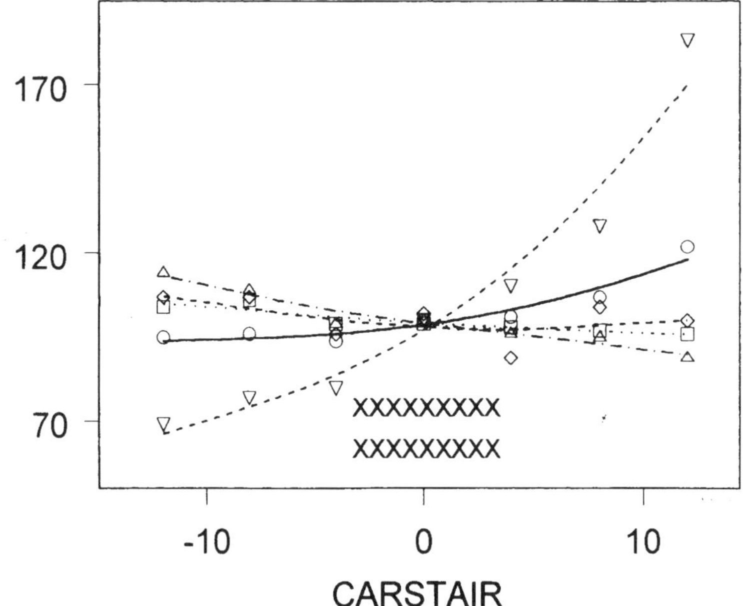

Fig 4.4.1 Variation of Standardised Incidence Ratio for cancer with CARSTAIRS scores for deprivation. Lung (inverted triangles), all malignancy (circles) show negative effects and breast (triangles), colon (squares) and leukemia (diamonds) show positive effects. The row of XXXX's define the range of deprivation measured in the Wales rural study area described later. (*Source:* Carstairs and Morris, 1991 and Small Area Health Statistics Unit, London)

4.5. Evaluating trends

One way in which we can examine the hypothesis that proximity to a nuclear site or other polluting source causes health problems is to compare two groups; the study and the control; the local with the distant, or the local with the whole of England and Wales. Often, this does not utilise all the information there is. Sometimes, if we have several different wards we can look for trends with distance from the point source. Lately, this approach (of examining trends with distance) has become the method of choice, but it can go dangerously astray for a number of reasons. One of these is that pollution does not conveniently emerge from a pollution source radially and contaminate the local environment uniformly. It might do this if it were a gas, and there was no wind, and the nuclear site was situated on a uniform flat plane, but these circumstances do not exist. In reality, the wind blows the pollution in certain directions and down winders are affected.

When there is no wind and there are anticyclonic conditions, temperature inversion layers constrain airborne pollutants in valleys to a narrow strip around the valley sides. So it is necessary to have an idea of the likely movements of discharges before deciding which are the contaminated and which the control group. Gould and Sternglass, in studying breast cancer near US nuclear sites used a simple but effective method of comparing population sectors in the prevailing downwind zones with upwind populations (Gould, 1996).

If we are trying to see if there are statistically significant trends in health detriment between groups who are believed to have decreasing levels of exposure, there are a number of methods, considerations and pitfalls to avoid. The main method used by almost all epidemiologists is a mathematical process called 'regression'. The rapid way in which regression methods have infested all disciplines has two sources. The first is psychological. Since the modern (but not post-modern) philosophers have emphasised the importance of objectivity in all attempts to tease out the truths and since this objectivity has been grounded firmly in mathematics, no one seems capable of deciding anything any more without looking to mathematics for support. Just as the inquisitors supported themselves with the teachings of Aristotle (and ignored what they saw in Galileo's telescope), modern epidemiology, sociology, psychology and economics (particularly economics) rely on multiple regression methods to find out what is going on. The fact that this routinely leads them into the swamp seems to make no difference. They clutch at the regression equations like drowning men at straws.

What is regression and what does it do? For a complete answer to this I'm afraid you have to do a bit of reading elsewhere, but I will try to give an outline. Regression is a method of looking to see if there is a relationship between two or more variables based on lots of data. When there are only two variables, we can plot them on a graph, as in Fig 4.5.1, which plots values of ground level ozone and air temperature. There is clearly a relationship. Linear regression assumes that a straight line represents the best fit to the data and calculates the equation of the best fit line using a statistical procedure that balances the number of points either side of the line. Regression is also used to look at a whole range of different variables at the same time. A regression equation for ground level ozone might involve examining temperature, wind speed and solar radiation intensity. If we assumed a straight-line relationship for the effect of all three on ozone the equation would be:

(Ozone) = a*(temperature) + b*(wind speed) + c*(radiation) + constant

The constant is there in case there is a residual amount of ozone even when the wind is not blowing, the temperature is zero and it is the middle of the night.

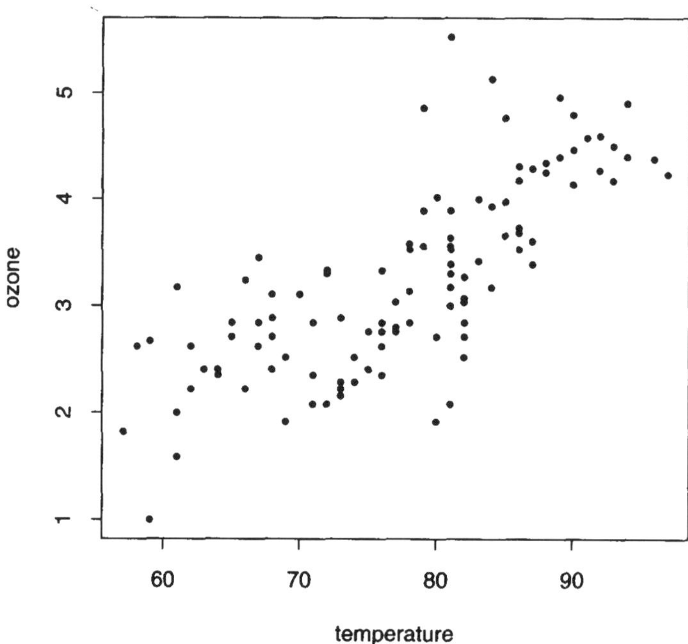

Fig 4.5.1 Scatterplot showing relationship between air temperature and ground level ozone from which a regression line may be deduced

The purpose of such a multiple regression is to see the effects of the three different causes, expressed as the coefficients a, b and c. Hundreds of different sets of measurements of temperature, wind speed, radiation and ozone are made and a computer program is set to work calculating the coefficients and also the statistical significance of each coefficient. If there is too much scatter or if an easy straight line cannot be drawn through any of the individual relationships, taken one at a time (and freezing the others), then the significance statistics shows this and the relationship does not exist. This is the theory. Many people think this theory itself is invalid (since there are some deep philosophical problems with fixing some variables whilst allowing others to move) and, in practice, multiple regression is fraught with technical and conceptual and philosophical difficulties if we want to be certain that it is even approaching something useful. This can be seen by comparing results for one variable with results for two and then three variables. So these methods are best avoided. There are two other major problems. First, we do not really know the relationship between the dependent (ozone) and the independent variables. There is no reason why it should be a straight line; it could be a smooth curve or even a wiggly curve. Assuming a straight line and modelling as if there were one may tell us there is no relationship when actually it is only telling us that there is no straight-line relationship.

A good example of this is afforded by a recent linear regression of cancer incidence in Somerset on distance from Hinkley Point nuclear power station, presented by Dr Julia Verne at a public meeting in Burnham on Sea in 2003. The graph is shown in Fig 4.5.2. Here, Dr Verne, who is anxious to show that there is no effect from Hinkley Point on local cancer rates, has plotted standardised incidence for every ward in Somerset by distance from the nuclear power station and (in this figure) the centre of the contaminated mud flats. This includes wards in Yeovil, some 60km away. How could anyone imagine the effect of the power station operating over 60km?

Figure4: Standardised Registration Ratios (SRR) for Somerset wards by distance from mudflats. All cancers 1990-1999

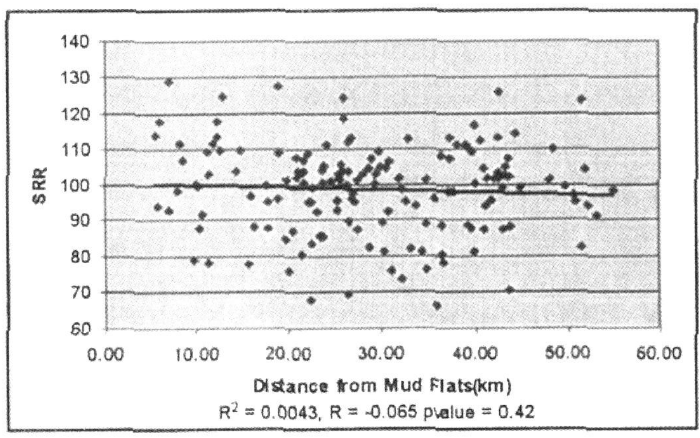

Fig 4.5.2 Regression straight line calculated by Dr Julia Verne of the South West Cancer Intelligence Unit in her September 2003 report of cancer near Hinkley Point. She has ignored the clear upward trend in the risk as the mud flats are approached but has spread the study area out as much as possible and averaged all the wards out to 60km in her attempt to show there is no statistically significant effect (see text). This allowed her to argue that there was indeed no effect. Following this Dr Verne was invited to join COMARE. (*Source Verne 2003*)

However, close examination of the graph in Fig 4.5.2 will show that between 0 and 30km, there seems to be a significant sea coast effect (I have determined the statistically significant straight line using the statistics package S-Plus). More likely, however, is that the relationship is a complex one and not linear at all. This is a further problem with regression and establishing relationships. You can fit a line or all sorts of curves to scattered data and the resultant fits can be described by statistics that estimate how good the fit is or whether it could have occurred by chance. Often, these *goodness of fit* statistics are used to suggest that there is a significant relationship between the causal determinant and the dependant effect. All that regression statistics tell us is how good a fit there is for the line or curve. Following this triumph of obfuscation, Dr Verne was elected to COMARE in 2004.

It is an interesting fact that the same goodness of fit statistic will be given by the statistical significance of a regression line fitting the series 12,15,17,18,21 as for the series 120,150,170,180,210. If these were numbers of cancer cases, there would be considerably different statistical significances between them. Imagine the last two represented numbers of cancer cases in the closest and next close wards near a point source and that we wanted to know if there was a statistically significant excess in the nearest ward by comparing the two. Poisson Tables tell us that 21 is not statistically significantly different from 18 (RR = 1.17; p = 0.2693) but 210 is certainly statistically different from 180 as $\chi^2 = 5$ (RR = 1.17; $p < 0.05$). Thus there are many occasions where regression tells us there is no significant effect because the overall numbers are not employed by the procedure. There is, however, a good method for examining trends, which does evaluate the significance of the trend line, and this is called 'Chi-squared for linear trend in proportions'. To use it you need a statistics package, and the best and easiest one for this and also the other Chi-square calculations is Epi-Info, which has the added advantage that it is entirely free. To use it you merely have to call up the 'STATCALC' routine and type in the data, observed and expected. The computer then does the rest.

4.6 Computer methods

I began by using a BBC 64 computer and writing all the programs I needed. This was the BBC that lived in my pre-fabricated concrete garage in Mallwyd and had to be dried out each morning with a hair dryer or it produced insane reams of output. I discovered a tremendously useful and powerful statistics teaching program developed at Reading University by Joan Knock called INSTAT, and all my early research in this area used this. I still have it. But now the BBC is outgunned and sits on the shelf. The PC is the essential tool for these studies (I suppose an Apple Mackintosh would do the same trick, but I don't know much about Mac's). With a cheap computer from the high street, or a secondhand one for a hundred pounds, you have the computing power of the average government department in 1992. The Small Area Health Statistics Unit (SAHSU), set up in 1984 after the Sellafield Enquiry, boasted in 1991 a DEC 5500 super computer running at 24MHz with data storage of 10,500MB (Elliott *et al* 1992). What a joke! Most children now have access to a computer that outperforms such a machine, running at speeds greater than 3000MHz and with storage capacity greater than 120,000MB. In addition, many programs exist now that can deal with epidemiological data and are cheap or free. Microsoft EXCEL is a spreadsheet package that will do nearly all the tricks necessary to calculate expected numbers of cases and compare them with observed numbers (although it has limitations for really huge datasets). In addition, the internet has made it possible to download files in formats that can be imported into EXCEL. For more advanced work, the free epidemiological package EPI INFO can be downloaded from the website of the 'Centre for Disease Control' (CDC) in Atlanta Georgia (www.cdc.org). This package used to be somewhat impenetrable, but has improved a lot recently and has all you need; it will do regressions, logistic regressions, statistical calculations, trend calculations and even has a very good instruction manual. For more advanced analysis, there are many commercial software packages. I use SPSS (a statistics package favoured by sociologists and psychologists, which has a tremendously valuable ability to dissect out what you want from enormous datasets) and I also use S-Plus, which is a programmable package that seems to have been developed (by IBM) for data mining. There is a new, simple, fairly idiot proof package called Sigmastat which even leads you through the jungle by asking you what data you have and suggesting tests. My daughter Araceli, who is employed as an epidemiologist, uses STATA. The big programs cost money, thousands of pounds, and you don't really get much more than a combination of EXCEL and EPI INFO, although EXCEL won't handle very large files. Don't be fearful or think you can't do any of this. I have talked about statistics with many epidemiologists. The truth is, epidemiologists are not usually statisticians or mathematicians and usually know less than I do. They are mostly frightened that someone will suss out their ignorance. It is an Emperor's New Clothes affair. They have statisticians working for them in the big departments. But here's another thing: The statisticians don't know epidemiology. The mathematicians may have taken over the world of objectivity, but they are not that good at seeing the real picture.

4. 7 Why epidemiology?

I have tried to give an overview of the ideas and processes involved in epidemiology, and I have also shown how it is possible for anyone with a basic understanding of maths to find out whether a point source of pollution is causing illness in the local population. This is partly because much of what I have to say in this book relies on this kind of reasoning and partly because I want to empower everyone and help them to take control of their environment and the risks it poses to their health. We are all observers and we all learn to avoid harm. We teach our children what our parents taught us, but the world is becoming increasingly complex and dangerous and the new dangers are not things we are immediately able to comprehend. Simple hunter-gatherers could look at the sky and predict rain. They taught their children to avoid poisonous snakes or plants. They did not need to know about road traffic, but would probably stay well clear of the noisy roads and fast cars if they were transported to our developed countries. Today, dangers are posed by environmental pollutants and much nonsense is spouted by government and industry about the safety of the new processes. You will see reports of epidemiological studies that claim to show that risks are low, or non-existent. You should be very, very cautious about such studies and look beyond the surface. Think independently and carefully about what is said and the evidence it is based upon. As I shall argue later on, epidemiology is an area that is pre-eminently disposed to bogus analysis and biased conclusions. This chapter was intended to supply the basic machinery for examining such claims and the basic toolkit for carrying out simple studies to answer such questions about risk. These are the new snakes in the new jungle. But they are invisible: we have to infer their presence from epidemiology. This is why it is a critical discipline for our survival, and why it is being distorted to persuade us there are no snakes, and that when we are bitten, or one of our children is bitten, it is not a bite but just an accidental play of chance.

We are ready now to look at the results of the first piece of research I did to investigate the distribution of cancer near a source of risk: Green Audit's study of cancer in Wales near the Irish Sea..

5
The Irish Sea Part I. Cancer in Wales 1974-89

5.1. Wales

In *Wings of Death*, in 1995, I predicted a cancer epidemic in England. At the time, it was being argued by the government that there were no increases in cancer in real terms. The basis of my argument was the increase in cancer in Wales which began in the late 1970s and which national data showed to accurately follow the cumulative dose to the Welsh population from Strontium-90. The graphs are shown in Fig 5.1.1 below.

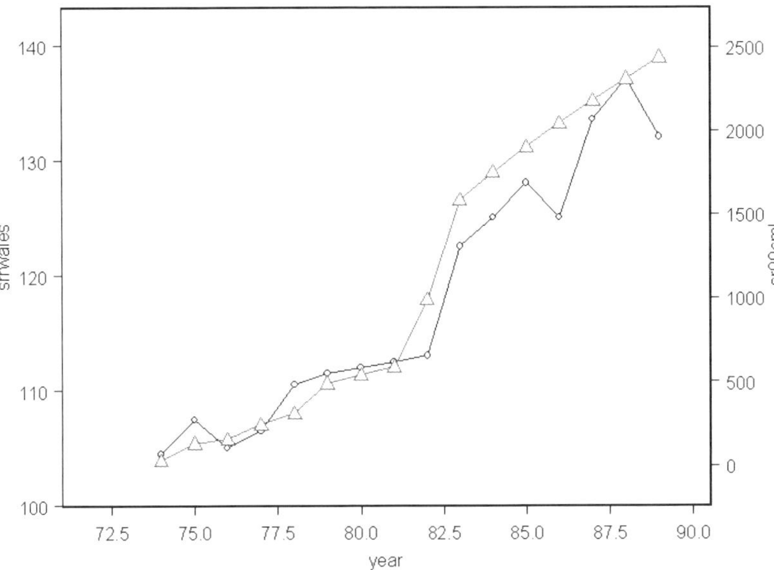

Fig 5.1.1 Cancer in Wales (circles, SRR, all malignancies M+F) and Strontium-90 cumulative dose (triangles, microSieverts) twenty years earlier i.e. lagged so that the dose in 1960 is plotted in 1980 to allow for its effect on the cancer rate (Busby, 2004, BNES).

Of course, there was not just Strontium-90: There was Caesium-137, Barium-140, Iodine-131, Ruthenium-106, Plutonium-239, on and on and on: a list that includes a host of new radioactive substances capable of being incorporated into human tissue and causing genetic damage to cells. The reason for the higher levels of radioactivity in Wales was rainfall. Wales has three times the rainfall of England and the levels measured in the milk and the food by the Ministry of Agriculture (MAFF) were two to three times higher than in England. But this was not the only radioactivity in Wales. There was also the material that fell with the rain after the Windscale fire in 1957. There was also the material from Sellafield washed up on the coast. There were three questions. Were the increases in cancer shown by the national aggregated data in *Wings of Death* uniformly spaced over Wales in the disaggregated small area data? If not, then where would the highest levels of cancer be found, if radioactivity were the cause? Finally, what would be the effect of living near the contaminated coast, if any?

Sellafield released material over the whole period covered by the data at a much greater level than there had ever been before or since. There were huge discharges, which increased from the beginning of the period and peaked towards 1979. If there was a 1-year lag between the contamination leaving the pipeline and fetching up on the coast of Wales then, allowing a few years for the start of the clinical expression of cancer from this source, and walking into the problem like the TV detective Columbo with a naïve air of ingenuous bewilderment, we could expect two things. First, there should be higher levels of cancer near the coast in the north, which was closer to Sellafield. Second, the trend in cancer risk over the period should increase more rapidly near the coast than further away. These would seem reasonable 'prior hypotheses'. But at the beginning we didn't know what we should find and, at that time, we didn't know either about the concentration of the material in estuarine and inter-tidal sediment, nor did we know anything about the trend in air concentration away from the coast. We found all that out later when we were trying to explain the (initially) curious results. Originally, when we were thinking about the atmospheric test fallout, we thought that the highest levels of cancer would be in the areas of highest rainfall, but that there might be some coastal effect from Sellafield superimposed on this and increasing over the period.

The idea was to look at the small area distribution of cancer in all of Wales over the period 1974-89 and this is what we did. Some of these results can get a bit technical. Don't bother to try and follow it all if it gives you a headache. I have put a lot of the results in this book as reference material for those who want to dig deeper. The gist, however, is clear to all.

5.2 The data and the exercise

Between 1974 and 1995, when they were closed down, Wales Cancer Registry collected details of all cancer cases in Wales by address at the time of diagnosis, sex, age at diagnosis and site of cancer (or what I shall call cancer type). For historic reasons to do with the population divisions of the country and for purposes of statistical analysis, the numbers of cases were aggregated by WCR to small areas called Areas of Residence (AOR). These areas varied widely in area, but each consisted of a small number of census wards. Appendix B lists the names of all the AOR's in Wales with their 1981 population. In 1998, we began research for the Irish Court case, which was still running when I began this book. The case *Short and Others vs. BNFL* began in the early 1990s and dragged on painfully, being stalled in the Courts by BNFL with tedious arguments on points of law. These eventually wore everyone down and the case was recently (the summer of 2006) knocked on the head by the Irish Supreme Court which changed its mind about being able to prosecute a foreign company, BNFL, for trans-boundary pollution. Such is politics. This was a serious cop-out. There are plenty of instruments the Irish could have used, but clearly there was some political deal behind-the-scenes. As you will see, the Irish State has let down its citizens who are dying in their thousands because of Sellafield.

To inform the case, the idea was to examine cancer incidence risk by distance from the Irish Sea and also look for any changes there might be over the period 1974 to 1989, the period covered by the data. We had all the different cancers. We had all the age groups. The most difficult part at the beginning was converting the text-based files we were given into a form that could be sorted on the computer. Because they were too large for EXCEL, we had to use SPSS for this procedure. The first file we were given was a compressed data file named *A-2218.exe*, which had been extracted from the mainframe computer at the Welsh Office by Susan Frost on 25th May, 1995. It had an on-board unpacking program but when it unpacked it was too large for any program we had on the computer we had then: they promptly locked up. As you will see later on, this turned out to be valuable, since I asked for the file to be split into two and Wales Cancer Registry sent me the divided file on a separate disk. Unfortunately this was also too big. By late 1996, (and not unconnected with stable doors and horses) Wales Cancer Registry had been closed down. However, the Welsh Office cancer data collection was now being carried out by the Statistics Division and I phoned Heather McGrane, who was part of this operation, and asked if I could have a different version of the cancer files and one which was updated as far as possible. She was helpful and organised to send me a complete set of the data back to 1974. This was extracted, by Hugh Warren, from the mainframe computer using a different method on 12th June 1996. This file included the latest data year 1990 and was labelled *A-2883.*

We had to wait until 1998 to start examining all this. The Irish State bought us a bigger PC, a Gateway 2000 (a machine which is still running) and they also paid for software that enabled us to begin organising and analysing the data. In addition, we obtained two second-hand backup 486 machines, which were used by the data processing assistants. You may laugh, but this was quite significant computing power back then.

Ecological analysis

The basic method we used to investigate the hypothesis that exposure to radioactive discharges had caused excess cancer on the Irish Sea coast of Wales is termed by epidemiologists, 'ecological'. It cannot, even after a discovery of a very strong association, prove a causal relation, but may provide supporting evidence, strong negative evidence or, on the other hand, may generate new hypotheses. The best form of such analysis would be the comparison of radioactive exposure levels for the isotopes of interest, perhaps measured as doses, with subsequent levels of cancer. However, here we had only the measured levels of radioactive pollution in the inter-tidal sediment for certain points on the Welsh coast and data on activity levels of man-made radioisotopes in soil. We could also identify the coastal populations and our initial hypothesis, as described below, was merely that such people have a higher risk of cancer than those living inland.

The most useful form of cancer incidence data would be post coded cases, so that an accurate mapping of cases to distance bands from the coast could be compared with populations in such bands. Post coding only began in the middle of the period we were examining and, anyway, the data we had been given was not post coded. So, in practice, we were constrained to examining the smallest areas that cases are coded to by the Wales Cancer Registry database, the AOR. In any event, the ability to usefully examine case numbers would depend upon having suitable population data. What we were essentially doing was comparing observed rates with expected rates. To generate rates for an area we needed the population of that area.

Hypothesis

The hypothesis being tested was that coastal populations are at greater risk of cancer than inland populations. The null hypothesis, that there is no difference, was tested using a chi-square statistic where numbers of cases were greater than 50 and cumulative Poisson probability where the numbers were smaller. The trend with distance from the sea and also trends in time in distance bands were examined using a Relative Risk based on the England and Wales populations for 1979. This is because this 1979 population was used as a base for trend analysis by the Office for Populations, Census and Surveys, OPCS in their annual publication Cancer

Statistics Series MB1 and also because we had used this base year in other analyses and publications, notably in Wings of Death. It also enabled us to examine trends in time relative to data from England and Ireland. In addition, certain other statistical procedures were used to examine the data and these will be described in due course.

Populations and Areas of Residence

The best available source of population data for small areas is the decennial census, and so we were forced to identify the smallest area we could examine with the smallest census unit. In this case, however, the AORs used by the Welsh Office for health administrative purposes were slightly larger than these. They varied in area and population, but these AOR populations could be obtained by aggregating 1981 census wards so long as we could find what the wards were.

This resulted in a 1981 population for the AORs. It was this population, and its distribution by 5-year age group, that was used to approximate the population for each year from 1974 to 1989. Cancer incidence generally increases exponentially with age and so it was necessary to allow for the ageing of the population between 1974 and 1989. This is a problem, however, for ward level data, since population data from the 1991 census was based on new wards due to boundary changes, which occurred between the 1981 and 1991 censuses. Normally, the best method to allow for changing population demography is to generate a trend line between the 10-year census populations. Because of the boundary changes, this was not possible. However, we were able to use the larger areas in Wales to examine the level of error that was introduced by using the 1981 census figures alone and show that, for Wales, for the summation of effects from the whole age range, the alteration in population from 1974 to 1981 exactly balances that from 1981 to 1989 and that the error was negligible. This is shown in Table 5.2.1. below. It had also been possible, in the case of some of the AORs, because of minimal changes in the ward boundaries, to examine the effect of the changing populations. Such analyses confirmed that the 1981 populations were a suitable approximation for the population at risk over the whole period. Table 5.2.1 also shows the change in expected numbers of 'all malignancies' in Bangor, North Wales, based on 1981 and 1991 populations although this comparison has to be considered with caution owing to slight changes in the ward boundaries between the two years.

After some considerable digging and telephoning, the ward composition of the AORs was obtained from the Office of Population Census and Surveys (now the Office for National Statistics (ONS)), Titchfield, Hants. Census figures also were obtained from OPCS and separately on floppy disk from the Statistics Division of the Welsh Office. AOR maps were generated from the ward lists we obtained from OPCS using County maps of the 1981 wards supplied by the Cartography Division of the Welsh Office, who also kindly supplied 1991 ward boundary maps. A digitized map of the AORs was produced using the program EPIMAP. This map is used throughout for presentation of geographical data and as a coloured descriptor of disease rates or pollution. The basic map of AORs in the study area used is given in Appendix A and Plate 4.

Table 5.2.1 Variation in expected numbers of 'all malignancy' based on 1979 England and Wales rates using 1974, 1981 and 1989 estimated populations for Wales. *(Source: Welsh Office Statistics Department)*

Population	Expected number 'All Malignancies'
a. All Wales 1974 only	10879
a. All Wales 1981 only	11522
a. All Wales 1989 only	12284
b. Population at risk: all Wales 1974-89	185203 by linear interpolation
c. Population at risk: all Wales 1974-89	184352 by approximation on 1981 population
Bangor MB 1981 census year only	47.07
Bangor town wards 1991 census	46.20

a Based on Welsh Office figures (Welsh Office 1994)
b Summation of annual totals produced by linear interpolation between the data years.
c 11522 x 16 years

Distance from sea, SEADIST

Our identification of population distance from the sea was similarly constrained by the data. What we did is to calculate approximate centroids of population for each AOR and to use these as the distance from the sea labelled SEADIST in our working files. The centroids of population were obtained by the following method: The main centres of population in an AOR were identified on a map and a line was drawn between the two largest. A point was positioned on this line such that the distance from the two ends was in proportion to the relative populations. This point and its calculated virtual population were then used as a centre of population in a subsequent similar exercise involving the third centre of population. The process was repeated until the centroid was obtained. In practice, the centroids for most AORs were easily determined since there was only one centre of population, usually a large town. In the case of the coastal towns within 1km or less of the sea there could be no error. Centroids of population for AORs in Gwynedd had been published by the Wales Cancer Registry in their 1994 Report on Trawsfynydd Nuclear Power Station (Welsh Office, 1994). This paper is discussed later but the centroids given in that publication substantially agreed with those obtained by the method outlined. Distance from the sea was measured from the map in any direction to the nearest sea coast.

Origin of cancer data

The Wales Cancer Registry Database (which I will refer to as WCR1) was obtained in 1995 (see above). An account of the acquisition of WCR1 and an entirely separate layout of the same data including the year 1990 which was given to us by the Statistics Division of the Welsh Office in 1996 (which I call WCR2) is also discussed later in this book. It is the data from WCR1 that was used throughout the study as the primary source. However, WCR2 has been extracted and coded for the age groups 0-4, 5-9, 10-14 and 15-19 in order to provide a check for the childhood cancer analysis. Both these databases were provided as text files extracted from the Welsh Office mainframe computer. The text files were separately compressed using different compression routines at an interval of one year. They were extracted in the Welsh Office from the SPSS data file on the Welsh Office computer by two different people, using different routines, working a year apart. The first pages of the text files of WCR1 and WCR2 are reproduced in Appendix A together with pages of data from the two separate databases referring to a case of childhood cancer in Bangor. This is to illustrate the point that the two databases may be used as a check upon each other to show that at the point that they were handed over to us, except for certain anomalies relating to leukaemia, which will be discussed later, they largely agreed with each other.

Software and routines

The data supplied by the Welsh Office, WCR1, was decompressed using the on-board routine supplied and then imported into MS Word 6 for preliminary examination or comparison with WCR2. This text file was then stripped of initial text lines and imported into either MS EXCEL or Mathsoft AXUM. The EXCEL/ AXUM files were then filtered into cancer site files for each year but containing columns for each 5-year age group. These were then exported to SPSS or S-PLUS programs and saved as SPSS and S-PLUS files. Population data were reconfigured to AORs using the disk versions of the 1981 census ward populations supplied by the Statistics Division of the Welsh Office and imported to EXCEL. The aggregations of AORs in terms of their constituent wards had been a problem at first. Initially, the new cancer registry that replaced WCR in 1997, the Wales Cancer Intelligence and Surveillance Unit (WCISU) was approached for assistance, but they had no idea what the makeup of the AORs was, and still don't know. In fact, as I will show later in this book, when making calculations on cancer risks WCISU virtually made up the populations to suit their beliefs. To obtain the true ward aggregations for the AORs I had to contact the Office for National Statistics in Titchfield and eventually they supplied me with two separate files and an invaluable table of equivalent ward names and AOR names that enabled me to collect the constituent wards of the AORs together. It turned out that the AORs were based on 1974 local government boundaries whose constituent wards were largely unchanged by the 1981 census. Following the acquisition of the aggregate ward names and designations, and employing these populations, the expected numbers of cases were then generated within these files by applying the age-related incidence rates for the cancer site in question recorded in the OPCS 1979 cancer incidence Volume (OPCS, 1994). The expected numbers for each AOR were then exported to the relevant SPSS and S-PLUS cancer site file for final analysis. In order to examine the effects of the various possible casual parameters, e.g. rainfall, deprivation etc. dummy variables relating to the AORs (a dummy variable is an indicator of some categorical description e.g. near the coast = 1, remote from coast = 0) together with data on Plutonium pollution, rainfall, socio-economic descriptors etc. were imported or coded into the SPSS and S-PLUS master area files. Finally, following the analysis of these files, any AORs with significant excess cancer risk were checked against the separate text file WCR2 in case the result was an error picked up in the various manipulations.

This work was massively tedious and hugely complicated. I supervised, planned and checked it but much of it was carried out by a number of young men and women who worked for me for small sums. We only had small sums, because the Irish State did not pay up until the end of the three years so I was paying these people with plastic and borrowed money. One of these assistants, Alasdair Stocking, did the work in an Internet Café between serving coffee and helping out. A very clever, intense young man with a degree in computer sciences, Alasdair solved many of the programming difficulties we had, accurately converting the text files to useable data. Another, Bruce Kocjian (Plate 23) a Scot with Brazilian father, had a degree in geographical mapping. At one point, Bruce had to sleep in a tent (this was in winter). He also did some of the work in our house in Queen Street whilst the windows were removed (they were being replaced on a council grant and I was living in a small flat with Molly and the children). He sat at the computer for three weeks wrapped up in a sleeping bag whilst snow blew in from the street. This is bare-foot epidemiology for sure.

Area chosen for study

The area of Wales chosen for the study was rural mid- and north Wales north of a parallel drawn through St David's Head. We also initially looked at a study area which was slightly larger and which included Pembrokeshire and Carmarthen in the South and Wrexham in the North. The justification for reducing the area was that the OPCS classification of the County Districts containing the Areas of Residence (AORs) should be uniform in order to exclude, as much as possible, confounding causes of cancer from industrial pollutants. The final AORs included in the study area were thus all those classified by OPCS as 'Type I (Rural Areas)' and all 'Type V (Mining and Industrial Areas)' were excluded. In addition, the AORs south of St David's Head which included the areas near Milford Haven and Llanelli were excluded for two reasons. The first was that there is considerable petrochemical pollution associated with the refinery at Milford and the chemical and steel factories in the area. The second was that measured Sellafield radioactivity concentrations were very low in the Bristol Channel and South Wales silts, and effects from the Bristol Channel nuclear sites may have confounded any results. A map showing the AORs with their names is given in Appendix A Figure 1 and the AORs with their total populations in Appendix A Table 1.

Method

For each AOR in the study area, the expected number of cancer cases in each sex and 5-year age group was calculated by multiplying the 1981 census population in each sex and 5-year age group by the rate for that cancer site published for the 1979 population of England and Wales. This provided the expected number of annual cases of that cancer for any aggregate group of persons in the AOR. In general, for all ages, the sex and 5-year groups were then summed to give the total expected numbers and this was multiplied by the appropriate number of years to give the total expected number of cases, termed 'E'. The Relative Risk (RR) was then obtained by calculating the ratio Observed/ Expected or O/E. For some cancer sites, a socio-economically adjusted Relative Risk was also considered. This was obtained by adjusting the expected number of cases by a factor derived from the Carstairs Index of Deprivation as described elsewhere in this book.

Having calculated Relative Risks for any site, population age group or period, the next stage was to examine the data for trend with distance from the sea. This was initially done by generating a scatterplot of Relative Risk by distance from the sea, or RR by SEADIST. There is a problem, however, in interpreting such a plot or in using the RRs for each AOR as individual data points in any regression analysis to examine causes. This is due to the widely different population sizes in the different AORs. Some of the rural AORs in Powys have very small populations; this lead to a much larger scatter of values for RRs in these areas, especially for low incidence cancer types and for children where the natural rates are very small. This could have resulted in one such AOR having a single case by chance but causing a very high RR and the resultant scatterplot or regression would thus convey undue weight to this point value. The problem is discussed in Elliott *et al* (1992) where a number of solutions are suggested, including the method of Bayesian smoothing. We adopted a different approach. Scatterplots may be weighted by the size of the AOR to produce what is called a 'bubble plot'. In such a plot the size of the data point represents the weight to be ascribed to it. Thus an area with a large population has a larger bubble and the eye is led to see the relationship between cancer risk and SEADIST.

Besides the graphical use of 'bubble plots', to analyse the relationship qualitatively we also decided to overcome the problem in two other ways. The first was by aggregating AORs into grouped bands at different distances from the sea with approximately the same number of AORs. For the high incidence- all ages analyses, seven such bands were used. The distances were not linearly defined since the main purpose was to establish sufficiently large populations in each band to reduce the variance in Relative Risk. The following distance (km) bands were used:

Group I0~SEADIST<0.8
Group 2 0.9<SEADIST~2
Group 3 2. l<SEADIST<5
Group 4 5.1 <SEADIST<11
Group 5 11.1 <SEADIST<20
Group 6 21<SEADIST<40
Group 7 SEADIST>41

In addition, for comparison, RR values were computed for three other groups;

- All study area
- All South Wales
- All Wales

Population data averages and mean values of SEADIST and number of aggregate AORs for the groups are given in Appendix B.

The second way of examining the effect of SEADIST and also other possible explanatory variables was by regression analysis. I asked Professor Diggle of Lancaster University, an expert in this area what to do. He suggested using as a general equation of trend the following:

$$\text{Relative Risk} = Ae^{\alpha S + \beta D + \dots}$$

or

$$\ln(RR) = \alpha S + \beta D + \dots + \text{constant}$$

Where for each AOR, RR is relative risk, S is SEADIST, D is deprivation, and other covariates can be examined. The basic regression on SEADIST and the p-value of the t- statistic for the coefficient α answers the question of whether there is a significant trend away from the coast although it constrains the answer to an assumption that the form of the relationship over the whole range of distance is logarithmic (see the arguments about regression in Chapter 5). In order to overcome the problem that small areas carry equivalent weighting with large population areas, the values of RR were population-weighted by the expectation values. Inclusion of socio-economic deprivation coefficients in the equation of risk (as β) enabled this factor to be examined. However, as already noted, there are problems of interpretation with a multiple regression approach, which increase with the number of covariates in the equation. There are also statistical pitfalls associated with autocorrelation, heteroscedasticity and multi-collinearity. Furthermore, regression and correlation only measure association. Interpretation depends on inputs of other factors, areas of knowledge and causal mechanisms. One important area where the results must be considered with caution is that of illness and socio-economic deprivation. This has already been considered in Chapter 5 and in order to make certain that deprivation was not at the base of the effects we discovered in Wales, a number of different techniques and indicators were used.

Socio-economic deprivation

In an attempt to resolve the problem of standardising for deprivation, we obtained two sets of deprivation indices. First, we contacted the Small Areas Health Statistics Unit (SAHSU) at Imperial College, London. Their deputy director, Dr Jarup, agreed to supply us with Carstairs scores for the 1991 Welsh census wards but was unable to help over the problem of devising a standardisation routine. He suggested using the cancer rates in all the AORs in the whole of the study area to obtain a correlation that would enable us to devise a standardising factor. But this approach would lose any comparisons with England, something we were not prepared to do as England in 1979 was our base. Second, we discussed the same problem with the statistical division of the Welsh Office and they supplied copies of 1981 ward-level maps together with a list of values for deprivation in the 1981 wards calculated using a more comprehensive deprivation index: the Welsh Index of Socio-economic Conditions.

Our final procedure was to calculate two different deprivation indices for the AORs in the study area using the 1991 Carstairs index ward-level data for wards that approximated to those boundaries in 1981 wards. The ward data was a population-weighted aggregate of these 1991 wards approximating in boundary to the 1981 AOR boundary. These values were coded as CARSTAIRS. The Welsh Index of Socio-Economic Conditions was a population weighted aggregate to the exact AOR level and was coded as DEP1. We then ran simple linear or log regressions between the Relative Risks and deprivation scores as suggested by Jarup.

In a second approach, which I prefer as it seems more rational, we examined the relation between cancer incidence and the Carstairs index found by Carstairs herself in Scotland, and generated standardisation factors for the main cancer sites we examined. They were applied to certain cancer sites to see if the magnitude of any effect could explain all or part of the results. The effect of deprivation on cancer trends can be teased out in another way. We know, for example that lung cancer has a strong positive relationship with deprivation. The more deprived, the greater the lung cancer: this is what is universally found. On the other hand, leukaemia and breast cancer operate in the opposite direction. So if there is a sharp excess of lung cancer in a small area (over the national average) and also an excess of leukaemia and breast cancer, then the primary reason cannot be deprivation. This approach showed that our sea coast effect was not a deprivation one, as both lung cancer and breast cancer increased sharply near the contaminated coast in north Wales.

5.3 Results

In the following pages I will show the results of this exercise. Each pair of pages represents the results we obtained for each of the main cancer types we examined, first in adults of all ages, then in children. For some of these a coloured map of relative risk over the larger study area is displayed in the Plate Section. These maps have to be approached with caution since in many of the large rural areas there are very few people and so a high RR may not be statistically significant and is probably a chance finding. This is unlikely to be true for the towns and the more populated areas. In each results section I show a bubble plot of risk for the cancer in all the AORs in the study area by distance from the sea. This is followed by a table of risk in each of the aggregated bands and in Wales and South Wales. These values are then plotted and a local regression LOESS line fitted to examine any underlying associations between risk and distance from the sea. I then plot the trend in cancer over the period 1974-1989 for aggregated groups at three distances from the sea, in order to examine whether there has been an increase in cancer close to the sea relative to groups far from the sea. Finally, for each cancer I give a summary of the results of regression analysis on the various possible confounding causes that we examined. At the end of this section, I look separately at the confounding causes and describe them in greater detail.

5.3.1 Adults: all malignancies

The most common malignancies in men are lung, skin, prostate, bladder, stomach and colo-rectal (large bowel) cancer. In women the common cancers are breast, skin, lung, colorectal and stomach cancer. . Lung cancer accounts for 22 per cent of male cancers whereas female breast cancer accounts for 22 percent of cancer in women; one in 12 now develop it at some time in their lives. In examining the trends in cancer in Wales by distance from the sea, we were anxious to examine all cancers aggregated together because the increase in real terms of all cancers had been already shown to follow the increase in cumulative doses from weapons fallout Strontium-90. The hypothesis was that genetic damage introduced by the weapons fallout had led to an increase in all cancers some twenty years later. But, of course, there are some very large question marks over such a hypothesis. Different cancers develop with different lag times; in putting all the cancers together we are looking at the sum of many effects, but these effects are mainly driven by the high incidence rate cancers like lung and breast etc, which probably do have roughly similar development period from initial exposure. The results for Wales from 1974-89 show that there was a significant sea-coast effect with significantly higher rates of cancer in the 0-2km group of areas (Table 5.3.1.1, Fig 5.3.1.1 and Fig 5.3.1.2). In addition, the levels of cancer in this coastal population were higher than in industrial south Wales or Wales as a whole and that the overall increases which were found in Wales as a whole increased most rapidly in this coastal group, particularly after Chernobyl in 1986 (Fig 5.3.1.2).

This result was the first of many that showed a very sharp increase in cancer close to the coast. From Table 5.3.1.1 we can deduce that, over the 16 year period, about 3000 people in the 0-0.8km plus 1000 people in the 0.8-2km strip developed cancer because they lived in these coastal strips, rather than living inland in the rest of Wales. Thus a total of about 4000 extra cancers in the 16-year period can be traced to the effects of the Irish Sea coast. Using the average incidence to mortality ratio for all cancer this implies a cancer death toll of about 2700 in this 16-year period. These increases were distributed amongst most (but not all) the cancer types.

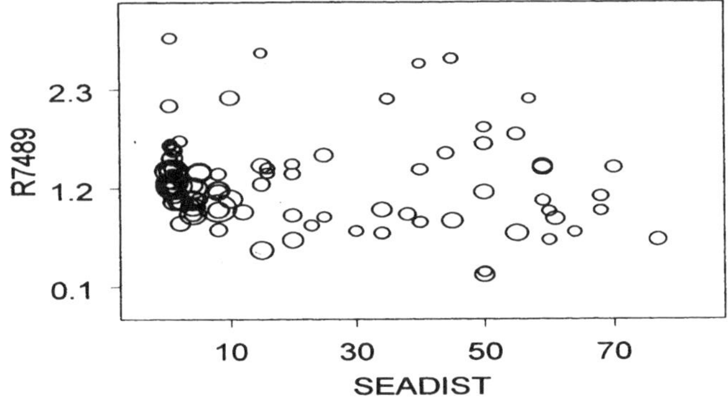

Seadist range Km	Average (SD)	N AORs	Oberved 74-89	Expected 74-89	Relative Risk	P value
<0.8	0.56 (0.17)	17	14445	10419	1.4	0.0000
0.9<x<2	1.38 (0.51)	13	11714	9559	1.23	0.0000
2.1<x<5	4.27 (0.47)	10	8283	7290	1.13	
5.1<x<11	8.44 (0.88)	10	8358	7388	1.13	
11.1<x<20	17.5 (2.32)	12	4294	4231	1.02	
21<x<40	33.67 (6.5)	12	2995	2524	1.18	
>41	55 (9.5)	23	7153	6579	1.09	
S Wales E=2		65	125054	105201	1.13	
Wales		193	207272	174675	1.12	

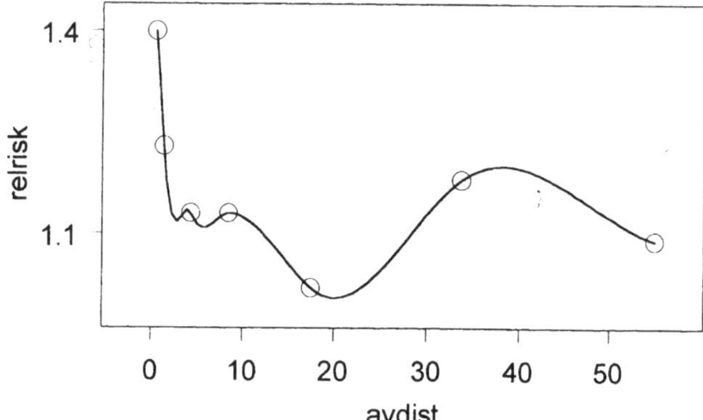

Fig 5.3.1.1 Top: Bubble plot of incidence risk for all malignancies in study area. Centre: Table of Relative Risks for all malignancies (ICD9 140-208) by distance bands showing details of bands. Bottom: LOESS plot of risk by distance form sea in km.

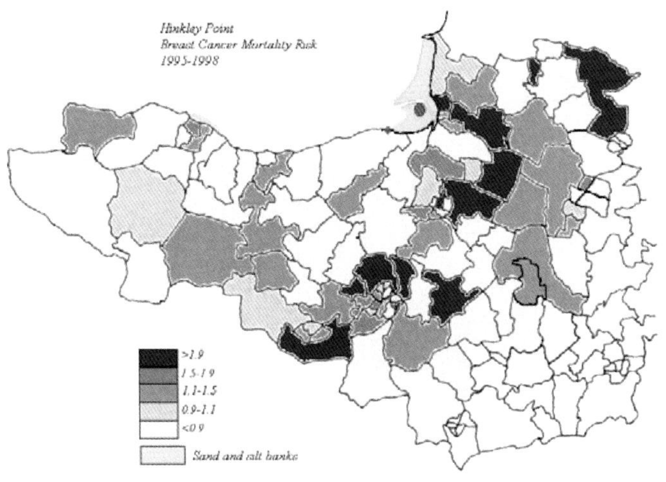

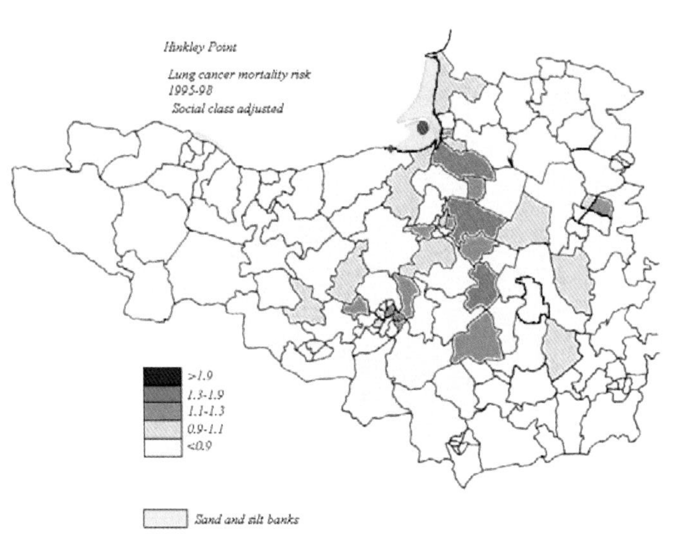

Plate 1 Maps of cancer mortality risk in Somerset 1995-98. Upper: breast cancer. Lower: lung cancer. Note the higher risks follow the tidal river Parratt; all the higher lung cancer risk is on the flood plain (see text)

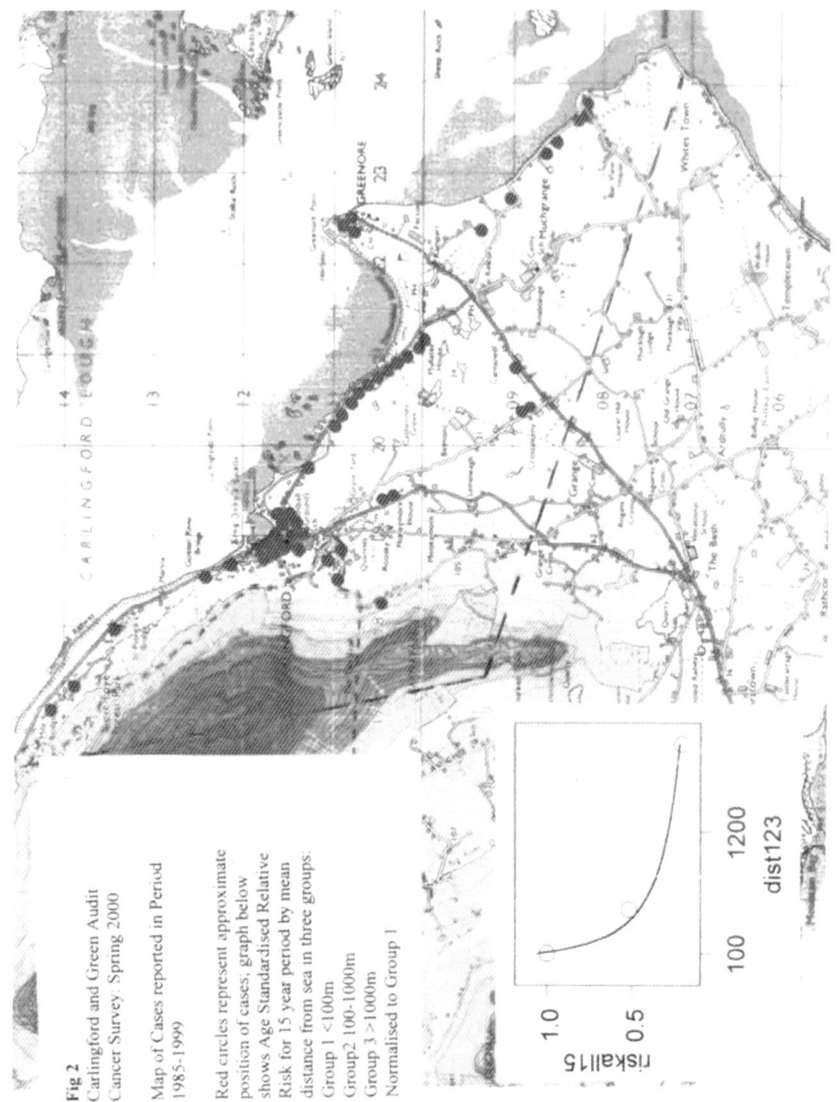

Plate 2 STAD/Green Audit cancer survey of Carlingford and Greenore, County Louth. Red circles are cancer cases. The area surveyed involved all the houses in the area within the dashed line. Inset are the relative risks of cancer incidence in three distance bands from the contaminated mud flats (shown on the map as blue areas). The risks are normalised to the proximal 100m strip =1.0 (see text).

Plate 3 Upper: Measuring radiation by collecting mud cores from the tidal accretion zones on the mudflats on the river at Dundalk, Co Louth. Lower: lots of radioactive mud and a long way to the low water mark when the tide is out. Dundalk Bay looking north from Blackrock. Ironic sign from 'Europe against Cancer'.

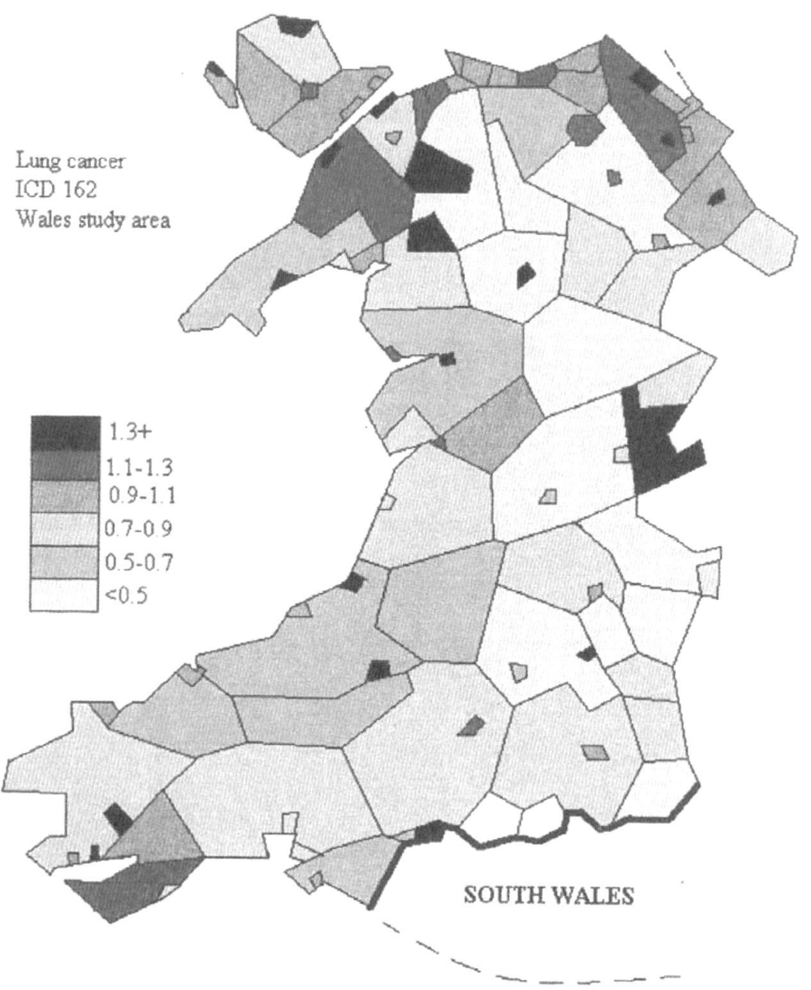

Plate 4 Wales study area showing Areas of Residence and Relative Risk from lung cancer ICD 162 in both sexes all ages from 1974-89. Note higher risks along north Wales coast and near sea generally (see text).

Plates 5 and 6 Non-violent direct action at Trawsfynydd nuclear power station in 1992. We chained the main gate shut so no-one could get in or out and called the TV. The station was due to restart after the discovery of cracks in the pressure vessel. After this it was closed down. Above: Joe Busby. Below: Chained to the gate.

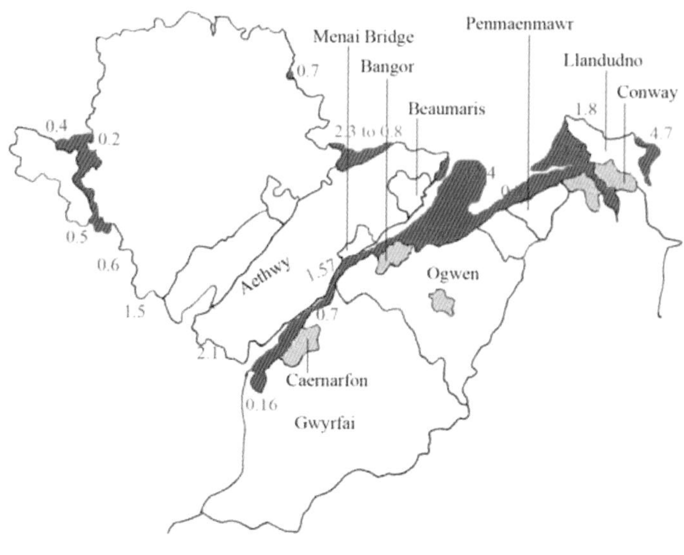

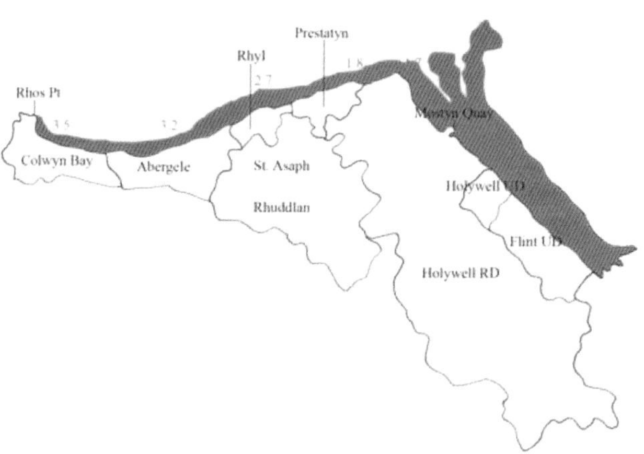

Plate 7 Plutonium in intertidal sediment (red and orange) Becquerels per kilogram. SEAPU. Above: Gwynedd and the Menai. Below: Clwyd coast and the Dee estuary (different scale). AORs are named.

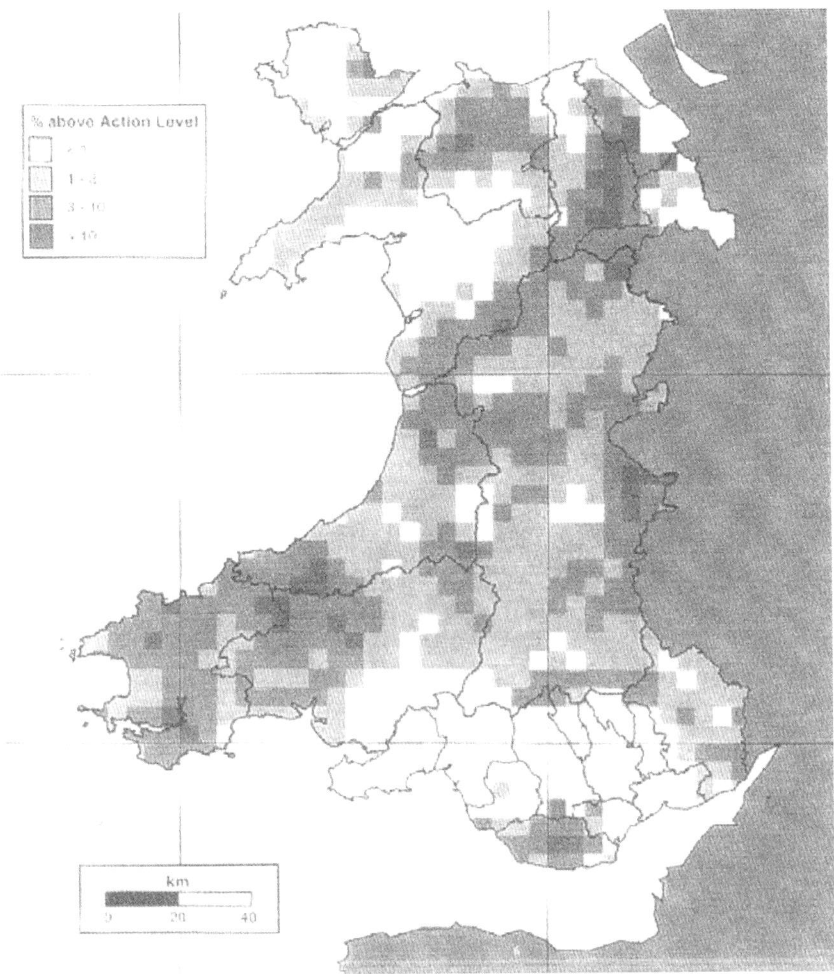

Plate 8 Radon levels in houses in Wales from NRPB study. Percentage of homes in the area above the NRPB action level 400Bq/cu:m. Note the generally low levels in the AORs around the north Wales coast where the levels of cancer are high (Map from NRPB).

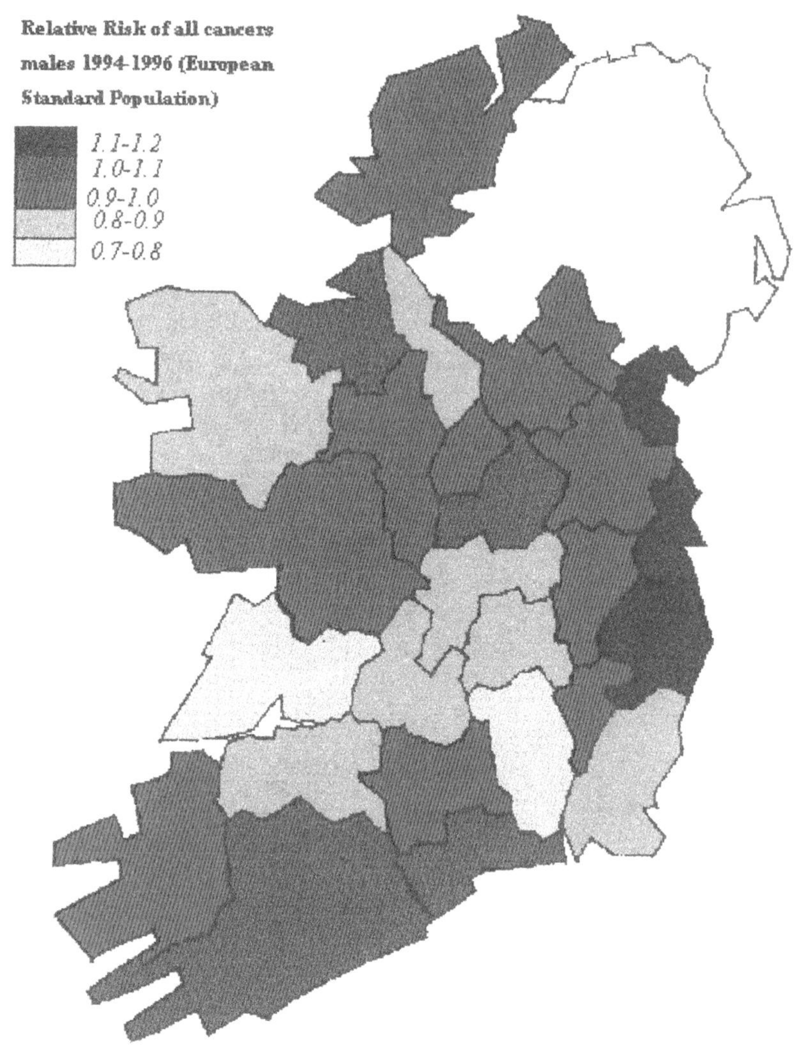

Plate 9 Cancer in Ireland 1994-96: all malignancy RR incidence in males by county (source: National Cancer Registry). Note highest levels on east coast, particularly County Louth (but these also contain the highest levels of industry).

Plate 10 Top: The mud flats in Carlingford Bay in Ireland contaminated by radioactivity from Sellafield. Bottom: Molly and Rosa on the beach at low tide. Carlingford Castle and village in the background.

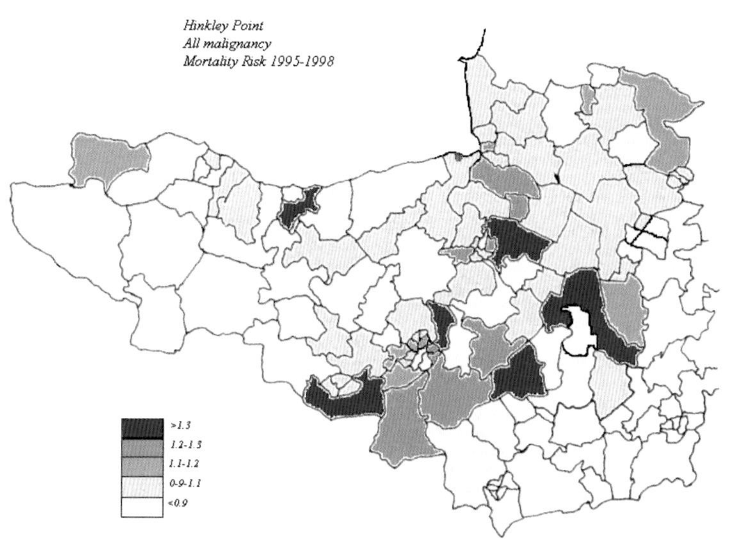

Plate 11 Top: Landsat photograph of Hinkley Point nuclear power station (white block lower left) and estuary of River Parratt. Burnham on Sea is the town on the right of the picture on the coast. Lower: All malignancy mortality risk 1995-98 in wards in Somerset. See also Plate 1 which shows lung cancer and breast cancer risk.

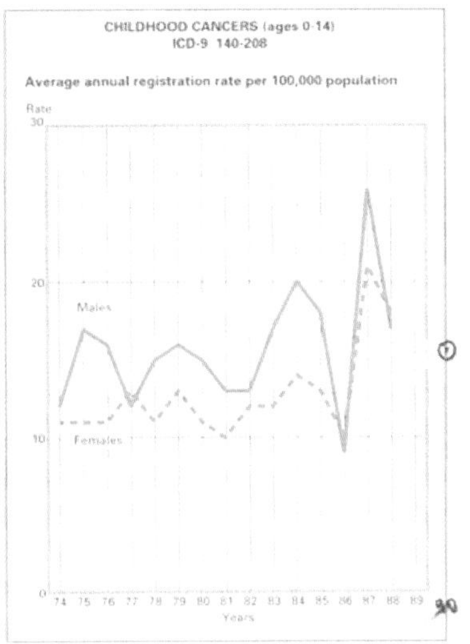

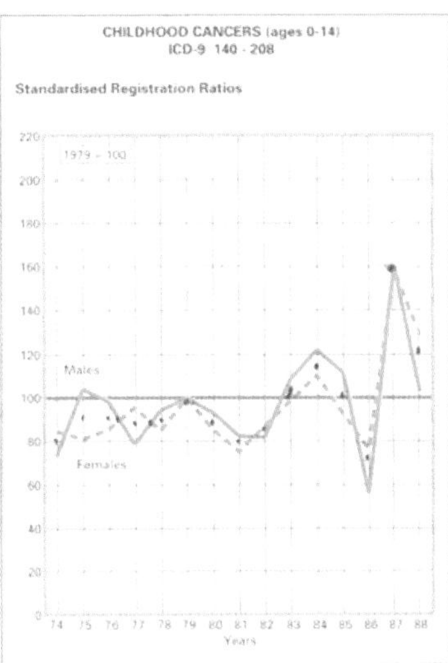

Plate 12 Top: Copy of the graph showing increases in childhood cancer in Wales published by Wales Cancer Registry in 1994 shortly before it gave the small area data to Green Audit, was closed, and the new Wales Cancer Intelligence Unit directed by Dr John Steward (below) took over and removed children from the database (see text). Note the increase after Chernobyl.

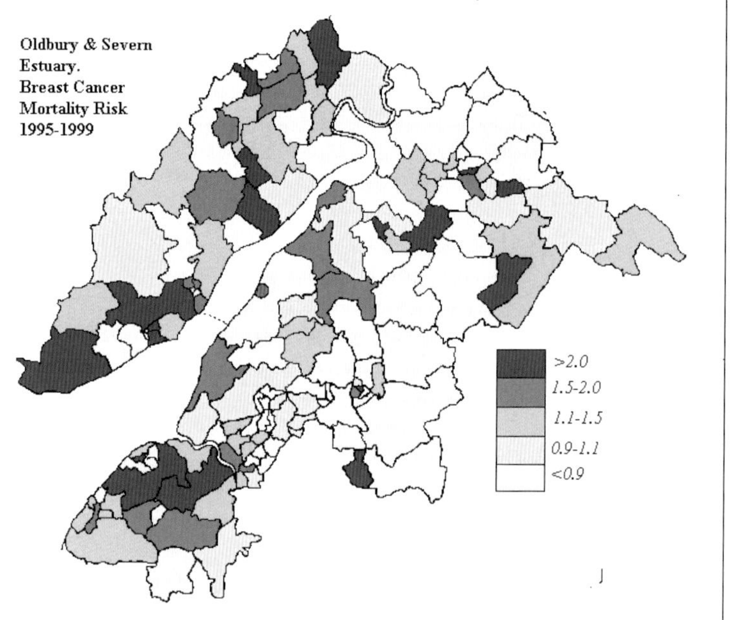

Plate13 Top: (Natural Background) Gamma radiation levels measured by NRPB for south west England. Map shows that the background around the Severn estuary is quite low. Bottom: Breast cancer mortality risk around Oldbury Nuclear Power Station (red spot) 1995-99 in wards on the English and Welsh coasts. Note high levels on mud flats below Severn Bridge (dotted) and along rivers Wye and Avon.

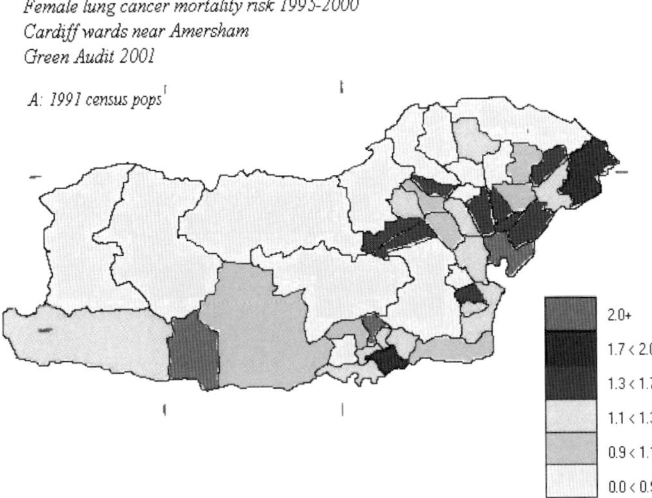

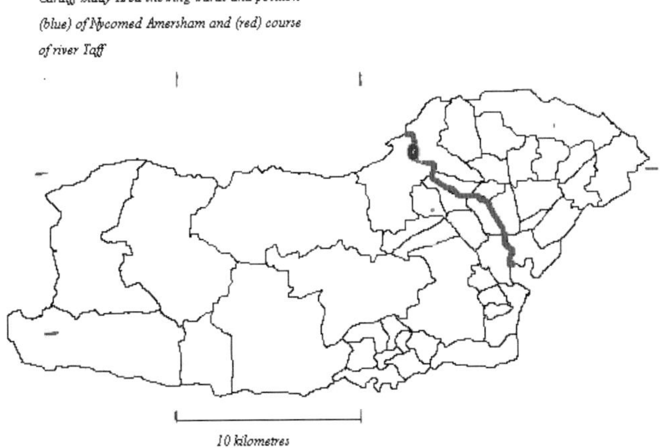

Plate 14 Female lung cancer risk in wards near Cardiff 1995-1000. Note higher risk near river and coast. River Taff is shown on the lower map which also located (blue spot) site of the Amersham isotope production factory which releases Tritium and other isotopes to the river. The M4 runs across the north of the area: there is no cancer excess risk associated with it.

Plate 15 The Dundalk BNFL litigants triumphantly leaving the Irish High Court. Left to right Mark Deary, Mary Kavanagh, James Mc Guill (solicitor) and Ollan Herr. Ten years on, this case has now run into the ground due to legal stalling by the defendants, BNFL and the weakness of the Irish State.

Plate 16 Trawsfinished, Dungenext. The *Green Committee of 100* in action at Dungeness nuclear power station in Kent in 1994. The electric gates were chained shut and the TV called in to explain why.

Plate 17 Top: Strange secret structure in Hafren Forest, Powys. What is under the concrete slab? Bottom: Green Committee of 100 in action again: Richard Bramhall chained to the stage as *Seventh Seal* Death at the British Nuclear Energy Society International Conference 'Health Effects of Low Dose Radiation: Challenges for the 21st Century' during keynote speech by Sir Richard Doll at Stratford on Avon in 1998.

Plate 18. Depleted Uranium measurements and dead tanks. Top With Al-Jazeera Satellite Channel in southern Iraq on the Kuwaiti border, September 2000; Bottom with Nippon TV in western Kosovo January 2001. I am using an Electra scintillation counter to measure betas. There was a human leg in the hedge.

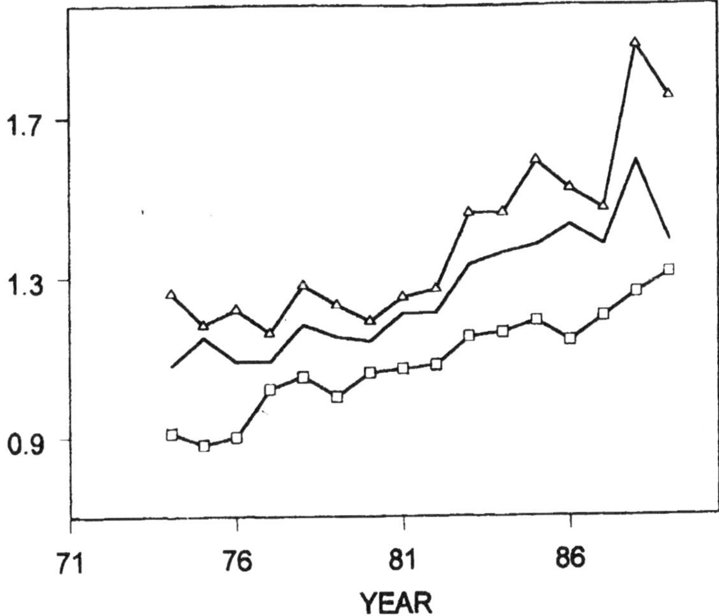

Fig 5.3.1.2 Trend over the whole period 1974-89 of Relative Risk of all malignancy (ICD9: 140-208), all ages, by seaside (<0.8km, triangles), coast (<5km, line) and inland (>5km, squares).

Table 5.3.1.1 All malignancy (ICD140-208) in Welsh AORs. Summary of regression and other statistical results.

EFFECT	??	RR; (p-value)	Regression Slope p-value	Comment
SEADIST (RR for <0.8km)	++	1.4 (0.0000)	0.004	significant in multiple regression
deprivation DEP1	0			
Deprivation CARSTAIRS	+			
Coastal vs. inland 5km cut	++	1.22 (0.000)		99% Confidence 1.16<RR<1.28
Plutonium in soil	0			
Plutonium in sediment SEAPU	0			
Rainfall RAIN	0			
Trend 74-89	+			
vs. South Wales	+	1.24 (0.001)		
vs. All Wales	+	1.24 (0.001)		

5.3.2 All leukaemias in adults ICD 204-208

Leukaemias are a diverse group of malignancies arising from the precursor cells of blood cells and tissue white blood cells. They have been associated with ionizing radiation exposure since the beginning of the radiation age, but acute lymphoblastic and acute myeloid leukaemia, diseases which account for the major part of childhood cancers, have been connected to radiation exposure more than the chronic leukaemia, which are essentially diseases of older people. Indeed, it was the increase in childhood leukaemia at Sellafield in the 1980s that rekindled the concerns about the effects of nuclear pollution and led to the formation of the various committees and organisations that have been responsible for the cover-ups that I am addressing.

Leukaemia was a major and early feature of the Hiroshima survivors study and various other external radiation studies, which have been used to assess radiation risk. Rates in Wales, which are higher than in England, have been rising consistently since 1982 and more sharply since the Chernobyl accident in 1986 (Welsh Office 1994, WCISU 2003). The lag between exposure and expression of the disease varies with the size of the exposure and, as I argue elsewhere, there is always an immediate response also. The distribution of leukaemia in adults (i.e. all ages) with where they live in Wales and its trend over the period 1974-1989 should be a pointer to the cause of the disease. As with the 'all malignancies' category, results for Wales from 1974-89 show that there was a significant sea-coast effect on leukaemia, with significantly higher rates in the 0-5km group of areas (Table 5.3.2.1, Fig 5.3.2.2 and Table 5.3.2.1). As with all malignancies, the levels of leukaemia in this coastal population were higher than in industrial south Wales or Wales as a whole, and that the overall increases that were found in Wales as a whole increased most rapidly in this coastal group, particularly after Chernobyl in 1986 (Fig 5.3.2.2). The trend in development of the disease, by distance from the sea over time, shows graphically how the effect is driven by proximity to the sea (Fig 5.3.2.2). We see that there is little change over the period 1974-89 in leukaemia in adults in the people living more than 5km from the sea yet, in those living in areas less than 0.8km, the risk doubles over the period from about 1.2 in 1974 to 2.4 in 1988. If we assume a lag of about 5-8 years then this result directs the cause of the sea coast effect to an exposure that is linked to leukaemia and one which involves events in the period 1975- 1983. The effect seems to be driven by coastal towns and small areas on the north Wales coast. Thus the AORs of these towns, close to the highest measured levels of radioactivity from Sellafield trapped in the coastal and estuarine sediments are significantly high compared with inland town areas as I show in Table 5.3.2.2 below.

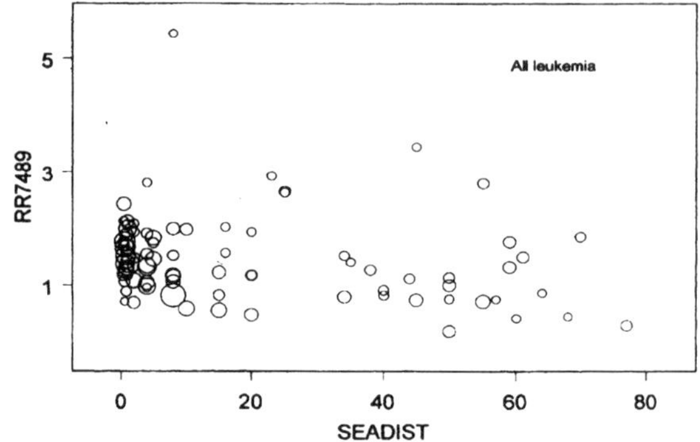

Seadist range Km	Average (SD)	N AORs	Oberved 74-89	Expected 74-89	Relative Risk	P value
<0.8	0.56 (0.17)	16	325	202	1.61	0.0000
0.9<x<2	1.38 (0.51)	13	288	189	1.52	0.0000
2.1<x<5	4.27 (0.47)	11	207	147	1.41	
5.1<x<11	8.44 (0.88)	10	167	148	1.13	
11.1<x<20	17.5 (2.32)	10	68	70.8	0.96	
21<x<40	33.67 (6.5)	12	73	50	1.4	
>41	55 (9.5)	20	130	120.3	1.08	
S Wales E=2		65	2545	2042	1.25	
Wales		193	4511	3446	1.31	

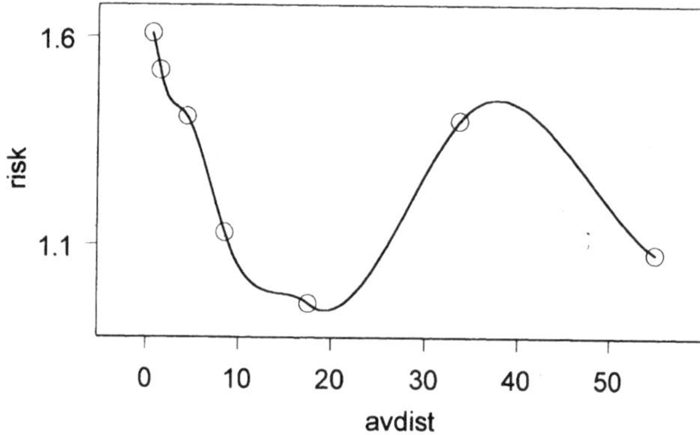

Fig 5.3.2.1 Top: Bubble plot of incidence risk 1974-89 for all leukaemia (ICD9: 204-208) in study area. Centre: Table of Relative Risk all leukaemias by distance bands showing detail of bands. Bottom: LOESS plot of leukaemia risk by distance from the sea by AOR groups.

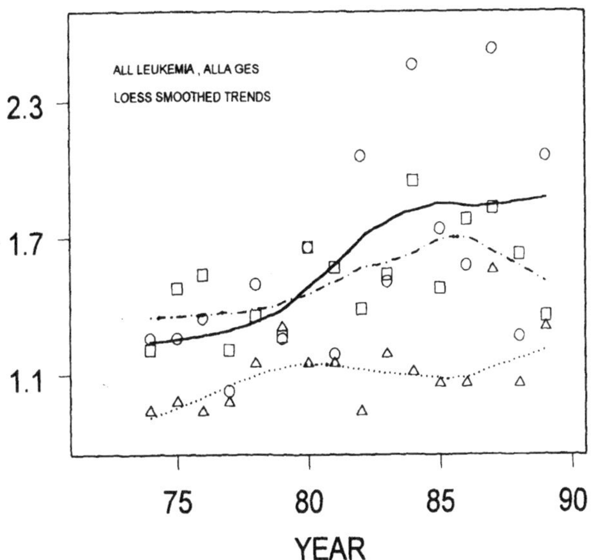

Fig 5.3.2.2 Trend over the whole period 1974-89 of Relative Risk of all leukaemia (ICD9: 204-208), all ages, by seaside (<0.8km, circles, line), coast (<5km, squares, dotdash) and inland (>5km, triangles).

Table 5.3.2.2 SRRs for all ages leukaemia incidence 1974-89 in north Wales coastal town AORs compared with some comparable inland town AORs

Coastal Areas	**O/E = RR**	**Inland Areas**	**Relative Risk**
74CA Bangor	37/15.9 = 2.44***	71GA Denbigh	15/12.3= 1.2
71CC Colwyn Bay	67/48 = 1.4 ***	76AA Brecknock	12/8.4 = 1.5
71JA Prestatyn	51/30.8 = 1.7 ***	76AA Builth Wells	2/2.6= 0.8
71JC Rhyl	65/36.7 = 1.8***	3 Newtown AORs	11/21.3= 0.5
71CA Abergele	53/26.6 = 2.0 ***	76CG Welshpool	13/9.9 = 1.3
1.374AE Llandudno	51/33.6 = 1.5***	76ET Rhayader	8/6.31 = 1.2
74AG Llanfairfech'n	11/5.7 = 1.9	76EC Llandrindod	7/6.2=1.1
71EA Flint	32/19 = 1.7**	76CB Llanidloes	6/4 = 1.5
All coastal above	367/216.3 = 1.7***	All inland above	74/71.1 = 1.04

Table 5.3.2.1 All leukaemias (ICD204-208) in Welsh AORs. Summary of regression and other statistical results.

EFFECT	**??**	**RR; (p-value)**	**Regression p-value**	**Comment**
SEADIST (RR for <0.8km)	++	1.61 (0.0000)	0.0005	significant in multiple regression .0007
deprivation DEP1	0			
Deprivation CARSTAIRS	0			
Coastal vs. inland 5km cut	++	1.60 (0.001)		95% Confidence 1.22<RR<2.09
Plutonium in soil	0			
Plutonium in sediment SEAPU	0			
Rainfall RAIN	0			
Trend 74-89	+			lags Sellafield emissions at coast
vs. South Wales	+	1.29 (0.001)		
vs. All Wales	+	1.22 (0.001)		

5.3.3 Breast cancer in women

Breast cancer is the most common cancer occurring in women and has received the greatest attention as to its cause, since the disease began to increase rapidly in the mid 1970s and is now at epidemic levels. Unlike lung cancer, but like leukaemia, the trend with Social Class is negative, i.e. there is higher risk in high Social Class. Breast cancer rates are higher in Wales than in England and highest in North Wales. In 1995 and 1996 I analysed the age profile changes over the period of the increases in the mid 1970s. I concluded (Busby 1995, 1997) that there was a cohort effect that identified women who were progressing through puberty at the peak of the weapons fallout as most at risk. These women would have been aged between 40 and 54 in 1980.

Because there was more than twice the fallout in Wales, especially north Wales, we would expect the onset of the overall national increase to begin in Wales, which it did and we should expect north Wales to be most affected, which it is. We might also expect highest levels of fallout Strontium and other isotopes to be washed to the sea and result in exposure near the coast, and also to be augmented with material (including Plutonium, Uranium, Caesium and Strontium) from Sellafield. Therefore it would not be unexpected for there to be a sea coast effect, and indeed, the results show that this is exactly what there is. However, there is also an increase in incidence in areas between 50 and 50km from the sea, a result that is also found in other cancer types studied. Results for Wales from 1974-89 show that there was a significant sea coast effect on breast cancer with significantly higher rates in the 0-5km group of areas (Table 5.3.3.1, Fig 5.3.3.1 and Fig 5.3.3.2). As with all malignancies the levels of breast cancer in this coastal population were higher than in industrial south Wales or Wales as a whole. The trend in development of the disease by distance from the sea over time shows graphically how the effect is driven by proximity to the sea (Fig 5.3.3.2), where we see that there is little change over the period 1974-89 in the people living more than 5km from the sea yet in those living in areas less than 0.8km, the risk doubles over the period from about 1.2 in 1974 to 2.4 in 1988. If we assume a lag of about 5-8 years then this result directs the cause of the sea coast effect to an exposure that is linked to leukaemia and one which involves events in the period 1975- 1983. Regression results show a high level of significance for the seacoast effect ($p = 0.0002$) and for no other covariant, including deprivation.

Again, risks are high in the north Wales coastal towns e.g. Bangor (O/E = 120/79; RR = 1.52), Caernarfon (O/E, 98/66; RR = 1.5), Conwy (O/E = 194/109, RR = 1.8), Prestatyn (O/E = 231/154, RR = 1.5), Rhyl (O/E = 280/187, RR = 1.5) and Menai Bridge (38/21, RR = 1.8).

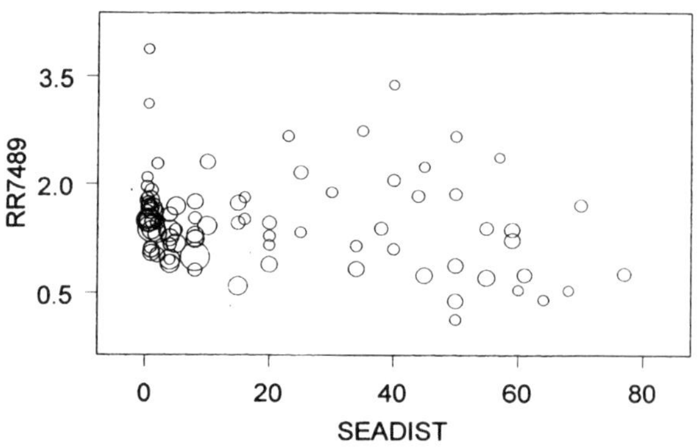

Seadist range Km	Average (SD)	N AORs	Oberved 74-89	Expected 74-89	Relative Risk	P value
<0.8	0.56 (0.17)	16	1646	1035	1.59	0.0000
0.9<x<2	1.38 (0.51)	13	1372	972	1.41	0.0000
2.1<x<5	4.27 (0.47)	11	995	777	1.28	
5.1<x<11	8.44 (0.88)	10	1045	188	1.32	
11.1<x<20	17.5 (2.32)	10	456	374	1.22	
21<x<40	33.67 (6.5)	12	431	263	1.64	
>41	55 (9.5)	21	689	638	1.08.	
S wales E=2		62	10907	9274	1.18	
Wales		189	23333	18421	1.27	

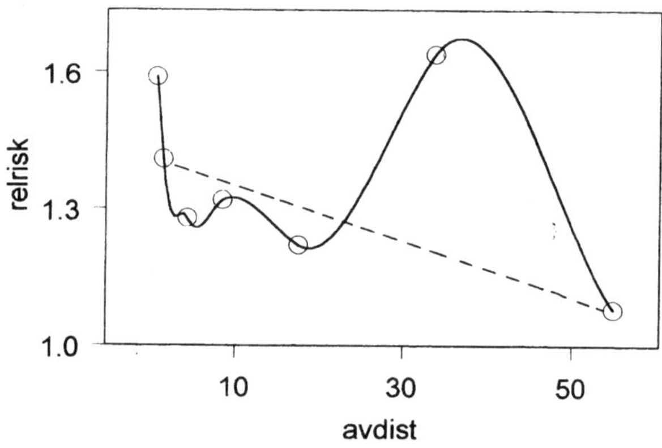

Fig 5.3.3.1 Top: Bubble plot of incidence risk 1974-89 for breast cancer (ICD9: 174) in study area. Centre: Table of Relative Risk breast cancer by distance bands showing detail of bands. Bottom: LOESS plot of breast cancer risk by distance from the sea by AOR groups.

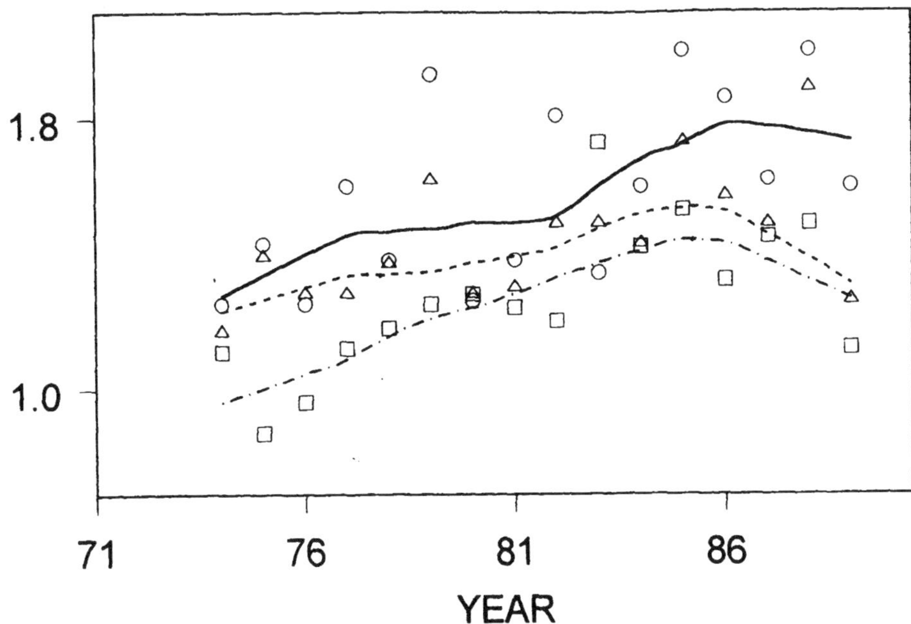

Fig 5.3.3.2 Trend over the whole period 1974-89 of Relative Risk of breast cancer (ICD9: 174), all ages, by seaside (<0.8km, circles, line), coast (<5km, triangles, dash) and inland (>5km, squares, dotdash).

Table 5.3.3.1 Breast cancer (ICD9:174) in Welsh AORs. Summary of regression and other statistical results.

EFFECT	??	RR; (p-value)	Regression p-value	Comment
SEADIST (RR for <0.8km)	++	1.59 (0.0000)	0.0002	significant in multiple regression .0007
deprivation DEP1	0			
Deprivation CARSTAIRS	+		0.03	anomalous positive slope (wrong direction)
Coastal vs. inland 5km cut	+	1.23 (0.01)		95% Confidence 1.1<RR<1.4
Plutonium in soil	0			
Plutonium in sediment SEAPU	0			
Rainfall RAIN	0			
Trend 74-89	+			
vs. South Wales	+	1.29 (0.001)		
vs. All Wales	+	1.22 (0.001)		

5.3.4 Lung cancer

Lung cancer is the most commonly occurring cancer. Since a great deal of epidemiological work in the post war period, it has become associated with cigarette smoking and, following health education, the reduction in smoking had begun to reduce the levels of lung cancer in men (though not in women) over the period of these results. Because of its link with smoking, the disease shows a strong association with Social Class, with almost a doubling of risk between the highest and lowest Social Class, and it is this link that drives the general positive association of all malignancy with Social Class such that the lowest Social Class have the highest cancer risk. However, the results of this study indicate very strongly that lung cancer in Wales is determined by where you live rather than by what you do. Rather than declining slightly after 1980, as the disease was in England, in the coastal groups in Wales it was increasing. Results for Wales from 1974-89 show that there was a significant sea coast effect on lung cancer with significantly higher rates in the 0-5km group of areas (Table 5.3.4.1, Fig 5.3.4.1 and Fig 5.3.4.2). In general, in the inland part of study area the risks were significantly lower than in England but they increased sharply near the coast. This is clear from the map shown in Plate 4. Levels were highest in Bangor (O/E = 189/142, RR = 1.33) and Caernarfon (O/E = 168/118, RR = 1.4). Compare the inland towns of Newtown (O/E = 106/195, RR = 0.5) and Welshpool (O/E = 82/91, RR = 0.9). Logarithmic regression showed a very significant association with sea-distance (p = 0.003), with Plutonium in Air (p = 0.04) and with Carstairs deprivation (p = 0.001), though not with the Welsh Office Deprivation DEP1 (p = 0.14). I conclude that these results suggest that the generally clean air of the region results in low levels of lung cancer relative to England and Wales, but that inhaled radioactive material from the sea causes an increase in the disease in the coastal areas close to the pollution. The Carstairs association may show that deprivation is also a component but, if this is so, the lack of association with the DEP1 covariant is puzzling. This sea coast effect in lung cancer was the first time we found such an interesting result. However, we were to find this lung cancer sea coast effect in most of the mortality studies we did, as I shall describe later in the book.

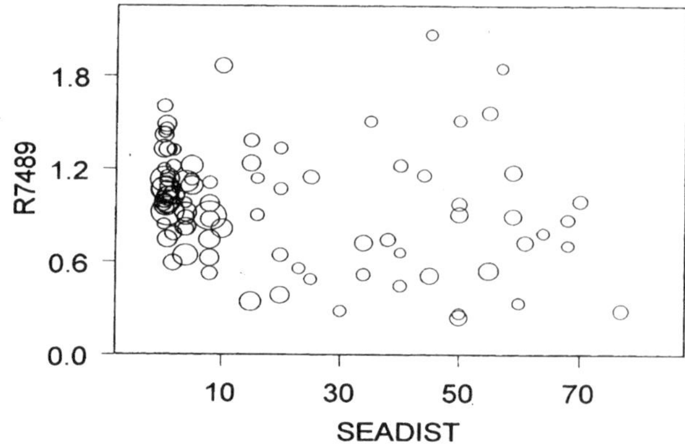

Seadist range Km	Average (SD)	N AORs	Oberved 74-89	Expected 74-89	Relative Risk	P value
<0.8	0.56 (0.17)	16	2259	1961	1.15	
0.9<x<2	1.38 (0.51)	13	1743	1789	0.97	
2.1<x<5	4.27 (0.47)	11	1305	1361	0.96	
5.1<x<11	8.44 (0.88)	10	1265	1379	0.92	
11.1<x<20	17.5 (2.32)	10	537	671	0.80	
21<x<40	33.67 (6.5)	12	401	474	0.85	
>41	55 (9.5)	21	954	1171	81	
all wales			32731	32487	1.007	
S.Wales (E=2)		66	20140	19208	1.05	

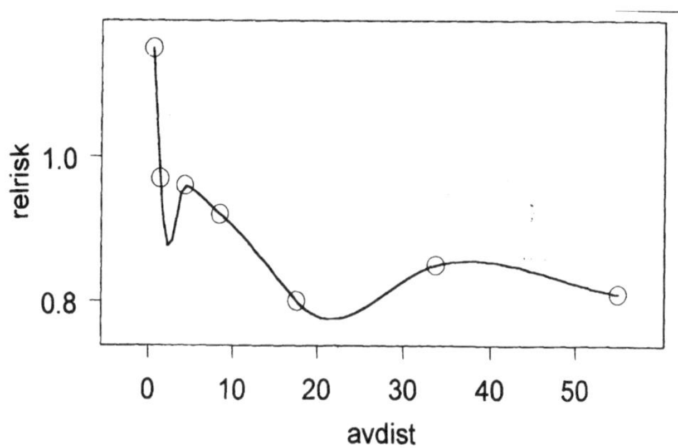

Fig 5.3.4.1 Top: Bubble plot of incidence risk 1974-89 for lung cancer (ICD9: 162) all ages both sexes in study area. Centre: Table of Relative Risk lung cancer by distance bands showing detail of bands. Bottom: LOESS plot of lung cancer risk by distance from the sea by AOR groups.

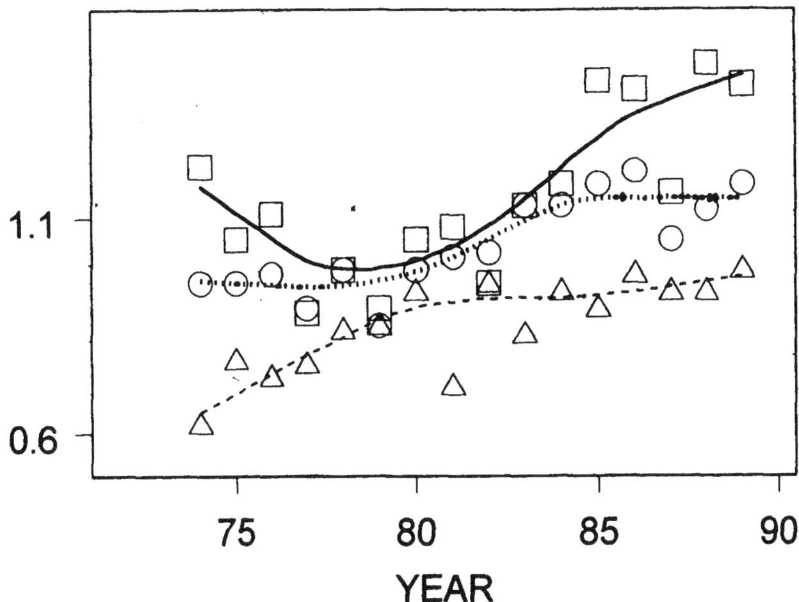

Fig 5.3.4.2 Trend over the whole period 1974-89 of Relative Risk of lung cancer (ICD9: 162), all ages, by seaside (<0.8km, squares, line), coast (<5km, circle, dots) and inland (>5km, triangle, dash).

Table 5.3.4.1 Lung cancer (ICD9:162) in Welsh AORs. Summary of regression and other statistical results.

EFFECT	??	RR; (p-value)	Regression p-value	Comment
SEADIST (RR for <0.8km)	+	1.15 (0.0000)	0.0003	significant in multiple regression .0007
deprivation DEP1	0		0.14	but see Carstairs below
Deprivation CARSTAIRS	+		0.000	correct slope for lung cancer
Coastal vs. inland 5km cut	+	1.22 (0.005)		see loess graph
Plutonium in soil	0			
Plutonium in air AIRPU	+		0.04	
Rainfall RAIN	0			
Trend 74-89	+			sharp increase near coast after 1980
vs. South Wales	+	1.29 (0.001)		
vs. All Wales	+	1.22 (0.001)		

5.3.5 Colon cancer in adults

Cancer of the colon (colorectal cancer) is the second most common cancer after lung cancer in the UK. It accounts of about 12 percent of all cancers in Wales with few cases at ages below 40 and rates in women being slightly higher than rates in men in Wales. Like other cancers, the rates are higher in north Wales and also highest close to the coast. There is a clear sea coast effect in colon cancer as can be seen by the results in Fig 5.3.5.1 and Table 5.3.5.1 which gives the data on distance groups and risks. Fig 5.3.5.2 shows the trend by distance over time, Table 5.3.5.2 gives statistics of comparisons of the coastal and inland groups by 5km break, and a summary. Risks are driven mainly, as usual, by the coastal towns e.g. Bangor (O/E = 113/56, RR = 2.0) Caernarfon (O/E 71/46, RR = 1.53) but there are also high risks in some inland towns e.g. Denbigh (O/E = 82/45, RR = 1.8). Regression (Table 5.3.5.2) shows significant association with SEADIST ($p = 0.001$) and also AIRPU ($p = 0.0002$), but there is no association with deprivation ($p = 0.2$).

Colon cancer is associated with meat eating (Cairns, 1988) and presumably therefore the exposure of cells in the large intestine to mutagenic materials. These would be higher in coastal populations if they ate local food, including meat, seafood (shellfish) and vegetables that are contaminated with resuspended contaminated sediment.

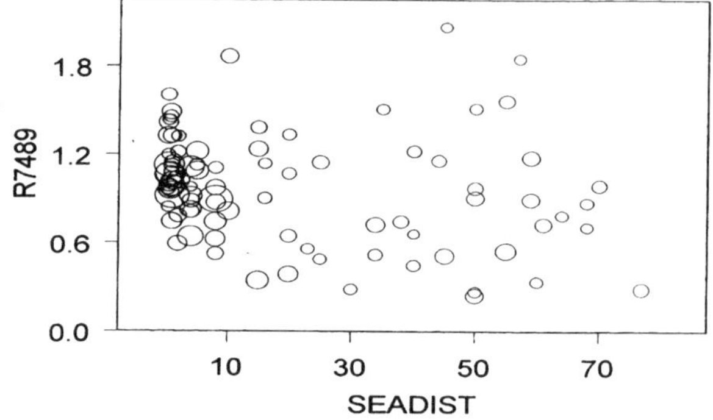

Seadist range Km	Average (SD)	N AORs	Oberved 74-89	Expected 74-89	Relative Risk	P value
<0.8	0.56 (0.17)	16	1187	781	1.52	0.0000
0.9<x<2	1.38 (0.51)	13	963	717	1.34	0.0000
2.1<x<5	4.27 (0.47)	11	710	538	1.32	
5.1<x<11	8.44 (0.88)	10	577	527	1.1	
11.1<x<20	17.5 (2.32)	10	268	262	1.02	
21<x<40	33.67 (6.5)	12	223	186	1.2	
>41	55 (9.5)	21	511	443	1.15	
S wales E=2		65	7774	7311	1.06	
Wales		193	14374	12491	1.15	

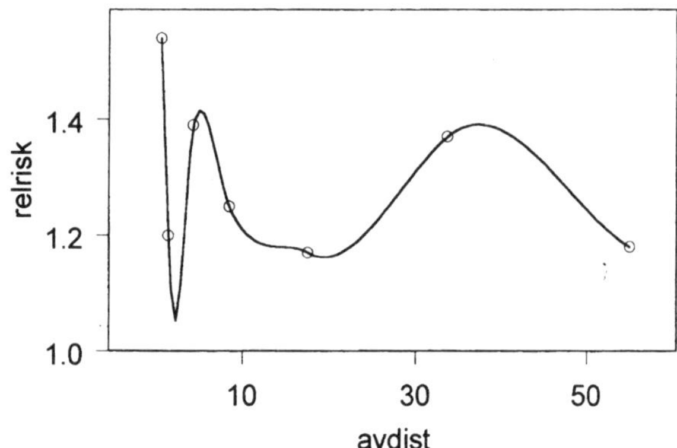

Fig 5.3.5.1 Top: Bubble plot of incidence risk 1974-89 for colon cancer (ICD9: 153) all ages both sexes in study area. Centre: Table of Relative Risk colon cancer by distance bands showing detail of bands. Bottom: LOESS plot of colon cancer risk by distance from the sea by AOR groups.

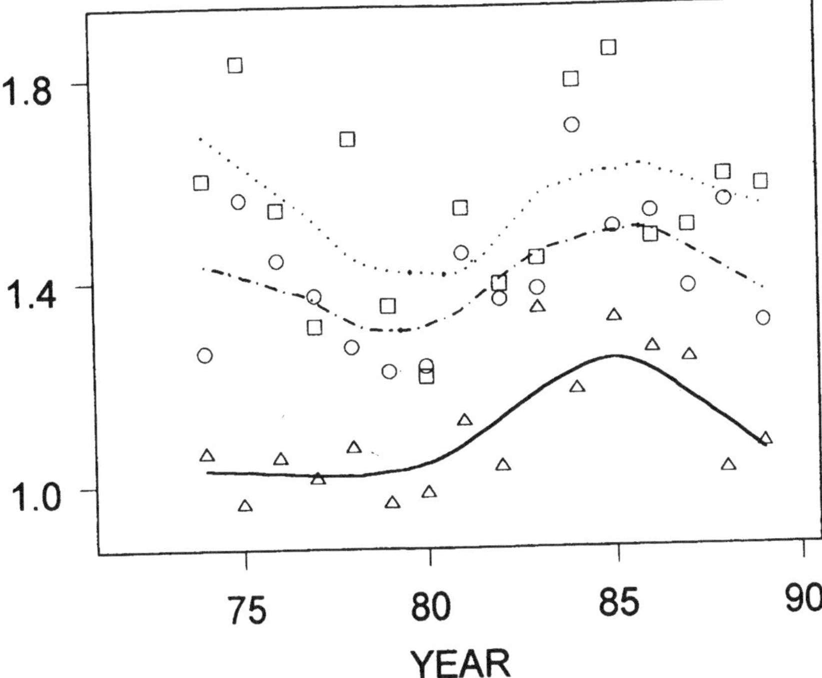

Fig 5.3.5.2 Trend over the whole period 1974-89 of Relative Risk of colon cancer (ICD9: 153), all ages, by seaside (<0.8km, squares, dots), coast (<5km, circles, dotdash) and inland (>5km, triangles).

Table 5.3.5.1 Colon cancer (ICD9:153) in Welsh AORs. Summary of regression and other statistical results.

EFFECT	??	RR; (p-value)	Regression p-value	Comment
SEADIST (RR for <0.8km)	++	1.52 (0.001)	0.001	significant in multiple regression .0007
deprivation DEP1	0		0.17	but see Carstairs below
Deprivation CARSTAIRS	0			
Coastal vs. inland 5km cut	++	1.26 (0.01)		see loess graph
Plutonium in soil	0			
Plutonium in air AIRPU	++		0.0002	highly correlated
Rainfall RAIN	0			
Trend 74-89	vary			peaks in 1985 in all seadist groups
vs. South Wales	+	1.43 (0.001)		
vs. All Wales	+	1.32 (0.001)		

5.3.6 Prostate

Cancer of the prostate is a common cancer in men accounting for 9 percent of all new registrations in Wales. It has been increasing in Wales since 1974 when data was first being collated. It also has been associated with working in the nuclear industry among those who are contaminated with internal fission-product isotopes (Beral *et al* 1993a). This led to my associating the increases in prostate cancer in Wales with the weapons fallout in 1997 (Busby 1994), drawing a comment from the nuclear industry that such a conclusion would demand an enhancement of radiation risk over that which was assumed by a factor of about 1000-fold (Atkinson 1994). Although prostate cancer has increased sharply in Wales, the distribution by distance from the sea is not as clear-cut as with the other common cancers, as the results show. Fig 5.3.6.1 shows the basic results as a bubble plot, with the loess plot and the table showing distances and risks. Fig 5.3.6.2 shows the trend by distance over time, Table 5.3.6.1 shows the regression results and the summary. The lack of clear cut association with sea coast in the case of prostate cancer is also found in the mortality studies and requires an explanation, which as yet, I cannot supply. Prostate cancer has a very long lag time and so it seems that the increases probably relate to events that occurred before the peaks in weapons fallout as well as to later exposures, and this may be part of the explanation for the less clear correlation. Nevertheless, there is a weak association, as the regression results show ($p = 0.02$). In a multiple regression on 5 covariates, the only significant association was with SEADIST and AIRPU (the Plutonium in air function).

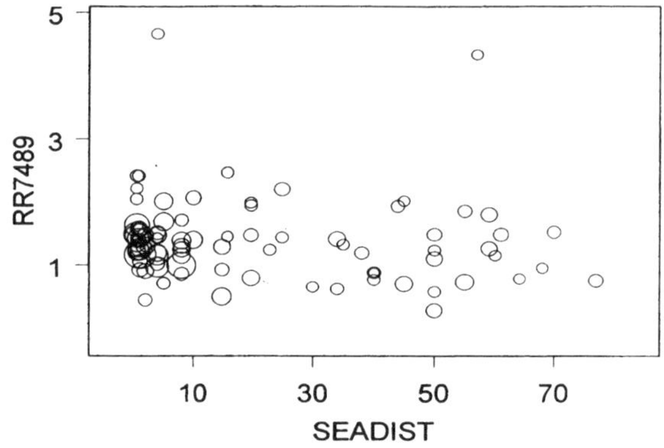

Seadist range Km	Average (SD)	N AORs	Oberved 74-89	Expected 74-89	Relative Risk	P Value
<0.8	0.56 (0.17)	16	750	488	1.54	0.0000
0.9<x<2	1.38 (0.51)	13	534	446	1.20	
2.1<x<5	4.27 (0.47)	11	454	325	1.39	
5.1<x<11	8.44 (0.88)	9	391	312	1.25	
11.1<x<20	17.5 (2.32)	10	186	158	1.17	
21<x<40	33.67 (6.5)	12	153	112	1.37	
>41	55 (9.5)	20	324	266	1.18	
S wales E=2		65	5207	4285	1.21	
Wales		193	9451	7240	1.31	

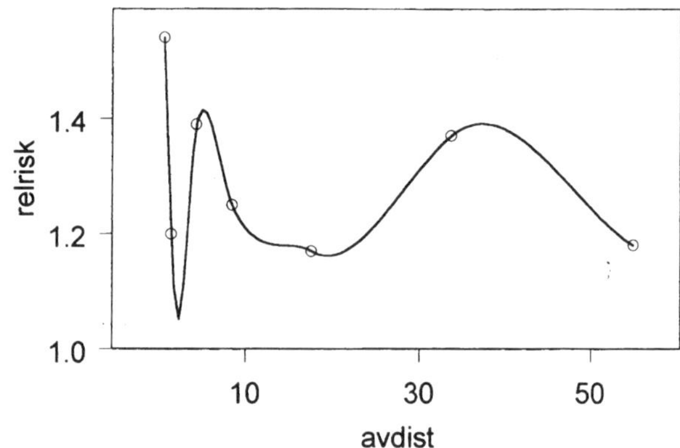

Fig 5.3.6.1 Top: Bubble plot of incidence risk 1974-89 for prostate cancer (ICD9: 185) all ages in study area. Centre: Table of Relative Risk prostate cancer by distance bands showing detail of bands. Bottom: LOESS plot of prostate cancer risk by distance from the sea by AOR groups.

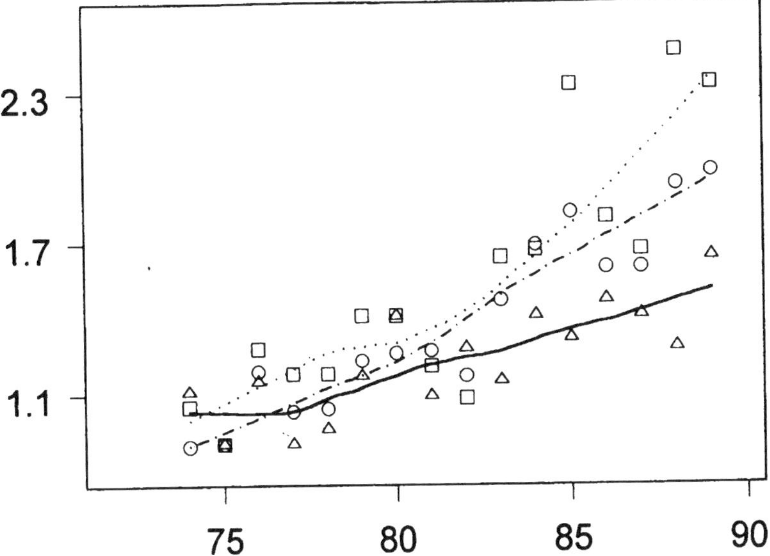

Fig 5.3.6.2 Trend over the whole period 1974-89 of Relative Risk of prostate cancer (ICD9: 185), all ages, by seaside (<0.8km, squares, dots), coast (<5km, circles, dotdash) and inland (>5km, line, triangles).

Table 5.3.6.1 Prostate cancer (ICD9:153) in Welsh AORs. Summary of regression and other statistical results.

EFFECT	**??**	**RR; (p-value)**	**Regression p-value**	**Comment**
SEADIST (RR for <0.8km)	+	1.54 (0.0000)	0.02	
deprivation DEP1	0		0.3	but see Carstairs below
Deprivation CARSTAIRS	0		0.6	
Coastal vs. inland 5km cut	+	1.12 (0.01)		see loess graph
Plutonium in soil	0		0.3	
Plutonium in air AIRPU	++		0.004	highly significant in multiple regression
Rainfall RAIN	0		0.1	
Trend 74-89	vary			peaks in 1985 in all seadist groups
vs. South Wales	+	1.21 (0.0000)		
vs. All Wales	+	1.31 (0.0000)		

5.3.7 Oesophageal cancer, thyroid cancer, cervical and stomach cancer

Cancer of the oesophagus has increased over the study period in Wales, particularly in men. It was of interest to see if it also exhibited a sea coast effect, and indeed it did do so, as can be seen by the bubble plot and loess results given in Fig 5.3.7.1. However, although the levels are high close to the coast, they also increase in the more remote inland areas so the regression results do not show a significant effect.

Stomach cancer, which now accounts for about 6 percent of all cancers, has been falling nationally over the period 1974-89, possibly due to the development of anti-ulcer drugs in the anti-H(2) histamine series like ranitidine and cimetidine (e.g. Zantac). These were drugs that I did some research on when at Wellcome. Another possible cause for the decline in stomach cancer is the use of antibiotics that are capable of (often as a side effect) decreasing levels of the types of bacteria which are associated with the inflammation of the stomach that increases the likelihood of the disease. Although the levels were falling in Wales, the levels were highest in north Wales where there was still a sea-coast effect on the risks. Note the interesting trend over the period, with a bump in the coastal groups some ten years after the Sellafield peaks (Fig 5.3.7.2 and 5.3.7.3). Levels were significantly high in Caernarfon (O/E = 82/40, RR = 2.10) and Bangor (O/E = 90/48, RR = 1.9) and in other coastal areas.

Thyroid cancer results are interesting (see Fig 5.3.7.4): the highest levels might be expected to follow radioiodine exposure. If this were from weapons fallout then the high levels seen in the mountainous areas can be explained. Care should be exercised though as it is a very rare disease and the numbers are small. The cervical cancer seems to be highest in the wider coastal strip (0-10km) but the multiple regression results showed a positive effect of deprivation with no SEADIST effect but a statistically significant p-value for Carstairs of 0.03, is in agreement with the literature on the association.

Seadist range Km	Average (SD)	N AORs	Oberved 74-89	Expected 74-89	Relative Risk	P value
<0.8	0.56 (0.17)	16	335	218.3	1.54	
0.9<x<2	1.38 (0.51)	13	282	200.4	1.41	
2.1<x<5	4.27 (0.47)	11	199	150.4	1.32	
5.1<x<11	8.44 (0.88)	9	172	147	1.16	
11.1<x<20	17.5 (2.32)	10	89	73.22	1.21	
21<x<40	33.67 (6.5)	12	65	52	1.25	
>41	55 (9.5)	21	181	127	1.43	
>61	68 (6.1)	5	40	25.3	1.58	
S.Wales (E=2)		66	2667	2041	1.3	

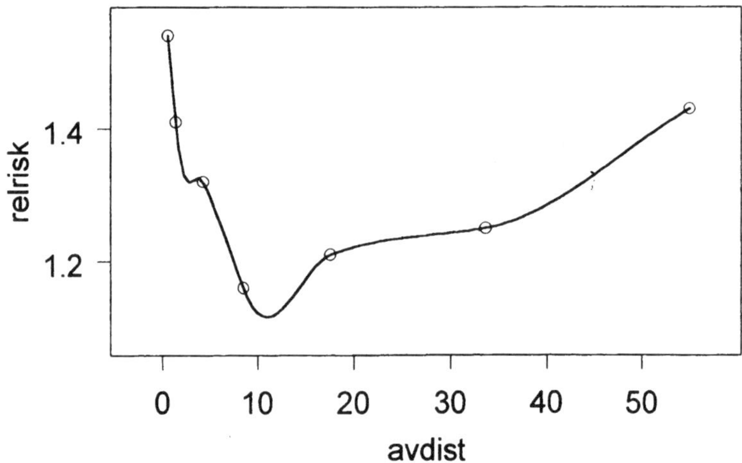

Fig 5.3.7.1 Upper: Table of data and lower: LOESS lot of incidence risk of cancer of the oesophagus (ICD9: 150) in study area by distance from the sea 1974-89.

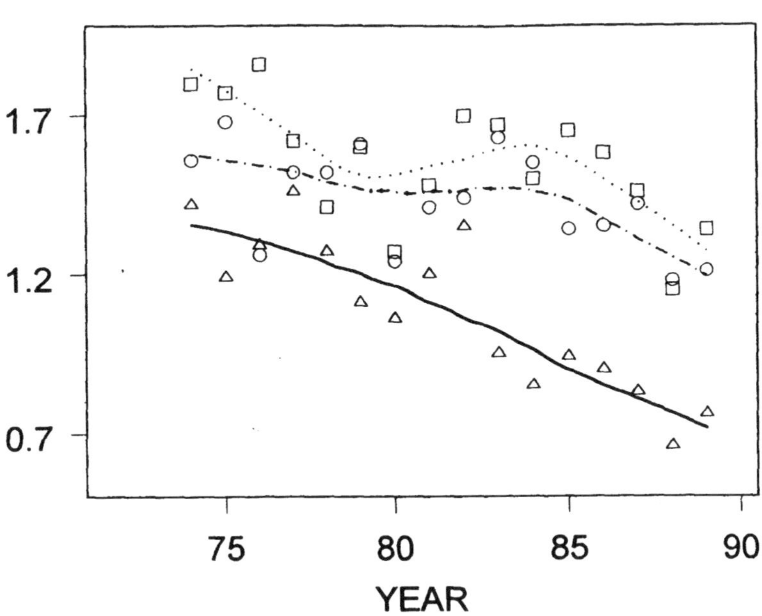

Fig 5.3.7.2 LOESS regression temporal trend over whole period 1974-89 of Relative Risk of incidence of stomach cancer all ages (ICD9:151) by seaside (<0.8km, squares and dotted line), coast (<5km, circles and dot-dash line) and inland (>5.1km, triangles and full line).

Seadist range Km	Average (SD)	N AORs	Oberved 74-89	Expected 74-89	Relative Risk	P value
<0.8	0.56·(0.17)	16	1057	678	1.56	0.0000
0.9<x<2	1.38 (0.51)	13	789	621	1.27	0.0000
2.1<x<5	4.27 (0.47)	11	677	465	1.46	
5.1<x<11	8.44 (0.88)	10	541	454	1.19	
11.1<x<20	17.5 (2.32)	10	251	226	1.11	
21<x<40	33.67 (6.5)	12	186	191	0.97	
>41	55 (9.5)	20	449	320	1.40	
S wales E=2		65	8191	6264	1.30	
Wales		193	14473	10753	1.35	

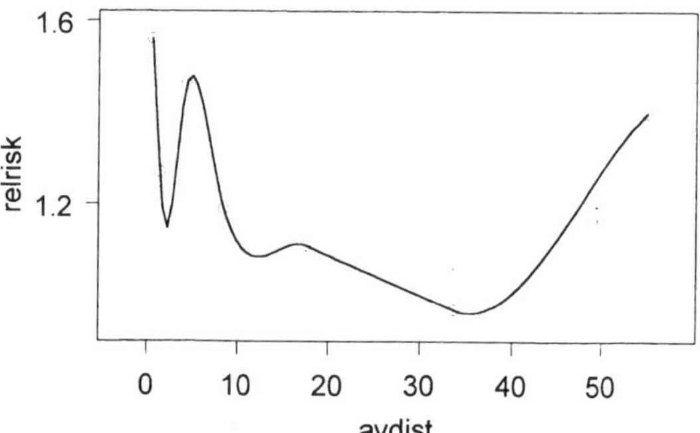

Fig 5.3.7.3 Upper: Table and lower: LOESS plot of incidence risk of cancer of the stomach (ICD9:151) in study area 1974-89.

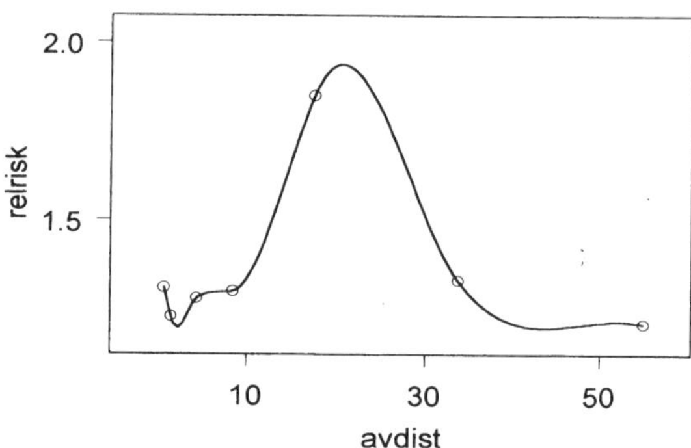

Fig 5.3.7.4 LOESS plot of incidence of thyroid cancer ICD193 all ages and both sexes by AOR distance groups from the sea. Highest level is in the mountain region.

5.3.8. Other cancers in adults

In addition to the cancers in adults that I have listed, we also examined the area distribution of some other cancers, which we felt might be of interest from a radiological viewpoint. These were brain, thyroid, cervix uteri and pleura. For these, the results were either equivocal with regard to a sea coast effect or else there was definitely not one. Results are summarised below in Table 5.3.8.1

Table 5.3.8.1 Risk Effects by area in cancer of brain, cervix uteri, thyroid, pleura in Wales 1974-89.

Cancer	**Seacoast effect cut at 5km?**	**O/E (RR) <0.8) km**	**Regression p value on SEADIST**	**Regression p value on DEP1**
Brain	0.92 Not significant	158/112 (1.4)	0.58	0.80
Cervix	1.0 Not significant	305/158 (1.9)	0.2	0.8
Thyroid	0.97 Not significant	47/36.6 (1.3)	0.3	0.47
Pleura	1.5 Not significant	12/19.7 (0.6)	0.14	0.4

6
The Irish Sea Part II
Childhood Cancer in Wales and Other Relevant Studies

6.1 Introduction

Childhood cancer, although rare, is the third most common cause of death in the age group 0-14. There are major differences in tumour type and primary sites in childhood cancer compared with adult cancer. In England and Wales, leukaemia is the commonest childhood cancer, responsible for a third of all cases, with a preponderance of acute lymphoblastic leukaemia, which peaks in the age group 0-4. The two other main types of childhood cancer are brain tumours and lymphomas. Table 6.1.1 shows the distribution of these cancers in England and Wales in the 0-14 year old group between 1971 and 1980 (Draper, 1995).

The risk agencies and the nuclear industry have always concentrated on leukaemia as the main indicator of radiation damage to populations, despite the clear evidence that ionising radiation causes increase in all cancer types. The Gardner study of Seascale showed a three-fold excess of non-leukaemia cancer in children, as well as the ten-fold leukaemia and lymphoma excess (Gardner *et al.*, 1990). Leukaemia was the basis of the legal action regarding radiation effects from Sellafield (Reay and Hope *vs.* BNFL, 1993) and was bound to be an important consideration in the litigation for which the present results were obtained.

As a result of the Hiroshima and other studies, leukaemia in children had come to be firmly associated with radiation exposure by the late 1960s and so when, in 1983, a cluster of childhood leukaemia was discovered near the Sellafield plant, with relative risk of about ten times the national average, public concern was that the plant emissions were the cause of the illness. The risk agencies argued then, and continue to argue, that their risk factors, obtained by linear extrapolation from the yield in the Hiroshima survivors, could not predict the effect, and therefore that there must be some other cause (COMARE, 1996). Shortly after this, studies were published that showed excess risk in children near the reprocessing plant at Dounreay of eight times the national average (Heasman, 1986). This was followed by the discovery of a significant, though modest excess near the atomic weapons factories at Aldermaston and Burghfield (Roman, 1993, Busby and Scott Cato, 1997). More recently, the French reprocessing plant at Cap de la Hague has been the focus of studies showing excess childhood leukaemia risk associated with both playing on the beach and also eating shellfish (Viel, 1994, 1997).

Since Chernobyl, there have been reports of leukaemia increases in the affected territories (Savchenko, 1995; Nestorenko, 1997; Busby and Yablokov 2006) and also reports of no stepwise leukaemia increases in the entire aggregated European population (Parkin *et al.* 1996). However, I had drawn attention to increases in childhood leukaemia in Wales and Scotland after Chernobyl at the House of Commons symposium we organised (Busby 1996a, 1998a) And, in particular, Molly Scott Cato and I had recently argued that risk factors adopted by the ICRP (and used by the UK National Radiological Protection Board) fail to predict the significant 3.3-fold excess leukaemia incidence in those infants (age 0-1) in Scotland and Wales exposed *in utero* or with fathers whose sperm was exposed before conception. (Busby and Scott Cato, 2000)

The error involved is of the order of hundreds of times, a number that is sufficient to explain the Sellafield leukaemia cluster and also those at other nuclear sites. Similar increases in infant leukaemia after Chernobyl have been reported from Greece (Petridou *et al.*, 1997), the USA (Mangano, 1997), Germany (Michaelis *et al.*,1997) and in a preliminary report from Scotland (Gibson *et al.*, 1988). I shall return to these.

Table 6.1.1 Distribution of the main childhood cancer types in England and Wales in 1995.

Type	Numbers (% total)	Crude rate per 100,000
All cases	11,479	10.3
Leukaemia	3857 (33.6)	3.47
Brain and spinal	2685 (23.3)	2.42
Lymphomas	1314 (11.4)	1.16
All other sites	3623 (31.7)	3.25

Source: Draper, 1995.

For childhood cancers we will report here the results obtained in the original, slightly larger, study area that we began looking at in 1997, since there was no significant difference in the trend in childhood cancer between this and the restricted area that we used for the adult cancers. The results we obtained for leukaemia in children in our initial study of the Wales Cancer Registry first database (A2218.exe) gave rise to enormous controversy when I first reported it in 1998. It showed a very high rate of child leukaemia in north Wales and was picked up by the BBC who made a half hour TV documentary called *Sea of Troubles*. This drew attention to the high levels of leukaemia and also other cancers in adults in the coastal areas of mid and north Wales and resulted in the Welsh Office calling in COMARE. It also switched on a searchlight that illuminated the earlier questions over cancer incidence in Wales and the closure of the Wales Cancer Registry just after they released to us the small area data. It began a fight over the truth of the cancer increases in Wales that continues to the present day. I will devote some space to these arguments in Part III but here I will present the results of the studies into childhood cancer in the area.

6.2 All cancers in children ages 0-4 and 0-14

Results by distance from the Irish Sea are given for the whole period in Table 6.2.1 and in the bubble plot Fig 6.2.1. The trend over the whole period was interesting: whilst there was a sea coast effect throughout the period, it became significantly high in the last thirds between 1984 and 1988, by which time the relative risk in the coastal strip <0.8km was 3.6 with 17 cases observed and 4.8 expected; p = 0.0005. The effect existed but was less obvious in the 0-14year olds, where over the whole period 1974-89 there were 56 cases of cancer observed and 40.9 expected (RR= 1.4, p = 0.01). By 1984-88 the 0-0.8km coastal strip had 22 cases observed and 12.8 expected (RR = 1.7, p = 0.01). So the effect was driven, as with the Sellafield children, by the 0-4 year olds. The trend over the whole period was interesting: whilst there was a sea coast effect throughout the period, it became significantly high in the last thirds between 1984 and 1988, by which time the relative risk in the coastal strip <0.8km was 3.6, with 17 cases observed and 4.8 expected; p = 0.0005. Fig 6.2.1 shows this effect graphically in the sets of points for 1984-88 added to the LOESS graph. Tables for the three periods 1974-78, 1979-83 and 1984-88 are shown in Table 6.2.1

Table 6.2.1 All malignancy risk ICD9:140-208 in children 0-4 in Welsh study area by distance bands from sea coast. From top to bottom: 1974-89; 1984-88; 1979-83; 1974-78

Range of distance from sea,<sd> (km)	Mean distance (std. dev)	Observed Cases	Expected Cases	Relative Risk	P value (Poisson)	Number of areas aggregated
<0.8	0.56(0.16)	34	15.3	2.2	0.0000	18
0.9<sd<2	1.4 (0.5)	33	21.8	1.5	0.009	17
2.1<sd<5	4.2 (0.4)	23	20	1.1	-	15
5.1<sd<11	8.2 (0.66)	36	33	1.1	-	17
11.1<sd<21	16.4 (2:8)	7	13.5	0.5	-	14
21.1<sd<40	34.7 (5.8)	24	20	1.2	-	17
Sd>41	55 (9.3)	20	17.9	1.1	-	27
All South Wales		270	195	1.4	-	61

Range of distance from sea,<sd> (km)	Mean distance (std. dev)	Observed cases	Expected cases	Relative Risk	P-value Significance (Poisson)	Number of areas aggregated
<0.8	0.56(0.16)	17	4.8	3.6	0.0000	18
0.9<sd<2	1.4 (0:5)	17	6.8	2.5	0.0007	17
2.1<sd<5	4.2 (0.4)	6	6.5	1	-	15
5.1<sd<11	8.24 (0.66)	12	10.4	1.2	-	17
11.1<sd<20	16.4 (2.8)	2	4	0.5	-	14
21.1<sd<40	34.7 (5.8)	8	6.3	1.3	0.28	17
Sd>41	55 (9.3)	9	5.6	1.6	-	27
All South Wales		106	61	1.7	-	61

Range of distance from sea,<sd> (km)	Mean distance (Std. dev.)	Observed cases	Expected cases	Relativ e Risk	P-value Significance (Poisson)	Number of areas aggregated
<0.8	0.56(0.16)	7	4.8	1.5	NS	18
0.9<sd<2	1.4 (0.5)	7	6.8	1	-	17
2.1<sd<5	4.2 (0.4)	8	6.5	1.2	-	15
5.1<sd<11	8.24 (0.66)	6	10.36	0.6	-	17
11.1<sd<20	16.4 (2.8)	4	4.2	1	-	14
21<sd<40	34.6 (5.8)	7	6.25	1.1	-	17
Sd>41	55 (9.3)	4	5.6	0.7	-	27
All South Wales		69	61	1.1		61

Range of distance from sea,<sd> (km)	Mean distance (Std. dev.)	Observed cases	Expected cases	Relativ e Risk	P value Significance (Poisson)	Number of areas aggregated
<0.8	0.56(0.16)	9	4.8	1.9	0.056	18
0.9<sd<2	1.4 (0.5)	11	6.8	1.6	0.08	17
2.1<sd<5	4.2 (0.4)	8	6.5	1.2	-	15
5.1<sd<11	8.24 (0.66)	15	10.36	1.5	-	17
11.1<sd<20	16.4 (2.8)	1	4	0.25	-	14
21<sd<40	55 (9.3)	6	5.6	1.1	-	27
All South Wales		78	61	1.27	-	61

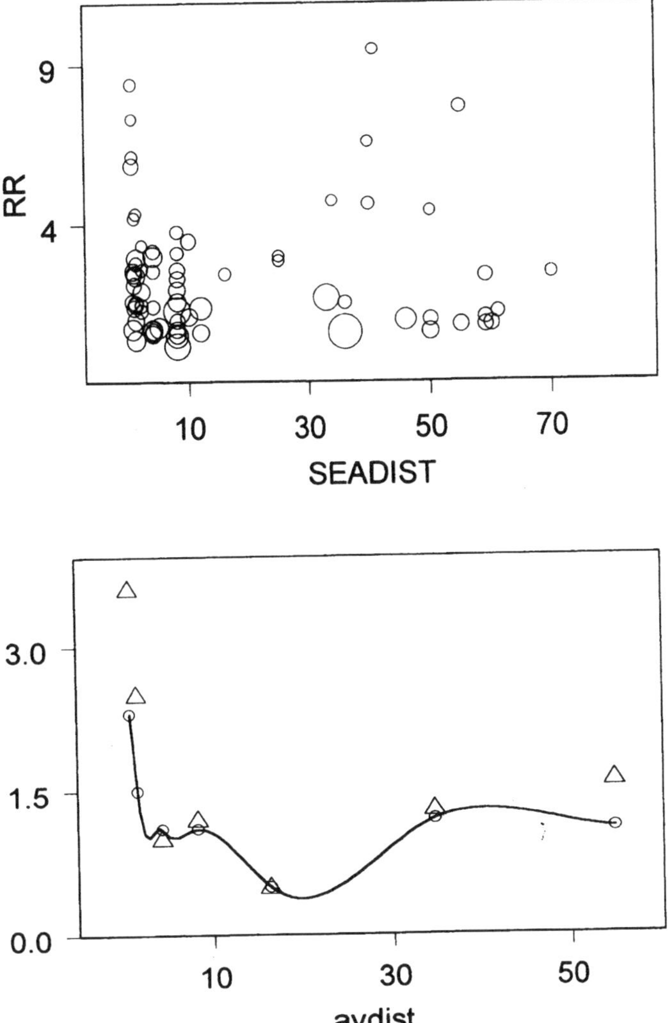

Fig 6.2.1 Top: bubble plot of childhood cancer risk ages 0-4 (ICD9; 140-208) by distance from the sea in AORs. Bottom: LOESS plot of risk of childhood cancer 0-4 in distance groups of AORs. Line represents whole period 1974-89. Triangles are for 1984-88. Note increase in effect near coast.

6.3 Leukaemia

The Wales Cancer Registry data for childhood leukaemia caused us a great deal of difficulty from the beginning. The first set of files we were sent (the A2218 exe files) contained separate columns for all leukaemia to those that were listed as ICD 204-208, the code for all leukaemia. I took this to mean that there were separate listings in the database for child leukaemia and, in the initial analysis, added the two columns of leukaemia data together. This was because there was no overlap. If a case appeared as 'all leukaemia' it did not appear as 204-208. I return to this issue later in this book. But, as far as the results were concerned, we reported results for two separate analyses. The first was the analysis of the Wales Cancer Registry first file A2218.exe, which I call WCR1. The second was the analysis of the second Wales Cancer Registry A2283.exe (WCR2) file that I obtained from the Statistics Division of the Welsh Office after the registry had been closed down.

The result that caused all the trouble was the leukaemia incidence in the 0-4s indicated by the WCR1. This is shown in Fig 6.3.1. Also shown is the same analysis but this time using the WCR2 file. Fig 6.3.1 also shows the plot of risk by distance from the sea over the whole period for the two databases. The sea coast effect is present in both datasets but the numbers of cases are far greater in the WCR1 dataset. I will return to the controversy about these numbers in Part III. Initially, when the arguments over the issue of the two files came to a head following the BBC documentary, it was agreed by the new cancer registry, the Wales Cancer Intelligence and Surveillance Unit (WCISU), that the WCR2 data was accurate. This second file shows a sea coast effect that increases in the second half of the period 1982-90. Cutting the coastal groups at 2km we find that over the whole period 1974-90 the relative risk was 1.5 ($p = 0.004$) and in the second half, 1982-90, this increased to 2.9 ($p = .001$). So even in the agreed dataset, without the extra cases tabulated in the first dataset, there is a significant sea coast effect on child leukaemia. Childhood leukaemias are very rare, so a single case in an area might give a high relative risk and yet be a chance finding. However we can look to see areas where there are multiple cases over the period. We find that these areas are all the same coastal towns in north Wales that showed the high levels of adult cancer. Fig 6.3.1 also shows AORs in the study area with more than one case of child leukaemia 0-4 and the calculated relative risk.

Range of distance from sea,<sd> (km)	Mean distance (std. dev.)	Observed cases	Expected cases	Relative Risk	P value significance (Poisson)	Number of areas aggregated
<0.8	0.56 (0.16)	27	6.01	4.5	0.0000	18
0.9<sd<2	1.41 (0.51)	28	8.54	3.27	0.0000	17
2.1<sd<5	4.2 (0.41)	24	8.12	2.95	0.0000	15
5.1<sd<11	8.24 (0.66)	31	13.0	2.4	0.0000	17
11.1<sd<21	16.4 (2.8)	17	5.31	3.2	0.0000	14
21.1<sd<41	34.7 (5.8)	20	7.93	2.5	0.0005	18
41.1<sd<61	51.8 (5.8)	9	5.91	1.5	0.203	20
51<sd<71	61.4 (4.8)	3	3.41	0.9	0.660	14
South Wales		118	76.6	1.54		65
All Wales		285	145	1.96		192

Source: Wales Cancer Registry, *Welsh Areas of Residence Datafiles 2218*. May 1995.

Distance	Number of Areas	Average sea distance	Observed cases	Expected cases	Relative risk	P value (Poisson)
<0.8	18	0.56	10	6.4	1.56	-
0.9 to 2	17	1.41	10	9.08	1.1	-
2.1 to 11	29	6.31	18	20.9	0.86	-
11.1 to 40	29	27.3	11	13.2	0.83	-
>41	23	54	6	5.25	1.15	-
All Wales	182		159	149	1.07	-
South Wales	66		104	94	1.10	-

Source: 2283 and 2218 common cases checked against totals from WCISU 1998 files.

AOR[a]	Number observed cases	Relative Risk
71CC Colwyn Bay	3	5.64
74CA Bangor	3	11.2
74CE Caernarfon	2	8.12

[a] refers to a coastal Area of Residence.

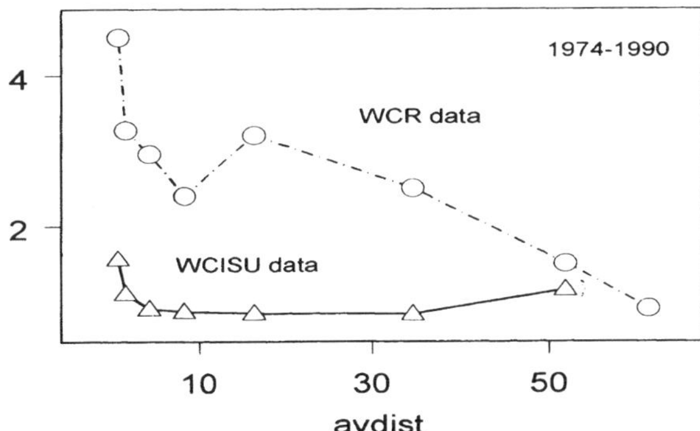

Fig. 6.3.1 (From top) 1. Table of risks of child leukaemia 0-4 in AOR groups by distance from sea in the disputed WCR1 data. 2. The same results for the WCR2 data (see text). 3. Effects in individual AORs near the coast in the validated WCR2 files. 4. Plot of risk by distance from sea in the two databases.

6.4 Brain tumours, lymphomas and cancer of the eye.

Brain tumours represent the second most common childhood cancer. In England and Wales about 13% of all tumours were brain tumours. The incidence has been increasing steadily in England and Wales between 1962 and 1991, with the greatest increases (50%) in the 0-4 age group. About half of these are fatal. Cook Mozzafari found excess brain tumours around nuclear installations in 1987 (1987). Recently (2005) I have been involved in a court case in Florida with a cluster of children with brain tumours near the St Lucie nuclear power station. We found a significant excess of brain tumours in Wales in children 0-4, 0-9 and 0-14 in the coastal groups with the excess driven by the usual coastal towns with contaminated beaches and local sediments. Fig 6.4.1 shows data for the 0-4 age group by distance from the sea. In the Table I show the analysis for the 0-9 age group. The effect was not significant in the 0-14s suggesting that it was driven by exposure occurring in the middle of the period of study (which is when Sellafield releases became significant).

I also give results for the coastal towns and compare 11 coastal towns with 11 inland towns. These results show high risk from brain tumours as well as leukaemia in the coastal towns, at levels that approach those found at Seascale near Sellafield in the 1980s. Since non-Hodgkin lymphoma (NHL) was also a feature of the Seascale cluster, we looked at NHL in Wales. The numbers are very small and so we had to split the area into three sections cut at 2km, 11km and greater than 11km. When we did this, we found a significant excess (RR = 2.73, p = 0.06) in the coastal 2km strip. This effect was not there for all lymphomas combined.

Because the well described genetic eye cancer retinoblastoma is associated with Sellafield pollution, as I have described earlier, we also examined the few cases of eye cancer in the 0-4 year olds over the period. Although the numbers were very low, there were higher risks in the coastal areas in the north of Wales. Out of the 10 cases in the entire study area over the 16-year period, four cases were in coastal AORs Flint, Llandudno, Pwllelli and Valley on Anglesey. The coastal effect was not statistically significant for eye cancer in the 0-4s.

The excess risk of brain tumours in children near the coast which we found in the 1974-89 period we also later found in children living near the Menai Strait in the study we carried out with the HTV researchers in 2004, and by then the Relative Risk in the coastal Menai towns had become very high indeed. I return to this issue.

Range of distance from sea,<sd> (km)	Mean distance (std. dev.)	Observed cases	Expected Cases	Relative Risk	P value Significance (Poisson)	Number of areas Aggregated
<0.8	0.56 (0.16)	9	1.92	4.7	0.0002	16
0.9<sd<2	1.4 (0.51)	3	2.12	1.41		13
2.1<sd<5	4.27 (0.47)	1	2.04	0.5		11
5.1<sd<11	8.4 (0.84)	4	2.35	1.7		10
11.1<sd<40	27 (8.3)	1	1.4	.71		22
>41	56.3	4	1.63	2.45		21
All South Wales		42	30.2	1.4		66

Source: Wales Cancer Registry, *Welsh Areas of Residence Datafiles 2218,* May 1995.
Note: NEWCLAS area excludes Wrexham and South of St Davids Head

Range of distance from sea,<sd> (km)	Mean distance (std. dev.)	Observed cases	Expected cases	Relative Risk	P value Significance (Poisson)	Number of areas aggregated
<0.8	0.56 (0.16)	12	4.04	3.0	0.0009	16
0.9<sd<2	1.38 (0.51)	7	4.4	1.6		13
2.1<sd<5	4.27 (0.47)	6	4.38	1.37		11
5.1<sd<11	8.24 (0.66)	8	4.67	1.71		10
11.1<sd<40	27 (8.3)	3	3.0	1.0	-	22
>41	56.3 (9.3)	8	3.3	2.4	0.02	21
All South Wales		88	61	1.44		66

Source: Wales Cancer Registry, *Welsh Areas of Residence Datafiles 2218,* May 1995.

AOR	Observed cases			Relative Risk		
Northern Coastal	0-4	0-9	0-14	0-4	0-9	0-14
Entire Group of 11 AORs	9	13	15	3.9	2.7	1.9
*71JA Prestatyn	2	4	4	9.5	8.9	5.1
*74AE Llandudno	3	3	4	13.7	6.5	5.0
*74CA Bangor	2	2	2	11	5.1	3.0

AOR	Observed cases			Relative Risk		
Inland	0-4	0-9	0-14	0-4	0-9	0-14
Entire Group of 11 AORs	1	3	3	0.85	1.22	0.53

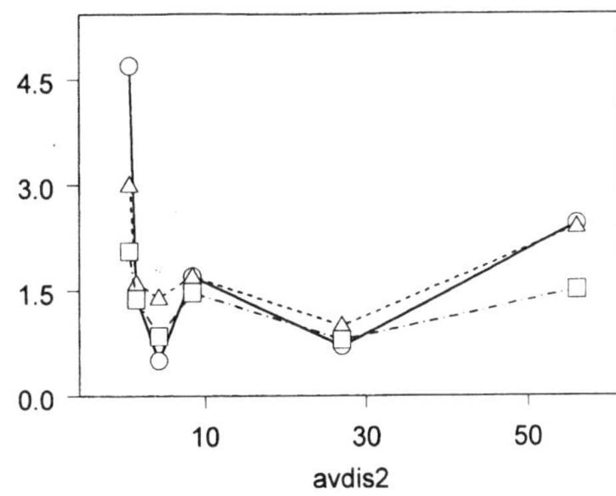

Fig 6.4.1 Top to bottom: Risk of brain tumours in children 0-4 by distance from sea in AOR groups 1974-89; same for children 0-9; comparing northern coastal AOR towns with 11 inland matched AORs; trend with distance from sea (0-4 circles; 0-9 triangles; 0-14 squares).

6.5 Trawsfynydd and Wylfa study (Welsh Office, 1994b)

The results found by us were electrifying in their significance. They showed that the operation of Sellafield had resulted, not only in local effects at Seascale, but also deaths along the shores of the Irish Sea. The implications for the authorities were immense and so they moved swiftly to counter the accusations implicit in the results. Of course they must have known that there was such an effect when they rapidly closed the Wales Cancer Registry after the cat was out of the bag in 1995. But, interestingly (and useful to our position), there was earlier data that showed the existence of the same sea coast effect which we had uncovered. This was, ironically enough, contained in a report intended to exonerate the nuclear industry. This first study to investigate cancer incidence in Wales in terms of possible causes was undertaken in 1994 by the Wales Cancer Registry. It followed the 1992 General election and our 1992 Non-Violent Direct Action against Trawsfynydd nuclear power station and its subsequent closure. The direct action was undertaken in conjunction with the publication of the books *Low Level Radiation from the Nuclear Industry: Biological Consequences* and its Welsh language translation *Pelydriad Level Isaf o'r Diwidiant Niwcliar: yr Canliniadau Biolegol* (Busby 1992). This book argued that cancer in Wales was largely determined by low-level radiation exposure and focused partly on the radioisotopic pollution of the lake at Trawsfynydd nuclear power station.

The Wales Cancer Registry study (Welsh Office, 1994b) published in May 1994 was entitled 'Investigation of Incidence of Cancer around Wylfa and Trawsfynydd Nuclear Installations, 1974-1986 A-EMJ-28'. There was no author listed, but in 1998, the present director of the Wales Cancer Intelligence and Surveillance Unit, Dr John Steward, admitted to me at our first meeting in Cardiff that he had been the main author of the report. Later, he retracted this admission. I have tried many times to get the Welsh Office and Welsh Assembly to let me have the names of the authors of this study, but with no success.

For full details of the report and a critical review of its methods and results refer to the original report and to Busby, 1994b. Briefly, the finding was that there was no significant excess cancer risk that fell off continuously with distance from either Trawsfynydd or from Wylfa nuclear power stations.

The analysis for risk near a putative point source used the method of Stone (Stone 1988). This is a statistical procedure in which continuous fall-off of relative risk in annular aggregates of wards at increasing distances from a single point source of pollution is used as confirmation that there is a problem. The method itself is subject to criticism (Busby 1995). Its use in the Welsh Office paper was spurious since there were two sources of risk: Wylfa and Trawsfynydd. Therefore, if there were an increase in risk near each site due to radiation, risk would increase as the wards distant from one site approached the second site and the Stone procedure would signal no effect, even if there were one. However, the importance of the study is that the same Area of Residence (AOR) cancer incidence data for Gwynedd was used, together with centroids of population for seven groups of cancers, for the period 1974-86.

'All leukaemias' was among the cancers analysed. Results were presented together with a map of the AORs and their centroids of population. In Busby 1994b, which reviewed the analysis, it was observed that cancer incidence relative risks shown in the report increased close to the shores of the Irish Sea. The numbers of cases of the seven groups of cancers tabulated in the results section of WCR, 1994 agree closely with the data contained in the two files WCR1 and WCR2, with the exception of the contested child leukaemia data. The 'all leukaemias - all ages' totals given in the Trawsfynydd study can easily be shown to demonstrate the sea coast effect. A plot of Relative Risk for 'All Leukaemia - all ages' in the areas of Gwynedd and western Clwyd reported in WCR, 1994, with distance from the sea, obtained from the WCR, 1994 map is given in Figure 6.5.1. Both the effect of the proximity to the Irish Sea and also the effect of Trawsfynydd power station are clearly visible. Because the cancer sites chosen for the study were small incidence sites, it was not possible to effect the same analysis for the other sites or more restricted age groups. However, in the case of the leukaemia, the WCR 1994 study shows a result very similar to the general finding, that is: increasing risk close to the coast.

The study is valuable evidence because it shows that already, in 1994, Wales Cancer Registry data showed the existence of a coastal effect on leukaemia. The Trawsfynydd study was a demonstrably flawed attempt to exonerate the nuclear industry sites at Wylfa and Trawsfynydd from causing increases in cancer in their neighbourhood. That the author of the study was Dr John Steward, Director of the WCISU, the organisation set up to take over from the Wales cancer Registry was our first suggestion of Dr Steward's sympathies. However, as I will relate in Part III, Dr Steward later denied ever having been involved in the report and my enquiries to the Welsh Office met with the statement that the report was produced by 'Wales Cancer Registry', and no individual author would be named.

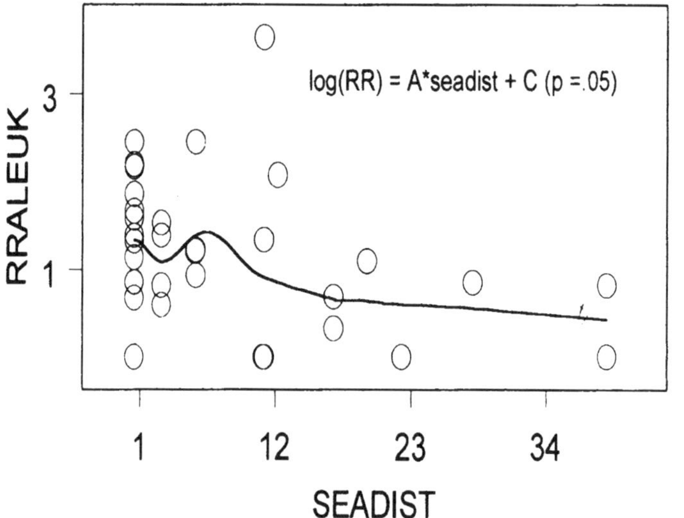

Figure 6.5.1 Scatter plot and local regression (LOESS) of Relative Risk of all leukaemia in all age groups by distance from Irish Sea. Data from Wales Cancer Registry Study of cancer near Trawsfynydd and Wylfa nuclear sites, WCR, 1994. The peak in the line represents wards around Trawsfynydd.

6.6 Other possible reasons for the effects found in the Wales data.

6.6.1 Confounding causes

The hypothesis at the beginning of this study of cancer risk in Wales was that man-made radioactive isotopes had been released from Sellafield under license and had migrated to the coast of Wales and caused increased exposure to coastal populations, which resulted in increases in cancer. Finding higher levels of cancer near the coast might, however, have been due to other confounding factors and these needed to be examined.

The first possibility was radioactivity from global weapons fallout in grassland and soil throughout Wales, ignoring the materials that had been washed to the sea and had become fixed in estuary sediment. These substances were measured by teams from Harwell in 1984, and again in 1986, following Chernobyl. (Welsh Office, 1988) Tables and maps of concentrations of Strontium-90, Caesium-137 and Plutonium-239+240 in Wales are thus available. The fallout from weapons testing correlated with rainfall. Rain in Wales washes much of the particulate fallout to the rivers and thence to the estuaries of these rivers, many of which empty to the Irish Sea. The east and south flowing rivers, draining the eastern parts of the Cambrian Mountains, take a circuitous path to empty into the Severn estuary and Bristol Channel (Wye, Usk and Severn) and part of the fallout isotope burden will have taken this route to the sea. The ecological correlation with cancer risk may be modelled from the rainfall data and from the fallout data itself. We calculated and coded two variables, PLUTO, Plutonium in soil from the Welsh Office Harwell report (Welsh Office, 1988) and RAIN (rainfall maps from the Meteorological Office, Bracknell). Both were coded to the AORs by map superposition and geometrical square averaging. A map of PLUTO is shown in Fig 6.6.1.

Of course, the Irish Sea coast in Wales thus has inputs from weapons fallout and Chernobyl, as well as from Sellafield, and the various proportions of these in the silt in parts of north Wales have been determined by Assinder *et al.* (Assinder *et al.*1994). In general, Assinder found that the weapons fallout and Chernobyl fallout predominated at the inshore end of estuaries whereas the Sellafield radiation contributed most to the seaward end of estuaries and in the coastal sediment. Measurements made by the Harwell teams (Garland *et al.* 1989) show that 80% of the Sellafield radioactivity in Wales is in silt between the Menai Strait and Llandudno, together with material trapped in the Dee estuary. The highest concentration was in the Lavan Sands near the town of Bangor. The remaining 20% is distributed along the shores of West Wales, with higher concentrations in the silt of estuaries of the rivers. This material and its concentration was coded to the coastal AORs and labelled SEAPU.

The sea-to-land transfer of radioactivity from Sellafield was discussed in Chapter 3. Several studies of Plutonium-in-air concentrations by distance from the Irish Sea show a quite specific type of behaviour. There is a very rapid increase in concentration close to the sea, in the 0-1km range of distance, with a sharp flattening out in concentration from 5km to 200km. This suggests the existence of two ranges of particle behaviour based on the mass of the particle with larger particles dropping out under the influence of gravity in the first 1000m. Using data from various sources, but based largely on the work of Eakins and Lally (1984), we used the program 'MATHCAD' to derive an empirical relation between Plutonium in air and distance from the sea. This is coded to the AORs as the variable AIRPU.

Data was available on the levels in Wales of the natural radioactive gas Radon-222. This variable was coded to the AORs as RADON.

In addition to the variables already described, I used two socioeconomic variables DEP1 and CARSTAIRS. A list of the variables that were coded and considered is given below in Table 6.6.1

Table 6.6.1 Descriptive regression variables coded to each AOR and investigated for correlation with distance from Irish Sea and cancer risk in this study. Results of these regression analyses will be described.

Variable name	Description	Origin
SEADIST	Distance from Irish sea (km)	Mapping (see text)
RAIN	Average rainfall 1960-1995 (mm)	Metereological Office
PLUTO	Activity of Plutonium in soil (Bq/kg)	Harwell (Cawse *et al.*1988)
SEAPU	Activity of Plutonium in inter-tidal sediment. (kBq/kg)	Harwell (Garland *et al.* 1989)
AIRPU	Activity of Plutonium in air (nBq/cu:m)	Harwell (Eakins and Lally, 1984)
RADON	Activity of Radon in dwellings (Bq/cu:m)	NRPB 1999
DEP1	Welsh Index of Socioeconomic Deprivation (see text)	Welsh Office 1981
CARSTAIRS	Carstairs Index of Socioeconomic Deprivation (see text)	Census 1991, Small Area Health Statistics Unit

6.6.2 Rainfall

The variation of average rainfall with distance from the coast is given below in Fig 6.6.2.1 None of the simple two covariate or multiple log regressions gave significant association between any cancer risk and RAIN.

6.6.3 Plutonium in soil.

It had been hypothesised that increased risk might be associated with increased levels of Plutonium in soil. The relation with distance from the sea, given in Fig 6.6.3.1 below, suggests that this simple relationship is unlikely and indeed no cancer risk regression results gave any significant beta coefficient for such an association. However, the averaging process that led to the construction of the Plutonium maps could not show differences on a small scale and thus could not distinguish elevated levels of isotopes in river valleys. There was a significant and moderate rural/urban split in cancer risk in the whole of the study area but mostly in the eastern low-risk areas, where most of the towns are built on rivers e.g. Builth Wells on the Wye.

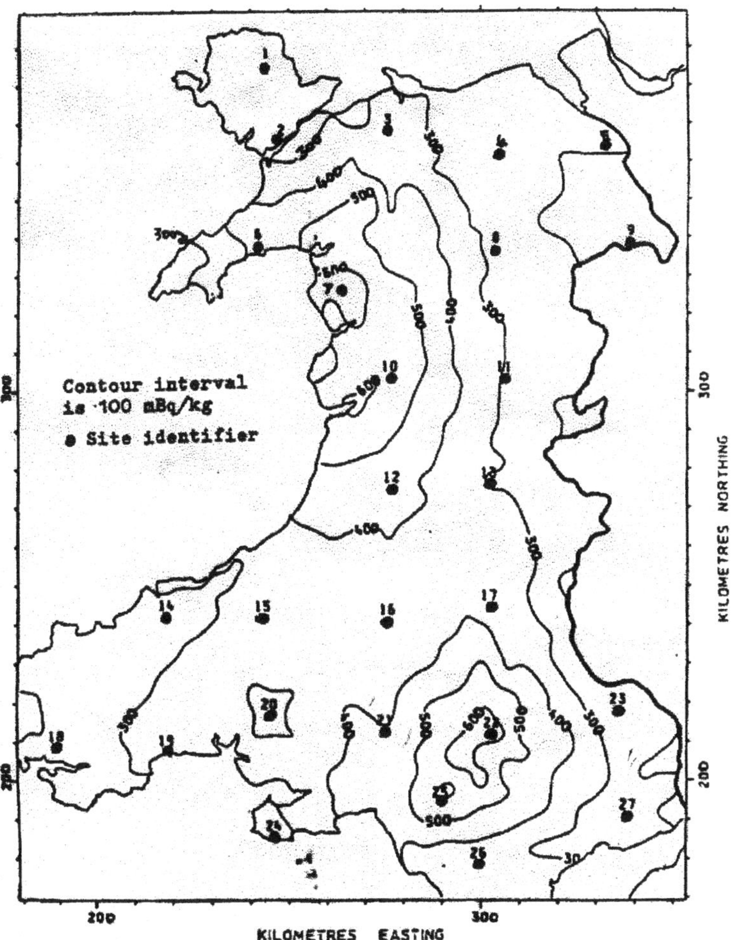

Fig 6.6.1 Map of Plutonium in soil (Bq/kg) in Welsh AORs
(*Source:* Welsh Office, 1988) Note the interesting contours around the Trawsfynydd region (near Point 7) and at the inner end of the Dyfi estuary (Point 10).

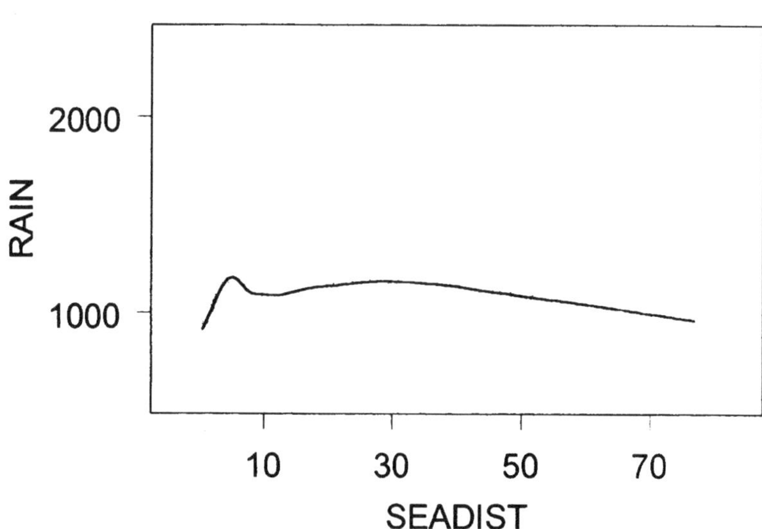

Fig 6.6.2.1 LOESS fit of RAIN (mm annual precipitation) coded into the AORs with distance from Irish Sea in study area (source: Met Office).

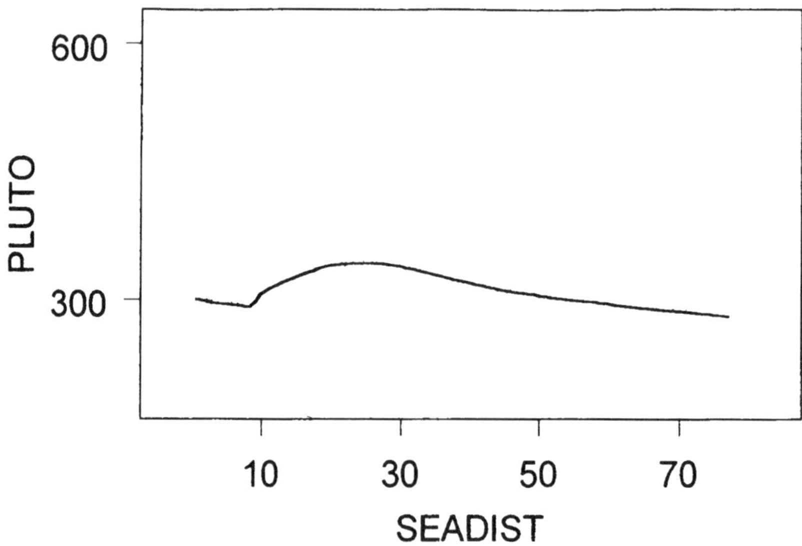

Fig 6.6.3.1 LOESS fit of PLUTO, Plutonium in soil (mBq/kg) on distance from sea in study area. It appears from the trend that the highest levels are in the mountains, and this would follow the higher rainfall that occurs there.

6.6.4 SEAPU

The Plutonium concentration in inter-tidal sediment (which I have termed 'SEAPU') was mapped on the basis of measurements made by Harwell (Garland *et al.*, 1989). This map is shown in Plate 7. Coastal AORs were coded for the levels indicated on the map that were either measured or extrapolated linearly from measurements made by this Harwell study. The higher levels of cancer, particularly childhood cancer, were generally associated with the AORs in the north where the value of SEAPU was high, e.g. Bangor to Llandudno and Colwyn Bay to Flint. Indeed, it was possible to show that there was a correlation between the value of SEAPU for these coastal areas and the relative risk of cancer of most types. For example, scatter plots of relative risk for adult all-malignancy, leukaemia and colon cancer against SEAPU is given in Fig 6.6.4.1 In the case of some cancer types, e.g. colon cancer and leukaemia, the correlation was statistically significant at the $p<0.05$ level.

In the overall regression of weighted relative risk of the cancer sites investigated in all the 94 AORs in the study area, the beta- slope coefficients for SEAPU were not statistically significant. This was because the value was only defined for about a quarter of the total AORs. Nevertheless, the discovery that the highest cancer relative risks were on the coast and in the north enabled the secondary analysis using the SEAPU variable and this pointed to the source of the high relative risk in the existence of high levels of Sellafield radioactivity, modelled here as Plutonium, in the coastal or estuarine sediment.

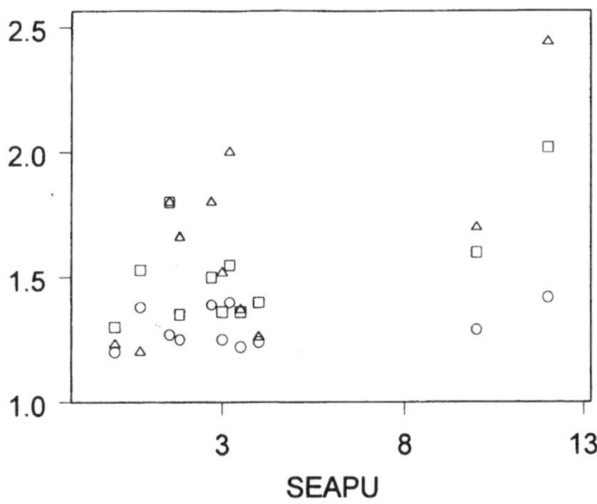

Fig. 6.6.4.1 Relative Risk of all malignancy (circles) colon cancer (squares) and all leukaemia (triangles) by SEAPU, concentration of Plutonium in inter-tidal sediment (kBq/kg) (*from Garland et al., 1989).*

6.6.5 AIRPU

The sea-to-land transfer of radioactive material from the Irish Sea has been measured. In order to examine the effect of such transfer, the concentrations in air with distance from the sea measured by Eakins and Lally (1984) in Cumbria were converted into a general function to describe the fall-off of air concentration with distance from the sea. This function was obtained by mathematically fitting the empirical result and generating a trend curve. Values of Plutonium in air at different distances on this sea distance trend line were then assigned to the AORs on the basis of their SEADIST value. (These values were termed 'AIRPU') We modelled the trend in AIRPU by distance from the Irish Sea using these empirical measurements of Eakins and Lally. This function was then used as a covariate in the multiple regressions for cancer risk.

In the logarithmic regression of cancer risk in the study area, AIRPU was generally a highly significant covariate, and often more significant than SEADIST. This was because of the sharp increase both in cancer risk and in Plutonium in air in the 0-5km coastal region. For example, in the case of all leukaemias, all ages, AIRPU correlated with Relative Risk with a p value of 0.001. Fig 6.6.5.1 shows the trend in AIRPU with distance from the sea in the coastal region up to 10km.

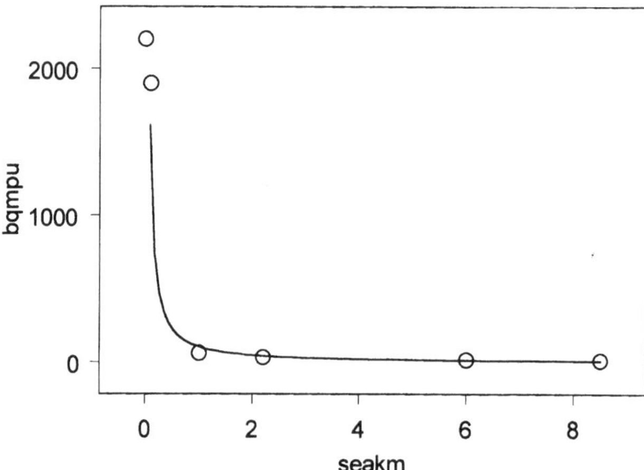

Fig 6.6.5.1 AIRPU trend with distance from sea, based on empirical measurements by Eakins and Lally 1984.

6.6.6 RADON

There has been considerable concern over exposure to the radioactive alpha-emitting gas Radon-222, which is a daughter product of the decay of naturally occurring Radium-226, the fifth daughter of Uranium-238 (see e.g. BEIR V, 1988).

This gas seeps through Uranium containing rocks in granite areas and becomes concentrated in homes, particularly those modern homes, with low ventilation rates. The main concern is that Radon may cause lung cancer and evidence for this comes from Uranium miners, although these are also exposed to solid radioactive dusts. Wales is not considered to be a high Radon area, like Devon and Cornwall, nevertheless, the NRPB, at great expense, have mapped Radon concentrations in homes in Wales and recently (2000) published a Radon map. This is reproduced in Plate 8.

In view of the risk that is believed to exist between Radon exposure and cancer, particularly lung cancer, we coded the NRPB map to the AORs and examined the data for correlation. There are no cases of correlation between Radon levels and any cancer type in the study area. Indeed, the areas of highest risk, Bangor to Llandudno in the north have the lowest levels of Radon in Wales. Fig 6.6.6.1 below shows the levels of Radon (% of homes above action level of $400Bq/m^3$) in AORs by distance from the sea. Fig 6.6.6.1 also shows a bubble plot of lung cancer risk versus Radon level. The relation, if there is one, is negative: this is because the high Radon levels are remote from the sea and therefore carry lower risk.

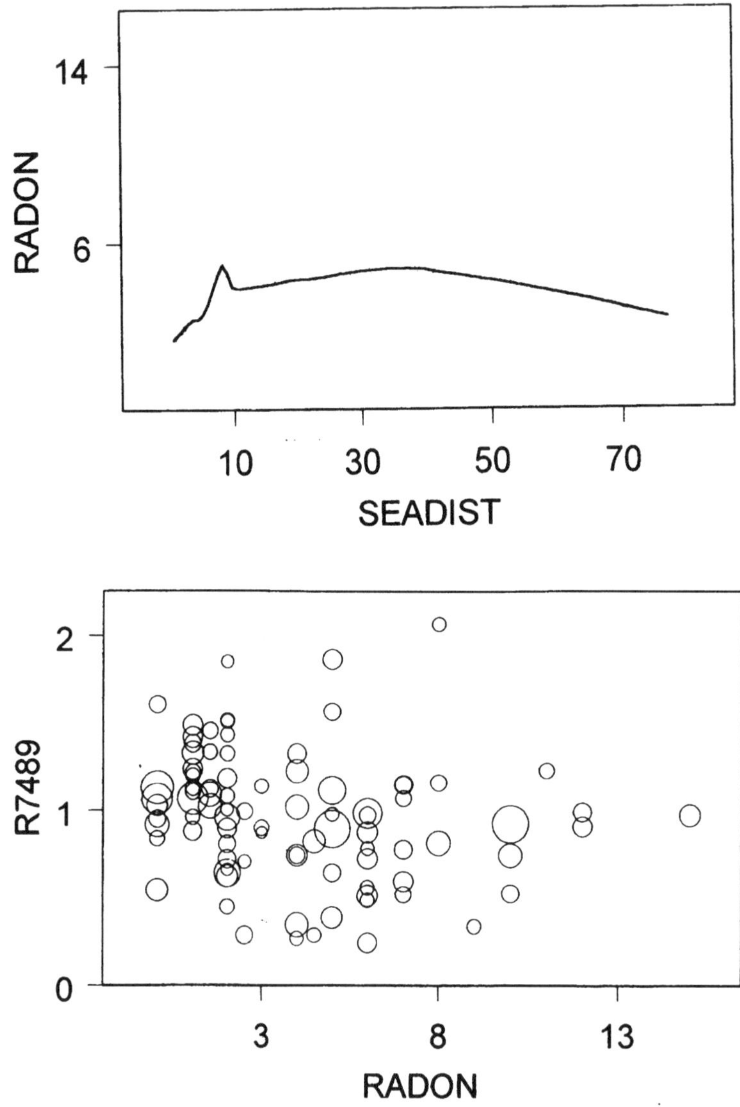

Fig 6.6.6.1 Top: Trend in mean Radon in homes in Wales study area in AORs by distance from the sea. Lower: bubble plot of lung cancer risk 1974-89 in AORs weighted by expected cases, versus mean Radon levels in homes in the AOR. Note negative correlation; more Radon, lower lung cancer risk.

6.6.7 Deprivation DEP1

The DEP1 deprivation index was described earlier. None of the cancer Relative Risks could be correlated with DEP1. The DEP1 index is one-sided, unlike the CARSTAIRS index. That means it does not have a negative range: populations are described as being un-deprived or having varying levels of deprivation. Thus the greater part of the population of the study area, particularly those in the eastern region of Powys, were described by DEP1 as being un-deprived. Their low levels of cancer were not able to weight any regression line in favour of a significant correlation. The pattern that emerged in the results was one in which deprivation had no effect on cancer rates in Wales. This is clear in the marked difference between cancer rates in the north of Wales compared with the socio-economically deprived south of Wales. The variation of DEP1 and SEADIST in the study area is shown below in Fig 6.6.7.1. There is clearly little difference in DEP 1 with distance from the sea.

DEP1 is believed to be a more comprehensive and appropriate index than the simpler CARSTAIRS index and indeed the values of DEP1 were calculated for the exact ward aggregates of the AORs used in this study by the Welsh Office in 1981. This is explored further in the analysis of the results for CARSTAIRS below.

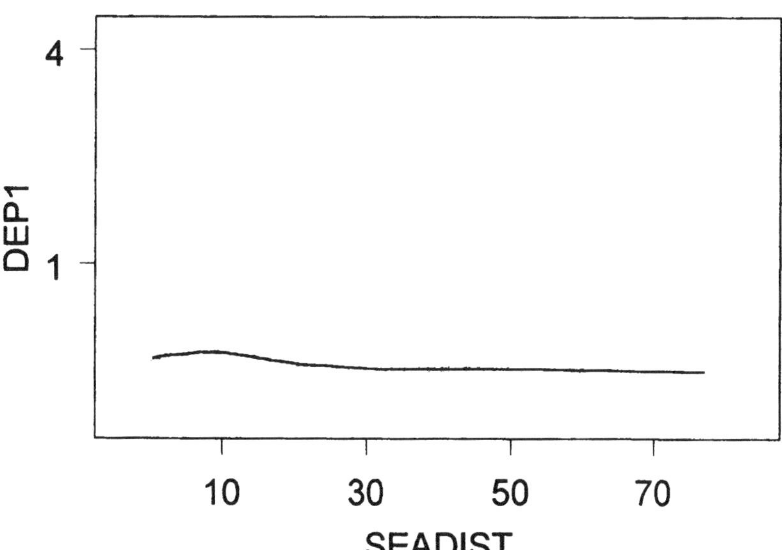

Fig 6.6.7.1 DEP1 deprivation index by distance from the sea in the study area AORs.

6.6.8 CARSTAIRS

This index, and its correlation with cancer rates, has also been discussed earlier. The index has a slightly different relation with distance from the sea to DEP1, for reasons that are unclear. One possibility is that many of the coastal towns are either sea-side resorts or university towns and both have a large proportion of rented accommodation either for students or for holiday makers and CARSTAIRS gives a different weighting to overcrowding and car ownership than does DEP1. It is for this reason, given the peculiar urban rural mixture of Wales, that the Welsh office favour DEP1 to the rather blunter CARSTAIRS index. However, most important, CARSTAIRS shows a small increase in the coastal 0-5km AORs. This is shown in Fig 6.6.8.1 below. Is this the explanation for the coastal effect we find? The answer is no. The range of this increase in CARSTAIRS units is from about 0 at the 5km line to +1 at the 0km line. If this increase in socioeconomic deprivation were affecting cancer rates, the correction to the Relative Risks found would be modest and in some cases would increase them. The correction factors based on the results from Carstairs and Morris in Scotland (1991) and Leon in England and Wales (Leon, 1988) are calculated and given in Table 6.6.8.1

It is clear that CARSTAIRS variation cannot explain the magnitude of the coastal effect. In addition, given the increases in child and adult leukaemia and adult breast cancer found near the coast, the CARSTAIRS increase would predict higher risks that we have found. This inability of CARSTAIRS or DEP1 to explain any part of cancer in Wales is clearly demonstrated by examination of the overall rates in the counties. Except for a low level of cancer in Powys in the east, the other counties, in the highly deprived south of Wales to the less deprived north of Wales, show little correlation with deprivation. Results are calculated for the Counties and are given in Table 6.6.8.1 and Table 6.6.8.2. It is clear that deprivation is of secondary importance to cancer risk in Wales, where proximity to the sea is a much larger indicator of risk.

In passing, isn't this an interesting finding? The cancer charities are forever writing about healthy living, eating well, fresh fruit and vegetables, not smoking, not being fat and so forth. It is now the fault of the cancer sufferers that they fell ill. But from what we found here, this is not the true explanation. These people who died (and actually about 3500 people died of cancer in the coastal AOR group in Wales over the 16 years of the study) did not die because they did not eat broccoli. They died because of the nuclear industry and its radioactive releases.

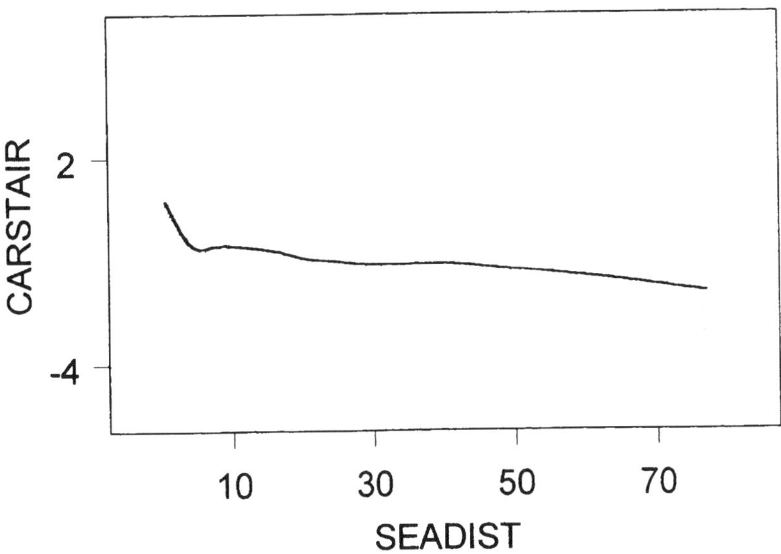

Fig 6.6.8.1 Variation in CARSTAIRS index of deprivation by distance from the sea.

Table 6.6.8.1 Calculated expected variation in Relative Risk in coastal AORs based on CARSTAIRS index and correlations between CARSTAIRS and standardised cancer incidence found in Scotland and in England and Wales.

Cancer Type	Correction Factor to Relative Risk in Coastal AORs
all malignancy	1% decrease
Leukaemia	1% increase
breast cancer	0.5% increase
lung cancer	4% decrease
colon cancer	no difference
cervical cancer	4% decrease
prostate cancer	no difference
Childhood cancer	2% increase

Table 6.6.8.2 Variation in all malignancy SRR in Welsh Counties 1984-88 with mean CARSTAIRS index. (*Source: Welsh Office, 1994 and Small Area Health Statistics Unit)*

County	Type	No. of wards	SRR all maligs. 1984-88	Carstairs means (Standard Deviations)
Gwynedd	North rural	139	103	+0.32 (2.7)
Mid Glamorgan	South industrial	120	100	+2.37 (3.03)
Clwyd	North mixed	150	103	-0.21 (2.64)
East Dyfed	Mid rural	162	100	-0.45 (2.13)
Pembroke	South west rural		98	-0.14 (2.5)
Gwent	South industrial	111	103	+0.8 (2.9)
South Glamorgan	South industrial	47	93	+0.38 (3.58)
West Glamorgan	South Industrial	84	105	+1.12 (3.05)
Powys	mid rural	84	84	-2.07 (1.95)
all Wales	-	1066	100	0.02 (2.85)

6.7 Conclusions from the Welsh studies

At the end of this section of results I will briefly draw together what we believed the data showed us at the end of the study of the Wales Cancer Registry data. First, there was clear evidence that something was causing a sharp increase in most cancer rates in coastal populations of Wales. The effect was there for most of the cancers we studied and the effect got worse over the period of the study. It could not have occurred by chance since the statistical power and significance were high. This was because the analysis was of a very large population over a sixteen or seventeen year period. This also enabled us to show that the effect was there in children, particularly the 0-4s. A pointer to the cause of the effect was the sharp increase very close to the coast: clearly it was something happening very close to the coast that was the cause or related to the cause. What could this be? We examined all the possible causes we could imagine, coding disadvantagement, rainfall, radioactivity in soil and Radon. The only factors that could explain the sea proximity effect were Plutonium in air, or sea spray, or the level of contamination of inter-tidal sediment, SEAPU. In other words, the regression was telling us that the trend in cancer risk with distance from the sea was the same as the trend in Plutonium with distance from the sea, as measured by the Harwell scientists Eakins and Lally in the 1980s. A separate regression told us that, among the sea coast AORs, those with the highest risks were those with the highest levels of Plutonium contamination. Finally, examination of the development of the increases in risk over time showed that the overall increases between 1974 and 1989 were in the coastal strip, particularly after 1982. This was some five years after the Sellafield material washed up on the coast and began to expose local people who would have inhaled the airborne sea spray and resuspended radioactive particles, or eaten the contaminated local food. The data for adult leukaemia is most interesting. We can see the development of the risk in the coastal strip relative to the inland areas in Fig 6.7.1.

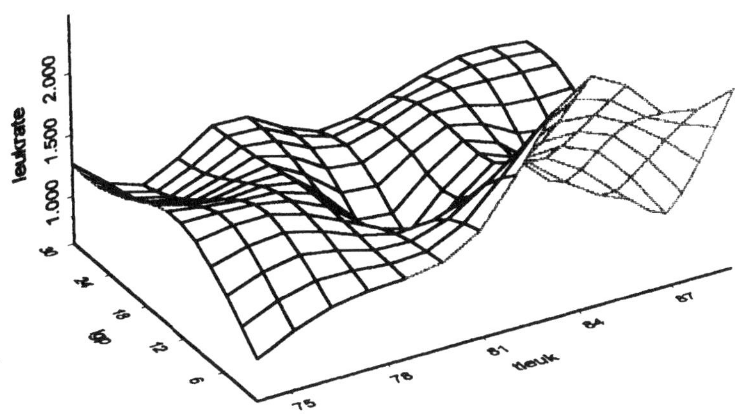

Fig 6.7.1 Changes in relative risk for adult leukaemia by time and distance from coast. Note increase near the coast in period 1981 to 1984 and compare with Sellafield pollution trends shown in Section 2. (*Tluek is the year for which the relative risk of leukaemia (leukrate) is plotted, by distance from the sea lgp (kilometres)*)

The response of the authorities was to deny the data in the case of the child leukaemia and brain tumours and then, because the WCR data had apparently been wiped from the computer when WCR was closed down, to undertake a different analysis based on wards in bands by distance from the sea. In the case of the adult cancers, their response was to ignore the assertion that the adult cancer sea coast effect existed and concentrate on the children. I will return to these responses and to the bad news in Part III, and will now turn to evidence from Ireland. Before I do so; I will just relate an incident in North Wales.

In 1999, after the denials by WCISU that there was an increase in childhood leukaemia in North Wales, I spent some time driving about the north to look for independent evidence. I was reduced to asking priests and looking at ages on gravestones. In fact I eventually found someone who knew about the many cases of children with leukaemia but, before I did so, I was in Llanrwst one day looking for the cemetery to see if there were any children's graves and to talk to the vicar. I fell in with some workmen who were digging up the road. One of them, who turned out to be the head of the construction company told me the following tale:

I took my children last year to Disneyland in Florida. They were always pestering me to go and so at last I gave in. When we checked in at the door and bought the tickets, we were asked where we came from. 'I don't suppose you have heard of it', I said,' but we come from Wales'

'Of course we have heard of it', they replied. They added.' That's the place where there is that awful Sellafield atomic plant where the children catch leukaemia'. Astonished, I asked how they knew this. The answer was grim. 'It's because every year we have these children from the area come here to see Disneyland. The local people have got together to donate money to send these dying children for a last treat.'

And so there they stand, conjured immediately in our minds, sad happy little creatures with their bald little heads and white faces, shining with hope and despair, cosied along by their desperate mothers and fathers, visiting Mickey Mouse and Donald Duck, perhaps for the last time, courtesy of Sellafield and British Nuclear Fuels.

If these results represented evidence of an effect on the coasts of the Irish Sea, then we would also expect to find similar effects on the Irish coast, where there are estuaries and inlets, contaminated mud banks and coastal populations. Although Ireland had no cancer registry until 1994, some data became available for the three years 1994-6, and in addition, in 1999 I devised a cancer questionnaire study which was undertaken in Carlingford in early 2000. The results of these Irish studies confirmed the existence of the sea coast effect, and I will briefly describe the history and the consequences of our researches in Ireland.

7
Ireland

Ich am of Irlonde
Of the holy lande of Irlonde
God Syr I pray Thee
For of Saint Charitie
Come and daunce with me
In Irlonde

7.1 Background

People living in the north east of Ireland have believed that the operation of Sellafield has caused increases in cancer in their locality for a very long time. I was first there in the late 1990s when I was invited to give a contribution to a conference organized by the Association of Irish County Councils in Galway. I heard many people who attended this meeting give vent to their concerns about the health effects of the Sellafield pollution. The problem was that there was no national cancer registry operating over the period of peak output from the plant from 1974-90, and so no one really knew. This is a common condition these days since the data is not available either because it is kept secret, or in this case, because it was never collected. Of course, the Radiological Protection Institute of Ireland (RPII) maintained, whenever the question arose, that the doses were too small. But no one at the conference paid them any heed.

In 1996, at a second public meeting on the subject of Sellafield (called by the Mayor of Drogheda, Fergus O'Dowd), I first met Grattan Healy. He was energy researcher for the Greens on the European Parliament and has since become a great friend and helper in this matter of nuclear risk. Grattan suggested that I ask the Minister, at the conference in front of all those attending, to support the Welsh Cancer data research. Ultimately this led to the contract that enabled us to carry out the work, but an initial follow up to this first meeting with the Minister, Avril Doyle, was not encouraging. Following publication of my report `Nuclear Waste Reprocessing at Sellafield and Cancer near the Irish Sea, arguments for an Independent Collaborative Study' (Busby, 1996b), correspondence between Green Audit and the Irish Minister for Energy, Emmet Stagg, made clear that the Department of Health was advising the government that there was no excess risk near the coast. This was despite the fact that no real study had been done except for one.

Mr Stagg sent us a copy of a report by an expert committee commissioned by the Department of Health way back in 1986. This showed results of a study of incidence and mortality from acute lymphoid leukaemia in the 0-14 age group over the period 1971-83. Although it was presented as evidence that there was no problem, the following extract from the conclusion section of the report suggests otherwise:

More detailed examination of mortality showed a small excess in coastal strips approximately three miles wide on the east and south coasts for the period 1971-86, but not for the period 1977-82. Deaths were evenly distributed along these coastal strips and no particular area of coast had higher rates than another. On the east coast in 1971-76 an average of 2.7 deaths per year occurred whereas 1.5 would have been expected if the rate there had been the same as the rest of the country. On the south coast 0.8 deaths per year occurred whereas 0.5 would have been expected. A strip of approximately 18 miles deep inland of the coastal strip in both areas had fewer deaths than the national average prior to 1977, and when this was combined with the 3 mile strip, death rates from ALL[Acute Lymphoid Leukaemia] in children there were identical to the national average. (p. 8)

Here we see immediately that the effect is similar to that in Wales. Note that the committee are looking at the 0-14 age-group, which reduces the relative risk, to 2.7/1.5 = 1.8 and also that 3 miles is six times wider than the strip than that within which we find our main excess effect in Wales. The committee continued:

When incidence rates were examined for the two time periods 1974-76 and 1977-1983 the east coast showed an excess of new cases of ALL [Acute Lymphoid Leukaemia] for the earlier period but not for the later; the south coast showed no such increase. For the 3-mile deep east coast strip, 5 new cases were seen annually whereas 2.7 would have been expected. (Page 8)

If this represented $5 \times 10 = 50$ cases in the ten-year period with $2.7 \times 10 = 27$ expected, it implies a relative risk of 1.85 with Poisson significance level of $p = 0.00005$. Even if it referred to the period 1974-76 the observed over expected of 15/8.1 gives a Poisson significance value of $p = 0.01$. How this could have been presented as a sign of no problem is hard to see.

The committee concluded:

1. *A national cancer registry should be established to monitor cancer incidence.*
2. *A Board, composed of representatives of appropriate government departments and scientific experts should be established which would have statutory responsibility for the monitoring and control of all environmental hazards.*
3. *An epidemiological research programme enquiring into incidence, trends and causation of cancer should be undertaken.*

It is not clear whether these conclusions have been paid attention to. It would seem not. However, a national cancer registry was established in Cork in 1994 and the first report of this registry, which related to data for 1995 and 1994, was published in September 1998.

By the end of the period we had put aside for the funding; we had been able to persuade the new National Cancer Registry to give us some small area data aggregated to areas that we had made up out of District Electoral Divisions. We were thus able to look at cancer incidence effects for 'all cancers' and 'leukaemia' only by distance from the sea over the three-year period 1994-1996. I will present some of these results in this chapter. But before we received these data we had been able to look at two other sources of information. One was an extremely valuable dataset that had been presented to a small meeting in Carlingford, County Louth in 1997 by a local GP, Dr Andy MacDonald. I visited Andy in Greenore and was able to get a copy of his report together with a breakdown of his practice population.

I wrote to Dr Harry Comber, the Director of the Irish National Cancer Registry, which had just been set up in Cork and had published data from 1994-96 (Refs INCR 95,96). The reports had enabled us to look at the County level for incidence rates. The highest Relative Risk for All Malignancies and All Ages for both sexes separately for the whole of Ireland was in the Eastern Counties closest to Sellafield: County Louth and County Dublin. The incidence rates for many types of cancer in these two counties are among the highest in Europe. These two eastern counties also have the highest population density close to shoal beaches with large areas of drying mud and silt covered flats, tidal inlets or river estuaries. This is a common feature with the Welsh result. Maps were not provided in the reports and so I coded the 'all malignancy' and 'leukaemia' standardised ratios. I show risks for all malignancy in males in Plate 9.

I explained in my letter to Harry Comber that what was needed here was to obtain data for small areas so that we could see if the coastal effect was there. He replied that he was prepared to release it to *Green Audit* but only in a form that involved aggregation of cases to levels defined as respecting confidentiality in a protocol devised and adopted by the Association of UK Cancer registries. This meant that data could only be provided for areas with base or denominator populations in any group being considered more than 1000 persons. This was extremely irritating. We had already been tied up in our ability to analyse small areas in England and Wales by this ludicrous rule (which I shall have more to say about). In my reply, I questioned why Ireland had to be bound by UK regulations that, in any case, were absurd. How could Comber argue that UK rules should be used to cover up effects caused by UK nuclear pollution? I received a shirty and outraged reply to this. Was I suggesting that he was deliberately covering up an effect? I thought that maybe I was. But we eventually found a compromise. If we at Green Audit aggregated the District Electoral Divisions (for which census populations were available) into larger units then they would let us have data for all malignancy and for leukaemia. *Green Audit* obtained ward maps of Ireland from the Ordnance Survey in Dublin in 1999 and Helen Rowe and Evelyn Mannion made up an EXCEL file with an aggregation of wards into new areas called GADEDS or (Green Audit District Electoral Divisions). This enabled the analysis of all cancers in the 0-4 and other and all age groups by proximity to the Irish Sea with control wards from counties on the west coast and inland. These aggregate small areas are slightly larger than the Welsh AORs but would provide, it was believed, a similar result on trend in cancer rate. Our analysis of these results formed part of the STAD court case against Sellafield and this case only fell very recently. Because of this I will present the full results separately in another paper and can only broadly overview what we found. But before I move on to that study I will describe the results of the most interesting study we did on this matter and one that forms a prototype for a new kind of citizen epidemiology. This was the STAD Carlingford cancer questionnaire.

7.2 Cancer in Carlingford and Greenore

The absence of a national cancer registry in Ireland for the period corresponding to the peak output of discharges from Sellafield represented an impediment to the collection of convincing data to support the case, *Short and others vs. BNFL*. This meant that Welsh data was all that could be used as a surrogate for Ireland over this period. However, one very important indicator for the situation on Ireland's eastern coast over the period was the cancer incidence data collected by Dr Andrew MacDonald in Carlingford, Co. Louth.

Carlingford Lough is a wide, shallow sea inlet, noted for its oyster beds and also for its drying mud flats (See Plate 10). The area has attracted radioisotopic pollution from Sellafield since the beginning of the discharges, and measurements of the levels of radioisotopes in the silt in the Lough contain the highest concentrations of Sellafield isotopes in Ireland (RPII). This is probably the result of the peculiar tidal conditions in the area, as I explain in Chapter 3.

The paper *A twenty year survey of a Rural General Practice in Ireland* by Dr Andrew MacDonald of Greenore, Co Louth, tabulated incidence and mortality for cancer in a rural medical practice covering 3000 persons. A copy of this report was been placed by us in the House of Commons library but has recently mysteriously disappeared. An analysis of this data represents a very significant source of supporting evidence that there is an excess of cancer in the Carlingford area. The main cancer findings are shown in Table 7.2.1 below. The importance of the data is that they cover the period of peak output of Sellafield 1970-1980. Although the numbers from the Carlingford practice are small, they are more reliable than cancer registry data, which is subject to bureaucratic inaccuracies, such as recoding errors (and as we will see, some other errors of less ethical provenance). The ten-fold excess of childhood leukaemia at Seascale near

Sellafield was based on very small numbers. In the 34 years between 1950 and 1983, Gardner and colleagues (1990) established that 1068 children were born (about 30-40 per year) to mothers resident in the Seascale parish and 2614 children in the age-group 0-14 between 1950 and 1983 were followed up. This base population yielded five deaths from leukaemia and one non-Hodgkin lymphoma in the 34 years in children aged 0-14, a relative risk of 9.36. In addition there were four deaths from other cancers, a relative risk of 3.76.

Using census data for Carlingford and figures supplied by Dr MacDonald we have estimated the base population of 0-14-year-olds in the practice at 850 children. Thus the 3 cases of leukaemia in the 0-14 age-group in Carlingford is of the same order of significance as the Seascale excess of 5 deaths from leukaemia in the period 1950-1983 analysed by Gardner and colleagues. The Carlingford cases occurred in 1971, 1972, and 1973, the period when alpha releases from Sellafield were at their peak.

These are similar findings to those we obtained in the northern coastal towns of Wales, Bangor, Caernarfon etc where there were similar levels of contamination.

Table 7.2.1 Cancer rates in Carlingford: various sites, 1965-1986 calculated from data supplied by Dr Andy MacDonald, local GP.

Site	Obs. no	Expected number	Relative risk	Poisson p- value
		All malignancy		
1965-85	411	358	1.15**	P<.01 ($\chi2$)
1986-96	148	115	1.3**	P<.005 ($\chi2$)
Colorectal				
1965-86	35	28	1.25	Not significant
		All leukaemia		
1965-75	10	2.36	4.24***	.0002
1965-85	11	4.7	2.33**	.009
		Leukaemia 0-14		
1965-85	3	0.66	4.55*	.03
		Thyroid		
1965-86	2	.87	2.3	Not significant
		Brain		
1965-85	12	3.06	3.9***	.0001
		Gastric		
1965-85	69	14.6	4.7***	.0000
		Skin		
1965-85	*131*	*23.9*	*5.5****	.0000

[a] Base population: England and Wales 1979.
Source: MacDonald, 1997.

7.3 A Cancer Questionnaire

How could we augment Dr MacDonald's data for the period of peak output from Sellafield and see what was happening today? We decided to approach the population of Carlingford and nearby Greenore with a cancer questionnaire: Why not? Why rely on the cancer registry, who, in any case, would only give us data to quite large areas. We knew that any effect would be very local to the contaminated coast (we didn't at that stage realize quite how local!). It seemed to me that it would be possible to find out about levels of cancer by asking people in houses if there had been any cancer diagnosed in the household in the last five or ten years. The key to a subsequent analysis for risk would be to obtain a base population by also asking for the number, sex and ages of each person in the household. This would enable us to calculate the expected numbers in such a population (using appropriate national rates) and compare the reported numbers for each cancer type. I designed a questionnaire that asked for this data and also asked for information on smoking (Andy MacDonald thought that smoking levels were higher in Carlingford). We also asked whether people were involved in activities that meant they would be near the contaminated coast and if they had any general comments. I printed the questionnaire of nice bright yellow paper on the printing press that Sir James Goldsmith had bought for us in 1996 and sent it off to the STAD group for distribution in Carlingford and Greenore.

The purpose of the questionnaire was three-fold.

- First, we wished to examine whether there seemed to be a higher than expected incidence of all cancer, or any particular cancer type or site, or any particular age group in those people living in the area.
- Second, we wished to examine the apparent risk trend of cancer by distance from the sea, that is, in the Carlingford area, where the mud banks are known to be contaminated by discharges from Sellafield.
- Third, we wished to gauge the level of concern about Sellafield in those people living in the area.

It was intended to be filled in for each household on the electoral list for the two areas of Carlingford and Greenore by the head of - or some responsible person in - the household, with the assistance of an interviewer. The questionnaire asked for the sex and age of all persons living at the address. It then asked if any person at that address had been diagnosed with cancer in the previous ten years. Details of this person were then asked for, such as the type of cancer (site), their sex, the age at diagnosis and the year of diagnosis. This data enables the direct calculation of relative risk in the sample population, relative to the national population.

In addition to the fundamental questions above, the questionnaire also asked about the lifestyle of the cancer cases, whether they smoked, whether their habits put them in proximity to the beaches or the sea, whether they ate fish or shellfish regularly and other questions that might throw light on the cause of the cancer. In particular they were asked if they lived near the sea, defined as less that 500m since it was of interest, following the discoveries in Wales and elsewhere, to establish risk by distance from the coast. In the event, an exact positioning of the cases was made possible because the arrangement of distribution of the questionnaires by the STAD team and their helpers ensured that coded with the returned questionnaires was the exact location on the map of the house in which the cancer cases lived.

Respondents were asked if they thought that the Sellafield operation might pose a risk to the people of Ireland and whether they felt it had caused ill health to the people of Ireland. Finally, they were asked to make any comments they wished and also if they were prepared to help with further interviews if necessary.

The questionnaire itself is reproduced below. It formed the basis also of the later questionnaires we carried out in Burnham-on-Sea in Somerset near the Hinkley point nuclear suite, in Plymouth near the naval nuclear sub dockyard and, recently, in Llan Ffestiniog near Trawsfynydd for the Welsh HTV company (where we found a 6-fold excess of breast cancer in the down-winders). I have presented the method now at various conferences, including one on citizen epidemiology in Chicago in 2005. The questionnaire may be used by any group wishing to discover effects near a putative source of risk.

The questionnaire was introduced by STAD:

STAD comprises the support group for four citizens of County Louth who are proceeding with a Court action against British Nuclear Fuels who operate the Sellafield reprocessing plant. This plant, which is situated in Cumbria about 60 miles from County Louth, has discharged radioactive waste to the Irish sea since 1952 and the radioactivity has been measured in samples of fish, shellfish, mud, seawater and air on the East Coast of Ireland.

There is concern that the exposure of people living on the East Coast of Ireland to Sellafield radioactivity may be having a harmful effect on health. Radiation exposure causes cancer and for this reason STAD is working with the independent environmental group Green Audit, based in Wales, to examine the possibility that there may be increased risk of developing cancer in areas of Ireland close to the coast.

As part of this survey, Green Audit has devised a short questionnaire, which follows. We would be very grateful if you could find time to answer the questions. Your answers will be held in complete confidence and no one will be identified. The results will be based on an aggregation of the data. If you feel you are able answer some further questions then we have asked you to indicate this. When you have finished the questionnaire, please return it to the interviewer who will collect it or post it to STAD, Backhouse Centre, Clanbrassil St, Dundalk.

The STAD action is intended to stop the further releases of radioactive discharges to the Irish Sea, and this information, which we are interested in, is being sought partly in relation to this case. We are also, however, concerned to find out if there is indeed a basis for the considerable anecdotal evidence of high levels of cancer in the area. Here is the questionnaire:

Questionnaire Identification Number...........................

Questionnaire

1. About the people living at your address.

(we need to know this in order to calculate rates in adults and in children).

1. How many people over the age of 18 live at your address?

………………………………………………………………………………

2. What are the approximate ages of each of the men over 18 living at your address?

……………………………………………………………………………..
(example: 24,48,67)
3. What are the approximate ages of each of the women over 18 living at your address?

……………………………………………………………………………..
(example: 23,49)
4 What are the sexes and ages of all the children under 18 living at your address?

………………………………………………………………………………
(Example: if there is a boy aged 4, and two girls aged 14 and 16 write 'M4, F14, F16'. If there are none then write 'none')

2. About cancer

1. Has anyone including yourself in your household been diagnosed as having cancer, leukaemia or lymphoma in the **last ten years?** Yes/No

2. If you answer is Yes then for each person please write down the following:
(1) Was the person Male or Female?
………………………………………………………………………
(2) Which year was the cancer or leukaemia diagnosed?
………………………………………………………………………
(3) How old were they when the cancer, leukaemia or lymphoma was diagnosed?
……………………………………………………………………….
(4) What kind of cancer or leukaemia or lymphoma was diagnosed?
…………………………………………………………………………
(5) How long had this person lived in the Carlingford area?
…………………………………………………………………………
(6) Where did they live before living in the Carlingford area?
…………………………………………………………………………

(7) Did/does the person receive treatment or surgery?

……………………………………………………………………………

(8) What is the name of the person's GP or doctor?

……………………………………………………………………………

(9) Does/did the person smoke more than 10 cigarettes a day before the cancer was diagnosed?

……………………………………………………………………………

(10) Is the person still alive?

……………………………………………………………………………

3. About lifestyle and location

1. Is your house close to the sea i.e. within 500yards or an easy walk? By the sea we also mean Carlingford Lough.

……………………………………………………………………………

2. For all the people diagnosed with cancer in the first section above please tell us:

(1) Do they eat fish regularly i.e. more than once a week?

……………………………………………………………………………

……………………………………………………………………………

(2) Do they eat shellfish more than once a month?

……………………………………………………………………………

……………………………………………………………………………

(3) Do they have any hobby that regularly places them close to the sea e.g. sea fishing, bait digging, coastal walking, yachting?

……………………………………………………………………………

……………………………………………………………………………

(4) Does their job, if they have one, place them mostly outdoors or mostly indoors?

……………………………………………………………………………

……………………………………………………………………………

(5) If their job is mostly outdoors does it place them regularly close to the sea or seashore?

……………………………………………………………………………

……………………………………………………………………………

3. About what you think about Sellafield

(1) Do you think the existence of the Sellafield plant poses any risk to the people of Ireland? Yes/No/Don't know

……………………………………………………………………………………………
…………

(2) Do you think that discharges from Sellafield may have caused ill health to people in Ireland? Yes/No/Don't know

……………………………………………………………………………………………
…………

4. About further help

Would you be prepared to help us further by answering some more questions about what you have told us? Yes/No

……………………………………………………………………………………………
…………

5. Is there anything else you feel we might be interested in knowing?

……………………………………………………………………………………………
…………

Thank you for your time: your answers might prove very valuable. Now please return the questionnaire to STAD. We will contact you with the results of this survey when they have been analysed.

The project was set up assuming a 50% response rate. This gave a population-at-risk of approximately 1000 persons. The survey assumed that such a population would have roughly the same age structure as that of all Ireland and, on this basis, using the mortality rate of about 400 per 100,000 population we should expect about 4 cases per year, or 40 cases in 10 years. The exact number of cases expected was calculated from the actual numbers and age distribution of the questionnaire respondents (see below). The age breakdown of the respondents is given in Table 7.3.1, which also gives the respondents in different age groups as percentages of the census population in those groups.

Table 7.3.1 Numbers and age breakdown of questionnaire respondents with totals expressed as percentage of the 1996 Census population of the two electoral divisions

Age group	Male respondents	Female respondents	Persons respondent as percentage of Census population (%)
0-14	119	145	54.5
15-24	136	126	72.4
25-44	165	174	62.7
45-64	146	149	69.9
65+	69	75	46.1
All	635	669	46.1

Population leakage

The questionnaire asked for details of cancer incidence in the 'last ten years'. In the event, respondents gave cancer details back as far as the late 1970s. However, it is clear that the inclusion of cancer cases diagnosed in the area for earlier periods runs the risk of missing cancer cases or deaths for the same early year which were not reported because the house where they lived was sold and new people live there who are not aware of the cancer case and therefore did not report it. This is a problem with such a retrospective study. The loss of cases from earlier years is termed 'population leakage' and may be examined by looking at the trend in Relative Risk by different period of time prior to the survey. Information may also be obtained by examining Relative Risk by age group, since older people are more likely to leak out of the study population because they are more likely to die of cancer and their houses sold.

Distribution of the questionnaire

The distribution and collection of the questionnaire was organised by STAD workers over two weekends in May 2000. Fourteen survey teams each consisting of a STAD member and also a local guide (a person who lived in or knew intimately the layout of the section, and who would reassure the householder) were assigned sections of the survey area of Greenore and Carlingford. They were supplied with a large-scale map of the section and of the area and also with the appropriate part of the electoral register. The teams then visited all the houses in their section and gave the questionnaire to a responsible person in each house with instructions and an explanation of the project. If necessary, the survey person ensured that the respondent filled in the questionnaire.

Before the questionnaire was given, the respondents were assured that the information they gave would be kept strictly confidential. This was arranged in the following way: Each household was allocated a number and two letters. The letters identified the STAD local guide: the number identified the house. These codes were recoded by Green Audit into the database that was used to analyse the data. The STAD guide also located the house on the large-scale map of the area. The total number of questionnaires filled in and returned was 415, of which 282 were from Carlingford and 133 from Greenore. Only three people refused to fill in the questionnaire. It was intended that all the houses in the area would be canvassed but restriction on time meant that if people were not at home they were not followed up.

Methodology

The sample of the population of the study area who responded was assumed to be the population at risk. The total numbers of cancer cases expected in one year was calculated by multiplying the population at risk in each sex and 5-year age group by the 1994-1996 average national rate for the cancer type or site calculated from the Irish National Cancer Registry data. The total numbers expected over 5-year, 10-year and 15-year periods was then obtained by simply multiplying the annual expectation by the appropriate number. This was then compared with the observed number of cases over the same period. This process was employed for various age groups to examine the possibility that younger people were at greater risk or to look for any trend that might suggest population leakage (see above).

To examine the effect of proximity to the sea, the sample population was divided into three groups. These were allocated on the basis of the mapped position of the house and placed the house and its inhabitants in Group 1, 2 and 3 according to their location inside 100m, between 100 and 1000 metres and above 1000 metres from the Mean High Water Spring Tide line.

Results

Overall the levels of cancer indicated by the questionnaires were about what would be expected, allowing for population leakage over the ten year period. There were two important results. The first was the clustering of the cancers close to the shoreline. This can be clearly seen in Plate 2 and it is not a consequence of there being more people living close to the shoreline because we were able to allow for this statistically. The inset in Plate 2 shows the relative risk of cancer in the three proximity groups and Table 7.3.3 gives the trend statistics and also compares group 1, close to the sea, with the two inland groups combined. The second interesting result was the clustering of cases in the 40-44 age group. These were those individuals who were born around the time of the Windscale fire. They are collected together in Table 7.3.2. What these results suggest is that a further study of this cohort using a larger number of individuals from the north east of Ireland might be valuable.

Finally, there was no correlation with smoking. The number of smokers in the cancer cases was slightly lower than the number expected on the basis of Irish national statistics.

Table 7.3.2 Cancers in the 5-year Windscale fire cohort born 1956-1960

Cancer site	**Cases in 10 years (RR)**	**Cases in 15 years (RR)**
Colon	8 (RR = 1.90; p =0.6)	9 (RR = 1.43; p =0.18)
Lymphomas	4 (RR = 2.35; p = 0.09)	4
Liver	4	4
Kidney	3	3
Lung	2	4

Table 7.3.2 Trend statistics for cancer risk by distance from the contaminated mud flats. Contingency tables for coastal groups tested against both non-coastal groups combined with and without skin cancers. Carlingford and Greenore combined 1990-1999.

Exposure score	**Odds Ratio relative to baseline**	**Cases**	**Controls**
1 (<100m)	1.0	24	486
2 (101-1000m)	0.62	13	423
3 (1000+m)	0.17	3	368

Chi-square for linear trend in proportions = 11.03
p value = 0.0009

Excl. NMS 10-yr	**Cancer**	**Control**	**Total**
Coastal group 1	24	486	510
Non-coastal 2+3	16	806	822
	40	1292	1332

Relative Risk = 2.42 ; 95% confidence limits 1.30<RR<4.51
Chi-square (Uncorrected) = 8.23
p-value = 0.004

Did the people with cancer smoke cigarettes more than the national average?
The results of this question indicated that there were 15 smokers in the total number of people with cancer, some 27%. 73% of the cancer cases were reported to be non-smokers. Data from the Irish National Cancer Registry gives the

proportion of smokers among cancer patients as 25% and non-smokers at 33.6%. In this national survey the smoking status of 30% was not established. On this basis we feel that the population studied were not heavier smokers than the national average and were likely to be less heavy smokers.,

7.4 Irish National Cancer Registry small area study 1994-6

I mentioned earlier that over the course of the period of the Welsh study I had been trying to obtain small area data on cancer from the new Irish National Cancer Registry. I eventually succeeded but, owing to the usual tedious arguments about confidentiality, was only able to obtain data for aggregations of wards that we made up, blocks of wards, which we named GADEDS or Green Audit District Electoral Divisions (which were slightly smaller than the AORs used in the Welsh study).

By inspection of the DED map of Ireland, supplied by the Ordnance Survey, 23 counties were divided into 270 GADEDS. Table 7.4.1 shows the DED composition of two examples, the GADEDs labelled A1 and A2 in County Carlow. These groups and their DED composition were supplied to the Irish National Cancer Registry (NCRI) in Cork in 1998, who agreed to process their post-coded data so as to supply the numbers of cases registered in the period 1994-1996 in these GADEDs. The work was apparently carried out by a separate organisation but was checked by NCRI. The final files were given to Green Audit in June 2000. Table 7.4.2 shows the numbers of cancer cases used in the study to determine risk by distance from the sea.

Table7.4.1 DED composition of GADEDS A1 and A2 in County Carlow

County	GADED	Constituent DEDs	DED Number
Carlow	A1	Ballintemple	1013
Carlow	A1	Ballon	1014
Carlow	A1	Clonegall	1021
Carlow	A1	Cranemore	1023
Carlow	A1	Kilbride	1029
Carlow	A1	Myshall	1035
Carlow	A1	Rathrush	1040
Carlow	A1	Shangarry	1042
Carlow	A2	Clonmore	1003
Carlow	A2	Hacketstown	1005
Carlow	A2	Haroldstown	1005
Carlow	A2	Kineagh	1006
Carlow	A2	Rahill	1007
Carlow	A2	Rathvilly	1008
Carlow	A2	Tankardstown	1044
Carlow	A2	Ticknock	1009
Carlow	A2	Tullow Rural	1047
Carlow	A2	Tullow Urban	1048
Carlow	A2	Tullowbeg	1046
Carlow	A2	Williamstown	1010

Table 7.4.2 Registrations of all cancers excluding NMS in whole study area by sex and age.

Age	Females	Males	Persons
0-14	127	149	276
15-24	335	186	521
25-34	1243	274	1517
35-44	1681	505	2186
45-54	2310	1216	3526
55-64	2607	2754	5361
65-74	3626	4973	8599
75-84	3026	3554	6580
85+	855	738	1593
All	15810	14349	30159

The study examined cancer incidence in these 270 small areas in 23 counties of the Republic of Ireland for the years 1994-1996 inclusive. Data was made available by the National Cancer Registry Ireland by sex and ten-year age groups for all malignancies, brain tumours and all leukaemia. In addition, data was made available for children aged 0-4.

Using the area distribution of risk in the total cancer numbers given in Table 7.4.2, we sought to examine the hypothesis that living on the East Coast, near the Irish Sea, involved significant excess risk of cancer, due to internal exposure to man-made radioactivity from sea-to-land transfer of radioisotopes from Sellafield in Cumbria, UK. To this end, the total area was divided into three groups made up of small areas whose area centroids were at different distances from the East, South and West coasts of Ireland. By calculating Age Standardised Relative Risks for men and women of different ages in these areas it was possible to determine the trend in cancer risk for the three cancer data groups by distance from the sea coast. This was the main method we used in the Welsh 1974-89 study I presented in Chapters 5 and 6.

The results clearly demonstrated a significant cancer risk sea coast effect on the East Coast, but not on the West or South coasts for women of all ages combined. The effect was highly significant. For bands of increasing distance from the East Coast centred at 2.4, 3.2, 6.4, 8.1, 13.1, 31, 51, 71 92, 128km the relative risks for women of all ages were 1.4, 1.27, 0.86, 0.86, 0.9, 1.0, 1.03, 1.15 and 0.97. Chi-square for trend was 10.7; p = 0.001. Testing the coastal <5km group against the >5 km group gave Chi-square = 44.3; p = 0.00000. A curious excess risk existed on the eastern sea coast in younger women in the age groups 25-34 and 35-44. The trend with distance in the 25-34 group for the same distance bands as those listed above gave 1.66, 1.53, 0.53, 0.49, 0.73, 0.9, 1.02, 0.72, 1.14, 0.56. Chi-square for trend was 11.13; p = 0.0009. Test of coastal <5km against non-coastal in this age group gave RR = 1.62; p = 0.000025. This trend with distance is similar in shape to that which we previously found in Welsh incidence data for 1974-89, the cancer mortality data for Somerset from 1994-99 and the mapped questionnaire data from Carlingford and Greenore, Co. Louth.

The most interesting aspect of this was that for the South and West coast groups there was no discernible trend with distance from the sea in either women or men of any age group, suggesting that the cancer excess was due to an environmental agent present on the east coast. The effect was clearest in the comparison of County Louth with a control county using County Galway. Fig 7.4.1 shows the effect for all malignancies in women of all ages by comparing the trend along transects running from the east coast-west, the south coast-north and the west coast-east.

For some unknown reason, for men of all ages combined, the effect was absent on all three coasts although it is there for the age group 25-34 and 35-44 on the East Coast. This age group represents the cohort most affected by the releases from the Windscale fire in 1957, and these groups were identified as a high-risk group in the Carlingford and Greenore survey results also.

For children aged 0-4 and 0-14, there was no significant sea coast effect, nor is there any effect for brain tumours and leukaemia. However, we really didn't have statistical power for evaluating effects in this age group. The numbers needed to show an effect however over three years 1994-6 were very small and so perhaps the study could not really inform us about risk in the children either way.

We concluded that the results for all malignancies support the hypothesis that living near the East coast of Ireland carries excess risk of cancer for women of all ages and men of the age group 25-44, and that this excess risk was driven by some factor that is specific to the narrow coastal strip bordering the Irish Sea. The finding supports our hypothesis that exposure to radiation from Sellafield may be responsible. The full study was, until recently, still part of the STAD case and so I could not describe the results in full until recently. The case itself was bogged down in endless legal procedures and eventually, in this last Summer, was thrown out by the same Irish High Court that let it in. They decided that after all, they could not try an accused who was not part of the country where the effect was occurring. This is a dangerous precedent as pollution does not need a passport as we found out after the Chernobyl accident. But with my political hat on, I expect there were various horses traded for this as the British government wants to build new nuclear power stations and the Irish case is a thorn in their flesh. I hope that the evidence I show in this book, which was to be part of this case, may move the British government to closing the Sellafield pipeline independent of any legal action being brought.

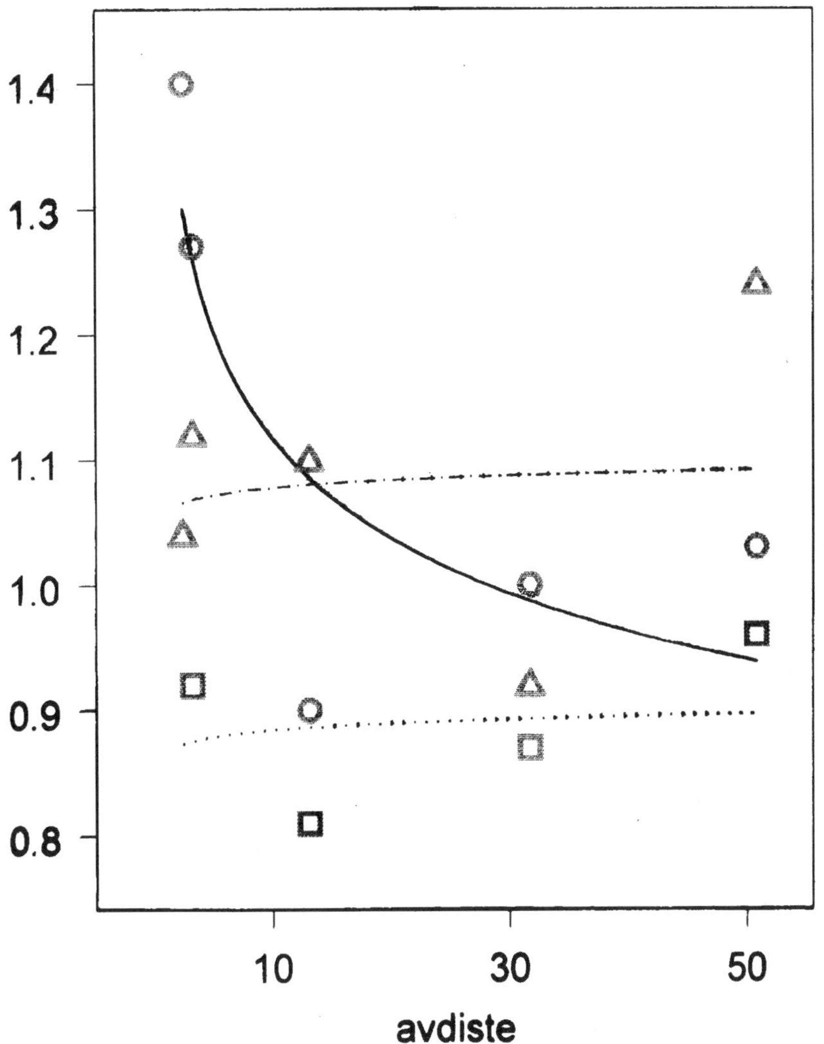

Fig 7.4.1 All malignancy cancer incidence risk on Irish small areas (GADEDS) for women all ages by distance from the sea on three transects east coast inland moving west (circles, full line), south coast inland moving north (triangles, dotdash) and west coast moving east (squares, dotted line). Data from Irish National Cancer Registry (Busby and Rowe, 2000)

7.5 Lancashire and Galloway

The other coastal areas that could be studied, if the data were made available, are the coasts of Cumbria, Lancashire and South West Scotland, the Solway Firth. I believe that to study the coast of Cumbria would be a waste of time. Why? Because if there is a cover-up in Wales (which we can be certain of, as you will discover in part III), then there is no way that the accurate data for cancer on the Sellafield coast will ever emerge. The relevant cancer registry is the Northern Cancer Registry based in Newcastle. I am told that nuclear workers with cancer get sent to Newcastle and registered there. Whatever the truth, I haven't been able to obtain data from this cancer registry. The Yorkshire TV childhood leukaemia programme speaks for the effect in children, and Janine Allis Smith, who indefatigably runs the local anti-nuclear group tells me that everyone there speaks of the high cancer rates in adults. For the nuclear workers themselves, there have been official studies (e.g. by NRPB) but the results have been presented as showing there is no effect when there clearly is one. Saoirse Morgan and I recently used the UKAEA obituaries, published in the house magazine *UKAEA Today* (and sent to me by my friend and colleague Wendy Gilford) to show that the Sellafield workers live roughly five years less than the other nuclear workers, a study which I will publish shortly.

As far as Galloway and the Solway Firth is concerned, I have managed to obtain small area data from the Scottish Assembly and I have a student looking at it but it is one of those studies that is on the shelf; there is so much to do and so little time!! But there is some evidence of a sea coast effect in leukaemia from Lancashire. The coast of Lancashire has many of the characteristics of North Wales and eastern Ireland. It is also subject to pollution from Sellafield. A study of leukaemia in all age-groups was reported as *Geographical Distribution of Leukaemia in NW England,* published by the Geography Department of Lancaster University in 1987. (Burch *et al.*, 1987)

The study looked at leukaemia incidence at all ages from 1982 to 1986 in wards in Lancaster in relation to proximity to the sea coast. Numbers of cases were about 600, enabling sufficient statistical power in the study to indicate if a coastal proximity effect existed. This coast is essentially a large drying bay, Morecambe Bay, and includes river estuaries of the Lune, Wyre and Ribble rivers. The tidal situation here is very similar to that in Dundalk Bay, although the tides run more strongly. The main finding was an excess of leukaemia in those wards close to the coast. At the Health District level, Relative Risk was as high as 2.5 for acute lymphoid leukaemia and 2 for chronic granulocytic leukaemia for those two health districts close to the coast compared with 1.5 for acute lymphoid leukaemia in the seventeen health districts remote from the coast, although three of the remote health districts had higher relative risks for chronic granulocytic leukaemia. Ward-level Poisson analysis shows that the highest risks are associated with the north-western part of the coast in the path of the prevailing wind. Statistically significant

Relative Risks as high as 4 are found in some coastal wards. In a ward-level overall analysis a chi-squared statistic was used to establish that there is a coastal ward excess (defined as wards with population centroid under 5km from the sea) of leukaemia that is significant at the 0.05 level. Table 7.5.1 shows the main result which is that the sea coast effect on leukaemia exists in Lancashire with a Relative Risk for wards of 2.3 (p = 0.01).

Table 7.5.1 Contingency table and statistics of risk for leukaemia in Lancashire. The number of wards where there is a significant excess risk 1982-86 was tested for coastal versus non coastal locations. (Burch *et al*,1987)

	Wards with excess leukaemia	**Wards without excess leukaemia**	**totals**
Coastal wards	14	112	126
Non coastal wards	19	376	395
Total	33	488	521

RR = 2.3 (95% CI 1.19<RR<4.47) ; p = 0.01; Chi squared = 6.4; my calculation

Leukaemia in Galloway

Dumfries and Galloway is an area that borders the Solway Firth and where the population mainly lives in the coastal plain. This is south facing, towards Sellafield, from which it is about 40km distant. There has been concern about childhood cancer and leukaemia in Galloway since the early 1980s. High levels of radioactive pollution have been measured (Baxter, 1989, AERE, 1991) especially in the tidal estuaries of the rivers Dee (Castlye Douglas, Kirkudbright) Fleet (Gatehouse of Fleet) and Cree (Wigtown). In 1993 the Galloway and Dumfries Health Board examined the rates of leukaemia in adults and children over the period 1975-90. The method used utilised post coded areas rather than wards and did not examine smaller areas close to the coast. However, local concerns forced the board to examine child leukaemia in the Castle Douglas and Kircudbright areas close to the estuary and the sea. In a letter I have, dated 25th March 1987, the Scottish Cancer Registry wrote to the Health Board and tabulated leukaemia in the 0-24 age group in the DG3.3 Castle Douglas area. (Note the dilution involved in using 0-24 instead of 0-4). Between 1968-84 there were 4 cases where 0.68 would be expected (RR = 6; p = 0.006). The letter attempted to reassure the Health Board over the 6-fold excess. It said:

As was said by Dr Heasman at the Dounreay enquiry, these cases represent the highest incidence relative to expectation in any postcode sector in Scotland. These figures should not be interpreted as a cause for alarm because the figures for the Castle Douglas and Dounreay areas are not comparable. An inevitable character of random distributions (such as those of leukaemia cases in postcode sectors) will occur by chance in some areas rather than others. The Dounreay investigation, on the other hand, centred on a hypothesis about a single geographical area in which a source of potential influence on leukaemia risk was known to exist. The observed figure for Dounreay could therefore legitimately be compared with that expected by chance.

The author of this letter was Mr David Adams Jones, who reappeared in the Wales Cancer Intelligence Unit as the man who was responsible for moving the Wales Cancer Registry data from the Welsh Office system to the WCISU computer. He was also the WCISU envoy who came to see us in Wales about the high levels of leukaemia in North Wales, and who then co-authored the airbrush study presented to COMARE which I will review in Part II.

Of course, the point about the prior hypothesis at Dounreay was absurd. Levels of sediment contamination from Sellafield in Galloway were far higher than anything there was near Dounreay. Sellafield had been spewing out huge amounts of radioactivity for forty years when the letter was written, dwarfing anything released from Dounreay. And the population of south West Scotland were right in the prevailing wind.

The 1993 Galloway Health Board report succeeded in glossing over the high levels of adult and childhood cancer in the area. They did this by running their significance tests on too small an area to obtain any result. Only three of the 165 postcode areas had significant excess risk but, for the total area studies, there were 137 cases of leukaemia in adults between 1975 and 1990, where only 88 were predicted, a Relative Risk of 1.54 ($\chi^2 = 27$; $p < 0.005$) a value roughly equal to the value we found for North Wales, and probably due to the same reason. Levels of risk in the children were not quite statistically significant owing to the small population.

8
Studies Near Coasts and Estuaries

Roll on, thou deep and dark blue Ocean-Roll
Ten thousand fleets sweep o'er thee in vain
Man marks the world with ruin- his control
Stops with the shore

Byron, Childe Harolde

8.1 Mortality studies

Byron would not have written those lines if he knew what we know now. Man's control no longer stops with the shore and his ruin has certainly extended to the Ocean. But to prove this by extending these studies to other parts of the British Isles was not an option at the time we were first examining the Irish data. This is because to examine environmental effects on health we must have data at the small area level. The Wales Cancer Registry data was leaked to us. This was a disaster for the authorities and they moved swiftly to limit by closing the registry and denying the figures. But the cat was out of the bag. These figures enabled us to discover the coastal effect on cancer, and this discovery was then backed up by the Irish National Cancer Registry study and also the Carlingford questionnaires. This is as far as we could go. Luckily in late 1999 the UK Office for National Statistics began to sell ward level mortality data for the main causes of death annually from 1995 onwards. These are the VS4D Tables of 'deaths by cause in census wards'. They contain the numbers of men and women of all ages who die in any year from one of a number of causes which include all cancers, lung cancer, breast, stomach and prostate cancer. So by 1999 there were the four years 1995, 96, 97 and 98. Every year after that we were able to buy the same data for 1999, 2000 and 2001, but there the process ended. In September 2002, as I was writing this book and also updating the studies I report here, ONS slammed the gate with a resounding crash: no more data would be given to Green Audit or to anyone else. The reason given was 'confidentiality'. The secrecy of the cancer registries had infected the vital statistics department and our little game was up. The official that wrote to me about this refusal was appropriately named 'Alison *Holding*'. Of course, I complained. In 2005 I began to use the new 'Freedom on Information Act' to attack the confidentiality arguments of the cancer registries and ONS. And interestingly it has paid off. In the last few months and towards the end of writing this book I was informed that the VS4Ds ward tables would now again be released. Maybe they have had time to adjust the deaths? No. That is surely going too far with paranoia. Isn't it?

However, by this time we still had seven consecutive years of data and had been able to look at several pollution sources in England and Wales. We were able to show that the effects we found in the earlier studies, the sea coast effect on cancer, existed around Hinkley Point, the Severn estuary (Oldbury and Berkeley nuclear power stations and Amersham radioisotope factory in Cardiff) and Bradwell nuclear power station in Essex. In this chapter I want to present some of these results. Later in the book I will examine the developments and the desperate responses to all these studies by the health authorities and the radiation risk committees and agencies.

8.2 Cancer near Hinkley Point in Somerset

In November 1999 I was telephoned up by a man who lived near the north Somerset coast. He told me that his dog had just died of cancer, and whilst talking with a neighbour he had been told that a friend of hers who had been diagnosed with breast cancer lived in the small coastal town of Burnham-on -Sea, which is just across the bay and downwind from Hinkley Point nuclear power station. This friend had remarked that many of the other women attending the hospital were also from Burnham on Sea. She wondered if there was a connection with the plant.

I was the first person to buy the ward level mortality data from ONS. I saw this new possibility as having similar status to having hooked a very large salmon whilst fishing for trout (which is something that happened to me long ago in Northern Ireland when I was 16). I thought that someone would realise what they were doing before they sent me the data and, so tenderly, asked for a pre-production copy. I could not imagine that there would not be a block put on these data when it was realized what could be done with them. Indeed, the CD that I have which contains the data was printed specially for me and has a handwritten label. At about the same time that I was negotiating for the mortality data, Jim Duffy, a Green Party friend who lived in Bridgwater and was associated with the local anti-nuclear group 'Stop Hinkley', was wondering if the work that we did on inter-tidal sediment in Wales might suggest that the very large amounts of inter-tidal sediment (or mud) at the mouth of the River Parratt might be having some effect on cancer near the plant. You can see this from the satellite photo in Plate 11.

Long before, in May 1996, we had once attempted to examine cancer risk in small areas around Hinkley Point and we had approached Dr Pheby of the Bristol Cancer Registry for data. The letter was referred to Dr Jennifer Smith, the director of a new Cancer Intelligence Unit based in Winchester. Dr Smith refused to release the small area data on the now standard excuse that it was confidential. This was one of a series of refusals to release data for small areas near nuclear sites and, not surprising in view of her earlier refusal to let us have data for the island of Alderney, near the Cap de la Hague site which I had visited and studied at the request of a local Alderney man Dr David Davies. But we knew that in 1988 Somerset Health Authority had conducted a study of leukaemia in parishes inside a radius of 15km from Hinkley Point, using data provided by the local large hospital, Musgrove Park (Bowie and Ewings, 1989). The study looked at data from 1959-1986 and concluded that following the commissioning and operation of the Hinkley 'A' station in 1964 there was a significant increase in the rates of leukaemia and non-Hodgkin lymphoma among under 25 year-olds living inside a 12.5km radius of Hinkley Point. A statistically significant Relative Risk of 2 to 2.5 times the national average was driven by cases in the 5-year period following the operation of the plant. This seemed to support the conclusion that, like Sellafield and Dounreay, it was the latter that was somehow causing it. Thus there was some prior evidence to suggest that the operation of Hinkley Point may have caused increases in leukaemia in its vicinity. If there was an excess of leukaemia, could there, asked Jim Duffy, also be excess of other cancer?

I said that if they paid us some money (about £600) we would take a look, using the new mortality data. We needed some money to pay for the census population data, which we had to buy from ONS, and also to pay for some work putting the data into the EXCEL files used to do the calculations. This was the first of the mortality studies and it showed us that cancer was indeed associated with living near the coastal mud. It also showed us that there was a significant increased risk, if you lived near a tidal river, for breast cancer, all cancer and interestingly and very clearly, lung cancer. I was helped in this study by Paul Dorfman, who was doing a PhD on aspects of the sociology of radiation risk at the University of the West of England and Helen Rowe, who did most of the mapping. The first cancer we looked at was breast cancer and we published the report in April 2000.

8.3 Results of the Hinkley Point studies

The method used for all these mortality studies was the same. I have described the method in Chapter 5. The basic calculation derives Social Class and age adjusted Standardised mortality ratios (SMRs) for each of the cancers being studied in each of the wards in a selected area around the putative source of risk. The area studied extended from Porlock and Exmoor in the West along the coast to Berrow, just south of Weston-super-Mare, and extended to Blackdown in the southeast and Wells in the north-east. We chose to exclude the large town of Weston-super-Mare and its immediate environs since its large population would have swamped any of the distance effects we were examining.

There were two questions we wanted the answers to. The first was whether there was a greater risk of dying from cancer near the coastal mud flats than inland; was there a sea coast effect centred on the contaminated mud or was there a general sea coast effect? The second was whether there was an increased risk of breast cancer or any cancer in Burnham-on-Sea, as the anecdotal evidence suggested. The results showed clearly that there was an increased risk of cancer mortality in those living near the mud flats with a similar fall-off of risk by distance.

For our main distance analysis we took as our point source the centroid of the offshore mud banks formed by coastal and tidal conditions at the mouth of the River Parrett. It is these mud banks that we believe to be the main source of radiation exposure, through sea-to-land transfer of radioactive particles, however, we also analysed the data using a point source 1.5km east of the Hinkey Point outfall pipe (ST240460), a location used by MAFF for taking samples of mud for analysis. For each point used as centre we constructed concentric rings at 5km radii up to 25km. Wards which were cut by these rings we partitioned according to the fractions of their area which appeared to be in each 5-km annulus. For example; if 30 percent of the area of a ward is in the 0-5km ring and the remaining 70 percent is in the 5-10km annulus we add 30 percent of the observed and expected numbers for this ward to the aggregate expected and observed numbers in the 5-km ring and the remaining 70 percent to the aggregate numbers in the 5-10 annulus. This assumed a uniform density of population.

For breast cancer we found that there was a sea coast effect which fell off with increasing distance from the centre of the mud bank. For populations living inside concentric rings, which were drawn 5,10,15,20 and 25 km from the centre, the SMRs were 1.43, 1.33, 1.24, 1.16 and 1.13, whilst the overall SMR for the 103 wards was 1.09. The most significant high-risk ward for breast cancer was Burnham-on-Sea North, closest to the mud bank and downwind of the station. Here, in this initial study covering 1995-1998 the relative risk was about twice the expected (8.7 expected, 17 observed, RR = 1.95, p = 0.02). This result was sent to the local media who reported it and started a sequence of denials and arguments involving Stop Hinkley, the Health Authority, the power station operators and ultimately the South West Cancer Intelligence Agency. What happened will be told in Part III, but we were to continue to check the breast cancer in Burnham and the cluster remained in later years. By 2003 we had three more years of deaths up to 2001 giving a total of 30 deaths for the seven years where 15 were expected (RR = 2.0; p = 0.001).

In addition to the breast cancer we also examined prostate cancer, lung cancer and all cancers combined, and we followed up the Breast cancer report (Busby *et al* 2000a) in May 2000 with separate results for prostate and for all malignancies and lung cancer (Busby *et al* 2000n, Busby *et al* 2000c). The coastal effects existed also for these cancers and the results are shown in Fig 8.3.1 below.

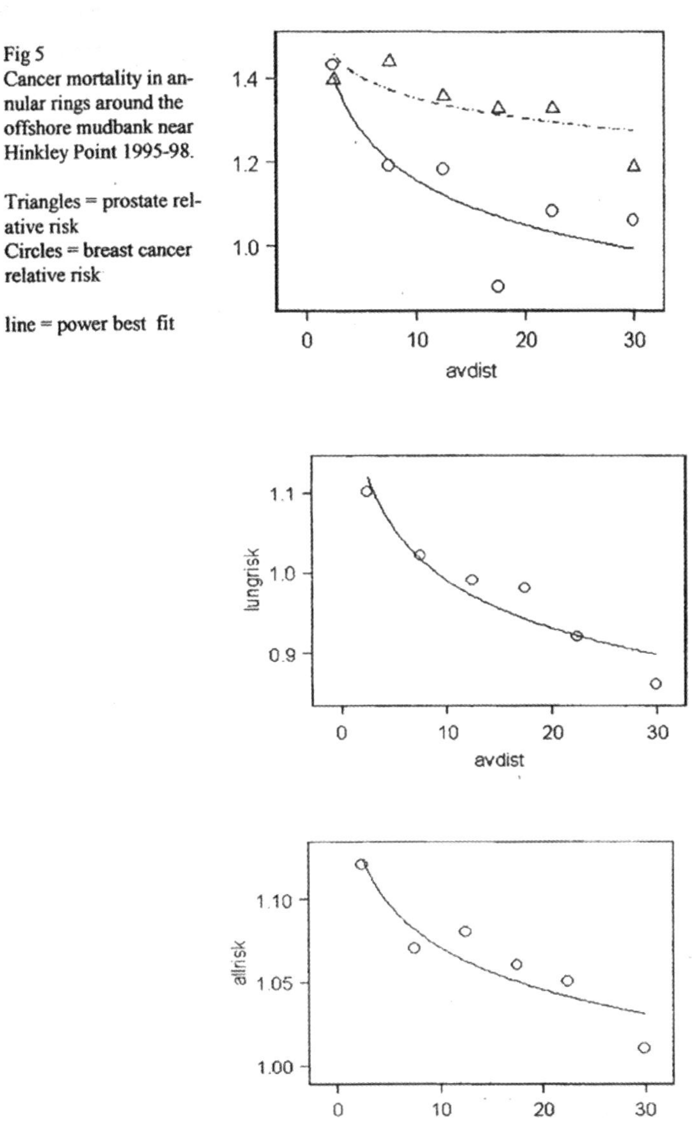

Fig 8.3.1 Risk of cancer mortality by distance from Hinkley Point; exponential fit to data.

As with the breast cancer, prostate cancer mortality showed a significant trend with distance, falling from 1.4 in the 5km ring around the centre of the offshore mud banks to 1.02 in the 25-30km ring (Chi square for trend 3.47, p = .05). Again, the down winders at Burnham-on-Sea suffered a significantly raised cancer mortality risk: for prostate cancer mortality in the two wards, Burnham North and Burnham South combined, the Relative Risk was 1.5 with p = 0.05 (14 expected, 21 observed)

The data also showed another interesting result. This was the clustering of the cancer near the River Parratt, which is tidal for almost 50 miles inland. This can be easily seen from the risk maps where almost all the cancer is in the flood plain of the river basin. A statistical test of cancer in areas below 200ft compared with areas above 200ft showed a significant 60% excess in the mortality in the low lying areas. The effect is most clear for lung cancer in women. The risk maps are given in Plates 1 and 11.

If we find that the contaminated mud appears to be a source of risk then we need evidence that the mud contains the radioactivity. This is there in the annual MAFF reports which also show that the gamma dose rates over the mud since the first releases for Hinkley (60-110μGyhr) are higher than the mean gamma dose rate inland (30-50μGy/hr) as measured in the NRPB survey of England and Wales (ref NRPB).

Table 8.3.2 Gamma background levels near Hinkley Point in 1994 compared with average levels for Somerset. (*Source: Nuclear Electric Annual Report 1994, NRPB, 1989)*

Location	**Gamma dose rate at height of 1m (nGy/hr)**
Hinkley point outfall beach dose	98
East of outfall, beach dose	68
West of outfall, beach dose	111
Burnham on Sea, beach dose	60
Combwich, beach dose	78
Average NRPB dose Somerset	34

So the conclusions from the first Hinkley Point studies were that the sea coast (or more strictly the sediment) effect on cancer risk we found in Wales also occurred near another reactor that released material to a muddy estuary and to offshore drying banks. Shortly after the Hinkley reports were released, we were asked to look at the situation near the two other local nuclear sites, at Oldbury and Berkeley, both on the eastern banks of the river Severn. This work was funded by Michael Holmes MEP, through the offices of David Taylor, another old friend and also the prospective Green Party MEP for the south West region. The study was complicated by the fact the wards involved were in several separate counties and also in Wales, which made the work trickier. But, in addition, we were able to use the 1974-89 Wales Cancer Registry data to examine effects on the Welsh side of the estuary. At about the same time as we were settling down to this Oldbury study, we were also asked by a citizen group on the other side of the country at West Mersea in Essex to look at health effects near Bradwell power station which discharged to the muddy and tidal river Blackwater. We decided to do both studies in parallel since this would save time by enabling us to do all the calculations in one combined file.

8.4 Oldbury and the Welsh leukaemias.

The Severn estuary discharges to the Bristol Channel and is joined by the estuary of the river Wye just above the Severn road bridge near the town of Chepstow. The estuary is tidal with a considerable rise and fall, some 20 feet, so the sea rushes in twice a day and rushes out again, carrying silt from the two rivers and distributing material along the banks of both and on the shores of the sea. Anyone who has visited the area will know that the sea is brown and mud coloured as far as Hinkley Point on the English Shore and well to the west of Cardiff on the Welsh shore. Visitors to the resort of Weston-Super-Mare will know of the miles and miles of fine mud and the enormous distances between low and high water. Anyone who wants to swim at low tide has a long walk. The coast is contaminated by discharges from Hinkley Point and also three other nuclear sites, the power stations at Oldbury on Severn and Berkeley and the Nycomed Amersham radioisotope factory at Llanishen in Cardiff, which discharges to the river Taff and Cardiff Bay. Levels of Tritium from this latter source are measured in seawater and in mud, but also at very high concentrations in fish and vegetation nearby, suggesting that there is some concentration mechanism that has been overlooked. After the publication of the Hinkley Point study, I was contacted by many people with tales of cancer in towns and villages on this coast and these estuaries. One man was from a dinghy sailing club near Oldbury and he told me of all the cancer cases in the club members.

This Oldbury study was a very complicated and difficult study and took about three months to complete. The reason was that in those days we created the ward maps by tracing them from boundary commission maps and then scanning the trace into a PC. We now have digitisers and digitised data but for the Oldbury studies Helen Rowe wielded her mapping pen and tracing paper. The maps were very beautiful. I have some on the wall here. The cancer results were published by us in April 2001 and they included a look at childhood leukaemia on the Welsh side of the estuary opposite the Oldbury plant which we could do using the Wales Cancer Registry data. Results showed that the sea coast effect on cancers existed below the Severn Bridge but not above it. In particular, there was a strong sea coast effect to the south of Avonmouth and also on the Welsh coast, both in areas where there were extensive mud banks. Cancer risk also followed the two tidal rivers of the Avon in Somerset and the Wye above its mouth in Chepstow. The breast cancer mortality map is given in Plate 13. Lung cancer was also higher along the coast, particularly on the Welsh side. There was also an interesting discovery. The Wales Cancer Registry data revealed a childhood leukaemia cluster in the Chepstow area of residence, just across the river from Oldbury and at the mouth of the river Wye. This caused considerable interest in the media since the Relative Risk on the basis of the 3 cases was over 11 ($p = 0.001$) comparable with Seascale. Remember, the latter Sellafield cluster was based on 4 cases over a much longer period. One enterprising reporter actually tracked down one of the children, who had survived the disease and who knew of the other cases, so the cover ups that were a feature of the earlier Welsh leukaemia analysis results were not possible. There was also a significantly raised level of prostate cancer in the 10km radius around the Oldbury plant.

We have to ask why it is that the coastal effect was not as clear in the upper reaches of the Severn above the Chepstow Bridge. We think that this is because the banks of the river above the bridge are far less muddy than below the bridge and this is because the tidal energy is very high. The funnel of the Bristol Channel has so tapered by this point that the waters roar up the Severn in the famous Severn Bore. Thus there is little chance for the smaller particles to precipitate and there is little chance for any activity to resuspend particles that have precipitated since the slope of the banks of the river is great. To see the effect, we hypothesise, there has to be a large area of drying contaminated sediment that is covered by the sea as the tide comes in. This gives a chance for bubbles to form in the incoming tide when the wind blows and it is the bubble formation that causes the resuspension of the radioactive material. An almost ideal example of such a system is the East Coast inlet of the Blackwater in Essex, which is fed by the discharges from Bradwell.

So at about the time we were examining Oldbury and the Severn we looked at wards around Bradwell. We were asked by the local group there to do this because there was a plan to burn radioactive waste there in an incinerator and local down winders were becoming concerned.

8.5 Bradwell

West Mersea is an island in Essex noted for yachting and surrounded by the tidal saltings and muddy creeks that make up much of the East Coast rivers of Essex and Suffolk. Yachts dry out at low tide and sailors in this area have to keep an eye on the depth of water under the keel and the state of the tide. In a previous life as a yacht delivery skipper I ran the old wooden 11-ton gaff cutter yacht 'Swift' aground off Bradwell whilst sailing from Rochester to Maldon in 1977 and had to sit out the night tide watching the lights of the power station. This station, like the others, pours its waste into the sea through a pipe. Here, however, the sink is the muddy estuary of the river Blackwater: not really a river at all but more like Carlingford Lough, a sea inlet which all but dries at low tide and which is extended by offshore sandbanks to the south (St Peter's Flats, Buxey and Ray Sands) and the north (Mersea Flats and Bench Head). Nearly all the material is therefore trapped in the mud and like all these systems is concentrated at the head of the inlet, in this case near the town of Maldon. This is because the finest silt is moved continuously up to the head of the tidal penetration.

The Ministry of Agriculture Fisheries and Food (MAFF) measure radiation in silt every year near UK nuclear sites. The concentrations of Caesium-137 are measured in mud at the pipeline outfall, at West Mersea 3km away on the opposite side of the river and at Maldon at the head and some 15km up tide. Levels are always highest at Maldon. In 1993, concentrations were 17Bq/kg at the pipeline; 19Bq/kg at West Mersea and 84Bq/kg at Maldon but these ratios are much the same every year.

Our study was undertaken for the West Mersea Residents Association who paid us about £800. Our initial report, which looked at 26 wards, was published in March 2001. It used data for 1995-1999 and showed that there was a significant excess risk of breast cancer in the wards adjoining the estuary of the Blackwater and that the highest relative risk was in the Maldon wards. In Maldon North ward the risk was more than twice the national average at 2.6 (O/E = 15/5.8; $p = 0.001$) and for all three Maldon wards the risk was found to be 1.62 (Obs/Exp 22/15.8; $p = 0.09$. The risk map is shown in Plate 20.

The newspapers had a field day over this and the local health authority brought in SAHSU to check out the situation, and this in turn later brought in COMARE (The government's Committee on the Medical Aspects of Radiation in the Environment) and the story of the Bradwell breast cancers forms part of the later section.

SAHSU (and COMARE) always use concentric rings in their analysis of risk, a truly ridiculous method that can only be there to ensure that there is no excess risk ever found. For situations where there are populations entirely surrounding a source of risk, higher rates of illness in down-winders will be offset or diluted by low rates in up-winders. In the Somerset coast studies, there were, of course, no up-winders since the region was that of the blue ocean. The up winders were the fish. Near Bradwell, the fact that the risk was close to the mud and not radial led us to carry out a second study of the slightly larger area which we heard that SAHSU were using. In this study we adjusted for Social Class. It was published just before the SAHSU study in July 2001. We examined 64 wards and tested Blackwater wards against non-Blackwater wards including and excluding Colchester. We also used a control. We tested the cancer mortality rates against wards adjacent to the River Crouch, another muddy estuary to the south of the Blackwater but isolated from it by the Foulness Sand. Measurements made by MAFF on the Crouch show that little radioactivity from Bradwell reaches the Crouch, so it can be used as a control, and specifically the town of Burnham on Crouch makes a good control for Maldon. We were able to show in this study that comparing populations living inside rings at different distances (4km and 17km) from Bradwell showed no effect (as SAHSU also found) but comparing the Blackwater wards with the non Blackwater wards showed an excess breast cancer risk. In the 13 wards adjacent the Blackwater (population 19326) there were 62 deaths observed with 44.9 expected SMR = 1.34; p = 0.003) In the 26 non-Blackwater wards (female population 51287) there were 133 deaths with 127 expected, SMR = 1.05). In the 5 wards adjacent to the Crouch (female population 7101) there were 11 deaths with 15.4 expected (SMR = 0.71). This enabled us to carry out a statistical test on the various populations, results of which are given in Table 8.5.1

With this paper and the opposition paper from SAHSU, which argued (on the basis of concentric rings) for no effect, a battle was begun which is still raging. Unfortunately (or perhaps fortunately in view of what transpires), both our results and that of SAHSU had included a few mistakes, so the figures were not quite correct in either study. COMARE could not resist attacking us for making a mistake and in checking out the figures found that SAHSU (whose study was reported to have cost North Essex Health Authority £30,000) had made a much bigger mistake.

After the errors in our first two reports had been pointed out by COMARE we recalculated the results using the correct data and published the corrected paper in December 2002. The result was that the effect was even more pronounced. The RR for the Blackwater vs. non Blackwater wards had increased from 1.32 to 1.6 (p = 0.019) and to 1.7 if the two extra years 2000 and 2001 were included (p = 0.0015). The test of Blackwater vs. Crouch wards for the period 1995-2001 gave RR = 2.1 (1.12<RR<3.98; p = 0.018) and the test of Maldon vs. Burnham on

Crouch for 1995-2001 gave RR = 2.1 with 34 deaths in Maldon (pop 5571) and 10 in Burnham (pop 3364) RR = 2.1 (1.02<RR<4.15; p = 0.04). The SAHSU study errors involved their having completely omitted some Maldon postcodes and so their entire conclusion was turned on its head, forcing them to change their methodology. This was so blatant, and was associated with so many twists and turns in direction that I will keep the story for Part III.

The yachtsman peacefully at anchor off Mersea or Tollesbury at nightfall listens to the ebb tide lapping at the hull and the sound of the sea birds wading at the waters edge and calling to each other. He believes he is one with nature and feels safe. The radiation is invisible; the micron sized specks of radioactivity float in the air to be inhaled. MAFF are aware of the existence of the radioactivity. They have measured it. They wrongly consider the critical pathway for exposure to be external radiation doses to the houseboat dwellers whose boat hulls are in contact with the contaminated mud. In an echo of the dinghy sailing club near Oldbury on Severn, after we published our results, Mr BJR Wright, Secretary of the Maldon Oyster Fisherman's Association, wrote to the Maldon and Burnham Standard on April 6th 2001:

'Trust the experts'. What a joke . . . I find it more than coincidence that in the last seven years four commercial fishermen who spent years working on the mud flats and fishing outside Bradwell Power Station have all had bone cancer. Three have died and I myself have survived owing to the brilliant staff at Broomfield Hospital. I have also been told that commercial barge skippers who regularly plied our river are affected by bone cancer.

So there we are. The people don’t trust the official scientists. The public think that science is used against them. Maybe they are right.

Table 8.5.1 Statistical significance of some tests of hypotheses that breast cancer risks are not elevated close to the Bradwell nuclear site or close to the river.

Test group	Relative Risk	95% confidence interval	Chi square	p- value 2-tailed
Radial 0-4km vs. 4-17km	1.06	0.47<RR<2.38	0.02	0.89
Estuarial: Blackwater vs non Blackwater	1.32	0.98<RR<1.78	3.24	0.07
Control: Blackwater vs. Crouch	1.93	1.02<RR<3.67	4.22	0.04

8.6 Cardiff and the Amersham isotope factory

I finish this chapter with a brief account of another study in this mortality series, that of the area around Cardiff. We have also now looked at Harwell, Aldermaston and three areas of Scotland, near Hunterston, Torness and Chapelcross. Indeed, we now have an automatic computer program for calculating SMRs in any ward of England, Wales and Scotland and, with the recent data we bought from ONS after their reversal of the decision to withhold the mortality ward data, we can look at years up to 2005. However, the Cardiff study is notable for its having not shown the effects it was designed to look for, but instead some other effects it was not designed to find. It therefore is useful for us in defending against the arguments advanced by the nuclear industry that we fix our methods and choose our study areas (exactly as they do, as it happens, an example of psychological transference). In 2001 we were asked by Eurig Wyn MEP to examine cancer near the Nycomed Amersham radioisotope plant in Llanishen, a suburb of north Cardiff. The plant releases various radioactive substances into the air and into the river Taff. The most activity is in the form of Tritium, an isotope of hydrogen, which produces very weak beta emissions. It has been discovered in the last few years that Tritium from the Amersham plant has been concentrating in plants, fish and shellfish to an enormous degree. In the 2000 RIFE report of the Food Standards Agency a map is given showing concentrations of Tritium in seawater. This is reproduced below (Fig 8.5.1) and shows the extent of the contamination along the shores of the Bristol Channel and Severn Estuary. This is in addition to all the other radioactivity from Berkeley, Oldbury and Hinkley Point. There seems to be some way in which the Tritium gets into living systems to a much greater extent than the Tritium released by Sellafield. For example in the RIFE 2000 report concentrations of Tritium in flounders caught near the pipeline were 105,000Bq/kg of which 51000Bq were organically bound, and therefore more dangerous owing to a longer biological half life. Fish caught in the river Taff contain 6000 to 23000 Bq/kg of organically bound Tritium. Land produce also contains Tritium. Cabbage contains 860Bq/kg of which about half is organically bound. Could this have caused any health problems? In 2001, the local health authority commissioned SAHSU to look. A large question over Tritium effects has to do with developmental anomalies. This issue was raised by my friend Hugh Richards, the secretary of the Wales Anti-Nuclear Association (WANA) who carried out some time series analyses on stillbirth rates near the plant in the late 1990s. He showed that peaks in Tritium emissions were followed by increases in stillbirth numbers, but there were various problems with the way in which the analysis was done. The main problem was that there was really only one Tritium excursion and the numbers were small so he attempted to carry out a complex devolution of the time series data which may or may not have shown something but which was certainly attacked by the establishment quite savagely. Nevertheless, since people are not gulled, there was sufficient concern for the SAHSU study (which was to look at cancer and also birth anomalies) and this was underway when we were asked to give an independent view. We looked at all malignancies separately for men and women, also lung cancer separately and breast and prostate cancer mortality. The period was 1995-2000. We also examined infant mortality and stillbirths over this period and in addition used the 1974-89 Wales Cancer Registry data to look at childhood leukaemia 0-4. The cancer results were adjusted for Social Class as usual, and in addition, we obtained a set of ward populations updated by the Welsh Assembly and Health Authority researchers from GP practice lists. This was because there had been some population changes in certain wards in Cardiff as a result of the Cardiff Bay developments and so we needed to be sure that any results we found were not due to incorrect denominators (if there are more people in the ward than the 1991 census records then there will be more cancer deaths automatically). SAHSU, as usual, drew rings around the Amersham plant.

The study area we used was chosen on the basis that releases from the Nycomed Amersham plant would concentrate in the valley of the River Taff below the plant and that exposure would be greatest in wards adjacent to the river Taff downstream of the plant and also the coastal wards of Cardiff and adjacent areas. For those who know Cardiff, the study areas contain all the wards from Llantwit Major and Llandow Ewenny in the west, to Trowbridge and Lisvane and St Mellons in the East, and were approximately bounded in the north by the M4 motorway and the wards of Peterston super Ely, Whitchurch and Rhiwbina.

We attempted to address the problem existing in Cardiff that there has been considerable population change since the census of 1991, especially near the dockside developments. We obtained National Health Service Activity Record (NHSAR) populations for each of the wards in the study area for 1998 and used a version of these that was adjusted for overall Cardiff demographic fractions based on the Office of National Statistics projections. NHSAR are populations based on the records of General Practitioners in the wards. We are grateful to Nathan Lester of Bro Taf Health Authority and to Chris Batsford and Shaun Ward of the Cardiff Research Centre for advice and for supplying data. Using these data we recalculated all the cancer SMRs to examine the effect of population increases.

Statistical analysis was based on three hypotheses.

1. There was no significant difference in cancer risk in people living in wards (A) adjacent to or within 2.5km of the sea or the tidal river Taff below the ward of Riverside and those people living in wards (B) which were further than 2.5km of the sea or not estuarial.
2. People living in the wards on Whitchurch and Tongrwnlais and Radyr and St Fagans, adjacent to Nycomed Amersham (LOCAL 1) had no higher risk of cancer than those living in the whole study area excluding these wards.
3. As for 2 above but including the two downstream wards of Llandaff and Llandaff North (LOCAL 2) in the target group.

To examine infant mortality and stillbirth, the numbers of cases of infant deaths below 28 days and in the first year over the period 1995-2000 were compared with the number of births occurring in this period in each ward to obtain a ward rate. This was compared with the national rate to establish a mortality ratio. In addition, stillbirths in the wards were examined.

Since we have access to Wales Cancer Registry incidence data for all cancers by sex and age and year from 1974-1989 to the small area codes used by the Welsh Office (Areas of Residence) we also were able to examine childhood leukaemia risk over this period, the latter half of which included operation of Nycomed Amersham. The area of residence 77AA CARDIFF CB is larger than the ward level areas used for the mortality study but might have been expected to show any gross effect on childhood leukaemia caused by releases from the plant were there to have been any.

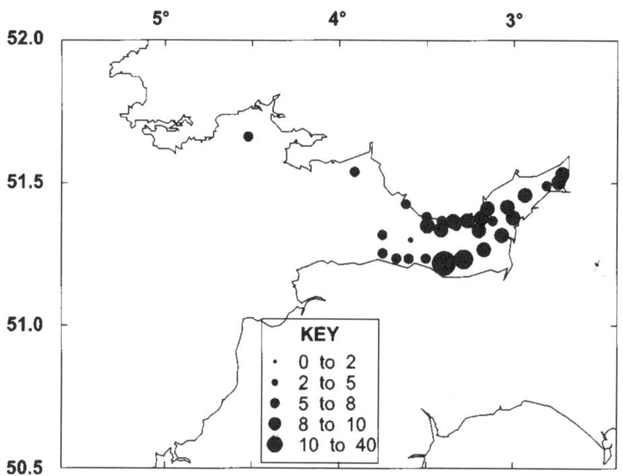

Fig 8.5.1. Concentrations of Tritium in surface water from the Bristol Channel, September 2000 (RIFE 2000)

While we were finishing off our research, the SAHSU study was released [SAHSU 2001]. Their approach was to examine risk for certain cancer incidence and mortality over the period 1968-97 for leukaemia in all ages and thyroid, breast and prostate cancer from 1991-97. In addition, they examined congenital malformation infant mortality (0-1yr) and stillbirths from 1983-1998. Their approach was based on their standard method: they set up two circles around the plant and established the relative risk based on national means for populations living within the inner circle and the annular ring between the inner and outer circles. The radii they chose were 2km and 7.5km. The reason for this choice was not apparent. It begs a number of questions about what would have happened if different radii had been chosen. For example, the radii used by SAHSU in their study of Bradwell Nuclear Power station were 4km and 17km. As I have already shown, in the section on Bradwell we were able to show that this choice of radii enabled SAHSU to show that there was no proximal effect of the plant. The question we asked then was whether the radii were chosen arbitrarily, or whether a number of different radii were chosen to see what would emerge, and those radii chosen which showed no effect from Bradwell? In any case, the whole theoretical basis for such a model is flawed since the radionuclides either go into the sea or a river, and expose those who live near the sea or river, or they go into the air and expose the downwind populations. A radial model would not find down winders since their risks would be balanced by the low risks in up winders, even assuming that the risks are linear, which is not shown by the data.

Unsurprisingly, the SAHSU study of Nycomed Amersham found that there were no increased risks from any of the cancers they studied and the only result of interest was a statistical excess risk of leukaemia incidence in adult females in the outer band (RR = 1.28). The study found a significant excess risk of infant mortality in males in the outer band (1.2 for males and 1.21 for females) and non-significant excess risk (RR=1.35 for males, 1.52 for females) in the inner band. There was also a significant excess risk of infant mortality in males in the outer band (RR = 1.14).

Thus there was some evidence from the SAHSU report that cancer near Nycomed Amersham is not a problem though there may be an effect on congenital malformation and infant mortality. In general it was impossible to analyse the report since no numbers were given either for populations or for cases. They could have made the whole thing up: it was left to us to see what was going on there.

When we used a concentric ring method we immediately saw that the result was very sensitive to which radii were chosen for the two rings. This was because the cancers seemed to be clustered in wards that were close to the river Taff, Cardiff Bay, where the river opens out and has muddy (contaminated) beaches and the coastal wards themselves. The effect was very clear for lung cancer. Plate 14 shows the map of lung cancer mortality risk in women. Plate 14 also traces the course of the River Taff below the Amersham plant. It is easy to see how a concentric rings approach would fail, as it did in the Bradwell study. The lung cancer effect in women is highly significant (RR = 1.4; p = 0.0002) but less so for men (RR = 1.14; p = 0.06). So the seacoast and river effect on lung cancer, which was there in the other mortality studies, is there in Cardiff. We did not find an excess risk for any cancer near the plant nor for infant mortality or stillbirths. Except for the coastal clustering, the Cardiff study did not reveal an effect from the Amersham plant, and therefore it was never released to the press by Eurig Wyn MEP, Plaid Cymru, nor has it ever been paid for (a miserable £550) despite the fact that it had taken three months of hard work and many phone calls to the MEP's office.

8.7 The small area mortality studies: conclusions

There is no need to labour on giving more and more of the same information and describing other studies we have made along these lines. We have an embarrassment of riches here. The results all confirm the simple points, which emerged from the Wales study. Cancer is an environmental disease; you get it if you are exposed to carcinogens. People who live near contaminated coasts and rivers have more cancer than those who do not. The bracing sea air carries death. In this chapter I have laid out the bare results of the first small area studies. There is more. When these results were first made known, we received extraordinary and violent responses, not only from the nuclear industry, but also from the public health agencies and departments, from the National Radiological Protection Board, from the government committee COMARE, and from the local health care systems in the areas studied. The battle lines were drawn up: local people and Green Audit versus the healthcare system and the nuclear industry. We intercepted emails between senior officials covering up data. We were leaked committee minutes. It was a media war, and very dirty. The newspapers carried articles based on nuclear industry Press releases; they carried our responses. I have divided these developments from the bare results of the studies as I want to examine the dirty war in Part III. Before I turn to the skulduggery and cover-ups I will try to draw all the results together in the next short chapter into an account of what I think we have found.

9
The Way to Dusty Death

Your shadow in the morning striding behind you. Or your shadow at evening rising to meet you;
I will show you fear in a handful of dust".

TS Eliot. The Waste Land.

9.1 Gathering it together

So I will now end section II of this book by drawing together what I believe we have learned. I started out showing that cancer was an environmental disease, that is to say that it is caused by damage to the DNA in cells, accumulated like the winning numbers on a Bingo card, where the unwanted prize is something which you cannot refuse. Although the precise mechanisms and probabilistic gates affecting this process are still to be entirely described, enough has been discovered now to know that this is so. Therefore, the increase in cancer rates in real terms, in young and old, which characterises the latter half of the 20th Century, is a consequence of some environmental agent or agents which came into being in increasing concentrations after 1950. This is not to deny the causative effect on lung cancer of cigarette smoking, or the effects of other earlier exposures, but we are dealing with a massive phenomenon, which goes largely unaddressed by the public health community. The great increase in cancer rates, which began in Wales in the late 1970s and in England in the 1980s, is mirrored in Europe and in all countries of the world that keep cancer incidence data. And the rates continue to rise. What is the cause?

In *Wings of Death* I argued that it was the man-made radioactive pollution from weapons fallout and nuclear plants. The work that I have done since writing that confirms this but at a much larger area scale in terms of description and at a higher resolution. I am looking now in space whereas before I was looking in time. The curious pattern of the trend in cancer risk by distance from the sea and coastal and estuarial contaminated mud, which appears in all the studies we have done, identifies the source of risk as radioactively contaminated particles. How do they cause cancer? Many studies show how these particles get from the mud to the bodies of the people who live close to the mud. There are measurements of sea spray concentration of salt and sea-derived particulates, trends of plutonium in air, of plutonium in children's teeth and in autopsy specimens. Radiation research shows how the high local ionisation density near the DNA results in the mutations and genomic effects that lead to cancer. We can follow the cause from its creation and then its release from Sellafield or some other radioactive site to the environment, then to the people, then to their bloodstream, then to the DNA.

9.2 Dust

Much of the dust in the UK derives from the sea. The Chair of the Airborne Particles Research Group, Prof Roy Harrison, asked by the government to find out the origin of the PM10 particles that were associated with the huge increases in asthma, stated at a meeting that 30% of particles in the UK are sea derived. When the winds blow from the west and the seas crash against our western shores, the silt is resuspended and electrically charged. It drifts across the whole of the country. On the west coasts of the UK and east coast of Ireland onshore winds carry the salt spray and whatever else that is attached to the salt. If the sediment contains radioactive particles, then this is what is carried ashore. Anyone who lives within a kilometre of the sea knows that their windows become encrusted with salt and their cars also. Wipe the salt away: it is brown. Look at it through a microscope at 1000X and you will see the particles. Many of them are not salt, but are made up of insoluble materials. Certain plants will not grow in this region or have to be protected.

Where does the pollution that is being continually released go? It goes to the sea. Rain washes out the material from the atmosphere, the organic chemicals, the radionuclides, and the heavy metals. The rivers flow to the sea. Factories, hospitals, research laboratories, domestic sinks and drains discharge into rivers: all flow to the sea. Landfill sites, waste incinerators, all the machinery of waste; ultimately result in materials moving to the sea. Of course, this is not the entire story: there are materials which concentrate in stopped valleys, or declivities in hilly parts of the countries. For example, after Chernobyl, NRPB stated that all the Caesium-137 that fell in Wales with the rain would be washed to the sea in six weeks. There are still contaminated parts of the upland areas more than 15 years after the accident, and sheep are still measured with more than the safe limit of 1000Bq/kg. However, the principle is sound.

There is a geophysical cycle in the dispersion and redistribution of the radiation that I argue is the determinator in space of the cancer epidemic. Radiation from fallout and Chernobyl is mostly washed to the sea and concentrates in parts of the coast that have low tidal energy conditions, inlets and estuaries. In the case of those coasts with their very own nuclear site, like the Irish Sea, this happened naturally. Material pumped into the sea is moved to these sites by natural physical action. The smaller sediment particles carry the radioactivity, and these particles end up on the mud banks and in the inlets and estuaries. From there, they are resuspended and blown by the wind across the country. Their concentration is highest close to the sea, within a few kilometres, but then, as they move inland, their distribution is interesting.

These particles are very small, less than a micron in diameter. Some are less than 100nm, nanoparticles. They are kept afloat in the air by virtue of their extreme smallness and the fact that they become electrically charged by sunlight (photoelectric effect) and perhaps by their own radioactivity. They are called aerosols, and they behave rather like a gas. They are extremely mobile. The Uranium Oxide particles produced when the uranium weapons were used by the US in the recent Iraq War (2003) were detected in the UK (Busby and Morgan 2006). The particles also can be attracted by electrical discontinuities in the earth's electric field. What is this? The earth has a permanent electric field of about 150 Volts per metre, negative at the ground and positive in the air. If this field were visible, then mountains, rivers and valleys would provide an awesome sight. There would be a forest of electrostatic lines of force radiating from the ground and curving over and collapsing near rivers or at the junction between different geological strata. I met a Chinese scientist at a conference in Vienna who told me of the activity of soil bacteria at the junctions between these strata and how the erosion of soil was a function of the electrostatic discontinuities caused by sudden variations in soil conductivities. The charged dust will also be attracted by such discontinuities and will concentrate in areas where the field collapses. The field also collapses when it rains and the ground becomes wet. The particles are then washed into the river valleys, but stick in certain parts of the valleys where they have become trapped.

High voltage electric power lines will also attract such particles, and in dry weather the ionising radiation levels in air below such power lines can be measured and shown to be higher than away from the power lines. This is particularly true near the power lines leading current away from nuclear power stations where there is considerable pollution. I have measured radiation under the power lines near Trawsfynydd power station in Wales. Professor Denis Henshaw, of Bristol University has been fascinated by the effects of power lines on dust and with co-workers has been able to argue that the daughter isotopes of Radon decay concentrate near such power lines. He has also found that lung cancer rates are higher just downwind of these high voltage power lines. There are many studies now which associate child leukaemia with living near high voltage power lines, and their ability to attract radioactive dusts may well be the cause of this effect. Research on this issue should be carried out urgently.

There are two types of long-lived environmental radioactive particle that are of great interest. They are the oxide particles of Plutonium and Uranium, which are the common forms of the contamination of the environment by these elements. The particles are smaller than one micron (one thousandth of a millimetre). Both Uranium and Plutonium oxide are very long lived in the environment and both are alpha emitters. Both bind to DNA and have high atomic numbers which enable them to amplify natural background gamma rays, a property which I have drawn attention to elsewhere (Busby 2005). Both oxide particles are the main form released by nuclear sites like Sellafield and the atomic weapons research establishment (AWE) at Aldermaston in Berkshire or the Atomic Energy Research

Establishment at Harwell in Oxfordshire. In the Nevada desert, after the weapons tests, these particles were found everywhere in the top layer of soil and also on foliage, where they were surprisingly difficult to remove. In dry desert conditions, artificial mixtures of plutonium oxide particles with dry sand were found to contaminate the leaves of plants grown in pots outside. But the same experiment done in a greenhouse resulted in no transfer of plutonium to leaves. This was not understood at the time. A likely explanation is that inside the greenhouse, the electric field has collapsed. In the open, the plant's leaves electrostatically attract the plutonium particles, which are resuspended by the earth's electric field.

We now have a model for the redistribution of radioactive dust. There is a huge and invisible engine at work pumping radioactive dust around the planet. In the UK, the particles come from the sea, from weapons fallout and from inland sites like Aldermaston or ranges where uranium weapons are tested. In sunny weather the particles are suspended and hover in the air. They move under the influence of breezes but are attracted by discontinuities in the electric field, by power lines or vertical metal objects, by discontinuities due to strata or other geology including underground watercourses. In sunny weather the dust can be seen. It is called 'smoke haze'. It is particularly clear when there has been a lot of it generated as in the aftermath of a war. In Kosovo, when I visited there in 2001 with Nippon TV looking for depleted uranium dust, you could barely see a kilometre for the scattering of light caused by the dust particles in Pristina, the capital. When it rains, the dust is washed out and the air clears. In Kosovo, in the town of Gjakove, I found depleted uranium (DU) dust under a snowdrift that had melted about a week earlier (Plate 18). I brought the dust home and the BBC paid for it to be analysed. I was interested in the concentration of the beta emitting daughter isotopes Thorium-234 and Protoactinium-234m relative to the parent Uranium-238. Because these daughters have rapid half-lives compared with the parent U-238, they should be in equilibrium, so that there is one decay of Th-234 for one decay of Pa-234m for one decay of U-238. But what we found was remarkable. The concentration of Th-234 and Pa-234m was about 4000Bq/kg but the concentration of U-238 was only 450Bq/kg. In other words, in the week between the melting of the snowdrift and the exposure of the DU particles to the sun, 90% of the DU had vanished from the sample, leaving the daughter isotopes (which would not have been particles, but must have been sloughed from the surface of the DU particles and adsorbed by the natural soil).

If this is so, then where you live is very important. If these particles are concentrated in certain areas through these mechanisms and can be resuspended in sunny weather and can be inhaled, then they can get into the body and cause cancer. In this case, we would expect cancer rates to be higher where these particle concentrations are higher, and for this variation to be on quite a small scale, even smaller than a ward. Certain types of area stand out immediately. They are:

1. Near nuclear sites
2. Contaminated coasts and estuaries
3. River valleys, but perhaps not at the bottom of the valley (see below)
4. Natural field discontinuities, e.g. along strata, over underground watercourses of fault lines.
5. Artificial field discontinuities, which may be active e.g. high voltage, power lines, buried power lines, radiating antennae etc. or passive, e.g. metal towers.
6. Areas where a great deal of dust is raised through soil disturbance, e.g. near building sites, new towns, farming.

There has been a great deal of argument about the clustering of child leukaemia. The child leukaemia clusters, say the nuclear industry, occur in places which are remote from nuclear power stations; therefore nuclear power station clusters may be merely examples for these other clusters for which there is at present no explanation. In addition, these clusters are taken as evidence for an infective origin for the disease; a cluster suggests that there is transfer of the disease from person to person. This is the Doll and Kinlen hypothesis (see references), the straw clutched at by the drowning nuclear industry. However, it could also result from concentration of the causative agent.

We have been involved in two cases where we have had access to child leukaemia data at the level where each case can be marked on a map. One of these was the Northampton 'Pembroke Road' leukaemia cluster where the cases run like a string of pearls along the side of a valley where a railway line and river run. We were involved in a complaint against the BBC over the coverage of this case, and I will return to this in Part III. The second child leukaemia cluster was in West Berkshire, between Newbury and Reading. Here the cases string out along the river valley of the Kennet where geological strata fulfil the requirements of the hypothetical plutonium particle pump, and Aldermaston provides a source for the plutonium and uranium particles. The river bed is Valley Gravel, then come the Reading Beds, the lower Bagshot Beds, chalk then London Clay, then Plateau Gravel. Tilehurst, where the highest level of child leukaemia was found, is at the junction of the Plateau gravel and the Reading beds. In Tilehurst, between 1971 and 1997 there were 9 cases in the 0-24 age group with 2.7 expected (RR = 3.3; p = 0.001).

In this area, the radioactivity in the dust has been partly characterised. This is because the chief perceived sources of radioactivity, AWE Aldermaston and Burghfield, were focuses of a public enquiry into their secrecy and radioactive releases, particularly since there has been a child leukaemia excess in the area that was discovered in the mid 1980s and has been confirmed by COMARE. Like the Sellafield cluster, COMARE have concluded that the radiation doses (based on ICRP models) cannot be the cause. However, AWE has been forced to measure radioactivity in the air, soil and dust and every year these measurements now are tabulated in their annual reports. They use two methods for the air concentrations. They use high volume air sampling (where a pump pulls a known quantity of air through a filter which is then ashed and analysed) and passive airshade sampling (where a piece of muslin is hung out on a pole and whatever sticks to it is analysed for radioactivity). It is the second of these techniques that give a clue to the nature of the airborne dust and its possible effect on child leukaemia.

AWE makes its measurements some distance away from the plant. The most remote site is Basingstoke, some 16 miles away to the southeast. The results show enormously high levels of radioactivity in the dust, levels that vary from month to month. Table 9.1 below gives some results. These results should give us the horrors. Remember that the levels of radioactivity that define low-level waste are 400Bq/kg and that sheep meat cannot be sold if it has more than 1000Bq/kg. This dust, with alpha levels of more than 1500Bq/kg, is floating about Berkshire and Hampshire being inhaled by children and adults. What does it consist of? Some of the activity will be from Radon daughters, but the ratio of average alpha to average beta rules out the Radon daughters as the main component. We are left with the Uranium isotopes, Thorium and Plutonium. Levels of U-238 in soil have been measured in the area: they average about 20Bq/kg or less. Thorium-232 levels are less than this. The Plutonium-239 in the soil has also been measured. Although there are some interesting anomalies (which I will look at in Part III) the soil levels are far too low (between 0.2 and 2Bq/kg) to account for the dust concentrations of radioactivity. AWE are also puzzled. They state: *Although the reasons are not fully understood, it is common to record higher activity concentrations from samples prepared from smaller than usual quantities of dust.*

Table 9.1 Average and peak monthly concentrations Bq/kg of radioactive dust particles trapped in passive airshades by AWE at various sites near Aldermaston and Burghfield (AWE annual report 1992)

Site	Annual average alpha	Peak alpha	Annual average beta	Peak beta
On site Aldermaston	1400	4800	11000	62000
On site Burghfield	1100	2800	11000	27000
Off site monitors				
1. Tutts clump	1900	6500	15000	47000
2. Sulhampstead	1500	4400	13000	25000
3. Stratfield Mortimer	800	1400	10000	17000
4. Sherfield on Loddon	1100	2100	11000	33000
5. Basingstoke	1700	4900	14000	42000
6. Hannington	2600	13000	19000	68000
7. Plastow Green	1100	1300	14000	42000
8. Thatcham	1300	4100	12000	68000
Average off site monitors	1500	4700	13500	42750

The measurements made by AWE show that the radioactive dust is not more radioactive close to the plant. Therefore it has its origin somewhere else. To this we can add another curious fact. Levels of alpha activity from Plutonium in the areas near Aldermaston have been steadily rising since 1986 when they were measured in the Harwell grassland surveys of Cawse and Horrill. Then the levels were around 0.02 to 0.07 Bq/kg (Cawse and Horrill, 1986). However, by the time of the Croudace survey in 1998, the levels were as high as 10Bq/kg, with ranges between 0.2 and 4Bq/kg. Nothing had happened between these dates to explain the increase. Chernobyl rainfall did not fall on this area and, in any case, levels of plutonium in the Chernobyl rain were low: the main component was Caesium-137.

There is a third relevant observation. According to surveys of the Irish Sea by MAFF (Kershaw *et al*),which I mentioned earlier, a significant proportion of the calculated Plutonium inventory of the Irish Sea is missing. That is to say, they know how much they put into it, but when they integrate the measurements of the plutonium in the sediment, there is not enough. Somehow, it has flown away.

The answer seems straightforward. The radioactive material put into the sea has come ashore and blown across the country. It is in the dust. This is the dust in the street, on your mantelpiece, on the car, in your lungs and in your body and that of your children. It is the dust on the plants that you eat. It is the dust on the grass that is eaten by the cows and made into milk, by the chickens and made into eggs. And if you live near the sea or near a concentration focus for the dust, look out! To paraphrase Roosevelt, 'If you cant stand the radioactivity, you'd better stay out of the environment'.

The radiation century has come to a close. In the children's encyclopaedias, Roentgen, who started it all in 1895, is pictured as a smug but benign looking Victorian scientist in a tweed suit. He demonstrates the bones of his wife's hand, the wedding ring dividing the third finger. Roentgen, the physicist, calls the invisible rays X-rays, because in mathematics, X stands for the unknown. Henri Bequerel, the other half of this first peek into Pandora's box, suffered severe skin burns whilst carrying a phial of radioactive material in his waistcoat pocket. Edison's assistant, Clarence Dallow, experimented with X-ray tubes and died of cancer after his arm had to be amputated. Tragedies piled up (Caufield 1989). The Radium Dial painters were dying horribly after moistening their brushes on their tongues and transferring the Radium to their bodies. Marie Curie, who discovered the element and has now appropriately been transmuted into a cancer charity, was dying of leukaemia. The trend in child leukaemia since 1900 exactly tracks the trend in Radium production (Busby 2002BNES).

I recall the Victorian illustration of Pandora's box in the book I had as a child. Maybe you know the one? An astonished and scatty looking young girl in a nightie has the lid of the trunk up. A host of unlikely bat-like creatures are whizzing about the room followed by Fairy Hope. There is a more appropriate tableau. You are in a darkened room. You look at a shaft of sunlight, on which dust motes dance, flicker and sparkle. Occasionally a pinpoint of dazzling light explodes and is extinguished. If we could see ionising radiation, this is how the dust would appear, even in the total darkness. Since 1945, through the atmospheric tests, nuclear accidents, licensed discharges and leaks, the dust, like everything else, contains the contents of Pandora's Box, and is invisibly killing young and old alike in horrible ways. The scientific and military experiment has released unstable and completely novel substances with numbers attached to them, like convicts: Strontium-90, Plutonium-239, Caesium-137, Iodine-131, Tellurium-132. They are out there, out here, and cannot be put back in the box. The contaminated food is eaten, the air breathed, babies drink the poisoned milk; inhale the particles in the air. The demons are now inside your body. Everything is invisibly sparkling: the food, the milk, the bones and teeth, all living tissue. I am reminded of the sparkly pink plastic that *Barbie's* artefacts were often made of. I am reminded of the Ruby Slippers of the wicked witch. In addition, and thanks to the military, we now have Depleted Uranium particles, a million particles for each citizen of Europe, floating about in the air. The cancer rates rise inexorably. Governments of the world advised by the bought, the biased and the stupid pour money into cancer research and continue to hold open the lid of the chest. Where is Fairy Hope? Perhaps we are Fairy Hope. Perhaps you are.

Help! Fairy Hope, Help!

Part III
Denials

But man, proud man
Dress'd in a little brief authority
Most ignorant of what he's most assured
His glassy essence, like an angry ape
Plays such fantastic tricks before high heaven
As makes the angels weep

(Isabella)
Shakespeare: Measure for Measure

Overview

I know it's clichéd but never was it more appropriate. Let's look at some of these fantastic tricks. What would we expect if governments realised, too late, that their antics had opened Pandora's Box and released the demons. What could they do? The demons could not be put back in the box, and everywhere people were being bitten, poisoned and beginning to die. Of course, at first there would be denial. Scientists would be bought who would employ bogus research to show that there were no demons, or that no one was dying at any greater rate than was normal. Committees would be set up to argue that demons could not exist, or that the government's policies could not cause their release from any box, or that even if they had been released, they were harmless.

I am writing this book to draw attention to a massive cover up of the causes of cancer. Since *Wings of Death* I have worried about the problem of how scientists, doctors and epidemiologists could continue to miss what is so clear, with regard to what has now become the largest single cause of death. I have deployed sociological arguments and psychological arguments. But maybe the answer is not so complex. Remember, nuclear equals atomic equals war equals power, influence and money. Nuclear energy is tied to bombs, warships, mining shares, and the ability to operate a society without coal miners who have an annoying propensity toward believing they should be paid a living wage. Nuclear is about the free world versus the Reds. Ernest Sternglass, the founding father of the anti-nuclear science told me that he had been told that the British Royal family have 8 Billion dollars invested in Rio Tinto Uranium shares. 'If nuclear power goes, the shares will turn to sand,' he said with a grin. Whether this is true or not, certainly somebody has large amounts of money invested in this area and people with money wield power and influence in order to keep their money.

Therefore I believe that the simple answer is that there is a systematic cover-up at the highest level, of the effects of radioactive pollution. And for fear of status, identity, job, money, or for some other reason, perfectly good individuals look the other way and continue to allow the children and their mothers and fathers to die. No one blows any whistles.

The reason I can afford to blow this whistle, sound this factory siren, engage this Queen Mary foghorn, is precisely because I have no status and no job. My identity is reasonably secure. I have nowhere further to fall! I get a little money here and there from a few of the green foundations, the Joseph Rowntree Charitable Trust, The Goldsmiths, Poulden Puckham, various other small trusts and a few pounds from the anti-nuclear citizens. I can get in amongst these cowards and moneygrubbers and expose them. I talk with them at the international meetings, and meet them on the government committees, grinning like apes, agreeing with each other, refusing to examine evidence which falsifies their beliefs, or pretended beliefs. In order to understand what happens to produce the lie that cancer is not an environmental disease, but is somehow the sufferers' own fault, through bad genes or eating habits or flying on too many holidays in the sun. After ten years of mixing with these people, man-watching, I have developed a theory about expert committees and government advisers. It is called BIW theory. The initials are for Bastard, Idiot, Wimp. You can work out the rest. I now apply it automatically, taxonomising the various scientists and experts I meet in this area.

What is apparent is that the anti-nuclear scientists, as a rule, have no jobs or are independent in income or retired. If they had jobs, they usually have been pushed out or threatened. Professor Jean Francois Viel, the eminent French epidemiologist who discovered the child leukaemia cluster near the Cap de la Hague reprocessing site (associated with playing on the beach and eating shellfish, note.) got into so much trouble with the authorities after publishing his results that he told me he could not have anything more to do with the issue and refused to help as an expert for the Irish litigants against BNFL. He was threatened with court action and wrote his story in a book (La Sante Publique Atomisee); he was (justifiably) afraid he would lose his job and his home and be unable to look after his family. More recently in Belarus, the eminent scientist Professor Yuri Bandashevsky was gaoled on a trumped-up charge after reporting his findings that in children in the Chernobyl affected territories there was a significant correlation between heart disease and Caesium-137 whole body counts. He is still in gaol and quite ill. So when I am asked (as I often am) how do members of the public choose between the arguments of the independent scientists and those of the nuclear industry I say, 'Why would anyone do this work for so little money and endless aggravation?' For myself, I'd far rather be in a deck-chair on the beach (except that is not a safe option as I now discover).

In Part III I will present some stories and some evidence showing how the trick has been done, and how it is still carrying on. In the final part, Part IV, I will look at some alternatives, and ask what our options are for a happy future. We can make a world without poisons, and even if we cannot put the demons back in the box, at least we can understand why they are there and keep the lid shut so there are no more. We can learn lessons that we can apply to other possible risks, from electric fields, from Genetic Modification. And those who develop cancer can stop blaming themselves and wondering if they should have taken more exercise or eaten more green vegetables. Even the cigarette smokers should know from the Somerset risk map that smoking is not the whole problem.

And maybe we can forgive the early scientists who cheated and tricked us long ago. And perhaps, if they are sufficiently abject, we can exile those who still argue for the safety of radioactive pollution, and play fantastic tricks before high heaven, to one of the French Pacific Islands where the testing was carried out. We can make a just and happy world if we decide to. For as Jesus apparently said (in the Gospel of Thomas, Nag Hammadi Texts, John Robinson):

The kingdom of the father will not come by waiting for it. It will not be a matter of saying: 'here it is' or 'there it is'. Rather the kingdom of the father is spread out on the earth, and men do not see it.

10
Post War Developments

I know that most men, not only those considered clever and capable of understanding the most difficult scientific, mathematical or philosophical problems, can seldom discern even the simplest and most obvious truth if it be such as obliges them to admit to the falsity of conclusions they have formed, perhaps with much difficulty-conclusions which they have taught the others and on which they have built their lives.

Leo Tolstoy, 1989

10.1 After the Bomb

The period which followed the use of the atomic bomb on Hiroshima and Nagasaki was one where the consequences of exposure to external and internal radiation were being discovered. It was not until the early 1950s that studies of the survivors began in earnest with the setting up of the Atomic Bomb Casualty Commission (ABCC), a body that transmuted into the Radiation Effects Research Foundation (RERF), which is still following the survivors and comparing their cancers with those of a control group who were supposed not to have been irradiated. It is these studies that define, for the purposes of legislation, the risks from radiation. I have examined some of the problems associated with these studies in *Wings of Death* but will briefly give three examples here of developments in the understanding of the flaws in these studies that I have discovered since that book. The first is fairly recent research carried by Professor Alice Stewart in the years before she died. Alice believed that the problem with the Hiroshima studies was that they were not studies of a homogenous sample and could not be used to predict or explain effects in a normal population even of Japanese genetic types. She managed to obtain data from the RERF which classified the individuals in the samples of irradiated and unirradiated in terms of their immediate medical symptoms and using some complex mathematics was able to show that her thesis was correct, and that the survivors were not a proper sample on which to make judgements about the effects of radiation on normal human populations. These were a sample where the less fit had already died, a sample of survivors. The manuscript was sent to one journal after another, blocked by referees and returned by editors. Many of the referees' arguments were trivial; some were laughable. One of the reviews she showed me, asked: what is her evidence that radiation causes skin burns? She became quite depressed about it, and almost gave up; she was very old, 93, and had spent all of her life fighting against the belief that low dose radiation is safe. Her first fight had been to gain acceptance for her discoveries that obstetric X-rays cause a high risk of cancer in the children who were X-rayed *in utero*. This was in 1957 and began her career as a radiation research heretic. Her story is well described in a recent book *The woman who knew too much* (Gayle Green, 2001).

Alice agreed to be the first Chair of the new European Committee on Radiation Risk (ECRR) but sadly she died before I managed to get the system operating and produce the first report in January 2003. Alice started the ball rolling as it were and she wanted it acknowledged. It was her obstetric findings, published in *The Lancet* in 1957 that influenced Ernest Sternglass to make his calculations of the consequences of the weapons fallout, and then go on to examine the other effects of the fallout, like those on infant mortality. This drew in John Gofman and Arthur Tamplin who argued that Sternglass's calculations were not quite correct but sufficiently worrying to indicate that there would be a serious increase in infant mortality and cancer following the fallout. Ernest told me that it was his article about the effects of weapons fallout that came to the attention of President Kennedy and led to the Atmospheric test ban treaty with Khrushchev. Shortly after, the warmongers killed Kennedy for this and his other inroads on their moneymaking projects. Ernest had been making these calculations, based on Alice's findings because he was wondering whether to buy a fallout shelter. He decided that it would be a waste of money as everyone would soon be dead, a scientifically validated version of Neville Shute's *On the Beach* or Mordecai Roshwolds's *Level Seven*. Arthur Tamplin, who was sacked from his job working for the US Atomic Energy Commission went on to figure out that hot particles represented a radiological risk. In the mid 1970s he put a figure of 115,000 on the enhancement factor for plutonium oxide particles. This figure may be about right under certain circumstances.

10.2 The control groups for the A-Bomb study

There was a great deal of messing about with choices of control groups in these A-bomb studies in order to make the results tidy and to show that there was very little problem with radiation. The US certainly did not want to believe their weapon had caused such long term effects on innocent people, and in addition, such effects would make it all too clear that no one could win an atomic war. The problem of the inadequacy of the controls was evident in the 1963 reports of UNSCEAR, where it was possible to see that there was a high level of leukaemia in the control group. I pointed this out in *Wings of Death* in 1995 but I now know it had been addressed by Pere Carbonell as early as 1983 at a conference in Amsterdam (Schmitz Feuerhake 1983, Carbonell *et al.* 1983) and was also implicit in calculations made by John Gofman through a comparison of the different dose classes in 1982 (Gofman 1982). Table 10.2.1 shows a profile of Standardized Mortality and Incidence rates for the 55,000 person 0-9 rad T65D and 26,500 person 'Not in City' (NIC) control groups relative to the Japanese national rates. Of the latter, only 4500 persons were early (3-days) entrants (NIC-EE) who would have been exposed to the higher levels of short-lived fission products and neutron activation products. Of these, 6 cases of leukaemia were found up to 1978 (Kato, Brown *et al,* 1982) which is about RR = 2. Japanese investigators found high levels of leukaemia in a greater collective of Early Entrants (Hirose 1968, Wanatabe 1974). The data of Hirose are from the Hiroshima and Nagasaki tumour registries up to 1968. 45 cases of leukaemia found in 25798 early entrants of Hiroshima correspond to a 3.7-fold excess on the Japanese national rate.

10.2.1 Standard Mortality and Incidence Ratios for Hiroshima-Nagasaki control groups compared with national rates for Japan (significant excess at the 95% level is indicated by *)

Cause	Group 0-9rad T65D (0-90mSv assumed)	Group Not in City (0mSv assumed)
All causes	0.9	0.87
All malignant neoplasms	1.08*	1.02
Leukaemia	1.5*	0.95
Respiratory system	1.35*	1.3*
Digestive system ex stomach	1.1*	1.1*
Benign and unspecified neoplasms	1.25*	0.9
Breast cancer 1950-74	1.5*	1.61*
Thyroid cancer	4.1*	3.4
Leukaemia Hiroshima 1971-75	1.8*	-

Carbonell *et al.* and Gofman both assumed that the doses from fallout were external doses. They attempted to estimate this dose on the basis of chromosome aberration analysis and arrived at a figure of 50 to 300mSv. But this seems rather high as an external dose and raises the question, for me at least, that we are seeing effects from internal exposure due to inhalation and ingestion, but at an enhanced level. In other words, the results are more easily accommodated by splitting the effects of the bomb into external and internal fallout effects. It is the latter that are increasing the leukaemia and other cancers in the NIC-EE group. However, Carbonell *et al* used their findings to re-assess a hybrid leukaemia risk factor upwards by a factor of between 1.5 and 5 rather than assuming that it was an enhanced effect of low internal doses. This is very important distinction as it has ramifications for those exposed to discharges from nuclear sites, and the fallout from weapons tests and accidents. The US military argued strongly that there was no fallout because it had been an air burst. But samples had been taken and the fallout isotopes measured in the vicinity of the cities and indeed later on in Arctic ice cores.

Genetic effect differences are also seen in the control groups. This aspect of the Hiroshima studies emerged recently through the research of my good friend, the Indian scientist VT Padmanabhan. VT became involved in the issue of low dose radiation through working with Rosalie Bertell in the study of the high background radiation area of Kerala in southern India. In considering various indicators of genetic damage in the Kerala study he was led to examine the A-bomb effects. The genetic effect of the A-bombs had been something that was examined for the ABCC-RERF by James Neel (who recently died). VT was interested in sex ratio. That is the number of boys born relative to the number of girls. It is known that this ratio is a sensitive marker for genetic damage, and Neel had originally included sex ratio as one of the indicators. However, there was a sex-ratio effect discovered but it was not in the direction that had been anticipated, so Neel abandoned the sex-ratio study. What the result was showing was that the exposure had had some harmful effect on the children born to the study group relative to the controls. But Neel would not accept that this was possible so he quietly shelved the evidence. Neel incidentally has recently been brought into the limelight as the man who was involved in the genetic experiment on the Yanomami Indians in South America. Apparently he collaborated with the American anthropologist Napoleon Chagnon in a human experiment (worthy of the Nazis) to prove their thesis that the fittest (in their belief the men who were leaders, chiefs and so forth) would also be the ones who would survive an epidemic. They engendered an epidemic of a particularly nasty strain of measles through an inoculation programme and found that their thesis was wrong, though not before most of the tribes people had died (Patrick Tierney: *Darkness in Eldorado,* 2001)

10.3 Genetic effects at Hiroshima/Nagasaki and the sex ratio test

The sex ratio is merely the number of males born per thousand females. It has been shown by animal studies and by genetic arguments (because there are two X chromosomes in women but only one in men, so that there is no back-up for the X-chromosome in the male foetus) that sex ratio is a very sensitive indicator for genetic damage. In almost all groups studied there is a higher masculinity at birth, believed to be due to an excess of female embryonic and foetal loss. SR was commonly used as an indicator of genetic detriment caused to a species by radiation. It is a quantitative variable and significant deviation both above and below about 1055 is an indicator of mutagenic stress. Padmanabhan studied SR as one of the end-points in the population living in his native Kerala in south India where there is an area of very high natural background radiation in the monazite sand. This research involved an enormous amount of work. Results showed an effect on SR in the high dose group. But this interest of his extended to the Hiroshima survivors and he began to mine the data to see if there were any SR effects. He discovered that, before 1965, the GE3 genetic study of the Lifespan group looked at 70,000 children born between 1948 and 1953. They were looking for increases in stillbirth, neonatal death, malformation and sex ratio. SR was expected to increase (positive effect) after paternal exposure and decrease following maternal exposure. Results available in 1953 showed changes in SR consistent with the genetic hypothesis SR regression coefficient (decrement of male births per Sv maternal exposure = - 0.0105, $p < 0.05$). However, in the period 1954 to 1962, the period of the weapons testing fallout, the effect, though still significant, sharply reversed in direction relative to the controls (SR coefficient = + 0.035, $p < 0.01$), which left the researchers rather confused. We can now see what happened. The exposures against which the effects were being correlated were the exposures of the original bomb flash, so the result would be based on whether the immediately exposed parent was male or female. But the effects of the weapons fallout would not operate in such a way, since the new exposures from residual radiation and fallout would operate on the basis of the diet of both parents, including the controls who were, of course, living in a contaminated area eating contaminated food and drinking contaminated water. The fallout effect operated whether the parent had been originally acutely exposed or not and indeed, since it is the birth outcome that is of interest, the exposure of the foetus in the womb to fallout substances like Strontium-90 would be the determinator of sex ratio irrespective of which parent was irradiated at Hiroshima. But what the ABCC researchers under Neel did was to combine the two sets of data: after 1965, the dosimetry was reassessed and the two sets of effects were combined to cancel out. The residual effect (still significant) was discounted since it was against the prediction of theory. Sex ratio was dropped by the establishment researchers after 1981 without explanation. The genetic results of the A-bombs were believed to be non existent because of these studies. For this reason, we have had to wait until the development of the minisatellite electrophoresis to discover genetic effects of low dose radiation. The exposures from Chernobyl showed real effects, which I will describe later.

In trying to discover the source of the curious sex ratio results, Padmanabhan re-analysed the data and showed that all the exposed groups experienced sex ratio changes in the direction of the genetic hypothesis if the Not in City (NIC) control group (which swamped the study in terms of total births) were excluded from the picture. And he found that, as with many results in the area of low-level radiation (and indeed many of the dose response curves of the Hiroshima results for cancer and leukaemia), the degree of change was inconsistent with dose. The discovery of the problems with the not in city NIC group led him to look more closely at this group, which is made up of the early entrants (NICEE) and late entrants (NICLE). He discovered that there was a significant degree of difference in the ultimate health of these two groups, in terms of cancer and other diseases. So again we see that the NIC control group was not a true control group, and the discoveries of Padmanabhan could be interpreted in terms of the internal exposures received from the residual radiation and fallout.

In Table 10.3.1 I have drawn together some of the sex ratio results in a way that I hope points to what was happening. Note the highly significant aberrant sex ratios in the offspring of two NIC control group parents in children born after 1952, when the internal exposures from the fission products would have accumulated.

I have some more evidence that the choice of Hiroshima controls was flawed. This comes from a New Zealand friend, Kate Dewes, who visited Japan and talked with the *Hibakushas*, victims of the bombing of Hiroshima and Nagasaki. The Japanese word translates literally to "explosion-affected people." Her account is so important and interesting that I will devote some space to it.

Kate Dewes story: Women *Hibakusha* from Hiroshima and Nagasaki Talk about Genetic Effects

In June 2001, Japanese peace activists organised a speaking tour of eight cities for Mary Silk from the Marshall Islands and myself, to launch the Japanese version of the book Pacific Women Speak Out for Independence and Denuclearisation. [Zohl de Ishtar-Ed WILPF (Aotearoa), Disarmament and Security Centre and Pacific Connections; Christchurch, 1998]. As mothers, we spoke of our ongoing concerns about the genetic effects of nuclear radiation. Specifically, we highlighted the stories of women who had given birth to 'jelly-fish babies' and 'bunches of purples grapes' in the Marshall Islands following the US Bravo nuclear tests in 1954. As a result of the media attention and our openness in discussing these sensitive issues, first and second generation women hibakusha (atomic bombing survivors) approached us with stories of the cover-up which continues to take place in Japan over the genetic damage caused to their children. After speaking in Nagasaki, a young woman called Kimie, aged about 23, gave me photos of her young son and asked me to share his story with anyone who would listen outside Japan. She told me that she was a second generation hibakusha, and that during her pregnancy she had been warned by two older doctors that her baby might be deformed. When her son was born with a deformity to his hand, her husband blamed her grandparents' exposure to radiation and immediately divorced her. He does not keep contact with his son. Like many other hibakusha women before her, she continues to suffer discrimination because she is speaking out. She was told by other doctors that genetic damage is not normally attributable to radiation, and that therefore her son would not be eligible for compensation

However, when I met Dr Mori – who had made diagnoses of 400 hibakusha – in Kochi City, he confirmed that there are now 34 different illnesses recognised as radiation-induced. Having been to the Marshall Islands in the 1970s to help with compensation claims, he provided me with papers which proved that *the US government paid compensation to Marshallese who gave birth to deformed and mentally retarded children born after the nuclear tests. For example, a boy born with a tumour on his spine, and those who had stunted growth due to effects on the thyroid gland, were each given US $100,000. He told me of research done on a few men from the 856 Japanese fishing boats exposed to radiation during the Bikini tests in 1954. Those who were hospitalised were tested for their sperm counts. There were 10 men without any sperm and, of the others, the number of sperm was 570, 140 and 120. A healthy man's semen would normally contain 50-100,000 sperm per cu ml, so these results showed less than 1% of the average. After eight years the men had children, but the sperm was not healthy. There was no follow-up study done on these men.*

As we traveled around Japan, we spoke with older women hibakusha, with second generation women hibakusha as interpreters. The interpreters explained that we were also mothers, we were genuinely interested in their stories, and we believed there was a link between radiation and genetic damage. The women therefore trusted us and talked openly about issues which they had often not dared mention since 1945.

Some of them had given birth to 'bunches of purple grapes'; some had been forced to have abortions even years after the bombings; most had stopped menstruating for up to eight years, and they knew of many deformed and intellectually handicapped children who had been hidden away. They spoke of friends concealing the fact that they had been hibakusha from their own husbands, children and grandchildren. They said researchers had rarely asked about menstruation problems, miscarriages, or deformed children. The women had often lied to protect themselves from further discrimination, and because it was culturally inappropriate to talk about these sensitive issues with men.

Some brave women were prepared to have their names published. For example, Bun Hashizume knew of babies born with small heads. Nagano Hatsue has 3 daughters and 2 sons, 5 grandchildren and 2 great grandchildren. She and her late husband were both hibakusha from Hiroshima. She said her second son was really small and very weak when he was born – he looked black and very wrinkled. The midwife was very surprised because he looked so unusual. She had to take him to the hospital every day for 3 years. Another son suffers from diabetes. One of her daughters still suffers from anaemia and gets very tired – she also has thyroid problems. The doctors say these illnesses are not related to radiation. She said that doctors never asked her about the health of her children or anything to do with her fertility and miscarriages – it was therefore not documented. She was pregnant with her first son when the bomb was dropped. He has liver problems which his current doctor refuses to acknowledge as attributable to radiation. The first doctor she saw with him admitted that it was radiation-related. Teruko Yokoyama of Nagasaki has written about her youngest sister born in 1948. At the age of 7 she developed purpura (or red blotches) all over her body and suffered bad stomach aches. Some hibakusha experienced the same symptoms soon after the bombing.

Haruko Manzen was 9 years old when the bomb was dropped on Hiroshima. She gave evidence in the Hiroshima District Court in August 2003[,] to the effect that, although she had been 2.6 km from the hypocentre, her parents-in-law told her to have an abortion when she became pregnant in 1960. She had several miscarriages and in 1962 had her ovaries removed to prevent pregnancies. After the bombings, midwives in Hiroshima and Nagasaki became very concerned about the number of deformed babies being born. In the September 1954 issue of Health and_Midwifery, *it was reported that about 30,150 births were observed in Nagasaki from 1 January 1950 to 31 December 1953:*

Before the bomb was dropped the proportion of abnormal children to those born healthy was very low, but in the nine years since the bomb was dropped this proportion has changed enormously. Of 30,150 babies born, 471 were stillborn and 181 abortions. Of those born alive, 3,630 were abnormal and the abnormality was divided as follows:

- 1046 children suffered from degeneration of the bone, muscle, skin or nervous system
- 429 from deformation of organs of smell and hearing
- 254 from malformation of lip or tongue
- 59 had a cleft palate
- 243 suffered from malformation of the inner organs
- 47 from deformation of the brain
- 25 children were born without a brain
- 8 without eyes and sockets of the eyes.

In recent years hibakusha, keen to get this information out to the wider community, have sent me details of other Japanese research into this issue. For example, Mr Tajima Yatarou evaluated that there were 63,000 (Hiroshima) and 42,000 (Nagasaki) babies born to hibakusha between 1946 and 1980. He stated that there was a potential increase in the number of abnormal babies due to genetic effects of 11-16% in Hiroshima and 5-7% in Nagasaki [Tajima Yatarou, 'Genetic Effects of Radiation: The Cases of Hiroshima and Nagasaki', Nagasaki Igakukai Zasshi, *47, 1972, p. 336.]*

Professor Yoshikazu Sakamoto observed that "foetal exposure to radiation in Hiroshima and Nagasaki brought about a higher rate of congenital deformation, particularly microcephalia and mental retardation as compared with those who have not experienced such exposure." He confirmed that it was "not easy to say anything definitive on the 'second generation' on the basis of statistically reliable data, because a large number of survivors and their children have not disclosed information on their experience and they... fear that they would lose their

opportunity for employment, marriage and bearing offsprings". He suggested that "the second generation and the generations to come have to live under the constant fear that they, after the interval of decades, would suddenly be afflicted by fatal diseases." [Yoshikazu Sakamoto quoted in an article by Dr Syed Sikander Mehdi, 'No More Hiroshima, No More Nagasaki', Third World International, *Vol 9, No 4, August 1985, pp 21-22. Professor Sakamoto cites*
Hiroshima and Nagasaki: The Physical, Medical, and Social Effects of the Atomic Bombings, *by the Committee for the Compilation of Materials on Damage Caused by the Atomic Bombs in Hiroshima and Nagasaki (Tokyo, Iwanami Shoten Publishers, 1979), pp 706, and especially Chapter 9 ' After Effects and Genetic Effects,' pp 217 ff]*

Table 10.3.1 Review of sex ratio effects in the children of A-bomb survivors (*source Table 6 of TR7/81, my calculations for Chi-squared, two sided Goodness Of Fit, based on calculating expected numbers in the total births in each category if SR = 1055 (all Japan); critical value for p = 0.05 is 3.84, p = 0.01; 6.6; 0.005, 7.8)*

Father	Mother	Male birth	Female birth	SR	Sign	*Chisquare
Early period 1943 to 52						
High	High	762	787	968	Negative	2.8
NIC	High	2959	2891	1024	Negative	1.3
Low	Low	2816	2724	1034		
Low	High	582	556	1047		
Low	NIC	1736	1653	1050		
NIC	Low	7747	7115	1089	Positive	3.6
NIC	NIC	17785	16332	1089	Positive	8.3***
High	Low	884	802	1102	Positive	
High	NIC	1042	909	1146	Positive	3.3
Total		**36313**	**33769**	**1075**	**Positive**	**6.16***
Fallout period 1953-62						
High	High	521	466	1118	Positive	0.8
NIC	High	2839	2484	1143	Positive	8.2***
Low	High	653	547	1194	Positive	4.4*
High	NIC	2257	2061	1095	Positive	1.4
High	Low	1146	989	1159	Positive	4.5*
NIC	Low	7338	6711	1093	Positive	4.4*
NIC	NIC	16959	15138	1120	Positive	28****
Low	Low	2805	2415	1161	Positive	11.6***
Total		**38195**	**33897**	**1126**	**Positive**	**75.6******

So the Hiroshima study is flawed, it does not even show the accurate effects of external acute radiation. It reports no genetic effects by employing controls who were irradiated. Nevertheless, it is the yardstick for assessing the effects of internal radiation and has been since the 1950s. By the late 1950's the Strontium-90 was getting into the milk and the Medical Research Council was getting jittery because childhood cancer seemed to be increasing. They produced a paper; 'The hazards to man from nuclear and allied radiation' in which Richard Doll argued that the exposures associated with the fallout were safe (Loutit, et al 1960)

Doll by then knew of Alice Stewart's results but must have been discounting these findings. Alice's work showed a 40% increase in childhood cancer after an irradiation of about 10mSv, which in those days was considered to be a meaningless dose. But if there was a linear relationship, this did suggest that a dose of 1mSv might produce a 4% increase in childhood cancer, or even other effects which might emerge later in life. So this was a time when many were holding their breath. Bombs were being exploded all over the globe and the yields were getting bigger. British servicemen were being exposed in Australia; down winders were being exposed in Nevada; Soviets in Kazakhstan; and various members of the US military and local islanders in the South Pacific. In 1957, there was a fire at Windscale and radiation leaked all over the country. The first real evidence I was able to gather that there was a cover-up of radiation effects was the affair of the winds over Windscale.

10.4 The winds over Windscale

If you create the genie you have to control it, or it destroys you. All over the world, the indescribable energy locked into the fabric of the Universe is constrained in massive metal and concrete cubes or spheres, and is being tickled and irritated by technicians who force it to divert some small fraction of its awesome power into heating water for electricity generation, into boiling vast kettles. In the early days of the research that led to this happy state, there were some mistakes made. Things got out of hand. The first accidents were in 1957, at Kyshtym in the Soviet Union, where a waste tank evaporated, reached critical mass and exploded, and at the accident at Windscale, now Sellafield, where Wigner energy, which at that time was not understood, caused the reactor to catch fire.

On the 10th of October 1957, following a routine shutdown, the No.1 unit, an air-cooled graphite moderated reactor used for the production of Plutonium, caught fire. It burned for two days. The burning fuel elements released fission-products to the atmosphere: radioactive smoke from the fire was dispersed over England, Wales, Scotland and Ireland. Or was it? The accident has been described in detail in two government enquiry reports (CMMND 302 and 471). In addition there have been a number of studies both of the composition of the radioactivity and of its dispersion (e.g. Baverstock and Vennart 1976, Burch, 1959, Blok *et al*, 1958, Chamberlain, 1957, Chamberlain and Dunster 1958, Clarke 1974, Crabtree, 1959, Taylor, 1981, Dunster *et al.* 1958). There is reasonable agreement about what happened that led to the reactor fire, but less agreement about where the radiation went. It is this question that led me to the discovery that the area of nuclear risk is one where there are strange happenings. The Windscale fire was a very serious radiological problem and its profile was kept very low.

When I was an expert witness for Helen John who spray painted the House of Commons entrance, Tony Benn also gave evidence and referred to his experience as a Minister of the secrecy surrounding the nuclear project. He told the Court that he only learned of the fire from the Japanese Prime Minister whilst on a visit to Japan, rather than from his own civil servants; an interesting window into who it is that is running the country, and one which I have also found through my dealing with the environment minister Michael Meacher. The cross-boundary contamination was an embarrassing problem: if there were consequences for health in the UK, well this could be dealt with, as it could be seen as a domestic matter involving cost and benefit. The same was not true, however for the country that would have received the greatest potential exposure, Ireland, or for the Isle of Man, which stood squarely in the path of the radiation, if the wind had been easterly.

In 1996, I visited the Island of Alderney, 12km to the east of the La Hague reprocessing plant. I was invited by a local man, Dr David Davies, who I met in Aberystywth. David had been a medical anthropologist; his grandfather had founded the National Library of Wales but he had retired to Alderney. He noticed that all his neighbours were suddenly dying of cancer, and also that the trees on the island which faced the direction of France (and the nuclear plant) were turning brown and dying. Despite considerable obstruction by the authorities, I managed to copy out (by hand) all the death certificates from 1972 to 1994 and subsequently show that there was a sudden doubling in the cancer mortality rate after 1990. So Davies had a point. I also took samples and using gamma spectroscopy found fairly high levels of Krypton 85, a radioactive gas released by La Hague in vast quantities: hence the dying trees (Busby 1996). I was chased off the island after various interviews with the BBC who flew out to interview me about the problem, and later Davies was also squeezed off the island by the island tax authorities. Funnily enough, David has moved to the Isle of Man, 55km to the east of Sellafield, the obvious place to look for any effects of a major release like the Windscale fire.

I began corresponding with the Isle of Man authorities in 1996 and received interest and help. They sent me a complete copy of their mortality records, and statistical reviews back to 1952. In addition, the Director of Public Health, Dr P Powell authorised the Merseyside Cancer Registry (who administered the cancer statistics on the Isle of Man) to give me the cancer incidence data from 1974-93.

Hence, I was able to examine the mortality during and following the period of the Windscale fire and also have a look to see if there were any effects later on. But first we had to know whether the fire contaminated the island. This depended on the weather conditions, so I obtained the various reports and began trying to figure out what happened. What I discovered was that there seemed to be considerable confusion.

The releases from the core fire appeared to begin in the morning of the 10th October. By 1600 hrs, inspection of the core through a plug hole in the charge face showed glowing fuel cartridges. Attempts were made in the night of the 10th to reduce the temperature by blowing carbon dioxide into the core, but this didn't work so by Friday 11th they began to pump water into the core. Luckily for them, and all of us, this worked. By the afternoon of Saturday 12th the reactor was cold. Therefore the period of releases was between the morning of the 10th and midday on the 12th. Dunster (1958) reported that winds on the 10th were from the south or else were light and variable. On the 11th they shifted to the north and then to the west. This would suggest that the radiation went inland. However, he also states at one point, '(initially) one of the survey vehicles was able to get under the plume at a point approximately 1 mile downwind on the coast'. This would make the wind easterly and the plume would be blowing out to sea.

The Atomic Energy Authority press release agreed: the radiation was blowing safely out to sea (Taylor, 1981). In 1959, Crabtree, of the Royal Meteorological Society, examined the weather patterns and drew various conclusions about the plume direction. His conclusion was that at 1200 on the 10th, 'a cold front lay over central Scotland and northern Ireland with low pressure to the north, Winds were light S to SW over north west England, but a small area of low pressure lay off south west England and by 1800 on 10th this had moved to South Lancashire producing light east to north east surface winds. By the beginning of the 11th October this low pressure area had moved away and the winds had shifted to the South West. So Crabtree has the wind blowing out to sea on the 10th. His paper also gave a sequence of synoptic charts illustrating the point that, 'A cold front moved SE early on the 11th Oct passing the site at about 01 to 02 hr. Material released into the atmosphere before the passage of the cold front would be carried mainly NE by the SW wind, it would then be swept SE as the front approached.' The radioactivity was measured in various parts of England; eventually the plume reached Europe and measurements were made there also.

The 1959 picture given by Crabtree was reversed suddenly in 1973 with the publication of a paper by Roger Clarke, who was then working at Berkeley for the CEGB. Clarke pointed out that the temperatures in the pile at 2200 on 9th October were alarmingly high, so releases may have already begun as early as the evening of the 9th: certainly there was a problem by 0800 on 10th. Clarke, who became Director of the National Radiological Protection Board and then the ICRP, abruptly reversed the wind direction. Referring to earlier studies he decided that 'during the early part of the releases, the wind at ground level appears to have been from the North East, but the activity was discharged from a 400ft stack and there was an inversion layer at about this height. Above the inversion layer, the wind was apparently SWly. At about 0100 on the 11th, the wind veered NWly becoming stronger.' So who are we to believe? Was the wind blowing out to sea (and Ireland) or was it blowing inland? I have tabulated the various versions of the wind direction in Table 10.4.1, where I also add in the results of our own researches, which I shall now describe.

Table 10.4.1 The winds over Windscale according to various authorities

	Dunster 1958	**Crabtree 1959**	**Clarke 1973**	**Busby 1996***
October 10th				
0600	S			ESE 5knots
1200	Variable	S to SW	SW	SE 5knots
1800	Variable	E or NE	SW	SE 5knots
2400	SW	E or NE	SW	S 5knots
October 11th				
0600	N	NW	NW	Calm
1200	NNW	NW	NW	NW
1800	NW	NW	NW	WNW

*from Air Ministry daily synoptic chart kept at Bracknell.

Richard Bramhall and I contacted the Meteorological Office and arranged to examine the historical records at Bracknell. When we got there, we asked the archivist to see the anemometer records for the Windscale station. These were duly produced. The volume that dealt with the period was a 3 inch thick blue book about 8 inches by 14 inches into which the original record sheets were bound, The sheets themselves, made of thick blue card, were entitled, 'Form 3431 (1955), Air Ministry Meteorological Office, anemograph tabulation, hourly values. There were 14 days to a sheet giving wind direction and speed, entered in various shades of pen by different people. But to our consternation, the cards that dealt with the period August 26th 1957 to 1st December 1957 were empty. Written across each one was 'NO RECORD, MAST DISMANTLED.' We asked to see other years of data. We couldn't find any other block where there was such a gap in the data. But while putting the book away, I noticed something very curious. When looking at the side of the book, it was apparent that the cards that covered the second half of the data were all new, and of a clearly different shade of colour. And on closer examination, whereas the real records were a bit worn and dog-eared, as might be expected for a record card that is handled and written on 24 times a day for fourteen consecutive days, the card for the period of missing data, which referred to the dismantled anemometer, were pristine and shiny. Someone had gone to the trouble of removing the old cards (which no doubt gave the correct wind direction) and re-binding the volume with new and altered cards. Unfortunately they couldn't get the correct shade of card, and were not sufficiently careful to try to age them, as any good forger would.

There was one other way we could check the weather. This was to call up the huge Air Ministry plotted synoptic charts from the records. These give the wind direction from various weather stations and also the prevailing weather, barometric pressure and isobars. Since I have sailed various yachts and boats I had learned to read these things. The charts gave a reasonable picture of the weather in the early part of the Windscale releases. The key to understanding the situation was the cold front, which lay at 45 degrees from Northern Ireland to Scotland at the beginning of the fire. This front drew air from the southeast towards it as it moved across the area slowly. Rain fell heavily from the front as it moved and in the rain were the volatile radioisotopes and radioactive gases like Te-132, I-132 and I-131. I show the position of this front at the start of the fire in Fig 10.4.1 and track its progress in Table10.4.2.

The warm and contaminated wind from Windscale travelled at 5 to 10 knots in a north west direction towards the cold front where it met cold wind from the north and the resulting hard rain fell on Ireland and the Isle of Man and Scotland as the front moved slowly south east. At 5-10 knots it takes 5 to 10 hours for the radiation to reach the front at the Isle of Man. The heavy rain that fell in the night will have carried the activity from the plant to earth and irradiated the people of the Isle of Man and southern Scotland. There was some attempt to cover this up by altering the anemometer records. So what effect did this radioactivity have?

The cancer data for the Isle of Man starts in 1974 and, and I looked for effects on childhood leukaemia. The pattern of childhood leukaemia on the Isle of Man between 1974 and 1993 is unusual in that the trend with age shows higher levels in the older children. Normally the peak in childhood leukaemia is in the 0-4 year olds as I show in Table 10.4.3.

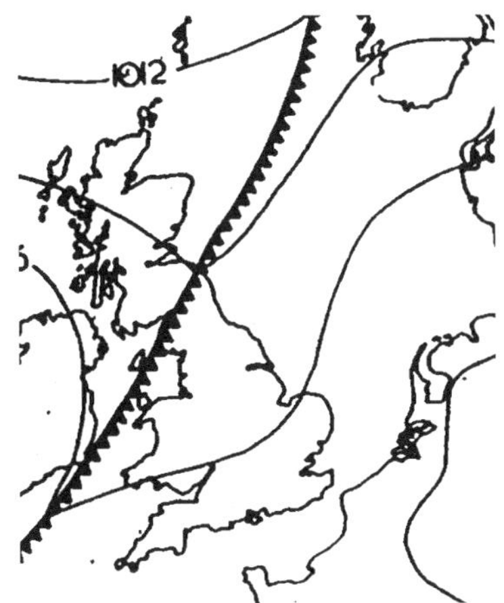

Fig 10.4.1 The cold front and isobars at the beginning of the Windscale fire.

Table 10.4.2 The progress of the front and the winds at Windscale and the Isle of Man at the time of the reactor fire in 1957. (Source: Air Ministry Charts, Bracknell).

Time	Wind scale	Rain WS	Isle of Man	Rain IOM	Notes
10th Oct					
0600	ESE 5	No	S 5		
0800	SE 5	No	S 5		
1000	SE 5	No	SE 5	Rain	
1200	SE 5	No	SE 5	Rain	Wind E in Dundalk
1400	E 5	No	E 5	No	Rain Whitehaven
1600	SE 10	No	SE 10	Rain	Winds E across area
1800	SE 10	No	N 5	Rain	Wind N in Dundalk
2000	SE 5	No	NE 5	No	
2200	Calm	No	Calm	No	Front reaches Isle of Man
2400	SW 5	No	N 5	Rain	Heavy rain in IOM for 6 hrs
11th Oct					
0200	SE 5	Light	NNW 5	Heavy	Rain Ireland to Cumbria
0400	SE 5	Light	NNW 5	Heavy	Rain North Wales to Tyne
0600	Calm	Light	NW 5	Rain	Rain Wales (Snowdonia)
0800	W 5	No	N5	No	Front lies Cornwall to Humber
1000	NW5	No	NW5	No	
1200	NW 10	No	NW 10	No	Front lies lands End to Wash
1400	NW 15	No	NW 15	No	Front is moving SouthEast: Rains in Holland/ Denmark by 2000

Table 10.4.3 Childhood leukaemia on the Isle of Man, 1974-93, with rates for England and Wales, 1991

Age group	England and Wales rates per 100,000 1991	Isle of Man, 1974-93 expected (1986 census)	Observed 1974-93	Poisson p-value
0-4	5.4	3.6	2	.9592
5-9	3.3	2.4	3	.4303
10-14	2.2	1.9	3	.2963
15-19	1.6	1.52	3	.1912
20-24	1.65	1.47	0	1
25-29	1.7	1.2	3	.1205
30-34	2.15	1.6	2	.4751
Total 0-34		13.7	16	

The numbers are small, but it is clear that the leukaemia are in the children older than 0-4, and also are higher than expected in the young adults. If this is our hypothesis we can test it my multiplying the Poisson probabilities together to get p = 0.001. Why are the leukaemias in this period concentrated in the older children?

If the contamination had caused an increase, it should be people who were children at the time of the fire or born immediately after it. We only had data from 1974-93 so, as far as this idea was concerned, this restricted us to looking at certain age groups. A child born between 1954 and 1960 would be either aged 4-5 at the time of the fire, exposed in the womb or born to parents who were exposed just before conception. These children would be in the age ranges given in Table 10.4.3 over the period of the cancer records we have. We can test the hypothesis by calculating the number of leukaemia and non-Hodgkin lymphoma cases expected over these 11-year periods, and I do this in Table 10.4.4

The result is that there is a 50% to 90% excess risk of leukaemia and non-Hodgkin lymphoma in those exposed as children, but that the result has a 20% probability of having occurred by chance. This is mainly due to the small numbers and it would be of interest to examine the fate of these children in more recent incidence statistics. In the Carlingford questionnaire analysis, carried out in 1999 (see Chapter 7), there was an excess of cancer in this cohort who lived in Ireland, and who by the time of the questionnaire were aged about 40-44 and just beginning to enter the period of life when cancer rates increase. In addition, the Irish national small area data for 1994-6 showed a significant sea coast effect in this cohort, then aged 35-39.

Patricia Sheehan, the Dundalk GP, certainly believed that Windscale had produced the effect she discovered in Ireland and reported in the Lancet in 1984.

This was the cluster of Downs's Syndrome babies born to girls who attended St Louis boarding school in Dundalk and were exposed to rain at the time of the fire. In 26 women who were schoolgirls together in 1957 they agreed that they had suffered an illness similar to influenza at the time of the fire. Among these 26 women there were 6 Downs syndrome babies. The normal rate in this age group was 1 in 600 births, so their excess Downs risk was 23-fold. Patricia went on to discover that these women, and also a very large number of other women in the whole area who were exposed to the Windscale rain were suffering from anomalously low levels of Vitamin B12. Patricia Sheehan was deeply involved in researching the effects of Windscale on north eastern Ireland. Early in 1994 she was working on a new study linking the deaths of eighteen Irish children, and birth defects in 38 others, to the Windscale fire. She died unexpectedly in a car crash near Athlone in 1994. Apparently her car ran off the road: there were no witnesses. At the time of her death she was working on information and evidence for the legal case against Sellafield *Short and Others vs BNFL.* Her work has been taken up by another Dundalk GP, Mary Grehan.

My intention here is not primarily to look at the effects of the fire, but more to show that the wind direction, which was a critical element of any claim from Ireland that their population had been affected, was reversed by Roger Clarke in a 1973 paper and that the background data was tampered with. Roger Clarke went on to become perhaps the main figure in a group supporting the assertion that low dose radiation is safe. He became head of the National Radiological Protection Board (a post he held until this year when he was followed by Roger Cox). Clarke became truly the keeper of the sacred scroll, since he was also head of the ICRP.

Table 10.4.3 period in which diagnosis of leukaemia or non-Hodgkin lymphoma is in an individual exposed to radiation from the Windscale fire born on the Isle of Man between 1954 and 1960 together with observed numbers of cases diagnosed in that period.

Age at diagnosis	**11y Period of expected diagnosis (from 1954-60)**	**Number of cases observed, L and NHL**
15-19	1969-1979	1: L75
20-24	1974-1984	2: NHL82, NHL84
25-29	1979-1989	2:L79, L82
30-34	1984-1994	2: L90,L93
Total	1974-93	7

Table 10.4.4 Observed and expected cases of leukaemia and non Hodgkin lymphoma in the Isle of Man in children and young adults exposed to radiation from the Windscale fire.

Age	Rate leukaemia and NHL	Expected in 11 years	Observed	RR (p-value)
15-19	2.2	1.15	1	0.9
20-24	2.1	1.03	2	1.9
25-29	2.6	1.07	2	1.9
30-34	3.8	1.58	2	1.3
All		4.83	7	1.5 (0.2)

The reason why no one looked too closely at the link between ill health and exposure to radioactivity is that in 1959, when such evidence began to emerge through the fog of lies and deceit, an agreement was made between the World Health Organization (WHO) and the International Atomic Energy Agency (IAEA). This document laid down the rules for examining the health effects of low dose radiation. The rules stated that radiation effects were out of bounds for the medics in the WHO; they could worry about epidemics of smallpox and malaria, they could spend fortunes examining malnutrition and AIDS, but what they could not do was to examine the radiation. This was the remit of the IAEA, the physicists. And what was the main remit of the IAEA? The development of peaceful uses of the atom: nuclear energy.

This agreement has prevented the emergence of what is probably the biggest public health cover-up and scandal of all time, the systematic genetic poisoning of the human race. It is still in force, as those who have studied the consequences of the Chernobyl accident or looked at the effects of Depleted Uranium in Iraq, will testify.

10.5 Cancer in England and Wales after Chernobyl

Among the various categories of black operations associated with the assessment of cancer risk are the data transformation scams. Some of these are subtle, some appear blatant. In the latter category is 'The Strange Case of the Standardised Incidence Ratios after Chernobyl'. I have already trailed this issue in Chapter 1, when I looked at the increases in cancer in Wales and their relationship with weapons fallout. The Standardised Incidence Ratios, or Standardised Registration Ratios as they are named by ONS, are invaluable indices of what is happening to trends in cancer rates in real terms. They are the instrument on the panel of spaceship Earth that we need to keep an eye on. SRRs are given in the annual

OPCS/ONS cancer statistics, Series MB1, blue books which have been published annually since 1974 but have now been discontinued, the data appearing instead in a shortened form on the ONS website. They were presumably intended to present the cancer data so that doctors and epidemiologists could spot any sudden increase in incidence rates and try to discover what the cause was. Or perhaps it was to evaluate trends so that local health authorities could budget ahead. After all, why collect the data if no one can see it? This is national data mainly, although rates in regions are also given. In order to evaluate real trends in cancer, each of the books used to have a table showing Standardised Registration Ratio (SRR) by year. This is the most important table and is put right up front as Table 1 in all these volumes up to the one covering 1990. Curiously, there was a big gap between the publication of the 1989 tables in 1994 and the publication of the 1990 tables in 1997. By this time the gap between the data and the publication was seven-years! In 1990 the SRR tables began being left out (as the increases are becoming embarrassing).

This is how the SRR works. The index year after 1979 is taken to be 1979 and for each following year SRRs were based on 1979=100. So if there is an increase of 10% in real terms over some period, i.e. age standardised, the SRR is 110. If the increase was 20% the SRR was 120. When based on the whole population of England and Wales an increase of even 10% is highly significant and represents about 23,000 extra cases in a year, about 15,000 of whom will die. So this is a big deal. My thesis was that there is a cancer epidemic, which began in Wales in about 1979, and began in England later, in the mid 1980s, because of the lower fallout doses. I based the latter on the OPCS SRRs, which, in 1995 when I wrote *Wings of Death,* had only been published up to 1987. But exactly when did the England increase begin? Because in 1986 there was the Chernobyl accident, and if the cancer suddenly began to appear to rise following this year, it might look as if the radiation from Chernobyl caused the rise. But relax. The blue books show that the cancer began to rise in 1985, the year before Chernobyl. Or did they? Table 10.5.1 below gives the sequence of SRRs for all malignancies as they are presented in each of the different annual reports, before and after Chernobyl.

Table 10.5.1 Mean values of the male and female SRRs for all malignancy as they appear in the Annual ONS Cancer Statistics Reports Series MB1 for the years after Chernobyl, 1986-90. The columns represent the year which the blue book covers, and the first row the year this volume appeared. The last column shows the true value calculated by me from the raw data presented in the books.

	1986	**1987**	**1988**	**1989**	**1990**	**Busby**
Published	1991	1993	1994	1994	1997	
1977	102.5				No table	***102.5***
1978	101	101			No table	***101***
1979	100	100	100		No table	***100***
1980	100	100	100	100	No table	***100***
1981	101.5	101.5	101.5	101.5	No table	***101.5***
1982	102	102	102	102	No table	***102***
1983	102	102	102	102	No table	***102***
1984	103	103	103	103	No table	***103***
1985	**100.5**	**100.5**	**109**	**109**	No table	***100.5***
1986	**102**	**102**	**108**	**108**	No table	***102***
1987		**106.5**	**113**	**113**	No table	***106.5***
1988			118	118	No table	***118***
1989				115.5	No table	***116***
Values in the following years were calculated from the raw data						
1992						***123.5***
1994						***124***
1997						***117***

This table shows that the volumes published before 1993 gave different values for the SRRs across the period of the Chernobyl accident. The value for all malignancies for 1987, the year after the Chernobyl accident is either 106.5 or 113, depending on whether we believe the 1993 or 1994 publication. The values for 1985 are either 100.5 or 109. You may say, 'what a nitpicky point!' But it is a serious question. The trend in cancer either appears to increase after Chernobyl, or according to the revisionists, before Chernobyl. Which is the true trend? Well it is a simple (though tedious) matter to do the calculations and find the truth. The answer is in the final column of the Table, and follows the SRR trend through to 1997, the latest data year. Incidentally, the sudden increase in cancer in the year after Chernobyl was well documented by Wales Cancer Registry, before they were closed down. As Bramhall's song (to the tune of the Wombles and presented in Appendix B) puts it, together with the explanation:

After Chernobyl we finally hear
All kinds of cancer went up the next year
Hard to explain it says OPCS
Can't understand it well here is a guess
Nuclear isotopes from the Ukraine
Fell to the earth with the wind and the rain
Rainfall is higher in Bangor than Kent
Cancer in Wales is up 30 per cent.

The effect in time of a sudden injection of radiation like the Chernobyl rain in Wales is now a well kept secret. I spoke recently with a biodosimetry researcher with the IAEA who told me that, in terms of the Chernobyl accident, the effects in the affected territories mirror the effects in time trend of low dose radiation on cells to give chromosome aberrations, one of the end points of biodosimetry. That is, there is a sudden decrease in effect, followed by a large increase and then a fall-back to the zero effect line (and see this in Plate 12). This is followed considerably later by a slow rise in effect due to genomic instability. The effect is seen in the cancer rates in the Chernobyl affected territories but is suppressed by the IAEA and UNSCEAR and also by the authorities in the countries most affected, as I know from my dealings with these people. The proceedings of the IAEA Chernobyl meeting in Vienna in 1996 have not been made public even now. This is because that meeting was inundated by contributions from the floor giving reports of increases in cancer and other illnesses. There was an alternative meeting in Vienna at the same time, organised by the IPPNW, the Permanent Peoples Tribunal, which reports many of these findings (IPB 1996).

The Chernobyl rain, the black rain, fell in Wales. I know: I was rained on. My dog died of cancer shortly afterwards. The rates dipped then increased alarmingly, then fell back to the baseline and are now increasing again. The new cancer registry have airbrushed much of this, as I will explain in the next chapter, but the trend is the same as the chromosome aberration trend and the Eastern Europe trend described by my IAEA friend. The IAEA, of course, know all this, but will not publish it or concede it publicly. Of course, the authorities in Wales said that the lag was too quick, and so it couldn't be the effect of Chernobyl.
However, for now, I merely want to point out that the figures in the official annual database have been changed to show that the increases were before, and not after Chernobyl. For those who, like Thomas, need proof, I put the calculation for 1986 in Table 10.5.2.

Let's be clear about this. What it looks like is an attempt by someone to imply that the cancer increase (which no one now seems to deny) didn't follow Chernobyl but already began before it. We are looking for a sudden increase. Let us forget the aging population (which is happening slowly and not suddenly in

1986) and examine the rates. I have plotted the rates for all malignancies by year from 1981 to 1997, taken from the Series MB1s in Fig 10.5.1

So there we have it. A 20% increase in rates. In case you think there was a sudden change in the population size that accounts for this increase, then think again. The numbers for the critical years are plotted in Fig.10.5.1. *After Chernobyl we finally hear, all kinds of cancer went up the next year*. Not the year before.

Who was in charge of producing the post 1987 ONS volumes? In the 1986 volume, published in 1991, enquiries were referred to the Cancer Registration Section of OPCS. In the 1987 volume, held back until 1993 (there is a little sticker), we hear of a new body, The National Cancer Registration Bureau, OPCS. The Director of this bunch is a certain Dr Mike Quinn. If you are confused, write and ask him what is up. I'm sure there will be an explanation: there always is. Quinn is a big cheese in cancer statistics and will appear in this work later on, also in connection with Bradwell and in connection with rules of confidentiality in releasing cancer data.

Table 10.5. 2 Expected and observed numbers of all cancers for 1986. Populations (thousands) from the 1986 data, Ser.MB1 No 19 Appendix A. Rates for 1979 from Ser MB1 No11.

	Males	**1979 rate**	**Expected**	**Females**	**1979 rate**	**expected**
0-4	1632.2	.000144	235	1551.0	.000129	200
5-9	1553.3	.000108	166	1471.3	.000061	90
10-14	1651.9	.000096	159	1565.6	.000082	128
15-19	2004.5	.000149	299	1906.7	.000121	231
20-24	2130.4	.000193	411	2072.2	.000176	364
25-29	1877.0	.000275	516	1847.0	.00035	646
30-34	1683.0	.000432	727	1658.3	.000746	1237
35-39	1851.2	.000682	1263	1848.7	.001214	2244
40-44	1593.2	.001115	1776	1570.1	.002036	3196
45-49	1394.2	.001962	2735	1382.0	.003213	4440
50-54	1334.0	.003846	5130	1332.7	.004344	5789
55-59	1328.9	.006643	8827	1374.0	.005855	8045
60-64	1299.4	.010855	13845	1415.1	.007595	10748
65-69	1071.5	.015397	16498	1279.3	.00933	11936
70-74	897.2	.021462	19255	1210.1	.011219	13576
75-79	625.9	.027416	17160	1014.0	.013567	13757
80-84	325.9	.03066	9992	688.6	.015765	10856
85+	150.0	.03245	4865	489.0	.018724	9156
All ages			103863			96641
Observed			103495			102309
SRR			**99.5**			**105.8**
Mean SRR for males and females combined = 102.7						

Note: The 1986 Ser MB1 No 19 gave the SRRs as 99 for Males and for 105 Females in substantial agreement with the above calculation.

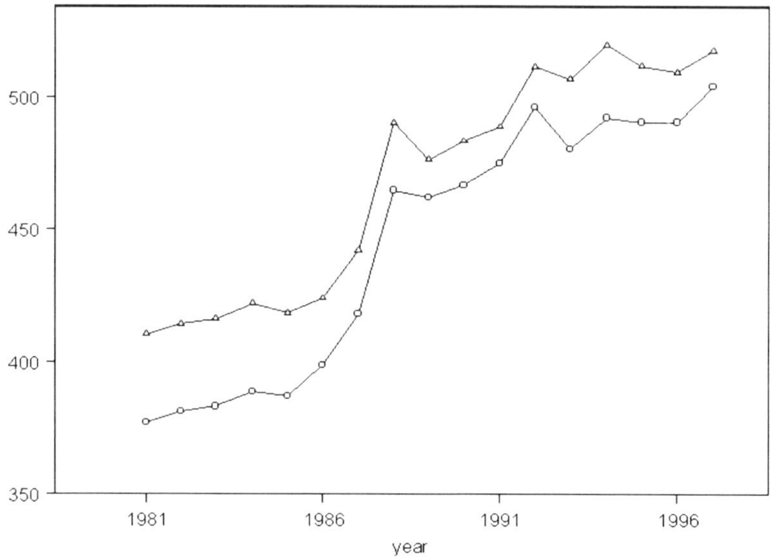

Fig 10.5.1 The effect of Chernobyl. Rates per 100,000 men (triangles) and women (circles) for all malignancies in England and Wales 1981-97 (Source: OPCS/ONS Ser MB1 Cancer Statistics Registration)

The trends I have shown here are plotted directly from the annual blue books, the Series MB1s. There is a kind of compilation of data, produced by Quinn *et al* in 2001, which shows graphs that bear little similarity to the data I have used (Cancer trends in England and Wales, 1951-1999), any more than the strange narrative that accompanies the lovely coloured graphs. But I leave it to you to make up your mind. But a word of caution: I have looked earlier at the idea that in cancer there is a lag between exposure to the carcinogen and expression of the disease. But this is not the whole story, since there will always be people who already have all but one of the genetic errors and only need the last number on the Bingo Card. This is why there is a sharp rise in cancer after Chernobyl.

11
The Nuclear Mafia

Bryn Bridges: The childhood leukaemia clusters we have in this country are around sites where reprocessing is carried out, Sellafield and Dounreay. What is common about these? Well, yes, there are various radiation and radioactivity things going on, but they are both in isolated rural areas, they are both subject to this other phenomenon of population mixing.
Reporter: Surely the population mixing has been going on for fifty years. Should it still be showing itself as a higher incidence of these illnesses?
Bryn Bridges: Our view is that it is surprising if it does. Yes, I think the population mixing can account for the Dounreay cluster, but it seems strange that it should go on for 40 years around Seascale.

Bryn Bridges, Chair of COMARE; BBC Radio 4, June 1998

11.1 ICRP, NRPB, COMARE and SAHSU

This chapter is about what my friend the late anti-nuclear activist and French ex-MEP Solange Fernex (and other anti-nuclear activists) calls 'the nuclear mafia'. To follow the arguments we now need a little more background. John Gofman once said, 'The nuclear industry is conducting a war against the human race'. For many the centrepiece and metaphor for this war has become Sellafield. The war is fought with words and research studies, with ideas and beliefs. I was asked some time ago to speak on this issue by some artists and film people in a London Art Gallery. These were the art intellectuals; the men had shaved heads and earrings, the women, cool little black skirts or black velvet trousers. The lights were low and everyone was Foucault, Barthes or Beaudrillard. Everything was up for grabs, concepts, beliefs, facts, nothing was allowed to be real. I was asked at one point if the nuclear industry was 'evil'. Great question! But I didn't have to answer it: the best reply came from one of the café philosophers. Evil, he said, is control. Good, he continued, is freedom; is chaos. Well, think about it: do you agree? I believe that if there is a straight choice, perhaps I do. I believe that this is just the point, the crossing of the two straight lines, the nexus. This point will certainly separate people in a dinner party. Chaos does not have to be bad, but for some, it is now axiomatically bad. They can't deal with it. Yet life is apparently chaotic, or more important, it seems chaotic to the physicists who seem to need order and equations. Look inside a rat or a duckling- go on, open it up with a knife and see if you can find any straight lines. Their system (the rat, the duckling) seems to work well when alive, despite the chaos and coloured liquids. It certainly doesn't look like a machine, anyway.

Primitive peoples impress order on their chaos through spiritual connections with their landscape and its events. If a tree falls on you, it is because you haven't propitiated the correct demon. Levy Bruhl the anthropologist found only two types of thinking, primitive and Western intellectual. But the West is not immune. We live in a Christian country. But look here: Jesus died on the cross to save us from our sins, even the sins of my daughter aged 9! And the sins of the children at Seascale who are dying of leukaemia, their sins also. Perhaps you believe this. Do you also think the Azande are primitive? Read Jung.

There is a passage in the latest book about the 'Science Wars' by Bruno Latour (1999). Latour is upset because some scientist has had a go at him about whether he believes that all science is cultural. 'Do you believe in reality?' asks the scientist. Latour points out (and I agree) that the problem is to do with the fear of rule by the mob and began with the Greeks. If there is no objectivity, then we cannot know anything. Then no one is right and anything is possible. We surrender to the chaos of the mob. Of course the Greeks actually had a very well-defined mob. Socrates invites Callicrates to agree: A single clever person is almost always bound to be superior to ten thousand fools; political power should be his and they should be his subjects. This was an ironic statement about power made in a discourse with a fascist, but as Latour argues, Socrates has his own version of this argument and espouses in his case, 'the power of reason, the force that rules over gods and men'. I leave Latour to his conclusions, which I hope you will examine (Latour 1999). Perhaps, the scientists are those who are fearful if they cannot control and understand. This idea (of objective rationalist logic based on mathematics) rode to the rescue of the toffs who were besieged following the Victorian overthrow of God. The scientists define objectivity through numbers. Spray painted on the walls of the bridge: 'The reductionists rule OK'. But the pinnacle and zenith of reductionist science is the nuclear physicist. In this chapter, I shall lay out the ultimate piece of reductionism. This is the calculation that lies behind the position that the radiation from Sellafield could not have caused the child leukaemia. It took me a long time to figure out this nonsense, mainly because I could not believe that anyone would swallow such a ludicrous calculation; I assumed there must be something clever behind it. But there is nothing behind it. It is the booming idiocy of the Wizards of Oz.

But first, who are these Wizards of Oz? Those scientists who have been engaged in this war for the truth about radiation and health refer, like Solange, to the system as the Mafia. This Mafia is made up of the networks and organisations that control the risk model. They begin with the International Commission on Radiological Protection (ICRP), but include the original US parent company, as it were, the National Council on Radiation Protection (NCRP). They include the United Nations Scientific Committee on the Effects of Atomic Radiation, (UNSCEAR) and the Biological Effects of Ionizing Radiation subcommittee of the US National Academy of Sciences, (BEIR). There is then also the International

Atomic Energy Agency (IAEA), a United Nations affiliated organisation. There is the EURATOM treaty group of scientists, the shadowy 'Article 31 Group' who advise the European Union. In the countries of the world there are then the national radiation risk advisory bodies, like the National Radiological Protection Board (NRPB) in the UK. On occasion, when the system strains credulity, reserves are called in, like the recent Royal Society committee on Depleted Uranium who Seventh Cavalried along to argue that there was no case to answer. Very often, although the committees have different names, the same people run the show. ICRP is a British-based operation: its head was the head of NRPB, Roger Clarke. Now that he has retired from NRPB, the new Director, Roger Cox, is also on the ICRP. The Chair of CERRIE, Prof. Dudley Goodhead is ex-COMARE and also sat on the Royal Society Depleted Uranium Committee, mainly responsible for the substance of its report. Goodhead retired last year but ran the Medical Research Council radiation research at Harwell, where the Atomic Energy Research Establishment is. Next door (walking distance) is NRPB, at Chilton. The address, 'Chilton', is just to advertise that there is no connection with Harwell where the nukes did all their research, but actually it is the same place. If this isn't bad enough, the independent COMARE also operate out of the NRPB building and their secretariat is run by NRPB. It is a joke. When my friend Kit Lisle wrote to the Department of Health about low-level radiation he got a letter from Roy Hamlet, signing himself as Department of Health, Radiation Protection. Hamlet states in his letter that he, as DoH, gets advice from the 'independent' COMARE. Well, he doesn't have far to walk, as he is their secretary. The Chair of COMARE, Bryn Bridges (ex-Atomic Energy Research Establishment, Wantage) is also one of the three-man Medical Research Council committee on the health effects of Depleted Uranium. They recently found that there is no need for any further (further??) research on the health effects as the Royal Society found there were none. The other two members of this coven are (again) Dudley Goodhead and Prof David Coggon of the MRC epidemiology unit at Southampton. Coggon is famous for having written in the British Medical Journal in 1994 that there was no epidemic of cancer. When I accosted him with this howler recently, he was clearly embarrassed but tried to maintain that this was still the case. Coggon took over from Martin Gardner, the epidemiologist who confirmed the Sellafield leukaemia cluster and found it was associated with parents who worked for the nuclear site. Gardner died suddenly of cancer at the age of 50. Coggon shut down the research. He is now a favourite of the establishment for Chairing committees on ill health and pollution, e.g. the Advisory Committee on Pesticides (ACP) and the Depleted Uranium committee of the Ministry of Defence (DUOB). Goodhead got an OBE recently and so did Coggon and so did Bridges. I hope it makes them happy. These three will turn up at times through this book. My point in introducing them is to begin to show that, actually, there do not need to be so many operators to keep the system going: Just a few people in the right place. Nor am I saying they are anything but perfect gentlemen, who believe what it is they say. It is merely that when someone talks about the science of radiation risk, what is there in practice is actually the beliefs and activities of rather a few individuals.

Remember, also, that in the nuclear war nations, the US, UK, France, Israel, USSR and China, behind all of these front men are the secret services, the military psychological operations battalions and, ultimately, James Bond 007. Remember when the French bombed the Greenpeace ship when it was involved in opposition to nuclear tests? Fernando Pereira was killed. They control a huge and powerful lobbying operation and use it (but not, as it turns out, very cleverly).

But we are more interested in the front end, the visible. The UK is in the interesting, novel (and arguably inefficient) position of having several different bodies who are all apparently looking at and advising on the same thing. The way this has come about is a pointer to the status and credibility of radiation risk advice in general. In the UK, if you want to know whether some low dose radiation exposure is safe, the first port of call (if you know no better) is NRPB. They will almost always tell you that it is safe. But if you don't believe them (and no one does) you may turn to another equally unbelievable committee, funded by the Department of Health, the Committee on Medical Aspects of Radiation in the Environment, COMARE (appropriately, *Godmother* in Italian). If their response also seems hard to swallow, you could then turn to CERRIE, the Committee Examining Radiation Risk from Internal Emitters (which I sat on). There seem to be an endless spawning of committees. As each one shows itself to be laughably wrong, another one has to be set up. CERRIE may be the end of the line in this regard as it was an experiment in the idea of oppositional committees (see later).

The reason why the UK has suffered such a runaway process of committee production began with the child leukaemia cluster at Seascale near Sellafield, and the rapid further discovery of other similar child leukaemia clusters near nuclear sites. NRPB responded to the initial discovery with various blusters, encapsulated in a 298-page report NRPB R171 (1984) but Sir Douglas Black, who Chaired the enquiry in 1984, was clearly unconvinced. He clearly could not believe that leukaemia in children living near the largest source of radiation in Europe was not a causal process when the only known cause of leukaemia was radiation. He wisely recommended that a proper epidemiological study be carried out. It was, and Martin Gardner confirmed the cluster and found the association with parental preconception radiation. He then asked for a new independent committee to examine NRPB's thesis that radiation was not the cause. In addition, because the cluster had been turned up by Yorkshire TV and not the local public health department, he asked for a new body to be founded to examine small area health statistics. The first of these became COMARE, the second SAHSU.

11.2 COMARE's Sellafield calculations

The initial NRPB report on the leukaemia at Seascale, R-171, which was produced in July 1984, set the stage for all the denials that followed. The methodology was based on the calculation of doses *apparently* using the ICRP system of averaging. The idea was to show that the doses were too low to cause the leukaemia on the basis of the Hiroshima risk factors. When Jakeman's new information became available that the contamination at Seascale was much greater than had been incorporated into R-171 and that the plant had been covering up the releases, a new calculation was made in 1986 and released as R-171 addendum. The new report stated:

For the leukaemia to be attributed to the operations at the Sellafield plant, the calculated (Hiroshima) average risk would have to be increased about 250 times.

Black, making the obvious application of Occams Razor asked for a new committee to review this position. COMARE was established in 1985. The pressure was on. In principle NRPB now had someone looking over their shoulder. By 1995 NRPB had produced a new set of calculations of absorbed doses, R-276. They abandoned the absolute calculation of risk. The new approach was to compare natural and man-made exposures. Note that in this context, 'natural' meant Uranium. And the Uranium concentrations on the sea coast near Sellafield were very high indeed and by no means natural. NRPB now conceded a connection with COMARE:

Close liaison was maintained with COMARE. . . the general approach and data were endorsed by COMARE.

Their conclusion was effectively unchanged. In addition, the calculation showed that 'natural radiation' (i.e. mostly Uranium and decay products) contributes more than 80% of the dose.

It is not then surprising to discover that the COMARE report on the issue, which came out one year later, depended on the calculations made by NRPB in R-276. COMARE IV, 1996 concluded that NRPB were correct in their analysis. Surprise, surprise! Among the 14 members of the committee responsible for this report were Professors Bryn Bridges, Ray Cartwright, Sarah Darby, Gerald Draper, Dudley Goodhead and Jolyon Hendry. Many of these actors have already made appearances here or will do so later on.

What I am concerned with here now is mainly the dose calculation. Because, in the late 1980s, sea-to land transfer of Plutonium (and Uranium) had become a proven fact, and it was known by the autopsy studies that these microscopic hot particles ended up in the tracheobronchial lymph nodes, the NRPB/COMARE arguments had to deal with doses to these organs. The trouble is that these organs are very small, a few grams. That is to say they have low mass, and in the dose formulation of Dose = Energy divided by Mass; a small mass

means a large dose. So what did they do? On p76 of COMARE IV the committee acknowledges:
Both the Black committee and COMARE had looked at dose to the tracheobronchial lymph nodes as it was known that these could be the site of origin of leukaemia and lymphoma in laboratory animals, and they are sites which could be exposed to inhaled radionuclides.
COMARE apparently asked NRPB for the calculation, the results of which are also given on p 76. They show the dose to the TBN of a 1-year infant, integrated to 25 years. In the worst year this dose came to seven times that from Natural Background. There are some immediate problems with this calculation. The first is that an infant is a strange choice since the parameters for infants are very different from those aged 2 to 25 years. Infants breath through their noses, are very small and live indoors. Older children are mouth breathers, stay outdoors more and have larger lungs. There is another problem, which arises out of comparing natural and man-made doses and that is the Uranium point I made earlier. Uranium levels in the atmosphere at Sellafield are very high, owing to the fact that Uranium is the main source material for the entire Sellafield operation and huge amounts of it being tipped into the sea. Although Uranium is natural, Uranium near Sellafield is not. So the real doses, even using NRPB averaging are the highest found in any organ. The calculation results are in COMARE IV and the conclusion of that report is based on these doses, but the calculation is not a document that is available. So I wrote to Bryn Bridges, the Chair, asking how COMARE did the calculation. He wrote back that COMARE did no calculation. The calculations are in NRPB's R-276. But no, they are not, I replied. Bridges apologised, I was misinformed (by Hamlet). They are in a report by JR Simmonds, 'NRPB 95/40'.
'Can we have a copy?'
'No you can't!' was the reply, 'it is a private report of the NRPB'.

So the denial of the causality in radiation of the Seascale leukaemia is now based on an unpublished report which is internal to NRPB and cannot be checked according to the Chair of the 'independent' committee set up to examine the issue. I wrote to Frances Fry of NRPB: 'Can I see this report?'
'No! The report is not available, it hasn't been internally reviewed.'
'Good, put that in writing and sign it please and I'll go to the media with it.'
The report appeared the next day. It consisted of one page, containing the message that the doses had been calculated. No details whatever. The covering letter stated that the results should not be cited because the calculation had not been checked.
Can you believe this? The big fat COMARE IV report, all 180 pages, Price £15, massively 'Press Released' and bruited as the last word on the possibility of a radiation link between the child leukaemia and the radioactivity depended in its conclusions on an NRPB calculation, which was (a) confidential and (b) had not been checked. Why were there no details of the calculation? What was there to hide? For the answer we must recall the size of the tracheobronchial lymph nodes.

A clue is to be found in NRPB R276. In that, the doses to the lymphatic system (where they admit lymphoma and leukaemia may originate) are to be calculated, according to NRPB, by dividing the energy from the inhaled and trapped radioactive particles into the lymphatic system which they modelled (p86) (and note this) as:

. . . the thoracic and extra thoracic lymph nodes, the liver, spleen, kidneys, pancreas, uterus, thymus, thyroid, stomach, small intestine, upper large intestine, colon, red bone marrow, and cells on bone surfaces.

This is a curious description of the lymphatic system, one not to be found in any textbook of physiology. It is only in the deranged consciousness of NRPB that such a description can emerge and, as far as they are concerned, for good reasons. They must have panicked when they realised the magnitude of the true dose to the TBNs and invented Seascale Man, *Homo Radioactivus Obliterans*. According to ICRP Standard Man, (ICRP23, 1975) this bag of guts and assorted organs in an adult comes to about 11kg. On the other hand, the tracheobronchial lymph nodes in an adult are about 10g each according to George Ham of NRPB who helped with the Popplewell autopsies and whom I spoke with. So if I am right, the doses to the TBNs calculated by NRPB in the secret report should be increased in the ratio 20g to 11kg i.e. 550 times. Wait on! Isn't this approximately the error factor needed to explain the leukaemia?

This TBN calculation, first mobilised for the Seascale children issue, has now become utilised to deny the lymphomas in the Gulf War and Kosovo veterans exposed to Depleted Uranium and suffering excess of lymphoma. When I return to this issue later, I will do the calculations and show the difference in the doses. In the case of the Seascale children, NRPB should, at minimum, have used the masses in ICRP Reference Man. They had no business modelling the lymph nodes as an enormous bucket full of organs and can only have done so to reduce the doses. COMARE (assuming they were not in on the scam) should have examined the study and questioned its parameters.

If the radiation didn't cause the leukaemia, the favourite alternative theory is that they were caused by population mixing and an unknown virus. This is the famous Kinlen Hypothesis. It was actually originally a suggestion by Richard Doll, an explanation for the observation that child leukaemia cases had a tendency to cluster in space and also in time but Leo Kinlen set out to investigate new towns and various other places where population mixing might occur and has found modest increases in child leukaemia in such places. I address this in *Wings of Death* and the various alternative explanations for Kinlen's discoveries. However I recently found (from J.Clemmesen in Copenhagen) that adult leukaemia also occurs in clusters, so the idea of children's developing lymphatic system being particularly susceptible to a novel leukaemogenic virus is a red herring. By now, you will be well aware of our explanation, that it is radioactive dust in the lymphatic system. This idea explains the coastal leukaemia, the nuclear site leukaemia, the Aldermaston leukaemia, the new towns and also farmers and builders who also suffer higher levels of leukaemia. But Doll still banged his drum. In 1999 he was saying, in a forward to a paper in the British Journal of Cancer (Dickinson et al, 1999): *the time may now have come when Kinlens's hypothesis. . . can be regarded as established.*

Both Sir Richard Doll and Alice Stewart died recently, during the period I was writing this book. So I suppose I should be kind about Doll and not speak ill of the dead etc. But Doll, who I have crossed swords with several times in public, was a very important figure in this argument about radiation and towards the end of his life continued to argue vehemently that the child leukaemia at Sellafield were not caused by radiation. He had to do this. The alternative, accepting that he was wrong, would have taken him back to a decision made in 1959, when he advised the Medical Research Council about weapons fallout effects regarding Strontium-90 in milk. His whole career in the radiation risk debate subsequent to that fatal error was aimed at justifying it. This is why he must have (perhaps unconsciously) biased his scientific studies and those he was associated with (of the Nordic leukaemia, of the atomic test veterans) to conclusions which supported his original thesis. Otherwise, he would have to concede that he had given the wrong advice, and countless millions would have died because of this. The error he made was easy to understand, and not one which he was knowledgeable enough to detect. Doll was a medic, remember, in his initial training. His work on the radiation treatments for ankylosing spondylitis and subsequent cancer assumed that there was such a thing as 'dose' and this is the unit you measured radiation in. The basis of 'dose' was physics, and Doll was not a physicist. And he must have assumed the physicists who measured 'dose' knew what they were talking about. So maybe we should forgive him. I talked with Alice Stewart about Doll. He was very hard on her. Read about it in the Gayle Green book. Well, they are both gone now.

12
Cover-up in Wales

A major exercise to validate this data [on childhood cancer in Wales] is being carried out . . . it is intended that this exercise will explore why the rates reported for Wales in this publication are higher than those in regional registries in the UK.
Cancer Registration in Wales 1984-88 (1994, Cardiff: Welsh Office)

12.1 A long and complicated story begins

Nowhere is the story of the cover up of the relationship between illness and radiation more obvious than in the story of the Wales Cancer Registry and its leaked data.

Wales is important as a study area. There are two reasons why Wales is an interesting laboratory for examining the effects of radioactive pollution and health. It rains more than in England and so there was more exposure to global weapons fallout in the 1960s and then again exposure to Chernobyl fallout in 1986. In addition, its coastline is situated on the Irish Sea, which is contaminated with fine radioactive Plutonium-bearing silt from Sellafield, and is West-facing, into the prevailing winds. There are two nuclear power stations in Wales, and one of these - Trawsfynydd- is the only inland nuclear power station in the UK. But it is the pollution from fallout and Sellafield that is by far the greatest component of exposure. Much of my early study was of the overall time trend effects of the weapons fallout. It was later on, after 1995, that I was able to look more closely at the effects in terms of area, and this was made possible by the acquisition of the Wales Cancer Registry small area datafiles. These were crucial to our understanding of the situation, but they were also crucial to those who wished to cover up radiation effects. In this chapter I will tell the story of how the release of these files, and what they showed, was dealt with by the various organisations whose job it is to protect the public but whose real agenda seems to be to airbrush any evidence that we are all being systematically poisoned. It is a long and complicated story, but I need to put at least the main points down, because it is a major feature of my long chess game with the nuclear establishment and their supporters.

The story began in 1994 with the publication, in Wales, of *Cancer Registration in Wales, 1984-88* by the Welsh Office. This was a regular publication by Wales Cancer Registry (WCR) a division within the Welsh Office responsible for obtaining, collating and ordering cancer data as one of the UK regional cancer registries. Two earlier publications in this series covered the period through for 1974 to 1984 and 1984-86. I was studying these in connection with the work I had been doing on the 4.5-fold excess of bone and other cancer in Wales, which I believed was caused by the weapons fallout (Busby 1995 BMJ). The 1994 publication showed a sharp increase in cancer in Wales after Chernobyl, but it also drew attention to high levels of childhood cancer. These high levels, it said, were being examined and validated by the Childhood Cancer Research Group in Oxford. This outfit is the operation of Dr Gerald Draper, who has made himself the foremost expert on childhood cancer in the UK. Draper originally joined Alice Stewart's research group in the 60s when she was obtaining the childhood cancer data, which became the Oxford Survey of Childhood Cancers, but moved off to set up his own operation (the CCRG) with mysterious amounts of government funding. Alice told me a few years ago that she did not trust him and thought that his agenda was suspicious. After all, she asked, why did the money for this research not come to her, since she had started the whole thing off?

In 1995, the arguments about bone cancer in Wales (see Wings of Death) had resulted in pressure to meet with WCR to ask what was going on. I had a letter about cancer in Wales published in the British Medical Journal [Busby, 1995BMJ]. The Director of WCR, Mary Cotter, had replied to this, also in the BMJ [Cotter, 1995]. Apparently, a WCR bone cancer revalidation had shown that the excess we were arguing was caused by Strontium-90 was a mistake. However, I had made a presentation to the Welsh County Councillors in Bangor, and they exerted pressure for us to have a meeting with the Medical Officer of Health for Wales, Dr Deidre Hine and the Cancer Registry directors, Mary Cotter (Medical) and Reg Fitzpatrick (Statistical). This meeting went ahead, with Richard Bramhall, myself and Stuart Kemp of the Nuclear Free Local Authorities (NFLA). At this meeting we asked several searching questions about how the bone cancer revalidations had been carried out. We received no reply, but instead a prepared lecture on the work of the cancer registries. I interrupted this and asked if we could have the data down to small areas, as, if I were correct about the fallout, the cases would be in the wet areas. No, we couldn't have the data to small areas, said Mary Cotter. 'Why not?' I asked. 'Because it would enable you to identify individuals', she replied. 'But how could I identify an individual if I knew that there were five cancers in a population of 1200 people in an area near Bangor? Why should I wish to?' This argument is now a common one. There was one other conversation we had, which is worth recording. While we were talking about validation of the bone cancer figures, she told me how careful they were to ensure accuracy. The childhood cancer excess reported by WCR in their 1994 report had been extensively revalidated, she said, by Gerald Draper of CCRG. The figures were accurate: the excess was real.

Regarding the small area data Deidre Hine, the Medical Officer for Wales was quite supportive, 'Can you not give data to a small area which is larger than one in which people can be identified?' Eventually, it was agreed that WCR would give us data to the County District level, for all the different cancers by 5-year age group and sex and year from 1974 to 1989, the latest year that they had processed. County Districts are quite large areas, and so this wasn't going to help us much. To our surprise, shortly after this, there appeared in the mail a floppy disc from WCR. The files on it were compressed and when I tried to open them, there was not enough space on the PC that I then had, and it locked up. I described the data and how we acquired it and used it in Chapter 5 where I reported the results of the analysis but I will briefly repeat the story here as it is relevant to the political implications, the cover-up and the arguments, which is the aspect I turn to here..

The data in A2218EXE was for the sixteen years 1974 to 1989. There were numbers of cases for all the ICD9 cancer sites, by sex, 5-year age group, 194 small areas annually from 1974 to 1989. In principle this gave 50 x 2 x 14 x 194 x 16 = 4,345,600 cells, over 4 million numbers to deal with in one file. No wonder smoke came out of the computer. Buried in all these numbers was the answer to what we were looking for. In 1996 I decided to see if I could obtain a more user-friendly version, split down by counties. I contacted the Welsh Office in May 1996, shortly after we (the Low Level Radiation Campaign) had organised a symposium at the Houses of Parliament on radiation effects. What's happening about cancer data? I was put through to Heather McGrane, of the statistical division, who explained that they were gathering the data whilst it was decided what to do about a new cancer registry. She agreed to let me have a new file, extracted differently county by county and to let me have the extra year 1990. This file duly arrived in June. It was titled A2883EXE and was extracted by Hugh Warren on 12th June. By 1996 Richard Bramhall, Molly Scott Cato and I had set up the Low Level Radiation Campaign and obtained some financial support from the Goldsmith Foundation, but we were not able to examine the files properly until 1997.

12.2 Ireland pays to study the data.

In 1996 I had been invited by Fergus O'Dowd (related to ‘Boy George’), the Mayor of Drogheda, on the east coast of Ireland to give a presentation on low level radiation. I took Molly and my daughter Rosa, then aged 2. There was a great deal of argument and energy about Sellafield; the locals were greatly exercised about the imposition of radioactivity on the coast and in the fish and shellfish. The Radiological Protection Institute of Ireland sent their director Tom O'Flaherty to make soothing noises. BNFL sent Richard Wakeford to attack me (which he did with great gusto but little science). The high spot was when the Minister Avril Doyle said that she would support research into whether there were any effects. Unfortunately, Ireland had no national cancer registry so figures were unavailable. I was standing with Grattan Healy, who was a researcher for the Green Party MEPs Nuala Aherne and Patricia McKenna. Both had made a major platform of their election the existence of Sellafield as a threat to the Irish constituencies they represented. Grattan said, 'Why don't you ask her if she'll fund studying your Welsh Data? So I jumped up and put the question in front of all the assembled and angry people. She agreed to look into it. Later when I talked with her she picked up Rosa (as politicians do) and had chocolate smeared all over her face and nice suit. She seemed a nice person, and took it very well. Later I received a letter from Emmett Stagg, her colleague and the Minister for Energy. I wrote an outline of a protocol for a collaborative study. He passed this to his civil servants, who were negative and dismissive. What did emerge was that there had indeed been one study of childhood leukaemia in eastern Ireland, conducted by researchers from University College Dublin. This had been carried out by the Irish Department of Health in 1986. It showed the existence of an excess leukaemia mortality risk in the 0-14 year old children in a coastal strip 3 miles wide on the east coast and south coast for the period 1971-86. Although this was a statistically significant finding, the committee who published the report were not alarmed. They did, however, suggest the founding of a national cancer registry, and also that an *epidemiological programme enquiring into incidence, trends and causation of cancer* be undertaken. Nothing had been done to follow up this work, and Emmet Stagg resigned shortly after this exchange. But in the autumn of 1997, the litigants in a court case against BNFL, four individuals from County Louth named Mark Deary, Constance Short, Mary Kavanagh (Plate 15) and Ollan Herr (Plate 33) managed to obtain a High Court ruling in Dublin that they could take BNFL to court law for polluting the coast of Ireland. The State agreed to fund the research needed for this case and I was approached to see if I would look at the Welsh data. This was the breakthrough that was needed. By the end of 1997 I had obtained a new PC and software able to cope with the file conversions. We set to work, in January 1998, to look at the data.

In the event, the State did not pay for the study until long after we had been working on it. The initial work was all done on the cheap, although we were later able to pay for the results to be checked independently. There were very few mistakes. The first cheque, for part of the work, appeared in June 1999, 18 months after we began. I was helped initially by a succession of recent graduates who I employed to attack various aspects of the case. Because there was no money from Ireland, I had to pay them with promises and handouts. As I mentioned earlier, one of them, Bruce Kocjian (Plate 23), who was a mapping expert, worked at the PC in the attic room where we lived whilst the builders were removing the window. He sat in front of the PC for three weeks in freezing weather, in a sleeping bag, typing in gloves with the fingers cut out. It was like a scene from Chekov or Dickens. For a while, he slept in a tent in the woods; this was winter. Luckily he was Scottish and inured to cold. Alasdair Stocking, who sorted the data worked in the local Internet café, and did the work between serving cups of coffee. Mapping was done by Helen Rowe and Evelyn Mannion. The small Areas of Residence were coloured with coloured pencils on photocopied enlarged maps pasted together like a giant jigsaw on card. I still have them. They look quite beautiful. There was no question of digitised maps or GIS in those days (too expensive), although we eventually moved to more advanced technology (thanks to ebay). I have always been cynical about such technology anyway. Very often it is such super art that obscured the findings, or else is used to show results that are very weak or non-existent.

12.3 First meeting with the new Wales Cancer Intelligence and Surveillance Unit WCISU.

At the beginning of this study the first problem was the identification of the exact boundaries of each of the small Areas of Residence (AORs). I list some of these in Table 12.3.1, together with the wards that make them up and their 1981 census populations. This was the first problem we came up against. No one in the Welsh Office knew what these AORs were all about, or had heard of them or their designations. They seemed to be something that Wales Cancer Registry had used, and a hangover from their early period of operation in the 1980s. I contacted the new cancer registry, WCISU. 'What are the geographical and ward boundaries of the AORs?' I asked. I spoke with Helen Beer, a researcher there who apparently was looking at exactly the same thing, since WCISU had the same problem of dealing with the WCR data. 'We don't know either', she said, 'We are talking with the statistics department about this'. I decided to come and see the WCISU and ask about the data and the AORs. I also did a great deal of phoning round. A Green Party colleague, Mal Evans, worked for the Welsh Office mapping department. He was unable to help. I talked with the Statistics people there. They couldn't help. After a great deal of research I eventually struck lucky. There was someone at the Office of National Statistics at Fareham in Hampshire who knew what these names represented in terms of wards. John Walsh sent me a table where the AOR names were lined up with ward names, parishes and communities. It was then a relatively simple (though tedious and lengthy) matter to collect together the census wards and assemble the populations. This was something that WCISU never achieved. In 2002, when I was involved in looking at cancer near the town of Mold in North Wales, where there is a cluster owing to pollution from the government war gas repository at Rhydamawyn, it became clear that WCISU had no idea at all what the AORs comprised and still do not. I return to this.

My meeting with the WCISU introduced me to their Director, Dr John Steward. Steward was affable and full of bonhomie. He would help us in every way. He introduced himself as someone who had always been interested in radiation and health and told me he was the author of a study of cancer and leukaemia near Trawsfynydd (*Report A-EMJ-28 Investigation of the incidence of cancer around Trawsfynydd and Wylfa nuclear installations,* 1994). This was quite interesting since, if it were so, he must have known the composition of the AORs all along since the Trawsfynydd report used these same AORs. Why then did both he and Helen Beer say they knew nothing about the AORs? Perhaps he had forgotten. Without these AOR designations I was stuck: no research on the WCR files could be carried out.

Steward also gave me a copy of a paper by Ray Cartwright that found excess child leukaemia near estuaries [Alexander *et al*, 1990]. Cartwright has since got into considerable trouble over this paper, as I will relate. Steward also told me that the data that I had been given by WCR had been wiped from the mainframe computer. This was rather extraordinary, and I said so. He agreed, and had no explanation. He smiled the whole time.

The populations of the AORs had to be constructed from the 1981 census, but this was now possible since I had their make-up from John Walsh. Luckily, 1981 fell in the middle of the period we were studying. The work crawled along slowly. It dawned on me what I had been leaked and what it could show. I began to feel paranoid about these discs. After all, if the data was wiped from the mainframe, and the whole of WCR had been sacked, someone was taking a great deal of trouble to ensure that whatever cat was out of the bag should be knocked on the head. I made several copies of the original discs and sent them to as many people as possible. I kept one of the original discs; the other I sent to Richard Bramhall who lodged it in a solicitor's safe, where it still is. It seemed to me that there might be some question about veracity, about altered data. This was prescient. My own disc mysteriously disappeared from my house shortly after this.

Table 12.3.1 Some AORs in Clwyd and their ward composition.

Wales Cancer Registry AOR	Civil parish	County/Local Authority
71AA BUCKLEY UD	Argoed	Buckley UD pt
	Ewloe Wood	Buckley UD pt
	Bistre East	Buckley UD pt
	Bistre West	Buckley UD pt
	Ewloe Town	Buckley UD pt
	Pentrobin	Buckley UD pt
71AC CONNAHS QUAY	Central Ward	Connahs Quay UD
	Golftyn Ward	Connahs Quay UD
	South Ward	Connahs Quay UD

12.4 Two sets of data: a Sea of Troubles

The first dataset, A2218 EXE, was a text file, with the left hand column giving, by year, the AOR and cancer site, and the rest of the columns the number of cases in each 5-year age and sex band (Appendix A). The final two rows after the AOR, gave totals for all malignancies and all leukaemias, because this is what I had asked for. The cancer sites were designated by their ICD9 code, for example, Breast cancer is 174; lymphoma is 202. In this code, 204, 205, 206, 207 and 208 are all types of leukaemia. So there were two places in the data where leukaemia was tabulated, in the row 'all leukaemias' and also in the row alongside the specific leukaemia type, e.g. 204 is acute lymphoid leukaemia. I approached the problem of what to do with this in two ways. First I added all the leukaemias. Second I used only the ICD 204-208 leukaemias. I thought that the 'all leukaemias' file was a shadow file that had been kept apart from the others, particularly since it seemed to have cases mainly in North Wales. The second dataset A2883 did not contain these 'all leukaemias' rows. It was most mysterious but also very interesting. It seemed to confirm what Wales Cancer Registry had been saying in their 1994 report, but placed the children near the sea, near the radioactive pollution in North Wales. We were at the position in late 1998 to know that there was a statistically significant sea coast effect in both adult and childhood cancer. Over the 16-year period, children in the coastal strip had more than twice the chance of being diagnosed with cancer than the national average rising to almost 4 times in the last four years of the period. For brain tumours, the relative risk over the whole period was almost 5-times the national average in the coastal strip. The data for child leukaemia from the combined data showed high levels of childhood leukaemia in north Wales coast - up to 4.5 times the expected number of cases with the distinctive trend which I described in Chapter 6. If we used only the ICD column data, the effect was still there although the actual values were much lower, with the coastal strip relative risk falling to 1.5 although the effect was higher (RR = 2.4) in the latter half of the time period.

I reported these results at the Standing Conference on Low Dose Radiation in Bromley in 1998. Shortly after this I was approached by BBC Wales who wanted to make a documentary. This was produced by John Fraser Williams and was in the series, *Week in Week out*. It was titled *Sea of Troubles* and was transmitted in February 1999. It made a big splash. Unfortunately, it focused mainly on child leukaemia since the BBC saw this as a good storyline. In fact, because the numbers are much larger, the adult cancers are much more horrifying. Between 1974 and 1989 more than 3500 adults died in the coastal strip from cancer that was related to where they lived and some environmental effect.

In the TV programme John Steward (Plate 12) was interviewed and denied the existence of elevated leukaemia in children in north Wales. The Welsh Assembly contacted COMARE to ask for an investigation. Steward was asked to do a study by COMARE to back up his assertion that there was no child leukaemia excess. No one seemed to be interested in the childhood cancers, or the adult cancers. Steward sent an emissary to Aberystwyth, one David Adams Jones, ex-director of the Scottish Cancer Registry and an epidemiologist who had been involved in the Dounreay child leukaemia cluster work. Adams Jones turned up for a meeting with the Green Audit team (myself, Bruce Kocjian and Molly Scott Cato). We naturally asked for the data they held. Adams Jones said that there was no WCR data on the computer so they did not have the data we had. He wanted our files. We refused. We wanted the WCISU files. He refused. Impasse.

Why did we refuse? Because if he had our files, Steward would know where the cases contributing to our excesses lived and he could then adjust his adjusted files to fit with our files. But if he didn't know where our cases were, he wouldn't know which cases to remove from his files to get the relative risk down to below statistical significance. If he let us have his files, then we would see which cases he had removed and go and find the people. He has never let us have his files, even after being asked to give them to us by COMARE. Steward decided on a way forward. We had used as a covariate the mean distance of the AORs we had received from WCR. At this time Steward refused to deal with the AORs, which were made up of the 1981 census wards and would not give us the numbers of cases he had in the AORs. Instead, Adams Jones suggested we define strips in terms of 1991 census wards, and WCISU would then aggregate the cases into these strips. Why not, I thought. At least we would get some information and maybe using simultaneous equations figure out what WCISU was up to. So I put Evelyn Mannion to the task of aggregating the census wards into strips at various distances parallel to the coast. This took some time but eventually the strips were constructed and sent to Steward. Steward analysed risk of child leukaemia 0-4 and 0-14 in the 'Busby Bands'. They also examined childhood cancer 0-14 and brain tumours in children 0-14. They did not find anything. Their paper actually showed fewer children with leukaemia in the coastal strip than inland. For brain tumours and all malignancies there was a weak coastal effect. They presented their results to COMARE at their 55th meeting in March 1999.

12.5 COMARE discusses the issue.

The furore in the Welsh Assembly caused by *Sea of Troubles* resulted in their asking COMARE to investigate. Several MPs, including the Chair of Plaid Cymru, Dafydd Wigley, asked for an enquiry. Of course, as MP for Caernarfon, one of the coastal towns identified in the coastal strip, he already had concerns about the high level of cancer there. This is local knowledge and has nothing to do with official figures. Asking COMARE to investigate is rather like asking the Mafia to consider a report of organised crime, and the result was as predictable. John Steward's

WCISU childhood cancer study for Wales, analysing the Busby Bands was presented in person by him. At no time did COMARE ask us to present our side of the case, nor were we to see Steward's paper until after the Press Release by the Welsh Assembly, which rubbished our position. Unluckily for COMARE, not everyone on that committee was as convinced by Steward, and the minutes were leaked to us. The confidential minutes of the 55th meeting held on 18th March 1999 arrived on my doorstep in a brown envelope. They made interesting reading. They began with an account of Steward's presentation. This concluded with Steward accusing us of scientific fraud. Not all the members went along with the belief that there was no effect. For example:

7.13: Professor MacMillan asked whether it was possible to be sure that there was no coastline effect on the incidence of leukaemia. Professor Clayton also thought it was premature to say that the coastline effect does not exist. He would support further coastal analysis. . . Professor Boddy commented that the public would think that COMARE were not carrying out their duties unless further action was taken to address Dr Busby's hypothesis.

The Chairman asked the committee whether they would wish to recommend a further study to test the hypothesis. At this point, Roy Hamlet (the secretary) steps in:

7.16 Dr Hamlet said that this would raise Dr Busby's credibility and would open the door to others to lean on COMARE to recommend research.

The final report on the issue from COMARE concluded that Steward's analysis was correct and that there was no problem. They apparently did this by asking Gerald Draper to compare the figures with his own Childhood Cancer Research Group figures. These data apparently agreed with Steward's and not with those of WCR that we had used. By this time, however, we had been able to look at Steward's totals and had worked out that he had taken 15% of the children with cancer off the WCR database as published by WCR. The total numbers given by WCR were the same as the total numbers we had in our A2883 EXE file, and the results we had for the analysis of this file showed an excess of leukaemia, brain tumours and all cancer in children in the coastal strip. I wrote to Bryn Bridges pointing out that Steward had removed children from the data. He ignored this. COMARE released their conclusions to the Welsh Assembly and Jane Hutt, Health Minister, released it to the Press on 21st July 1999.

National Assembly Health Secretary Jane Hutt announced today the results of an independent examination of the claims made by Dr Chris Busby and colleagues of Green Audit, which concludes there is no higher incidence of leukaemia among children living along the north Wales/Irish Sea coastline.

Although we were specifically excluded from seeing Steward's paper on which this was based, they had to send it to the media, and did so with a covering letter that it should not be given to us. This was unheard of. Naturally, all the newspapers faxed us the report and asked for our response. I went on the air saying that it was a cover-up. And, as I will relate, it clearly *was* a cover-up, since by late 2003, the TV company HTV had put a researcher in charge of investigating the children. Was there a cancer excess? Yes indeed. But what had happened to it?

12.6 Steward's report: a tale of two studies

Results of a preliminary study to test the Irish Sea proximity hypothesis of Busby et al. by Steward JA, Adams Jones D, Beer H and John G was presented as a re-run of the Green Audit study on which the TV program was based, but with WCISU data. It was not. In order to dilute out or remove the effect, every trick in the book was used. They used wrong populations, different distances from the sea, different age groups and removed cancer cases from the data. For the 0-14 age group and all malignancy we could compare directly with the WCR cases published in their various reports. These numbers agree exactly with the WCR data in the small area files used by Green Audit. The essential differences for 0-14 year olds are given in Table 12.6.1

Table 12.6.1 Comparing the Green Audit and WCISU studies of childhood cancer 0-14 in Wales by distance from the coast.

Green Audit study (WCR data)	**WCISU study (WCISU adjusted data)**
Period 1974-89	Period 1974-89
All malignancies	All malignancies
1981 census wards	1991 census wards
800 metre closest strip to coast	5km closest strip to coast
Significant excess found in coastal strip. RR in 800 metre strip = 1.4 (p = 0.01); RR = 2.2 in 0-4s	Non-significant excess found in coastal strip of 5km; RR = 1.1
1981 population of 564,870 children aged 0-14 and 169,200 aged 0-4	1991 population 569,900 children 0-14 and 204,800 aged 0-4 (21%higher than 1981 population)
Total cases 0-14 in WCR data was 1188	Total cases 0-14 in WCISU data was 1006; 182 cases or 15% less.

So what did they do to remove the result?

- First they used the wrong populations. Census populations are only available for 1981 and 1991. How can it be proper to use 1991 populations for a study covering 1974-89? Clearly the 1981 populations fall in the centre of the study period, so why not use them? In the 0-4 year olds, where the effect is largest, the 1991 populations are 21% higher than the 1981. So this would reduce any cancer excess in this age group by 21%, since the population is the denominator of the rate.
- Second, they increased the width of the coastal strip. We made very clear that the effect was located inside 2km from the coast and was highest in the 800m proximal strip. This is where the exposure to the Plutonium in the sea spray is at its maximum. By extending the width of the strip to 5km, any proximal effect is diluted *at least* by a factor of two.
- Finally, since even these shenanigans clearly were insufficient, they just took the cases off the WCR database. 15% of the 0-14s were removed from the WCR published data, the same data we were studying, agreeing in totals exactly. These involved 182 children. The children were taken from the coastal strip. How do we know this? Because we can see it by comparing their results with ours, setting up simultaneous equations for the AORs and the 'Busby Bands' and subtracting.

This final item where Steward *et al* removed the 182 cases from the total children with cancer given in the Welsh Office publications for 1992 and 1994 has been the subject of continuing demands by Green Audit for an explanation. Even COMARE were eventually bounced by us into asking Steward to give us the data. Of course, he refused. Eventually, very recently, he has come up with an explanation (2003). The cases were removed because they were adults who had been misclassified as children by WCR. Gerald Draper repeated this nonsense to me at a recent radiation workshop in Oxford. How come, I asked, these misclassifications only occurred for children living near the contaminated mud banks of the north Wales coast? The 182 cases include 50 cases that Steward had removed from his own April 1998 published database, which was published before the TV programme, and the level of argument meant he had to go back and take out some more cases. When I phoned and pointed this out, there was general consternation. I don’t think many people have had this early version of the WCISU data, which was such a hostage to fortune.

The correspondence and argumentation over these issues of whether there were excess cancers in North Wales’s coastal wards have continued to surface regularly since 1999, and became part of the CERRIE process also (which I shall describe later), since a major plank of our contribution to the CERRIE debate was the existence of excess risk near contaminated coastal areas. COMARE eventually decided that the child leukaemias in the shadow 'all leukaemias' file was an artefact of some sort. They tried every method to explain how the file came about. They asked me for the data; I refused to give them the entire file until I saw Steward's data for reasons that I have already described, but in the interests of truth and accommodation I gave them two years of data, 1984 and 1988. These two years taken together showed high levels of childhood cancer in the towns near the Menai Strait, as I show in Tables 12.6.2 and 12.6.3 where I compare with the numbers that underpinned the Sellafield cluster.

Extraordinarily, COMARE did not comment on the numbers of cases and risks in the north Wales area shown by these two files but said that they just wanted them to see if they could find the source of the problems with the shadow leukaemias. They were unable to solve the problem, and merely concluded that there was some error at the Wales Cancer Registry end. They accused me of using incorrect data and publicly called for the withdrawal of our claims, as we were 'scaremongering'. I refused to withdraw the reports. COMARE had never looked at the high levels of adult cancers in north Wales, nor had they succeeded in obtaining data from Steward, nor any explanation from WCISU as to how the children they had taken off the database had been originally misclassified. The whole process stank to high heaven of cover-up. We were to find that this was exactly what had happened from an unexpected source. Just as Yorkshire TV had been the first to discover the leukaemias near Sellafield in 1983, now Harlech TV in Wales was to do the same for the children of the coastal communities of north Wales.

The government-funded watchdogs, COMARE and SAHSU, set up in the wake of the Black report, were seen to not only be useless, but actually to represent an operation hand in glove with the nuclear industry. At a CERRIE meeting in 2003 discussing the Welsh leukaemias, and where now the Chair, Dudley Goodhead, was asking me to release the WCR files, I mentioned that I had already given two years of data to COMARE so that they could check. Richard Wakeford, BNFLs chief epidemiologist said, 'Ah but those two years were chosen by you because they exhibited a high risk for child leukaemia!' He was right, but how did he know this, unless COMARE had sent him the data? This links them all together. Are we surprised?

Table 12.6.2 Observed and expected numbers of childhood cancer cases in some Areas of Residence near the Menai Strait in the two years 1984 and 1988 combined. These are two of the years for which Wales Cancer Registry reported high levels of cancer in North Wales in their 1994 publication.

AOR	All maligs 0-4	Expect	Obs/Exp (RR)	p-value
74CA Bangor	4	0.17	23.5	0.0000
74CE Caernarfon	1	0.15	6.4	
74JL Aethwy	1	0.26	3.8	
74JJ Menai Bridge	0	0.044		
74JC Beaumaris	0	0.028		
74CN Ogwen	0	0.086		
74AC Conway	0	0.176		
74AE Llandudno	2	0.202	9.9	0.01
All AORs	8	1.122	7.13	0.0000

Table 12.6.3 Observed and expected numbers in 1984 and 1988 of all malignancy, all leukaemia and brain tumours in 0-4 and 0-14 age group in the AORs in Table 13.3, compared to Seascale and coastal villages.

Site and age	Observed	Expected	Relative risk	p-values
All malignancy 0-4	8	1.12	7.1	0.0000
All malignancy 0-14	12	1.4	8.6	0.0000
All leukaemia 0-4	3	0.44	6.8	0.0000
All leukaemia 0-14	3	1.02	22.9	0.08
Leukemia 0-4 + shadow file	5	0.44	11.3	0.0000
Leukemia 0-14 + shadow file	7	1.02	6.9	0.0000
Brain 0-4	2	0.15	13.2	0.0000
Brain 0-14	3	0.48	6.25	0.0000
Seascale + coastal villages All maligs. deaths 0-14 1963-82 (a)	4	1.36	2.9	0.04
Seascale + coastal villages All leukaemia 0-14 in children born 1950-83	3	0.32	9.35	0.004

12.7 Raising the dead: Byd ar Bedwar

So there we are. That is how it is done. Airbrush the data, remove the children who were ill or died in areas that are inconvenient for industry. In the case of adults, comparisons of the WCISU publications and those of WCR showed that besides the children, WCISU had also removed 3000 cases from the WCR data inherited by them. There is an interesting cartoon I saw in a French anti-nuclear magazine. Two guys are looking through a fence into a nuclear site where a lorry is tipping some stuff into a hole. One says to the other, 'What's that? Nuclear waste?' The other guy says, 'No! Cancer data.' WCISU had raised the dead, bringing the cancer patients back to life at the stroke of a Tippex brush.

But now there is the denouement. As St Mark says:
For there is nothing hid, which shall not be manifested; neither was any thing kept secret, but that it should come abroad. [Mark 4;22]

In 2002, Linda Parry, a young researcher for the Welsh Language Channel S4C based in Bangor, decided to start digging. Her friend had died from non-Hodgkin lymphoma and she had become concerned about the levels of cancer on the north Wales coast, particularly around Caernarfon and the Menai Strait between the island of Anglesey and the mainland. The Menai is particularly contaminated with material from Sellafield. Wielding a Geiger Counter over the mud there will convince you that you are inside the Chernobyl exclusion zone. Over two years, Linda managed to interview the parents of many children diagnosed with leukaemia and various cancers. She contacted the Low Level Radiation Campaign and Green Audit in the autumn of 2003. We collected her data together and analysed what we had in early 2004. The results were alarming. And this time there could be no argument about the cases. We knew where they were. Our 2000 report to the Irish Court Case, which used the WCR data, had identified the towns of Bangor and Caernarfon as having significant excess childhood leukaemia and brain tumours between 1974 and 1989. This area was one where Steward had to have removed the cases to reduce the coastal risk. Linda Parry's data showed a 21-fold excess of leukaemia in Caernarfon and 18-fold excess of brain and spinal tumours in the same town. In the 34 wards that back the Menai Strait, the leukaemia risk in children 0-4 was 6 times greater than the national average and 3.4 times the national average, if the Caernarfon cases were excluded. I show the numbers in Table 12.7.1

For brain and spinal tumours, the Menai Strait wards had more than 4-times the national expected numbers of cases between 1996 and 2003. There was an 18-fold excess of brain and spinal tumours in children in Caernarfon over the same period. These were just the cases found by Linda. It is unlikely that she got all of the children. There is more. Interestingly, WCISU published figures for cancer in Wales from 1992 to 2001 in 2003. These figures show rates for adults and although there are high levels of leukaemia in Wales, the highest in Europe, the high levels are not recorded as being in North Wales. For the whole of Wales, the numbers published show that there are no significantly high levels of leukaemia in children 0-4. In fact, although, according to WCISU the adult leukaemia in the whole of Wales from 1992 to 2001 is the highest in Europe, RR = 1.5 we are to believe that childhood leukaemia age 0-4 is exactly the same as in England, indeed to an astonishing degree: according to their data RR = 1.00.

Table 12.7.1 Childhood cancer in towns and wards near the Menai Strait as obtained through interviews by Linda Parry of HTV Wales televised as a documentary Byd ar Bedwar, Feb 10th 2004, Producer Tweli Griffiths.

Site, age group, period	Pop	Observed	Expected	RR	p-
Leukaemia 0-4. (2000-03)					
Caernarfon	528	3	0.142	21	0.0000
34 Menai wards	3824	6	1.02	5.8	0.0006
Leukaemia 0-14 (1996-2003)					
Caernarfon	1655	3	0.56	5.4	0.02
34 Menai Wards	12417	11	4.17	2.6	0.004
Brain+ 0-14 (1996-2003)					
Caernarfon	1655	5	0.28	18	0.0000
34 Menai wards	12417	9	2.1	4.3	0.0003

So, following this new information we are justified in asking a few more questions of those who were responsible for examining the levels of cancer in Wales, Dr Steward and the WCISU, and also a number of other players in this drama, including COMARE, Dr Gerald Draper of CCRG, and Dr Ray Cartwright of the Leukaemia Research Fund who will appear later on in this book.

By 2005 Steward had struck back again, but this time he made a fatal error. Clearly the TV documentary was an important piece of evidence and had scared everyone in the area. The analysis on which it was based had been peer-reviewed and presented in September 2004 at the International Conference of *Children with Leukaemia* in London. (Busby *et al* 2004). Steward and co-workers carried out a study for the Welsh Assembly and launched it in 2005 (Steward *et al* 2005). Steward could not deny the children, as we had their names. But these children were diagnosed recently, after 2000. Steward argued that this was a temporal cluster and caused by chance. With regard to the earlier cases which we had found in our Irish State report he now agreed these existed also, but had to get rid of their significance as it made nonsense of the claim that the children with cancer after

2000 were a chance cluster. So he reduced their statistical significance and Relative Risk by altering the base population by a factor of three. He did this by misapplying the ward population aggregates for the AORs. In fact, the way he effected this was so absurd and bizarre that it was easy to demonstrate the error. He used the population of Caernarfon wards plus Bangor wards plus Ogwen wards to represent the population of the town of Bangor (Busby and Howard 2006, Busby and Bramhall 2006). His calculation was farcical and desperate. Nevertheless, no one looked at it, COMARE rubber stamped it. The Assembly Government, the National Health Services for Wales organisation and COMARE all underwrote it and in a Press Release and COMARE statement, slated Green Audit for having made a mistake in the populations. We were asked to be more careful and not indulge in scaremongering. The laugh was that it was Steward and his gang who had made the mistake, in this instance it wasn't just taking a few children off the database, it was a complete howler.

I made a formal complaint to the Royal College of Physicians, to COMARE and to the *Journal of Public Health*. My letter with Vyvyan Howard to the *Journal of Public Health* was peer reviewed and accepted. It was published earlier this year (Busby and Howard 2006). COMARE apparently met to discuss their mistaken support of WCISU and eventually a letter accepting that there was a serious mistake made by WCISU was sent to me. But no apology. The new Chair of COMARE, Alex Elliott, quickly glossed over the howling error and went on to ramble on at tedious length about how the latest data from Steward showed there was no problem. What's this? More nonsense? Is there no end to the slipping and sliding? Well, no, actually there doesn't seem to be. Steward now has decided that in fact the children who he agreed earlier lived in Bangor and Caernarfon now seem to live elsewhere. And then here's the really extraordinary move. Steward decides to study only the towns themselves individually (rather than the Menai) and concludes that each town individually (Bangor and Caernarfon and Colwyn Bay) have too few children with leukaemia to demonstrate statistical significance. The RCP enquiry under their Chair, Prof. Rod Griffiths carried on for six months after the initial complaint and eventually resulted in a letter to me saying that the college's legal advisors recommended that they do not pursue it. I wrote an angry response to Griffiths who replied saying he sympathised and would put pressure on the editor of the Journal of Public Health to let me have a space to say all this. He advised me to complain to the General Medical Association who have criminal investigation procedures and can kick people out of their jobs. I shall.

The final scary thing is that following the publication of our letter pointing out Steward's mistakes, the Welsh Assembly clearly came under pressure from the North Wales Councils and various important individuals up there. The responded by commissioning a report on the possibility of radioactivity from Sellafield being the cause of the excess child leukaemias and brain tumours (even though they had maintained there weren't any). The study was up for tender. Who do you think made the winning bid? Who did the study? Who was paid £93,000 of public money to show that the doses (yes) were too low? Westlakes in Cumbria, the research subsidiary of British Nuclear Fuels, BNFL. Can you believe this? Their report was the basis for a recent press statement by the Welsh Assembly Health Minister that people in north Wales should not believe Green Audit, or HTV. All was well. No one was being poisoned by BNFL.

12.8 Decide on your own scenario.

Lately, there have been children's novels that give alternative scenarios, and so, in the spirit of modernity, I will place the sequences of events chronologically and leave you to draw your conclusions. Chernobyl occurred in 1986. No problem for health, said NRPB and the nuclear establishment. The radiation will soon disappear. Wrong on the second count (it is still there and sheep movements are still restricted in some parts). Wrong on the first count also. The fallout was highest in North Wales, contaminating the grassland and washing to the sea to join the material from Sellafield in the estuaries and coastal sediments. In the late 1980s, sea-to-land transfer had been discovered. Autopsies had shown the Plutonium in the lungs of people who lived near the sea. In the early 1990s, Ray Cartwright, Freda Alexander and others [Alexander *et al* 1990] published a study that asked a reasonable question: Do the radioactive pollutants which collect in estuaries cause increased levels of leukaemia in those who live nearby? They looked at estuary wards around England and Wales, but for some reason, not explained, cut out the estuaries in North Wales. North Wales has the highest concentration of people living near contaminated sediment on the shores of the Irish Sea after Seascale and the coastal villages. They found that there was indeed a modest, but significant excess of leukaemia in the combined estuary wards even excluding north Wales. John Steward knew about this paper because it was he who brought it to my attention. By 1994, WCR was publishing data that showed a significant excess of childhood cancer in North Wales. This was, their Director told me, validated by Gerald Draper of CCRG. After publication of *Wings of Death*, the political pressure forced a meeting with WCR at which the Medical Officer of Health, Dr Deidre Hine, told WCR to give us the data. We were leaked the small area data in 1996. Immediately, WCR was closed and its personnel scattered, and the data removed from the mainframe computer. Dr Hine was removed and her place taken by Dr Ruth Hall, hostile and dismissive to the Green Audit position. The new cancer unit, the WCISU, was headed by a man who admitted to being the author of a 1994 report exonerating the nuclear power stations in north Wales from any effect on health. Shortly after taking over, WCISU published a report showing that they had removed 3000 adult cancers from the WCR data and 15% of the children. No explanation was given, and the time period involved was too short for a major revalidation exercise. Funded by the Irish State, the analysis by Green Audit of the WCR data in 1999 showed the presence of high levels of child leukaemia in North Wales, also brain tumours in children and also a coastal cancer risk effect in children and adults. This effect became worse over the 16-year period of the data, 1974-89 and was driven by coastal areas and towns near contaminated sediment, particularly near the Menai Strait. BBC-TV did a documentary, *Sea of Troubles,* but the results were rubbished by the WCISU and by COMARE. At that time, two of the members of COMARE, who were part of the meeting making the decision not to follow up the research and to deny the existence of the effect, were Gerald Draper and Ray Cartwright.

13
More Cover-ups in England

Q. *"Radiation is the only established environmental cause of leukaemia in children within the limits of present knowledge." What do you say about that?*
A. *I would agree with that.*

-Transcript of cross-examination of Prof SJ Evans
Sellafield leukaemia trial, 18th day; Thursday Nov 26, 1992

The mystery is considered insoluble for the very same reasons that should lead me to consider it solvable.
Edgar Allan Poe: The Murders in the Rue Morgue

13.1 Nordic leukaemia study revisited

One of the most influential studies of the health effects of exposure to internal man-made radioactive isotopes was published in 1992, at about the time the discussions were taking place about how to fight the Sellafield leukaemia trial, *Reay and Hope vs. BNFL.* The prosecution lawyers were to have to explain how the 10-fold child leukaemia excess in Seascale near Sellafield could be caused by radiation from the plant. One explanation (the correct one, I believe) was that the ICRP risk model was incorrect for internal radionuclides. The other explanation was the one that the lawyers were advised to pursue, that it was caused by genetic damage following parental pre-conception radiation. This was bad advice, as it happens, and the case was lost. However, for the nuclear establishment this case was a potential disaster. They were well aware of the scientific weakness of the ICRP model for internal radiation. One of their experts told Bill Pritchard this over a pint during the Hinkley enquiry. Bill is a friend of mine who was there representing Greenpeace. Something was clearly necessary to block off this possibility and so something was done. Enter Dr Sarah Darby and Professor Richard Doll and the Nordic Leukaemia study. I had already criticized this study in *Wings of Death.* Because it reappeared during the deliberations of a new government Committee Examining Radiation Risk from Internal Emitters (CERRIE) in 2002-2003 as a major piece of evidence I looked more closely at the study. The story is quite entertaining, and gives an insight into the process of unravelling a system of scientific bias and the effort required to discover the truth.

First let me outline what I knew at the time of writing *Wings of Death.* The title of the paper, which was published in the British Medical Journal in April 1992, about a year before the trial began in earnest, was *Trends in Childhood*

Leukaemia in the Nordic Countries in Relation to Fallout from Nuclear Weapons Testing [Darby *et al*, 1992]. The authors were Sarah Darby, Jorgen Olsen, Richard Doll, Bharat Thakrar, Peter de Nully Brown, Hans H Storm, Lotti Barlow, Froydis Langmark, Lyly Teppo and Hrafn Tulinius. Most of these people were on the paper because they supplied the data. The calculations were done in Oxford by Sarah Darby. Results were based on a rather complicated time-series Poisson regression analysis involving a lot of mathematical manipulation and splicing together of data from Denmark, Sweden, Iceland, Norway and Finland. They appeared to indicate that there was *little evidence of increased incidence in children born in the high fallout period.* For children after birth, leukaemia incidence and red marrow dose were not related overall, but rates of leukaemia in the 'high exposure' period were slightly higher than in the surrounding medium exposure period.

Looking at the graphs of leukaemia rates *standardised for age, sex and country* it is difficult to see any change over the period of the weapons fallout. Fig 13.1.1 uses the data from the paper to show the rates for the 0-4s. But close reading of the text shows that this graph is a construction, a creation of mathematics and hope. It does not actually show the rates in the 'Nordic Countries' because up to 1958, only rates from Denmark were available. This is the major and lethal flaw in the study. What Darby *et al* did was to sell this as a study of child leukaemia in a homogenous population over a span of 36 years, children who were exposed in the middle of the period to internal man-made radioactive materials from weapons fallout. In reality it was a study of at least two distinct populations. Before the fallout it was a time series of Danish rates; after the fallout it was a time series of Denmark plus all the other Nordic countries, adjusted in various unelaborated and complicated ways. Anything that might have happened in Denmark after the fallout would be swamped by the big populations of the other Nordic countries. Anything that might have happened in the other Nordic countries would be missed because there was no pre-fallout baseline before 1960 to compare the rates with. The doses in the different countries are quite different due to patterns of rainfall and so the development of the illness would have a different lag time. The same process, carried out by IARC at Lyon, has successfully smudged out increases in childhood leukaemia after Chernobyl, another story.

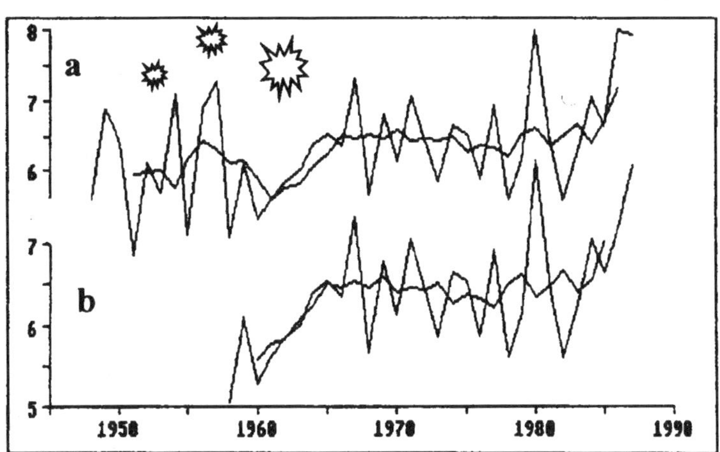

Fig 13.1.1 The time series of the Nordic leukaemia study for 0-4s as reproduced in *Wings of Death.* Also shown is the series for the Nordic countries with the Danish data removed. Note the apparent increase in leukaemia rates after 1959 if the early (Danish) data are cut out.

In 1995 I wrote to Sarah Darby to ask if I could have a look at the raw data. I wanted to see what had happened to the Danish series after it had been absorbed into the general Nordic population. She replied on 1st September 1995 that the data was not available. *I think it must have been destroyed when Dr Bharat Thakrar left our Unit.* But my daughter Celi, who worked as an epidemiologist at the London School of Hygiene and Tropical Medicine met Thakrar and spoke with him about the data. He told her that he certainly had not destroyed it. And there the matter would have ended had it not been for the CERRIE committee. I will give an account of the Committee Examining Radiation Risk from Internal Emitters in part IV as it is both a major triumph and a major event of our campaign, but here I will now relate how it came about that the plot of the Nordic Leukaemia study was finally unravelled.

13.2 Hakulinen sees: fallout brings disease.

Since the remit of the CERRIE committee was to look at internal radionuclides, it was inevitable that someone would advance the Nordic leukaemia study as proof that there was nothing to worry about, and that is exactly what happened. In this case, interestingly and unhappily for her, Sarah Darby had been brought into the committee at a late stage (after its members had been chosen) as a 'neutral epidemiologist' by the Chair, Dudley Goodhead. CERRIE itself had been forced into existence by the incontrovertible evidence of increases in infant leukaemia in the children who were in the womb at the time of the Chernobyl black rain. The effect occurred in five different countries and had to be an effect of Chernobyl; but if it were, then the ICRP risk factors were in error by about 100 to 500 times (which is about right, actually). The nuclear apologists on CERRIE fell back on the Nordic Leukaemia study. Why was there no effect there, they cried. The study looked at child leukaemia 0-4, but infant leukaemia would have shown up if there was an effect. So I countered with my arguments from *Wings of Death.* The series was bogus. The study population was changed in the middle of the series, at exactly the point something should happen. How was the series constructed, I asked Darby. Can we see the data? Can we look at Denmark only and see whether there was an effect there, in the only dataset that covers the whole period? No you can't, she replied. The data has been destroyed, removed, wiped long ago. It does not exist any more.

But some data did exist, and some studies of Leukaemia in Denmark had been made it seemed. I began to dig. And (strangely) thanks to Richard Wakeford of BNFL, we had our first break. Wakeford agreed to write to Jorgen Olsen of the Danish Cancer registry and ask for the raw data. But a few months after this he also turned up a fat report entitled *Trends in cancer incidence in the Nordic Countries* (Hakulinen *et al* 1986). This gave data on adult, infant and childhood acute leukaemia aggregated in five-year blocks. The authors noted that the only data that covered the period before 1960 was from Denmark. They showed that for acute leukaemia, there were significant increases in the incidence of infant, childhood and also adult leukaemia in Denmark over the period of the fallout. They noted (p92) *Hansen et al. (1983) concluded that the increases in acute leukaemia in age groups 50 years and over may not be an artefact. They suggest environmental factors are involved. Ionizing radiation is a well-known risk factor in leukaemia.*
They did not refer to the amazing increases in childhood acute lymphatic leukaemia plotted in their publication. I have plotted the rates of childhood acute leukaemia in Denmark given by the Hakulinen *et al* publication in Fig 13.2.1. I became quite excited by this and obtained the paper by Hansen *et al* referred to in the Hakulinen *et al* report. Sure enough, Hansen (1983) had examined leukaemia in Denmark and published in the prestigious *Journal of the National Cancer Institute* a paper entitled *Trends in the incidence of leukaemia in Denmark 1943-47: an Epidemiolgic study of 14,000 patients.* (Hansen *et al*, 1983)
In the abstract, Hansen *et al* stated; *An epidemiologic study of the total population of patients with leukaemia in Denmark during 1943 to 1977 was performed. The material stemmed from the National Danish cancer Registry and was believed to be complete. . . Over the 35 year period the incidence of acute leukaemia increased threefold in the age groups 0-9 and 50-70+ years; whereas the increase*

in the age groups 0-9 climaxed in the period 68-72, the increase in the age group 50+ was sustained.

Of course, a peak in incidence in 0-9 year olds in 1969 to 1972 points to an exposure in the womb or early childhood in 1960 to 1964, the fallout peak! These papers suggested that the Danish data showed an effect for acute leukaemia. Why had they not been referenced in the Nordic leukaemia study? After all, if you write a scientific or medical paper, you should include the work of other people in the area. I was confused and I decided to put some pressure on Darby and Doll to find their lost data. I contacted the Editor of the *British Medical Journal* and asked him to look into the matter of the Danish data, since the paper was very influential and had been published by his journal. I also wrote to the *Danish Committee for the Investigation of Scientific Dishonesty* in Copenhagen. I also wrote to the Fitness to Practice Directorate of the British Medical Association. The Hakulinen and Hansen data suggested that the fallout had caused significant increases in acute leukaemia in Denmark in children and also in adults. Neither of these papers had been cited in the Nordic study, which showed no increases in leukaemia in Denmark. What was going on?

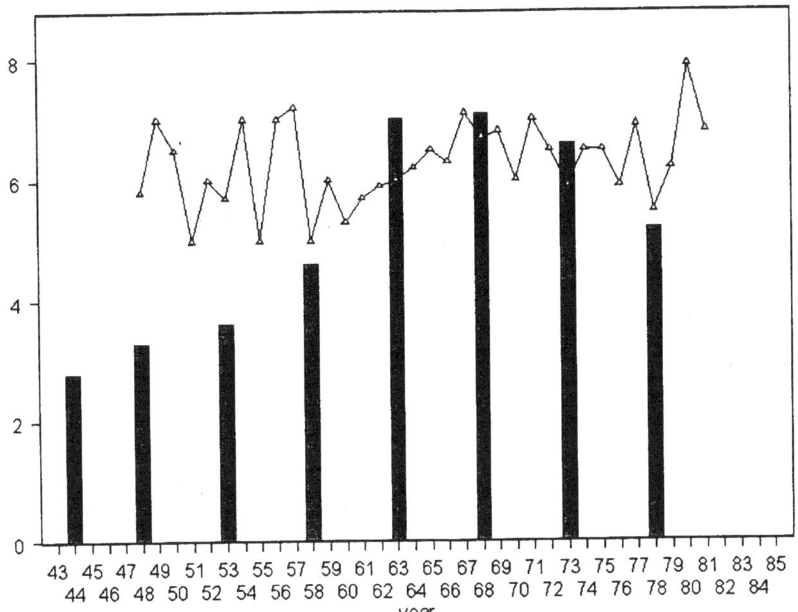

Fig 13.2.1 Childhood acute leukaemia 0-4 in Denmark 1943-77 from Hakulinen *et al* (1983) bars. Also shown is the Nordic leukaemia study trend (rates per 100,000)

13.3 The data magically appears

The Danish Committee on Scientific Dishonesty started digging. The British Medical Journal wrote to Darby and Doll. A miracle occurred. Dr Darby found a disc with the original data. This was sent to Prof. Roger Robinson of the BMJ and passed on to me by the editor, who declared that he was satisfied that the explanation given by Darby and Doll for the discrepancies between their graph and that of Hakulinen *et al* and Hansen had been justified.

Let me remind you what is happening here. I am questioning the validity, direction and honesty of one of the most important studies ever published on a question at the basis of the operation of the nuclear project. The authors are the most respected people in epidemiology. Their co-authors are directors of the various Scandinavian cancer registries. Olsen is Director of the Danish Cancer Registry, which was taken over by the State in 1997. He is presently the Head of the Institute of Cancer Epidemiology in Copenhagen with 40 researchers, 20 technical staff and a secretariat. Their research is based on extramural funding from the US National Cancer Institute and the International Agency for Research on Cancer in France and the Nordic Cancer Union (which he is also president of). Are they looking at the effects of radiation? Don't bet on it. Do we think the Danish Committee for Scientific Dishonesty will take on these people? They are Big Dogs. Forget it.

The Nordic study is regularly used as a cornerstone of the nuclear industry case. In 1993 NRPB wrote to Bramhall using this study to deny the existence of radiation related bone cancer in Wales. There is now a massive cancer epidemic. There is a lot at stake. The Danish Committee judge, Henrik Waaben, who had taken the case over, wrote to me and said that he couldn't investigate the paper because it was too long ago. A 5-year Statute of Limitations applied, apparently. I don't blame him for chickening out.

The explanation given by Darby and Doll was that Hakulinen and Hansen looked at Acute Leukaemia. Darby Doll *et al* looked at 'All Leukaemia' and that, in the early years before 1960, many children registered with leukaemia of unclassified type. The questions being asked implicitly and explicitly by Hansen and Hakulinen in 1983 and 1986 had apparently already been addressed in the International Journal of Epidemiology in 1989. The paper *Incidence of Childhood Cancer in Denmark 1943-84* was by Peter de Nully Brown, Henrik Hertz, Jorgen Olsen, Minna Yssing, Elma Schiebel and Ole Moller Jensen. De Nully Brown and Olsen were to reappear on the Nordic leukaemia study in 1992. The intention and purpose of the paper was clear from the final sentence in the abstract: *Our descriptive data suggest that environmental exposures do not play any significant role in the aetiology of the majority of childhood cancers.* Can you believe these people? What causes the childhood cancer then? Bad luck? Witchcraft? The only real data shown that could be used to underpin this inane conclusion was a three-

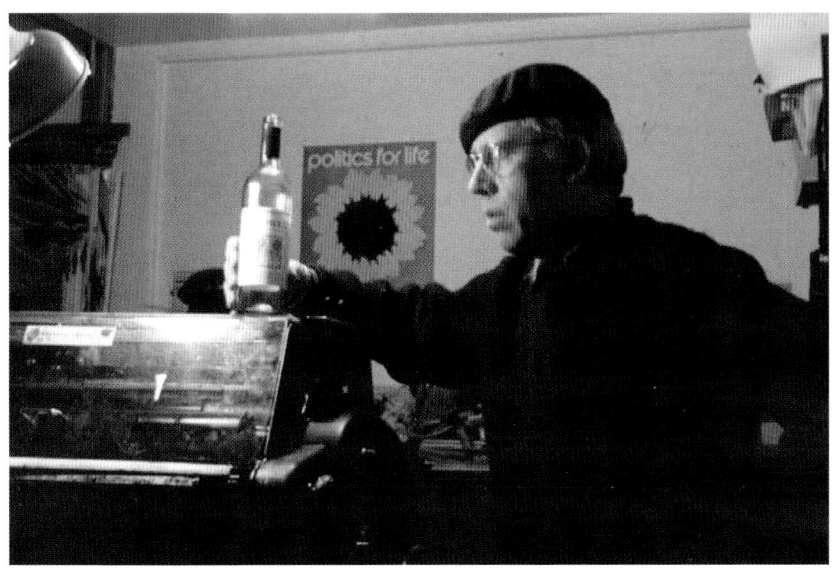

Plate 19 All in a day's work. Top: Printing all night on the huge AB Dick A2 Press at 38 Queen St. We had to reinforce the floor with steel pillars. The poster was printed on the (alcohol damped, as I was) press, which was a nightmare to operate and frequently reduced me to tears. Bottom: Richard Bramhall with the ex- Soviet Military Sodium Iodide crystal Gamma Ray Energy detector from East Germany.

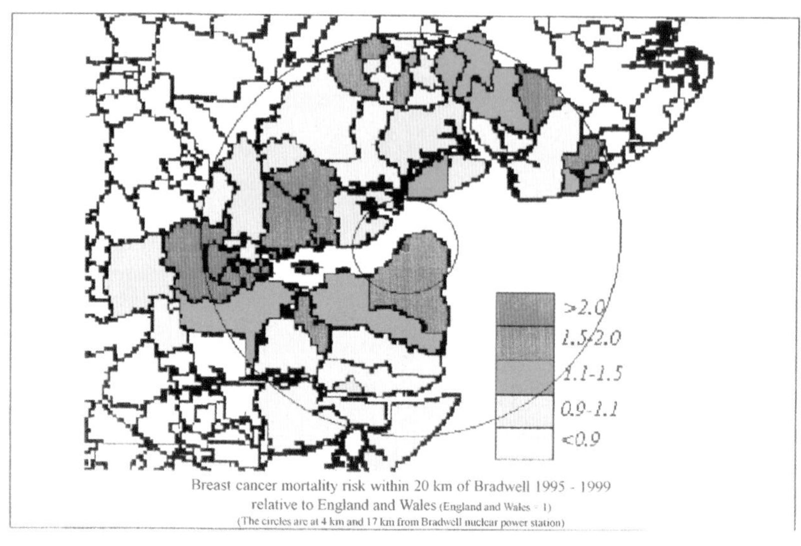

Plate 20 Top: Breast cancer mortality risk in North Essex near Bradwell Power Station and the estuary of the tidal 'river Blackwater'. Note low risk on the lower estuary where there is no nuclear site. Bottom: Metal Can label designed for the Euratom Campaign organised by Alex Begg of the Green Party.

Plate 21 *Sarj, there's a knife!* Richard Bramhall's Seargeant Mercer applies the ICRP averaging risk model to a murder investigation. Mercer was named after Dr Gerald Draper of the Childhood Cancer Research Group (Radioactive Times Vol 3 No 1 March 1999)

Causes of Cancer 3: Statistical artefacts

Causes of Cancer 2: Flying to Mallorca

Causes of Cancer 1: Population Mixing

Plate 22 My own cartoons from Radioactive Times. Top: Teddy and Dolly and The Causes of Cancer series. Bottom: Roger Radon, NRPB, ripped off from Dick Tracy.

Plate 23. Old and new independent researchers. Above: (L to R) Prof John Goldsmith (founded the International Society for Environmental Epidemiology), CB, Prof Ed Radford (resigned from the NCRP over health effects of radiation), Prof Ernest Sternglass (see text). Goldsmith and Radford are now dead. Below: Some of the Green Audit workers Jenny and Bruce Kocjian, Rachel Kaleta, Mark Carter, all now dispersed to make a living.

Plate 24 Top: LLRC/ Green Party Euratom Directive Campaign: South Lakeland Friends of the Earth in Kendal on April 1st 1998 obtained 552 signatures on the petition to oppose recycling nuclear waste into consumer goods. Nicola Davies (left centre) and Margaret Sanders (right centre). Bottom, Richard presents the petition to Baroness Symons in Cardiff with Richard (now Lord Livesey) and Jill Stallard of Welsh CND.

Plate 25 Independent Science from the ex-Soviet Union. Top: Professor Elena Burlakova from Moscow, University of Muenster, Germany 1997. Bottom: L to R Professor Alexey Yablokov from Moscow and Prof Wassily Nestorenko from Belarus, Ministry of Health, Kiev 2001.

Plate 26 Scary situations. Top: Calais 1981, taking the 87 ton ancient and leaky wood sailing barge *Revival* to Deauville. Below: toshed up and speaking at the Nobel Prize lectern at the Peace Institute in Oslo. The suit cost £6 from the Salvation Army shop in Aberystwyth. Note the bow tie which cost more!

Plate 27 Top: In the lock is the 65 ton Humber Keel *Nidd* which we converted to a yacht out of trade and lived on for 5 years. Celia and Lorraine on the warps, Frances and Araceli in hatch. Bottom: Trawsfynydd 1992: these are the people who change the world, the people who care.

Plate 28 Cause and effect. Top: Sellafield. Bottom: ICRF Charity Shop advertising Breast Cancer Day. All those pretty balloons!

Plate 29 Top: At the Big Green Gathering 2006: Saoirse Morgan, CB, Hugo Charlton, environmental barrister and ex-Chair of the Green Party. Bottom: members of the European Committee on Radiation Risk in Oxford (L to R): Richard Bramhall, Prof Inge Schmitz Feuerhake, Prof Elena Burlakova, Dr Paul Dorfman, Prof Alexey Yablokov, Prof Vyvyan Howard.

Plate 30 CERRIE at St Catherines College Oxford, 2003. L to R: CB, Dr Richard Wakeford, Dr Phil Day, Dr Eric Wright, Dr Colin Muirhead, Dr John Harrison, Prof Jack Simmons, Mr Pete Roche, Prof Dudley Goodhead, Dr Ian Fairlie, Dr Roger Cox.

Plate 31 Top: This low resolution picture was taken in Baghdad in Gulf War 2. We believe we have evidence of the use by the USA of uranium in missiles and bunker buster bombs. The temperature of a uranium explosion is over three thousand degrees causing a very white flash and the production of mobile sub-micron radioactive oxide particles. Below: a DU bullet from a A10 Warthog tankbuster gives a high reading on a Geiger counter (*Jo Baker)*.

Plate 32. Radioactive waste in middle England. Top: The weir below the Harwell radioactive waste outfall pipe to the Thames at Sutton Courtney. I measured high levels of gamma radiation on the river bank in 2002. Look at the willow tree. The part facing the spray from the weir seems to be dying. Below: The Aldermaston radioactive waste pipe to the Thames at Pangbourne. Green Party economist Miriam Kennet who lives nearby talks of children with cancer in the neighbourhood.

Plate 33. Top: in Aberystwyth with Ollan Herr, green activist, moral giant and hero of the Irish Sellafield case, which has now collapsed owing to the pusillanimity of the Irish State. Bottom: going down the sewer in Ray Fox's garden, Earley, Reading, for BBC Radio 4. The eerie echoing interview was repeated on 'pick of the week'.

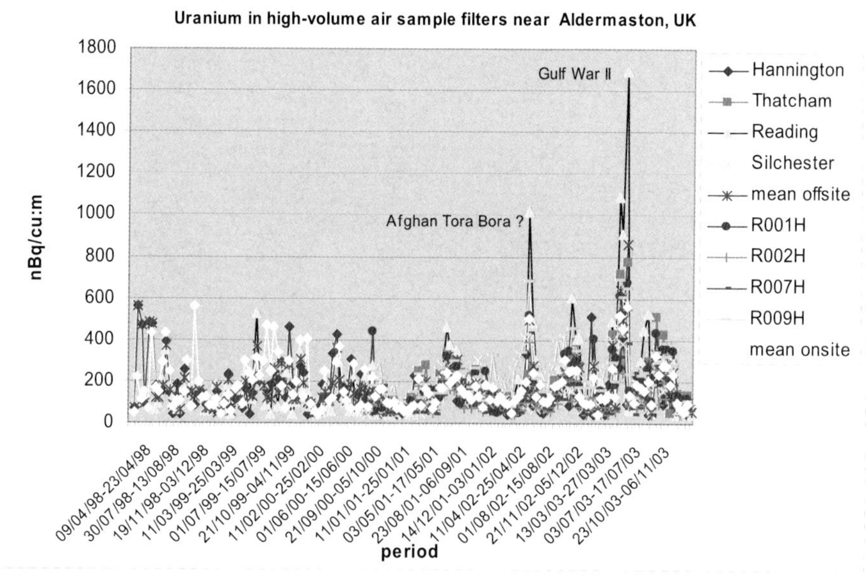

Plate 34 Saoirse Morgan (above) types in data obtained under the Freedom of Information Act from the Atomic Weapons establishment Aldermaston to produce the graph (below) showing the global dispersion of uranium oxide particles from Gulf War 2.

decade logarithmic trend graph of childhood cancer and leukaemia in the ages 0-14 from 1943 to 1984. Because they included neuroblastoma (rate 0.08 per 100,000) with leukaemia (rate 13 per 100,000) they were able to squeeze the leukaemia trend into the vanishing region of the log graph. This is a common ploy when embarrassing trends are displayed. Logarithmic graphs squeeze out any changes and should never be used for trend examination. Logarithmic display always should set off alarm bells, and three-decade log makes it virtually impossible to see an effect, particularly in the way it was plotted in this paper. Nevertheless, my photo-enlarging and careful measurements showed that there was a 20% increase in leukaemia between 1953-57 and 1968-72 for the 0-14 age group. Since this increase occurred after the fallout, it is hardly fair to say that they had shown no effect of the environment. Their result showed little resemblance to the Hakulinen/Hansen series or to the lost data, which I painstakingly typed into a computer program and began to unravel. Interestingly, the de Nully Brown paper did not reference Hakulinen *et al,* or Hansen *et al*. The airbrush was out.

13.4 Johannes Clemmesen and Otto Carlsen

In this search for the correct data, what no one had noticed was that there was another player in this area, Johannes Clemmesen, the original founder of the Danish Cancer Registry. Clemmesen was looking for the relationship between cancer and the environmental cause. Starting in 1943, he painstakingly collected cancer data and recorded the incidence rates in Denmark, together with essays and studies of the aetiology of cancer and leukaemia in five fat red volumes published between 1965 and 1977 covering the period 1943 to 1972. These volumes *Statistical Studies in Malignant Neoplasms* are an amazing source of information about cancer trends and cover the longest period of any cancer registry covering a large single genetic population. In order to examine trends, you have to have all of the five volumes. The Clemmesen series had been cited by Hansen *et al.* but none of the other papers had mentioned it. I began to obtain them from the British Library and to copy out the leukaemia data. Here at last was something I could trust. Apart from this, all there was were tables of numbers from people who were not high on my list of believable witnesses and which didn't generally agree with each other. After looking at and plotting the Clemmesen data on childhood leukaemia in the first four volumes I became stuck. The Fifth volume, needed to complete the study was missing from the British Library. I tried elsewhere, various Universities, the Internet, my daughter who is at the London School of Hygiene and Tropical Medicine. No luck. It had vanished into thin air. Why? It was actually possible that this was a piece of evidence available for anyone interested in checking out the effects of fallout in cancer, not just in children but also in adults. Maybe someone had removed it from the shelves of all these libraries. I had to have it. I telephoned my friend Otto Carlsen in Denmark. Could he get it from the National Library in Copenhagen? Was it there?

I had met Otto Carlsen when his political party *Folk-bevaegelsen mod EU* invited me to Copenhagen in 2000 to speak about the threat from the Euratom 'Basic Safety Standards Directive' which permitted the recycling of nuclear waste. He lives in Aalborg, on the northern tip of Denmark - 5 hours from Copenhagen by train. I emailed him my report on the issue and left it at that. A few months later, when I had largely given up, a box appeared by carrier on the doorstep. It contained all five of Clemmensens's volumes, and a letter from Otto. The letter said:

Dear Chris Busby,
The famous founder of the Danish Cancer Registry, now a very old man, this morning gave me two copies of his original work, one for you and one for me. I hope this allows you to decide upon the Twist that you described to me in your letter.
I couldn't reach the data through normal scientific libraries since restricted admission to the data is practiced. For certain reasons springing from my original research I chose to meet the founder personally, which I do not regret. Johannes Clemmesen, though of a very high age, is a person of integrity and dedication to his life work, described in his, several volume, written memoirs. Therefore I of course listened carefully to his expressing worries of the actual status of the institute (which may well be grounded?) that, 'research now has to follow 10 certain health lines instead of numerous more distinctly defined disease lines, of which some are seldom and rare'. These were Mr Clemmesens words to me yesterday. Do you have an opinion on this, or does it parallel tendencies elsewhere? My question for you.

I showed him my book on the investigations of the 'International Physicians against Nuclear Weapons' on which I am preparing the 2nd edition, and I guess this convinced him of you and I being worthy of him handing us over his work. After this meeting I picked it up today in the cellar of the Institute, with the help of Dr Hans Storm and Secretary Inge Bilde Hansen. Now as You can see, the one five volume copy I send to you as well as the same five volumes are to be considered our personal property, and I hope they shall help the common cause of preventing the diseases from low level radioactive pollution, certainly a noble purpose of decisive importance, and certainly a longsighted work in which you for years have been the forerunner. Many things have happened since my organisation, Folkebevaegelsen mod Unionen invited You to our country and You spoke in our Parliament, and I am sorry to say, that especially the Nordic countries have a lot more to be grateful for in regard of your research than has been outspoken. We ourselves had excellent scientists whose work had for years to wait

to meet acknowledgement. Niels Bohr is the best known. Me and my organisation wish you progress in your work to test and refine your theory,
Yours,
Otto Carlsen
Aalborg Oct 14th 2003

Well there it was, the whole dataset, one that I could believe since it was constructed printed and published before the arguments about Sellafield leukaemias after the Black committee in 1984 and well before the trial in 1993. What did it show? Was there an increase in childhood leukaemia in children or in infants in the Danish series? The answer is yes to both. And indeed, the increase is also there in the basic data that was miraculously found by Sarah Darby and arrived via the BMJ.

In Fig 13.4.1 I show this data from the Clemmesen series for the 0-4 year olds and plot it on top of the graph for the 0-4 year olds given by Darby *et al* in the Nordic leukaemia study paper in the BMJ. There is also an increase in infant leukaemia; a very significant point since we saw infant leukaemia after Chernobyl in England and Wales and the Nordic study was advanced in CERRIE as a reason why we should not believe the several studies that reported the increase in different countries. The big fat peak that is there in Denmark has been absorbed by mathematical magic into the Nordic trend shown by Darby *et al*. I still can't figure out how they did it as Sarah Darby hasn't given me the SAS program that they used (I asked her for it) but there you are.

13.5 Was there an increase in childhood and infant leukaemia after the weapons fallout?

Childhood leukaemia 0-4 is now believed to follow foetal exposure or exposure to the sperm. This is why it peaks in the age group 0-4. The increase of about 35% in childhood leukaemia follows a difference in absorbed dose to the foetus of about 80μSv so, if this was the cause, then we can compare the increase with the 40% increase found by Alice Stewart after 10mSv obstetric X-rays, which is now believed to be the best evidence of childhood cancer risk following exposure. The difference is about 125 times. That is to say that the Danish data suggest that 125 times more children developed leukaemia than would even be predicted by Alice Stewart's risk factors, never mind those of the ICRP which are much lower.

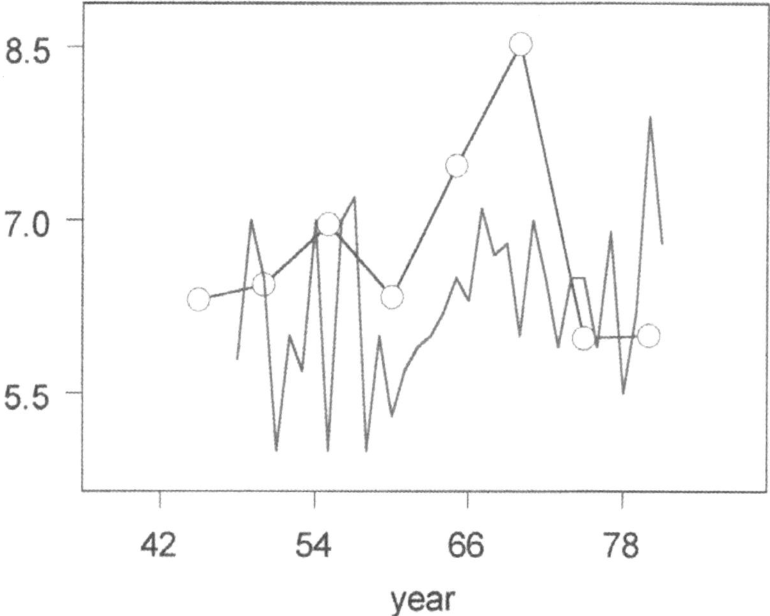

Fig 13.4.1 Rates of childhood leukaemia 0-4 in Denmark 1943-77 from Clemmesen publications (line with large circles) together with Darby *et al.* Nordic leukaemia study (1992) published trend (full line). Whoops! Of course, if we are looking at acute leukaemia, then the Hakulinen line Fig 13.2.1 is the true comparison.

But I am not really that interested in the calculation, because this involves more arguments about which dose, which risk factor, which age group, endless roundabouts of argument and counter argument which have been brought to CERRIE by the advocates of the nuclear industry: all very boring and complicated. All I wanted to report here was merely the way in which the Nordic leukaemia study was constructed to show that there was no increase in childhood leukaemia following the weapons fallout when the data showed there actually was. In fact, there was a very good study in England (Bentham and Haynes 1994) that showed that there was at least a 25% increase in childhood leukaemias between wet and dry areas of the country, and this result is in fairly good agreement with what the Clemmensen data and the Darby raw data from Denmark show. What of the other Nordic countries; what do they show? Well, I now have the data from the other Nordic countries also, but unfortunately they all begin their series at about the point you would expect there to be an effect. If you examine each country separately, then there are various peaks that occur at slightly different times and the overall average is smudged out. The best we can do is look and see what the other Nordic countries show after 1959, the earliest year for data for the whole bloc. When this is done (as I showed in *Wings of Death*) there is an increase there of about 25%.

Finally, when all this was revealed in the CERRIE committee, after all the work I did and the scurrying about by Otto and the pressure from the BMJ, what did Dr Darby and Professor Doll say? They said (and this is the honest truth, knock me down with a feather, you can ask them), *we knew all along that there was a peak in the childhood leukaemia incidence in Denmark. That is why we did the study: so as to see if it was there in the other Nordic countries also. And it wasn't, so it must have been a statistical blip.*

Well, there you are. End of story. So why did you not say this in the paper Drs Darby and Doll, and cite Clemmensen, Hakulinen *et al.*, Hansen *et al*?
Richard Bramhall jokingly composed a little Haiku which he called Hakku Haiku. It goes:

Hakulinen sees
Fallout brings disease; later
They cook the data

There are, of course, many problems with looking for an increase at the time of the fallout, 1959 to 1963. Lots of changes were occurring during the course of the time series. The fallout didn't arrive in one peak like it did with the Chernobyl epidemiology. There were large changes in birth rate in the early 1960s following the sexual revolution. There were very cold winters in the 1960s (due to the fallout in the stratosphere blocking out the sun, and the radiation affecting the ozone layer). There were many sources of radiation exposure in the late 1940s and early 1950s that would have increased the rates of childhood cancer in the early control period, e.g. obstetric X-rays, chest X-rays for TB screening, Radium dials on watches and wartime equipment like compasses. These radium dials were horribly radioactive and were clipped to the belt, giving a large dose to the testes. After the war, they were mostly sold in Army Surplus stores or just thrown away. I expect they gave much delight to children who acquired them and watched them (as I did) glow in the dark. The Army compass I still have (and use as a calibration source for our spectrometer) gives 50μSv per hour external dose. The large bubble in the card damping fluid is pure Radon. In one day, clipped to the belt, you get a whole year's equivalent of natural background. Perhaps this is the cause of the sharp increase in childhood leukaemia in the Shetland Islands during the influx of servicemen during the war, rather than the population mixing which Prof Leo Kinlen has based it on.

The increase in child leukaemia has been inexorable since the beginning of the last century. This actually supports the argument put forward by Sir Richard Doll that the radioactive releases from fallout and nuclear sites cannot be the cause of the increase in childhood leukaemia. But I complete this section with a graph I constructed following a suggestion by Richard Bramhall. In Fig 13.5.1 I plot world Radium production (which is the same trend as Uranium production) and childhood leukaemia mortality (which is the same as incidence up to 1960). Notice anything? We know now what is the basis of childhood leukaemia. It involves genetic damage *in utero* or around conception. The genetic damage causes chromosome double strand breaks. These rearrange and translocate to form new hybrid chimeric chromosomes that have sequences that code for new chimeric proteins. The translocations have been characterised and are found in child leukaemia cells. It is radiation that causes double strand breaks more than any other agent, particularly alpha radiation, or multiple tracks of beta or Auger radiation. The story is complete. It is only political power that forces it off the explanation list.

Finally, let me say that I am not really accusing anyone of dishonesty. I have had to do a lot of thinking about this since I met with and listened to Sarah Darby and her explanations. Bias, perhaps, and maybe the kind of unconscious bias that scientists suffer from like everyone else. The data they used was not altered; it was just selected. They accuse me of doing the same thing, and maybe I do. Maybe it's inevitable. I don’t try to do it and maybe they don’t either. If they had used acute leukaemia they would have found something quite different. If they had looked at Denmark alone they would have found something different. Why did they not draw attention to the earlier work? Well, this is more difficult to answer, but it isn’t a crime. I merely want to show that scientific studies do not always give the correct answer to the question they say they ask, and can be set up in such a way to affect the result in any direction. This is why it is so important to oppose every study with the opposite study before you make up your mind, particularly in an area that impacts on health with such awful consequences. The Nordic study is one kind of epidemiological twist. It ignored an uncomfortable result and absorbed it in a larger mass of data. Sometimes this cannot be done, and then there have to be other approaches.

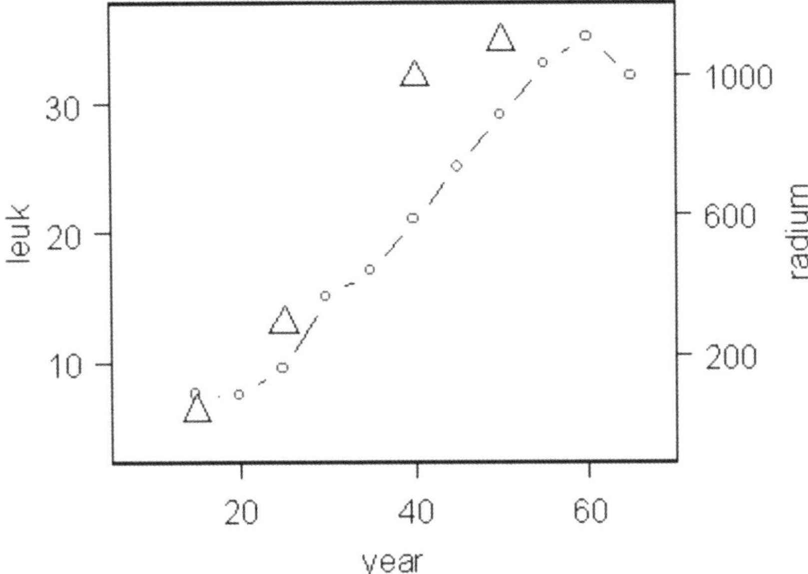

Fig 13.5.1 World Radium production and childhood leukaemia mortality trends (radium gramme, triangles; leukaemia death rates per million ages 0-4 in England and Wales, dots)

13.6 Darby, Doll and the Atomic Test Veterans

Sometimes it is possible to remove embarrassing cases from an epidemiological study to ensure that it shows nothing. We saw this happen in the Wales data. In the Nordic study, the cases were diluted out. In the story I now tell, cases were removed from a study after it began and although this did not succeed in changing the overall outcome, the conclusions of the first study were reversed by choosing a new period of comparison. The result was that a subsequent study reversed the findings of the initial one. I recently had to consider these studies in connection with a court case involving the widow of Gerald Adshead, one of the atomic test veterans, personnel who were drafted out to various parts of the world as part of Britain's testing of nuclear weapons. Mr Adshead died in 1999 from a malignant brain tumour and, if this might have been caused by exposure to radiation, then his wife Eva should receive a war widows pension. The pension was originally refused, however, on the basis that it was deemed unlikely that the exposure at Maralinga - which did not register on the (external) film badge dosimeter - could have been sufficient to result in the cancer. It is of interest that the US test veterans with cancer are automatically given pensions on the basis that their cancer may have been caused by the radiation; this mirrors a similar difference in behaviour over Gulf War syndrome between the US and Britain.

I have always argued that for the test veterans, film badge doses are irrelevant as the badges only register external radiation. The hazard was in the internal dose from fallout material. Maralinga is an extraordinarily contaminated place where uranium bombs were exploded. Gerald was a lorry driver. He drove equipment out to and back from the tower where the bomb was. He was a joker, a fun person according to his wife, Eva. He had no illusions about the effects of the tests and the exposures he had suffered, since although he had no record of exposure, he suffered a red rash on the back of his neck after one test. She told me that at one point he was the last person out and his lorry wouldn't start as the battery was flat. Everyone else had left and the clock was counting down. Luckily he had parked it on a hill and could bump start it after a push. Wow! After we won the case, Eva gave me his army doserate meter as a memento. It is on the shelf, reminding me of all the poor soldiers, sailors, airmen, technicians and national servicemen, defending their country standing out there in their khaki shorts with their backs to the flash and their eyes covered with their hands. They were all betrayed by the Ministry of Defence, by the scientists and by the health establishment.

So the exposure in this case was from material inhaled during the period Mr Adshead was in the test area. All this is familiar stuff. However, the arguments involved examining the two epidemiological studies of the UK Test Veterans undertaken by Darby and Doll *et al.* in 1988 and later by Darby and Doll *et al* in 1993.

Sarah Darby, lead author on these papers, collaborated with Richard Doll (again) and researchers from NRPB to examine the rates of cancer incidence and mortality in a sample of UK test veterans compared with a suitable control group. The result of the first study published in 1988, showed that there was a significantly higher level of leukaemia and multiple myeloma in the test veterans compared with the control (Darby et al 1988). This finding caused the MoD to decide to admit that the test veterans had a case and to presume that these diseases were radiation related. The success for the vets was short lived, however. In 1993 a new study was published by Darby and Doll and a new line up of NRPB researchers (Darby et al 1993). The new study used an 'expanded and altered study group' in which the excess leukaemia and multiple myeloma had apparently disappeared.

What had happened? Whatever it was, the MoD changed their decisions about awarding pensions and went back to denying any culpability. The tests caused leukaemia in 1988. By 1993 they did not cause leukaemia. The 1993 study was hauled out and dusted off and brought forward by AWE (the Atomic Weapons Establishment) to oppose the evidence I brought forward in the case of the late Gerald Adshead.

The first study, 1988

This study, one of the Darby and Doll radiation *ouvre*, was published in the *British Medical Journal* (Darby et al, 1988) and examined death from 38 causes in 22,347 men who participated in the UK atmospheric tests between 1952 and 1967 in Australia and the Pacific Ocean, according to MoD archives. Their mortality and cancer incidence was compared with 22,326 matched controls. The period of the study was up till 1984. Note the numbers which are given again in Table 13. 6. 1 The standardised mortality ratio from all causes was 1.01 and for cancers was 0.96: this just means that they were very fit men being compared with a general population, another favourite trick of the epidemiologists. But comparing with the controls for leukaemia and multiple myeloma there was a significant excess risk (RR, leukaemia = 3.45, 22 deaths observed, 6 in controls) (RR myeloma = infinite; 6 deaths observed, 0 in controls). For incidence, the risk from leukaemia was also high RR = 2.43 with 28 reported developing the disease compared with 11 controls and for multiple myeloma, 10 in the participants and none in the controls. On the basis of these findings, the military were forced to concede that at least leukaemia and multiple myeloma were caused by the exposures and give war widows pensions. Clearly this cost the military relatively little; however it had serious implications for radiation risk models since the participants should not have been developing leukaemia at the film badge doses involved, which were generally (like Gerald Adshead's) below 1 mSv. So something had to be done and it was.

The second study, 1993

This was apparently an update to the first study with seven extra years of data to 1991. It was published by NRPB (R-266-1993) and also in the BMJ [Darby et al 1993]. Its conclusions were different and it allowed the MoD to do a U turn on the leukaemia and the pensions. The argument was that the intervening seven years of data showed a very low rate of leukaemia in the irradiated group relative to the controls, and so therefore the initial study must have been a chance result. This second study involved largely the same individuals, though a reduced number - 21,358 vets and 22,333 controls. But here is the problem: there was a crucial difference in the study group and a mind numbingly stupid analysis. First, 1503 men had been taken out of the veterans group on the basis that these men 'had no more potential for radiation exposure than the general public'. The second change was that any leukaemias or cancer occurring in the first two years were assumed not to be caused by the tests and were discounted when analysing the extra period of 7 years. 6 leukaemia deaths had occurred in the extra five years according to the report. and 3 additional deaths from multiple myeloma. The abstract of R-266 concludes:

The suggestion from a previous study that participants may have experienced small hazards of leukaemia and multiple myeloma is not supported by the additional data and the excesses observed now appear likely to be a chance finding although the possibility that test participation may have caused a small risk of leukaemia in the early years after the tests cannot be ruled out.

It is now time to look at the numbers of leukaemia deaths. The second study lost 1503 men that were in the first study. The first study found 22 leukaemia deaths in the 22,347 participants in the entire period of follow up to 1983, with 6 deaths in the 22326 controls (RR = 3.45; p = 0.0000). The second study (1984-91) found an extra 6 deaths in the participants (after the three deaths in the excluded group had been removed) in the extra seven years and an extra one death in the earlier period which brings the total deaths in the participants for the whole period to 29. In the control group, in this extra 7 years, there were 11 deaths. At the tribunal I pointed out that it was bad practice to remove participants from the study after it had begun, especially since there were three deaths in only 1503 persons, a crude rate of 200 per 100,000 compared with the rate in the controls of about 67 (RR = 3.02). It looked like they were trying to get rid of cases. Why? Well one possibility was that these cases were in the extra 7 year period. If we assume this, then this period gives a RR about equal to unity. I pointed this out to the Tribunal hearing Gerald Adshead's case and also presented the new ECRR 2003 report (which I will review later) to back up the arguments. The MoD advisor called for a three month recess but the Tribunal found for the widow, a victory for careful examination of a scientific paper. But I hadn't thought the logic through. In fact, the main problem with the MoD arguments and the conclusions of the second study was one that was so enormous that it was invisible.

Men are irradiated during their tour of duty, either from internal radioactivity or from an external dose. This is mainly in the period 1955-60. If this was Hiroshima, then the results of the study of the survivors show increases in leukaemia peaking ten years after the exposure and decaying away relative to the controls after about twenty years. The first study examined the differences between the veterans and the controls up to 1984, i.e. about 25 years of follow up. By then, all the differences in leukaemia will have emerged between the irradiated and the controls. And they have: we see a three-fold excess in the 1988 paper, highly significant, not related to dose, indeed most of the recorded doses were below 1mSv. This would have been very bad news for the nuclear industry. In 1988 they were in the full throes of the Sellafield arguments. Leukaemia clusters were popping up near nuclear sites all over. Even if all the doses were 1mSv, a three-fold excess of leukaemia represents a jolly big error in the ICRP model.

Now here is the truly extraordinary development: Darby and Doll *et al* examined a small period following the end of the earlier period, the seven years from 1984 to 1990. After removing some cases (we don't know when these removed deaths occurred, but we would like to) it was found that the rate in the participants was now less than that in the controls. There were 6 deaths in the participants and 11 in the controls in this period. On this late 7-year basis they argued that the earlier 27 year span result finding was chance. But not only was the earlier period much longer with more deaths, it included the ten year lag peak when all the leukaemias would have presented themselves. The second study looked at a period from 27 years after the irradiation to 34 years after the irradiation. On this basis we could take a look at the difference in the leukaemia rates in the Hiroshima controls and irradiated group 30 years after the bomb and conclude that any large excess found ten years after the bomb was a chance finding. In addition, with a variation in the susceptibility in a fixed population, removal of a person by dying of leukaemia will make the survivors more resistant. Furthermore, by 1963, the controls were receiving large doses from northern hemisphere weapons fallout.

To reinforce what was done by Darby *et al*, I will give an example of the trend in risk from leukaemia in the irradiated. Boice *et al* (1985) shows that acute leukaemia increased in those patients treated with radiation for cervical cancer in the 10 years after the treatment. But after this increase, between 10 and 24 years after the treatment, the rate was actually about 50% lower than the control group. If Boice *et al* used the logic of Darby *et al*, they could have argued that the decrease in risk in the second period showed that the increase in the first period was a chance effect and that leukemia was not caused by radiation.

There were other major problems with both studies which I will just briefly review.

(1) Army men who were discharged on medical grounds were excluded from both studies The Army represented about 42% of the total. This introduced a serious bias at the outset.

(2) A further and admitted bias has to do with Social Security (DHSS) claimants. This would be concentrated in the early period. The authors claimed to have controlled for this bias by leaving out the Army men, but most of the Army were Royal Engineers, and a final quality control check involved only a 1% sample of RE records, turning up one further participant who had been missed. This indicated a further 100 DHSS claimants axiomatically likely to be sick, missing from the participants group.

(3) 40% of known participants could not be included as their service records were missing: these were known to be at dirty Maralinga, like Gerald Adshead, who was not included in the study. Another 47% were at Christmas Island.

(4) The studies made much of the fact that the soldiers had the same mortality as the general public. This is another trick. As with studies of nuclear workers, the comparison with the general public is irrelevant since the participants were chosen as healthy. The control group served in the 'tropics' but where they were serving is not noted. In view of the wide ranges of fallout contamination (like the serious contamination that occurred in the case of the Japanese fishing boat 'Lucky Dragon', hundreds of miles from the nuclear tests in the Pacific) the use of such people as controls was itself questionable unless we can be sure they were not

exposed to fallout from the tests. This is the same problem as that of the Marshall Island studies which I reviewed in *Wings of Death.*

So to summarise all this, I can say that the initial study (which may or may not have looked at all the people involved) nevertheless found that there was an excess of leukaemia and multiple myeloma in men whose external dose was too low, on the ICRP predictions to have been the cause. Therefore a subsequent study removed cases and focused on a short period more than twenty five years after the initial exposure, when all the leukaemia rates had fallen back to normal, to argue that the initial finding was due to chance.

13.7 SAHSU, random clusters and Bayesian smoothing

I want to turn now to some epidemiological scams developed in the 1990s to get rid of uncomfortable evidence of cancer near point sources of pollution. You will recall that in 1983 it was Yorkshire TV who discovered the Sellafield child leukaemia cluster. At the subsequent enquiry, Sir Douglas Black recommended setting up a group to check for childhood leukaemia and cancer clusters so that it wouldn't be the TV reporters who found them. The HTV researchers recent discovery of the child leukaemias near the Menai in north Wales, reviewed in the last chapter, shows that the attempt failed. This is not surprising. What Black was hoping for is that such a group would get to the clusters before the TV did. What the group that was set up, the Small Area Health Statistics Unit (SAHSU), decided to do was something much cleverer: theoretically dismiss the concept of causal clusters altogether. The existence of the clusters would then be unknown since no data would be allowed out for small areas under the excuse of patient confidentiality. If anyone flagged up a problem, a local doctor perhaps, then the health authority would call in SAHSU, and they would carry out an expensive study that would conclude that there was no problem. No figures would be given, just a conclusion.

Following Black, SAHSU was set up and funded by the government. Its boss is Professor Paul Elliott and it is presently based at Imperial College in London, though for a time it was at the London School of Hygiene and Tropical Medicine. These people have become called 'cluster busters' because of the tangled and complex mathematical sophistry they have developed to argue that there is no such thing as a point source related cancer cluster. They use two methods for this, which they developed or adopted soon after they were set up. The first was the Poisson analysis of random clusters: the *a priori* hypothesis and the concept of the Texas Sharpshooter. The second was Bayes smoothing. Both techniques are now taught to all epidemiologists at school and they take these in with their mother's milk, so to speak. It is next to impossible to demonstrate the existence of any effect in the face of these procedures. If you want to know what is going on, don't call an epidemiologist. They will be able to deny the existence of the rising sun.

To illustrate the kind of thing that happens I shall give two examples from our own work.

The Texas Sharpshooter strikes in Northampton.

The first example illustrates the 'Texas Sharpshooter' argument and was deployed in a BBC documentary called *Street of Doom (18 June 1996)* about the child leukaemia cluster in Pembroke Road, Northampton. Green Audit, acting on behalf of the parents of two of the children formally complained to the Broadcasting Standards Authority about this BBC programme and its content. We lost the case because the issue was too technical, and the board accepted the explanations of the advisors of the programme (including Ray Cartwright).

The 'Texas sharpshooter' is said to draw a target around the point that his bullet struck. That is to say, in epidemiology, you must make a hypothesis before you make a discovery. Paul Elliott actually discounted the Sellafield leukaemia cluster on this basis. He argued that the fact that there was a high rate discovered there by the TV crew could not be used as evidence because they did not have a prior hypothesis (BMJ 313, 1996, 863-6). This is nonsense, incidentally, Cutler went there to dig around because radiation causes leukaemia and Sellafield is the largest source of radiation. But he did think that it would be in the workers themselves, not the children. There is a major problem with this approach: it excludes the known environmental cause; you are not allowed to look at the data to see what is there. That is called data mining. The argument is that in any large data set, there is bound to be something on the basis of the play of chance. You can then grab that and decide it is linked to the agent you wish to implicate. In the case of the Pembroke Road cluster, it was the intention to address the very real concerns about cancer and leukaemia clusters in the mind of the public by arguing that they were all due to the play of chance. In the programme, the BBC and their advisors set out to contrast the 'ignorant parents' (who naturally and correctly believed there might be some common cause for their children's deaths) with the analysis of the clever scientists who maintained that the cluster was entirely due to chance. The Northampton Health Authority's own report, which the BBC drew on heavily, began with the fact that any truly random dispersion of points on a map would naturally have some points which were close together or clustered. Drawing a circle around these points after the event would be like the Texas Sharpshooter. In this report they reproduced a 10x10 grid in which the random distribution of 40 points was apparently calculated and shown on the TV screen. I reproduce it in Fig 13.7.1

X		X					X		
	X		XX						
	X				X				
X		X	X			X			
	XX					X	X	X	
X			X		X				
	XX XX	XX			X	X			
X		X	X		X				X
	X		X			XX X			
		X							X

Fig 13.7.1 Bogus mapping of randomness to "prove" that in a dispersion of 40 points in a grid of 100 squares can give four points in one square by chance. The four crosses in the same square are very unlikely, but the BBC program incorrectly argued that they could have occurred by chance (see text).

I was fascinated by this cluster, where there were four points in one cell of the grid. Our attempts to use Poisson statistics to reproduce the effect failed. This is because such a cluster is actually very unlikely. Not only that, but the Pembroke road data had 28 cases in the whole area, not 40. Why did the advisors to the programme makers not distribute 28 points randomly? The answer is that this would have made it even more unlikely. For a 28-event situation the probability is 0.016 or 1 in 63 that there will be four cases clustered in a single cell of a grid of 10x10. And if this was not enough, the programme did not even show the real map of cases, which shows them strung along the side of the valley that carries the trains, the power lines and the river, and most important, the sidings where the nuclear trains waited with their leaky containers of spent nuclear fuel en route to Sellafield. The complete map was obtained by us from John Parfitt, director of Health of Newbury District Council, who had been using the Northampton report and the BBC programme to argue that the child leukaemia cluster in Newbury was also a random cluster. Parfitt showed the BBC video to parents in order to allay their fears that the leukaemias might actually be caused by the high levels of Plutonium in the soils nearby.

In our complaint to the Broadcasting Standard Authority, made on 23 June, 1997 we argued that the case was made erroneously and failed under the following headings:

- Biased selection of scientific opinion
- Flawed statistical analysis, in that the map of the cases was not shown, the Poisson statistics were not accurately calculated, the relative risk at Pembroke road was given as 6-fold whereas it was actually over 100 fold, that known causes of leukaemia were ignored and that the nuclear train connection was not mentioned.

We argued that the computer screens generating the random clusters of dots and showing them falling occasionally in the same grid square were mathematically wrong. We argued that the actual distribution of the real cases, in a string along the river valley, was not a random pattern and asked why they did not show this map. The interesting thing in all this is that it is really quite elementary to show that the grid they showed on the programme to demonstrate the point about clusters was not mathematically correct. In fact it was wrong. In an exam they would have failed. But this was not enough. The real world is not a school and there is no teacher to appeal to. The ideology and the programme were certified by real epidemiologists. The Broadcasting Standards people were not going to get out their calculators. Probably they wouldn't know how, but you'd at least think they would ask someone about it. But no! They threw out our case.

And guess who appeared in the programme to say that the cause of childhood leukaemia was unknown and that all studies had failed to determine it (ignoring the only known cause and the Hiroshima studies)? Ray Cartwright.

Thomas Bayes and the Bradwell cancers

When I first heard about the technique of Bayes smoothing of mapped risk data I thought it was a joke. Now that I understand more about what it sets out to do, I realise that there may be a need for something like this, but it seems to me that the way in which it is carried out is basically in the wrong direction. What is it? Well, it is a general method for dealing with risk maps. The problem with risk maps (and you can see some of these in the Plates section) is that if you just plot risks in small areas as varying shades of red and green say, then you can get some small areas showing very high risks in low population wards just because there are only a few people; in these cases the statistical significance is low. On the other hand, if you decide to plot statistical significance to get round this, there can be high statistical significance in areas of high population, even though the risks are only slightly raised. The Bayes approach is essentially to map risks but assume that any sudden change in risk across an artificial border (like a ward boundary) is 'unlikely' and to reduce it towards the mean for the whole area by some amount (making the red pink). Araceli Busby sent me this:

Bayes methods involve a specification of the SUBJECTIVE prior knowledge of the Relative Risks that must be estimated. Essentially the method involves correcting the area SMR towards the mean, with the size of the correction depending on the size of the population in the given area. Thus an area where there is a larger population will be corrected to a lesser degree than one with a smaller population. If the population is small the posterior estimate will be close to the overall mean.

Well that's OK then. If we find a leukaemia cluster in Sellafield we can say that the population is small and adjust the relative risk towards the mean, i.e. 1.0. We don't have to worry about the existence of a source for the risk. We have already seen that, in fact, we are not even allowed to. In case you think this is all academic, I will just relate what happened to the breast cancer cluster in Maldon, Essex, which we laid at the door of radioactive pollution from Bradwell nuclear power station.

The story of the Bradwell breast cancer mortality study has already been given in Chapter 9, section 9.5. Green Audit carried out a mortality study on the wards within 17km of the nuclear power station at Bradwell, which discharges to the muddy estuary of the river Blackwater. The radioactivity is trapped in the mud and is carried inland by sea spray and by the sea to land transfer. We found that, like Hinkley Point, the wards near the estuary had higher risks from Breast cancer. SAHSU were called in and paid to do the same study. As I mention in 9.5 there were some errors in the Green Audit initial study and also some errors in the SAHSU initial study. When COMARE pointed these out, we corrected them and in the second report showed that, in fact, the effect we discovered was unchanged, even that it had become more significant. However it turned out that the same was not true for the SAHSU errors. Whereas we had shifted some cases from one ward to the next accidentally, they had omitted a whole load of cases entirely, due to a problem with their system not using certain postcodes. The result was that their conclusion *no wards had a significant excess risk of breast cancer mortality* was no longer true. The wards of Maldon, at the head of the Blackwater, and where the MAFF measurements show the highest levels of radioactive contamination, now had significant doubling of breast cancer deaths in the period we studied. When the correct figures were used, SAHSU must have discovered this also, and that their original paper to the health authority had been wrong. What could they do? Well, apologise and give the money back would have been a start. What they did at this point was bring in Bayes smoothing. On the basis that such a statistically significant excess was unlikely, they brought all the risks in the wards down to the mean so that they could still say that there was no ward with a statistically significant excess. And so they produced a second paper acknowledging the earlier mistake, but maintaining that there was still no problem. We would never have heard of this, incidentally, except for a conversation I had with Bryn Bridges, Chair of COMARE.

The Bradwell studies contain one other interesting piece of information that suggests that the whole business is a conspiracy to cover up the effects of radioactive discharges. This is the evidence of the links between the various players that we were able to discover through judicious use of the Data Protection Act. Before I review this there is one last twist to the Bradwell studies worth relating. In the CERRIE committee, it was agreed at an early stage that the way forward to resolve the arguments about whether there is or is not a coastal effect on cancer was to re-run the Bradwell study using incidence data as well as mortality data for a longer period than that available to our original study. At this early stage, in December 2001, most of the nuclear industry and NRPB side of the committee still thought that we had made a mistake in the figures, and that in reality there was no effect. So they were anxious to prove this under conditions where we would have to agree that there was no problem, i.e. with the same (but new) data. It emerged, after we had agreed to this joint study that the mistake made no difference to the result for us, though it certainly did for SAHSU. Consternation. However, the project could not easily be stopped by them at this stage without admitting that it was always a ploy to discredit our calculations. So they stalled, and although the wards and protocols were agreed by both sides, no data came from the Office for National Statistics. We were told by the Secretariat that there was no reply from ONS to a number of letters sent. This went on for more than eighteen months. After Michael Meacher, who set up the committee, was sacked as environment minister by Tony Blair in July 2003, the CERRIE committee was given a deadline by the new Minister, Elliot Gould, for finishing its discussions and projects. ONS eventually replied and a meeting was set up. Despite the ONS agreement to let the committee have the data, aggregated to appropriate levels, the Chair, Dudley Goodhead, cancelled the study on the spurious grounds that there was no agreement about the ward identities, something that had been agreed (and which we taped) in early 2003. So the study was not to go ahead. If it had, then the result would be that a government committee would find that there was a sea coast effect on cancer associated with radioactive discharges. This would have opened the floodgates to litigation and goodness knows what.

13.8 The UKCCCS study, Ray Cartwright and childhood leukaemia

On the 29th May, 2001 Richard Bramhall wrote a letter to the Fitness to Practise Directorate of the General Medical Council at 178 Great Portland Street in London. It was a request to examine the behaviour of Prof. Ray Cartwright of Leeds University then head of Epidemiology at the Leukaemia Research Fund.
Bramhall wrote:

We are writing to you to make a formal complaint and ask you to investigate Professor Raymond Cartwright's role in the current study of childhood cancer in the United Kingdom (UKCCS), which involves large amounts of public and charitable funds. We are concerned that during a decade of research intended to discover the cause of childhood leukaemia it seems that Raymond Cartwright has consistently directed attention away from radioactive pollution, thus subverting the study's ability to test one of its basic hypotheses. When challenged to explain his behaviour in this respect he has told untruths in public. We are also concerned that he appears to be involved with the British Nuclear Energy Society, which raises issues of conflict of interest, which should also be investigated.

The details were straightforward. Childhood leukaemia, the largest illness cause of death in children under age 4 has steadily increased in the developed world since about 1910. Massive amounts of money and energy have been poured into the investigation of the problem of the cause. The UKCCS study, begun in the early 1990s, was a huge prospective case control study of all the children born in England and Wales. It cost the government and the cancer charities about £15 Million. Ray Cartwright was a senior figure in the study design, if not the most senior. I spent some time in *Wings of Death* drawing attention to the correspondence I had with him over this design in March 1992 and how he had stated that he did not intend to look at fission product isotopes like Strontium-90 and Plutonium (despite the evidence at the time that this substance was associated with increases in leukaemia). He wrote to me in April 1993:

...it had not been thought appropriate to study such sources until answers were available in respect of radon and natural gamma exposures

According to the protocol of the study (a document dated 14th September, 1992) five hypotheses were *worth testing*. The first of these was that:

Childhood cancer may be caused by exposure of the child to ionising radiations, either in utero or postnatally, including both radiations ***from manmade sources*** *and from terrestrial low-LET gamma radiation and high-LET alpha particle radiation from natural sources, either individually or combined*

What I was unaware of in 1995, but had been brought to my attention by Dr Steward in Wales, was that in 1990 Professor Cartwright was one of the authors of a study which found a positive association between leukaemia incidence and residence near estuaries, where the hypothesis was that radioactive contamination of the estuarine mud was a causative factor in the aetiology of leukaemia (Alexander, Cartwright *et al*, 1990)

Cartwright did also seem to be somewhat close to the nukes. When we carried out our direct action and Bramhall dressed as Death, chaining himself to the stage at the British Nuclear Energy Society conference in Stratford on Avon in 1997 (Plate 17) and got thrown out, we noticed that the British Nuclear Energy Society listed Professor Cartwright as a member of its 'organising committee'.

On April 1, 1998 Richard Bramhall was at another conference in Keble College, Oxford organised by the Health and Safety Executive in partnership with DTI, DETR and DoH. He asked Dr Hilary Walker of DoH about the scope of the UKCCCS study and its capacity for determining the impact of manmade radioactive contamination. In a carefully worded reply Dr Walker said that the study "still covers the original five hypotheses" and that, in respect of manmade radioactive contamination, "the data could be dredged at a later date." Richard decided to follow this up.

In May 1998 he wrote to Cartwright to ask him to confirm Dr Walker's assertion. In August 1998 the reply said that ... *the study has made no attempt whatsoever to ascertain exposure from the trivial levels of artificial radioisotopes consequential upon atmospheric and aqueous discharges*. In November 2000 Richard attended a meeting at Harwell at which Professor Cartwright discussed his research. He stood up and asked from the audience:

It is true, isn't it, that you were one of the authors of a paper on leukaemia and estuaries; and that the prior hypothesis of that study was that the estuaries contain man-made radioactivity from Sellafield and other sources, and that radiation was a known cause of leukaemia; and that you did find a significant increase? Now, if all that is true - and it is in the literature - the question is: Why did the UK Childhood Cancer Study, which you designed, make no attempt whatever (I am quoting a letter you wrote to me) "to ascertain exposure to man-made radioactivity?"

Replying, Cartwright agreed that the 1990 paper had shown a positive association but that it had not been confirmed by subsequent studies *including one currently in press*. He said he would send the citations. On November 28, 2000 Bramhall wrote to Professor Cartwright, recorded delivery, asking for the citations. The letter was signed for in Leeds November 30, 2000. There was no reply. He wrote again on February 2, 2001. There was no reply. On March 5, 2001 he wrote again. On March 30, 2001 Cartwright replied sending a partial copy of an unpublished BSc thesis by one of his own students, Frances Lloyd dated May 1999

This paper was subsequently examined at the CERRIE committee and shown to be worthless, even laughably so. Tables of numbers of cases made no sense. The estuaries used by Lloyd were not the same as those in the original paper; the time periods were different and were after Chernobyl. It seemed to have been cobbled together in a hurry to cover the fact that there was actually no new work on the original hypothesis. And in any case, the question is how a paper written by a student in 1999 could have informed the decision not to look at man-made radiation in the UKCCS study which had by then been crystallised at least five years earlier and which had, as far as Cartwright's letter to me was concerned, crystallised in 1993, six years before the Lloyd's paper was produced in desperation.

Bramhall's letter to the BMA said:

The UKCCS, after almost ten years of work and expense, has completely failed to test its first hypothesis. When its emphasis on radon and natural gamma was questioned in 1993 Professor Cartwright's reply suggested that it might be possible to examine manmade radioactivity at a later date, an opinion echoed by Dr Walker of DoH in April 1998. However, Professor Cartwright's letter of August 1998 reveals that the UKCCS has collected no data on exposures to inform such an examination. In view of the amount of persistent evidence of associations between nuclear installations and cancer this is a serious failing in a study that had set out to investigate radiation from manmade sources.

We have asked Professor Cartwright for an explanation. The question is: what evidence had come to light by September 14, 1992 (the date of the UKCCS Protocol) to persuade the author or authors that it was unnecessary to ascertain such exposures. Professor Cartwright's assertion at the Harwell meeting in November 2000 appears to be an untruth - there were no "subsequent studies", and nearly seven years were to elapse before one of his own students had written a thesis which is far from conclusive and remains unpublished.

Whether or not this is the case, the evidence makes it difficult to escape the conclusion that Professor Cartwright has skewed the UKCCS in order to avoid revealing associations between radioactive pollution and disease. We do not know why this is. We asked him about his connection with the British Nuclear Energy Society but he has made no response other than to state that he is "not a member of BNES".

It may be thought that the forthcoming study of childhood cancer incidence relative to proximity to nuclear power stations which the Committee on Medical Aspects of Radiation in the Environment is about to undertake using data collected by UKCCS will adequately inform about risks from radioactive pollution. This is not so. The first hypothesis of the UKCCS requires a different approach. There is in addition abundant evidence that the disease is associated with radioactivity in the environment, which is distributed unevenly by a number of mechanisms. Such a hypothesis was explicit in the 1990 study we have referred to and was positively demonstrated.

The UK Co-ordinating Committee on Cancer Research has, for no clear reason, declined to give us detailed information about the contributions made to the UKCCS by various funding bodies until they have seen the substance of our concerns. They have confirmed, however, that the bodies to whom we are copying this letter are involved (except DETR and the National Audit Office), and that the study has cost some £11½ millions of which £½ million has come from the Department of Health.

During nearly a decade of research millions of pounds have been spent, some of it from government revenue, but with a large proportion given by members of the public who are anxious to find the cause of childhood cancer. We believe that Professor Cartwright has neglected a major aspect of the UKCCS, in that respect wasting those resources. We feel that this is a very serious matter, and we seem to be unable to obtain a satisfactory explanation from Professor Cartwright. Please ask him to account for his actions.

This letter was copied to:
Hon Michael Meacher, DETR, Rt Hon Alan Milburn, DoH, Douglas Osborne, Chief Executive, Leukaemia Research Fund, Sir Paul Nurse, Director General, Imperial Cancer Research Fund, Professor Gordon McVie, Director General, Cancer Research Campaign, Eddie O'Gorman, Chair of Trustees, Foundation for Children with Leukaemia, Michael Pattison, Kay Kendall Leukaemia Fund, Miss Julie Hearn, UKCCCR, Sir John Bourne, Comptroller and Auditor General, National, Audit Office, Dr Penny Snell, Medical Research Council
Health and Community Care Committee, Scottish Parliament

The BMA took this seriously but clearly were in a pickle about what to do. This was high politics and serious stuff. They eventually wriggled out of having to do anything. They wrote back and explained that because the complaint was not one involving clinical practice they would pass the complaint on to Leeds University, where Professor Cartwright worked. (You bet this is what will happen over the Steward complaint). Leeds University apparently examined the issue and felt that the problem was that Cartwright had misled us (and a public meeting) about the publication dates of the Lloyd paper (which by then had still not been published). They asked Cartwright to write to us and apologise (which he eventually did) but only about misleading the public over the date of a publication. But the complaint was not about the publication date of the Lloyd paper. It was about how the UKCCS study seemed to have been directed away from one of its defining questions and it is outrageous that the BMA committee passed the buck on such an important issue.

The UKCCS study, for all its huge expense, turned out to be so surrounded by establishment figures like Carwright and Doll that, in the end, nothing much was apparently either looked for or found. Our explanation for the increases in childhood leukaemia is straightforward. I presented it earlier in this chapter

13.9 The Section 7 Data Protection Act requests

In 2003 I was asked by the comedian Mark Thomas to help with a TV programme about a radioactive house in Earley in Reading. While we were together he told me of a method which could be used to obtain information from anyone who was writing letters about you using email. It is to make a request under Section 7 of the Data Protection Act 1998 for information about you that is held by anyone in electronic format. You can write to the Health Authority, or BNFL, or SAHSU or whoever you think you want to find out more about and send £10 stating that: *this is an official request for information that I am entitled to under Section 7 (1) of the Data Protection Act 1998. If you need further information from me, or a fee, please let me know as soon as possible. If you do not handle these requests for your organisation, please pass this letter to your data protection official.*
Actually, I was already on to this as I had watched him use the technique in an earlier series of his programme. I have sent such requests to various organisations involved in the arguments we have had relating to cancer in small areas, and received some very useful and interesting information, usually torn from them through fear of legal reprisals and appearing at the last minute (they have to reply with the information within six weeks). But none of these have been as interesting as the reply I received from the data protection officer at Imperial College London in response to my request for any emails that mentioned me by name from the Small Area Health Statistics Unit (based at St Mary's Hospital, part of IC). The response, from Mr CP Ince, sent me paper copies of 17 emails that existed in the system of Imperial College between individuals, all of whose names were blacked out. I show an example in Fig 13.9.1

Paul Aylin

Subject: RE: Busby/S

SAHSU

Mike Quinn (NCIC) . big fish 2.

sign of ----

detective

Good detective work by Mike....

National Cancer Intelligence Centre.

Subject: RE: Busby

Paul Aylin (SAHSU)

Subject: RE: Busby!!!

Elliott. Paul (Director SAHSU).

-----Original Message-----

Subject: RE: Busby!!!

wording

Essex

CERRIE (which has been set up by COMARE to look at health effects near nuclear sites, and includes Busby).

problem

received

NOT

N.ESSEX

Fig 13.9.1 Two emails released to me under Section 7(1) of the Data Protection Act 1998, apparently containing my name. My notes on these identify some of the words blacked out.

These emails were about Bradwell and I later realised that they referred to the major and fatal mistakes made by SAHSU. Not only were the authors of the emails blacked out, but so were the texts, except for a few scraps. One scrap said, among twenty blacked out lines (shown ===):

Subject: Busby!!!!

==============================and has Busby on his back to release all correspondence and details concerning our discrepancies. This obviously reinforces Busby's conspiracy theory, and=======================

Unfortunately (for them), this one had not been adequately blacked out at the top where the author and recipient were listed and use of a magnifying glass enabled us to read the tops and tails of the letters. They were Paul Aylin (SAHSU), presumable the author of the mistake- ridden Bradwell study and Paul Elliott (SAHSU boss) the biggest fish in this pond. In another email, also blacked out but not quite well enough, we note another big fish, Mike Quinn of ONS, the man who runs the 'National Cancer Intelligence Centre', and who oversees the production of the annual cancer incidence data. Remember the various shenanigans associated with the backdated Chernobyl cancer increases I found in the annual cancer incidence data in the ONS blue book? Well write and ask Mike Quinn about this and see what he says. In this email, from Aylin to Quinn, where all the text is blacked out except the header, 'Re:Busby/S==== one line clearly can be seen to say, 'send detective'.

Another one, with 42 lines blacked out leaves one set hanging enigmatically in mid air in the centre. :

24 blacked out lines

========Governments CERRIE working group that is examining the risks of internally deposited radionuclides. You will be delighted to hear that Chris Busby is also a member of this group and==============

=========Busby==============

17 more blacked out lines.

Another copy email had:

9 blacked out then

======I understand they have invited Busby to the Press Conference,=================Busby will make the most of this opportunity to attack the SAHSU study and SAHSU generally in front of the media.=======

12 blacked out then

=====*because it will allow Busby an undefended swing at SAHSU.*
======*North Essex considered inviting Busby to their Press Conference,*
=============
33 blacked out lines

Well, enough of this foolery. I wrote to Mr Ince at Imperial College and asked whether he thought sending me pages of blacked out text was what the Data Protection Act required. He said that it was, as the blacked out text was not personal data about me. So there you are. Actually he was not telling the truth, as it is clear from some of the less well blacked out section that my name appears. In one email, the whole page, authors and title were blacked out: why was I sent that one at all? But clearly SAHSU and ONS found it important to keep their relationship and their discussions secret. To my mind this is a conspiracy, especially as it concerns covering up something so serious as the increase in death from breast cancer near a nuclear site. I complained about this to the Data Information Commissioner but heard no more.

I see this as evidence that the increases in breast cancer and other cancer in adults living near nuclear sites are real phenomena and that they are known to a certain section of the cancer research and cancer epidemiology community, particularly SAHSU and ONS. Indeed, given SAHSUs original remit, it is inconceivable that they would not have discovered such an effect at an early stage. They then transmuted their remit into methodology for discounting such evidence, Bayes and the like. ONS, for their part would also have seen the increases in cancer rates. What did they do? They removed the annual trend SRR tables from the annual blue book, and apparently backdated the rise in cancer after Chernobyl to the year before Chernobyl occurred. They developed reasons, spuriously arguing about confidentiality for preventing release of data to ward level where the effects could be discovered. In this they shut the stable door too late. The horse had bolted and we had seven years of mortality data. This enabled us to show that breast cancer was highest near the contaminated estuaries, a pointer to the real cause of the breast cancer increases seen in the last thirty years. Just as exposure to the weapons fallout isotopes caused this, similar exposure to the same fission isotopes, Sr-90, Pu239, Cs137 etc, released from nuclear plants and trapped in the sediment, cause it near the estuaries.

Part IV
Explanations and Resolutions

We have concentrated, so far, on the evidence that man-made radioactivity from weapons tests, accidents and licensed releases are collectively the cause of cancer and other serious illnesses. We saw in Part III how this evidence has been covered up at the highest level, that in fact there is a conspiracy to deny the effects, to keep the data secret, to block reports in journals, indeed to do anything that will keep from the public the fact that they are being systematically poisoned for profit. Although I have used Sellafield as a hook for my argument, I see enough to know that the tensions between economic progress and toxic releases are at the centre of policy in all areas, whether these releases have to do with nuclear radiation, genetically altered organisms or chemicals.

For me, there are two important questions that follow; the first is how do these people live with themselves? Some might say that this is a naive question. But it is one that fascinates me nevertheless. The scientist who knows that his advice is wrong but gives it in order to gain advancement cannot be unaware that he may be condemning as many innocent people to death as the General who ordered the fire bombing of a town in Germany in the Second War. And these scientists exist. I suppose they could have the same justification as the General: that it was for the greater good of the State (and therefore saved the lives of some other people). But these people should be aware that their advice can save lives or kill, just as if they looked though the telescopic sight, pointed the gun and pulled the trigger. These are interesting moral ideas. Remember Nuremberg? In Wales, in the coastal strip, more than 3500 people have died of cancer between 1974 and 1989 who would not have died if they had been living inland. The study I presented in the last few chapters showed this. The cause was mainly Sellafield. The scientists who deny the evidence, who control the data, have these numbers of deaths on their conscience.

The second question is: what can we do about it? How can we ensure that science advice to policy makers is not biased? In this section I continue the story of our attempts to shift policy. I show that there is no longer a viable argument denying both the reality and the causes of the effects I have drawn attention to. The Chernobyl accident has provided un-ambivalent proof of this. I finally move to address the other two issues, looking more closely at science, society and beliefs in general. This leads to what I think is an explanation of the (largely sociological) phenomena I have described, and also a way forward.

On the Beach 2005

This is the South Pacific
The hiss of the surf and the endlessness of it
The white sand
Take me home to Africa
The blue sky and its immenseness
Are not comparable to anything else on Earth
I lean against the bleached tree trunk
I make patterns in the sand with shells
Spelling my name: like children do
Soon to be washed away or
For any passing God or Goddess
Who may take an interest
In the distance, the horizon an infinite line
I look North: to Fiji and Samoa
Where civilization has overtaken the primitive
As it has here

From this extreme outpost of the sprawl
I view the economic system and its recklessness
Through the wrong end of a telescope
Icebergs melt and tectonic plates shift
I remain centred and grounded: here in the sand
Whose hundred billion grains equal the number
Of stars in the Galaxy
Of galaxies in the Universe
Of blood cells carrying life around my frame
I remain

Wolves of Water

Summer is ebbing here in this inverted April
Overhead, my old friend the Southern Cross
Pointer from my childhood to my future
Pointing the way of all our futures
Caught up in the rush to succeed, to own, to control
Fearful of chaos, of Nature, and the sweet things
that fill our souls with glee and sudden joy.
This is, perhaps, the most important generation
What is being done now cannot be undone
Our minds have made the greatest of machines
And fuelled them with lust and melancholy
To tear from our own breasts our living hearts
And throw them on the pyramidal altar
As many primitives have done before
But with this difference:
Magnitude

New Brighton, South Island, May 2005

14
The Litmus Test

An acid is a substance that turns blue litmus red. . .
All early chemistry textbooks

14.1 Political activism and recent developments

After the publication of *Wings of Death* the arguments began with the Wales Cancer Registry, COMARE, the NRPB, the Welsh Office, the Medical Director for Wales and the nuclear industry. Letters flew back and forth. Press releases were sent, and counter press releases. We won the media war easily because we were able to convince the reporters that what we had done was sound, whereas the opposition merely used invective and *ad hominem* arguments. They dismissed us on the basis that we were 'not real scientists', or we were 'Green Party Activists', or that I was not a 'qualified epidemiologist'. I was also called a 'scaremonger' and once even a 'sadist' by the nuclear industry because I was frightening people. I was told that Nick Hance of Harwell told someone he would punch me on the nose (although when I did meet him later when they invited me to inspect the site he was quite mild and seemingly friendly). We, on our part, began publishing *Radioactive Times*, operating the www.llrc.org website and also later www.greenaudit.org, which covered other areas of the environmental issue. We were helped in this by the Green Party, and by many individual people, who sent us small sums of money, and by two or three charities, notably the Goldsmiths and the Joseph Rowntree Charitable Trust and, also, with the help from the late David Gillett. I owe a great debt of gratitude to Teddy Goldsmith and to Zac for their kindness and assistance. We engaged with our detractors and critics on various fronts. We queried their science, we published our own studies, we lampooned them and put their concepts in cartoons and songs (Plates 21 and 22). We besieged their nuclear sites with our friends and sang to them. I climbed up on the table at the Trawsfynydd Visitor Centre with my 5-string banjo and sang the Strontium Wombles song (Appendix B). The media came to us for balance whenever there was a nuclear story. I became national speaker on Science and Technology for the Green Party.

We were able to enlist the support of two MPs, the Plaid Cymru MP Cynog Dafis and the Welsh Liberal Democrat MP Richard Livsey. In order to open the issue up, in April 1996 with the help of Cynog Dafis, we organised a low level radiation and health conference in the House of Commons. A large number of people attended, but there was insufficient time to cover all the issues and have a satisfactory debate. Nevertheless, we had four main speakers, Dudley Goodhead of the Medical Research Council, Colin Muirhead, the NRPB chief epidemiologist,

Ernest Sternglass who had come over from Pittsburgh and myself. In addition there were other contributions including one from Prof Inna Merlakova from Minsk. Penny Kemp of the Green Party had invited the Belarus Ambassador, Vladimir Shchazny, who turned up with a crate of green vodka and a hamper of caviar, and after the event we repaired to the Pugin room with the booze - much to the disgust of Cynog who is anti-drink. Shchazny opened up the vodka and gloomily told me that his government was not releasing the accurate cancer or health data because they had done a deal with the IAEA and the British Government to keep the lid on the problem in exchange for aid. A few years later I was to be asked to give a paper on Chernobyl effects at the Belarus Embassy on Chernobyl and I met the new ambassador. This one scared me to death: he sat with his team, like basilisks on the stage, listening to the talk, all dressed immaculately in black, expressionless and sinister. There was the most beautiful woman, tall and stately, among this bunch, also in black, with her hair pulled back severely. I'm sure she knew how to kill me with a special grip. Wow.

In Belarus they are trapped between having to cope with an enormous problem of health that absorbs about 10% of the gross national product, and having to get the balance of advertising their health problems right between desperate and not so bad. They must get aid from the independent aid agencies (Children of Chernobyl) whilst not actually saying that anyone has suffered from the radiation (so as to keep the International Atomic Energy Agency happy and the aid flowing from the United Nations). So naturally, when one of their own scientists starts to say there is a problem, they move quickly and put him in gaol. This is what happened to Professor Yuri Bandashevsky, as I will relate. However, the symposium was a success and Richard taped the whole thing and made a 'Proceedings' that I printed on our primitive press and which we published (Bramhall 1996). One of the items I included was the analysis of the post Chernobyl childhood leukaemia in Wales and in Scotland. There was a small, sharp, but statistically significant increase in both countries in the 0-4s if we compared before Chernobyl with the few years data we had then for the period after the contamination. This symposium, at Westminster in the House of Commons, opened the debate up. The general outline of the battle lines are familiar by now. The key questions were about the use of the external acute Hiroshima cancer yield to inform about chronic internal exposures from man-made isotopes. Prof Goodhead specifically addressed our 'Second Event Theory' (see Ch 2.6) arguing that it was not founded in biology and that it was improbable since a second decay from a sequential isotope would be unlikely to follow the same directional path as the first (this is wrong, by the way).

From this time on it became increasingly clear that we had developed a method for changing the world of ideas, one that worked. Between 1996 and 2004 we used this formula again and again, moving swiftly from one area to another, making a study, publishing it through Green Audit as an occasional paper and reporting the conclusions in *Radioactive Times,* on the website and finally sending it to the media. We generally did not bother with the peer-review literature except for a few letters to the *British Medical Journal* and, with one notable exception, which I will cover below. This was because this route was expensive in time and effort, and would in any case have been unsuccessful. In one bizarre development, Roger Cox and Alan Edwards of NRPB attacked the Second Event Theory in a paper in the *International Journal of Radiation Biology,* even though the same journal had rejected my own paper on the theory several years earlier. The editor wrote and asked me if I wanted space for a reply. I wrote back and pointed out the absurdity of what he was allowing to happen. Cox is now the Director of NRPB and a senior figure in ICRP. Cox and Edward's paper was laughably simplistic and also incorrect as I pointed out in the space I was given to reply.

In addition we often employed non-violent direct action. In 1994 Molly and I had been able to frame a Green Party conference proposal to advocate the use of direct action as a legitimate political means. We argued (and I was asked to give a paper on this to the famous *South Place Ethical Society* in London) that political theory held that the laws of government could be legitimately opposed if government could be shown to be incompetent (*Ethical Record, 1995.).*

The Green Party Conference proposal was passed along with another one we invented and advocated. This was *PS208.* This argued that everyone should re-appraise everything they did to see if it was helping or harming the people and the planet. If it was harming, then it should be abandoned or re-thought. This included everything from the direction you cut a loaf of bread, to how you addressed a bishop. Heady stuff! I once (as an error) was driving down a one-way street the wrong way. Someone shouted at me (of course). I shouted back, 'PS208'. He looked startled, and said, 'OK, fair enough!' Perhaps he thought I was an official. Anyway, I pass on PS208 to you. It is the sub-text of this book really, and my life. The electricity between Molly and me in those days could have powered a milk float. We walked past a table and pieces of paper flew off and stuck to us. The power of love.

The elections in 1994 had shown that the particular type of democracy we 'enjoyed' in the UK excluded large minority opinions, and that it was legitimate politics to try and change the world directly, as Gandhi had, the Civil Rights movement in the USA had and Bertrand Russell's Committee of 100 had in the 1960s. We formed the *Green Committee of 100* and, for security's sake, adopted various code names. I was *Wasp* after the Eric Frank Russell science fiction book. Molly was *Electra*. Celia, my daughter, the anthropologist, who had figured in the national papers whilst at Cambridge cutting her way into the US base in Lakenheath was *Kali.* I still have her bolt cutters on the wall. We had them all, *Pobble, Captain America, Max, Stevidge, Yellowgate, Desperate Dan*, about two hundred committed crazies prepared to lie down under trucks, get cut on razor wire, be stapled to concrete blocks and to chain themselves to nuclear power stations. Many of these brave people are still at it, bashing Hawk fighters or US bombers with hammers, cutting the fence at Aldermaston, spray painting the House of Commons, and so forth. Alex Begg of the Green Party was actually run over by a huge digger and squashed into the ground in a roads protest; he is lucky to be alive. I have this event on videotape, all the screaming and yelling and tears. The first Direct Action I organized was the chain up of Trawsfynydd Nuclear Power Station in Wales in 1993 (Plate 6) and then Dungeness Nuclear power station (Plate 16). The last direct action I was involved in was when we disrupted the British Nuclear Energy Society International Conference on Radiation and Health at Stratford on Avon in 1996 and chained Richard Bramhall to the stage dressed as Death (Plate 17). Nowadays, as a change from being Tintin, I also appear in court in a suit (Plate26), Professor Calculus, the expert witness, defending the activist's arguments and behaviour. This is often a scary business. I was interrogated in a deposition in New York recently for 8 hours by two high-powered attorneys representing the American Nuclear Insurers. I'd rather sail a leaky barge across a crowded shipping lane with no lifeboat (Plate26).

The strategy here was to influence the policy-makers. In this area, the policy makers are effectively the civil servants who advise the politicians, and those who legitimise the processes, the Ministers and the Cabinet. These civil servants (like Roy Hamlet and Hilary Walker at the Department of Health, or Robert Smith at the Environment Agency) are in turn dependent on NRPB and COMARE for advice. To do this, we had to have developed sufficient credibility in the teeth of the attacks by the nuclear lobby, and then get to talk to the politicians themselves (who generally know little science) and convince them of the problem. We had one advantage. The early part of the 1990s had seen the affair of 'Mad Cow Disease'. This had shaken the government's faith in the science advice procedure. Even better, the Chair of the committee that (wrongly) advised government that BSE could not pass the species barrier to humans (in the teeth of the evidence) was Sir Richard Southwood. At the time, and for the early 1990s, Southwood was also Chair of NRPB. The BSE/Mad Cow affair had cost the country huge sums of money and the process of advice construction was very similar to that in the field of nuclear risk. There were credible establishment scientists arguing that there was no risk; there were independent mavericks who were attacked and marginalized and later were shown to be right.

14.2 Greens in the European Parliament

Leading to our breakthrough was the connection with the Irish Green Party European MEPs Nuala Aherne and Patricia McKenna, and their clever and sparky energy researcher Grattan Healy. I had been in contact with the Irish Greens through my UK Green Party connections, and was a member of a new outfit, the

Green Islands forum, which included Scotland, Ireland, Wales and the Channel Islands, a kind of Celtic fringe green party group. Through this I got to speak about Sellafield and its effects at various conferences in Ireland, for the Association of Green Councillors in Galway, for the Drogheda conference on Sellafield, in Dublin and in Carlingford. As a strategic ploy, Grattan managed to get the Greens to organise the Science and Technology Options unit of the European Parliament to run a symposium on 'Criticisms of the ICRP Risk Model'. Grattan was arranging to have the conference organised and reported by a neutral body. However, by the time the meeting came about on 5th Feb, 1998, the Commission had moved swiftly to ensure that the organisers of this were people who would ensure the minimum of damage. The process was organised by Prof Assimakopoulos, a physicist, of the University of Ioannia. The original idea had been, and the Unit had been asked, to concentrate on the criticisms that suggested that there was harm occurring as a result of the failure of the risk model. Assimakopoulos opened this up and asked for criticisms from the opposite direction, from the crazies who thought radiation was good for you, and the nukes who thought the rules were too stringent. This was to become the next defence of the nuclear supporters, the idea being that those who argued that internal radiation had killed people at low dose were to be balanced by those who thought radiation was good for you and should be prescribed by doctors (as it was in the 1930s when everyone who tried it died rapidly of cancer). The idea was that the ICRP model then became the voice of reason, balancing its way through the centre of the madmen.

So the meeting went ahead with all sides represented. In the event there were more heavyweights arguing for the dangers: we had Alice Stewart, Rosalie Bertell, Jean Francois Viel (who found the La Hague child leukaemias) and myself. There were also Heiko Ziggel (the Kruemmel nuclear plant child leukaemias) David Sumner, Dudley Goodhead, Horst Kuni, Carmel Mothershill and Colin Seymour (genomic instability). Together we made a strong case. Rosalie pointed out the self selecting and closed nature of ICRP, the fact there were no women on it, its colonisation by people from the nuclear industry and medical radiation, the fact that there were no public health or epidemiology members. She said that the Hiroshima study was flawed and the reported results could not be believed. Alice drew attention to her objective proof of errors in the Hiroshima study, how the members of the study group had been selected into the study more than five years after the bombing, allowing all the weakest to have already died. Viel talked about his childhood leukaemia findings and how he had been attacked by the French government and threatened with legal action. I spoke about the Second Event Theory and other mechanistic errors in the model, and also about the epidemiology of cancer in Wales following the weapons fallout. But we had not allowed for the power of rapportage. By the time our presentations had been translated into the draft final report, most of what we had said had been slanted, attacked, misrepresented or omitted altogether. Assimakopoulos wrote what he thought himself about the ICRP model (which was that it was generally fine). Our changes to the report were not put in. This was our first taste of rapportage control. This is the power of the secretariat, which was to manifest itself in the battle for control of the new CERRIE committee. There was, however, one valuable development. Present at this meeting was the Scientific Secretary of the ICRP, Jack Valentin. In the meeting (though you would not guess this from the final report) he came under a lot of pressure. Eventually he cracked: 'ICRP is a Charity', he complained, 'and no one has to follow anything it states. If you don't like what it does, you are free to consult any other body or committee you choose.'

We were already there. In April 1997, the Greens had asked us to come to Strasbourg to discuss the new Euratom 96/29 Directive that had been passed by the European Parliament in 1996. They were unsure of its purpose and contents, particularly the tables of isotopes in Appendix A of the Directive. They were concerned that, since Euratom preceded the EU treaty, they had no power to alter the directive but could only make suggestions, which had been largely ignored. The Commission had adopted this directive and it had to be transposed into each member state law by May 2000. Was it a problem, asked the Greens?

14.3 The Euratom Directive

I was sent a copy of the Directive Euratom 96/29 by Paul Lannoye, the Belgian MEP who had been the Parliament's rapporteur on the subject. After careful reading, it was clear what its purpose was. Whilst masquerading as the unification of the rules regulating exposure across the EU, it was, in fact, a nuclear waste disposal charter. The 'Basic Safety Standards Directive' involved the regulation of all practices involving radioactive materials and exposure. It seemed to explicitly permit, without either authorisation or reporting:

- The disposal of radioactive waste into the environment
- The dilution of radioactive waste with ordinary waste and subsequent disposal into landfills or even on fields
- The recycling of radioactive waste into consumer goods
- Any practices involving radioactivity so long as the average concentration of radioactive substances was below the new threshold levels for each isotope as listed in the Annex A.

It stated (Section2, Article3):

No reporting need be required where the concentration of activity per unit mass of radioactive substances do not exceed the exemption values laid out in the Annex.

The tables in the annex gave these threshold values. Of course, to most people reading this stuff it was just a series of numbers. But to us it was a nightmare. The numbers were huge. At the time, the UK law, the Radioactive Substances Act, classified any man-made radioactive material with activity higher than 400Bq per kilogramme as radioactive and requiring reporting or authorisation. It was illegal to dispose of or use such a substance without a licence. In most EU countries the equivalent blanket value was 10,000Bq/kg. But the Directive specifically allowed reuse, recycling and disposal, and incineration of radioactive materials. Spokesmen from the nuclear industry, the regulators and the Commission, openly admitted that there was nothing to stop the radioactivity ending up in consumer goods, fertilisers, or (with a few bizarre exceptions) any product. There would be no tracking. The Commissions view, openly stated, was 'Let the buyer beware' if they don't want contaminated goods or raw materials. The concepts of 'exemption' and 'clearance' would lead to widespread dispersion of radioactivity, exposing the maximum possible number of people. This was admitted by the Commission. They claimed that, according to internationally accepted risk factors, it represented a trivial and acceptable health risk. The clearance provisions of the Directive meant that below certain thresholds ('clearance levels') contaminated material arising from dismantling nuclear licensed sites could be sold on the open market. Unsaleable items below clearance levels would be land filled and incinerated without restriction. The OECD estimated that in the next few decades dismantling hundreds of nuclear factories and power stations would generate 30 million tonnes of metals alone and assessed its worth at 15 billion dollars. With the disposal of all nuclear wastes becoming more contentious and expensive, there was a double incentive for contaminated waste to be classified as 'safe'. The Clearance provisions at the time were permissive and badly drafted. The directive led to wild enthusiasm within the industry, one journal stating, 'new standards for *de minimis* would be of considerable assistance to decommissioning'. After our campaign drew public and media attention to the Directive, the Commission got cold feet on this aspect and published a Guidance Note setting lower thresholds than the industry expected and preventing 'hot' materials being diluted. This was the first, and perhaps most important result of the campaign, since it put nuclear sites outside the framework for dispersal created by the directive, to the incandescent fury of the nuclear industry. However, the principle on which the directive was based represented a significant departure from previous structures in that it argued that so long as the concentration of radioactive material in any sample was below that which would cause an external dose of 1mSv in a year, the sample was to be considered safe.

This principle has been already extended in the UK and elsewhere to the release of radioactively contaminated sites for building development and public use. The best example is the large Harwell site of the United Kingdom Atomic Energy Authority (UKAEA) in South Oxfordshire, heavily contaminated with radioactive material from fifty years of atomic research and the source of radioactivity in London drinking water due to waste pumped into the Thames at Sutton Courtney. This site has been ploughed up and everything homogenised to get mean levels of radioactivity below the acceptable level. The way that the UKAEA have interpreted the idea in the directive is quite creative, but very bad for the poor people who will be living and working on the new released site. The development of the site began before the transposition of the directive, so they had to utilise the 400Bq/kg threshold laid down in the Radioactive Substances Act 1993 (RSA93). This would have been quite hard as the whole site was massively contaminated and the mean level of radioactivity was already 700 Bq/kg. We are talking about millions of tonnes of contaminated soil. So what they did was to assume that they were permitted to leave enough of the historic waste in the soil to maintain a new level of radioactivity at the historic level of 700Bq/kg *plus* 400 Bq/kg that they assumed was a 'bonus' permitted them by RSA93, that is 400 plus natural background. So their new allowance was 1100Bq/kg and this is what they have aimed for, taking the worst of the pollution away in bags to Sellafield or the Drigg site in Cumbria, and mixing the rest or covering it up with fresh soil. This magic was effected by the consultants Dames and Moore in a report to the Vale of the White Horse Council who sent the idea for 'peer review' to another set of similar consultants, 'Aspinwalls'. They agreed the 'Remediation Report' and planning permission was given for 275 houses and an amenity area with a shop, sports pavilion and play facilities to be built on a radioactively contaminated site. What neither report stated (perhaps these consultants were unaware) was that the background level at Harwell was not a background level for the area of the Vale, but was a measure of the tonnes of radioactive waste tipped on the site over the period of its operation since 1943. This is easy to demonstrate. NRPB, who have been measuring natural background all over the country, published a gamma dose map in 1989 showing the background dose rate on the chalk of the Vale of the White Horse to be about 20nGy/hr. But measured reported background doses on the Harwell site are 100nGy/hr. The extra 80nGy contains the gamma component of all the contamination and on its own would give an extra annual dose of about 0.7mSv to anyone living on the site. But this, of course, is not the problem. If there is historic contamination, this includes particles and the dangerous man-made isotopes like Strontium-90. However much you homogenise the soil, you will never be able to homogenise the particles, and they will be there to be inhaled by the children playing in the 'play facilities' and the people using the 'amenity areas'.

But to return to the directive, here was a new law from Europe that changed these numbers on an isotope-specific basis. It changed them to huge numbers, and the highest thresholds were reserved for the substances that the nuclear industry needed urgently to get rid of: Tritium (now 1000,000,000Bq/kg), Krypton-85 (100,000), Strontium-90 (10,000) Caesium-137 (10,000), Technetium-99 (10,000). I have listed some of the new thresholds in Table 14.3.1. The clue lay in the total in any single release permitted for Technetium-99. At the time, Sellafield was discharging vast amounts of this isotope into the Irish Sea. It was fetching up in Scandinavia in lobsters. The new Exemption Value for the isotopes was 10,000,000 Bq. Hurrah! A nuclear waste disposers charter. We were tempted to ask what there was to prevent the nuclear industry cutting up fuel rods and diluting them into infant food formulas so long as the Strontium activity was below 10,000Bq/kg. Happily, the Commission was not peopled by monsters: they had though of this. Section 5 stated: *Member states shall permit neither the deliberate addition of radioactive substances in the production of foodstuffs, toys, personal ornaments and cosmetics, nor the import or export of such goods.* Well that's OK then. Everything else, however, seemed fair game.

Table 14.3.1 Examples of new exemption concentration values (Bq/kg) from Annex 1. Table A of Euratom 96/29, The Basic Safety Standards Directive.

Isotope	1998 UK	1998 EU	Poposed Euratom
Strontium-90	400	100,000	100,000
Tritium	400	100,000	1,000,000,000
Plutonium-239	400	100,000	1000
Caesium-137	400	100,000	10,000
Krypton-85	400	100,000	100,000
Technetium-99	400	100,000	10,000
Iodine-131	400	100,000	100,000

The truth is that, by 1996, there was nowhere left to put the waste. No one would allow it in their backyard. All attempts to put it in holes in the ground had failed through the opposition of locals. The Seamen's Union and brave Greenpeace actions from the high-speed inflatables (where they interposed themselves between the drums and the sea) had stopped the sea dumping and the OSPAR Treaty had nailed the lid shut. All the nuclear plants were producing it but there was nowhere for it to go. So the bright idea was to put it back into the environment. Spread it on the fields with fertiliser. (Before you laugh, this was not only suggested but is actually happening in the USA). We had to address this, and we did. We stopped it becoming UK law, our first success. When May 2000 came around, to the fury of the nuclear industry, Meacher refused to implement the directive and kept the provisions of the old Radioactive Substances act of 400Bq/kg. The UK is currently being taken to Court for this by the European Commission.

I have to say that this success had less to do with our clever strategies and hard work than with the fact that the nuclear lobby had spent too much time in their own Alice wonderland to realise what the public would think of the idea of recycling nuclear waste into consumer goods. Imagine it! At first we had a job persuading any journalist that this was what the directive really permitted. No one would believe that any sane person could advocate such a thing. Even the MEPs had a job realising they had been scammed. When the Independent ran the story we sent them, Andrew Marr, the editor received a terse letter from Ken Collins of the EP Environment Committee saying that the story was wrong. But they ignored him: there it was in black and white. We fanned the flames and sent leaflets around to MPs and activists. We began a joint campaign with the Green Party and others, collecting signatures to oppose the transposition of the directive in the UK and in Europe. I stoked up the printing press and began to print. In 1998 Rosa was four. I would look after her in the building where I printed, the old malt house in Aberystwyth. She would sit on the floor painting pictures of rainbows and pigs whilst the Press, Sir James, whirred and clicked like a monster sewing machine producing leaflets and briefings for Richard to mail out. The Green Party designed a food can label, 'I can't believe its not nuclear waste' (see Plate 20). Activists took stalls and walked the streets obtaining signatures (Plate24). BBC TV (E-files, November 1997) did a documentary. I stood outside the Capenhurst nuclear plant where they had tonnes of radioactive aluminium waiting to be made into coke cans and explained the problem; my friend Joy Pagano from Manchester clattered about in the kitchen complaining about having to cook with radioactive saucepans. Paola Buonadonna, the presenter, filmed Michael Clarke of NRPB arguing how safe it all was, the washed-out colour, shape and angle of the clip making him look like something from the film of Orwell's '1984'. On the Welsh News, the presenter who reported the proposals raised his eyebrows so high they almost disappeared into his hairline. With Joy Pagano we organised an Ethics and Euratom Conference in Manchester Town Hall. An early day motion opposing the transposition was laid down by the Liberal Democrats. I wrote an article in 'The Ecologist', which ran a nuclear issue. The government agreed to a public consultation.

The campaign gathered momentum. I went to speak about it in Europe, Strasbourg, Copenhagen, Oslo, Bergen, Helsinki. Richard went to Vienna, Brussels and Amsterdam. By late 1998 we had over 30,000 signatures and we decided to hand them to someone in government at the EU summit in Cardiff in June 1998. Richard Livsey MP, Richard Bramhall, Jill Stallard of CND Wales and Per Hegelund, a director of Friends of the Earth Sweden came with me to hand in the petitions and make our case. As luck would have it, we got to meet with Baroness Symons who is a clever person and a political fixer. She listened carefully. She told me one of her relations had died of leukaemia, so she had a personal interest. I persuaded her that there was a case: the ICRP model was false. I wanted to meet the environment minister Michael Meacher to explain this. She believed us. She said she would help. This was the breakthrough.

14.4 Michael Meacher

On 24th November, 1998 Richard Livsey arranged for us to meet with Michael Meacher, then UK Environment Minister in the Tony Blair government of New Labour. We were to present the arguments about the Euratom Directive. At the first meeting, Livsey pointed out that the essence of the problem was that the scientific model underlying the directive was in doubt. We said that the genetic damage from the nuclear waste threatened to be a massive embarrassment similar to that from BSE/Mad Cow Disease. Meacher listened carefully and said that he had made no decisions. He arranged for us to come back at a bigger meeting and face the NRPB. This meeting took place on the 8th February, 1999 around the big maple table at Ashdown House just after the BBC *Sea of Troubles* documentary about the Welsh childhood leukaemias was broadcast. It was snowing heavily. I was there with Molly and Richard Bramhall. The big guns were there: Colin Muirhead and Roger Cox from NRPB, Hilary Walker from the Department of Health, Chris Wilson of DETR, various secretaries and Press Office people. The meeting lasted hours. I outlined the case. I drew attention to the Irish Sea cancers caused by Sellafield. I described the weakness of the case supporting the radiation protection standards. I was pretty scared. This was the big table. What no one knew is that I had brought a bag of radioactive mud from the beach at Sellafield. It contained 22,000Bq/kg of plutonium-239. I was going to dump it on the table if things began to get difficult and ask NRPB if they thought it was safe. Watch them dive for cover. In the event, there was no need.

NRPB were asked to respond. They turned out to be even more scared. They stuttered and choked their way through the old arguments. The Minister seemed to be enjoying their discomfiture. He seemed disinclined to accept their dismissive attitude and at one time became quite irritated. Cox had held up his finger and thumb close together: 'The amounts we are talking about are tiny, Minister, tiny!'

'I think that's Dr Busby's point', responded Meacher. He wondered why NRPB were not investigating the issue on their own initiative.

This began the relationship with a most powerful actor in this area in the UK beneath the cabinet. It led to the effective refusal by the UK government in May 2000 to implement the EC directive and to the setting up of the new Committee Examining Radiation Risk for Internal Emitters, CERRIE. It shoehorned me into the Royal Society high table determinations of the health effects of Depleted Uranium weapons and ultimately on to the Ministry of Defence Depleted Uranium Oversight Board. Michael Meacher is a star, and an unusual politician. He is clever, political, technically competent, honest and (until recently) a survivor who maintains the moral traditional values of the Labour Party. He is a Socialist dinosaur. Eventually they got him, of course, and he was sacked in July

2003; but not before he succeeded in providing the basis for the end of the nuclear power industry in CERRIE.

The reason Meacher was sacked is thought to be because of his successful opposition to the introduction of GM crops, a kind of rearguard action he was carrying out to keep these Frankenstein products out of the UK. My own belief is that it had more to do with other activities: his powerful presence behind the manoeuvrings of the CERRIE committee, and the fact that we had him at the end of the phone to attend the various problems that arose there. Also, the point where he got the boot occurred at the end of a two-year battle by him, advised by us, over the release of small area cancer incidence data. This battle had begun at the start of our meetings. We said that the only way to discover anything about radiation from the nuclear industry and cancer risks was to have the cancer incidence data to small areas released for independent scrutiny, i.e. by us. Meacher agreed. We told him that the cancer registries refused to give it to us. Could he get it? Well he tried and tried and tried but he never did get it. But, by then, there was nowhere for the cancer registry supremos to turn. They had been backed into a corner constructed out off their own arguments and were going to have to disgorge the data. I believe that this would have shown that the effects we found in the Irish Sea and near nuclear pollution sites were real and had been covered up by SAHSU and ONS, as the intercepted emails over Bradwell suggested. They could no longer hold out and refuse to give the data to the Environment Minister. And they will have known that the data was for us. These data would, no doubt, have shown health consequences of many polluting operations, apart from nuclear ones, and so the problem for the authorities was much more general and far reaching: So he was sacked.

I learned a great deal from Michael Meacher about the ways in which control is exercised in government, through the civil servants and pressure from the Cabinet. My naïve idea had been that if you were the Environment Minister, you just clicked your fingers like Captain Picard of the *Star Ship Enterprise* and said, 'Make it so!' It turns out that it is far more like the TV series, 'Yes Minister!' The first line of defence by the Civil Servants against change is to contact their opposite number in another Ministry and set up a system of Ministerial tension that stalls any progress in the matter. I have seen this in action through various leaked memos relating to the cancer registry data releases. Of course, this is assuming you get past the civil servant gatekeepers to begin with. We would never have got to Meacher by writing to the Department. Our letter would have been shunted off to Roy Hamlet; to send us an anodyne reply. Such letters used to be our lot at the beginning of our campaigning before we switched strategy. 'Write to your MP' is the common cry of all campaigns. Forget it. It is like petitioning the King. In fact you are probably better off petitioning Prince Charles. And in an area of science as complicated as radiation protection, it is easy for the civil servants to make you out to be a flat-earth loony or crystal forces aura-reader, and they commonly do. And the other problem is that the Minister has so much to do. It beats me where they get the energy, certainly where Meacher gets the energy. So any argument longer than one third of a piece of A4 is too long; it is all done on the basis of face-to-face trust. This is the essential problem.

I will return to these issues, but here I will move to a second and very powerful strategy that we developed out of the STOA workshop and the Euratom meeting in Strasbourg. It is the development of alternative institutions, in this instance a balance against the ICRP committee. We called it the European Committee on Radiation Risk, ECRR.

14.5 The European Committee on Radiation Risk

The essential problem in trying to change minds in complicated areas of science (or anything else) is that you have to have credibility. The widely held belief is that your scientific credibility is measured by your university or government position, the number of degrees you have and the number of research papers you have published. The most credible person in the hypothetical area of asterometrical medicine would be the Kleinian Professor of Asterometrics in Cambridge, who did the asterometrics option of a science or medical degree, then a PhD in the same subject which added to the existing beliefs, was elected a Fellow of the Royal Society and has published 50 research papers on the subject, is the author of the standard text, editor of the International Journal of Asterometry and so forth. If the hypothetical mother of a child who had developed an asterometric disease after bathing in a river contaminated with Rhodium (a suspected cause) decided to do some research and found a clear link, she would make little headway against advice from such a person, or worse, a committee chaired by such a person and staffed with his colleagues, selected by him. This has little to do with the security of her case in reality or the number if deaths occurring. Indeed, they would be more likely to scupper her case, since it would become clear that the good Professor and his team had missed the connection and would be implicitly to blame for the dead babies. She would be told to get back in the kitchen, that epidemiology was a complex science, that clusters of asterometric disease were common as a result of the play of chance, or if they were not, then it was some other cause yet to be identified and that her beliefs were being coloured by her emotions.

But if we look closely at the trajectory of such people from their schooldays, or even from their birth, it is more often that they achieve these positions, certainly that they get to sit on the science committees, as a result of being a safe pair of hands, rather than being so clever. These days it is not so hard to get papers published if your status is high, and your status gets higher the more papers you publish. The papers can be any nonsense and they often are. Molly used to be copy-editor for Oxford University Press and I would see all the European sociology papers as she painstakingly drew the bad English together to make it into sense. They were almost all of them useless pieces of stupid research proving (and often not proving but stating nevertheless) fatuous conclusions obtained through complicated mathematical regression methods and questionnaire data, results that any child would be able to predict (or the opposite). The studies themselves were usually reflections of the particular psychological hang-ups that the researchers themselves had dragged through from childhood and attempts to justify themselves through reductionist data analysis. I have met a lot of important people in this game, and the majority of them are not very clever. So are we likely to find brilliant and ethically pure scientific Knights of the Round Table in the ICRP or in UNSCEAR or IAEA or NRPB? Answer: No. But in the case of these nuclear risk committees they are not even Fellows of the Royal Society or Cambridge Dons. They are only important determinators of public exposure to radiation and the public's cancer risk merely because they are on the committees. They are safe pairs of hands and the committees are safe committees, not rocking the boat, because they are selected for just that quality, ballast. It is very rare that a real scientist who has something important to say gets on one of these committees, unless a big cheese like Michael Meacher appoints him or her. So we had to develop a strategy to deal with this problem and once we began to think in these terms the answer was clear. Just as we bypass the media and the science journals with *Radioactive Times,* we can bypass the science committees also. We can set up our own risk committee. Grattan Healy, Molly and I developed what we call the 'Golden Crown' strategy. No one will listen to anyone but the King. The King is the king because he has a golden crown. We create a golden crown out of thin air by magic and crown our own king. This is what they did when they started ICRP. It is no different. Look at Abel Gonzalez, look at Roger Clarke. Do they strike you as clever? Have you read their scientific papers? Check them out.

We will set up our own alternative institution, we thought. If they ask: *Who are you?* And, *How come you are a radiation risk committee? What degrees do you have? What are your affiliations etc.?* They fall into a trap since we then respond with the same questions, to which they have no better answer than we do, indeed their answer shows their affiliation and lack of independence. We decided in 1997 to create an alternative to the ICRP and in 1998, at the STOA workshop, when the secretary of ICRP himself said that his body was only a charity and anyone was free to consult other groups he fell into our trap. Thus was begun the ECRR, also called the Comitee Europeen Sur le Risque de l'Irradiation (CERI).

Initially it did nothing at all. This is because there was no money and I was busy organising the analysis of the Irish data. The developments in the arguments about Euratom began to make it clear that the world needed the alternative scientific viewpoint, all the research and the arguments drawn together and encapsulated in a single report. This would be the reflection of the Report ICRP60, which had been published in 1990 and was the gold standard of risk assessment for the various agencies and departments advising governments on policy.

14.6 Making it happen

It seemed to me that if I didn't start it off, no one else would, but I can tell you, I was not keen. I am essentially lazy, though you may not think so from reading this book. I'd rather be floating about in the sun on a boat or sitting on the beach with a bottle of Rioja, or with my head on the lap of my beloved by a river, dreaming. I felt like Frodo the Ringbearer; it was a job I'd rather have someone else do. But no one else would do it. There were two initial problems. The first was money; I had to live for 3 months as I drafted the basic structure. The second was the production of the book itself; the printing had to be paid for. This was not the most worrying though; my time in the Green Party had taught me the impossibility of getting even the members of a single committee of alternative types to agree on wording or indeed anything. Imagine trying to get a large number of independent scientists to agree. Well, as Chairman Mao said, a long journey starts with a single step. I asked Caroline Lucas MEP to see if the Greens in the European Parliament would pay £3000 for six months of my time (Yes, that is the level of income I survived on then). In the end, she and her UK Green Party colleague Jean Lambert paid £1500 and Jill Evans of Plaid Cymru and Paul Lannoye of the Belgian Greens also stumped up a few hundred. I began to write. I also contacted Dr Rosalie Bertell in Canada and Prof. Alexey Yablokov in Russia. I had met Alexey at a conference in Oxford some years earlier and was impressed by his largeness of vision and his political analysis. He was a scientist, had been advisor to Presidents Gorbachev and Yeltsin, and had a good idea of the territory. I thought that the Chernobyl effects in the ex-Soviet territories would be valuable, and the presence of a strong Russian voice on the committee would draw attention to the US and UK domination of ICRP (and annoy them). I talked with Ernest Sternglass and Joe Mangano in the USA, with Prof.Wolfgang Koehnlein, Dr.Wolfgang Hoffman and Prof. Inge Schmitz Feuerhake in Germany, with Dr.Vyvyan Howard in the UK. I talked with anyone who was interested and might have some good suggestions.

I listed all the scientists who I knew who had criticised ICRP, many of whom I knew personally or had met at conferences like the one in Muenster in 1999. I also thought we should have experts in ethics, experts from the NGOs like Greenpeace and Friends of the Earth, politicians who had studied the subject, epidemiologists, clinicians, doctors, indeed everyone who had something useful to offer. I wrote to them all asking for input. I sent off the draft chapters and altered the chapters as suggestions were made. I asked Molly to look at the ethical aspects and gave her £600 to spend some time on this since she had studied philosophy at Oxford and is a clever woman. I took on the scientific philosophy myself, with some help from my daughter Celia, the anthropologist, and Paul Dorfman who was finishing off a PhD on the sociology of risk and knew the field and the players. In the end, I was only just finishing off the initial draft a year later. I had been given another £3000 by the Poulden Puckham Trust, thanks to the late David Gillett. The

ECRR report would not have happened without his help. Rosalie Bertell had been quite ill in Canada and had time on her hands to think about the report. She had sent in much valuable material. Professor Inge Schmitz Feuerhake from Bremen had also engaged with the project very positively, sending work she had done and valuable research reports. She, Alexey and Rosalie turned out to be the star components of the project. I had no access to big libraries and all the papers we looked at had to be bought from the British Library at £5 a photocopy. However, thank goodness this service was available, thank God for libraries and helpful librarians. Interestingly, NRPB library was also very helpful. The fears I had about arguments were not borne out. There had been few critics and many positive and helpful contributions. Prof Alice Stewart had agreed to be the first Chair early on, but sadly she died before the report was completed. Richard Bramhall and Molly did the copy-editing. Another Quaker trust (who prefer to remain anonymous) paid for the final printing. The project had originally been for a book called ECRR 2001. Eventually it was launched in January 2003 in Brussels at a Press conference organised by Paul Lannoye, MEP and head of the Green Group in the European Parliament. I was there with Inge Schmitz Feuerhake, Alexey Yablokov, Caroline Lucas and the other Greens who had helped us. I had worked on it for three years, splicing together all the contributions. It is the hardest thing I have ever done and sometimes I thought my poor head would explode.

The main problem was solved after thinking about the issue for six months. We originally decided to discuss new ways of characterising radiation doses to cells, which we called celldose (with units 'Rats' or Radiation Absorbed Tracks). One *Rat* would be one track per cell per day, normalised for ionisation density. This would modify the tissue absorbed dose as a 'power to give an effect' dose. But, although we made some progress in this, and developed a new method that was more real, it was complicated by the fact that all the tables and reports that were already there (historically) dealt with doses from the various releases and the laws, also, were framed in terms of the conventional 'energy per unit mass' calculation. That's what 'dose' is: Joules per kilogram. But what causes the trouble is not energy, but ionisations along a path. Eventually I figured out a way to deal with the internal isotope risk problem, which I thought (and still think) was creative and fatal for ICRP. It developed the method originally suggested by ICRP itself of adding weighting factors for certain types of exposure. The ICRP model deals with the different radiobiological effectiveness of alpha and gamma exposures with a weighting factor. They invented the concept of 'equivalent dose' to allow for these variations in cancer producing effects. It is the equivalent dose in Sieverts (or Rems) that is the determinator of risk, and the unit that decides policy e.g. you are not allowed to receive more than 1mSv a year by law. One Gray of gamma rays is one Sievert of equivalent dose but one Gray of internal alpha radiation is 20 Sieverts because a weighting factor of 20 has been applied. All I had to do was to introduce a new set of weighting factors which distinguished external and internal doses, and doses from DNA binding isotopes from non-binding isotopes and so forth. It was an inspiration. Immediately we could use epidemiology of internal exposure to drive the risk of cancer from internal exposure, but remain within a framework that was already legally in existence. There was a 300-fold error in the ICRP risk for cancer shown by the correlation of cancer in Wales and earlier Sr90 doses. So all we have to do is put a weighting factor for Sr-90 that will convert a dose of 1mSv (ICRP) to 300mSv (ECRR). The result is that wherever you employ the new ECRR method you get the correct number of cancers and leukaemias; naturally, since it is these numbers (rather than the Hiroshima external irradiation numbers) that determine the equivalent dose. Incidentally, it doesn't even have to be that the Sr-90 is solely to blame for the risk enhancement since the Sr-90 doses can be used as a flag for 'fission product fallout', since generally all the isotopes are roughly in the same proportion in fallout. The final red book was the same size and shape and covered the same territory as ICRP60, but there the similarity ended. The battle of beliefs had begun in earnest.

The report made a huge impact, much greater than I had anticipated. Realising the importance of the internet, we had secured the website www.euradcom.org and obtained the unpaid assistance of my friend Dr Alice Todd, a very competent and clever (enigmatic, artistic, bohemian, retiring and shy) individual who lived in the hills of mid Wales. She knew about website design and was deeply committed to our position perhaps because her daughter had suffered an inherited problem which she suspected was caused by an environmental exposure. *ECRR2003, The 2003 Recommendations of the European Committee on Radiation Risk; Health Effects of Ionising Radiation Exposure at Low Doses for Radiation Protection purposes; Regulators Edition* rose on the horizon of the risk agencies with the brightness of a thousand suns. The French Nuclear Industry ordered ten copies. The entire print run sold out. Paul Lannoye organised its translation and we launched the French version in March 2004. It had been translated into Japanese in 2003. There is now a Spanish Translation and in 2004 we financed a Russian translation, printed in Moscow. The English version is in its second printing. New scientists, some of them very big names, contacted us and asked to be included in the committee. I will leave out further description of the ECRR report and its findings and recommendations. You can buy a copy and, if you are interested in all this, I suggest you do. Much of what it has to say is contained in some way in the present book. But what is important is the basis for the proof that the ICRP model is wrong, and this is what the ECRR report is based on. There is evidence that has turned the tables on the ICRP model and shown it to be false, unequivocally. These are two pieces of evidence that cannot be incorporated, spun, covered up or explained away. They are the Waterloo of the nuclear industry and all those who support it, the litmus test that shows that the ICRP model is falsified for internal radiation in the strict sense of Sir Karl Popper's definition of Science.

The ECRR set up three sub committees, one on Chernobyl, one on Uranium and one on dosimetry. The sub-committee on Chernobyl organised a review of all the Russian language literature on Chernobyl in English and I worked with Alexey Yablokov to produce the results as a book ECRR2006, Chernobyl 20 year On. This 280 page book contained over 750 references to the terrible problems in the Chernobyl affected territories of the ex Soviet Union. It was printed here in Aberystwyth and published by Green Audit in April 2006, the 20th anniversary of the accident. I launched it in Berlin at an international conference organised by the Strahlenschutz. The ECRR has now become accepted as the alternative risk model. The UK Committee on Radioactive Waste Management CORwM was set up by the government to advise on options for disposal of radioactive waste. The way in which this committee was set up, and the membership, made it clear that the committee was just a front for a government decision that had already been made, to dump the waste into a hole in the ground. But they had to say they had consulted everyone. So eventually I was asked by the Chair, Gordon McKerron to advise on the risk analysis of the hole in the ground option as it would be affected by the ECRR2003 model. I met with them in Birmingham and stated that I would only become involved if they agreed to include the ECRR analysis in their final report to government. They said that they would commission an independent analysis that used the ECRR risk factors and that I could collaborate and advise on what these were. I agreed. They agreed to include the results of this joint exercise. The 42 page report, by Mike Egan, of Quintessa, was very fair. I pointed out that he had used the wrong values for Uranium, a major component of the calculation. We had a second meeting to sort this out. The result of changing the values for Uranium (which carries a weighting factor because it binds strongly to DNA) made a significant difference to the exposures that resulted from the deep disposal. The Chair went back on his word, refused to include the calculation or any reference to the ECRR in the final report. Oh, and no one has paid me for my time or the fares to Birmingham for the meetings. These people are ill-mannered bounders. But what it does show is that they are taking ECRR seriously.

In January 2006, to my astonishment, the French Nuclear Risk agency IRSN (Institute Recherche Surete Nucliare) weighed in and released a report of three years of deliberations on the ECRR model and report (IRSN 2006). I only discovered this because I was phoned up by *le Monde* for a quote. IRSN concluded that ECRR was *right* in most of its criticisms of ICRP. However they stopped short there and said that the ECRR approach to the risk modelling was unsubstantiated and that new research was needed. However, clearly IRSN, the risk agency of the biggest nuclear power nation in the world, France, not only took ECRR2003 seriously but also agreed with its analysis. Blimey. So this just shows you. The World as Will and Representation.

14.7 Litmus tests

Students of chemistry will know that acids are defined by their behaviour to make blue litmus red. The indicator will always change colour in the presence of an acid. We do not need to enquire further. Though of course we can now talk about hydrogen ions, protons and so forth and describe the complex electrolyte equilibria, none of the workings, the mechanisms, if you like, are necessary. This is an example of the scientific method of induction. Whatever there is in common between the antecedent conditions of a phenomenon can be supposed to be the cause, or related to the cause of the phenomenon: John Stuart Mill's *Canon of Agreement*. Thus all substances of class *acid* cause the effect. That which does not cause the effect is not an acid. The same is not true, unfortunately, for childhood cancer and nuclear installations. And we cannot mix a child with radiation in a test tube and observe leukaemia. If it were possible to do this ethically, it wouldn't work as the effect is probabilistic. And even the probabilistic argument breaks down since usually there are confounding causes. But, although it is well accepted that radiation causes child leukaemia, we are told to believe that the clusters of leukaemia near sources of radiation are not caused by the radiation. Why? Because of the ICRP model which is based, not on child leukaemia near nuclear sites, but on adult leukaemia in Japan following a huge acute external dose. If we complain at this extraordinary use of deductive logic, we are told that there may be another explanation, population mixing (as if this doesn't happen in places where there are no leukaemia clusters). Two different possible causes are now available: it is as if we are told that both acid and oil can make litmus red. The ship motors on, killing more children. But after Chernobyl, two tests of the ICRP model became available. The first and major one was the observation of a sharp, statistically significant increase in infant leukaemia in five separate countries in children who were in their mother's womb at the time of the contamination.

Following the Chernobyl accident in 1986, the cohort of children who were exposed in their mother's womb to radioisotopes from the releases suffered an excess risk of developing leukaemia in their first year of life. This 'infant leukaemia' cohort effect was observed in five different countries. It was first reported in Scotland [Gibson *et al.*, 1988], and then in Greece [Petridou *et al.*, 1996], in the United States [Mangano, 1997] and in Germany [Michaelis, et al.. 1997].

We examined the relationship between the observed numbers of cases and those predicted by the ICRP model. For the first time, the specificity of the cohort enabled us to argue that the effect could only be a consequence of exposure to the Chernobyl fallout. There could be no alternative explanation. Because the National Radiological Protection Board had measured and assessed the doses to the populations of Wales and Scotland and because they themselves had also published risk factors for radiogenic leukaemia based on ICRP models, it was a simple matter to compare their predictions with the observations and test the contemporary risk model. The method simply assumed that infants born in the periods 1980-85 and 1990-92 were unexposed and defined the Poisson expectation of numbers of infant leukaemia cases in the children who were in utero over the 18 month period following the Chernobyl fallout. This 18-month period was chosen because it was shown that the *in utero* dose was due to radioactive isotopes which were ingested or inhaled by the mothers. Whole-body monitoring had shown that this material remained in the bodies of the mothers until spring 1987 because silage cut in the summer of 1986 had been fed to cattle in the following winter. The result showed a statistically significant 3.8-fold excess of infant leukaemia in the combined Wales and Scotland cohort (p = 0.0002). The leukaemia yield in the exposed *in utero* cohort was about 100 times the yield predicted by the ICRP model. Table 14.7.1 compares the effect in the three main studies. In this table, the B cohort were those children exposed to the internal exposure from Chernobyl *in utero* in the 18 month period following the event and born between June 1987 and January 1988. These exposure periods were defined by the whole body monitoring results. The control periods A and C were the ten years before (1975-85) and the four years after 1988 for which data was available.

We argued that the possibility of the effect being due to chance may be obtained by multiplying the p-values for the null hypothesis that the effect was due to chance in each of the separate countries to give an overall p-value less than 0.0000000001. Thus it was not a chance occurrence: it was a consequence of the exposure to low-level radiation from Chernobyl.

Since the World Health Organisation has given approximate exposure levels in Greece, Germany and the United States, it was also possible to examine the leukaemia yield in the infant 'exposed cohort' reported by the several other studies and establish a dose response relationship. It was found that the response was not the straight line of the ICRP assumptions but a biphasic one, like that described by Professor Elena Burlakova and also for different reasons by me in various papers dating from 1999.

We argued that the infant leukaemia results represented unequivocal evidence that the ICRP risk model was in error by a factor of between 100-fold and 2000-fold for the type of exposure and dose, the latter figure allowing for a continued excess risk in the cohort being studied and for the effect in populations where the doses were very low. This paper was published in the journal Energy and Environment and we were also invited to present it at the World Health Organisation Conference in Kiev in 2001.

Table 14.7.1 Unequivocal evidence of ICRP risk factor errors: comparison between infant leukaemia rates after Chernobyl in Wales and Scotland and similar data from Greece and from the former Federal Republic of Germany

Group	[a]Wales and Scotland	[b]Greece	[c]Germany
Exposed cohort B			
Cohort size	156,600	163,337	928,649
Number of cases	12	12	35
Rate	7.67	7.34	3.77
Unexposed cohort A + C			
Cohort size	835,200	1,112,566	5,630,789
Number of cases	18	31	143
Rate	2.15	2.79	2.54
Risk Ratio	3.6	2.6	1.5
Cumulative Poisson Probability	0.0002	0.0025	0.02

[a] *See text for A B and C periods*[b] *Petridou et al..(1996)*[c] *Michaelis et al..(1997)*

I was monitoring leukaemia data in Wales after Chernobyl, and had already presented evidence of a sharp increase in Wales and the House of Commons conference in 1996 [Bramhall ref]. I heard about the Petridou paper in *Nature*, which drew attention to infant leukaemia in Greece and wondered of there was anything in Wales. I noticed the sharp increase in the Welsh figures when I asked Helen Beer for the 0-5 data in 1998 and subsequently I contacted the Scottish Information and Statistics Department. Putting the two together was interesting. I show the series in Table 14.7.2, which makes it clear that there is an effect, without doing any statistics.

In each of the two-year periods from 1975 to 1986, the year of Chernobyl, the mean number of infant leukaemias had been 2.0. In the two years following the fallout, 1987 and 1988, the period in which the children in the womb had been exposed to internal irradiation, the number was 14. There was a 3.5-fold increase (p = .0001) Yet NRPB had told us that there was no risk, the water could be drunk; the milk could be made into ice cream.

Table 14.7.2. Numbers of leukaemia age 0-1 in combined areas of Scotland and Wales over the period of Chernobyl. Note sudden rise in 1987,88.

Year	**79**	**80**	**81**	**82**	**83**	**84**	**85**	**86***	**87**	**88**	**89**	**90**	**91**
Leuk.	0	2	4	1	1	3	2	1	**6**	**8**	3	3	1
	2		5		4		3		**14**		6		1

* Chernobyl accident

When I first made these calculations I saw immediately that this was the litmus test we required, the smoking gun. The doses were known, the risk factors were published, so the expected numbers could be calculated and compared with the observed numbers to show an error in the risk factors, that is the ICRP model. And the fact was that the error was the same size as that needed to explain the Sellafield child leukaemias. This was very big; this was dynamite. Elena Petridou had not made these calculations so someone had to. I obtained the whole-body monitoring data from NRPB to see over which period the internal radiation was exposing mothers. It included up to the middle of 1988, and so children born in 1987 and 1988 would have been irradiated in the womb. I wrote a Green Audit occasional paper in June 1998 and sent the calculations to COMARE to see what they would do. They eventually replied. Bridges had sent the paper to the 'transgenerational subcommittee'. I waited. I chivvied Bridges. What was the outcome? He eventually replied. The transgenerational subcommittee had looked at the paper and 'found it interesting', however the numbers were small and the effect could have been a chance one. They would, he added, keep the matter in mind for future reference. What did they mean? In case there was another Chernobyl to study? I asked who the members of this subcommittee were. Eric Wright, Ray Cartwright and Gerald Draper, was the answer. I phoned Eric. What did you think about our paper? What paper? The one on the Chernobyl Infants. Oh, I never saw that, they met when I was away. It must have been Cartwright and Draper. Well, there we are. So much for COMARE, watchers of the public risk from radiation; when informed of the failure of the NRPB that led to increases in leukaemia and probably deaths in Wales and Scotland they did nothing. Although I don't usually bother with the journals, I had to get this one out. I sent it to the *British Medical Journal* as a letter, an urgent communication. No reply. I phoned them up. Oh, we threw it away. I complained and sent it again. Liz Crossan wrote (14 September 1998):

We stand by our decision not to publish. There are several reasons. Firstly it is not the type of subject that we usually publish as a letter (despite the fact that we published the last one by you--which led to a hugely critical response from our readers as you know); second we actually found it extremely difficult to follow. . .

I phoned up the editor of *The Lancet*. Would they look at it? Yes, said John Bignall. He sent it to a referee (I wonder who this was). The referee stated:

It is quite hard to know exactly how he has managed to construct significant excesses in both Scotland and Wales. My guess is he has chosen the time period to be considered and the age group after looking at the data and specifically in order to show an excess. In addition he has given little information about the geographical area included, or the method of calculation of expected deaths. I am sorry to sound so sceptical but I personally would wish to see a lot more detail before believing evidence of this nature.

If I had to guess, this sounds like Sarah Darby; it has her edgy tone, but maybe I'm wrong.

So Bignall rejected it also. This is the kind of thing we have to put up with. What does the referee mean, 'He has chosen the time period'? The time period we chose was that of the prior study by Elena Petridou *et al*, and the period following the exposure. They were not deaths but cases. The areas were Scotland and Wales: how else could I describe Scotland and Wales? Does she want the latitude and longitude? Are you surprised that the radiation risk model has not been unmasked before now? How many papers have been rejected by referees who are either similarly biased or dim-witted?

But luck was with us. In 1999 I was contacted by Rebecca Harrison, one of the Low Level Radiation Standing Conference organisers. She had been handed the temporary editorship of a nuclear power issue of the peer review journal *Energy and Environment*. There would be gung-ho nuclear papers addressing global warming. Would I like to send in anything? Did I have anything? I certainly did! I wrote the paper and sent it off. I asked her to send it to referees who were not pro-nuclear, and so it bypassed the fixers and was published in June 2000. Shortly after this I was asked by Professor Angelina Nyagu, the organiser of the World Health organisation Chernobyl effects conference in Kiev in 2001, to give the paper there. The Chernobyl Infants argument had arrived. The ICRP model was finished. NRPB had no answer to the accusation that their advice, after Chernobyl, that in Wales there was nothing to worry about and no increases in cancer would be seen. They went to their chief epidemiologist, Colin Muirhead, for something to plug the leak and stop them sinking. He gave them a statement, based on his epidemiology textbooks, which was an extraordinary own goal. Their statement was a denial that the increases in the infant leukaemias could be used as evidence for failure of their model and incorrectness of their advice. It was based on Muirhead's argument that:

Overall the current evidence for increased leukaemia risks associated with environmental or occupational exposures from the Chernobyl accident is not convincing. It is not possible to tell using correlation studies whether the persons who developed the disease in question received higher exposures than the population as a whole.

What this can only translate into is that Muirhead is saying that, if there is a 300-fold error in the ICRP risk factors, the children may have actually received 300 times the doses that NRPB calculated. This we might agree with if it was cell dose that was the factor. It is clearly impossible that the mothers received 300 times the average dose in Wales. And the whole statement makes the method used to calculate the health consequence of an exposure useless. If politicians are framing policy on the basis that ICRP model can show the health effects of some small release, from Sellafield say, will cause no harm, then it is no good coming back afterwards and saying, well actually, all the dead children that have happened may have had a larger dose than the average dose on which the policy is based.

I wrote to NRPB pointing this out. I also decided to put a shot across the bows of the Environment Agency, who, in the UK, are the people who are at the sharp end of policy in the area of licensing discharges. I decided the time had come to bring in the law. If these people were sanctioning the release of substances that killed people then they were, like my friend Bill Pritchard believed, murderers and should be locked up. (Bill once went to the police to ask if they would arrest the operators of Trawsfynydd nuclear power station!). In fact, there were precedents. One was thalidomide, the teratogenic drug that was kept on the market to make money after it had been shown to be a problem. Another was asbestos. There was also cigarette smoking. Cases focussed on whether the people selling or sanctioning these had known about the evidence. I thought I would identify, by name, the single person that was responsible for signing the papers to allow the discharges and send him a solicitor's letter with a copy of the Chernobyl Infants paper (and other stuff). I would inform him that he had now been made clearly aware of this evidence and would not be allowed, in a subsequent court action against him (for murder or manslaughter) after this date, to plead ignorance of the evidence.

I went to see Hugh Parsons, a solicitor in Machynlleth who had helped us in earlier Direct Action protests. He drew up the paperwork without charging us and served it on the head of the Environment Agency. This frightened them to death. They asked for a meeting with us and I went along with Richard Bramhall to meet Robert Smith in Bristol. However they decided they could legally pass the buck to NRPB and are still signing the discharge papers, their own warrants I believe.

The Chernobyl Infants (as I call this situation) represents the end of the ICRP model and the end of the nuclear project as we know it. Their ship is holed beneath the waterline and will eventually sink, however many pumps they materialise. And they certainly try any argument to evade the inevitable foundering of their vessel. Muirhead's initial argument was changed by the time he contributed to the CERRIE conclusions in their final report. The matter is returned to when I discuss CERRIE, where I will show the lengths to which they have gone to, to avoid the inevitable. The point is this. Cancer and radiation are linked, but stochastically, probabilistically. There has always been a time lag of several years between exposure and expression. This is even true in the leukaemia studies, where often the lag is assumed or introduced in the analysis (as it was in the Hiroshima survivors and the A-bomb veterans) to lose cases. And in the lag period, there can be other occurrences: population mixing, exposure to chemicals, whatever can be grabbed at to avoid the radiation causality argument. With the Chernobyl Infants, there is no lag. There is just cause and effect. The children are irradiated, they get leukaemia: bam, bam. And the effect is wildly in excess of the expectation based on the external ICRP model: Check Mate.

There was one other significant argument that ICRP model was wrong which emerged around this time. This was the minisatellite DNA mutations in the children of Chernobyl.

14.8 Minisatellite DNA mutations

The ICRP model of genetic mutation after irradiation is based, like ICRP's cancer risk model, on the Hiroshima LSS yield of gross genetic effects and studies of radiation effects in mice.

Although subtle genetic effects on sex ratio were apparent in the LSS offspring, the RERF researchers excluded them from the study because they did not accord with their notions of the expected direction of such an effect [Padmanabhan, 1997]. Neels's exclusion of the sex ratio effects resulted in the belief that the genetic effects of 10mSv in the first generation would be unmeasurable. Thus BEIR V gives the incidence of total genetic effects including chromosomal effects (unbalanced translocations and trisomies) at 6 per million offspring compared with the natural rate of 4,200. It predicts a 10mSv excess risk of 10 cases of congenital malformation in a natural rate of 25,000 per million offspring and similar vanishingly small increases are given for autosomal dominant, X-linked and recessive disorders. Using a combination of mouse studies and the epidemiology of the LSS, the doubling dose for spontaneous genetic burden has been estimated to be 1 Sievert [e.g. BEIR V, 1990 p 70].

However, the development of molecular techniques in the last 15 years enabled objective measurements of the consequences of irradiation to be investigated in human populations. There have been several studies of minisatellite DNA mutation in children living in parts of the ex-Soviet Union and exposed to radiation from Chernobyl. Using the technological development of 'DNA testing' in which minisatellite DNA is separated into bands which are characteristic of its genetic identity, it has been possible to show that children living in Belarus and exposed to radiation from fission-product isotopes which contaminated their environment suffered a doubling in genetic mutation [Dubrova, 1996, 1997]. Similar work with barn swallows exposed in Belarus showed that these genetic changes were also present in these birds and were associated with phenotypic changes in their plumage patterns as well as reduced survival, therefore underlining the potential importance of such mutations [Ellegren *et al.* 1997].

Most recently, the minisatellite DNA tests have been applied to the children of Chernobyl liquidators who were born after the accident compared with siblings born before the accident [Weinberg et al. 2001]. There was a seven-fold increase in genetic damage found in the post-exposure children. By comparison with mutation rates for the loci measured, this finding defined an error of between 700-fold and 2000-fold in the ICRP model for heritable genetic damage. In addition, the research results could be stratified by dose range and this resulted in a biphasic or Burlakova type response. It is remarkable that studies of the children of those exposed to external radiation at Hiroshima show little or no such effect, suggesting a fundamental difference in mechanism between the exposures. [Satoh and Kodaira, 1996]. The most likely difference is that it was the internal exposure to the Chernobyl liquidators that caused the effects.

Bryn Bridges himself has been getting cold feet about this new evidence. In a review article [Bridges 2001] he conceded that the time may have come for a paradigm shift. In his outline of concerns, he has focused on the bystander effect whereby intercellular communication between cells traversed by an ionising track communicate a message to nearby cells which causes these to exhibit genomic instability resulting in genetic mutation in a large number of cells which are not subject to initial ionisation injury [Azzam *et al.* 1998, Hei 2001].

Together these represented unequivocal evidence that the ICRP model was flawed. The EU Parliament passed a resolution in May 2000 calling for a reassessment of the model. In the UK, Michael Meacher set up CERRIE.

Table 14.8.1 Studies which show unequivocal evidence of error in the ICRP models.

Study	Shows
1. Minisatellite DNA mutation after Chernobyl	Objective scientific measurements of children born after Chernobyl accident have shown a 7-fold increase in mutation relative to siblings born before. Error in ICRP 700- to 2000- fold for this end-point.
2. Infant leukaemia in five countries	Increases in infant leukaemia in children who were in utero over the exposure period for internal radiation define error in ICRP risk factor from 100- to 2000-fold for this end-point.

The Committee Examining Radiation Risk from Internal Emitters CERRIE was an idea based on the research done by Richard Bramhall, Molly and me on the question of science advice to government, reported in the book *I Don't Know Much About Science* (Green Audit 2000). The three of us had been involved through the Green Party in campaigns relating to Mad Cow Disease and as Speaker on Science and Technology for the Greens I had been also involved in other areas, GM foods, Ozone layer, Mobile Phones, Power Lines, Depleted Uranium weapons; all the continuing and well known wars between the Greens and Industry. How were political decisions made? Who was on the committees and how did they get appointed? Did the decision makers, the MPs, understand the science? How could we improve the process whereby scientists advised policy so that the public were protected?

15
Science and Society

We listen very carefully. I am not a scientist. A lot of this has to be informed by the science. We have listened to what the medical community, what the Chief Medical Officers and others have to say to us. Then we take the appropriate steps.

Mr Alan Milburn
(Minister for Health)

I don't know much about science, but I know what I like
Martin Amis

15.1 Rapportage

In the time of the Cold War, it was possible to control research evidence by funding, and any evidence that slipped past this, because the scientist was independently funded (like Alice Stewart) or financially independent (like Ernest Sternglass) could be excluded from peer-review publication through control of the Journals. Once the results were beginning to appear at conferences, meetings or on committees that might influence decisions, a new strategy was called for. If the committee or meeting or conference could not be controlled (through who was invited and who was excluded or the high cost of attending) then the focus of attention for saving the day moved to the secretariat and the rapporteur. In the area of nuclear risk, it was of paramount importance to control the belief that internal radiation was safe through the writing up of the proceedings: the manufacture of scientific consent about the safety of radiation. This meant that you had to have your people in the right places, or move them swiftly to the right places when there was a threat. We saw this happen in 1998 with the European Parliament STOA report, which I described earlier. For the truth is what is written down, not what is said at the time, which is ephemeral, however accurate or wise. I will briefly describe some other recent examples and then I will move on to describe how scientific belief is constructed and how we have to develop a way of making a new type of scientific committee that has, built into it, safeguards that ensure that the results of its deliberations provide the best approximation to the truth of an issue for politicians to make a judgment. This new type of committee has had its prototype in CERRIE, but, as I will explain, the desperation of the nuclear lobby ensured that all the stops were pulled out to make CERRIE ineffectual and its conclusions biased and misreported. This will have lessons for the future that we need to learn.

The Chernobyl disaster was a disaster for the nuclear industry: there is no doubt about that. What the nuclear lobby had to do was control any evidence that the radioactive pollution was causing illness in the affected territories; this meant mainly in Belarus and Ukraine. In the early period after the accident they were helped in this by the Soviet authorities, in whose interests it was to downplay the significance of the event, and to cover up the reports of illness. After all, it was a failure of a Soviet reactor system that caused the accident. As Alla Yaroshinskaya tells in her book (*The Forbidden Truth*), there was a move to deny the existence of any ill health by refusing to allow doctors to report radiation related diseases like leukaemia. As she says:

The most dangerous isotope to escape from the mouth of the reactor did not appear in the Periodic Table. It was Lie 86: A lie as global as the disaster itself.

The lie, which is about the true health consequences of the accident, was (and still is) promulgated by the nuclear industry and their apologists. A good example is the big glossy book *Chernobyl Record. The Definitive History of the Chernobyl Catastrophe* by Dr R.F.Mould (Institute of Physics Publishing 2000).

This book is a fascinating example of expensively produced biased reporting. In the looking-glass world of nuclear, black is white, or even colours that have not yet been described by Physics. Dr R.F.Mould's Chernobyl Record, despite its claimed 14 years in the research, 400 glossy pages, eight colour plates and hundreds of tables, maps, diagrams and analyses, is finally just a pro-nuclear industry talking-down of the dangers of nuclear power and the consequences of the accident. In case you think this is too harsh, here is a quotation:

The incidence of thyroid cancer is the most notable health effect of the Chernobyl accident, especially for children and adolescents in the Gomel region of Belarus. In terms of other cancers in Chernobyl populations, no significant increases in their incidence has been observed. (p 260).

Dr Mould is described in the blurb as an internationally known author, medical physicist and cancer statistics specialist. With wild disregard for any post-modern critiques of communication he jumps in:

What I have borne in mind throughout the research for this book have been the words of Thomas Gradgrind in the Charles Dickens novel, 'Hard Times': 'Now what I want to hear is Facts. Facts alone are wanted in life.'

His book is certainly not short of facts: it is brim-full of interesting, useful, curious facts and also incorrect facts, spun facts, and facts from which false conclusions are drawn and then presented as facts. In terms of what that we most wanted to know about Chernobyl, the facts are marshalled to produce the opposite of the truth.

For example, what are the important questions? How did the accident happen? Could it happen again here? Are the radioactive releases going to cause ill health in the world? How many people will die as a result of exposure? Is nuclear power safe? Dr Mould's arguments, his ordering and choice of facts, answers these questions implicitly. The explosion, we are told (incorrectly), was not even a nuclear explosion but was a steam explosion (like a kettle or a boiler). The radioactive contamination doses are mostly much less than natural background (and therefore safe) and the cancer yield, except for thyroid cancer in the most affected populations close to the plant, too small to measure. Reported increases in non-cancer (and even cancer) illnesses are apparently due to better ascertainment, or if verified, due to 'radiation phobia'. In the Kiev conference I attended, one ex-Soviet scientist argued that the cancers were the result of malnutrition, which drew an angry response from the floor. Mould's book was upbeat about nuclear. Nothing had happened. What was all the fuss about? Nuclear power had not been set back at all. It was the shining future, and should be allowed to expand and save the planet. The book was an expensive glossy production, costing a fortune to print. Who paid? Why? Will they get their money back? I doubt if they will from the book sales, but, on the other hand, maybe the nukes will all buy a copy to keep by the bed in case their conscience begins to trouble them; that would equal a good number of sales.

The International Atomic Energy Agency, the IAEA, have been consistently behind the control of the Chernobyl results. They are believed to have tied aid to the control of the data in Belarus. In 1996, their joint conference with the WHO in Geneva was a potential disaster for the nuclear industry. So many independent doctors, epidemiologists and scientists came there to present evidence that people were dying from radiation poisoning in the affected territories that the proceedings, which were to have been published, have not appeared to this day. This is not true of the alternative Chernobyl conference in Vienna, the Permanent Peoples Tribunal whose proceedings contain testimonies from many experts and contributors from the affected territories drawing attention to thc serious health problems.

So with these controls and Stalinist legitimization of lies it was business as usual for the nukes. And the next problem was to be an overall analysis, provided by the United Nations Scientific Committee on the Effects of Atomic Radiation, UNSCEAR. Dr Keith Baverstock, (who was sacked from the WHO for disagreeing with their reporting of the effects of Chernobyl and the effects of low dose radiation from Depleted Uranium) told me an interesting story. By the time of the new millennium, the head of IAEA, Dr Abel Gonzalez, temporarily took over the United Nations committee UNSCEAR for the period of the production of the definitive official report covering the radiation effects, UNSCEAR 2000. This report devoted huge amounts of space to the accident, but, like Mould's book, gave out facts about the releases, numbers of Bequerels of this or that isotope. The health effects were downplayed or, as in the case of many published reports in English and in Russian, just omitted. As with Mould, there was a great deal of space arguing that the only problem was an increase in thyroid cancer, which in any case may have been a consequence of pre-existing iodine deficiencies, without any real attempt even to relate the doses to the ICRP risk factors and previous beliefs.

Although there was a huge amount of evidence of serious health problems in published Russian language reports (hundreds of papers) not only cancers, but effects across the whole range of health deficits; none of these were reviewed or cited in UNSCEAR 2000. We ourselves had received many of these papers and had to struggle with the translations and the abstracts in poor English. There was one very alarming study that caused so much embarrassment for the authorities in Belarus that they struck savagely at the author. We received data from Professor Yuri Bandashevsky, Director of the Gomel Medical Institute that showed that children were suffering cardiac problems associated with measure whole body contamination of Caesium-137. Bandashevsky was arrested by the Belarus government on trumped up charges of fraud and gaoled for eight years hard labour. The children's contamination was measured by Prof. Vassily Nesterenko, using whole body monitoring equipment that he had devised himself and which he took around the country. Nesterenko, who I met in Kiev in 2001, is a physicist who also studied ill health in children and had prepared a report on the situation in Belarus. In this report Nesterenko stated:

In the period 1988 to 1995 the [childhood] tumours rate has grown by 2.4 time, the rate of malignant tumours by 13 time, endocryneous [sic] system diseases rate- by 4.5 times-illness of nervous system and organs of sense- by 3.5 times, illnesses of blood circulation organs- by 4-times, etc. was registered. Gross infringement of the immune, digestion, antioxidant and other systems were also discovered amongst children and teenagers. [Nesterenko, 1998. p32]

Nesterenkos' assistant was murdered recently; some feel that it was a missed attempt on Nesterenko who had survived an earlier attempt on his life. There are some serious players in this game. In addition we had also the testimony of some very eminent scientists. Professor V.K Savchenko, also of the Academy of Sciences, Belarus, recorded for UNESCO in 1995:

Medical data show that in the zone of strict control, during 1986-1990 there was a 50% increase in the average frequency of thyroid disorders, malignancies and neoplasms (leukaemia increased by 59%) a serious increase in the number of miscarriages, stillbirths and congenital malformations.[Savchenko, 1995]

Of course, what was needed was the translation, and/or some independent review of the Russian language literature on the health of the populations affected. By the time of the 20 year anniversary in 2006, the health problems reported had reached the level of meltdown, yet in the West, it was still being said by the politicians and by the risk agencies like UNSCEAR and IAEA that the accident had had no victims except a few of the liquidators and some children with thyroid cancer. To counter this, I worked with Alexey Yablokov in Moscow to obtain review articles in English written by senior research scientists in Russia, Ukraine and Belarus. With no funding to produce the book, apart from a small gift from a friend in the Green Party, I managed, with the help of another friend, Mireille de Messieres, to produce a 250 page book- *ECRR, Chernobyl: 20 years On*, which we published in April 2006. I launched the book in Berlin, with Professor Yablokov. We had contributions from eminent scientists who cited hundreds of references to research studies reported in Russian language literature. The contents make grim reading and show, without doubt, the serious results of contamination of an area with man-made radionuclides. I refer you to the book for the details (ECRR 2006).

What I wish to say here is that all this information, and also data from individual cancer registries from Poland and Bulgaria to Wales, show that the overall cancer yield of the accident will be very high, greater than the 970,000 calculated by Dr John Gofman in 1990. The WHO response was to set up an aggregate study of child leukaemia operated from the International Agency for Research on Cancer in Lyons, run by Max Parkin, husband of Sarah Parkin of Green Party fame. This outfit put all the child leukaemias together in a vast aggregate database from every country in Europe and found that there was a steady increase over the period of Chernobyl, but no sudden step change, such as those we have seen when we look at the individual registries. They conclude in this study that there has been little or no effect, in line with the ICRP expectation . Of course, since different countries received vastly different doses, and the highest doses were in countries in the ex-Soviet bloc, where the leukaemias were covered up, we should not expect much from such a study even if we trusted the people doing it. I recently had confirmation that, following our analysis of the infant leukaemias, ECLIS were hastily cobbling together a study of infant leukaemia of their own, but guess what? The Greek data would be excluded because of doubts about the accuracy.

So through this rapportage we are left with two entirely antithetical pictures of the aftermath of Chernobyl, exemplified by the pro-nuclear descriptions, presented by Dr Mould and his friends and the IAEA and UNSCEAR, and the second from the cries and screams of the poor people on the ground, and the reports of the doctors and scientists who study them. I was to meet many of these in the second WHO conference on the Health Consequences of the Chernobyl Accident held in Kiev in June 2001 when I was invited to present our paper on the Chernobyl Infants. I was able to see there at first hand, again, the way in which rapportage was used to alter the results of a conference. This time it was recorded on film by Wladimir Tcherkoff of Swiss TV, so you don't have to take my word.

The Low Level Radiation Campaign has now made a DVD of this amazing documentary if you want to watch it. Order it from the website.

15.2 Atomic Lies

The first WHO conference on Chernobyl health effects was jointly organised with the IAEA in Geneva in November 1996. Over 700 doctors and scientists attended and made representations. These were a potential disaster for the development of the nuclear industry and the proceedings were suppressed by the IAEA. This was stated in an interview between Prof Michel Fernex and Prof Hiroshi Nakajima filmed in Kiev at the beginning of the second conference. Nakajima, who was Director General of WHO at the time of the Geneva conference, says, *Six years ago we tried to have a conference. The proceedings were never published. This is because in this matter the organisations of the UN are subordinate to the IAEA.*
Fernex, retired now from the University of Basle in Switzerland, and who worked with the WHO remarks: *Since 1986, the WHO did nothing about studying Chernobyl. It is a pity. The interdiction to publish which fell upon the WHO conference came from the IAEA. The IAEA blocked the proceedings; the truth would have been a disaster for the nuclear industry.*

After our paper on the Chernobyl infants was published, we were invited to come to Kiev for the second of the WHO conferences. It was hoped that this conference would see a freeing up of the information about the true consequences. The association: Physicians of Chernobyl, which jointly organised the affair, asked Nakajima to be Honorary President of the meeting. At the start of the conference, on the first day, Fernex hoped this would help the truth to emerge. Nakajima said: *Although the agencies of the United Nation are in principle equal, for atomic, military and civil use of the atom, the IAEA command. The agencies are all subordinate to the Atom.*
Fernex said: *The IAEA signed an agreement with the WHO in 1959. They are prevented from researching health in this area or even from warning exposed populations. The IAEA will be here. And to buy scientists in poor countries is cheap. 100,000 dollars buys a lot of scientists.*

We had to go. But the cost would involve fares, accommodation and the £500 conference fees. We applied to the Joseph Rowntree Charitable Trust who agreed to fund our trip. All this happened at the last minute, and I had to rush down to London to organise Ukrainian Visas. I emailed the Green Party of the Ukraine to find somewhere Molly and I could afford to stay. They organised for us to stay on a steamboat, the Maxim Rilsky, moored on the river Dnieper. This is the advantage of the Green Party: there are always friends in every country! We were helped enormously by the Ukraine Greens in Kiev.

The conference was extraordinarily illuminating. I will give some examples here since it is an account of how the truth becomes created or changed and how messages appear that have little to do with reality. Imagine then the Health Ministry building in Kiev, a rather drab building set in the centre of a park. Hundreds of internationally renowned scientists appear here to present papers on their findings or discuss these from the floor. There are also physicians and researchers from the affected territories. Many cannot come, as it is too costly. On the stage sit five or six Soviet style men in suits, perhaps there is also a woman at times. There are translators and everyone has headsets. They look grim. They also look nervous and shifty. At the start, Abel Gonzalez of the IAEA, smooth and bonhomonious, is at the microphone:

The known effects of the Chernobyl accident are 31 deaths in liquidators and 200 thyroid cancers in children. Whether any other effects have occurred is an epistemologically insoluble problem, we just don't know. There are no other internationally agreed effects.

The IAEA data he is talking about is that validated by the US Los Alamos Laboratory and the French Nuclear industry, the CEA. Other reports are ignored. There is uproar from the floor, also applause from the men in suits. Dr D Zupka of the United Nations (OCHA) goes to the microphone, tall, earnest and concerned:

The consequences of Chernobyl do not fade away. They are only just beginning. There are 9 million victims. The tragedy is only beginning.

More applause, more shouts and headshaking. This is science in the making. This is as much science as the studies themselves and their reported results. Did you think science was about nature having the truth wrested from her by experiment? Oh, Naïve!

Up gets Norman Gentner of the United Nations Scientific Committee on the Effects of Atomic Radiation, UNSCEAR, a short balding Canadian. He looks as if this is some game:

The risk of leukaemia does not seem to be elevated even in the liquidators. I agree with the IAEA, positive perspectives exist. For those who believe, no explanation is necessary; for those who do not believe, no explanation is possible. (He should know) *We use the most rigorous possible data so that the people and the decision makers can get the right information.*

Prof Alexey Yablokov of the independent Centre for Russian Environmental Policy (kind of a Russian Green Audit) is there at the microphone, angry, bearded, like a biblical prophet:

This is Shocking, Shocking! An impudent presentation of non-objective data. What scares me is it's said openly, presented as scientific conclusions. There were irremediable falsifications of official health data. Don't you know that the leaders of the State Committee for Statistics were arrested two years ago for falsifying data?

UNSCEAR knows it. They know the data were falsified! They use them to say that the consequences of Chernobyl were not so serious. They say there are no genetic effects after Chernobyl, but the genetic effects are the most serious. Tens of papers in serious scientific journals show this, Bandashevsky shows the effects in children, sudden deaths, organ damage. Increases in mortality, cancers, congenital malformation, immune system disorders, exhaustion, slow growth. How is it possible to reject this? Silencing these facts is incorrect! It is science.

There is loud applause from the audience. The men in suits look unwell. Gentner looks terrified. Yablokov is a member of the Russian Academy of Sciences and was advisor on environmental matters to Presidents Gorbachov and Yeltsin.

Up gets Prof S.Yarmonenko from Moscow, author of a standard textbook on radiation and health, short, stocky, fuming and bustling:

In the name of the radiobiological community of Russia I want to apologise to the international community. I apologise for Mr Yablokov who is not a radiobiologist or a radiologist.

The audience shouts at him to sit down. A blonde woman doctor in a coat gets up and shouts: *Who paid you to say this!*

From the audience Prof Rose Goncharova, a biologist and geneticist, author of studies showing significant genetic effects in fish from the Chernobyl fallout some 200 miles from the plant, moves to the microphone. She is intense and angry, her eyes gleam:

As scientists we are dealing with a new phenomenon and will have to accept new information! The Radiation Effects Foundation in Japan have found that radiation effects general somatic mutation, this is a new phenomenon.

Loud applause.

Chair, Prof Oxana Garnets: *Sit down. This is absolute nonsense! This session is about social phenomena.*

Audience: *Shame, let her finish!*

Goncharova: *I will finish what I want to say. This is a social phenomenon.*

The meetings and presentations went on in the same vein throughout the conference. All the reports that were invited showed no effects (with the curious exception of ours). At the same time, arguments from the floor suggested terrible and widespread effects. After a presentation suggesting that the ill health was a consequence of malnutrition an infuriated woman doctor jumped up and said: *We are not ill because we have no bread. It is news that lack of food causes brain tumours.*

At the point where I was listed to give the Chernobyl Infants paper, Yarmonenko, who was before me, tried hard to extend his time at the microphone. The Chair allowed this, indeed seemed to encourage it. He ignored my interruption. I could see that this was an attempt to squeeze my presentation of our results out altogether and stood up and complained to the chair again. Nothing happened; Yarmonenko went on and on and on. I got up and walked to the microphone and took it from him. This took some nerve, I can tell you, but no one arrested me. I gave the paper. He jumped up and said the results were impossible. I said they had been reported from five countries by different research teams.

The most important item was the final resolution of the conference, for whatever that stated, would be an official line that the agencies would have to consider. It was vital for the nuclear mafia to control this. This is where rapportage comes in. The Chair stated that they were grateful for the assistance given by Norman Gentner in preparing the draft resolution. Yes, that's right; the draft resolution was prepared by Norman Gentner of UNSCEAR. It completely ignored the presentations of ill health and took the line that there were no effects apart from those already accepted by IAEA, the nonsense spouted by Gonzalez. At this point, five of us (Yablokov, Solange Fernex, Michel Fernex, Nestorenko and Yablokov and I) went to the microphone, one after the other, and attacked the draft. It was an outrageous misrepresentation of what had occurred. What about the Chernobyl Infants? It was as if I hadn't given this paper! Nakajima was in the Chair. He concurred. Change the draft, he said to me, the conference will accept your alteration. I quickly re-wrote the draft and altered it to say that there were significant health consequences and that research should continue (Gentner's version said that the research was no longer necessary, there was nothing to find). I gave my handwritten version to Nakajima. The apparatchiks looked sick. Gentner looked furious. But had we won?

The Swiss camera crew were still active. They hovered discreetly around the conference organiser looking down the viewfinder of their Canon XLS camera. Prof Angelina Nyagu, the organiser was in a heated conversation with Prof. Yarmonenko.

Yarmonenko: *It was a catastrophe, undoubtedly, but not a radiological one. My new edition of my handbook! Everything is in chaos!*

Nyagu: *Please calm yourself. You are like Dr Guskova, a worried soul.*

Yarmonenko: *How can I be calm? I am working on the next edition of my book. My handbook. And here everything ends in chaos.*

Nyagu, putting her arm around him and turning away from the camera: *There will be a great turmoil over the draft of the resolution. We will work on it with you this evening. . .*

Yarmonenko (looking relieved): *With pleasure*

Nyagu: *Even the IAEA understands that they must turn around difficulties, but you, you are shooting right away.*

Yarmonenko: *That is true; one needs diplomacy.*

Nyagu: *Do you think that it is not a radiological accident?*

Yarmonenko: *The radiological factor exists, it is true, but it is the smallest.*

Nyagu (takes his arm and laughs conspiratorially): *Very well!*

At this point Yarmonenko notices the cameraman. He is alarmed: *Who is this?*

Nyagu: *Television.*

Yarmonenko: *Television???*
Nyagu: *Swiss Television.*
Yarmonenko (relieved): *Oh Swiss Television. Swiss Television is like ours.*

Well, he was wrong, the whole affair was captured on videotape and became a Swiss documentary, *Atomic Lies* and we have now put it on to DVD and recently posted it to every MP in the UK Parliament. But Nyagu was correct. They got together and changed the resolution, or someone did. The final conference resolution did not contain the material I wrote down for Nakajima and which the whole conference had voted on accepting. It was a slightly modified version of Gentner's attempt to change reality. The rapportage had again triumphed. Gentner was to do the same thing at the 2002 British Nuclear Energy Society conference at Keble College Oxford when he was rapporteur and analyst of the debate over low dose radiation between myself (advocating the position that low doses were dangerous) and the position of the hormesis scientist Myron Pollycove (who honestly believes that small doses of radiation are good for you). Gentner's discussion of our two positions ignored most of what we said in our presentations and merely delivered the party line, his own position, and his presentation was longer than each of ours; Assimakopoulos all over again.

For light relief I must just mention what happened to us one night when we came back from the State Opera House in Kiev where we had listened to *La Traviata* (amazingly cheap). It was 11pm and the boat, with all our things and our cabin, had sailed off without us. We were left forlornly on the quay. Two sharp young men came and asked us what the matter was. We told them. They said that the boat was taking a party of KGB officers for a party on the river and would be back after midnight. We hung about. Eventually it appeared and tied up. Various black limousines appeared with a different set of smooth young men with pistols. We tried to creep on board. Another pair of young men with pistols stopped us. There were handsome, well-dressed and dangerous looking young men everywhere. Our two new friends, the first ones, suddenly pulled pistols of their own and began to shout at the two young men guards. Everyone was getting heated. Various officers walked about with red tabs on their collars. There was a strong smell of vodka and strains of distant music from within the boat. Our two friends eventually won the argument and escorted us to our cabin. We thanked them weakly and hid in there like Hansel and Gretel while the party slowly finished amidst thuds and screams and drunken yells. Blimey!

So, implicit in these accounts of how the truth is changed and scientific advice to policymakers is constructed, is a question. How could we devise a system where policymakers were given the best evidence or advice on any scientific issue? How can we bypass the rapportage and the other shenanigans? This was a question that we first pondered at the turn of the century in 1999. It seemed that the human race needed to find an answer to this question rather urgently. The three of us,

Molly, Richard and me, devoted some time and thought to this issue. We decided to look at three areas. These were:

- The ability of MPs and policymakers to understand scientific concepts
- The philosophy of scientific method
- The construction of an arena where differing views on a scientific issue could be reported agnostically

15.3 I don't know much about science

We eventually published our researches and conclusions in a small book *I don't know much about Science; political decision making involving science and technology* (Bramhall, Busby and Scott Cato, Green Audit 2000)

When Martin Amis says, *I don't know much about science, but I know what I like*, we laugh. But why? It is because the original is *I don't know much about Art, but I know what I like*. We laugh nervously. He is pointing out that Science and Art have the same subjective component. Science is Art. More recently, the philosopher Mary Midgley has pointed out that Science has now become Religion too (Midgley Science and Poetry) although its proponents become quite exercised by their belief in Science as Truth. In any event, we were more interested in Science as Communicated Truth. Communicated to policymakers, that is. To help us understand what was going on, in 1999 we sent a questionnaire to all MPs, outlining our research project and asking them what scientific, mathematical or statistical qualifications they possessed, or whether they had any experience or had worked in any capacity which they felt might help them understand scientific matters. Had they, for example, conducted any research in a scientific or medical field? We asked them if they had obtained O-level Maths or studied any O-level science subjects at school. About 150 of the 600 or so replied with completed questionnaires. Some refused to rcspond. A few were angry, and stated that they did not need to have any science or maths qualifications to make decisions about scientific matters as they either had advisors or they could consult people who did. We next went to the main publication containing CV information on MPs, *Dod's Parliamentary Companion*, and used this information to classify them in terms of sex, age and their general area of expertise or life experience. For this we used the 11 categories shown in Table 15.3.1.
In analysing the questionnaire returns, the educational levels of MPs were classed by stages from no O-levels in science through to PhD level in science.

The results of our analysis of MPs' are presented in Table 15.3.2. In Table 15.3.3, I show the scientific qualifications of the MPs in the sample who returned the questionnaire. In Table 15.3.4 the results return to the total database and attempt to indicate the university degree status of all MPs by science, arts or no degree.

Table 15.3.1. Categories for classifying MPs' area of knowledge and expertise

Area of main experience	**Classification label**
No details	0
Politics only	1
Media and PR	2
Blue-collar industrial	3
White-collar industrial	4
Computing/ admin./ secretarial	5
Civil service/ trade union/ NGO	6
Lawyer	7
Education/ academic: non-science	8
Education/ academic: science	9
Management/ business/ finance	10
Health	11
Agriculture	12
Mixed	13

It is clear from comparing the results of the sample of those 93 MPs who returned the questionnaire that the sample was biased strongly in favour of those who did have science or maths qualifications. For example, 42 per cent of the questionnaire respondents had science degrees of some kind compared with an estimated 20 per cent for the population of all MPs. This made it even more interesting that, in this sample, 28 per cent of the respondents had no qualifications in science or maths whatsoever, not even maths 'O' level. We might estimate from this that at least one third of all MPs are not scientifically or mathematically literate. People who do not have O-level maths may find themselves struggling with concepts such as ratios and percentages, never mind such technicalities as statistical significance of research findings or the more arcane niceties of inferential statistics.

Does this matter? For many of the political decisions that have to be considered, perhaps not. But in a world that is increasingly affected by scientific and technological knowledge, those who are unable to understand basic scientific or mathematical concepts are at a great disadvantage. In particular, they are prisoners to advice that is given by scientifically literate civil servants, expert committees, and lobbyists whose interests may be tied to trans-national corporations. And such advice is increasingly biased towards permitting questionable or hazardous procedures and processes where the result is likely to increase profit or employment.

Table 15.3.2 Classification of MPs areas of expertise

Category	Value	Frequency	Percent
No details	0	2	0.3
Politics only	1	21	3.2
Media and PR	2	66	10
Blue collar industrial	3	30	4.5
White collar industrial	4	42	6.4
Computing/ admin./ secretarial	5	24	3.6
Civil service/ trade union/ NGO	6	95	14.4
Lawyer	7	75	11.4
Education/ academic non-science	8	108	16.4
Education/ academic science	9	16	2.4
Management/ business/ finance	10	92	13.9
Health	11	36	5.5
Agriculture	12	9	1.4
Mixed	13	11	1.7
Missing	0	33	5.0
All	All	660	100

We gave a good example of this afforded by the decision made in 2000 to withdraw the contract for the operation of the Atomic Weapons Establishment (AWE), Aldermaston, from Hunting Brae Ltd and give it to a joint team from British Nuclear Fuels, the present operators of the Sellafield reprocessing plant in Cumbria and Lockheed Martin, a US firm with experience of operating nuclear plants. Both the old firm, Hunting-Brae, and the new firms had poor safety records, but the decision to bring in BNFL/Lockheed was made at the time of international scandal following BNFL's admission of routinely falsifying safety data on MOX fuel elements that had been sent to reactors in Japan and Germany. At the same time, evidence became available showing that the US government were refusing to give Lockheed Martin any more contracts because of their consistently poor safety record and management attitude to nuclear safety. For this reason, a BBC TV 'Panorama' reporter interviewed Defence Minister Baroness Symons in a programme televised on 27 March, 2000. He asked her why the government was using companies with such poor safety records to administer a nuclear plant where nuclear weapons were fabricated. Had she read the reports criticising the safety records of the companies?

In her response, Baroness Symons said:

I wouldn't necessarily understand the individual bits. I have the humility to say that I am not a nuclear scientist, but there are those who are and who understand the reports in full. I have to rely on those with real expertise.

The implicit assumption made is that these 'nuclear scientists' who understood the individual bits would be unbiased either as a consequence of their connections with the nuclear industry or following their education or experience in the field of nuclear physics. It is unlikely, for example, that Baroness Symons consulted with experts who may also have 'understood the individual bits' but whose provenance or background was with the Low Level Radiation Campaign, Greenpeace, Friends of the Earth, or the Nuclear Awareness Group in Reading, the town most likely to be affected by the operation of the plant.

There is also the question of the culture of the MPs who make decisions in the area of science. Two professions dominate our legislature: lawyers and teachers. Perhaps for a law-making body that is keen to tell us how to behave this is not surprising. But are these people best equipped to make decisions about practical matters? At very minimum, their respective cultures of 'certainty' or 'proof' differ greatly from those of science. A close third to these two dogmatic professions is the media and PR sector. Between them these three career backgrounds account for 40 per cent of our elected representatives in the House of Commons. Other, more practical, backgrounds are consequently under-represented.

This is a distinct pattern from the population at large, where only 1 per cent are employed in 'legal activities' and another slightly over 1 per cent work in marketing, consultancy, and the media. So these two sectors, which represent only 2 per cent of the working population of Great Britain (*Digest of Economic Statistics 1996*: Table 6.2), contribute 21 per cent of members of the House of Commons. In the UK population as a whole, 8.4 per cent of employees work in the educational sector, so, although this sector is over-represented amongst MPs, it is not as massively over-represented as the communications sectors. Under-represented sectors include particularly production and construction, which account for nearly 23 per cent of the UK workforce, while amongst MPs only 11 per cent have a background in industry as a whole, whether white- or blue-collar.

Table 15.3.3. Science qualifications of the sample of 93 questionnaire respondents

Qualification	Number	% of sample
Science 'O' levels		
0	26	28.0
1	6	6.5
2	12	12.9
3	49	52.6
Science 'A' levels		
0	46	49.5
1	7	7.5
2	12	12.9
3	27	29
4	1	1.1
Degree		
No	51	54.8
Yes	42	45.2
Higher degree		
No	74	79.6
Yes	19	20.4
Scientific publications		
None	72	77.4
Few	11	11.8
Some	2	2.2
Many	6	6.5
No answer	2	2.2

Table 15.3.4. University education of all MPs: results by type of degree

Degree	Frequency	Per cent
No degree (0)	173	26.2
Hard science (1)	56	8.5
Soft science (2)	74	11.2
Arts (3)	309	46.8
Not known	48	7.3
Total	660	100

Note: Hard sciences are physics, chemistry, mathematics, and medicine; soft sciences are computing and economics.

The age distribution of MPs is also instructive, as is their distribution by gender and by party. However, the question we wished to examine is how scientific advice on policy issues is generated and is converted by scientifically illiterate MPs into statute and whether the present process is the best one to ensure that the members of the electorate are protected from the consequences of wrong decisions made on the basis of inaccurate or biased advice.

In order to better illustrate the problem, we focused on the government backbench Environment Committee and asked how it might consider scientific advice given to it in areas where the consequences of policy might result in hazard to human health. The Environment Committee is routinely required to consider information of a mathematical and scientific nature and to make decisions that could affect the health and well-being of very large numbers of people for a very long period of time. The environment is where we all live and where our children will have to live in the future. Technological developments regularly occur where possible subtle toxic or environmental effects of by-products released from a production processes (dioxins, CFCs, radioactive discharges, nanoparticles, pesticide spraying, incinerators) or in some cases, subtle long-term toxic or mutational (cancer) effects resulting from exposure to the new agent itself (BSE, GM foods), may occur. The Environment Committee has to advise on draft legislation that ensures that progress in efficient use of resources is not blocked by irrational fears. We need to accept that history teaches that many of these fears are later discovered to be all too well grounded. Who do the committee listen to and how can they decide? We looked at the make-up of the 2000 Environment Committee (Table 15.3.5)

Of the eleven members of the committee, not a single one had a degree in a science subject or in mathematics. There were two with ‘A’ level maths and one with ‘A' level physics, none with post-O-level qualifications in chemistry or biological sciences. Examination of the MPs’ areas of expertise and qualifications enabled us to see that those who were selected onto this committee could have been more scientifically qualified. I would not wish to disparage the contributions made by the members of the Environment Committee. But it is their job to scrutinise legislation in this area and presumably to take responsibility when errors occur. It is surely unfair to expect such responsibility to be taken in highly technical areas without adequate background knowledge.

Table 15.3.5. The Commons Backbench Environment Committee

Name	Scientific education	Career background
Andrew Bennett (Chair)	Refused to respond	Social Science degree
Thomas Brake	3 science O-levels; maths and physics A-level	IT Manager
Christine Butler	O-level maths	Pharmaceutical, NHS, lab technician. Sculptor, management
John Cummings	O-level maths	Miner and colliery electrician
Brian Donohoe	O-level maths and physics	Apprenticed engineer; Hunterston nuclear power station; ICI
Gwyneth Dunwoody	None	Film production
Louise Ellman	O-level maths	Education; Social policy/ local government
James Gray	3 science O-levels; maths A-level	Shipping broker
Bill Olner	None	Apprenticed engineer; skilled machinist
Hilary Benn	O-level maths	Russian studies.
Alan Whitehead	4 science O-levels	Education; public policy

Source: Constituency offices; authors' questionnaire; *The Vacher Dod Guide to the New House of Commons* (1997).

What is the problem with this lack of scientific education? Surely we do not want our democratic representatives to be academic-oriented scientists or technocrats. But on the other hand, it is clear that without sufficient grounding in the basics of mathematics and/or science our politicians simply cannot judge the quality of the scientific information they are given. This makes them vulnerable to one-sided lobbying. It makes them accept information on the basis of the credibility of the person communicating it. In this world, Professor Plum must be more right than Dr Foster and no one listens to Mary Green. What should be done to ensure the best outcome? Surely, as a minimum, the 'other side' of any issue should be presented at an early stage in the process. Whatever their scientific education we can assume that politicians are adept at reading human cues, since this is a fundamental requirement for success within a political structure. So the politician's role might be to judge the validity and integrity of information presented. This would presuppose only a basic level of scientific knowledge on the part of the MP. But it raises new questions. Who is to provide the scientific information, and what is that information worth? This leads to the questions about science and scientific philosophy which form part of the present book also, and introduced much of the ECRR report which I move to later. The question is: What is good Science?

Science, as practised over the last 300 years, was a philosophical development which looked primarily to experiment and to the empirical data to provide evidence about truth. Its divergence from previous philosophical methods was fundamentally this: that beliefs began with objective consideration of the results of experiment rather than with statements about what seemed likely or about religious expectations or Holy Writ. In its basic form the method is based upon the principle of scientific induction. This states that there exists a form of inference by which laws can be inferred from particular facts, unequivocally.

The classical exposition of the inductive method (originally due to William of Occam) is what are now called Mill's Canons, the two most important of which are:

- The Canon of Agreement, which states that whatever there is in common between the antecedent conditions of a phenomenon can be supposed to be the cause or related to the cause of the phenomenon.
- The Canon of Difference, which states that the differences in the conditions under which an effect occurs and those under which it does not must be the cause or related to the cause of that effect.

In addition, the method relies upon the 'Principle of Accumulation', which states that scientific knowledge grows additively by the discovery of independent laws, and the 'Principle of Instance Confirmation', that the degree of belief in the truth of a law is proportional to the number of favourable instances of the law.

In addition to the inductive method outlined above, the scientific method includes the range of analytical methods subsumed within Popper's 'Doctrine of Falsifiability'. This regards science as moving forward through the experimental falsification of existing belief structures. Finally to the methods of inductive reasoning we must add considerations of 'Plausibility of Mechanism'. These are the methods of science (Mill, 1879; Popper, 1962; Harré, 1985; Papineau, 1996). Those who seek to apply these methods to the examination of a number of contemporary questions might be understandably confused. A good example, which is the matter of this book, is the question of increases in childhood leukaemia associated with nuclear sites. According to all of the routines of science outlined above it should be now universally conceded that low-level radiation exposure to man-made radioactive substances released from nuclear plants like

Sellafield, Dounreay and Cap de la Hague increases the incidence of child leukaemia in those exposed. Application of Mill's Canons all point to this. The Principle of Accumulation points to this. The Principle of Instance Confirmation is applicable. The continued assertion by the nuclear industry and by government that exposures are too low on the basis of studies of Hiroshima survivors have been (Popper) falsified by many researchers and through many studies. Yet the statutes that permit the releases, and allow fresh child and adult leukaemias to be induced, continue in place. Why? The answer relates to science's attitude towards evidence, significance, and truth and the legal attitude to the same things. These are not the same.

Let us look more closely at the concept of evidence. The dominant position taken by lawyers in our legislature becomes of specific relevance when we consider this question of 'evidence'; because what lawyers and scientists think of as evidence is entirely different (this point was first made explicitly by Michael Mansfield QC). In a legal context, stating that there is no evidence about, say, a crime is to make a strong statement. For example, the sentence 'There is no evidence that Mr. Blair was present at the scene of the crime' is to be taken as analogous to the statement 'Mr. Blair was not at the scene of the crime'. It is therefore a statement of his absence, not a mere acknowledgement of ignorance.

In science the position is entirely different. When a government scientist reports to Michael Meacher that 'there is no evidence that genetically modified crops are damaging to health', he is simply stating that none of the research studies conducted have found 'significant' answers to this question, or even that no studies have been carried out at all. If Meacher were to interpret this in the sense of legal evidence he might well take the statement as reassurance as to the negative consequences of genetic modification, rather than the statement of total ignorance it really represents. This important point indicates the crucial importance of the arts, and specifically legal, rather than scientific background of the majority of our decision-makers. Scientists seem to be unaware of this and will generally leave it to the policymakers to deduce what they can from the scientific advice thcy have been given. They argue that they are not expert when it comes to determining policy, and will not advise that such and such a process should not be legalized because children will die. Or not die. *If the rockets go up who cares where they come down: that's not my department says Werner Von Braun*, sang Tom Lehrer. Quite so.

The nature of scientific evidence presented to government committees and thence to ministers is also limited and biased in another way. Most of the scientific research carried out in universities today has been part funded by industry. As a result of the Thatcherite push towards 'market-driven research' only research programmes that can eventually yield a profit are likely to be funded. So what is the university scientist to do if s/he undertakes a research project and finds results that would undermine the product of the very company that funded the research? We illustrated the point by means of a fictitious case study.

Nuclear Futures Ltd. is interested in obtaining evidence that shows that there is a threshold of exposure to low levels of ionizing radiation below which there is no harmful effect. This 'threshold' hypothesis may follow from the discovery that damaged cells can repair themselves. Why, then, is it believed that low levels of radiation exposure may cause cancer? Camford University Radiation Biology department has a long history of doing funded work for Nuclear Futures Ltd (NFL). After some discussion, Dr Whizzhead is awarded a two-year contract to examine the hypothesis that there is a threshold for exposure dose below which there is no discernible effect. Dr Whizzhead and his team decide to irradiate cell cultures with alpha particles from Plutonium. In earlier experiments, he had found that there was no effect, below a certain quite high threshold. But this time, using new techniques that have become available, he follows the cells after exposure through several replications. His results suggest there is a threshold in the first irradiated cells but below this threshold serious genetic effects appear in the descendants of the irradiated cells. The results are not conclusive, however. What is he to do? Clearly, NFL are unlikely to fund further work that will result in their own demise. And this would result in no more contracts for his department. Maybe the work is quietly shelved. Maybe a preliminary paper is prepared for the *International Journal of Radiation Biology* but when it is sent maybe it is returned by a referee who wants further confirmatory results before passing such a contentious and potentially explosive report. Maybe the report describes the results in the body text but the conclusions and abstract are at odds with the detailed result. This latter is becoming a favourite method for providing acceptable reports without actually telling lies. Dr Whizzhead is a member of a government advisory committee. He is asked if the installations belonging to NFL may be responsible for increases in childhood cancer nearby. What does he reply? Does he exercise scientific caution? After all, his results were only preliminary. They required more work to confirm. No one has paid for this work.

We described in this small book a recent study involving research into the possible harmful effects of mobile phone radiation. In the study, published in the journal *Epidemiology*, the results were reported of a study of 195,775 employees of the company Motorola, who develop and manufacture mobile phone equipment (Morgan *et al.,* 2000). The study was part-funded by Motorola and carried out by a non-university organisation Exponent Health Group and examined all causes of mortality, with brain cancers, lymphomas and leukaemias as major *a priori* outcomes of interest. The study seemed to report no excess risk from any cause of death among the workers. We may be suspicious that such a study was funded with the express purpose of reassuring the public and those involved in legislation over mobile phone radiation exposure that there were no harmful effects. What are we to make of this? The raw data were not tabulated, nor made available for independent

examination, so we have to assume that the processed results were accurately reduced from the data. Furthermore, no one has access to such data except the company. The abstract of the results states:
Our findings do not support an association between occupational RF exposure and brain cancer, lymphoma or leukaemia.

However, close inspection of the paper reveals a quite different picture. The study compares mortality risk in the highly educated, upper social class, electronics workers with members of the *general public* in four States of the USA, Arizona, Florida, Texas and Illinois. Comparison of the death rates reveals that although the Motorola employees enjoy lower death rates (owing to their higher socio-economic status), their death rates from all causes were significantly lower than their death rates from leukaemia and lymphatic system cancers and most other cancers (but not brain cancers). The effect was particularly clear in the case of the lymphatic system cancer Hodgkin's disease, a result which was not mentioned at all in the Abstract. If the overall mortality risk from all causes is used as an internal control for the 'healthy worker effect' there was a higher risk of dying of most cancer types. And how do we know what the result would have been if Arizona and Texas were not used as external controls, but instead, Ohio and Tennessee were used? In fact, it was possible to use data reported in the paper to argue that there was a strong excess risk of most types of cancer in the workers, since standardised risk by period of employment consistently showed a 50 to 100 percent elevated risk in those who had worked more than 5 years with the radiation relative to those who had worked from 0-5 years. Nothing was made of this result either.

As I have shown in this book, there is a great deal of scope in epidemiology for tailoring the results to fit the hypothesis. Yet the results of this mobile phone paper and others like it, reporting studies which were funded by industry and showing results which counter any suggestion that these industries may be causing harm, are commonplace in the reference section of review committees which give advice to government. Do the government committee members (many of whom have only 'O' levels) look through the original papers? Would they know what to look for?

Aside from the biased research findings government experts do receive, there is also a limitation on what is available to them brought about by the system of peer review, a necessary hurdle for publication in an academic journal. Any researcher on the fringes of the scientific establishment, or whose findings fall outside the accepted scientific paradigm, might find him or herself asking 'Who is my peer?' A peer is usually defined as 'a person of the same age, status, or ability', which is unlikely to be the case when a young researcher submits a paper for review. But even more serious is the fact that the reviewers seem to assume that what should be the 'same' between reviewer and reviewed is their own view of scientific truth. Many reviewers seem to see their role as the reinforcement of the view of the world they themselves hold. So alternative theories are unlikely to be published. When all accepted authorities ruled that the sun revolved around the earth, Galileo was unlikely to find his paper on 'Let's Twist Again: The Need for a Real Copernican Revolution' accepted by *Acta Catholica Astronomica*. And the same situation persists today. The so-called peers who are allowed to judge what should be published may exercise their private theoretical prejudices at the expense of new ideas, and in the security provided by the system's secrecy.

According to concerns expressed by the editors of some of Britain's medical journals, the system of peer review is not effective even in weeding out fraudulent papers whose conclusions are based on bogus research. In the modern competitive academic environment, where researchers are desperate for advancement, evidence of fabrication and falsification of results is growing. Richard Horton, editor of *The Lancet*, was concerned that 'the public was increasingly aware that fraud existed and there was a risk that the scientific community, in not acting, would be thought to be sweeping it under the carpet' (Boseley, 1999: 8). The evidence accumulating about the quality of academic review suggests that the system of peer review is about the exercise of power and prestige within academia, not about a selfless search for scientific truth (Judson 2004, Washburn 2005).

So when government ministers make claims about their decisions being made on 'the best available scientific evidence' we should be cautious. This will probably mean that it results from a consensus view of the state of scientific knowledge as agreed by the senior academics who operate the peer review system. It may even mean that their decisions are based on nothing more than arm-waving by their advisers, no genuine evidence being available to consider. Or, worse still, it may mean that decisions are being made on the basis of information provided only by the corporations whose interests are served by a decision in favour of the process or product under examination.

Arpad Pusztai, the man at the centre of the media frenzy over GM foods in late 1998, described the threat he considers is posed to academic freedom by political and industry pressure in a recent article in *The Ecologist*. In response to his undertaking and reporting of objective scientific findings he was sacked and slandered, his reputation and scientific career destroyed. His employers abandoned and betrayed him once the political problems posed by his research became clear. But beyond this, he was also maligned by three committees which should be independent but which in this case were almost certainly acting under political pressure: the House of Commons Science and Technology Committee, the Royal Society Committee on Toxicology, and the Advisory Committee on Novel Foods and Processes. Such a savage response to unpalatable scientific results not only succeeds in undermining the researcher himself, they also give a clear signal to other scientists, who are quick to follow the cues about which results are acceptable and which not.

Pusztai himself said:

It seems that, in the eyes of many senior scientists today, the future of science lies with industry. When scientists who apparently have no obvious financial connection with the biotech industry defend GM crops so blindly, and attack even the mildest critics, slandering their work and abilities in the process, we must ask ourselves what motivates them. And one possible motivation is that, with the rapid disappearance of the State patronage of science, many of these people are genuinely worried about the future funding of scientific research itself.

Having dealt with the problem of evidence, what of science itself? What is Scientific Truth? The basic philosophical method has been described, but this is to assume that in some way the scientists themselves are somehow the cold thinking machines that the stereotype describes, translating Nature's secrets directly into laws and theorems with steely precision. Although scientists may believe that science moves forward through this formal philosophical framework, reality seems rather more down-to-earth. In the last twenty years, sociologists and social anthropologists have begun to direct their critical gaze at scientists and their real world. Much of what I have learned in this area has been from my daughter Celia, who is well qualified to say. After two years, she abandoned Natural Sciences at Cambridge to become an anthropologist. Our discussions concluded that it was a historical development. Fundamental questions about human behaviour led, after the Second World War (and its inexplicable horrors), to the examination of objectivity and the application of reflexive methods. We cannot escape from our culture, claimed the philosophers. What we appear to find when we look at other societies and cultures is largely a reflection of our own subjective view. And this interpretation is so embedded in the way we ourselves think about or understand the world that what we find is only our own picture, based on our own culture, of what we would be doing or thinking if we were the person being studied. Thus, what we find is essentially what we put there ourselves through our interpretative assumptions.

The early search for objectivity led to the belief that science was the most objective description of the physical world, particularly if the descriptions were mathematical. This was because it was believed that there were somehow 'scientific facts' wrested from Nature and elevated to the level of 'physical laws', like Newton's Laws of Motion. However, recent close examination of scientists at work and study, and of how their theories and discoveries come to eventually be accepted in their own and the wider community came to show that science is not as objective as it believes. 'Science studies', as this sociology has come to be known, finds that science is not free from the bias and inaccuracy that permeates all other areas of knowledge, for many of the same reasons. Scientists are human beings like non-scientists. And scientific facts are not the unassailable result of forcing Nature to reveal her Truths, but are assembled from the interplay of many different items, actors, machines and procedures, all of which may be faulty, biased, inaccurate or uncertain.

The situation is outlined by the philosopher Bruno Latour, in two books, *Science in Action* (1987) and more recently, *Pandora's Hope* (1999). Latour's conclusions are very relevant to our enquiry. He finds that scientific truths are not unassailable, nor final, nor always without components derived from muddier sources than Nature herself. He also finds that what is accepted at any period of history is a scientific world-view that consists of a system of 'black boxes'. These are accepted encapsulations of earlier theory that are then used as machines to understand and interpret new discoveries. Most significantly, he finds that as time passes and more knowledge is included in these 'black boxes' it becomes increasingly difficult for any scientists to open up or attack the complex system of connections that maintains the 'black boxes' or is within them. The current problem is that those who are building the present scientific consensus are those who are funded to do the research by those who have need of the results of this same research to make money. It is therefore quite reasonable to assume that this process leads to the construction of 'black boxes', which contain false reasoning, false connections and even false experimental results (Judson 2004, van den Hazel et al 2006).

If Latour, and the 'science study philosophers' are correct, then what emerges is a need to question the very advice given to government by its expert committees. This is because it is not 'the best scientific advice'. It is merely the contents of the particular black box that the particular scientific committee made up out of those particular experts they chose to believe. Are these experts unbiased? According to Latour, this is not a question about whether they are slipped buff envelopes containing fivers or dollar bills. It is an inevitable consequence of the fact, as we have pointed out, that they work in an area dominated by funding which is all aimed towards increasing profit and research.

The way that policy is presently driven by expert advice is through the science advisory committees. I have shown in this book a great deal of evidence that in this area of radiation risk, the relevant advisory bodies, COMARE, NRPB and so forth have signally failed to distance themselves from the nuclear industry when it comes to commenting on evidence. But they have not yet been so clearly shown to be as wildly incorrect as the classic example of an advisory committee that was too close to industry, the SEAC committee. The antics of this committee led to the delay in banning contaminated beef and the deaths of many people. Members of this committee are still walking around. Why are they not in gaol?

The story of BSE starts before the establishment of SEAC in 1990. It is a long and depressing narrative, investigated by the Phillips Enquiry, demonstrating a frightening ignorance on the part of MPs and their 'experts', combined with an even more terrifying complacency. The result has already been over 200 confirmed deaths, with an unknown number of UK citizens still incubating the human form of the disease. A readable version of this saga was offered in paperback form by Stephen Dealler, who, along with Richard Lacey and Helen Grant, were the heroes of this sad tale. These three acted as 'good' scientists should, informing themselves, drawing conclusions based on the best available facts, and then alerting government to the risks. The response was ridicule, humiliation, and the destruction of careers. Richard Lacey was insulted by Lord Soames in the House of Commons, told to 'keep taking the pills'. More seriously, his research unit was destroyed around him until he no longer had any staff to manage and was out of a job.

One quotation from Dealler's book serves to illustrate the attitude towards science of the Backbench Agriculture Committee under its Chairman Gerry Wiggin, who represented an agricultural constituency in Somerset. The meeting took place at the House of Commons in June 1990 when Dealler, Lacey and Grant presented evidence. The following is an account of the reception given to Lacey's evidence:

The questions asked seemed to be of minor significance - mostly about whether he had enough knowledge of the subject or whether he should speak about things that were really somebody else's province. . . The chairman, Gerry Wiggin, was determined to hear what risks Lacey felt were possible in the short and longer term. Lacey told him directly that this sort of disease could become a major cause of death in Britain, and said we should take action to prevent such a calamity. Wiggin made it clear that he felt that scare stories got nobody anywhere. As I had feared, the committee did not know enough to ask the right questions of Lacey anyway. They did not appear to know that there was no method of testing anything for the presence of infection without actually inoculating it into the brain of a cow. They did not seem to realise that animals inherently lacked any way of forming immunity to the agents of TSEs, nor that the disease could not be destroyed by cooking.

In view of the information provided in the previous section about MPs' level of scientific education it is not surprising that they could not ask useful questions. But what is shocking about this account is the arrogance and complacency shown by representatives in an area of critical importance to public health.

We can take no comfort from the fact that this was a few years ago, and the hope that the new intake of MPs will be better motivated. Recent evidence suggests that little has changed. In response to our scientific questionnaire, which focused on the BSE issue, one current Liberal Democrat MP representing a rural constituency replied as follows:

I would have to say that the questions you ask [regarding his scientific qualifications] are entirely irrelevant to the latest BSE arguments. The Liberal

Democrats oppose the ban on beef on the bone and led the debate against it in the House of Commons.

I represent a rural constituency and have seen first hand the damage done, by the present and previous Governments mishandling of the crisis, to my own constituents. I am here first and foremost to represent my constituency and do not feel I need any special qualification to comment on any particular issue that affects those in it.

Presumably, the 'constituents' this MP is representing are only those with an interest in farming, not those who have died from eating its products.

Of greatest interest to us, however, is the way in which government obtains advice on radiation risk. I have discussed this earlier in the book and drawn attention to the multiplicity of committees engaged in the exercise of advising on policy in this area. The reason for such a plethora of advisory bodies is the clear failure of any of them to persuade the public that releases for nuclear sites are safe. Government (and the nuclear industry) spend enormous sums on psychologists and sociologists attempting to figure out how they can communicate the science in a way that will overcome what they see as irrational or emotional fears.

COMARE has been mentioned at several points in the book so far. The Committee on the Medical Effects of Radiation in the Environment was set up in the wake of the Black Report into the Sellafield leukaemia cluster. Sir Douglas Black, who chaired the 'Independent Advisory Committee' was clearly unconvinced by arguments made by NRPB that the largest source of radioactivity in Europe could not be somehow associated with the discovery of a cluster of childhood leukaemia when radiation was the only proven cause of the disease. Environmentalists and anti-nuclear activists had long argued that the government's advisory committee on radiological protection, the National Radiological Protection Board (NRPB), was not independent of the nuclear industry. In 1977 one of NRPB's own senior researchers wrote in a letter to *New Scientist,* 'The Royal Commission on Environmental Protection criticises the NRPB for bias towards underestimating radiation risk and of not being seen to be independent of the UKAEA' (quoted in Busby 1995, p. 23).

So the purpose of the establishment of COMARE was for the government to have advice that enabled it to protect the public health from the dangers of radioisotopes, one that was independent of both the nuclear industry and the NRPB. The problem is that COMARE is based at the NRPB offices at Chilton, Oxfordshire. If you phone the COMARE telephone number it is answered with 'Hello, NRPB'. What is more the three-person secretariat that organizes COMARE's agendas are all on the NRPB payroll. This point has been raised with various leading members of NRPB and the COMARE Chairman as being worrying but they cannot see a problem. When asked why it was necessary for COMARE to be based at NRPB one replied that it enables members to use the NRPB library. But none of the COMARE members themselves are based at Chilton.

COMARE's three Secretaries: Roy Hamlet and John Cooper (Scientific), plus a currently empty post as Medical Secretary (formerly C. Sharp), are all NRPB employees who spend a proportion of their time conducting research for NRPB - the rest of their time being spent preparing paperwork for the members of COMARE, whose raison d'être is to be independent of NRPB. The Secretary we spoke to was unwilling to say how much time was spent with which hat on. We were recently amused to have copied to us a letter from the Department of Health in London advising an enquirer into radiation and health that the DoH took this area very seriously and were advised by the 'independent committee COMARE' on the effects of radiation. The letter was signed by Dr Roy Hamlet, who signed himself, Radiation Advisor, Department of Health. He does not have far to walk to get advice from the 'independent committee' since he is, himself, their secretary.

It seems apparent that in an area of such crucial importance as the medical effects of radiation in the environment it is wrong that there is no full-time member of staff even administering the Committee, never mind carrying out the independent research that all our lives depend on. Its meeting schedule of only four meetings a year also seems entirely inadequate for members to even discuss cursorily the vast number of papers published in this field around the world.

The consistent refusal of COMARE to distance itself from the industry line has meant that, since the discovery of the leukaemia cluster at Sellafield in 1983, nothing has been done to protect the children and adults, with the consequence that Sellafield has been permitted to continue to release its radioactive poisons for another thirty years. Thousands more cancer cases have resulted and, as we saw from the new data obtained by HTV, more children have died. The members and operators in COMARE should be held accountable for these deaths and the attendant misery that their failure to act (or their actions to support the nonsensical ICRP model) has brought about. Eventually we persuaded the minister Michael Meacher of this, and we set up yet another committee to look into the matter. This committee was CERRIE, (Committee Examining Radiation Risk from Internal Emitters) and I will report what happened in the next chapter. In his discussion with Yvette Cooper, the Health Minister, about setting up CERRIE jointly between the Ministries of Health and Environment, she asked what the purpose was of having a committee that would not agree, and he passed the question on to me. I answered that the politicians then would have to make up their own minds about who they believed, and, at minimum, would see that there was a large question mark over the issue. If the SEAC report had adequately addressed the information given to it, there would have been less of a problem with BSE. However, the new committee CERRIE did not, as it happened, have sufficient safeguards built in, as we shall see. And if this method is to work, important lessons must be learned from the CERRIE process.

16
The Oppositional Science System Experiment: CERRIE

Opposition brings concord; out of discord comes the fairest harmony
Heraclitus of Ephesus (535-475BC)

16.1 New mechanisms for arriving at the truth

I was told that the Iranians have a *Committee to Examine what is the Truth of the Issue and What is the Best Thing to Do About It.* Even if this is apocryphal, it is still an impressive idea. The citizens of the UK have lost faith in the scientific establishment. According to a recent ICM poll, public trust in scientists is now lower than trust in policemen. Only 35 per cent of those questioned said they trusted scientists 'a lot'; 54 per cent trusted them 'a little'; and 12 per cent did not trust them at all. The only professions to come lower in the trust ranking were politicians and journalists. On specific issues levels of lack of trust rose as high as 49 per cent on the issue of cloning animals and 40 per cent on the issue of genetically modified food (Travis, 1999).

This loss of faith has not occurred because of intellectual arguments about philosophy. The horrors of the real world ranging from defective medical treatments receiving scientific support to the destruction of the farming industry by pusillanimous government advisers have irreparably undermined faith in the ability of scientists to offer final and absolute judgements. In 1999 there was a total solar eclipse in southern England. The government spent a great effort telling people not to view the eclipse with the naked eye. The Chief Scientist or Medical Officer was trotted out and he told everyone to use smoked glass to look at the corona and to be ever-so careful. It was as if people were somehow unaware that the sun was bright and that they needed a 'scientist' to tell them this. The hilarity which greeted these pronouncements about the devastating potential health consequences of the solar eclipse indicates the level of esteem accorded to the scientific expert.

There seem to be two problems with the system of government scientific advice: appropriate evidence does not reach the expert committees; and the members of the committees are not in a position to independently assess the evidence and pass it on to decision-makers. Long before CERRIE, Richard Bramhall, Molly and I made a study of the issue and pointed out that these problems were deep-seated and required a complete overhaul (Bramhall *et al.* 2000) At the time, the official publication on this issue, *The Use of Scientific Advice in Policy-Making*, was laughable. It contained only 5 pages of double-spaced text, plus a list of references only one of which was not a government publication. The paper consisted of a series of legalistic principles, without any analysis or evidence of understanding of the complexity of the nature of scientific research and debate. Although it did contain some principles which might have improved the system - including the stated willingness to address issues raised by lobby groups and the importance of including experts from non-scientific disciplines - it did not address the question of the restructuring of scientific committees, which seemed so urgent.

The distorted idea that filtered through to those who were responsible was not that scientific advice was failing because the advice itself was wrong (biased by connection with industry funding), but that somehow the public, in their quaint and uneducated way just didn't believe the science and therefore some way was needed to educate them. This heralded the beginning of the stakeholder dialogues, where the public or their representatives were invited to meetings and the authorities pretended to listen to them. An early example of this absorption of the non-scientist representative was the introduction of two non-scientific advisory committees in the area where most hot potatoes had recently emerged, that of genetic engineering. The Human Genetics Commission and the Agriculture and Environment Biotechnology Commission would be responsible for the formulation and delivery of advice to ministers and were intended to ensure that 'both scientific and non-scientific views are brought to bear'.

The early part of the new century also saw some moves to incorporate citizen representatives in similar bogus dialogues concerning matters involving radioactivity. Examples included the 'Safegrounds' dialogue, for dealing with radioactively contaminated land, and the MAGNOX (nuclear power station) decommissioning dialogue. These were more sops to the view that it was necessary to consult with the public. The cynics in the anti-nuclear movements labelled this development UNCLE, which stands for *Unlimited Nuclear Consultation Leading to Exhaustion*. This was to replace DAD, or *Decide, Announce, Defend*. I kept well away from these new moves, but Richard Bramhall and Paul Dorfman went along, as did other members of the Greens and the anti-nuclear movement, my friends Jim Duffy (Stop Hinkley), Hugh Richards (Welsh Anti-Nuclear Alliance). As far as I was concerned, the only 'Stake Holder' situation I could see myself in was as the man holding the sharpened stake for the 'B' movie hero as he opened the coffin of the (nuclear) vampire at dead of night. Anyway, it soon became clear that these operations were indeed mainly a scam, there to cover up the lack of democracy in the area. Jim was leaked a memo from the nukes chortling about how their dialogue with the activists over the nuclear trains at Cricklewood in London seemed to have defused the situation, and congratulating everyone concerned. The intention was also to appear to consult, while actually enrolling some of the less knowledgeable members of the anti-nuclear community as special advisors so that the processes could be developed with a green fig-leaf and the opposition was split. Some of the positions were well paid, and in many cases, the anti-nuclear citizens were paid £200 or more plus expenses including a stay in a posh hotel to just turn up to the dialogue meetings. This is a lot of money for many of the poor people who are usually in this category. There is some glory (for a while) in being special advisor to the nukes, or Chair of some 'Uncle Tom' Committee with a grand name like 'The Environment Council'. This latter actually exists and fulfils the role.

The technique is being refined now. Whereas at first it was naively thought that all the establishment scientists had to do was educate the stakeholders, it was soon discovered that too many of the stakeholders were already educated and could address the science as well as (and often better than) those who were doing the educating. In setting up the Committee on Radioactive Waste Management CoRWM, it was advertised that this new committee should consist of those members of the public who were concerned about the issue (of dumping radioactive waste in the ground) and that these 'stakeholders' would make a collective decision. That is to say, the government was not making the decision, but the people were. Since the committee members were well paid, everyone applied to be on CoRWM. I did. Bramhall did. Dorfman did. All the people we knew who were 'concerned about the issue' did. But the committee was made up of people we never heard of, people who knew nothing at all about the issue, about the science, or even about science! Keith Baverstock, who had been Radiation Advisor to the WHO, managed to get on, but as soon as the powers discovered that he was too knowledgeable and not sufficiently malleable, he disappeared.

The process then went forward with the 'stakeholders', who knew nothing, being educated by the scientists who represented the official risk model (e.g. Dudley Goodhead). The opposing view was excluded. So, naturally, the committee of greenhorns was easily guided to agreeing the outcome that the government wanted all along, which would enable them to develop nuclear power again and hide the waste in some holes in the ground.

The latest stage in this project to dump nuclear waste in a hole near you is an organisation called 'New Leaf', set up to choose sites where the radioactive waste is to be dumped. It is headed up by Fred Barker, another ex-green who is rather close to the establishment. Paul Dorfman went along for an interview. His job was to sell the idea to local authorities and tempt them with the advantages attendant to having nuclear waste dump in their area. Lorry loads of money were to be given as incentives. Note that the local people here were not to be consulted. It was the local Authority Council that would decide and have control of the money. Of course we all know what that means. Paul refused the job, but it would have been well paid, £30,000 for three days work and, no doubt, a secure future. The 'New Leaf' organisation will be stuffed with dodgy greens making money. You watch. They will justify their positions.

This ploy for splitting the green opposition was developed in the US and it seems to have had a limited success here, with the green and anti-nuclear movement having been split between those of us who argue that low dose radiation from internal fission products is killing people (manifestly true) and those who have been gulled by the nuclear industry pretence of listening. Some are flattered by the attention, the money and the promises that they will have some influence on the process. The argument is old. Do a little good from the inside rather than standing outside and shouting and having no effect. The idea that standing outside and shouting with conviction and having a considerable effect might be an option seems to have passed them by. Maybe it was for this kind of reason that Tony Blair joined George W Bush in the Iraq war, hoping he could somehow head it off or have some beneficial influence. At least this is what Blair's supporters said at the time. But how much more powerful would have been a stand by the UK against this project?

Whatever the real influence of these new citizen dialogues, the real scientific influence still remains with the scientific advisory committees, who are closest to the policy makers. These are the people who advise that the process is or is not dangerous in the first place. And it is here that real changes are needed. The existing structure of these committees has grown out of the post-war culture of paternalism and secrecy: hence the obsession with reassurance. If we take the case of Mad Cow Disease, it is as if the emergence of news that a fatal, degenerative brain disease could be caught from eating beef might cause public panic and anarchy on the streets (and why not?). The natural response within this culture was to cover up and reassure; scientific truth was a secondary consideration.

While it is easy to be disparaging about the paternalism of the British decision-maker, the positive side of *noblesse oblige* was the requirement for decency and honour. This only now persists in the absurd notion that corporations who want to make vast profits by selling something are none the less likely to tell the truth to a government committee deciding whether to license it. While this faith in the honour of gentlemen is quaint and touching, it is incompatible with the cut-throat globally competitive world these corporations operate in and therefore, in itself, represents a threat to public health.

As an alternative to the perspective of trust for the scientist and the producer which has thus far determined the existing structure of advice, we proposed in *I don't know much about Science* a perspective wherein the corporation seeking permission for its product is characterised as driven by the profit motive, without any concern for the well-being of the citizen, represented by pressure groups. The old-fashioned view might have been of two naughty children arguing, with a benign father figure (democratic governance) wisely judging between their competing claims. Given the gross inequality of power and money between corporations and pressure groups this view is well out of date. The father has long since been judged senile and packed off to an old folks' home. Meanwhile, back at home, big brother has grown up greedy and over-sized, and finds no difficulty in abusing and exploiting his younger sibling.

To defend the weaker sibling we suggested a new structure based on the opposition principle so fundamental to the UK constitution. Just as in the House of Commons, the government, as protagonist, is opposed axiomatically by the Opposition, so the corporations, as developers of new processes and products, should face opposition by government scientists on behalf of the citizen. While the problems associated with an oppositional system - especially its engendering of an antagonistic rather than cooperative polity - have been emphasised in recent years, its main benefit has been ignored. This is the strengthening of legislation by means of a process of bombardment to identify any weaknesses. And just as in the House the most effective route to promotion for an ambitious back-bencher is to pick a sizeable hole in government legislation, so in an oppositional scientific environment, any new process or product would be subjected to a barrage of research by the young scientist eager to make their name. This would guarantee the genuine scrutiny of technological advance that the effete committees of eminent academics have so clearly failed to provide.

These two different perspectives on government scientific advice have been illustrated in the figures: Figure 16.1.1 shows how the existing system of science advice is supposed to work, while Figure 16.1.2 shows our characterisation of that situation. The proposed structure shown in Figure 16.1.3 indicates the new role for the government advisory committees as referees between the evidence provided by the corporations, on the one side, and the counter evidence provided by government-funded independent scientists on the other. This new role is the main strength of the proposed new system. As identified above, the combination of increasing teaching pressure and corporation funding has undermined the ability of the academic to carry out powerful and independent research. By contrast, these citizen scientists would be funded by public money to do just that. They could continue in their own university, or even work outside the university structure altogether, but compete with each other for fixed-term government-funded contracts within designated areas of public concern. They would then be required to produce and publish research and to provide information and advice to ministers and expert committees. This was our suggestion in 2000.

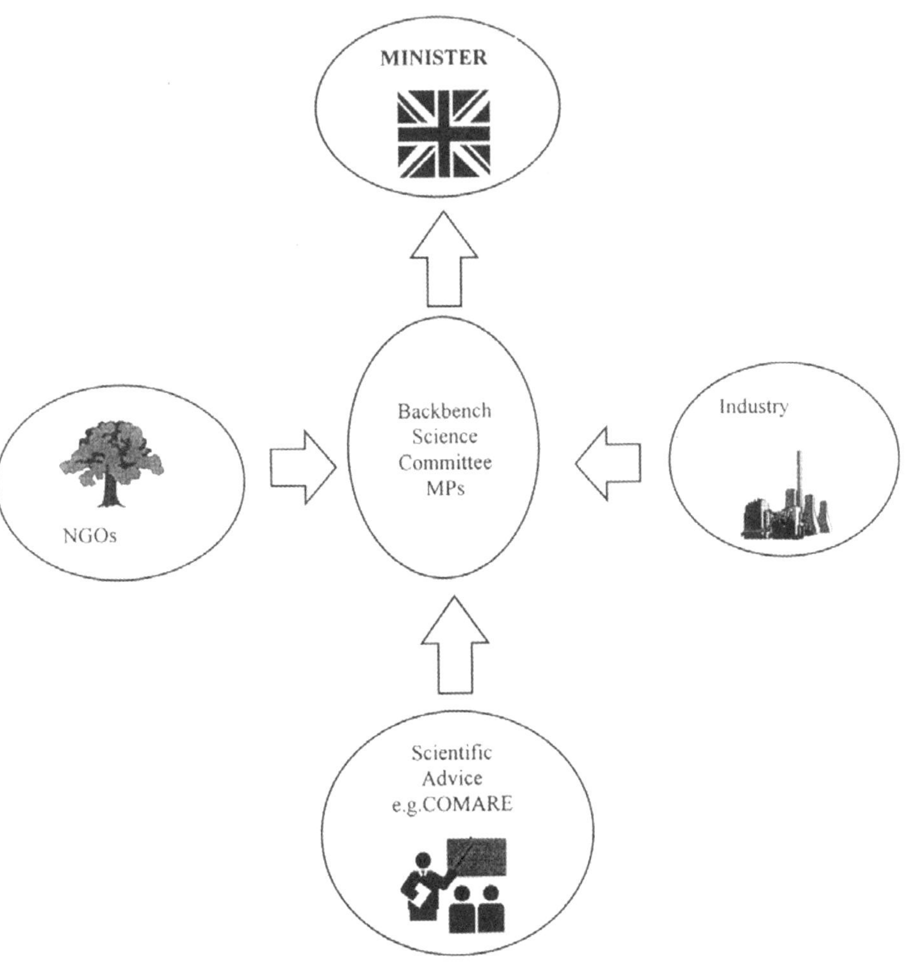

Fig 16.1.1 The official view of the existing scientific advice system. Industry and pressure groups are assumed to have equal and balanced input. The considered view of the objective scientific advice committee is passed to the backbench MPs who combine it with industry and pressure group views to arrive at a consensus, a 'scientifically agreed' position.

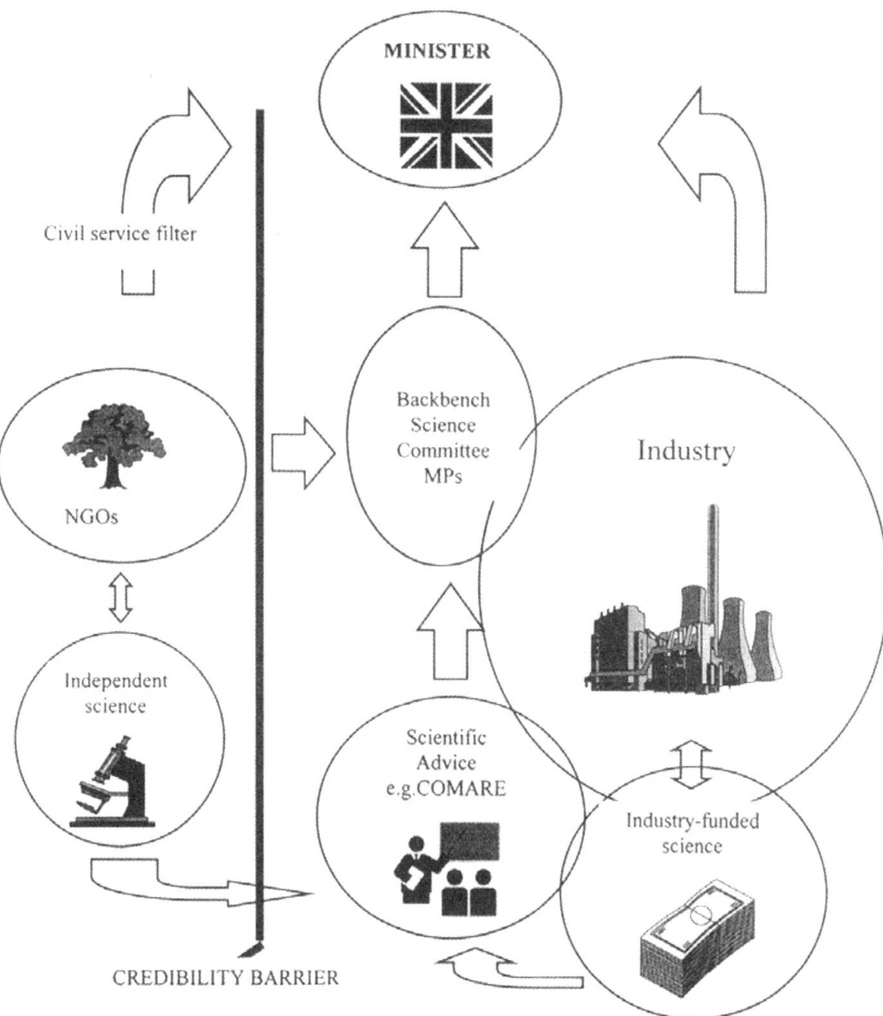

Fig 16.1.2 The reality of the present system. Industry, the research it funds, and the government committees are considered to have an unhealthily close relationship. Meanwhile, pressure groups and the small number of independent scientists are prevented from gaining access to the political process because of a credibility barrier and civil service filters.

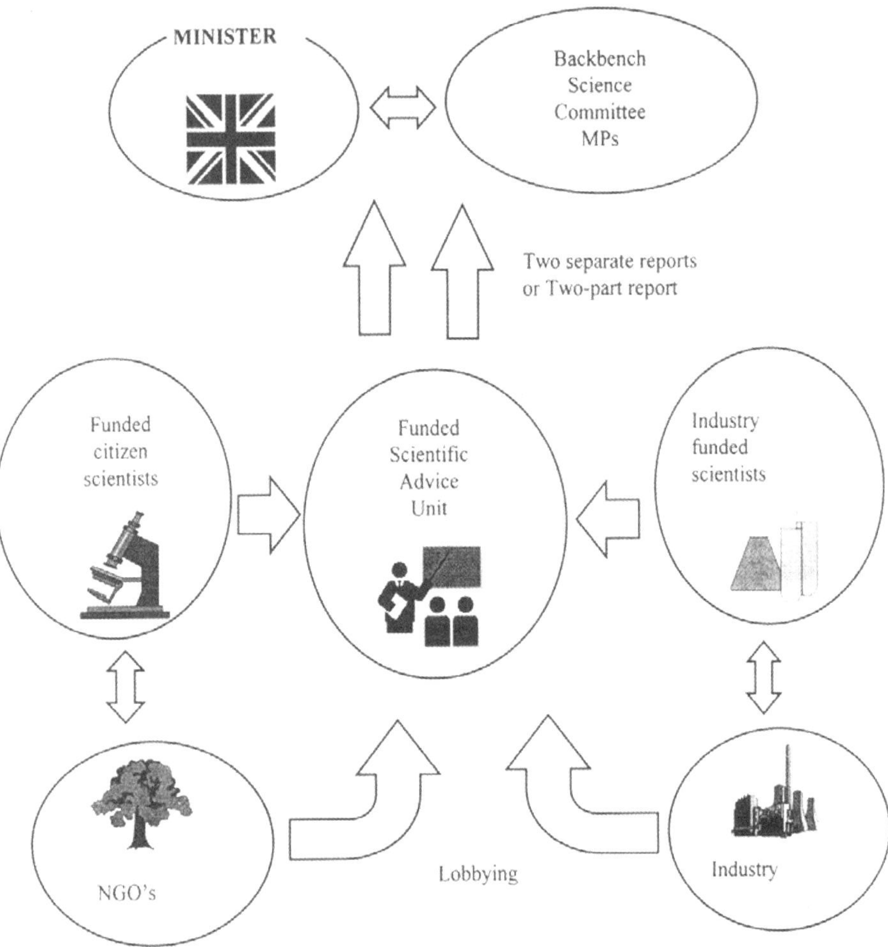

Fig 16.1.3 The proposed framework of oppositional scientific advice. Government funds a Scientific Advice Committee which in turn commissions and funds 'Citizen Scientists' to undertake studies and review all the evidence in specific areas where scientific advice is sought. The system must ensure that the final decision makers have seen reports from all sides of the issue.

Democratic governance requires that policy reflect the will of the people. In democratic countries this has been interpreted in various ways and practical procedures may reflect this ideal to a greater or lesser extent. However, the development of policy in the area of environmental risk has yet to significantly accept that, in many areas, people have often and apparently 'irrationally' rejected the development of certain policies that carry what may seem to be very small risks. This has resulted in a great deal of despondency among the proponents of new scientific and technological programmes like nuclear power and genetically modified foods. Large sums are devoted to analysing the psychology of the public and developing methods to overcome such irrational behaviour, all to little avail. The reason for the clash between the world pictures of 'ordinary irrational people' and those scientists who like to think that their beliefs are predicated on rational analysis has much to do with the way that humans view risk.

If mothers were asked if they would allow their children to play in a park where a poisonous snake had escaped, and they were told that the risk of their child being fatally bitten was 1 in 1 million would they let their children play in the park? The answer, of course, is No! The reason is clear: we are averse to risks, however small, if they result in death. By a similar token, we will take a chance, however small, if the prize is winning £1 million. In the case of the radioactivity from nuclear power and the resulting risks following exposure, the numbers are similar to the case of the snake in the park, with the difference that the park is the whole world and the snake is invisible. This snake is fed on the very doorstep of some. This is also the reason for the massive rejection of beef following the revelation that the various BSE committees had been mistaken. In this latter case it seemed that the 'irrationality' of those who stopped eating beef when the first suggestions of a problem had emerged had turned out to be good sense.

MPs are elected to represent their constituencies and to protect the well-being and health of their constituents. To do this they should ideally reflect in their parliamentary behaviour the way in which their constituents see the world. Our analysis of the backgrounds of the present MPs suggests that not only are they generally unable to understand the science, but that the way in which they see the world is far removed from that of the people that they represent. Some are lawyers and see a courtroom where radiation is safe until proven guilty. Others were teachers, who have their own distinctive view of truth; some are media people, some are ex-business people. All interpret the world differently.

We believe that ordinary 'irrational' people are often more able to analyse and avoid threats than the 'rational' scientists because they weigh all the data and respond to all the cues. Science does not do this. Science is atomistic and isolating: it has to exclude many important cues in order to function. William Blake's famous painting of Newton, measuring a small area of illuminated sand with dividers, on the dark shores of a Sea of Truth, is a very accurate one. The human way of avoiding risk is not constrained like this. It has developed over evolutionary time scales and has served the human race well. It would be served better by a system that took this approach into consideration and provided an arena in which all the data were made available, not just digested versions of it. The oppositional system that this report recommends would provide the basis for just such a process and enable everyone to make up their mind about the many actors, facts, speculations, data and theories that are involved in producing beliefs in science which inform policy.

16.2 CERRIE: a first attempt at an oppositional advice committee

16.2.1. The formation of CERRIE

Marx famously said 'philosophers have interpreted the world: the point is to change it.' Our first attempt to put something into practice in this area was when we persuaded Michael Meacher to set up CERRIE, the Committee Examining Radiation Risk from Internal Emitters. Richard Bramhall and I were at the House of Commons in London talking with him about the general problem of the cover-up in Wales, the sacking of the entire Wales Cancer Registry and how the Minister could get COMARE to re-examine the issue. It slowly dawned that this was only a part of the problem we wanted to address and that there was no point in asking COMARE to address it as they had already been set up for this as their original remit and had spectacularly failed to distance themselves from ICRP/NRPB or think independently, as Black had hoped they would. The real answer was to bypass COMARE altogether and get a new independent deliberative committee to examine the whole issue of risks from internal radioactive isotopes. The key was to set it up with the greens facing the ICRP advocates, with a remit to report all sides of the issue. The points of agreement and points of disagreement would be exactly delineated in its final report and research would be recommended to resolve issues. This was to be its remit. Meacher talked this through with Yvette Cooper, the Minister for Health, and she agreed to its formation. Since radiation protection was already something that was supposed to be done by COMARE, which was a committee of DoH, the line of control had to go through COMARE; however, they were not allowed to alter anything in the final report, and could merely comment on it. The report was to be for the two Ministers, Health and Environment. You would think that this was watertight wouldn't you? Meacher guaranteed that we would have our say in the final report, that as an oppositional report, all sides would be represented. Since the Chernobyl Infants showed unequivocally that the ICRP risk factors (and those of NRPB) were out by hundreds, we couldn't lose. We would state this in the final report and that would be the end of the nuclear pollution and the dead children. Checkmate. Or so I fondly planned. The formation of the committee was announced in July 2001.

Meacher announced that there would be *a review of models used to estimate health risks from radioactive emitters taken into the body. The new committee's remit would be to consider the present risk models for radiation from internal radionuclides in the light of recent studies and any further research that may be needed.* He added: *The committees review takes account the views of all parties in the debate on the risks of radiation. It aims to reach consensus where possible. On topics where differences of view remain after its deliberations, it will explain the reasons for these and recommend research to try to resolve them.*
He continued: *CERRIE will produce a report that is agreed by all its members. The report will not be subject to amendment by COMARE, the Department of Health or DEFRA and will be published. COMARE will consider the CERRIE Report and advise government on it.*

As you might imagine, this was potentially a major nightmare for the nuclear industry and their cronies. I can just see them scurrying around figuring out how to deal with the likely collapse of their safe paradigm. The telephones must have been incandescent. So, as expected, there was trouble right from the start. Meacher had decided on a full deliberative committee, independent of COMARE: this is what we agreed with him. We suggested the name as CORRIE (Committee on Radiation Risks from Internal Emitters), indeed, my first paper to the Chair before the pre-meeting we had in late 2001 was a paper for 'CORRIE'. We were alarmed to discover rather late in the day (just before the first full meeting) that the Civil Servants (no doubt COMARE) had demoted the status of the process by discourse manipulation. Without asking Meacher or telling him, they had named the new committee the *Consultative Exercise* on Radiation Risk from Internal Emitters, implying that what was happening was that the great COMARE would be listening to the quaint views of all the little woodland creatures before benignly dismissing them. I phoned Meacher. He talked with his civil servants who said that the name could not be changed as they had already secured and paid for the Internet website, www.cerrie.org.. In the event, Yvette Cooper, the Minster for Health cleverly saved the day by suggesting *Committee Examining* instead of *Consultative Exercise.*

The Chairman of the committee had been decided. Meacher had told me that Professor Dudley Goodhead had agreed to head up the committee and I was fairly happy with this. Goodhead had been one of the first to argue that tracks were more important than dose, and led the team at Harwell that discovered the new phenomenon of genomic instability (and the dangers from internal alpha emitters). So at the beginning I was happy enough with this. After the Chair, the problem was the appointment of the Secretariat, which we had made clear was a very sensitive issue. Who would run the show? Who would be in a position to adjust, trim and alter reports, minutes and agendas? Most important, who would draft the final report? As we saw in the STOA, Kiev/ WHO and then the BNES meetings, the key position in such an operation was that of secretariat and rapporteur.

I suggested some names, including Hugh Richards, of the Welsh Anti-Nuclear Alliance and Paul Dorfman, who was then finishing off his PhD on the sociology of radiation risk beliefs at the University of the West of England. In the event we were told that there would be a 3-person secretariat comprising Dr Ian Fairlie, Dr Katherine Mondon and Dr Marion Hill. I believe that this choosing was done by the COMARE team, Bryn Bridges and Roy Hamlet with Dudley Goodhead. Fairlie is a Canadian who had done some work on Tritium and was peripherally associated with the anti-nuclear movement because of his status as a PhD scientist who had criticised the risk factors for Tritium. At the time, I put him in the class of the other pale green, vaguely anti-nuclear scientists such as Dr Barrie Lambert and Dr David Sumner, who had been consulted by the (largely scientifically illiterate) anti-nuclear groups. I had met Fairlie a few times. I didn't know the other two in the new Secretariat. Katherine Mondon had apparently done work in an earlier 'consultative exercise' relating to radiation. I learned later that she was married to Barrie Lambert. Marion Hill I saw as a straightforward, nuclear-industry-friendly, agency researcher and organiser of long standing. She had worked for NRPB, for WS Atkins (who had been associated with the industry for many years) and for Enviros Ltd. These were all operations that put her in the enemy camp as far as I was concerned. However, I was pleased that there were two women. I always find women easier to deal with: there is usually less of the macho tangling that seems inevitable with men. Women are usually more sensible and more approachable and there are far too many men in radiation science anyway. ICRP is all men and nearly always has been.

But I was concerned about a secretariat that consisted of these three and said so. I asked Meacher to get our man Paul Dorfman on the secretariat, as we wanted even-handedness. Meacher tried. He reported back that Goodhead had threatened resigning as Chair if Dorfman was put on the secretariat (he had been interviewed by Paul as part of Paul's PhD work and so he knew who he was and guessed his connections). I suggested that Michael call the bluff, accept his resignation and appoint Hugh Richards or one of our friends. Goodhead quickly accepted the appointment of Dorfman and we had a foot in the secretariat. The next question was who would be on the committee? Meacher had argued for a three way split in membership in this new oppositional committee: a division into Critics, Defenders and Neutrals - four of each. I was not sure about this, since it would be hard to find anyone neutral on this issue and so we would be outnumbered. In the event, this was how the committee was ordered. I divide them in my head into what are, nominally, the blue, red and grey camps. These are made up as shown in Table 16.2.1 Most are shown together at the Oxford conference in Plate 30 (except for Bramhall who was busy preparing his ethics presentation whilst this photo was being taken).

Table 16.2.1 Members of the CERRIE committee; Dr Sarah Darby was added later by Goodhead without consultation and placed in the neutral camp and, although I opposed this, Meacher said there was nothing he could easily do.

Member	Affiliation	Comment by me
Prof. Dudley Goodhead	Chairman	Medical Research Council, Harwell; puts himself in the neutral camp, but later on we were not so sure (see text).
Blue Camp		
Dr Roger Cox	NRPB	Radiation biologist, now Director NRPB, now ICRP. Bluff and hearty. A politician. Openly more supportive of the 'all sides of the argument' approach than the Chair.
Dr Colin Muirhead,	NRPB	The senior epidemiologist with NRPB. A likeable but remote person. Everyone's idea of a committed scientist.
Dr John Harrison	NRPB	The senior biokinetic modeller with NRPB, jovial, likeable and generally helpful.
Dr Richard Wakeford,	BNFL	Self styled BNFL health effects Rottweiler. A formidable, clever, target oriented and occasionally frightening character.
Nominal neutrals, grey camp		
Prof Jack Simmons	Westminster University	A perfect gentleman. Very pleasant and approachable. Critic of the concept of 'dose' and in this agrees with us, but believes radiation is actually safer than models say.
Prof. Eric Wright	Dundee University	Was part of Goodhead's Harwell operation; now a world expert on genomic instability.
Prof Sarah Darby	Oxford University	Far from neutral; was the main radiation epidemiologist for studies supporting ICRP (see text).
Red camp		
Mr Richard Bramhall	Low Level Radiation Campaign	Bramhall is a Buddhist, ex- Double Bass player for the LSO, was not trained as a scientist, clever, moral, dependable and committed.
Dr Chris Busby	Green Audit	You know about me, I guess.
Dr Philip Day	Manchester University not FoE	Chemist who measured radioactivity near Sellafield. We wanted Dr Rachel Western but in the end FoE chose Phil Day. Immediately after joining CERRIE he disassociated himself from FoE.
Mr Pete Roche	Greenpeace	Not a scientist. Appeared tired and cynical. Pete left Greenpeace in the middle of the committee period .

16.2.2. The process itself

It was quite clear to all at the outset that the whole affair was being driven by our criticisms of ICRP so the deliberations began with a pre-process meeting between Goodhead, Fairlie, Bramhall and I. This was arranged in The Bull hotel in Crickhowell on the Welsh borders. Everyone was jolly. I wrote a paper with a shopping list of what we expected to address and presented it. The areas ranged from theoretical to epidemiological. At the start I was aware of how people who do not want to accept an unpalatable fact can avoid it and so each area of discussion had, associated with it, a list of questions that had to be answered. The idea was that each member of the committee had to put down in the final report exactly why they thought what they did. They must not be allowed to avoid doing this and fudging the issue. It was not enough for them to say, for example; *Oh, I just don't agree with that*, they had to say why. The main items that I felt had to be discussed are given in Table 16.2.2. Some examples of the questions that I drafted are given in Table 16.2.3.

Table 16.2 Main items to be addressed by CERRIE in its deliberations and to be included in the Final Report.

Concern	Note
Scientific method not used by ICRP in applying external risk model to internal exposure	This was never addressed as the Chair ruled we were not philosophers.
Variation of cell sensitivity over cell lifespan; Second Event Theory	This was the most discussed and most fiercely attacked by the radiobiologists including Goodhead.
Cell Field effects, genomic instability, bystander effect	These are crucial in the examination of high local doses from hot particles.
Transmutation from one element into another e.g. Tritium into Helium	Was presented by me but didn't make it into the final report
Particle Transfer across placenta	Was discussed. Evidence appeared to show that placenta was an adequate barrier but bystander effects could not be ruled out although this was not in the final report.
Cancer epidemic is consequence of weapons fallout exposure e.g. Wales	Was discussed. No agreement
Nuclear sites, reprocessing plants, child leukaemias, e.g. Sellafield	Was discussed. No agreement
Green Audit Irish Sea coastal effects studies, adult cancers, child cancers. Sea-to land transfer of particles. Coastal mud banks and particle transfer.	Was discussed. Data was attacked by BNFL rep. No agreement
Green Audit nuclear site cancer mortality studies (Hinkley, Bradwell etc.)	Was discussed. Joint study agreed by committee was developed but cancelled by Chair at last minute.
Chernobyl Infants	Was discussed. England and Wales data obtained from Childhood Cancer Research Group and joint study undertaken. Misreported in final report
Minsatellite mutations after Chernobyl	Was discussed. No agreement
Childhood leukaemia and 1960s weapons fallout (e.g. Nordic)	Was extensively discussed. Data obtained. No agreement.
Depleted Uranium	Presented but excluded from final report
Non cancer effects	Were discussed but misreported.
Natural vs. man-made isotopes; specific isotopes e.g. Tritium	Was discussed but misreported.
Auger emitters	Was discussed but misreported.

Table 16.3 Examples of 30 defining questions laid down at the start of the CERRIE process to be individually answered in the final report. Although agreed initially, all the questions were thrown out at the end of the 2-year deliberations, as it would have been too embarrassing for most of the members to have to answer them and explain how they could disagree with something that was manifestly true (see text).

Concern	Questions
ICRP model	1. Is it scientifically valid to extrapolate from high dose to low dose using a linear model and if so why? 2. Is it scientifically valid to use average spatial doses to tissue as a measure of doses to cells for internal irradiation? 3. Is it valid to do the same averaging over time?
Genomic instability/ Dose response	1. What is the significance of the effect for radiation protection? 2. What evidence is there that there are not sub groups of cell lifespan phases which are very sensitive to radiation?
Sellafield, La Hague etc.	1. Has scientific method been used properly in evaluating evidence from the nuclear site child leukaemias? 2. Should COMARE have published a report on the issue that was based on an unpublished, unchecked and confidential paper from NRPB?
Irish sea	1. Does plutonium from Sellafield end up in the bodies of people living near the Irish Sea?
Chernobyl Infants	1. Does the observation of increased infant leukaemia in 5 countries following Chernobyl show that the risk model of ICRP is in error by more than 100-fold?
Weapons fallout	1. Is there sufficient scientific evidence to exclude the exposure to Strontium-90 in fallout as a part cause of the present cancer epidemic?
Infant mortality	1. Does ICRP address infant mortality from exposure to ionising radiation?

The first full committee meeting was held in London on 4th December 2001. Paul had not yet been appointed to the secretariat and the affair of the name (CERRIE or CORRIE) had just begun. On the morning of the first meeting we learned that the committee was called Consultative Exercise on Radiation Risk from Internal Emitters. Bryn Bridges, Chair of COMARE explained how CERRIE was being modelled on the Consultative Exercise on Dose assessments (CEDA). Representatives from COMARE, DEFRA and DoH would sit in as observers. These turned out to be himself, Andy MacPherson and Hilary Walker. At this first meeting the fun began immediately. The papers drawn up by Goodhead and the

Secretariat, which we had received shortly before the meeting, were unlike anything that had been discussed before and laid out a route that marginalized the concerns we had discussed at Crickhowell. I sat up late in the hotel in London the night before and wrote out in pen a revised work schedule. I interrupted the meeting at the beginning and said that the proposals they had made were unacceptable and that I wanted to discuss the ones I had written out. I asked for these to be photocopied. Following some heated discussion, our suggestions were agreed and the original schedule thrown out.

This was to be the first example of the battles we had to fight in an endless war of attrition we had with the secretariat. Every meeting was minuted incorrectly, sometimes in a subtle or sometimes quite flagrant way. The minutes were biased, left items out, put in statements that were never made and seemed to re-order the past in a way that was hostile to the suggestion that the ICRP model was wrong. This became immediately clear at the second meeting when Bramhall and I looked at the minutes and found it hard to imagine that we had been in the meeting they described. It was Soviet Russia. We decided that the only way forward was to tape record the meetings and asked if we could do this. Goodhead and Fairlie opposed this but the committee voted to let us and from the second meeting on we built up a complete set of tape recordings. We used a very expensive Sony Digital Tape Recorder, a SONY DAT (digital-Analogue-Tape), the same model that the BBC uses, together with an extremely expensive SONY (ECMS 907) microphone. I had bought this outfit for Green Audit in 1999 with the Irish government money to make recordings in Ireland. The DAT broadcast quality recording tapes cost between £7 and £9 each and over the course of the 16 meetings and 4 epidemiology sub-committee meetings we made 47 tapes, which have on them, in extraordinary clarity, everything that was said. The system picks out the whispered asides and conversations that we never could hear at the time and makes for fascinating listening. It should provide a research source for sociologists and psychologists for many years. So when it came to arguments about the minutes (and it certainly did, at nearly every meeting) we were able to say for certain what had happened.

But this did not seem to have any effect on Dudley Goodhead and Ian Fairlie. They merely stated that they had made notes which they believed to be true and usually did not accept revisions from us. At this early point, Fairlie obtained a tape recorder also, and then a more expensive one (the first one seemed unable to cope for some reason) but we never heard what happened to the tapes. Richard Bramhall spent two or three days after each meeting sitting with headphones and the DAT tapes restoring the truth to the minutes. It was soul-destroying work. He asked Goodhead if there could be some funding for this, but Goodhead said no. Eventually we obtained some money for Richard from the Joseph Rowntree Charitable Trust. I asked the committee if we could have the transcripts of the tape recordings that Fairlie made, and the committee voted for this to happen, but

Fairlie said: *Over my dead body* (we have this on tape) and we never received any transcripts. The minutes were generally a travesty of what happened and by the end of the process, after Meacher had been sacked, became truly laughable and bizarre. Whole sentences were inserted into the mouths of random people, usually to make some point against our position. On occasion when it seemed important, we would provide changes to the minutes but, even when we did so, they were never completely accepted. It was all truly Kafkaesque.

There was also a CERRIE website. Versions of the minutes were placed on the website, www.cerrie.org, and this was arranged by Marion Hill until her resignation, when they stopped altogether. In general, the accounts on the website were fairly accurate, albeit condensed. In the event, Marion, whom I had placed (on the basis of her history) as the nuclear biased member, turned out to be scrupulously fair and honest, and she soon began to clash with Ian Fairlie. After Paul Dorfman joined the secretariat, he would tell us what went on behind the scenes. Katherine Mondon resigned early on; apparently she could not work with Fairlie. Paul also found him impossible to deal with. Paul was never able to penetrate the inner control loop of the secretarial operation, which he saw as a link between Goodhead, Fairlie and possibly others. Paul's revisions of the minutes of each meeting (from his own notes) were largely ignored; he was kept out of the decision making process. He told me that everything would be controlled by Ian who would even photocopy the papers himself and mail them out. And this exclusion and control eventually also extended to Marion, who had been given the task of preparing the initial report. As the scientific evidence we brought to meetings piled up, Marion became friendlier toward us and more scrupulous. She began to be no longer accepted by the inner control loop as a trustworthy part of the operation. This soon came to a startling conclusion.

It had been decided that we had to consult with other scientists in the world. CERRIE clearly could not just decide on the validity of the ICRP model on its own in a vacuum. So it was decided to have a 3-day meeting in Oxford towards the end of the process and canvass views and inputs from other concerned experts. The CERRIE website also asked for inputs and views to be emailed in, but there were, apparently, few contributions. However, there had to be an initial report of our deliberations, a ‘First Report’ that could be sent out to the invited scientists so that they could bring their observations and criticisms to the Oxford meeting. Marion was tasked with preparing this initial report. We had made much of the need to ensure that all sides were reported (as the committee remit had demanded). Marion was approachable and we had been sufficiently impressed by her work and we thought that her involvement in preparing this first report would ensure that all sides were adequately represented, so we agreed that she should be allowed to assemble this report. It would be a trial run for the final report which we trusted that she would also oversee. Paul was in close contact with her, and Bramhall and I had prepared various papers and comments. Marion eventually produced a version of the First Report. Fairlie and Goodhead changed it without consulting her. She resigned. Her resignation was the first provable confirmation of our suspicions that the project management had a darker side. Her resignation letter was leaked to us and made interesting reading.

16.2.3 Marion Hill's resignation

I received a copy of Marion's resignation letter in the post. I don't know who sent it. It was postmarked London. Since it is of significant interest in a situation that involves public health, and since she has allowed me to, I will reproduce the text here (my underlines):

Our ref. DOH 6423
DE0847000

Dr Hilary Walker and	*Dr Andrew Macpherson*
Department of Health	*DEFRA*
Radiation Unit	*Radioactive Substances Division*
Skipton House	*4/F8 Ashdown House*
80 London Road	*123 Victoria Street*
LONDON SE1 6LH	*LONDON SW1DE 6DE*

20 February 2003

Dear Hilary and Andy,

Resignation from the CERRIE Secretariat

I am sorry to inform you that I shall be leaving the CERRIE secretariat at the end of this month. The main reason is that I am unable to work amicably and efficiently with the other members of the secretariat (Ian Fairlie and Paul Dorfman) and with the chairman (Dudley Goodhead). I also have severe problems with the way that the committee has been set up and the way in which it is doing its work.

My difficulty with Ian Fairlie is that he refuses to consult other members of the secretariat about important issues. This has been going on for months in the case of Paul Dorfman and has now extended to me. The latest incident is one in which he altered a committee document that I had written and distributed it to members without referring back to me. This compromised my professional reputation, was discourteous and is completely unacceptable. He is also unwilling to delegate, despite being overloaded with work.

My problem with Paul Dorfman is that, because he is not a professional consultant, he has great difficulty in producing work of the required standard and to deadlines. This leads to other members of the secretariat, and also the chairman, re-doing his work. There are continual arguments between Paul and Ian about the way in which the secretariat works, and issues between Paul and Dudley. Further, there are doubts as to whether the contribution that Paul makes to the secretariat justifies the money he is being paid.

Dudley Goodhead is aware of the difficulties within the secretariat but does nothing to resolve them. Instead, he works closely with Ian Fairlie and together they exclude Paul and myself. <u>The most serious consequence of this is that it biases the work of the committee towards the scientific issues in which Dudley and Ian have an interest and (unwittingly) towards their own points of view on these issues</u>. The result is that the committee members from the Low Level Radiation Campaign and Green Audit do not trust them and the chances of reaching an agreed report at the end of the committee's work are remote.

The major problem with the way that the committee has been set up is that it is unable to pay unsalaried members for the time they have to spend writing papers. This disadvantages those who hold the most divergent views on internal radiation risks, that is those whose views the committee was established to address. Not surprisingly, the unsalaried members are very dissatisfied with this situation. They would be even more dissatisfied if they realised that by mid-2003 Ian Fairlie will have been paid more than £100,000 for his work for CERRIE, and that Enviros has already been paid over £50,000 for my time (although, of course, I have personally received much less than half of this sum).

The committee's way of working is old-fashioned and too heavily reliant on the production of long papers. There have also been too many digressions to topics that are peripheral to its main purpose. The result is that after more than a year of meetings the range of views on the committee has scarcely narrowed at all.

Overall, it has become very clear to me that my technical input to CERRIE is not required by the chairman or the other members of the secretariat. It would be a waste of tax payers' money to employ me only to carry out administrative, contractual and book-keeping tasks, and a complete waste of my time. So the best course of action is clearly for me to resign from the secretariat.

I will send a short note of apology to CERRIE members for any inconvenience my resignation may cause them. Others in Enviros will be in touch to sort out contractual matters.

Yours sincerely,

Ms Marion Hill
Technical Director
Enviros Consulting

This was sent a few days before a meeting of CERRIE. What would happen? What could they do to limit the damage? Remember, they did not know that I had a copy of the letter. At the meeting Goodhead told us that Marion had resigned 'for personal reasons. . . 'She has been under a great deal of strain in her personal life', he said. The tone was one of understanding and sympathy: the committee was invited to commiserate and send her our best wishes. This was too much. I jumped up and waving her resignation letter asked Goodhead to explain the true reason why Marion had resigned: that she was fed up with the way the committee was being run and had accused Fairlie of paying himself huge amounts of money and Goodhead of bias. There was general panic. Goodhead shouted 'Where did you get that letter. . . I demand you tell me where you got that letter! . . . I forbid you to read it out. . . It is a personal letter. . etc.'

'But is it true what she said?'

'No, no it is not true, she was upset etc.' (all this is on broadcast quality tape recordings).

'If you won't apologise for misleading the committee about the cause of Marion's resignation, Dudley, then I will read out the letter myself. I don't believe that you should misrepresent Marion and imply that she was not up to the stress of the work due to personal problems. This is sexist and morally questionable'.

At this point, Phil Day jumped up and said he would walk out if I read out the letter, as he didn't want to be involved in such an argument. (This was interesting in view of what happened later). Other members of the committee jumped up also. It was spectacular theatre. Everyone was on their feet around the table. Dudley Goodhead was ashen. The sky was falling in. I backed off. I told Dudley that I would give him until the following meeting to set the record straight about Marion's true reasons for resigning. If he did not, then I would. After the meeting I wrote to him and repeated this threat. I was angry. There had been a serious accusation from a senior member of the secretariat about the way in which the committee was being handled. No one seemed to want to acknowledge this or to do anything about it. Worse: Marion herself, in her absence, was being characterised as a dilly secretary having a fit of the vapours about something in her personal life. This was appalling stuff.

Dudley did nothing. There was no apology; there was no setting the record straight. The only result was that I was told by Paul that he would be doing more of the work and that Fairlie would be taking a back seat. This was wishful thinking as it turned out.

So we published a brief account of Marion's letter and her accusations in the next issue of *Radioactive Times* and we put it on the LLRC website. This led to incandescent outrage at the following meeting. Goodhead was threatening and bullying. He demanded to know who was responsible, who was the editor of RaT. Bramhall and I said we both were: I was the author of the piece: Bramhall had edited it. We stood by what it said. We were then accused of breaking the

'Chatham House' rules, which we had agreed to sign up to. These rules state that no-one is allowed to quote any committee member outside the committee. Goodhead thundered from the pulpit. Unless we apologised and retracted in the next issue, we would be chucked off the committee. We would be sued for libel. Would we apologise and retract? We were given 2 minutes to do this. Everyone sat aghast. The clock was ticking. High Noon. I told Goodhead that we would not: that it was a serious accusation in a letter and was of public interest. I had spoken to Marion on the phone. He could do as he pleased. And if it was a case of being chucked off the committee, then it was not in his gift, but was a committee matter and, in any case, I had specifically refused to be bound by the Chatham House rule at the outset, saying then that if there were a public interest aspect I would follow my conscience. Bramhall concurred. This was another showdown: the ball had been returned. Now Dudley sat still. Phil Day pointed out that technically, despite the 'tasteless and bad form' aspect of our story, we had not broken Chatham House, since nowhere had we actually said what any committee member had stated in a meeting. Whew! This gave Goodhead a way out of a situation he was not going to win; he backed off with threats of eventual libel actions and so forth.

These meetings of CERRIE required a strong head, and were ferociously and terrifyingly stressful. They were all like this. It was Daniel in the Lion's Den, or rather Daniel and his friend Richard. The other two greenies on the committee were sometimes helpful, sometimes unhelpful or even strangely negative but most of the energy was directed at the two of us. We had to provide the case for the prosecution, as it were, single-handedly. Richard helped enormously in taking the weight of ensuring that the minutes were corrected and the proceedings taped. He would see that I had the papers I needed and he and Paul would feed me with the required bits and pieces to ensure I could follow the plot, since most of my own energy was devoted to preparing scientific papers and arguments for the prosecution of the case that called into question the ICRP models for internal radionuclides. These would be 20 or thirty pages of A4, tightly argued, referenced and often involving considerable research and thought. Some of them took two weeks or more to prepare. Then I would have to defend the arguments against a shattering cross-examination by three or four or five people at the same table, one after the other, each preparing his or her argument whilst I addressed the argument of the earlier one. It was as I might imagine an interrogation in the Lubyanka, aimed to break the spirit of the prisoner, or make his mind crack. I would grit my teeth, conjure up Gemma Darcy's ghost and soldier on.

Every area that the committee examined would have to have a prosecution paper drawn up. Without this work, and these papers, there would be no committee. There would be nothing to argue about. Yet I was paid nothing for this work. Members of the secretariat were paid consultancy sums from the central budget. This meant that, as Marion pointed out, Fairlie was paying himself £700 a day for photocopying and sending out papers that I had spent weeks working on for nothing. Because Bramhall and I were in such a war zone, we had been unable to get enough issues of *Radioactive Times* out and asked for financial help. Long before Marion's letter, I asked Goodhead if there was any money in the kitty to pay for my time. No there wasn't, but he did agree to pay me for one piece of work. Apparently there was enough to pay me £2300 and £600 to Bramhall. So we got this, but that was all we got in the whole three years. The work was endless and it came to a climax when we had the Oxford Workshop in the summer of 2003. I had to present the case for the prosecution, on the stage, every day, usually twice a day, to 120 radiation experts from all over the world, at St Catherine's College. I had to have the papers. I had to have the overheads. I had to have the presentation. I had to field the arguments and the attacks as they came, which they did. I now think that this meeting was set up (at great expense) to destroy our case. If it was, it backfired. I didn't die of a heart attack, and enough of the delegates were sufficiently supportive of the case that the ICRP model was nonsense. We brought along some senior members of the European Committee on Radiation Risk, including our supporters and friends the Russian radiobiologist Professor Elena Burlakova (Plate 25, 29), Director of the Semenyov Institute of Radiation Biology, and the ecologist Professor Alexey Yablokov (Plate25,29) both members of the Russian Academy of Sciences, the Chair of ECRR Prof. Inge Schmitz Feuerhake from Bremen and Dr VT Padmanabhan all the way from India (see also Plate 29). I have to say that between us we routed the opposition on the science. Goodhead made a whole presentation, inviting members of the audience to agree with his analysis of our arguments but, apart from Norman Gentner of UNSCEAR, there were no takers. They all sat stunned.

Just before this conference happened, we lost our main source of power; Michael Meacher was sacked by Tony Blair and replaced by Elliot Morley, perhaps a more controllable number. This did not bode well for the finalisation of the CERRIE report. The revised Preliminary Report to the Workshop had been badly mauled by the invitees. In taking out the substance of the issues of contention, it had been made so bland that the consensus was that it was a meaningless piece of nonsense, with nothing in it to agree or disagree with. Some said this and some said that, was the tone of it. So what? Said the delegates. Why? Said the delegates. Understandably, since they were not to know that to have written it properly would have made implicit the idiocy of the ICRP position and the huge amount of evidence for its wild errors when applied to internal radiation.

Now that Meacher was out of the picture, they could also fudge the issues in the CERRIE committee without a Minister looking over their shoulder and they could ensure, through the Chair and Secretariat, that the final report would not contain the two sides that it had been set up to represent, but would present the usual story. The rapportage filter was back in position. As soon as we heard of Meacher's dismissal from government, we knew this would happen and our lives would become more difficult: And so it proved, but in a very different way to that which we had anticipated.

16.2.4 CERRIE, the end of the oppositional committee experiment

The full story of the CERRIE committee is too long to fully report, but you need to be told the gist of what happened in order to understand what the blocks are to discovering the truth about complex scientific issues. I have argued that the period 1950-2000 was one in which the truth about low level radiation and health was shielded from the public through the system of controls that were put in place by the authorities as a result of the connection between the military and the nuclear power lobby and their powerful supporters. CERRIE was one of the first possibilities that this truth would emerge at last because, for the first time, the actual remit of an official scientific advice committee was to report all the sides of the arguments and to assume at the outset that there would be a debate. The problem was that our view was so manifestly and demonstrably the correct one that to allow us even to have a minority section would make it clear that the nuclear industry and its military brotherhood had been killing and would (if allowed) continue to kill innocent children and their parents. We thought that we would be allowed to say our stuff in the final report; we thought that the joint epidemiological studies that we would do with data obtained by the committee secretariat would show that our findings (on the Chernobyl infants, on the Bradwell coastal breast cancers) would be demonstrably correct. But with the loss of Meacher, the fixers could shift gear and ignore the remit of the committee.

I had argued in various papers to the committee and to the Chair that the final report should be written in two or in three columns; each would be written by the secretariat in collaboration with the members espousing various sides of the argument. This way there would be a clear debate and those reading the final report would be able to make up their own minds. We had half of the Secretariat, Paul Dorfman: he would be in charge of the dissenting column. Fairlie would do the other column. Goodhead didn't agree to this, and basically didn't want us to have our own space at all. But he was overridden by the committee who voted for us to have at least a space for a 'dissenting statement'. Bramhall and I condensed our arguments into such a dissenting statement and sent it in. Despite strong opposition from the Chair and Ian Fairlie, at the 15th meeting it was agreed by all on a vote (only the BNFL member Richard Wakeford, voted against) that our statement (with a few changes which I agreed) would go in. Between the 15th and 16th meeting Goodhead and Fairlie got to work to stop this happening. First Goodhead kept changing the requirements in term of length and content. Then we were told the report was libellous and contained errors, but we were never told what the errors were. Kafka again.

It was a bizarre situation. We kept revising our minority report to make it acceptable but every time we did this there was some new problem with it. Out of the blue, Peter Roche, the committee member appointed by Greenpeace, offered us an alternative version of it, which he had made, apparently on his own initiative. It was far shorter and left out all the important items. We refused. We were continually revising our minority report to meet various new demands by the Chair. Just before the 16th meeting we had put our final version in the hands of Paul Dorfman who said he would give it a final clean up to make it acceptable to Goodhead. I had run out of energy for this by then. Then came the first intimation of their strategy. We received an email from Goodhead saying that he was meeting with government lawyers to ask if individual members of the committee would be individually liable in a court action for damages against the committee if they allowed the publication of 'negligent misrepresentations'. In other words, if our dissenting statement was allowed into the report, the nuclear industry or Prof Doll or whoever, could sue the government so long as our report contained 'negligent misrepresentations'; at the 16th and final meeting we were each handed a short note, purporting to have been written by DEFRA and DoH lawyers, stating this. We in our turn had consulted with our own lawyer, my friend Hugo Charlton, Chair of the Green Party (see Plate 29) who said that this was nonsense. He said: 'Whoever heard of a debate over a scientific matter being categorised as negligent misrepresentation?' They don't agree that the significant excess of infant leukaemia after Chernobyl represents evidence that the ICRP model is wrong, so they call it a negligent misrepresentation. If this is possible, it is the end of scientific advice, since the industry just has to threaten to sue the committee members. However, some more fixing had clearly taken place behind the scenes. The event that scuppered us occurred at the point where Bramhall was asking Goodhead for an example of a 'negligent misrepresentation' in our dissenting statement. Goodhead referred to our complaint that the joint Bradwell cancer study that had been agreed (and which a great deal of work and money had already gone into) had suddenly been cancelled at the last minute for no reason. Goodhead was in a corner and Bramhall was politely but icily persisting in his questioning on this issue. Suddenly, Phil Day (the no-longer FoE representative) intervened. 'Lets have a short recess for tea, and when we return', he said, 'there may be a proposal to shorten this argument.'

There certainly was: Day, Roche, Eric Wright and Jack Simmons sprang up as if pulled by a single string and put a motion to exclude our statement. The grounds were given: we had not adequately outlined our differences with the main report. This was new. All of these characters had, at the immediately preceding meeting, voted to have our statement included. Now they all wanted it excluded. The only thing that happened in between was the legal threat. But apparently it wasn't that that made them change their collective minds; Oh, No. Now they all suddenly saw something that they had overlooked in the various drafts and arguments that had been circulated and debated. It was that we hadn't 'clearly articulated our differences'. Articulated Our Differences. Blimey! Never mind that our whole dissenting statement was a condensation of all the differences that we had endlessly maintained and fought over. Well, there we are. That was the end of the idea of a deliberative process with the two sides of the scientific arguments being debated and reflexively and agnostically reported.

The legal threats were, or course, not credible. Indeed, they were not even real since the lawyers who gave them had not read our dissenting statement that they were advising on; they had merely been told that it contained negligent misrepresentations by Goodhead and Fairlie. This is clear when we read the statements.

In the first legal statement the DoH lawyers say: *What follows is necessarily general as the facts are not clear.* Also, *bear in mind that it is a defence to an allegation of defamation to show that a statement is true.* The DEFRA lawyers say: *In advising, I make the assumption that the offending passages are (a) not true and (b) liable to cause damage to professional reputations rather than being robust academic disagreement.* What they were referring to in the latter case were items where we drew attention to the fact that the Nordic leukaemia paper by Darby and Doll did not reference earlier research that showed increases in childhood leukaemia and that Dr Darby had said that the data was no longer available to check the childhood leukaemia in Denmark at the time of the weapons fallout. Later, as I stated earlier, she said, and placed on record that the reason the study had been done was because 'she knew that there was an increase in childhood leukaemia in Denmark'. All this is on tape and in the minutes, so if it is defamation, it is something she would be unwise to pursue according to the advice of the DoH lawyers. However, we took out this paragraph in the final version, so as to get our argument in a truncated form. But this was not enough, and subsequent events suggested that the legal arguments were irrelevant. We had been stabbed by the other Greens.

Why was this? How can I make sense of it? It clearly wasn't anything to do with the proposal that was put, as our statement had been little altered from the one that was agreed by them (and all the other members of CERRIE except the BNFL representative) at the previous meeting. At this previous meeting, Phil Day had said that, along with Voltaire, *I may not agree with your position, Sir, but would defend to the death your right to maintain it.* I emailed him about this after he stabbed us. He replied saying that he felt bad about it. But I note he didn't allow this feeling to interfere with his change of heart. So what happened? Meacher immediately said *they were nobbled.* Well, maybe, but how? Used fivers in a brown packet? I can't see it. Maybe they were offered positions on some of the influential bodies that were being set up to deal with nuclear power station decommissioning, or nuclear waste disposal, but they haven't yet appeared on such committees. Neither of them have a very good political analysis. However, they both think that I don't have a good political analysis, that Bramhall and I are too extreme. Roche believes in dealing and realpolitik. He is not a scientist and feels that our extreme scientific beliefs about radiation and health are not helpful as they just get us classed as lunatics and he doesn't want to be associated with such people). Because he is not a scientist he has to rely on others and, in this case, he used Ian Fairlie as his advisor. This was a bad mistake, as Marion's letter implicitly shows.

Phil Day doesn't like our swashbuckling approach. He sees it as bad form. To my mind, he is not himself a very powerful person and the one time I saw him come under direct attack by the nukes on the committee (over some tritium calculations he made, and some quite clever arguments that followed from them) he backed off very fast. He was quite shocked. So, as I see it, he feels that he can influence these people through measured argument and gentlemanly debate. A mistake.

However it happened, happen it did, and we were left to decide what to do. Of course, we went to the newspapers. *The Observer* agreed to run it but chickened out at the last minute for some reason. But by August 1st the *Sunday Times* carried a full page article *Government gags experts over nuclear plant releases.* This story is not over yet and continues, but I have to finish this book and you will have to wait or watch Radioactive Times or the www.llrc.org website for the news. Important lessons have been learned and I will now turn to an outline of how CERRIE failed and how such a committee must be set up in order to prevent such a thing happening again. We are half way to sorting out the problem. Let us grasp the nettle and go the whole way. Our lives and those of our children depend on it.

16.2.5 How to obtain the best scientific advice: lessons from CERRIE

I will conclude this chapter with an overview of the problem, showing how the oppositional solution failed in the case of CERRIE and suggest the solution to this.

There are three requirements for such an oppositional science advice committee to succeed. First we assume that there is some truth about the issue that is being discussed that we the public and our representatives the politicians wish to get as close to as possible. We further assume that none of the scientists actually know the answer, or can accurately show what this truth is. Each of them is culturally affected by their history, their psychology, their affiliation, their research funding, all the baggage that everyone carries that colours their response. This response is there to secure their personal identity, the person they meet in the mirror each morning. So what we do is what Molly suggests, we set up an oppositional arena and let them fight it out. The first requirement is to acknowledge this and set up a science advice committee, which has on it scientists whose job it is to attack the proposition. These people are, for preference, those who already attack the proposition, as they are the ones who (presumably) have the best arguments. Then you put in those who defend the proposition. You also may decide to appoint some neutrals (but as we saw in CERRIE, no one is neutral). Now, since scientific truths cannot be made by a vote, you cannot allow decisions to be made by votes. Indeed, you have no way of knowing what level of credibility, what weighting, to give to a vote. So all positions have to be respected and reported, however mad they may seem to be to others on the committee.

Second, you have the problem of resources and support. Members from Industry or from University may have salaries, but not everyone is paid to do this work; in particular we are not, the citizen scientists are not. Molly suggested we call these people Jedi scientists. In addition, we had little access to libraries and data. Before I was given a Fellowship at the University of Liverpool in 2002 I had to actually buy research photocopies from the British Library at about £5 a throw. I had to buy the data for studies of cancer from ONS for about £400 a study. And I had to pay for the ward populations for each study: this cost about £250. So most of the studies we did for the small grants like Stop Hinkley, or the Mersea Residents, actually paid nothing at all to me. They paid a small amount to Helen or Rachel or whoever I asked to do the mapping and data processing, and the rest went mostly on data from ONS. We had to buy statistical software or use freeware from the Centre for Disease Control. Whilst SAHSU produced maps of cancer levels using expensive GIS mapping packages, our ward maps were carefully traced by Helen on to tracing paper and scanned into bitmaps that were imported into Microsoft 'Paintbrush', the program that comes free with all computers.

Half way through CERRIE, our finances were, individually and collectively, in dire straights. We had to beg from the charities and the anti-nuclear groups, a few pounds here and there. The pressure on us was great. The pressure on me was enormous. After two years of this, toward the end of CERRIE my personal affairs were in a mess. Molly had taken a job in Cardiff two days a week so that we could eat. She had had enough of the bits and pieces of money that came in from her odd bits of work and mine: there was no security and she worried and worried. This job in Cardiff, however, meant a drive of three hours and a stopover for a night. I had always looked after my daughter Rosa, who was 9 in 2003, but now I had to increase the amount of domestic work and cook for everyone (we had Molly's two boys aged 13 and 16). We were desperate and ratty with one another: the relationship became worse and worse. Eventually Molly and I split up. We were both victims of the pressure there is on green activists. It is punishing. From then on for a year I had to juggle all this work for CERRIE with surviving in an attic looking out over the Irish Sea, surrounded by books and papers all stacked up in plastic boxes. I was in this attic when the TV people trooped in to do the documentary about the Menai leukaemias.

The reason I say all this is to give a flavour of what it means to do all this work and put out all this energy without institutional support. It was particularly galling, as Marion Hill suggested it would be in her letter, to hear that the secretariat were paying themselves huge amounts while Bramhall and I did all the work. More recently, Paul tells me that Ian will have paid himself about £250,000 over the period of the CERRIE committee. We are asking for a breakdown of the CERRIE budget to see if this is true.

So the second requirement for such a committee to function is to fund the members adequately. And this includes allowing them to draw from a separate budget to obtain help or obtain research data and maybe some equipment or software.

The third necessity is, of course, a truly independent and agnostic secretariat whose job it is only to act as such. Again and again we saw, at Kiev, at the BNES conference, at the STOA workshop, how the rapportage altered the message from the debate. There is also the possibility of a biased secretariat beginning with agendas that bias the proceedings. Maybe this cannot ultimately be allowed for. But we can try. We can recruit a secretariat from people who have little knowledge of the issue, who are from an entirely different discipline. Or perhaps make it from psychologists or the people who do mediation. After all, the job of the mediation experts is to get to the truth and guide the exchanges. Maybe the committees should be arranged and directed by Marriage Guidance Counsellors? However, so long as it is agreed at the outset that each side can have its say, there can be no way that the alternative views can be excluded, as they were in the case of the CERRIE fiasco.

I suggested quite early on in CERRIE that it would be impossible for one discourse to accommodate all the sides of the argument and that the issues should be addressed in two (or maybe on occasion three) columns. This was overruled by the Chair, but I still think that this is the best method. And finally, everyone on the committee would be obliged to state, in writing, the reasons for their beliefs regarding the substantive issues. This was to have happened, and was agreed, at the beginning of the CERRIE process. Indeed, I have answers to the questions written by most of the committee members. But they clearly saw later on that these answers were hostages to fortune. And in the case of the Chernobyl infants question, those of the committee who refused to see what was so clearly obvious were not prepared to put their reasons down, because, in this case, there werc no reasons and this would make them look daft.

At the end of such a process, carried out with these safeguards, the best scientific advice will be there. Indeed, all the scientific advice will be there. At this point research can be recommended to examine differences, if there are any, and ultimately the politicians will have to make decisions on behalf of those they represent, on the basis of all the data. If such an advice committee had been in place at the time of the Mad Cow disease affair, many deaths would have been avoided and huge amounts of money saved. We cannot afford not to have such a safeguard, since the next collision with reality as a result of biased scientific advice may be our last.

16.3 The Minority Report at the child leukaemia conference.

In torpedoing us in CERRIE, the nuclear apologists on COMARE could not have imagined we would quietly sink. We have played chess with them too long not to have seen this coming in one form or another. We had anticipated all this and made contingency plans. The main report of CERRIE was due to be published in October 2004. Since it would not contain our side of the arguments we intended to put them in our own Minority Report and publish this ourselves. In the event, this had to be done quickly. Here is why: After CERRIE's last meeting I spent some time writing this present book, as it was overdue by about a year. In early 2004, I had been contacted by my friend Alasdair Philips who is a leukaemia researcher and works part time for the charity founded by Eddie O'Gorman, the millionaire, whose son Paul died of leukaemia. This charity is now called *Children with Leukaemia.* Alasdair told me that they had decided to hold a very large and expensive child leukaemia conference. Eddie wanted to get to the bottom of the cause. Everyone was to be allowed to come, indeed to be encouraged to come. All possible reasons for the increase in child leukaemia were to be looked for. No stone would be left unturned etc. Would I be a member of the scientific steering committee, would I speak and could I suggest other speakers from the radical wing of science? I agreed to speak and help as a member of the scientific committee and I suggested Vyvyan Howard at Liverpool as another speaker. Alasdair's idea was that we had to break the monopoly on the issue held by the authorities. This meant the nuclear mafia. However, after agreeing to all this, I heard no more. Then I heard from Richard Bramhall that there were difficulties. Some scientists had refused to have me on the organisation committee and others had refused to come to the conference if I was listed as a speaker. The reasons were that I was not a real scientist and so forth.

By June I talked to Alasdair and told him that I had been invited to speak by the nukes themselves; I had been a plenary speaker at their British Nuclear Energy Society International Conference in Oxford in September 2002; I was also on two government committees; was a fellow of the University of Liverpool; had a major published paper on infant leukaemia after Chernobyl and had just been made Workpackage 6 leader of the EU Policy Information Network on Child Health and Environment following my invited contribution to their (PINCHE) London conference in April. It was hard to argue that I was not a scientist, or had sufficient status to be asked along to speak. In the end, Alasdair kept me a slot on the Friday (September 10th) to talk about the European Committee on Radiation Risk and the ICRP.

The ionising radiation day at this conference was Tuesday the 7th. He carefully listed the Friday slot as 'speaker to be announced' and this was advertised on the glossy flyer for the conference, which was held at Church House, Westminster, just behind Westminster Abbey. By the week before the conference, an amended agenda appeared: the slot had vanished and was replaced by some guy from Australia talking about mobile phones. The Tuesday, which was for ionising radiation, was filled up with presentations from Dudley Goodhead, Bryn Bridges, Richard Wakeford (BNFL), Eric Wright, and John Harrison (NRPB). The Chair alternated between Goodhead and Bridges. 'Control' is the word that comes to mind. The conference would hear the official view. The day before, Monday, had Leo Kinlen and some other guy, arguing that it was all population mixing.

I was angry about this. Here is this millionaire, Eddie, a nice old geezer, trying to throw money at the problem and discover why his son died, and the result is: he gets infiltrated by the nukes. There is no balanced view, since I have been squeezed out. I called Alasdair. This is what he told me. The previous week he had phoned the new Health Protection Agency, the big government organisation that would be incorporating all the functions of the NRPB and other agencies. It was headed by Sir William Stewart, the man whose committee decided the safety of mobile phones. (They were 'safe'). Would Sir William come and open the conference? They phoned back, 'Would Chris Busby be speaking?' Alasdair was taken aback. 'Well yes, he is due to speak on the Friday. Is that a problem?'
'No, of course not,' was the reply.

In the next hour, out of the blue, he and Prof Denis Henshaw at Bristol (another guy on the committee) received emails from nine plenary speakers, stating that, if I were allowed to speak, they would boycott the conference. In addition, two members of the scientific committee stated that they also would resign if I were allowed to speak. There would be no conference if this happened. He said that he had to remove me from the agenda and cancel my contribution. He contacted me at the last minute; he was very apologetic and said he was very angry at what they had done. I could still present the two posters that I had prepared and I could ask questions in the plenary discussion sections. Oh sure, I thought, with Bridges and Goodhead in the Chair.

We had anticipated something like this happening, but not the degree of central orchestration that seemed to be behind it. I had worked night and day for two weeks to get the minority report finished and boxed for publication. I had contracted the printers and persuaded them to print it as quickly as they could. They were very good. The report was printed by the Friday before the conference, 180 pages with a bright red cover. Leaving it till the last minute, so that the nukes didn't get wind of our cunning plan and pull out of the conference, or slap an injunction on us, we launched the Minority Report on Tuesday 7th, the day that had been hi-jacked at the conference. We launched it at the House of Commons; Meacher was there as well as Richard Bramhall, Paul Dorfman and myself. The report was featured in the *Independent* (Marie Woolf) and the *Guardian* (Paul Brown). I attended the rest of the leukaemia conference. Richard and I made some leaflets calling attention to the suppression of free scientific debate, but when we tried to leave them for the delegates, Alasdair and the conference organisers ran around after us picking them up. I told him that this was a matter of children's lives and that if he wanted me to be quiet about what had happened he would have to throw me out bodily. As far as my talk was concerned, Vyvyan had been listed to give a presentation on the Friday: he suggested that he give my presentation. Once he was up on the stage, there was little they could do. I gave him the slides. He gave the talk. Unfortunately, I was unable to be there as it was a day of the week I had to look after my daughter Rosa.

The reason I tell this story is that it shows the lengths that the authorities will go to suppress the truth. Well, I say 'the truth', but what I mean is belief that they disagree with. But you have to ask why they don't want this out there if it is all nonsense and I am a faulty scientist. To my mind, as a chess player, I have to say that they made a strategic mistake. They would have been better off allowing us to have our say in their Report and allowing me to speak at the leukaemia conference.

Oh, who were the nine emailers, the nine *Ring Wraiths*? Good question. I asked the organisers for the details. Alasdair identified two of them, Dudley Goodhead and Richard Wakeford. I wonder who the others were. I tried to find out using the Data Protection Act, but they were on to me. I got nothing.

16.4 Some good news

In 2004 I was invited to be leader of the Science Policy Workpackage of PINCHE, the Policy Information Network for Child Health and Environment, a million euro EU funded operation based in Arnhem in the Netherlands. I obtained this job (which paid hardly anything, but was very interesting) almost by accident. I had been invited to give a paper at a meeting in London on child health. I arrived there late and fell into the wrong meeting. It took me a while to figure this out, but the meeting was a meeting of this outfit PINCHE. Since I had developed radar for this kind of thing it didn't take long to see that there were some guys in among the contributors from the floor trying to alter the directions of the process regarding chemical exposures. The PINCHE operation is based on the idea that a lot of experts from different universities in Europe should review all the scientific literature on child health and environmental exposures and write a report for the Commission recommending legislation or research. After a while I couldn't bear it any longer so I stood up and told the meeting that they needed to be aware of the infiltration and the extra-scientific [or trans-scientific as Ruden (2002, 2003) calls it] processes that were involved in science advice. There ensued an interesting debate and I was asked to stay behind and talk with the management team. To my astonishment, a month later I was invited to be leader of the most important group, Workpackage 6, which was to advise on the science policy interface itself. There is insufficient space to recount all the adventures that this job involved. Most of the political manoeuvres that existed on the CERRIE and STOA processes turned up also in PINCHE, but in a milder form. The participants (perhaps because they were doctors) were generally more honest and unbiased. And, in the end, I did manage to get everyone to agree that there was significant bias in the present system of scientific advice and also that this could be dealt with by oppositional science. For me, this was an uphill struggle but worth it since it was finally agreed. Thus this idea of committee bias, industry control and the use of oppositional committees is now in an official report of a prestigious EU funded group and it has been accepted and published in a major peer-reviewed journal, *Acta Paediatrica.* In the paper, which I was responsible for a large part of (van der Hazel *et al* 2006) it states:

*However, more unconventionally, PINCHE examined the process itself [*of science advice] *looking behind the decisions. . . and came to variously significantly novel conclusions. PINCHE concluded that the interface between Science and Public Health policy and the important role that scientific assessments play in this interface are important issues and challenges. . . PINCHE recognised and cited evidence in its WP6 report that the acquisition of and the handling of scientific environmental data may be culturally biased by the needs of the institution handling the data and making representations about its meaning.*

The paper continues:

PINCHE, for this reason, developed a recommendation that scientific advice committees on specific exposure questions be set up at the beginning as discursive or oppositional committees, with institutional funding to include independent scientists to examine issues of environmental health. Reports of these committee's discussions would include all sides of the issue where there is some argument as to the health consequences of policies involving these substances of processes. It would then be for the policy makers to decide. . .

So there has been some success. The idea is officially out there. The key is to ensure that the secretariat is agnostic. I myself would suggest using sociologists or psychologists. There are of course limits to how watertight you could make this process. But if everything is reported and everything is transparent, at least you can come along later and see exactly what happened and find someone to blame.

There was one other recommendation that I managed to get accepted by the group. This was that children who lived near some putative source of risk should have their medical cards 'flagged' so that if they later moved away, or if, as adults, they developed some disease that might be linked to their exposure, this could be examined by retrospective studies. This will, if implemented, make the polluter think twice about what they release, as these retrospective studies will clearly represent a basis for litigation.

16.5 Conclusions

In this chapter I have presented a solution to a problem that has slowly and invisibly developed in democratic politics. Historically, democracy was a solution to the complex tensions that occur in large collections of individuals living in societies. (Ideally) the representatives of the people could debate what the best system was for all the people and put it in place, so far as that were possible. It was predicated on perfect knowledge. So it assumed that everybody knew what is going on. But in the 20th century this slowly changed. It became increasingly the case that the people and their representatives no longer knew what was going on or how to interpret what they were told. To understand what was happening, you increasingly needed specialist knowledge and often expensive and complex instruments. In such a situation politics is no longer democratic: it is hostage to the expert. And these experts are mostly tied in some way to the economic success of the country, the university or industry. And since these three are all tied together anyway, no one is looking after the people and their health. Sellafield is given as an example, but there are others. Mad Cow disease would not have broken out if we had an oppositional committee. Most recently, my friend Georgina Downs spent a huge amount of effort to draw attention to the risks to health from crop spraying of pesticides. She has a list as long as your arm of sick people who live near the sprayed fields. She has convinced a Royal Commission on Pesticides (RCP) that this is so. But the government's Advisory Committee on Pesticides (ACP) has in turn advised the government that the RCP's conclusions are wrong, and so the government has ignored the RCP and we have spraying as usual. So local people continue to be sprayed and to get ill and die so that farmers can grow more contaminated food and make more money. Is the ACP an oppositional committee? No. Its Chairman is David Coggon, also Chair of the Depleted Uranium Oversight Board, who we will meet in the next Chapter.

The human race has fallen into a trap of its own making, and unless it realises this and digs itself out, it will finish itself off, and everything else we love, in the name of progress. This is true of radioactive pollution, of chemical pollution and of the general destruction of the biosphere, the global temperature balance, the genetic integrity of life, any of the many developments that we have seen in the last 100 years which are built on Science. Science has been elevated to a Religion, and Science has become identified with Truth. It is not. It is now a muddy, money-grubbing and often suspect operation. The people are right to fear and disbelieve scientists, and to see Science as a confidence trick. I am a scientist and this is my conclusion, and the evidence (in terms of one such development) is here in this book. This is the real Third World War, and we, the people, the animals, your children, your grandchildren, the trees, the grass, the beautiful world we inherited, are losing it.

17
Lessons

What is Truth, says Pilate
Waits for no answer
Double your stakes, says the clock
To the ageing dancer
Double the guard, says authority
Treble the bars
Holes in the sky, says the child
Scanning the stars

Louis Macneice

Information is not power. Power is the ability to act effortlessly with sweeping impact.

Carl Cook,
President, BioComp Systems Inc.
Aug 1999

17.1 Apology

This book has become far larger than I intended, much more fragmented and perhaps irritating. For this I apologise. The reason is that I wrote it over the CERRIE and ECRR periods, leaving it and coming back to it in a deranged tango, each time seeing it afresh, with new information which slightly altered the viewpoint of the earlier version of myself, the previous (and slightly younger) author. More accurately, during this period, new evidence kept emerging that I felt had to be incorporated to give an understanding of the situation, and also to provide a history and testament of the extraordinary shifts and alterations of reality accommodated by those who were desperate to exclude the truth (or perhaps I should say evidence). This fourteen-year investigation into radiation and health, into the reasons for people's beliefs, into science, into the destruction of the human environment for profit has cost me a lot. In the last year I have lost Molly and my daughter Rosa, who I brought up for 10 years. The manuscript and I moved home three times, together with a staggering amount of paper, box files, books, computers, radiation detectors, banjos and guitars, my bandoneon, electric drills, oscilloscopes, microscopes, motorcycles, poetry books, gamma ray spectrometers, chemicals, my violin, the list is endless: all the paraphernalia one acquires and drags about over the years alive on earth. As Thoreau says we put all this stuff in barns and then when we die, it is then sold to go into the barns of other people. All that is left is what we write down. Although there are lots of other things I had intended to put in, I will have to draw this book to a close with this chapter. In any case, *now is the time*, as one of the Tarot cards signals - I forget which. They are gearing up for a recovery. Just as the Dark Lord always makes a comeback in the children's stories, the nuclear industry is back again, against popular demand. Here to save the planet from global warming. Hurrah! Fade in thematic linking music. The clicking Geiger accompaniment to *Radiation: the Bringer of Death*.

Is this the discourse of a Scientist? I can see you looking thoughtful here. What I want you to understand is that Science is more than just cold blooded, rational analysis and laboratory experiment. The laboratory is just that. It is a place. It is actually quite a strange place, not part of the real world. It is an artificially created place where influences are controlled, away from the world. But the world and its dynamic are also (or should be) our laboratory: that is why I am attracted to epidemiology. But we must be ethnographers also, faithful recorders of detail. Our epidemiology must not *a priori* exclude any evidence as second order. We must become as little children and see everything and accommodate everything. We must be aware that, as Marilyn Strathern puts it (After Nature, 1992):

It is an anthropological axiom that however discrete they appear to be, entities are the product of relations; nothing is not embedded in some context or worldview that gives it its special shape.

And in another essay she makes explicit her answer (and mine) to this problem, the problem of culture and scientific belief (in her case, social science). How do we get at the truth in these areas of scientific analysis in situations where we cannot exclude possible mechanisms because we don't know what they are. She writes (Commons and Borderlands 2004):

What research strategy could possibly collect information on unpredictable outcomes? Social anthropology has one trick up its sleeve: the deliberate attempt to generate more data than the investigator is aware of at the time of collection. Anthropologists deploy open-ended, non linear methods of data collection which they call ethnography. Rather than devising research protocols that will purify the data in advance of analysis, the anthropologist embarks on a participatory exercise which yields materials for which analytical protocols are often devised after the fact. The ethnographer may work by indirection, creating tangents from which the principal subject can be observed. But what is a tangent at one stage may become central in the next.

Of course, the modern epidemiologists would not let us get away with this. This is why they miss all the real evidence. They won't allow themselves to see the evidence. But I think I have made this point in this book again and again: we cannot assume that any evidence can be ignored on the basis of some pre-existing theory. And the way Science has developed and is developing (not just in this area, but in all areas) gives me great cause for concern. This process may have done a great disservice to mankind in the way in which it has been used as a political tool, a tool of power. It may be worse. It may have determined the very way in which we now think. As Herbert Marshall McLuhan once used to talk about the 'Medium being the Message' and the way in which the printing of beliefs on paper by Gutenberg *et seq.* organised the minds of the people who read, so in the 20th Century we all had to think 'Scientifically'. 'Scientific' had come to mean 'True' and was used as equivalent to 'I am right (and you are wrong)'. Along with the technological advances, the digital watches and lasers, we have developed a kind of science-induced blindness that arises out of the belief that we can atomise observational facts and deal with them as separate entities in a cultural vacuum and then reassemble them to obtain the truth. In this way we now have to imagine we understand how thought itself works, as a kind of more complicated version of the behaviourist's rats and their mazes. The process leads its proponents to tell us that we are at the end of science. Similar thought processes, scientific rational thought processes in others, tell us that the 'Market' represents the end of economics. We are at the end of History. All is understood.

In this, our own self created labyrinth, non-scientists, members of the public, even policy makers cannot now believe the evidence of their own eyes. They have to say, 'well, of course, I am not a scientist, and so I cannot comment' even where the evidence is screaming at them. Many of the arguments that I have related in this book are arguments between individuals who have chosen to adhere to some theory or other and have had to ignore or exclude observations that do not fit. Ordinary people (among whom I place myself, incidentally, hence the Tarot card) look out of the window, make observations, and draw conclusions, a response that has kept the human race surviving hazards throughout evolution.

There are a few things that I really must place on record before I go - a few little anecdotes and a conclusion that I wish to draw (which is the reason, I suppose, for writing the book in the first place). So I am going to lay these out in this last chapter for your entertainment and edification. If you have made it to this point, thanks for your patience. If you have jumped into the book and arrived here, well, Hello!

I will relate two stories that are about the real world; about things that happened. Having read what I have written earlier, you will be able to interpret the way in which the illnesses are linked to radiation, and how the authorities have covered them up, and why. The first is about childhood leukaemia clusters again. Again, it illustrates the nature of risk from invisible radiation in the real world and the methods used to cover up such risk. This is the invisible point source problem. How will you ever know that there is not one near you? The answer is that you will not; unless something is done about the secrecy of the cancer registries; unless there is someone to look on your behalf, someone you can trust: a Champion. The second is about the latest global threat. This is the most recent example of a radiation risk from discharges to the environment, Uranium Weapons (or some say, 'Depleted Uranium' weapons, as if this makes them less problematical).

These stories, and those I have told in this book, are always of situations that follow the way in which Science has been twisted to the shape desired by industry and the military.

What shall we do? What can we do? There is, happily, an answer along the lines I have indicated earlier. First we need oppositional science advice; second we need alternative and independent institutions, like the European Committee on Radiation Risk. Since industry does the pollution, it should be industry that pays for these safeguards, perhaps in the form of taxes. But failing that, the people themselves can fund the foundation of such alternative institutions; it is not that costly. But now here is a diversion…

17.2 Ray Fox and the Leukaemia Triangle

The Leukaemia Triangle

It is commonly argued that childhood leukaemia clusters occur all over the place, and therefore have some cause entirely separate from ionising radiation, the clustering behaviour suggesting that there is an infection involved. This is a theory first advanced by Leo Kinlen, and backed up by him through research showing modest increases in child leukaemia in country districts where there has been an influx of new people because of expansion of the town to accommodate increases in population (Kinlen 1988, 1993, 2001). Relative risks found in connection with his 'population mixing' scenarios were modest, about 1.1 to 2, rarely greater than that. An example is in Scotland where the North Sea oil discovery resulted in a rapid influx of workers and their families. The argument is that 'population mixing' increases the chance of infection, and that the child leukaemia is associated with this. And I have also given the example of the child leukaemia cluster in Pembroke Road, Northampton. I have also discussed Kinlen's hypothesis. The truth is that the only reason it is not laughed out of court is that it represents a convenient refuge for the nuclear mafia. At the recent Leukaemia conference in London, Kinlen was there to review and defend his position. His ears were closed to the many criticisms levelled by the scientific delegates. The most powerful of course is the observation (which he never alludes to) of the clustering of leukaemia cases in adults as well as children (Clemmesen, 1961), which suggests an environmental cause. The immune system of adults is completely formed, unlike that if children.

The nuclear project, however, has left behind some dark secrets. And without sophisticated radiation measuring equipment, the exposures are invisible. The most bizarre example is the buried Shell reactor in Reading, a large town in Berkshire. All the evidence points to the existence, several metres underneath a normal, quiet suburban housing estate, of a buried nuclear reactor, corroded and leaching its contents into the groundwater. The locals say that there is a high level of childhood leukaemia in the area; but no one really knows, as the health authority and the cancer registry will not release data to examine the assertions.

First some background. The area around Reading has a statistically significant excess of childhood leukaemia, first flagged up by the local paediatric specialist at the Reading Royal Infirmary, Dr Carol Barton. The matter has been the subject of several studies in the 1980s following the Seascale child leukaemias and was examined also by COMARE, who concluded (as you would expect) that the doses from the weapons factory at Aldermaston (20 miles to the West) and the bomb factory at Burghfield (a few miles to the South West) were too low to cause the leukaemias (Roman et al 1993). Nevertheless, the locals continued to argue that there was a concern regarding the release of large amounts of Plutonium and Uranium (Tritium and Krypton gas) into the environment. The releases were both from discharges into the air and also from liquid waste into the Kennet and Avon Canal and river Thames through a long and leaky pipeline.

In the mid 1990s, the focus of interest in this affair moved to the west of Aldermaston, to the USAF Airbase at Greenham Common a few miles east of Newbury, and some twenty miles West of Reading. A reporter, and CND advisor, Eddie Goncalves, had examined official documents released from secrecy after the 30 year rule. One was a report written in 1961 by two scientists, Cripps and Stimson, showing that there was an anomalous butterfly shaped pattern of enriched Uranium deposition around the USAF airbase at Greenham Common and that this pattern could have resulted from the burning of a nuclear bomb. It seems (and this is well documented) that a USAF plane had jettisoned a fuel tank and that this had caused a fire on the runway and destroyed some planes. It was believed that these planes carried atomic bombs. The contamination found in the Cripps and Stimson report was centred on USAF Greenham Common Airfield. The report was part of Operation 'Overture', an exercise for measuring Uranium isotope ratios, which had been thought, might be a useful way of detecting Soviet nuclear installations through analysis of plant and soil residues sent back by agents: all good Cold War stuff.

Anyway, there was a terrific row following the release of this information to the Press. The Ministry of Defence and the USAF both denied that any atom bombs had burned. I undertook a study of leukaemia mortality in children in the area. Using National Statistics data I was able to show that in the seven County Districts defined by the triangle between Oxford, Reading and Newbury, there were significantly high levels of childhood leukaemia only in those County Districts that contained nuclear sites. These were South Oxfordshire (Atomic Energy Research Establishment Harwell) and Newbury (Atomic Weapons Establishment, Aldermaston). Because of the strange influences on child leukaemia, we called this area, between Newbury, Reading and Oxford, the

'Leukaemia Triangle'. I sent a letter to the British Medical Journal and they published it (Busby 1998). It was picked up by all the major newspapers and became a *cause celebre*.

I had used mortality- all that was available. I asked the local cancer registry for data to see if incidence of child leukaemia was raised in specific wards; the director of the Oxford Cancer Registry, which held the data was Dr Monica Roche, She refused on the basis that the data was confidential. The Director of the Oxford Health Authority at the time was Dr Peter Iredale, who was ex-Director of the Atomic Energy Research Establishment at Harwell. (No doubt it seems natural to you that running a nuclear site is a good background for running a health authority: indeed, when I questioned the matter, this is exactly the response I obtained). So I went to the local Ethical Committee to ask for the data. It was refused. The Greens on Oxford City Council arranged for a meeting with the Ethical Committee Chair. It was truly bizarre. I struggled all the way to Oxford from Wales for this meeting, taking Rosa, who was only four at the time - car sick and vomiting all the way. Richard Bramhall came along to help look after Rosa. They sat outside the meeting in Oxford Town Hall playing with dolls. At the meeting, the Chair seemed nervous and continued to refuse the data. He ended up shouting at me that I was a scaremonger and not a scientist. He rushed off from the meeting before I could respond. This was the Ethical Committee that covered the area of the nuclear site at Harwell.

Although the Oxford ethical committee had refused on the grounds of confidentiality, strangely, the Reading ethical committee (where there was no big-deal nuclear site like Harwell) agreed to let me have their leukaemia data, so it did seem to me that there was some cover up taking place around Harwell.

But to return to the Greenham Common bomb story, because of the publicity and public concern, and because one local Newbury parent Richard Capewell whose daughter had developed leukaemia was mapping the leukaemias himself by asking questions of parents, Newbury Council commissioned a huge study of Uranium and Plutonium levels in soil in the area. This was carried out by a joint team from the University of Southampton (Dr Ian Croudace) and the Scottish University Research Reactor (Dr Ian Sanderson) (Croudace et al 1997). The former team analysed soils, and the latter engaged in an aerial survey using a complicated gamma ray camera. I have referred to this survey earlier in connection with the plutonium from the Irish Sea. The area covered was quite large, from the West of Newbury to just East of Reading and North as far as the perimeter of Harwell (the government did not allow them to measure over Harwell). The results showed much higher levels of Plutonium than were expected based on earlier grassland and soil survey carried out by Harwell scientists in the 1980s (Cawse and Horrill). Uranium isotope ratios were also measured. At this point I must say something about the Uranium isotopes, since it is part of this story and also the next one.

Uranium is a natural element on Earth and has been here since the beginning of the planet. The main isotope, Uranium-238, has a half-life of 4.5 billion years, so it will be around forever. Let me remind you about half-life: the concept is easy to understand. Half of any quantity of U-238 will have given off radiation and changed into another element in 4.5 billion years. In the case of U-238, the first decay (of an alpha particle) changes it into two very short lived isotopes Protoactinium-234m and Thorium-234, both beta and gamma ray emitters and these, in turn, decay into Uranium 234, another radioactive element but with a shorter, very long half life, 250,000 years. The decay products are called 'daughters' and, since each has a shorter half-life than the parent U-238, after a very long time they are in what is known as secular equilibrium. That is to say, on average, that for each decay of the parent there is a decay of a daughter: the isotopes have the same activity. A sample of U-238 left for long enough will have an activity of 'B' decays per second of U-238, 'B' decays per second of Pa-234 and 'B' decays per second of U-234. So in the natural state on earth, in minerals containing Uranium, there is a 1:1 ratio of activity of U234 and U238. However, there is another Uranium isotope, the source of all the trouble. It is the fissile isotope U-235. It is present in very small quantities in natural Uranium, 0.72 % and, because the masses are almost the same (238 and 235, only about 1%), they are very difficult to separate. In fact it was the Uranium isotope separation that was the biggest problem in developing the atomic bomb in the mid 1940s.

For atomic bombs and for nuclear reactors, there has to be a fuel that has a high concentration of the fissile isotope, U-235. The normal ratio of isotopes (in natural Uranium, mined from the ground) is 137.88 (atoms of U-238 to atoms of U-235). For a reactor, the ratio has to be less than about 50. For bombs it is usually about 25. The isotopic ratio of material in the soil pattern discovered by Cripps and Stimson was about 25. This is why they thought a bomb had burned on the runway during the fire in 1959. The codename of the fire was (appropriately) *Broken Arrow*. These military people! Aren't they something? The Israelis called their latest bombing campaign of the Lebanon '*Summer Rain*'.

So the big Southampton study was carried out. Samples of soil and vegetation were taken and examined for Plutonium and Uranium isotopes. The estimate was that it cost about £200,000 of taxpayers' money. Boiled down to basics, the results showed two things. First, the levels of Plutonium-239 were far higher than they had been reported by earlier studies of the same area - about ten-fold - with much higher levels near the Aldermaston perimeter fence (where a contaminated pond had overflowed). Second, that there was no longer any pattern of enriched Uranium deposition such as had been reported by Cripps and Stimson. Uranium isotope ratios were mostly quite close to the value 137.88 for the natural material, except near Aldermaston and Burghfield where there were some samples with low levels of enriched Uranium and some with small amounts of Depleted Uranium (used for anti-tank armour piercing shells). The lowest value (the most enriched) sample had a ratio of 98. This was taken from near the Aldermaston perimeter fence. The conclusion was that there had been no bomb fire at Greenham (just as both the UK and US military people stoutly maintained). The increases in child leukaemia were a mystery, in the same way that the Sellafield ones were. Dr Bithell of the Oxford Childhood Cancer Research Group examined the census figures and showed that population mixing had not occurred. Leo Kinlen argued that it was commuters: business as usual.

Enter Ray Fox

Ray Fox wrote to me sometime around 1997 to ask my advice. He sent me photographs of his body, which showed large areas of red rashes and blistering. 'Could it have been caused by radiation?' he asked, and told me his story. Ray is a short, tough-looking, but also unwell-looking character with a cockney accent, a tenacious attitude (as well he might have, given his experiences) and a kind of desperate angry energy. He lived, until recently, in Earley, near Reading, Berkshire at 337 Wokingham Road. In the mid 1990s he dug up a drain at the bottom of his garden to clear a blockage that was flooding his garden. The land drain crossing the corner of his property was blocked with some tarry black material, which Ray cleared away. Shortly after this he became seriously ill. His body became covered in what appeared to be burns and blisters. The symptoms (including other symptoms which he recounted) appeared to be those of radiation poisoning. He had urine analysis done in Germany where slightly increased levels of Uranium and Plutonium were detected. Following Ray's complaint about the drain, the plutonium and his illness, Shell immediately arranged for contractors to visit the property and dig up the drain, water jet the remaining sewer and close the system up, replacing all the material they removed with fresh soil.

There began several years of struggle to obtain an explanation for his illness and its origin, a struggle that has slowly revealed elements of what appear to be a most extraordinary cover-up - a secret underground atomic research site operated in Reading in the 1960s by the Shell Oil Company as part of a research effort into the development of atom bombs. As a result of the energy Ray put into investigating the cause of his illness, he managed to get all the evidence he had collected and all the results of the measurements that were made to the media. Quite a few programmes were made, including prime time documentaries on TV and a BBC Radio 4 piece called 'In The Bunker', which was a highlight of the week it was broadcast and was repeated by popular demand. In this documentary, I went down a sewer behind Ray's house (where the trouble had begun) with radiation monitoring equipment, the echoing commentary as I crawled underground, kitted up in gas mask and all the measuring gear, was reminiscent of a science fiction movie sound track (Plate 33).

The drain Ray had unblocked was an illegal connection to the public land drain to the River Loddon draining material from the Shell 'oil depot'. I first visited the house and garden and employed our gamma spectrometer to make radiation measurements of Ray's house and garden as part of the Mark Thomas investigation on Channel 4 TV. Beta and alpha scintillation counting showed very slightly raised levels and there were slightly elevated levels of radiation, mainly gamma signals from natural Thorium 234. The house itself had slightly high levels of radiation, particularly the lower block work in some rooms, but none were high enough to be considered a health risk in themselves. Samples were taken on behalf of Ray's insurance company and sent by their advisor, Dr Karta Badsha, to be analysed by LGC in Teddington. Results showed the presence of various toxic organic chemicals and heavy metals, as would be expected from groundwater near an oil depot, but there were also some very interesting radiochemical results which connect us with the Greenham fire and the leukaemia triangle. These are shown in Table 17.2.1.

Table 17.2.1 Plutonium and Uranium Isotopes in dust and soil at 337 Wokingham Road, Reading, found in samples taken by Dr Karta Bardsha and analysed at the Laboratory of the Government Chemist (LGC) Teddington.

Isotope	**First series, house dust (Bq/kg)**	**Second series, garden soil (Bq/kg)**
Plutonium 239+240	54.9	9.8
Uranium 238	18	10
Uranium 235	4.7	2.6
Americium	-	6.3

These measurements indicate the presence of material from a nuclear reactor for the following reasons. With regard to the Plutonium, prior to 1945 the background level of Plutonium would have been zero. Since global weapons testing the background level in soil and grassland should be about 0.02 to 0.7 Bq/kg, as measured by Cawse and Horrill in the 1970s. Since then, the sea to land transfer of plutonium from Sellafield has increased these values to about 1-2 Bq/kg and in the area near Aldermaston readings as high as 5-10Bq/kg were found in a few samples near the perimeter fence. However, in the largest analytical exercise run in the area of Berkshire, the Newbury survey of 1997, very few samples gave levels higher than 2Bq/kg. Thus the house dust sample of 54.9Bq/kg shows a level 100 to 500 times higher than expected on the basis of weapons fallout. Plutonium 239 comes from the fission of Uranium 235 in a reactor or a bomb, or from reprocessing of spent fuel.

The Uranium levels are not high overall but the isotope ratio U238/U235 is an unmistakeable fingerprint for material from a nuclear reactor or reactor fuel. This is enriched Uranium. Of the 516 samples taken by the Newbury survey (Croudace *et al* 1997) and analysed, all of the samples from the control areas (12), rural Berkshire (27), Greenham Common Outer (56), Greenham Common inner (137) and Greenham Common airbase (216) gave values within 3 standard deviations from the U238/U235 natural ratio of 137.88, i.e. they were all between 137.36 and 138.40. The 68 samples from Aldermaston included 11 samples outside this range and lower than 136.94, indicating slightly enriched Uranium. There was one sample only that gave the lowest ratio of 98.03 and this was from woodland soil at the Atomic Weapons Establishment Aldermaston.

I calculated the Uranium mass ratios from the house at Wokingham road and show them in Table 17.2 2.

Table 17.2.2 Uranium ratios in samples from Mr Fox's house and garden, 337 Wokingham Road, Reading, Berkshire

Sample	U238 Bq/kg	U238 ppm	U235 Bq/kg	U235 ppm	Ratio U238/U235
House dust	18	1.45	4.7	0.059	24.5
Soil	10	0.807	2.6	0.033	24.45

The very anomalous low value of 24.5 indicates enriched Uranium, either from reactor fuel or spent reactor fuel. There is also a reference value for this in the tables of the United Nations Scientific Committee on the effect of Atomic Radiation (UNSCEAR 2000). Table 15, p124 gives values of the activity (Bequerel) ratio for the two isotopes in air, water and various foods. The reference ratio for all is about 20:1, whereas the Wokingham Road bequerel ratios are 3.82:1 and 3.86:1 respectively. Thus is it is clear that Ray's house and land had been contaminated with enriched Uranium and also Plutonium. The similarity between the ratios for the two samples, from the house dust and garden suggest strongly that the source of the contamination is the same and would be a general contaminant for the house and garden. The ultimate origin of this material must be a nuclear reactor although we cannot say where this reactor is. I speculated at first, that solvent used for cleaning a nuclear reactor or some part of a nuclear reactor might carry the material and deposit it after a fire.

However, there appears to be other evidence. In the course of investigating this strange story, we found that there was independent evidence of an experimental nuclear reactor beneath the ground at the Earley depot. It was visited by Dr David Greenwood who worked at University College London. Greenwood sent an affidavit to the European Commission describing an extraordinary underground research laboratory complete with experimental nuclear reactor, buried in the heart of Reading. According to his statement, this was a graphite-moderated reactor of about 30 feet diameter. It was buried several metres deep and was apparently used for nuclear research in connection with the Manhattan Project and later nuclear developments.

But before the site closed something happened: there appears to have been an accident at this reactor site. In 1987 there was a fire and an explosion, which was recorded locally as a minor railway accident involving a diesel spillage. However, local people reported that the earth shook and that manhole covers blew off. What Ray's discovery suggests is that the reactor is still there and is leaking and contaminating the local area.

After the closure of the depot following the fire, the land remained derelict until acquired by a developer in the late 1990s when it was 'remediated' by removing a metre of topsoil and replacing it with fresh topsoil. A new housing estate was built on the site and people now live there. I have walked around the roads measuring background levels of radiation with a scintillation counter. There is some slight radioactivity elevation around the area at the bottom of Ray's garden, but on the other side of his fence; nothing very unusual. There is a fairly radioactive piece of road behind the site. But if the reactor is there it is deep underground and shielded. A magnetometry survey would find it, but the people who live on the new estate have refused to allow such a survey on their land.

With the Green Party MEP Caroline Lucas, Ray took the case to Europe. European radiation protection laws do not allow people to bury nuclear reactors and walk away. I went to Brussels and argued the case with the radiation protection head, Steven Kaiser. Wheels were put in motion. A letter was sent to the UK asking for an explanation of the radiation measurements. The UK stalled. Kaiser was moved to another department. In fact, the whole department was moved to another department. Radiation Protection moved from Directorate 'Environment' to Directorate 'Trade and Industry'(Just imagine the power these people have). Anyway, it seems that poor Ray has come up against a dead end in Europe, although he continues to worry away at the authorities here with writs, media items and new discoveries.

Here is my own interpretation of it all. Having met many of the people who knew and read all the documents that have been unearthed, this Earley story is part of a larger one, which is about the cold war research into bombs.

Leukaemia clusters, cancer clusters and the Cold war

When the first research into nuclear weapons and nuclear power, and the uses of radiation generally, was being undertaken, Shell was a big player. At Earley, they were examining the possibilities associated with radiation, radioactive materials and organic solvents. This would be almost impossible for them not to have done, since organic solvents are at the centre of their operation. From the nuclear research side, organic solvents are an integral part of the chemistry of Uranium and Plutonium processes, and would be used for cleaning as well as integral to the preparations. Shell would have had to research the effect of ionizing radiation on solvents. So where were the nuclear sites at that time (1950-1970) and where would these sites have acquired their solvents? The main research was carried out at Aldermaston and Harwell. The closest railway connected solvent depot to Aldermaston is the Earley depot. In addition, there was a huge amount of cooperative research with the Americans, the Manhattan Project and the subsequent research on H-bombs at the US sites Oak Ridge and Hanford. Material was sent from England to the USA. We know that Plutonium for US bombs was supplied by the UK. It was admitted in Parliament. The Shell site undertook research into the reactions between organic solvents and Uranium and Plutonium, to see if they could develop liquid nuclear fuels, creating organometallic compounds, chemical adducts of U-235 and hydrocarbons or ethers, solubilising the radioactive elements so that they would be movable by pumping through tubes. The Greenham Common fire was not a bomb fire, but was a fire involving just such a contaminated organometallic solvent, waiting to be flown out to the USA as part of a research collaboration. Map contours show that leakage of this stuff to the groundwater from the runway at Greenham Common airbase would have resulted in it being transported downhill into that part of Newbury where Richard Capewell's maps showed that the high levels of leukaemia were (including his own house). It was waste containing this stuff that was being discharged illegally to the River Loddon through Ray's garden. If you look at the map, the only other way Shell could have got rid of waste was to South Lake, to the north of the Shell site, and a radiological investigation of South Lake sediment might be instructive. If the research reactor at Earley was a big deal, then there should be more contamination from Caesium-137, which there is not, although it all happened a long time ago. The signature Uranium ratio found by Cripps and Stimson was also about 25:1. It is too much of a coincidence that the Overture fire ratio is the same as the Ray Fox garden ratio.

Since the authorities will not look, and we have run out of ideas, there the matter must remain until someone grasps the nettle and looks with a magnetometer. The buried reactor story is only one of similar Cold War inheritances. For example, a Mr John Dwyer contacted me some years ago about another research reactor operated by Shell on the Wirral near Birkenhead (where Shell have a big refinery and research setup and where I worked many years ago for a short time). Dwyer has evidence that Shell made a chemical reactor using Strontium-90 to beta irradiate solvents to see if there was any mileage in using radiation for chemical production. Mr Dwyer told me that the reactor had to be broken up in the 1980s and a team from Harwell turned up to advise. No one knew what to do. The whole affair was a nightmare of radioactivity. Dwyer alleges that it was taken away by private operators and buried in parts of North Wales. There are leukaemia clusters in parts of North Wales. The authorities say they are chance clusters.

Here is another story. I met a man in South Wales who told me that he was out late on the Heads-of-Valleys Road, courting. He described how a convoy of trucks with a police escort drove to the area above a local beauty spot and started unloading drums. This was in the middle of the night. The police blocked off the road and the drums were apparently emptied: he didn't wait to find out what was going on, but legged it smartly. Another story came from a gorgeous hippie woman called Marilyn, jangling with beads and flashing with colours and beauty. She lived in a derelict house in the middle of nowhere near Llanidloes and said that there was an experimental station in the Hafren forest where something was going on. Could I check it out for radiation, she asked, as she was a bit worried. For many months in the late 1990s convoys of ready-mix concrete lorries thundered into the forest in the middle of the night (she said) waking her up. No one was supposed to be living up there, so no-one checked her out. This went on for two months apparently. Later, when she decided to walk into the forest to investigate, she was stopped by a Ghurkha soldier who materialised from behind a tree with a sub machine gun. He sent her away. He said he was guarding the nests of the (then) rare Red Kite. Presumably a connection between the RSPB and the Ministry of Defence. She said that for at least a year after the concrete lorry episode, there were strange flashing red lights lighting up the whole sky over the Hafren Forest accompanied by rumbling. The ground shook. All this happened in the middle of the night. OK, I see you think, another looney. What next: flying saucers? But a number of other people had also noticed and had asked their MP, Alex Carlisle to make enquiries. He said that he had been told by the authorities that there was some experimental research being done on submarine communications. Of course, how silly. The Hafren Forest, 100 miles from the sea is the obvious place for submarine communication.

But like Strathern's ethnographer, we cannot assume that these people are mad on the basis of prior theories. About a year after all this, I figured out roughly where this would have been happening from Marilyn's description and approached the area from the south, penetrating the forest from the A44 end. This was 1994. I went with Molly and my friend Bill Pritchard. We found a huge concrete slab, maybe 100 metres across, with a vast wooden dome like structure. There was an aluminium laboratory, empty, but with some danger notices on it. There were very thick metal cables running into this tank and snaking out across the concrete slab, disappearing into the ground and vanishing. I have the photographs of us standing inside this science fiction contraption (Plate 17). There was obviously quite a lot happening underground, but all the entrances had been concreted up. There was no excess radiation anywhere. What was all this about? Who knows? Did it have an effect on health? Again, who knows? But why put it in the middle of nowhere? Why surround it with Ghurkhas with machine guns. Is Marilyn all right, or did she die of leukaemia, being told that it was a disease caused by chance, or population mixing? Perhaps she caught Kinlen's postulated leukaemia virus from the Ghurkha. Anyway, as you see, Marilyn was not a looney - or at least not that sort of looney. There was something there, just as there is something there in the case of Ray Fox.

The reason I mention these stories (just examples - there are more) is so that you can see that there has been quite a lot of secrecy, dissembling and unrecorded radioactive contamination in the period of the Cold War, and so the superficial dismissal of leukaemia clusters by the authorities and the arguments about Texas sharp-shooting I raised in the section on epidemiology should not be accepted without looking a bit more closely at the history of the neighbourhood, without being Strathern's ethnographers.

There has recently been a lot of fuss made about a big child leukaemia cluster in the little desert town of Fallon, Nevada in the USA. This (argue the nukes) is proof of population mixing, since the cluster began after the influx of a huge number of army personnel when the town was expanded to house them. But of course, this is Nevada, home of the atmospheric tests, home of the plutonium dusts. This is where the Cowboy and Indian films were made, rolling in the dust, riding the horses, and many of the crews (including many actors) later contracted lung cancer. The building works needed to house the 50,000 incomers would have raised all the radioactive dusts from the weapons tests and then the children and their parents would have inhaled the dusts. Not population mixing, but dust/ lymphatic system mixing.

Note also that it seems that it is not enough to virtually prove the existence of the hazard. This is where we can see that information is not power. Power is power. I wonder what would happen if I dug up the wretched reactor in Reading and placed a yellow flag on its surface. I expect I should be prosecuted for trespass.

17.3 Depleted Uranium

This is the latest radioactive hazard. The US have turned Uranium into a weapon of war, which has the added advantage that it is a way of getting rid of radioactive waste, which otherwise would have cost large sums of money to dispose of. What they do is they shoot it at tanks (and people, and buildings and just about anything that moves and that they don't like, so long as it is a long way away from the US). The subject could make another whole book like this one. I include a rough outline of the situation because it has many resonances with the subject matter, and because I have had quite a lot to do with the arguments and no doubt will continue to over the next few years. I am currently on the Ministry of Defence Depleted Uranium Oversight Board, whose job is to independently examine concentrations of Uranium Isotopes in the urine of the Gulf War 1 veterans and those who also served in the Balkans in the mid 1990s and early 2000s. I visited Iraq in 2000 for

Al Jazeera TV and made measurements in the south of the country (Plate 18). I also went to Kosovo with Nippon TV in 2001 and brought back DU contaminated dusts from areas where children were playing (Plate 18). What would the Martians say about us as a species, eh?
A Martian History Channel: *Oh yes, this race discovered radioactive material safely trapped and dispersed in ores in rocks. They dug it up, refined it to make it pure and as radioactive as possible, and then they developed a weapon where the impact caused the almost perfect dispersion of an aerosol consisting of pure uranium oxide, long lived, widely dispersible and respirable. Then they used the weapon on some thin excuse and dropped thousands of tons of it in populated areas of Europe, Iraq and Afghanistan.*

First, the war veterans themselves have been suffering from many strange diseases. The ensemble is known as Gulf War Syndrome. The vets (and I) think that DU may be a contributor. Why? Why is there concern about the health effects of Depleted Uranium? Would there be equivalent argument about the health effects following the use of Tungsten in tank shells or lead in bullets? The answer is straightforward: everybody knows that Uranium is radioactive and everyone knows that radiation exposure leads to cancer, leukaemia and genetic damage. No one wants to be exposed to ionising radiation.

So why is such a weapon being used, if this is the case? The answer is that DU is employed because the weapons are astoundingly successful and have revolutionised warfare, rendering the tank and its armour useless (Plates 18, 31). It also allows missiles to penetrate armoured bunkers. In addition, and perhaps most important, its use represents a route for the nuclear industry to rid itself of a waste product, which would otherwise be expensive to dispose of. But the downside is that the material clearly represents a radiation hazard that is indiscriminate: battlefields are going to be contaminated and civilian populations are going to be exposed. The stuff disperses over huge distances so we are all going to be exposed. There is an up-side and a down-side. The war will be won but the method will be illegal within contemporary accepted moral arguments. Human rights will be infringed by a randomly dispersed and thus indiscriminate radioactive weapon of mass destruction. This is clearly a war crime. The UN have judged it so.

Let us try to fit the dispersion of Depleted Uranium into the perspective of the other sources of nuclear pollution I have discussed. I remind you that in terms of disintegrating atoms, radioactivity is measured in Bequerels. One Bequerel represents one disintegration per second. This is a reasonable way of quantifying amounts of radioactivity. The average Natural Uranium content of soil is about 10-20 Bequerels per kilogram, including all the Uranium isotopes. Most people excrete less than 0.01mBq (0.00001Bq) per litre of urine as a result of absorption of natural Uranium in food they eat. (This tiny quantity is also called 10 nano Bequerels, nBq). Pure Depleted Uranium contains about 12,400,000Bq of U-238 per kilogram and, in Kosovo, some soil samples analysed by the United Nations

Environment Program (UNEP) contained 250,000Bq/kg (UNEP 2001, Annex). The 350 tonnes of DU used in the first Gulf War represents 4.3 TBq (4.3 x 10^{12} Bq) of Uranium alpha activity (13.0 x 10^{12} if the radioactive beta emitting daughter isotopes are included - more of these below). If researcher Dai Williams (2003) is correct and about 1700 tonnes were used in the latest Iraq war, then that represents 63 TBq of activity dispersed mainly into a populated area of perhaps 100km^2. This gives a mean density of deposition of radioactivity of 630,000Bq/m^2. These sums are instructive and are collected together in Table 17.3 1.

These activity comparisons are given just to get some feel for the amounts of radioactivity involved, and to show that the dispersion of Uranium in various recent battlefields is not trivial, as the military and some politicians regularly imply. But the comparisons are slightly misleading because we are not dealing with the same isotopes as were released by weapons fallout, which is composed of hotter alpha, beta and gamma emitters mainly in atomic or molecular forms. Battlefield DU fallout is in the form of microscopic alpha and beta emitting massive particles. That is to say, there are actually small particles made up entirely of Uranium Oxide, like flecks of dust, the kind of thing you see scattering light in the room when the sun shines through the window. U-238 is an alpha emitter. The U-238 daughters, Protoactinium-234m and Thorium-234 are beta emitters. Having short half-lives, they are in equilibrium and therefore have the same level of activity in a sample of DU. In an area contaminated by DU it is the beta radiation that is detected because it has a range in air of about 30cm unlike the alpha particles which are very short range.

We can find a better comparison for DU. As an alpha emitter and long-lived environmental particle, battlefield DU smoke is more comparable with Plutonium-239 particles from the sea. This, as I have already discussed in this book, is a material released by Sellafield and a major contaminant of the Irish Sea. Plutonium in the environment is also in the form of micron sized oxide particles.

Table 17.3.1. Mean density of deposition of radioactivity from DU in the two Gulf Wars and Kosovo including decays from U-238 and beta daughters Pa-234m and Th-234 compared with other radioactive contamination.

Event	Activity released or estimated deposited	Mean activity density Bq per square metre (area)
10 tons of DU in Kosovo	0.37TBq	3700*
350 tons of DU in Iraq 1	13 TBq	130,000 (into 100 km^2)
1700 tons of DU in Iraq 2	63TBq	630,000 (into 100 km^2)
Global weapons fallout Strontium-90 (Sr-90) Northern Hemisphere lat. 50-60deg (UNSCEAR, 2000)	73.9PBq	460
Chernobyl 30km Exclusion Zone *measured* Sr-90 (IAEA)		37,000 to more than 111,000
UK North Wales Radioactive Sheep restrictions *measured* Caesium-137 (Cs-137)		15,000 to 30,000
UNSCEAR definition of contaminated area. (Cs-137)		> 37,000
Irish Sea cumulative Plutonium from Sellafield 1952-1996 [Busby, 1995]	1350TBq	20,000

* *I measured 4000Bq/kg in Gjakove, Western Kosovo, in Jan 2001 in a car park, but these values are averages based on an assumption about the area into which the material has been dispersed.*

Like DU, these Plutonium Oxide particles are also long-lived and mobile. As I have already shown, Plutonium from Sellafield has been measured in autopsy specimens across the UK, in sheep droppings on the east coast of England 100 km from Sellafield at the same latitude and even in the teeth of children up to 200 km from the site in southeast England. Both Uranium-238 and Plutonium-239 are alpha emitters, although Plutonium has no beta emitting daughter isotopes in secular equilibrium. U-238 has a very long half-life, 4500 million years, so owing to its much shorter half life of 24,100 years; the specific activity of Pu-239 is far greater. It is 2.3TBq/kg. But this means that 350 tons of DU (or 4.30TBq of U-238) is equivalent in activity to about 2 kg of Plutonium-239. What would governments of the world say to a war in which one army caused the intentional scattering of 2kg of Plutonium-239 over a populated area? What would the ethicists and moral philosophers say? Or ordinary members of the public? What would happen in New York or in London if 2kg of Plutonium-239 was dispersed among the public? The emergency services are geared up in the UK to evacuate whole cities if such a 'dirty bomb' was exploded by terrorists. Actually, in terms of health deficit, what has been done in Iraq and Kosovo, possibly also in Afghanistan is much worse. (This has now been extended to Lebanon and Palestine, where Israel is using depleted Uranium shells and possibly DU tipped missiles, supplied by the United States of America, routed via Britain). Nothing is said by the regulatory authorities. Worse than this: they develop models and enrol scientists in an attempt to minimise any perception of harm and routinely deny or marginalize evidence that shows that the use of DU has had major and serious effects. I compare U-238 and Pu-239 in Table 17.3.2.

Table 17.3.2 Comparing Plutonium-239 and Uranium-238 in the environment

	Uranium-238	**Plutonium-239**
Environmental form	0.1-2μ oxide particles	0.1-2μ oxide particles
Density of material $g.cm^{-3}$	(UO_2) 10.9;(U_3O_8) 8.3	(PuO_2) 11.46
Solubility	Insoluble	Insoluble
Environmental Longevity	Long lived	Long lived
Main radioactive emissions	Alpha + beta + beta	Alpha
Alpha particle energy	4.19MeV	5.15MeV
Half life	4.51 billion y	24400y
Specific activity	37.2MBq/kg ($\alpha + \beta$)	2.3TBq/kg (α)
Main present contamination source	DU	Fuel reprocessing e.g. Sellafield
Mass for equal activity	175 tons	1kg

I have compared Plutonium and weapons fallout with DU to demonstrate that we are dealing with the same problem, the health effects of low level exposure to radioactive substances that irradiate our bodies from the inside.

As you now know, the weapons fallout and other pollution from nuclear sites like Sellafield has been responsible for the present cancer epidemic, the one that everyone has experienced. It has been a major project of the nuclear military complex, and for governments who have been involved in releases of radioactivity, to cover up the link between these exposures and cancer or other ill health. This is why all these committees are controlled and steered by the same people. Recognition that DU caused cancer, leukaemia or lymphoma at the doses experienced by those who were contaminated after its use would lead to inevitable recognition that the weapons fallout substances, the Strontiums and Plutoniums and Caesiums also caused cancer, leukaemia and lymphoma. The reverse is also true. Recognition of the cause of the Sellafield leukaemia/lymphoma cluster would lead to reassessing the risk models to the point where it would be clear that DU would have serious health effects. This is the origin of a massive cover up which extends to the cancer registries and the cancer research organisations.

I want to briefly consider the DU case under four headings. They are:

- The nature and dispersion of DU and its routes for human contamination.
- Theoretical radiation biology effects and science.
- Evidence of harm at the cellular level.
- Evidence of harm from epidemiology.

Particle doses and hot coals

To recapitulate, the ICRP model is the presently accepted risk model for radiation and health. It is based on the idea that radiation is external to the body. Examples of external radiation exposures are medical X-rays and gamma rays from atom bombs. The ICRP model bases the amount of ill health produced by doses of radiation of different sizes on a large study of the Hiroshima survivors. These people received a very large dose and some of them were incinerated. But among those that were not, some of them developed cancer much later on. The ICRP model relates the numbers of cancer to the large dose they received and argues that at half this dose there should be half the cancers and so forth. So, if the dose is very small there are very few cancers. The problem is that this model is not strictly applicable to internal radiation. Absorbed dose, in Grays or Sieverts or rads or rems is measured as energy per unit mass. Therefore it would not distinguish between a man warming himself in front of a fire and the same man eating a hot coal. The average energy per unit mass is the same. This is a good analogy for why the DU or plutonium situation is wrongly modelled. In the case of DU particles the decay energy is all absorbed in the local cells. So one single particle will give a big dose to the local cells and no dose to the rest of the body. The ICRP will say that the dose is very small, but because the alpha decay range is small, the dose to the cells nearby, is very large. This is a trick and I show how it is done for a 2-micron diameter particle of DU trapped in the lymphatic system of a person who inhaled it.

The calculation in Table 17.3.3 shows the dose to the tissue within range of the particle alpha decays and the dose to (a) the whole body and (b) the lymphatic system that NRPB and ICRP would calculate. [see e.g. NRPB, R-276 p 86 1995) The NRPB reference is to actual calculations made by NRPB on the doses from Plutonium particles to the public near Sellafield. Two things are immediately apparent. The cells close to the particle receive a significant dose and they also suffer an enhanced risk of receiving multiple tracks. The dose calculated by the ICRP model is vanishingly small, so it is easy to see how the Royal Society, the Ministry of Defence, the United Nations, the IAEA/ WHO say that DU cannot cause any cancer.

Table 17.3.3. Doses to local tissue within range of a 2-micrometer particle of DU compared with doses calculated using the ICRP model and an NRPB version of it.

	Value	**Comment**
Uranium oxide U_3O_8		
Density	8.6	
Decay energy/Bq	4.45MeV = 7.12×10^{-13}J	
Particle diameter	2μ (2×10^{-4}cm)	Common size
U-238 mass in particle	3.05×10^{-11}g	
Particle activity	3.79×10^{-7} Bq	
Mass of 30μ radius sphere of tissue (ρ= 1)	1.13×10^{-10}kg	
Dose to this tissue per Bq	6.3mGy	
Equivalent dose	126mGy	
Hits to tissue per day	0.03 α̃ and .06 β-tracks per day	11 α̃ tracks per year and 22β̃ tracks
Equivalent dose to this tissue per day	4.12mSv	Or 1500mSv per year
NRPB calculated equivalent dose to 'lymphatic system' per day	5.8×10^{-11}mSv (effectively no tracks)	*Assumes 8kg or 2.1×10^{-8}mSv per year
ICRP calculated equivalent dose to 'lymphatic system' per day.	5.8×10^{-10}mSv (effectively no tracks)	**Assumes lymphatic system as 800g (ICRP) 2.1×10^{-7}mSv per year
ICRP calculated dose to tracheobronchial lymph nodes per day	3.1×10^{-8}mSv (effectively no tracks)	**TBN Mass = 15g 1.1×10^{-5} mSv per year

**for lymphatic system modelled as lymph nodes, liver, spleen, kidneys, pancreas, uterus, thymus, thyroid, stomach, both intestines, colon, red bone marrow and cells on bone surfaces [NRPB, 1995]*

*** Values from ICRP standard man [ICRP23, 1975]*

Borrowing radiation energy from natural background: photoelectron amplification

I believe that there is a second source of error here and although it is difficult to quantify I am engaged in laboratory experiments to examine this. I mentioned it in Chapter 2 but will repeat it here since it is very relevant to the explanation of the anomalous health effects of Uranium. The absorption of gamma radiation and X-rays, the electromagnetic component of ionising radiation, is different for different substances. We all know that lead absorbs radiation and can be used as a shield. The reason for this is that the radiation is absorbed by the electrons, and a substance with a high density of electrons absorbs more radiation. There is a physical law that has been established to predict this effect. It is that the absorption is proportional to the fourth power of the Atomic Number of an element. The Atomic Number, Z, is the number of electrons orbiting the nucleus. It is the number given to the element in the Periodic Table, thus Hydrogen is 1 (one electron) and Helium 2 (two electrons), Lithium 3 (three electrons) and so forth. The mean atomic number of DNA is about 5.5 (the average weighted atomic number of the elements in DNA). The Atomic Number of Uranium is 92. Lead is 82, Mercury is 80. Both the latter are seen as 'heavy metal poisons' but no one has explained what the mechanisms of 'heavy metal poisoning' is. The ratio of the fourth power of 92 to the fourth power of 5.5 is 92^4 divided by 5.5^4 which is 71639296/915 = 78288. This represents the relative likelihood of absorption of a gamma ray by a Uranium atom relative to DNA, i.e. almost 80 thousand times more.

Now it turns out that Uranium binds very, very strongly to DNA. DNA has a very high affinity for Uranium in the form that the Uranium is in the body, the compound ion 'Uranyl' or UO_2^{++} . This has been known since the 1960s when Uranium was being used as a DNA stain in electron microscopy (Huxley and Zubay, 1961 also Busby 2005a and b for references). By the 1990s the affinity constant had been measured and was found to be greater than 10^{10} (Neilsen et al 1992). This means that at concentrations in the body of less than a tenth of a microgram of Uranium per litre, the Uranium is mostly on the DNA.

When the Uranium atom on the DNA absorbs a gamma ray, it converts the energy to a photoelectron or to several photoelectrons. These photoelectrons are the same as beta particles or auger electrons and can ionise the tissue elements in exactly the same way. So you can see that the Uranium has acted as a magnet for the natural background gamma rays and focused their energy on to the DNA. This, I believe, is a significant reason for the anomalous radiobiological effects of uranium and, for that matter, the toxicity of other heavy metals (Busby 2005a, 2005b).

The effect will also of course be there for the uranium oxide particles. These will intercept natural background gamma rays and the re-scattered and lower energy electromagnetic radiations from Compton and other processes and act as a secondary photoelectron source for natural background, focussing into points in the body like a magnifying glass focuses the sun. I met a scientist from Italy, Antonia Gatti who was looking at tumours with an electron microscope. She found particles of bismuth and other metals in many tumours. She argued that it was not the uranium from the battlefields but just the dust that caused high levels of internal particles and these produced irritation and inflammation. Bismuth has an atomic number of 83.

Particle environmental dispersion

The military and other authorities have dismissed the possibility of widespread dispersion of DU particles. The US Department of Defence papers make this claim but have not been able to justify it. The particles of less than 2μ diameter are easily resuspended by wind or by electrostatic repulsion in the earth's electric field. In addition they become charged by photoelectric effects owing to the low Uranium work function (see above) and these charges would assist their resuspension, although no experiments have been done to my knowledge. I discovered DU dust in western Kosovo one year after the war. It was in road dust at several sites under conditions where it was clear that the material had been washed out by snow. In addition the ratio of activity of the beta emitting daughter isotopes to the parent Uranium-238 showed that the U-238 was being preferentially resuspended. I gave this information to the Royal Society but their experts said that mathematical models showed that DU particles could not be resuspended and would remain where the targets were, a few metres from the site of impact. I gave a paper on this at a meeting organised in the European Parliament on DU. At this meeting I asked the head of UNEP, Dr Snihs, why UNEP had not examined air filters in their November 2001 survey of Kosovo. He stated that the DU would not widely disperse and would not be found in the air so there was no need. However, I note that UNEP did deploy air-measuring equipment later in Bosnia and Montenegro. This equipment detected DU in the air. The UNEP response was that the material had been resuspended by their disturbing of the soil. The UNEP Kosovo report tabulated the presence of DU in 46% of all the samples they measured but the tables were not given to the Press at the launch of the report in Geneva and the executive summary says *there is no widespread dispersion of DU.* If you read the report closely, their definition of '*widespread dispersion of DU',* was based on what they assume are the health effects (i.e. none) and not the absolute quantity in grams – i.e. considerable– and this subtle misdirection was, of course, missed by the journalists. Here again is an example of spinning a report. Since the results tables were not given out (and have since disappeared from the report on the website) no one was able to argue the point. For those who are interested, I have a copy of the UNEP Kosovo tables and have written a critique of the whole way the results were presented. The study also showed the presence of DU particles larger than 0.2μ in a rainwater pond in Vranovac (Busby 2001).

I also found widespread DU in southern Iraq when I visited there in September 2000, or rather; I found areas of high beta counts on the ground in the area of the 'Mother of All Battles' and saw a few A10 penetrators lying on the ground also. In Iraq, I found significantly higher alpha activity in the air in this area. Unfortunately, the Iraqi authorities would not let me remove any samples.

Aldermaston evidence of global dispersion

In 2005 I decided to follow up a request I had made in 2004 to the Atomic Weapons Establishment at Aldermaston for their annual data on Uranium in the filters they deploy around the site. I wanted to look at the trend in uranium in the filters to see if any of the Uranium from the use by the US in the 2nd Gulf war had made it all the way to England. By 2003, it had been widely suspected, on the basis of Patents for weapons researched on the internet by Dai Williams (see www.eoslifework.co.uk) that the US were putting large amounts of Uranium into bunker Busting bombs and hard target Cruise Missiles (GAAA 2004). AWE had ignored my letter, but in January 2005 the Freedom of Information Act became law in the UK. The data appeared but significantly, perhaps, what was missing was the six week period of the Gulf War. So I reapplied, and it duly turned up, this time from a different organisation based in Bristol. Saoirse painstakingly copied it into a database and we began to analyse the trends (Plate 34). AWE have, as required by law, measured uranium in filters deployed both close to their site in Berkshire and as far afield as Reading and Basingstoke since 1990. The readings are made every two weeks. We looked at the data from 2001 to 2004. Over this period there was only one clear excession, or divergence from the normal background level. This was for the six week period of the 2nd Gulf war. The Uranium went up in all the filters both onsite and offsite at the beginning of the war, and they came back to normal at the end of the war. The effect was statistically significant. The airflow was from Iraq to the UK over the period and we used the USA NOAA computer model to prove this. So this is proof that the particles are mobile. It surprised us that they were as mobile as this, but the mean diameter of these particles is about a tenth of a micron: the material is effectively a gas (Although the mean diameter is about 0.1μ , sizes range from nanometres up to around 2-5μ in diameter (Glissmeyer and Mishima 1978, Glissmeyer et al 1985). I calculated that over the six week period, an adult in Reading would have inhaled three million particles. The air route was north from Iraq and over southern Europe to feed into an anticyclone over the UK. The details can be seen in our paper, which was published and received considerable media interest (Busby and Morgan 2006).The trend in uranium in the filters in Aldermaston is shown in Table 17.3.1.

Table 17.3.1 Trend in Uranium in High Volume Air sampler filters deployed around the Atomic Weapons Establishment, Aldermaston from 2000 to 2004. Each plot represents a different filter location, the main peak is in Reading, some 12km away from the site and the period of the excession exactly coincided with the period of the bombing (see also Plate 34).

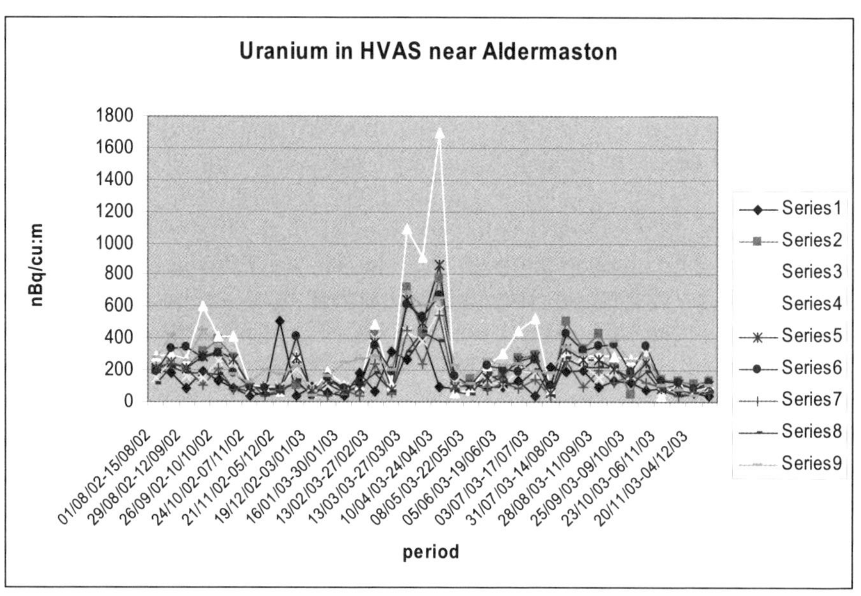

Human contamination and biokinetics

Shortly after my visit to Kosovo in January 2001, Prof Nic Priest visited the same region with BBC Scotland and took urine samples from some 20 people including his BBC cameraman. Priest has access to sophisticated mass spectrometry equipment and can measure Uranium isotope ratios in urine. He found that all the urine samples were contaminated, including the cameraman Donald Macleod who had only been there for five days. These results have now been published (Schroeder *et al*, 2003) and they show conclusively that the people in the area are contaminated with DU. We also have the results of measurements on the urine of Gulf War veterans by at least three teams. All show the presence of DU in the urine some ten years after the exposure.

The only way that this could happen is that there remains in these people some depot or store of DU which is slowly leaching out. At the time of the Royal Society's first report the biokinetic models of DU were based on the studies of natural Uranium in animals. It was conceded that DU particles were extremely insoluble and had a very long half-life in the body after inhalation. Recent studies

[Ansoborlo *et al*, 2001, Royal Society 2002] show half lives for the inhaled ceramic U_3O_8 and UO_2 particles to be of the order of 5000 days or 13 years.

If this is so, then the amount excreted per day in the 11th year after the initial loading can be determined from an exponential decay equation such as:

$$M = M_0[\exp(-0.693t_d/T_{1/2})-\exp(-0.693(t_d+1)/T_{1/2})$$

This gives a fraction of 0.03 of the initial loading being lost in the 11th year and a daily excretion of 8 x 10^{-5} (divide by 365) of the initial loading. So for an initial loading of 5mg, assuming a 10% translocation through lung and a 50% insoluble fraction there should be about 20ng a day of DU excreted in the urine if this half life is correct. However, it is not at all clear that there may not be material that has a very much longer half life, or more likely that with such high levels of insolubility the concept of half life breaks down and there remains DU trapped in certain tissue for the lifespan of the individual, which does not relate to the measured concentration in the urine. If, for example, 20% of the initial translocated material were trapped in the tracheobronchial lymph nodes and entirely inaccessible to dissolution and transfer to the greater system, this would leave 100μg of DU in an organ with a mass of a few grams irradiating cells over a period of ten or more years. We can calculate that this represents 2 x 10^9 particles of 0.2μ diameter, about one particle for each cell in the lymph nodes. For, even if the DU were trapped, the photoelectrons and beta or alpha particles would still cause damage to DNA in cells which were local to the trapped material. And uncertainties in the rate equations as applied to urine measurements over the periods involved in animal studies (mice live less than two years) would easily accommodate such a situation, so we should be cautious about using the results of urine tests to work back to initial contamination or its effects.

For 1 μ diameter DU particles biokinetic models employed by the Royal Society based on the ICRP66 human respiratory tract model suggest that 10 years after inhalation there would be a daily excretion of about 10^{-7} of the original loading, but I have been unable to replicate their calculations. (Royal Society 2001).

Since levels of 20ng have been reported for UK Gulf veterans some 10 years after their contamination, the value of 5mg may be a reasonable assumption for their initial contamination on the bases of my calculations.

Chromosome aberrations in Gulf Vets

The question of the levels of exposure and the level of resultant damage has been informed by an important set of measurements of chromosome aberrations in the peripheral lymphocytes of a group of UK Gulf War veterans, organised by Albrecht Schott. These results have now been published [Schroeder *et al* 2003]. It is possible to compare the levels of chromosome damage with the many earlier studies which related chromosome damage to earlier radiation exposure and conclude that the veterans received between 50 and 200 mSv. I have used a recent review of the relationship between chromosome damage and dose to back calculate [Hoffmann and Schmitz Feuerhake 1999]. The best value for the fraction of dicentric chromosomes (DiC) per cell per mGy obtained by regression is 5.21×10^{-5}. The Gulf veterans group showed a mean fraction of 0.0027 DiCs compared with 0.0005 in the controls. This suggests a mean dose for the group of 50mGy in the previous year, which I assume, must be from the 50% of the DU still in their system. For a relatively high 50mg initial loading in 1991 and 5mg getting through the lung we can calculate the mean ICRP dose to the 800g lymphatic system in the two years prior to the chromosome test.

It is vanishingly small: about 1.4×10^{-3}μGray. This suggests an enhancement of the radiation effect of about 500,000. (100,000 is the value that Tamplin calculated in 1971 for the enhancement of effects from hot particles).

On the other hand, comparisons with chromosome aberration studies of Chernobyl NPP workers who had film badges and therefore had recorded external doses [Shevchenko *et al* 1996] suggest more like 500mSv.

A value for particle dose effectiveness enhancement of 1000-2000 was adopted by the ECRR for their weighting factor for particulate DU enhancement in the recent 2003 report, but this may be a conservative value. Something seems to be going on here that is not adequately captured in present models and it may be that the ideas about scattering and secondary effects from background exposures need to be examined more closely. Such experiments are easy to perform and I am conducting some at present here in Aberystywth. However, these results do suggest that there should be increases in somatic genetic and heritable genetic damage and cancer in such individuals. Since the doses are mainly to the lymphatic system, some form of leukaemia or lymphoma would be the first evidence of such an effect.

Epidemiology from Iraq

I was invited to Iraq in 2000 and met with senior health officials in Baghdad and Basra. I examined cancer statistics from the Iraq cancer registry. There were sharp increases in leukaemia and lymphoma indicated, particularly in children born around the time of the 1991 war. The Iraqis have been accused of making up their cancer figures. However, there are pieces of data that they would not have thought of making up. The main problem with cancer data epidemiology is the population base. After a war, people are killed and move about the country; there are massive population upheavals. But you can still look at the cancer numbers and assume they are a sample from an unknown population. Then you can make comparisons within the sample. For example, we can look at the numbers of cases of childhood cancer in the period 1995-1999 [Iraqi Cancer Registry, Baghdad 1999]. I show some data in Table 17.3.4 for male children, where I compare the numbers of cancer cases with those expected on the basis of the England and Wales rates for the same cancers and in Table 17.3.5 show the relative risk in the war birth cohort, those aged 5-9 in 1995-99. This calculation uses the rates in England and Wales to predict the expected numbers of cases in each age group if the Iraqi children had the same rates as the England and Wales children.

Table 17.3.4 Male childhood cancer in Iraq, 1995-1999 (Source; Iraqi cancer registry, 1999)

Cancer site	**Male 0-4** Iraq, numbers *England and Wales* **numbers (rates)*	**Male5-9** Iraq, numbers *England and Wales* **numbers (rates)*	**Male10-14** Iraq, numbers *England and Wales* **numbers (rates)*
Lymphatic Leukaemia	69 *69 (7.1)*	112 *31 (3.2)*	70 *25 (2.6)*
Non Hodgkin's lymphoma	58 *58 (1.0)*	82 *75 (1.3)*	53 *75 (1.3)*
Hodgkin's Disease	7 *7 (0.3)*	52 *12 (0.5)*	42 *11 (1.5)*
All Cancer	279 279 (19.8)	399 171 (12.2)	354 158 (11.2)

Table 17.3.5 Relative risk of leukaemia, lymphoma and all cancers in the male children born during, or just after, the Gulf War in Iraq.

	Observed	**Expected**	**Relative Risk (p)**
Lymphatic leukaemia	112	31	3.6 (<0.0001)
Non Hodgkin's lymphoma	82	75	1.09
Hodgkin's disease	52	12	4.3 (<0.0001)
All cancer	399	171	2.3 (<0.0001)

We can conclude that childhood cancer increased in the war birth cohort. The effect was driven by lymphatic leukaemia and Hodgkin's disease, which is a cancer of the lymphatic system. As to the accusations of inventing the data to make a political point, there would be more mileage in making all the leukaemia numbers large immediately after the war. In fact, this was not done, although figures for different districts show a correlation in increased adult leukaemia with the areas where DU was mostly used.

Epidemiology in Kosovo: The Italian Kosovo Study
The question of whether there has been an increase in leukaemia/lymphoma or other cancers in occupants of or peacekeepers deployed in the Balkans has been a source of argument of a similar order and type as the question of increases in leukaemia/lymphoma and birth defects in Iraq. In the case of the Balkans, there is very little hard evidence (e.g. cancer registry data) which is available for independent scrutiny, and indeed some of the problems associated with the kinds of population movements that follow a major conflict would make such analyses very difficult. There was been a leak of a table of cancer incidence in Sarajevo from the cancer registry there which suggests a more than 10-fold increase in leukaemia and lymphoma even allowing for a doubling in the base population. This information was given to the Royal Society as evidence last year but was not included in their report or followed up by them [Busby 2002]. In addition, there has been anecdotal evidence of increases in leukaemia/lymphoma in the Italian and Portuguese peacekeepers and these have led to misleading statements from the authorities. Recently, in a letter to Caroline Lucas, MEP, a UK government minister, Dr Lewis Moonie, suggested that 42 leukaemia deaths per 100,000 peacekeepers was a reasonable sum and that, therefore, the handful of deaths observed should be seen as a normal situation. However, Moonie should certainly know better than to try on this rather silly attempt to blind us with numbers. It was easy to show that the 42 was a ridiculously incorrect number based on people of all ages and that the true figure (based on the actual age group of 20-40) defined a significant excess risk of about 1.5 deaths in every 100,000 persons.

In January 2001 Nippon TV, who took me to Kosovo, were told that there were 7 leukaemia deaths in Italian Kosovan peacekeepers (50,000) and, more recently, Eddie Goncalves, a journalist in Portugal, reported 5 deaths from leukaemia in the Portuguese Kosovan peacekeepers (5 deaths in 10,000 with two in the 20-30 age group). Thus in those groups we observe 12 leukaemia deaths where 0.9 are expected, a relative risk of 13. Even if we use a two-year period since the war the Relative Risk is still 6.5.

But in May 2001 the Italians commissioned a proper epidemiological study of their peacekeepers from Kosovo and Sarajevo [Italian report, 2001]. The study of 39,491 persons found a significant excess risk from Lymphoma, particularly Hodgkin's. The results are shown in Table 17.3.6.

Table 17.3. 6. Expected and observed numbers of lymphoma cases in Italian DU study group with statistical significance based on cumulative Poisson probability.

Disease	Expected	Observed	Risk Ratio	Poisson p-value
Non Hodgkin	4.1	4	0.97	NS
Hodgkin	3.38	10	2.95	0.003
Lymphoma	7.48	14	1.87	0.02

I obtained this study through the Italian Greens and used the data given to calculate the true relative risk after allowing for the 'healthy worker effect'. I could use the ratio of lymphoma to all cancers to show that the true excess risk was RR = 7.5. So the Italian veterans had a 7.5-fold excess of lymphoma, mainly Hodgkin's disease. The interesting aspect was that the disease had emerged a very short time after the exposure - a year or two later. I gave a paper on this to the Ministry of Defence DUOB.

Cancer in the UK Gulf Veterans

The UK government have been very poor at examining the health effects of DU. But various questions have been asked in Parliament by individual MPs and the Gulf Vets themselves and non-Governmental Organisations, like the Low Level Radiation Campaign, have put pressure on the Ministers to investigate risk. The MoD set up a Gulf Veterans Illness Unit and these people produced a report in November 2002, which compared deaths in all Gulf Veterans compared with deaths in a matched control group who were not deployed in the Gulf. Results show that there were 19 deaths from leukaemia and lymphoma combined, compared with 11 in the control group.

This is a statistically significant finding (p = 0.018) but nothing was said about it, and my attempts to obtain a breakdown by type of cancer have so far failed.

The US Department of Defence.

Because this book, in part, discusses the ways in which the establishment attempts to dismiss concerns about radiation, I will now turn to a widely quoted report about DU in the Balkans. This is the US Department of Defence report, *Depleted Uranium Environmental Surveillance in the Balkans* [US DoD, 2001]. The UK government Home Office uses this report to justify their own position on repatriating refugees to areas of Kosovo where DU was used and, as a result of various appeals cases, I have had to study the DoD report quite closely. I produced a critique for the Appeals Tribunal in 2002 [Busby, 2002]. The DoD document makes two assertions and bases these on 83 references, apparently to independent scientific work. The assertions are:

- The studies undertaken on DU in Kosovo have not detected any significant levels of DU.
- Studies have not shown any significant risk to health of the population of the province from the presence of DU.

Of course, both of these statements are incorrect. But all I wish to observe here is that the references on which the DoD report is based are almost all references to a NATO website or other NATO reports. I show the distribution of the sources of the conclusions of the DoD report in Table 17.3.7.

Table 17.3.7 Distribution of the sources of the conclusions about DU in the Balkans: Number of citations of specific sources in the 2001 Department of Defence report on DU in the Balkans [USDoD, 2001].

Source	Number of citations in DoD
NATO website	18
NATO report AHCDU-N (2001)38, April 3rd 2001	30
NATO letter IMSM-164-01, March 5th 2001	15
Royal Society Report, May 22nd 2001	4
UNEP environmental reports, Oct 1999, May 2001	3
WHO, DU report, April 2001	6
EC Article 31 group, March 6 2001	1
Available independent relevant studies	1
Peer reviewed studies	None

My conclusions are that the position taken by the establishment is not based on science, but on wishful thinking, or less charitably, on cover up. The NATO website and other NATO documents are reports of NATO meetings where everyone agreed that there was no problem. These positions were informed by a few meetings where military investigations agreed there were no problems. Other reports of the results of environmental surveys found no DU. This was probably because they were deploying Geiger Counters that only detect gamma rays. Later on, when there were some discoveries of DU made by the second UNEP survey, the statement 'no widespread dispersion of DU' was changed to, 'no widespread dispersion of DU at levels that would constitute a health risk'. And of course, these levels are those predicted by the ICRP risk models.

The authorities response: COMARE, NRPB, UNEP, WHO, The Royal Society, European Union Article 31 Group.

By now you will be able to anticipate this. These organisations all agree with each other that there is no health consequences from exposure to DU. They have all produced reports stating this. All of these reports are 'armchair' reports, based on the health model of the ICRP. None of them have used scientific induction to look at the health of people who are exposed and work backwards to the exposures. Instead they look at the cancer yield in the Hiroshima survivors and say that, at the doses imparted by the DU, there can be no ill health. This is not science, as I argued in my first paper for the Royal Society (Busby 2001). Scientific method is based on induction. The deductive conclusion about DU and health is similar to the deductive conclusion that the Sellafield leukaemia cluster is not caused by radiation from Sellafield. Both arguments are scientifically bankrupt.

The second Gulf war: Cancer in Basra Hospital, Iraq, 2003

I leave this issue with some new data supplied to me by Dr Jawad Kadhim Al Ali MRCP Consultant physician and oncologist, Oncology Center, Basra Hospital, Iraq (email: Jawadalali44@yahoo.com). I met Dr Al Ali in Hamburg in 2004; A short, sad-faced and cynical man (as well he might be) who has been travelling around Europe showing his evidence of the terrible effects of DU in his city, Basra. I visited Basra in 2000 and sat on the banks of the Shat al Arab, looking over the beautiful waters. I met a shoeshine boy and gave him a dollar (which probably kept him and his family for some weeks) and we talked. I wonder if that little boy was killed in the bombing recently. Jawad Al Ali is the cancer specialist at the Basra hospital and was trained in the UK. His observations included the following extremely rare events:

1. Familial clustering of cancer. More than one case of cancer in a single family in 58 cases.
2. Two different cancers in 9 patients.
3. Triple cancer in one patient.
4. Change in the age of cancer expression with cancer normally seen in the old being diagnosed in younger people.
5. Increased incidence of congenital anomalies, which he puts down to radiation exposure of pregnant women by DU.

Table 17.3.7 Incidence of malignant disease among children (0-14) in Basra

Site	1990	1993	1994	1995	1996	1997
Leukaemia	15	15	14	25	24	24
Lymphoma	2	4	1	5	8	8
Brain	1	4	3	2	5	6
neuroblastoma	0	0	0	0	0	3
Wilm's tumour	1	3	2	4	1	0
Others	0	1	1	0	0	2
All	19	27	21	36	38	43

Site	1998	1999	2000	2001	2002
Leukaemia	24	30	60	70	85
Lymphoma	9	19	13	18	35
Brain	2	2	3	3	7
neuroblastoma	4	6	3	2	12
Wilm's tumour	0	3	0	0	6
Others	3	5	13	7	15
All	42	65	92	100	160

Table 17.3.9 Incidence rate of malignant disease among children in Basra from 1993-1998 compared with 1990

Year	Population 0-14	cases	Rate per 100,000	Indexed to 1990
1990	476549	19	3.98	1.0
1993	518929	27	5.2	1.3
1994	533877	21	3.93	0.98
1995	459234	36	7.83	1.97
1996	565055	38	6.72	1.68
1997	581332	42	7.22	1.8
1998	627754	42	6.69	1.7
1999	605045	65	10.7	2.7
2000	604015	92	13.1	3.3
2001	792017	100	12.6	3.2
2002	863909	160	18.5	4.6

Conclusions
What can I say? By now, despite the cries of anguish and the deaths caused through cancer and the congenital malformations in Iraq, in Afghanistan, in Kosovo and Bosnia and in the veterans themselves - their own people, consecutive U.S administrations have been intent on contaminating the world with radioactive material. As Gofman pointed out long ago, the Nuclear Industry is conducting a war against humanity. As the civilian wing, the Sellafields, and Hanfords and La Hagues kill children in their own countries, the military kill the innocent in the rest of the world. None of this is entirely location-specific anyway. The Sellafield isotopes drift over to northern (and southern) Norway; the Nevada test material is found in Moscow; Chernobyl material kills babies in Wales; DU kills babies in Iraq and the particles arrive in the UK at Aldermaston, killing people on the way; the French tests kill babies in the Pacific; the English tests kill babies in Australia. Where will it end? Who can stop it? Well, I think that collectively we can. We, the people.

17.4 Wolves of Water

Look at the little girl on the cover. Gemma D'Arcy. Isn't she beautiful? I mean, wasn't she beautiful? Read about her short life in the book by Rob Edwards, *Still Fighting For Gemma.* Now multiply her by thousands, by millions. All the needless sorrow. What about the adults, living near the Irish Sea. What about the increases in cancer? What is to be done? Here is the end and conclusion of my book, my message to the planet. We have to take the matter into our own hands. We have to build our own institutions, which we can trust. We have to communicate with each other - and scientists with the public directly. It is no good assuming that those who govern us, those who work in industry and assess the effects of industry, will somehow become accessible to our arguments and will see the results of their processes. They will not. I have tried to talk to these people. The dialogue does not work. Their beliefs are fixed. They cannot afford to believe that what they have been engaged in is wrong, has killed children. They will never accept it. Building bridges is not possible. We have to make our own measurements, using our own instruments, however primitive. The Price of Freedom is Eternal Vigilance. Who said that? Lenin? Mao? Robespierre? It was Thomas Jefferson.

I came to much the same conclusion in *Wings of Death*. But since then, little has happened. There was no stampede to set up a real cancer research effort, as I had hoped and suggested in the conclusion. The pink balloons and circulars asking for money are all we still get (Plate 28). *Where there's a Will,* was a recent begging letter form the cancer charity machine that flopped on the floor. We must leave our money when we die for cancer research. They mean research to cure the disease. Not research to identify its cause. (Sir) Richard Peto, the surviving member of the Doll Peto team tells us that there is no environmental cause of cancer: it is a degenerative disease. Business as usual. Indeed, very much Business as Usual.

However, since *Wings of Death* I was helped by some people, the usual people, and through their support and encouragement was able to do what I could to research the issue myself, together with my old friends and the new friends I made. Research was done by single mothers, with little formal scientific training, in between bringing up their children on the dole or scrubbing floors to make ends meet. It was carried out by students living on shoestrings and sleeping in tents in winter, by committed middle-aged activists, serious people, intellectuals with little money, stretching their time to accommodate the work, walking the streets, knocking on doors. This cannot go on. There must be some focus for all this energy and some financial support for such a focus.

Having done the research, the other part of the formula to change the world, is to use the media to inform the public directly. I have always been attacked by the scientific establishment for this approach. But the truth is, no one reads scientific papers in learned journals and, if they do, most people - including the politicians - do not understand them. Then there is the problem of the control of what is published, a control exercised by the referees. If the media won't publish what you discover, then buy a printing press and print it and publish it yourself (Plate19). Use the Internet. If you want to draw attention to something then chain yourself to it and call the TV (Plate 6). If they won't come, take your own video camera and make your own film. Nowadays you can make a DVD and show it, send it round, put it on the Internet. If you can't get the authorities to give you small area cancer data, then collect it yourself from door to door. We have become accustomed to assuming that the State will do it all. We just sit back and watch TV where the State entertains us. Orwell got it wrong; Big Brother is not Watching Us. He doesn't need to. We are all watching Big Brother. And no, the State will not do it all, and our freedoms have been eroded to the point where we are being poisoned through pollution sanctioned by the State.

Through all this activity the message has become plain. We can change the world and refashion it in the image of our desire. We do this with alternative institutions, our own institutions and with our own responses, and by building all our own alternative systems. The European Committee on Radiation Risk was set up and produced its independent report ECRR2003 for less than £6,000. The research done by Green Audit on the cancer near the nuclear site at Bradwell was done for less than £900. The government SAHSU study cost the local health authority £30,000. What I am proposing now is the answer to the general problem of discovering the truth about the environment before it is too late, and letting the public know. This includes truths about all sorts of things, not just cancer. We must found alternative institutions. We must have our own researchers in our own institution examining the numbers and drawing conclusions based on quantitative evidence. In *I Don't Know Much about Science* Molly proposed the formation of oppositional science committees. CERRIE was just one of these and look at the pressure it brought to bear on the belief system. Look at the lengths that were gone to, to cover up the truth. And, in that committee, the alternative scientists (ourselves) were not funded by the system, although we did receive help from the Joseph Rowntree Charitable Trust.

Many years ago, during the time I was first thinking about these problems I had a dream. I really did. In my dream there was a big fence like the one around Harwell. There was a gate in the fence and the gate was fastened with an intricate golden padlock. All the clever people were examining this padlock and trying to open it. They were using everything to open the padlock, to understand the mechanism. All the cleverest thinkers were putting their minds to the problem. What no one had noticed was that the fence was not endless. It was really quite short. All one had to do was walk around it.

We cannot ignore any longer what is happening to the planet, to us all. In *Wolves of Water* MacNeice makes the cynical suggestion:

Come then all of you, come closer, form a circle
Join hands and make believe that joined
Hands will keep away the wolves of water
Who howl along our coast. And it be assumed
That no-one hears them among the talk and laughter.

This is what the State asks of us. The assumption is wrong. The joined hands, all the talk and laughter may continue, may even increase in some hysterical way, fuelled by TV. But this is the masque of the red death. One by one, the circle is broken; a reveller falls to the ground and is silent. There is a telephone call; the police knock on the door; the fateful telegram is delivered. Someone leaves the room of gaiety, white-faced and stricken. The laughter and talk stop for a little and resume; but there are fewer people. Fewer people. As well as the nuclear pollution, there is the genetic modification pollution, the economic pollution, the culture of desire of riches pollution, the culture of power pollution, the culture of cynicism pollution, the Science pollution, the objectivity pollution, and the inexorable filling up of the poor planet with global warming gases to fuel the big fat cars and the gratification culture.

We are living on borrowed time. From who have we borrowed this time? Time to go on holidays in the sun, flying thousands of miles; time to drive our big cars, to eat mangoes in Aberystwyth in winter, to put fresh tropical flowers on our mantelpieces. We have borrowed this time from our children. We have borrowed this time from their children. We are spending the Sellafield leukaemia children's lost lives. We are spending them ourselves as we join hands to keep away the wolves of water that howl along our coast, the Irish Sea Coast, the Somerset coast, the earth coast.

Yuri Bandashevsky, who discovered the Caesium-137 pathology in children after Chernobyl, and who was gaoled by the Belarus authorities for this discovery, put the results and the argument and the data in a pathetic paperback book with a pale blue cover (which was smuggled out to us and which is on my shelf here where I write). This little A5 booklet was printed on a samizdat press, just like the first A5 booklets I printed in 1994 on my little Vickers offset litho machine that was rescued from the skip. I recognize the print problems, the ink bleeds due to a poor water/ink mix. He ended this book with the following plea:

The health condition of the affected population is a disaster, but, being a physician myself, I cannot accept it as hopeless. With all my faith in God and life I appeal to anyone who can influence it: do your best to improve the situation. There is nothing more precious on this planet than life. And we should do everything possible to protect it.

Yu. I . Bandashevsky
Medical and Biological Effects of Radiocaesium
Incorporated into the Human Organism
Minsk: Belrad 2000

We are all the affected population.

Chris Busby
September 2006

References

Admiralty Hydrography Office, (1992) *Admiralty Tidal Stream Atlas for the Irish Sea and Bristol Channel.* Taunton: Hydrographic Office.

Aghamohammadi S and Savage JR (1992) The effect of X-irradiation on cell cycle progression and chromatid aberrations in stimulated human lymphocytes using cohort analysis studies. *Mutat. Res.* 268: 223-30.

Agricultural Research Council, (1958-73) Letcombe Laboratory Annual Reports (London: HMSO).

Airborne Particles Expert Group, (APEG) (1999) Source Apportionment of Airborne Particulate Matter in the United Kingdom (London: DETR).

Al-Achkar W, Sabatier L and Dutrillaux B (1988) Influence of time and cell cycle phase on radiation-induced chromosome lesions. *Ann. Genet.* 31: 87-90.

Alberts B, Bray D, Lewis JG, Raff M, Roberts K and Watson JD (1994) Molecular biology of the cell. New York: Garland

Alexander F E, Cartwright R A, McKinney P A, Ricketts T J, (1990) 'Leukaemia incidence, Social Class and Estuaries: an Ecological Analysis', *Journal of Public Health Medicine* 12(2)109-117.

Andersen H, Moeller T, (1997) Cancerinsidens omkring Barsebaecks Kaernkraftwerk, (Lund: Regionala Tumoerregistret Universitetssjukhuset).

Ansoborlo E, Hodgson A, Stradling GN, Hodgson S, Metevier H, Henge –Napoli MH, Jarvis NS and Birchall A (1998) Exposure implications for Uranium aerosols formed at a new laser enrichment facility: application of the ICRP respiratory tract model. *Radiat. Protect. Dosim.* 79 (1-4) 23-29.

Archer V E, (1987) 'Association of Nuclear Fallout with Leukaemia in the United States', *Archives of Environmental Health*, 42: 263-71.

Armitage P and Doll R (1957) A two stage theory of carcinogenesis in relation to the age distribution of human cancer.' *British Journal of Cancer* 11/2 161-9

Armstrong R, Doll R, (1975) 'Environmental Factors and Cancer Incidence and Mortality in Different Countries with Special Reference to Dietary Practices.' *International Journal of Cancer* 15: 631-717.

Assimakopoulos P, (ed.) (1998) *Survey and Evaluation of Criticisms of Basic Safety Standards for the Protection of Workers and Members of the Public against Ionising Radiations.* Proceedings of the STOA workshop held in Brussels, 5 February 1998 (Brussels: European Commission).

Assinder D J, (1983) 'Behaviour of Plutonium in the intertidal sediments of the eastern Irish sea.' in Ecological aspects of radionuclide release, Special Publication No 3 of the British Ecological Society, Eds P. J. Coughtrey, J. N. B. Bell and T. M. Roberts, 189-197.

Assinder D J, Mudge S M, Bourne G S, (1997a) 'Radiological assessment of the Ribble Estuary, 1. Distribution of radionuclides in surface sediments,' *Journal of Environmental Radioactivity* 36(1), 1-19.

Assinder D J, Mudge S M, Bourne G S, (1997b) 'Radiological assessment of the Ribble Estuary, 3. Redistribution of radionuclides.' *Journal of Environmental Radioactivity,* 36, 43-67.

Assinder D J, Robinson C D, Halsall J, Telford A, (1994) 'The distribution and behaviour of artificial radionuclides in sediments of the North Wales coast', Journal of Radioanalytical and Nuclear Chemistry, 182 (2), 225-235.

Atkinson W D, Marshall M, Wadc B O, (1994) 'Cancer Risk has no Effect on Mortality', BMJ, 308: 268.

Atkinson WD, Law DV, Bromley KJ (2002) A decline in the mortality from prostate cancer in the UKAEA workforce, In: Proceedings of the 4th International Conference on Health Effects of Low-level Radiation, September 2002, Oxford. Thomas Telford, London, Paper 08.

Atomic Energy Research Establishment AERE (1991), Radioactivity in Dumfries and Galloway, DoE Report No. HMIP/RR91/056 (Harwell: AERE).

Atomic Weapons Research Establishment (1992 through 2004) Annual Reports (Aldermaston: AWE)

Auvinen A, Hakama M, Arvela H, Hakulinen T, Rabola T, Suomela M et al., (1994) Fallout from Chernobyl and incidence of childhood leukaemia in Finland, 1976-92. *BMJ;* 309: 151-154.

Azzam E I, de Toledo S M, Gooding T, Little J B, (1998) 'Intercellular communication is involved in the bystander regulation of gene expression in human cells exposed to very low fluences of alpha particles.' *Radiation Research* 150, 497-504.

Bainbridge WS (1914) *The Cancer Problem*, New York. Cited by Steffenson.

Bandashevsky Y I, (2001b) 'Radiocesium and congenital malformations' *Int. J. Rad. Med.* 3 (1-2) 10-11.

Bandashevsky Y I, (2000) Medical and Biological effects of Radio-Caesium incorporated into the Human Organism (Minsk: Institute of Radiation Safety, 'Belrad').

Bandashevsky Y I, (2001a) 'Incorporation of Cs137 and pathology of the thyroid gland', *Int. J. Rad. Med.* 3 (1-2) 10-11.

Bandashevsky Y I, Bandashevskaya G, (2001c) 'Incorporated Radiocesium and cardiac pathology' *Int. J.Rad. Med.* 3 (1-2) 10-11.

Bandashevsky Y I, Nesterenko V B, (2001d) 'Cs 137 measures and public health' *Int. J. Rad. Med.* 3 (1-2) 10-11.

Barber R, Plumb MA, Boulton E, Roux I and Dubrova YE (2002) Elevated mutation rates in the germ line of first- and second- generation offspring of irradiated male mice. *Proceedings of the National Academy of Sciences* USA 99, 6877-82.

Barcellus-Hoff MH and Brooks AL (2001) Extracellular signalling via the microenvironment: a hypothesis relating to carcinogenesis, bystander effects and genomic instability. *Radiat. Res.* 156, 618-627.

Barcinski M A, Abreu M D C, Almeida J C, de Naya J M, Fonseca L G, Castro L E, (1975) 'Cytogenic Investigation in a Brazilian Population Living in an Area of High Natural Radioactivity', *American Journal of Human Genetics,* 27/6: 802-6.

Baverstock KF and Charlton DE (1988) 'DNA damage by Auger Emitters' London: Taylor and Francis

Baverstock K, Mothershill C, Thorne M *Radiological toxicity of DU* (Repressed WHO Document) 2001 5 Nov.
Baverstock KF and Vennart J (1976) Emergency refernce levels for reactor accidents: a re-examination oif the Windscale reactor accident *Health Physics* 30 339-344
Baxter M S, (1989) An Assessment of Artificial Radionuclide Transfer from Sellafield to South West Scotland, DoE report No PECD 7/9/343, (Glasgow, East Kilbride: SURRC).
Bedford J S, Hall E J, (1963) 'Survival of HeLa Cells Culture in Vitro and Exposed to Protracted Gamma Ray Irradiation', *International Journal of Radiation Biology Related to the Study of Physics, Chemistry and Medicine,* 7: 377-83.
Beebe G W, Ishida M, and Jablon S, (1962) Studies on the Mortality of A-Bomb Survivors; repr. in *Radiation Research,* 16, 253-80.
BEIR (Committee on Biological Effects of Ionising Radiation), (1990) The Health Effects of Exposure to Low Levels of Ionising Radiation, BEIR V, (Washington: National Academy Press).
Benfante R, (1992) 'Studies in cardiovascular disease and cause specific trends in Japanese American men living in Hawaii and risk factor comparisons with other Japanese populations in the Pacific Region.' *Human Biology* 64: 791-805.
Ben-Hur E, Elkind M M, Bronk B V, (1974) 'Thermally Enhanced Radioresponse of Cultured Chinese Hamster Cells: Inhibition of Repair of Sublethal Damage and Enhancement of Lethal Damage', *Radiation Research,* 58: 38-51.
Benn A, (1999) Statement under oath given in court in Regina vs. Helen John, Middlesex Crown Court, 15th December.
Bentham G, Haynes R, (1995) 'Childhood Leukaemia in Great Britain and Fallout from Nuclear Weapons Testing', *Journal of Radiological Protection*, 15/1: 37-43.
Bentham G, (1991) 'Chernobyl Fallout and Perinatal Mortality in England and Wales', *Social Science Medicine*, 33/4: 429-34.
Beral V, Inskip H, Fraser P, Brook M, Coleman D, Rose G, (1985) 'Mortality of Employees of the United Kingdom Atomic Energy Authority, 1946-79', *British Medical Journal,* 291: 440-7.
Beral V, Roman E, Bobrow M, (eds.) (1993) Childhood Cancer and Nuclear Installations (London: British Medical Journal).
Beral V, Rooney C, Maconochie N, Fraser P, Davies G, (1993a) 'A case control study of prostatic cancer in employees of the United Kingdom Atomic Energy Authority, 1946-79', *British Medical Journal*, 307, 1391-7.
Bergonie J, Tribondeau L, (1906) 'De quelques résultats de la radiotherapie et essai de fixation d'une technique rationelle', *Comptes Rendu des Séances de l'Académie des Sciences*, 143: 983.
Bertell R, (1977a) 'X-ray Exposure and Premature Aging', *Journal of Surgical Oncology*, 9(4).
Bertell R, (1977b) Written testimony on the hazards of low level radiation. United States House of Representatives, Committee on Energy and the Environment, Subcommittee of the House Interior Committee. Rep. Morris Udall, Chairman, August 6. 1975. Washington: US Congress.

Bertell R, (1978) Measurable Health Effects of Diagnostic X-ray Exposure. Testimony before the Subcommittee on Health and the Environment of the Committee on Interstate and Foreign Commerce, U.S. House of Representatives, July 11, 1978. Vol. 2. Effect of Radiation on Human Health. Serial Number 95 180.

Bertell R, (1981b) 'Radiation Exposure and Human Species Survival'. Environmental Health Review. 25 (2).

Bertell R, (1986) *No Immediate Danger: Prognosis for a Radioactive Earth* (London: Women's Press).

Bertell R, (1997) 'Low Level Radiation Exposure Effects in the Tri-State Leukemia Survey", pages 48-59, in 100 Years After Roentgen, edited by Inge Schmitz-Feuerhake and Edmund Lengfelder. Proceeds of the International Congress held in Berlin 1995 (Berlin: Ges. fur Strahlenschutz).

Bertell R, (1999) 'Environmental Influences on the Health of Children', Chapter 6 in Risks, Health and Environment, Editor M.E. Butter, Report No. 52, Science Shop for Biology, University of Groningen, The Netherlands.

Bingham D, Gardin I and Hoyes KP (2000) The problem of Auger emitters for radiological protection. Proc. Workshop on Environmental Dosimetry. Avignon, 1999. Radiat. Prot. Dosim. 92, 219-228.

Birch T M, Alexander F E, Blair V, Eden O B, Taylor G M, McNally R T, (2000) 'Space-time clustering patterns in childhood leukaemia support a role for infection', *Br. J. Cancer.* 82(9) 1571-6

Bithell J F, Dutton S J, Draper G J, Neary N M, (1994) 'Distribution of childhood leukaemias and non-Hodgkin lymphomas near nuclear installations in England and Wales', *British Medical Journal* 309 501-5.

Bithell JF and Stewart AM (1975) Pre-natal irradiation and childhood malignancy: a review of British data from the Oxford Survey. *Br J Cancer,* 31, 271-87.

Bithell JF, Dutton SJ, Draper GJ and Neary NM (1994) Distribution of childhood leukaemias and non-Hodgkin's lymphomas near nuclear installations in England and Wales. *Br Med J*, 309, 501-5.

Blok J et al (1958) Increased atmospheric radioactivity in the Netherlands after the Windscale accident. *Appl Sci. Res.* 7 150

Boice J D Jr., Land C E, (1982) 'Ionising Radiation' in D. Schottenfeld and D. Fraumeni (eds.), Cancer Epidemiology and Prevention (Philadelphia: W. B. Saunders).

Boice JD, Day NE and Andersen A (1985) Second cancers following radiation treatment for cervical cancer. *J Nat Canc Inst* 74, 955-975)

Bois PR (2003) Hypermutable minisatellites, a human affair? *Genomics* 81:349-355.

Bolch WE (1994) Physical and chemical interactions of radiation with living tissues. In: Internal Radiation Dosimetry. (Ed. O.G. Raabe.) Medical Physics Publishing, Wisconsin.pp.27-40.

Borek C, (1979), 'Neoplastic Transformation Following Split Doses of X-Rays', *British Journal of Radiology*, 50: 845-6.

Borek C, and Hall E J, (1974) 'Effect of Split Doses of X-Rays on Neoplastic Transformation of Single Cells', *Nature*, 252: 499-501.

Bourdieu P, (1972) Outline of a Theory of Practice (Cambridge: University Press).

Bowie C, Ewings P D, (1988) Leukaemia incidence in Somerset with particular reference to Hinkley Point, Taunton: Somerset Health Authority.

Bradford Hill (1965) "The Environment and Disease: Association or Causation?" *Proceedings of the Royal Society of Medicine;* 58: 295-300.

Bradford Hill A, (1966) Principles of Medical Statistics, (London: The Lancet).

Bradley EJ and Ewings LW (1995) The transfer and resulting radiation dose from polonium, thorium and other naturally-occurring radionuclides to the human fetus. In: Health Effects of Internally Deposited Radionuclides: Emphasis on Radium and Thorium (Eds G van Kaick, A Karaoglou, AM Kellerer.) World Scientific, Singapore. pp.19-22.

Brain JD (1988) Lung macrophages: How many kinds are there? What do they do? *Am. Rev. Respir. Dis.*, 137, 507-509.

Bramhall R, (ed.) (1997) *The Health Effects of Low Level Radiation: Proceedings of a Symposium held at the House of Commons,* 24 April 1996 (Aberystwyth: Green Audit).

Bramhall R, Busby C and Scott Cato M (2000) *I don't know much about Science. Political Decision Making in Scientific and Technical Areas.* Aberystwyth: Green Audit

Brecher R, Brecher E, (1969) The Rays: A History of Radiology in the US and Canada (Baltimore: Williams and Wilkins).

Brenner D, (1999) 'Commentary: Does fractionation decrease the risk of breast cancer induced by low-LET radiation?', *Radiat. Res.*, 151, 225-229.

Bridges BA (2001) Radiation and germline mutations at repeat sequences: Are we in the middle of a paradigm shift? *Radiat. Res*, 156, 631–41.

Brooks AL, Benjamin SA, Hahn FF, Brownstein DG, Griffith MW and McClellan RO (1983) The induction of liver tumors by 239Pu citrate or 239Pu)2 particles in the Chinese hamster. *Radiat. Res.* 96, 135-151.

Brooks AL, Retherford JC and McClellan RO (1974) Effects of 239PuO2: particle number and size on size on the frequency and distribution of chromosome aberrations in the liver of the Chinese hamster. *Radiat. Res.* 59, 693-709.

Bryant F, Chamberlain A C, Morgan A, Spicer G S, (1957) 'RadioStrontium in Soil, Grass, Milk, and Bone in the United Kingdom', *Journal of Nuclear Energy,* 6: 22.

Bryant F, Chamberlain A C, Spicer G S, Webb M S W, (1958b) 'Strontium in Diet', *British Medical Journal,* i: 1371.

Bryant F, Chamberlain A C, Spicer G S, Webb M S W, (1958c), Radioactive and Natural Strontium in Human Bone: UK Results for 1957, AERE.C/R.2583 (London: HMSO).

Bryant F, Morgan A, Spicer G S, (1958a) RadioStrontium in Soil, Herbage, Animal Bone, and Milk Samples from the United Kingdom: 1957 Results, AERE.HP/R.2730 (London: HMSO).

Bulkeley JL (1927) Cancer among primitive tribes. *Cancer* 4 289-295

Burch PRJ (1959) Measurements at Leeds following the Windscale Ractor accident *Nature* 4660 515-519

Burch J, Gorst DW and Whitelegg J (1987) Geographical distribution of leukaemia in NW England. (Lancaster: University of Lancaster)

Burlakova E B, Goloshchapov A N, Gorbunova N V, Zhizhina G P, Kozachenko A I, Korman D B, Konradov A A, Molochkina E M, Nagler L G, Ozewra I B, Rozhdestvenski L M, Shevchenko V A, Skalatskaya S I, Smotryaeva M A, Tarasenko O M, Treshchenkova Y A, (1996) 'Mechanisms of Biological Action of Low Dose Irradiation' in E. B. Burlakova (ed.), Consequences of the Chernobyl Catastrophe for Human Health (Moscow: Centre for Russian Environmental Policy).

Burlakova EB (2000) Low doses of radiation, are they dangerous? New York: Nova publishers

Burlakova EB, Antova Yu S, Goloshchapov AN, Gurevich SM, Zhizhina GP, Kozachenko AI et al. (1999) Mechanisms of biological action of low-dose irradiation. In: Consequences of the Chernobyl Catastrophe on Human Health, EB Burlakova (ed), pp 11-38, Nova Science, Commack,

Busby (1995) *Wings of Death. Nuclear Pollution and Human Health* Aberystwyth: Green Audit

Busby A L, (1993) Radioactive Fallout from Atmospheric Nuclear Weapons Testing and its Association with Infant Mortality in England and Wales from 1958-1970, M.Sc. thesis (London: Imperial College).

Busby C (1996) Recalculating the second event error. http://www.llrc.org/secevnew.htm

Busby C (2001RP) Health risks following exposure to aerosols produced by the use of Depleted Uranium weapons. Presentation to *Res publica* International Conference, Prague Nov 2001. Occasional Paper 2001/12 (Aberyswyth: Green Audit)

Busby C (2001RS) Science on Trial: On the biological effects and health risks following exposure to Depleted Uranium weapons. Invited presentation to the Royal Society London July 19th 2000 and also given at the International Conference on DU in Manchester Nov.4th 2000. Occasional Paper 2000/11 (Aberystwyth: Green Audit)

Busby C (2001UN) Depleted Uranium in Kosovo: Review of the UNEP Reportof 13 Mar 2001 Occasional Paper 2001/3 (Aberystwyth: Green Audit).

Busby C (2002IM) Lymphoma incidence in Italian Military Personnel involved in operations in Bosnia and Kosovo Occasional Paper 2002/2 (Aberystwyth: Green Audit)

Busby C (2002BN) *High Risks at Low Doses.* Proceedings of the British Nuclear Energy Society International Conference: Health Effects of Low Level Radiation. Oxford 22-24 September (London:BNES)

Busby C (2002CC) The Health effects of depleted Uranium weapons. Written Evidence to the US Congressional Subcommittee on National Security, Veterans Affairs and International Relations Hearing, London 18 June 2002.

Busby C (2002HO) Review of the Home Office statement on the health consequences of DU in Kosovo. Occasional paper 2002/2 (Aberystwyth: Green Audit).

Busby C (2003) '*Depleted Science: Health Consequences and Mechanisms of exposure to fallout from Depleted Uranium weapons.* In 'The Trojan Horses of Nuclear War; Proceedings of International Conference, Hamburg Oct 16th 2003 eds-Marion Kuepker and Dave Kraft Hamburg: GAAA; Evanston Ill: NEIS

Busby C (2005) Depleted Uranium Weapons and Radiation Dose. *European Journal of Biology and Bioelectromagnetics* Vol 1 No 1 p82-93

Busby C (2005) Does Uranium contamination amplify natural background radiation dose to DNA? *European Journal of Biology and Bioelectromagnetics* Vol 1 No2 p120-131

Busby C , Scott Cato M, (2000) 'Increases in leukaemia in infants in Wales and Scotland following Chernobyl: evidence for errors in risk estimates' *Energy and Environment* 11(2) 127-139

Busby C and Bramhall R (2002) Breast Cancer Mortality and Proximity to Bradwell Nuclear Power Station in Essex 1995-1999. Correction and Update to 2001 with a Commentary on Official Responses. Green Audit, Aberystwyth, December 2002 (Occasional Paper 2002/6).

Busby C and Fucic A (2006) Ionizing Radiation and children's health: PINCHE conclusions *Acta Paediatrica* 95 Suppl. 453 81-85

Busby C and Morgan S (2006) Did the use of Uranium weapons in Gulf War 2 result in contamination of Europe? Evidence from the measurements of the Atomic Weapons Establishment, Aldermaston, Berkshire, UK. *European Journal of Biology and Bioelectromagnetics* Vol 1 No 5 p650-668

Busby C and Rowe H (2002) Cancer in Cancer in Burnham on Sea North: Results of the PCAH Questionnaire. Green Audit: Aberystwyth, July 2002 (Occasional Paper 2002/5).

Busby C and Scott Cato M (2001) Increases in leukemia in infants in Wales and Scotland following Chernobyl: Evidence for errors in statutory risk estimates and dose response assumptions. Kiev WHO conference paper. Occasional Paper 2001/7. Aberystwyth: Green Audit

Busby C (1997a) 'Breast cancer in England and Wales and Strontium-90 in atmospheric weapons fallout', Proceedings of the World Conference on Breast Cancer (Kingston, Ont.).

Busby C and Howard CV (2006a) 'Fundamental errors in official epidemiological studies of environmental pollution in Wales' *Journal of Public Health* March 22nd 2006

Busby C, (1992) Low level radiation from the nuclear industry: the biological consequences. (Aberystwyth: Green Audit).

Busby C, (1994b) Radiation and Cancer in Wales (Aberystwyth: Green Audit).

Busby C (1996c) Nuclear waste reprocessing at Sellafield and cancer near the Irish Sea: arguments for an independent collaborative study Occasional Paper 96/1 (Aberystwyth: Green Audit).

Busby C, (1996d) Cancer and Leukaemia in Children born in Wales and Scotland after Chernobyl: Preliminary Note, Occasional Paper 96/2 (Aberystwyth: Green Audit).

Busby C, (1998b) Childhood leukaemia and radioactive pollution from the Atomic Weapons facilities at Aldermaston and Burghfield in West Berkshire: causation and mechanisms, Occasional Paper 98/1 (Aberystwyth: Green Audit).

Busby C, (1998d) 'Averaging Errors in the perception of Health Risks from Internal radioisotopes with specific emphasis on mutagenic enhancement due to 2nd

Event effects from sequentially decaying man-made fission-product beta emitters', in Proceedings of the European Parliament STOA workshop, February 1998. (Aberystwyth: Green Audit)

Busby C, (2000f) Radiation from Sellafield and Cancer near the Irish Sea. The Second Annual progress report from the Irish Sea Group in support of the litigation Short and Others vs. BNFL and Others. Unpublished report.

Busby C, Bramhall R and Dorfman P (2001) Environmental risk methodology and Breast cancer mortality near Bradwell nuclear power station in Essex 1995-1999. Occasional Paper 2001/8 Aberystwyth: Green Audit

Busby C, Kaleta R and Rowe H (2000), The effects of Sellafield on cancer incidence in Ireland from 1994 to 1996. Analysis of National Cancer Registry small areas data., Report 2000/12 (Aberystwyth: Green Audit)

Busby C, Scott Cato M, (1998c) Increases in leukaemia in infants in Wales and Scotland following Chernobyl: evidence for errors in risk estimates, Occasional Paper 98/2 (Aberystwyth: Green Audit).

Busby C C, Scott Cato M, Kocjan B, Mannion E, (1998e) Proximity to the Irish Sea and leukaemia incidence at ages 0-4 in Wales from 1974-89, Occasional Paper 98/4 (Aberystwyth: Green Audit).

Busby C, and M. Scott Cato, (1997)`Death Rates from Leukemia are Higher than Expected in Areas around Nuclear Sites in Berkshire and Oxfordshire', *British Medical Journal*, 315 (1997): 309.

Busby C, (1994) 'Investigation of the Incidence of Cancer around Wylfa and Trawsfynydd Nuclear Installations, 1974-86 Welsh Office Report A-EMJ28. An appraisal for Wales Green Party', (Aberystwyth: Green Audit).

Busby C, (1994a) 'Increase in Cancer in Wales Unexplained', *British Medical Journal,* 308: 268.

Busby C, (1996) Childhood Leukaemia and Radiation near Newbury, Occasional Paper 96/5 (Aberystwyth: Green Audit).

Busby C, (2000e) 'Reponse to Commentary on the Second Event theory by Busby' *International Journal of Radiation Biology* 76 (1) 123-125.

Busby C, Bramhall R and Dorfman P (2001b) Environmental Risk Methodology and Breast Cancer Mortality near Bradwell Nuclear Power Station in Essex, 1995-99. Green Audit: Aberystwyth, July 2001 (Occasional Paper 2001/8)

Busby C, Dorfman P and Rowe H (2000) Cancer Mortality and Proximity to Hinkley Point Nuclear Power station in Somerset, 1995-1998. Part 1- Breast Cancer; Part 2- Prostate Cancer; Part 3- All Malignancy, Lung Cancer, Stomach Cancer and Summary of Results. Green Audit: Aberystwyth (Occasional Papers 2000/2 and 2000/4).

Busby C, Dorfman P, Bramhall R (2001) Environmental Risk Methodology and Breast Cancer Mortality near Bradwell Nuclear Power Station in Essex, 1995-1999. Occasional Paper 2001/8. Green Audit, Aberystwyth, July 2001.

Busby C, Dorfman P, Rowe H (2000) Cancer Mortality and Proximity to Hinkley Point Nuclear Power Station in Somerset: Part I Breast Cancer. Occasional Paper 2000/2 Aberystwyth: Green Audit

Busby C, Dorfman P, Rowe H (2000) Cancer Mortality and Proximity to Hinkley Point Nuclear Power Station in Somerset: Part III All malignancies, lung and stomach cancer. Summary Occasional Paper 2000/4 Aberystwyth: Green Audit

Busby C, Dorfman P, Rowe H, (2000a) Cancer Mortality and Proximity to Hinkley Point Nuclear Power Station in Somerset: Part I Breast Cancer. Occasional Paper 2000/2 (Aberystwyth: Green Audit).

Busby C, Dorfman P, Rowe H, (2000b) Cancer Mortality and Proximity to Hinkley Point Nuclear Power Station in Somerset: Part II Prostate Cancer. Occasional Paper 2000/3 (Aberystwyth: Green Audit).

Busby C, Dorfman P, Rowe H, (2000c) Cancer Mortality and Proximity to Hinkley Point Nuclear Power Station in Somerset: Part III All malignancies, lung and stomach cancer. Summary Occasional Paper 2000/4 (Aberystwyth: Green Audit).

Busby C, Kocjian B, Mannion E and Scott Cato M (1998) Proximity to the Irish Sea and Leukaemia incidence at ages 0-4 in Wales from 1974-1989. Green Audit: Aberystwyth, August 1998 (Occasional Paper 98/4).

Busby C, Morgan S (2006) Did Chemical Exposures of Servicemen at Porton Down Result in Subsequent Effects on their Health. The 2005 Porton Down Veterans Support Group Case Control Study. First Report. Paper 2006/2 Aberystwyth, Green Audit.

Busby C, Rowe H, (2000d) Cancer Incidence in Carlingford and Greenore, County Louth: Results of the STAD/ Green Audit Questionnaire Report 2000/06 (Aberystwyth: Green Audit).

Busby C, Scott Cato M, (1998a) 'Cancer in the offspring of radiation workers:exposure to internal radioisotopes may be responsible.' *British Medical Journal* 316 1672.

Busby C. (2004) 'Childhood leukaemia and radiation' Presentation to Conference Child Health and the Environment Policy Information Network for Child Health and the Environment (PINCHE) London, 31 March 2004)

Busby C. Glyn E, Griffiths A, de Messieres M, Morgan S (2006c) A Survey of Cancer in the Vicinity of Trawsfynydd Nuclear Power Station. Commissioned by HTV for S4C TV progranmme. Report 2006/3 Aberystwyth: Green Audit.

Busby C.C (2001) ' Depleted Uranium in Kosovo: Review of UNEP Report of 13th March 2001' Occasional Paper 2001/3 Aberystwyth: Green Audit

Busby C.C (2002) 'Lymphoma Incidence in Italian Military Personnel Involved in Operations in Bosnia and in Kosovo' Occasional Paper 2002/2 Aberystwyth: Green Audit.

Busby C.C (2002) 'Review of the Home Office statement on the health Consequences of exposure to Depleted Uranium in Kosovo' Report 2002/2 Aberystwyth: Green Audit

Busby C.C, (2000) Radiation from Sellafield and Cancer near the Irish Sea. The Second Annual progress report from the Irish Sea Group in support of the litigation Short and Others vs BNFL and Others Aberystwyth:Green Audit

Busby C.C, Dorfman P, Rowe H and Kocjan B (2001), Cancer mortality and proximity to Oldbury Nuclear Power Station in Gloucestershire 1995-1999. Including all malignancies, female breast, prostate and lung cancer mortality. With an analysis of childhood leukemia incidence in ages 0-4 between 1974 to 1990 in Welsh Areas of Residence. Occasional paper 2001/6 (Aberystwyth: Green Audit)

Busby C.C. and Cato M.S. (2001) 'Increases in leukemia in infants in Wales and Scotland following Chernobyl: Evidence for errors in statutory risk estimates and dose response assumptions'. *International Journal of Radiation Medicine* 3 (1) 23

Busby CC (2000) From Sellafield to Chernobyl and Beyond: Exposure to man-made ionizing radiation as the primary environmental cause of recent cancer increases. ASPIS (European Commission DG XVI) Conference: Is cancer predominantly an environmental disease? Kos Island September 2000. Occasional Paper 07/00 Aberystwyth: Green Audit

Busby, C (1996) `Childhood Leukemia and Radiation new Newbury', Occasional Paper 96/5 (Aberystwyth: Green Audit).

Busby CC and Coghill R (2005) Are there enhanced radioactivity levels near high voltage powerlines? *European J. Biology and Bioelectromagnetics.* 1(2) Ch 7.

Busby Chris and Bramhall Richard (2005) Is there an excess of childhood cancer in North Wales on the Menai Strait, Gwynedd? Concerns about the accuracy of analyses carried out by the Wales Cancer Intelligence Unit and those using its data. *European J. Biology and Bioelectromagnetics.* 1(4) Ch 9

Busby, C. C. (1996), 'Cancer and Leukemia in Children born in Wales and Scotland after Chernobyl: Preliminary Note', Occasional Paper 96/2 (Aberystwyth: Green Audit).

Busby, C. C. (1996), 'Nuclear waste reprocessing at Sellafield and cancer near the Irish Sea: arguments for an independent collaborative study' Occasional Paper 96/1 (Aberystwyth: Green Audit).

Busby, C. C. (1998), 'Childhood leukemia and radioactive pollution from the Atomic Weapons facilities at Aldermaston and Burghfield in West Berkshire: causation and mechanisms', Occasional Paper 98/1 (Aberystwyth: Green Audit)

Busby C and Bramhall R (2006) Is there an excess of childhood cancer in North Wales on the Menai Strait, Gwynedd? *European Journal of Biology and Bioelectromagnetics* 1(4) 504-526

Cairns J, (1978) Cancer, Science and Society (San Francisco: W. H. Freeman).

Carbonell P, Schmitz Feuerhake I (1983) Evaluation of Low level effects in the Japanese A-Bomb Survivors after current dose revisions and the estimate of fallout contribution. IAEA-SM-266/23 Vienna: IAEA

Carbonell P, Krueger EH and Schmitz –Feuerhake I (1983) The cointirbution of fallout to the doses in Hiroshima and Nagasaki *Proceedings of 7th Int. Congress on Radiation Research,* Amsterdam July 308.

Carey A D, Barraclough I M, Mobbs S F, (1996) Radiological assessment of the development of Trawsfynydd lake for leisure activities. NRPB M755 (Chilton: NRPB).

Carpenter L M, Higgins C D, Douglas A J, Machonochie N E S, et al.., (1998) 'Cancer mortality in relation to monitoring for radionuclide exposure in three UK nuclear industry workforces.' Brit. J. Cancer 78 (9) 1224-1232.

Carstairs V, Morris R, (1991) *Deprivation in Scotland* (Aberdeen: University Press).
Casarett G W, (1964) 'Similarities and Contrasts between Radiation and Time Pathology', Advanced Gerontological Research, 1: 109-63.
Castellani A, (ed.) (1989) 'DNA Damage and Repair', International Congress on DNA Damage and Repair, Rome 12-17 July 1987, organized by the Italian Commission for Nuclear Alternative Energy Sources. (ENEA, Department of Environment and Health Protection, Rome, Plenum Press).
Caufield K, (1989) Multiple Exposure: Chronicles of the Radiation Age (London: Secker and Warburg).
Cawse P A, Cambray R S, Baker S J, Burton P J, (1988) Surveys of Radioactivity 1984-86: Surveys of Background Levels of Environmental Radioactivity in Wales (Cardiff: Welsh Office).
Cawse P A, Horrill A D, (1986) A Survey of Caesium-137 and Plutonium in British Soils in 1977, Report HL86/ 1030 (C10) (Harwell: Atomic Energy Research Establishment).
Central Statistical Office, (1967) Meteorological Office, Averages of Rainfall for Great Britain and Northern Ireland 1916-1950 (London: HMSO).
CERRIE (2004a) Report of the Committee Examining Radiation Risk from Internal Emitters (CERRIE) Chilton NRPB
CERRIE (2004b) Minority Report of the Committee Examining Radiation Risk from Internal Emitters (CERRIE). Bramhall R, Busby C and Dorfman P. Aberystwyth: Sosiumi Press.
Charles MW, Mill AJ and Darley PJ (2003) Carcinogenic risk of hot particle exposures. J. Radiol. Prot. 23, 5-28.
Charlton DE (1988) Calculation of single and double strand breaks in DNA from incorporated I-125. In Baverstock KF and Charlton DE 'DNA damage by Auger Emitters' London: Taylor and Francis
Chuang YY and Liber HL (1996) Effects of cell cycle position on ionizing radiation mutagenesis. I. Quantitative assays of two genetic loci in a human lymphoblastoid cell line. Radiation Research 146: 494-500.
Chamberlain AC (1957) Deposition of I-131 in Northern Englans in Octovber 1957 *Quart. J. Meteor. Soc. 351-361*
Chamberlain AC and Dunster HJ (1958) Deposition of radioactivity in Nort West England from the accident at Windscale *Nature* 4636 629-630
Clarke R H, (1974) 'An analysis of the 1957 Windscale accident using the WEERIE code.' Ann. Nucl. Sci. Eng. 1, 73-82.
Clemmesen J (1977) Statistical Studies in the aetiology of malignant neoplasms. Trends and Risks Denmark 1943-72. Danish Cancer Registry Munksgaard Copenhagen
Clemmesen J (1961) Statistical Studies in malignant neoplasms. Vol I. Review and results. Danish Cancer Registry Munksgaard Copenhagen
Coggon D and Inskip H (1994) 'Is there an epidemic of cancer?' BMJ 6923/308: 705-8
COMARE (1996) Fouth Report; The incidence of cancer and leukemia in young people in the vicinity of the Sellafield Site in West Cumbria (London: Department of Health).

COMARE (Committee on Medical Aspects of Radiation in the Environment), (1986) The Implications of the New Data on the Releases from Sellafield in the 1950s for the Conclusions of the Report on the Investigation of a Possible Increased Incidence of Cancer in West Cumbria, COMARE 1st Report (London: HMSO).

COMARE, (1988) Investigation of the Possible Increased Incidence of Childhood Cancer in Young Persons near the Dounreay Nuclear Establishment, Caithness, Scotland, COMARE 2nd Report (London: HMSO).

COMARE, (1996) The Incidence of Cancer and Leukaemia in Young People in the Vicinity of the Sellafield Site in West Cumbria: Further Studies and Update since the Report of the Black Advisory Group in 1984, COMARE 4th Report (Wetherby: Department of Health).

Committee on Medical Aspects of Radiation in the Environment (COMARE) (2001) COMARE statement. Further statement on the Incidence of Childhood Cancer in Wales.

Committee on Medical Aspects of Radiation in the Environment (COMARE) (1999b) COMARE statement. Statement on the Incidence of Childhood Cancer in Wales.

Committee on the Medical Aspects of Radiation in the Environment (COMARE) (2003a) COMARE Statement on Green Audit Occasional Paper 2002/5 Cancer in Burnham on Sea North: Results of the PCAH (Parents Concerned About Hinkley) Questionnaire.

Committee on the Medical Aspects of Radiation in the Environment (COMARE) (2003b) COMARE statement. Cancer mortality around the Bradwell Nuclear Power Station, Essex.

Committee on the Medical Aspects of Radiation in the Environment (COMARE) (1996) Fourth Report. The incidence of cancer and leukaemia in young people in the vicinity of the Sellafield site, West Cumbria: further studies and an update of the situation since the publication of the Black Advisory Group in 1984. Department of Health, London.

Cook-Mozaffari P J, Ashwood F L, Vincent T, Forman D, Alderson M, (1987) Cancer Incidence and Mortality in the Vicinity of Nuclear Installations, England and Wales 1950-80 (London: HMSO).

Cook-Mozaffari P J, Darby S C, Doll R, (1989b) 'Cancer near potential sites of nuclear installations' The Lancet ii,1145-7.

Cotter M, (1994) 'Bone Cancer in Wales Overestimated', *British Medical Journal* 6923/308: 859.

Court Brown W M, Doll R, Spiers F W, Duffy B J, McHugh M J, (1960) 'Geographical Variation in Leukaemia Mortality in Relation to Background Radiation and Other Factors', *British Medical Journal* (June), 1753-9.

Crabtree J, (1959) 'The travel and diffusion of radioactive material emitted during the Windscale accident'. Quart. J. Royal Metereological Soc. 85, 362.

Craft E.S, Abu Quare A, Flaherty MM, Garofolo MC, Rincavage HL and Abouu Donia MB (2004) Depleted and Natural Uranium: Chemistry and Toxicological Effects *J Toxicol and Env. Health* Part B 7: 297-317

Crick M J, Linsley G S, (1982) An Assessment of the Radiological Impact of the Windscale Reactor Fire, October 1957, NRPB R.135 (London: HMSO).

Croudace I W, Warwick P E, Taylor R N, Dee S J, (1997) An investigation of radioactive contamination at Greenham Common, Newbury District, and surrounding areas. Final Report. (Southampton: University of Southampton Oceanography Centre).

Croudace I, Warick P, Cundy A, Warneke T, Oh J-S, Taylor R, (2000) An assessment of radioactive contamination in the environment as a result of operations at the AWE sites in Berkshire. Report 2 (Southampton Oceanography Centre: Geosciences Advisory Unit).

Cutler J, (1983) Windscale - The Nuclear Laundry, documentary for Yorkshire TV.

Darby S C, Olsen J H, Doll R, Thakrah B, de Nully Brown P, Storm H H, Barlow L, Langmark F, Teppo L, Tulinius H, (1992) 'Trends in Childhood Leukaemia in the Nordic Countries in Relation to Fallout from Nuclear Weapons Testing', British Medical Journal, 304: 1005-9.

Darby SC, Kendall GM, Fell TP, Doll R, Goodill AA, Conquest AJ, Jackson DA, Haylock RGE (1993) Mortality and cancer incidence 1952-1990 in UK participants of UK atmospheric nuclear weapon tests and experimental programmes. NRPB R-266 Chilton: NRPB

Darby SC, Kendall GM, Fell TP, O'Hagan JA, Muirhead CR, Ennis JR, Ball AM, Dennis JA and Doll R (1988) Mortality and cancer incidence 1952-1990 in UK participants of UK atmospheric nuclear weapon tests and experimental programmes. Chilton: NRPB

Darby SC, Kendall GM, Fell TP, O'Hagan JA, Muirhead CR, Ennis JR, Ball AM, Dennis JA and Doll R (1988) Mortality and cancer incidence 1952-1990 in UK participants of UK atmospheric nuclear weapon tests and experimental programmes. *BMJ* 296 332-339

Darby SC De Nully Brown P, Hertz H, Olsen JH, Yssing M, Scheibel E and Jensen OM (1989) Incidence of childhood cancer in Denmark 1943-1984. Int J Epidemiol, 18, 546-55.

Darby SC, Kendall GM, Fell TP, Doll R, Goodill AA, Conquest AJ, Jackson DA, Haylock RGE (1993) Further follow up of Mortality and cancer incidence 1952-1990 in UK participants of UK atmospheric nuclear weapon tests and experimental programmes. *BMJ* 307 1530-1535

De Rooij D G, Roenbaeck C, (1970) 'The Effect of Sr-90 Given to Pregnant Mice on Spermatogenesis in the Male Offspring: A Comparison with the Effect on the Female Offspring', International Journal of Radiation Biology, 56/2: 151-9.

Department of Health, (1970) Confidential enquiry into postneonatal deaths 1964-66. Reports on Public health and Medical Subjects No 125 (London: HMSO).

Dickinson HO and Parker L (1999) Quantifying the effect of population mixing on childhood leukaemia risk: the Seascale cluster. Br J Cancer; 81: 144-151.

Dionan B, Wan S L, Wrixon A D, (1987) Radiation doses to members of the public around AWRE, Aldermaston, ROF, Burghfield and AERE, Harwell, NRPB-R202 (London: HMSO).

Doll R and Hill AB (1964) Mortality in relation to smoking: 10 years' observations of British doctors. Br Med J i, 1399-1410, 1460-7.

Doll R, (1957) The Hazards to Man of Nuclear and Allied Radiation, Second Report to the Medical Research Council Cmnd. 1225 (London: HMSO).

Doll R, (1993) 'Epidemiological evidence of effects of small doses of ionising radiation with a note on the causation of clusters of childhood leukaemia' *J. Radiol. Protect.* i3:233~24i.

Doll R, (1999) 'The Seascale cluster: a probable explanation' *Br. J. Cancer*; 81: 3-5.

Doll R, Peto R, (1981) The Causes of Cancer (Oxford: University Press).

Dorrian M D, (1997) 'Particle size distribution of radioactive aerosols in the environment' Radiation Protection Dosimetry 69(2) 117-132.

Draper G J, Little M P, Sorahan T, Kinlen L J, Bunch K J, Conquest A J, Kendall G M, Kneale G W, Lancashire R J, Muirhead C R, O'Connor C M, Vincent T J, Thomas J M, Goodill A A, Vokes J, Haylock R G E, (1997b) Cancer in the Offspring of Radiation Workers - a Record Linkage Study. NRPB-R298 (Chilton: National Radiological Protection Board).

Draper G J, (1991) The geographical epidemiology of childhood leukaemia and non-Hodgkin lymphomas in Great Britain 1966-83 (London: HMSO).

Draper G J, Stiller C A, Cartwright R A, Craft A W, Vincent T J, (1993) 'Cancer in Cumbria and in the Vicinity of the Sellafield Nuclear Installation, 1963-90', *British Medical Journal,* 306: 89-94.

Draper GJ, Little MP, Sorahan T et al (1997) Cancer in the offspring of radiation workers- a record linkage study. NRPB R298 Chilton: NRPB

Dubrova Y E, Barber R, Plumb M A, Boulton E, Roux I, (2002) 'Elevated mutation rates in the first and second generation offspring of irradiated male mice' *Proc. Nat. Acad. Sci.* USA May 7th 10.1073/pnas102015399.

Dubrova Y E, Nesterov V N, Jeffreys A J et al.., (1997) 'Further evidence for elevated human minisatellite mutation rate in Belarus eight years after the Chernobyl accident.' *Mutation Research* 381 267-278.

Dubrova YE and Plumb MA (2002) Ionising radiation and mutation induction at mouse minisatellite loci. The story of the two generations. *Mutat. Res.* 499: 143-150.

Dubrova YE, Bersimbaev RI, Djansugurova LB, Tankimanova MK, Mamyrbaev ZZ, Mustonen R, Lindholm, C, Hulten M and Salomaa S (2002) Nuclear weapons tests and human germline mutation rate. *Science* 295:1037.

Dubrova YE, Grant G, Chumak AA, Stezhka, VA and Karakasian AN. (2002a) Elevated minisatellite mutation rate in the post-Chernobyl families from the Ukraine. Am. J. Hum. Genet. 71: 801-809.

Dubrova YE, Jeffreys AJ and Malashenko AM (1993) Mouse minisatellite mutations induced by ionising radiation. Nat. Genet. 5:92-944.

Dubrova YE, Nesterov VN, Krouchinsky NG, Ostapenko VA, Neumann R, Neil DL and Jeffreys AJ (1996) Human minisatellite mutation rate after the Chernobyl accident. *Nature* 380:683-686.

Dubrova YE, Nesterov VN, Krouchinsky NG, Ostapenko VA, Vergnaud G, Giraudeau F, Buard J and Jeffreys AJ (1997) Further evidence for elevated human minisatellite mutation rate in Belarus eight years after the Chernobyl accident. *Mutat. Res.* 381:267-278.

Dubrova YE, Plumb M, Brown J, Boulton E, Goodhead D and Jeffreys AJ (2000) Induction of minisatellite mutations in the mouse germline by low-dose chronic exposure to gamma-radiation and fission neutrons. *Mutat. Res*. 453:17-24.

Dubrova YE, Plumb M, Brown J, Fennelly J, Bois P and Goodhead D (1998) State specificity, dose response, and doubling dose for mouse minisatellite germ-line mutation induced by acute radiation. *Proc. Natl. Acad. Sci* USA 95:6251-6255.

Dugan LC and Bedford JS (2003) Are chromosomal instabilities induced by exposure of cultured normal human cells to low- or high-LET radiation? *Radiat Res* 159, 301-311.

Dumfries and Galloway Health Board, (1993) Third Annual Report of the Chief Administrative Medical Officer and Director of Public Health (Dumfries: Dumfries and Galloway Health Board).

Dunster H J, Howells H, Templeton W L, (1958) 'District Surveys following the Windscale Incident October 1957' in Proceedings of 2nd International Conference on Peaceful Uses of Atomic Energy Vol. 18 (Geneva: IAEA)..

Dworkin R, (1977) Taking Rights Seriously (London: Duckworth).

Eakins J D, Lally A E, Cambray R S, Kilworth D, Morrison R T, Pratley F, (1984a) 'Plutonium in sheep faeces as an indicator of deposition on vegetation', *Journal of Environmental Radioactivity,* 87-105.

Eakins J D, Lally AE, (1984b) 'The transfer to land of actinide bearing sediments from the Irish Sea by spray.' *Science of the Total Environment* 35 23-32.

ECRR2003 (2003) 2003 recommendations of the European Committee on Radiation Risk. The health effects of ionising radiation exposure at low doses for radiation protection purposes. Regulators Edition ed-Chris Busby, Rosalie Bertell, Inge Schmitz-Feuerhake, Alexey Yablokov (Brussels: ECRR

ECRR 2006 (2006) Chernobyl 20 Years On. The health effects of the Chernobyl Accident. Ed Busby C, Yablokov A. Aberystywth: Green Audit

Cox R, Edwards A A, (2000) 'Commentary on the Second Event theory of Busby' *International Journal of Radiation Biology* 76 (1) 119-122.

Ehrenberg L, Erikson G, (1968) 'The Dose Dependence of Mutation Rates in the Rad Range in the Light of Experiments with Higher Plants', *Acta Radiologica,* suppl. 254: 73-81.

Elkind M M, (1991a) 'Physical, Biophysical and Cell Biological Factors that can contribute to enhanced neoplastic transformation by fission spectrum neutrons'. *Radiation Research* 128 S47-S52.

Elkind M M, (1991b) 'Enhanced neoplastic transformation due to protracted exposures to fission spectrum neutrons: biophysical model', *Int. J. Rad. Biol.* 59 (6) 1467-75.

Ellegren H, Lindgren G, Primmer CR and Moller A.P (1997) Fitness loss and germline mutations in barn swallows breeding in Chernobyl. Nature 389, 593-6.

Elliott P, Cusick J, English D, Stern R, (1992b), Geographical and Environmental Epidemiology: Methods for Small Area Studies (Oxford: University Press).

Elliott P, Westlake A T, Hills M, et al.., (1992a) 'The Small Area Health Statistics Unit: a national facility for investigating health around point sources of environmental pollution in the United Kingdom', *J. Epidemiol. Community Health*; 46:345.

Enesco M, Leblond C P, (1962) 'Increase in Cell Number as a Factor in the Growth of the Young Male Rat', Journal of Embryology and Experimental Morphology, 10: 530-62.

Eyring H, (1970a) 'The Dynamics of Life, II. The Steady State Theory of Mutation Rates', Proceedings of the National Academy of Sciences, 66/2: 441-4.

Eyring H, Stover B J, (1970b) 'The Dynamics of Life, I. Death from Internal Irradiation by 239-Pu and 226-Ra, Aging, Cancer and Other Diseases', Proceedings of the National Academy of Sciences, 66/1: 132-9.

Fialkow P J, (1974) 'The Origin and Development of Human Tumours Studied with Cell Markers', New England Journal of Medicine, 291: 26-35.

Fialkow P J, (1976) 'Clonal Origin of Human Tumours', *Biochemica et Biophysica Acta,* 458: 283-321.

Friends of the Earth, (1993) Sellafield, the Contaminated Legacy, ed. Nick Cassidy and Patrick Green (London: FoE).

Frolen H (1970)Genetic effects of Strontium-90 at various stages of spermatogenesis in mice. Acta Radiologica 9: 596-608.

Fry F A, Wilkins B T, (1996) Assessment of Radionuclide Levels around the Former Air Force Base at Greenham Common, Berkshire, Report NRPB-M752 (NRPB, Chilton).

GAAA (2004) The Trojan Horses of Nuclear War. World Uranium Weapons Confenece 2003, Hamburg Oct 16-19. Hamburg: GAAA, Chicago: Nuclear Energy Information Service.

Gadbois DM, Crissman HA, Nastasi A, Habbersett R, Wang S, Chen D and Lehnert BE. (1996) Alterations in the progression of cells through the cell cycle after exposure to alpha particles or gamma rays. *Radiation Research* 146: 414-424.

Gardner M J, (1992) 'Leukaemia in Children and Paternal Radiation Exposure at the Sellafield Nuclear Site', *Journal of the National Cancer Institute: Monographs,* 12: 133-5.

Gardner M J, Hall A J, Downes S, Terrell J. D. (1987) 'Follow-up Study of Children Born to Workers Resident in Seascale, West Cumbria', *British Medical Journal,* 295: 819-21.

Gardner M J, Snee M P, Hall A J, Powell C A, Downes S, Terrell J D, (1990) 'Results of case-control study of leukaemia and lymphoma among young people near Sellafield nuclear plant in West Cumbria', *British Medical Journal* 300:423-429.

Garland J A, Cambray R S, Burton P J, McKay W A, (1989) Artificial Radioactivity on the Coasts of Wales, Department of the Environment Report DoE RW/89/108.

Gartler SM, Gandini E, Hutchinson HT, Campbell B and Zechhi G (1971) Glucose 6 phosphate dehydrogenase mosaicism: utilization in the study of hair follicle variegation. *Ann Human Genet.* 35 1-7

Gibson BE, Eden OB, Barrett A, Stiller CA and Draper GJ (1988) Leukaemia in young children in Scotland. *Lancet*, ii, 630.

Gilman E A, Sorahan T, Lancashire R J, Lawrence G M, Cheng K K, (1998) 'Seasonality in the presentation of acute lymphoid leukaemia', Br. J. Cancer; 77: 677-8.

Glissmeyer JA, Mishima J (1979) Characterisation of airborne uranium from test firing of XM77 ammunition. Pacific Northwest Laboratory, Richland Washington 99352. US Army Document PNL-2944

Glissmeyer JA, Mishima J, Bamberger JA (1985) Prototype Firing Range Air Cleaning System. Proceedings of the 18th DOE Nuclear Airborne Waste management and Air cleaning Conference, Baltimore Maryland 12-16 Aug 1984. ED Melvin First. CONF 840806

Goddu SM, Howell RW and Rado DV (1996) Calculation of equivalent dose for Auger electron emitting radionuclides distributed in human organs. Acta Oncol. 35, 909-916.

Gogman (1982) Radiation and Human Health San Francisco: Committee for Nuclear Responsibility).

Gofman J W (1990) Radiation Induced Cancer from Low Dose Exposure: An Independent Analysis, (San Francisco: Committee for Nuclear Responsibility).

Gofman J W, (1995) Preventing Breast Cancer (San Francisco: Committee for Nuclear Responsibility).

Gofman J W, (1999) Radiation from Medical Procedures in the Pathogenesis of Cancer and Ischemic Heart Disease: Dose-Response Studies with Physicians per 100 000 Population, (San Francisco: Committee for Nuclear Responsibility).

Goldsmith J R, (1992) 'Nuclear installations and childhood cancer in the UK: mortality and incidence for 0-9-year-old children, 1971-1980', *Sci. Total Environ.* i27: 13-35.

Goncharova R I, (2000) 'Remote Consequences of the Chernobyl Disaster: Assessment after 13 Years', in Low Doses of Radiation: Are They Dangerous? E.B. Burlakova (ed.) (New York: NOVA Sci. Publ) 289 - 314.

Goncharova R I, Smolich I I, (1998) 'Chronic irradiation over many generations induces cytogenetic effects in populations of small mammals', Proc. Int. Conf. "Agricultural Biotechnology", December 14 - 17, Gorki, pp. 216 - 219.

Goodhead D, (1991) 'Biophysical Features of Radiations at Low Dose and Low Dose Rate', in New Developments in Fundamental and Applied Radiobiology, ed. C. B. Seymour and C. Mothershill (London: Taylor and Francis).

Gould J M, (1997) The Enemy Within (New York: Four Walls Eight Windows).

Gould J M, Goldman B, (1991) Deadly Deceit: Low Level Radiation, High Level Cover-up (New York: Four Walls Eight Windows).

Gould J M, Sternglass E J, (1994) 'Nuclear fallout, low birth-weight and immune deficiency.' *Int. J. Health Services* 24 311.

Gould J M, Sternglass E J, Sherman J D, Brown J, McDonell W, Mangano J J, (2000) 'Strontium-90 in Deciduous Teeth as a Factor in Early Childhood Cancer', *Int. J. Health Services,* 30, (3) 515 - 539.

Gracheva L M, Shanshiashvili T A, (1983) 'Genetic Effects of Decay of Radionuclide Products of Fission of Nuclear Fuel, II. Lethal and Mutagenic Effects on the Mutation of Cells of the Yeast Saccharomyces cerevisiae Induced by Sr-90 and Sr-89', *Genetika (Moscow)*, 9/4: 532-5.

Greaves MF (1997) Aetiology of acute leukaemia. *Lancet*; 349: 344-349.

Grosche B, Lackland D, Mohr L, Dunbar J, Nicholas J, Burkart W, Hoel D (1999) Leukaemia in the vicinity of two tritium-releasing nuclear facilities: a comparison of the Kruemmel Site, Germany, and the Savannah River Site, South Carolina, USA. J Radiol Prot; 19: 243-252.

Haenszel W (1970) Studies of migrant populations *J. Chronic diseases* 23 289-291

Hakulinen T, Andersen A, Malker B, Pukkala E, Schou G and Tulinius H (1986) Trends in cancer incidence in the Nordic countries. A collaborative study of the five Nordic Cancer Registries. *Acta Pathol Microbiol Immunol Scand Suppl*, 288, 1-151.

Hall E J, (1972) 'Radiation Dose Rate: A Factor of Importance in Radiobiology and Radiotherapy', British Journal of Radiology, 45: 81-97.

Hall E J, (2002) 'Cellular damage response', Proceedings of 4th International Conference on the health effects of low-level radiation. (London: British Nuclear Energy Society).

Hall E J, Bedford J S, (1964) 'Dose Rate: Its Effect on the Survival of HeLa Cells Irradiated with γ-Rays', *Radiation Research,* 22: 305-15.

Hall EJ (2000) Radiobiogy for the Radiologist. 5th Edition Philadelphia: Lippincott

Hall P, Adami HO, Trichopoulos D, Pedersen NL, Lagiou P, Ekbom A et al (2004) Effect of low doses of ionising radiation in infancy on cognitive function in adulthood: Swedish population based cohort study. *Br. Med. J.,* 328, 19-21.

Hamilton E I, (1981) 'Alpha particle radioactivity of hot particles from the Esk estuary.' *Nature* 290:3808, 690-693.

Hamilton E I, (1998) 'Marine Environmental Radioactivity - The Missing Science?' *Marine Pollution Bulletin* 36:1, 8-18, 1998.

Han A, Hill C K, Elkind M M, (1980) 'Repair of Cell Killing and Neoplastic Transformation at Reduced Dose Rates of Co-60 γ-Rays', *Cancer Research,* 40: 3328-32.

Hansen NE, Karle H and Jensen OM (1983) Trends in the incidence of leukemia in Denmark, 1943-77: an epidemiologic study of 14,000 patients. *J Natl Cancer Inst*, 71, 697-701.

Harada I., Ide M, Ishida M, Troup G M, (1963) Malignant Neoplasms in Hiroshima and Nagasaki, Atomic Bomb Casualty Commission Report 22-63 (Hiroshima: ABCC).

Harada T, Ishida M, (1961) 'First Report of the Research Committee on Tumour Statistics, Hiroshima City Medical Association, Japan', *Journal of the National Cancer Institute,* 29: 1253-64.

Harjelehto T, Aro T, Rita H, Rytomaa T, Saxen L, (1989) 'The Accident at Chernobyl and Outcome of Pregnancy in Finland', *British Medical Journal,* 298: 995-7.

Harre R, (1985) The Philosophies of Science (Oxford: University Press).

Hattchouel J M, Laplanche A, Hill C, (1995) 'Leukaemia mortality around French nuclear sites', *Br. J. Cancer;* 71:651-3.

Haviland A, (1888) 'The geographical distribution of cancerous disease in the British Isles' *The Lancet* Feb. 25th 1888; 365-367; March 3rd: 412-414; March 10th: 467-468.

Haynes R and Bentham G (1995) Childhood leukaemia in Great Britain and fallout from nuclear weapons testing. *J Radiol Prot,* 15, 37-43.

Heasman M A, Kemp I W, Urquhart J D, Black R, (1986) 'Childhood leukaemia in northern Scotland', *The Lancet*; 1:266.

Henshaw D L, Fews A, Keitch P, Close J J, Wilding R J, (1999) 'Increased Exposure to Pollutant Aerosols under High Voltage Power Cables' *International Journal of Radiation Biology* 75/12:1505-21.

High Background Radiation Research Group (1980), 'Health Surveys in High Background Radiation Areas in China', *Science*, 209/4451 (22 Aug.) 877-80.

Hill AB (1965) The environment and disease: association or causation? *Proc R Soc Med* 58, 295-300.

Hirose F (1968) *Acta Haematol Japan* 31 765

Hjalmars U, Kulldorff M and Gustafsson G (1994) Risk of acute childhood leukaemia in Sweden after the Chernobyl reactor accident. *BMJ*; 309: 154-157.

Hofer KG (1998) Biophysical aspects of Auger processes – a review. *Acta Oncol.* 35, 789-796.

Hoffmann W (2002) Has fallout from the Chernobyl accident caused childhood leukaemia in Europe? A commentary on the epidemiologic evidence. *Eur J Public Health*; 12: 72-76.

Hoffmann W and Schmitz-Feuerhake I (1999) 'How radiation specific is the discentric assay?' *Journal of exposure analysis and Environmental Epidemiology* 2, 113-133

Hoffmann W, Dieckmann H, Schmitz-Feuerhake I, (1997) 'A cluster of childhood leukaemia near a nuclear reactor in northern Germany', *Arch. Environ. Health,* 52:275-280.

Hoffmann W, Kuni H, Ziggel H, (1996) 'Leukaemia and lymphoma mortality in the vicinity of nuclear power stations in Japan 1973-1987' J. *Radiol. Prot.* 16 213-215.

Hoffmann W, Kuni H, Ziggel H, (1996) 'Leukaemia and lymphoma mortality in the vicinity of nuclear power stations in Japan 1973-1987' *J. Radiol. Prot.* 16 213-215.

Hoffmannn W, Greser E, (1998) 'Epidemiologic evaluation of leukaemia incidence in children and adults in the vicinity of the nuclear power plant Kruemmel (KKK)' in Schmitz-Feuerhake I and Schmidt M, Radiation Exposures by Nuclear Facilities, Proceedings of an International Workshop, Gesellschaft fuer Strahlenschutz, Portsmouth, England 1996 (Bremen: Gesellschaft fuer Strahlenschutz).

Hoffman FL (1915) *Mortality from cancer throughout the world.* Newark: Prudential Press. Cited by Steffanson.

Hohenemser C, Deicher M, Hofsass H, et al.., (1986) 'Agricultural impact of Chernobyl: a warning.' *Nature* 26 June p 817.

Holm L E, Lundell G, Wicklund K E, Boice J D, Bergman N A, Bjalkengren G, Cederquist E S, Ericsson U B C, Larsen L G, Lindberg M E, Lindberg R S, Wicklund H V, (1988) 'Thyroid Cancer after Diagnostic Doses of Iodine 131: A Retrospective Study', *Journal of the National Cancer Institute*, 80: 1132-6.

Howell RW (1992) Radiation spectra for Auger-electron emitting radionuclides. Report No2 of AAPM Nuclear Medicine Task Group No 6. Med. Phys. 19, 1371-1383.

Hursthouse R, (1999) *On Virtue Ethics* (Oxford: University Press).

Huxley HE and Zubay G (1961) Preferential staining of nucleic acid containing structures for electron microscopy. *Biophysical and biochemical cytology. 11(2) 273*

IARC (1976) International Agency for Research on Cancer: Cancer Incidence in Five Continents Vol III

ICRP (1989) Age-dependent Doses to Members of the Public from Intakes of Radionuclides: Part 1. ICRP Publication 56, Ann. ICRP 20 (2).

ICRP (1991) 1990 Recommendations of the International Commission on Radiological Protection. ICRP Publication 60. Ann. ICRP 21 (1-3).

ICRP (1993) Age-dependent doses to members of the public from intakes of radionuclides: Part 2 Ingestion Dose Coefficients. ICRP Publication 67, Ann. ICRP 23 (3/4).

ICRP (1994a) Human respiratory tract model for radiological protection. ICRP Publication 66. Ann. ICRP 24 (1-3).

ICRP (1994b) Dose coefficients for intakes of radionuclides by workers. ICRP Publication 68. Ann. ICRP 24 (4).

ICRP (1995a) Age-dependent doses to members of the public from intakes of radionuclides: Part 3 Ingestion Dose Coefficients. ICRP Publication 69. Ann. ICRP 25 (1).

ICRP (1995b) Age-dependent doses to members of the public from intakes of radionuclides: Part 4 Inhalation Dose Coefficients. ICRP Publication 71. Ann ICRP 25(3-4).

ICRP (1996) Age-dependent doses to members of the public from intakes of radionuclides: Part 5 Compilation of Ingestion and Inhalation Dose Coefficients. ICRP Publication 72. Ann. ICRP 26 (1).

ICRP (2001) Doses to the embryo and fetus from intakes of radionuclides by the mother. ICRP Publication 88. Ann. ICRP 31 (1-3).

ICRP (2003) Relative Biological Effectiveness (RBE), Quality Factor (Q), and Radiation Weighting Factor (wR) ICRP Publication 92. Ann. ICRP 33 (4).

ICRP, (1965) The Evaluation of Risks from Radiation, pub. no. 8 (Oxford: Pergamon Press).

ICRP, (1989) Age Dependent Doses to Members of the Public from Intake of Radionuclides: Part I, ICRP Pub. 56 (Oxford: Pergamon Press).

ICRP, (1990) 1990 Recommendations of the International Commission on Radiological Protection, ICRP Pub. 60, (Oxford: Pergamon Press).

ICRP, (1992) 1990 Recommendations of the International Commission on Radiological Protection. Users' Edition, (Oxford: Pergamon Press).

ICRP, (2002) Protection of non-human species from ionising radiation; proposal for a framework for the assessment and management of the impact of ionising radiation in the environment Draft 2002.08-26.

IPB (1996) Chernobyl: Environmental, Health and Human Rights Implications. *International Conference, Vienna 1996* Rome: Permanent People's Tribunal.

Independent Advisory Group (1984), Investigation of the Possible Increased Incidence of Cancer in West Cumbria, 'The Black Report', (London: HMSO).

Irish DoH (1986) Childhood leukaemia in the republic of Ireland; a report commissioned by the Department of Health (Dublin: Stationery Office)

Isaev S I, (1975) 'Reproduction Ecology of Wild Rodents in Relation to Habitancy of Strontium-90 Polluted Biogeocenoses', Ekologiya, 6/1: 45.

Italian Report, (2001) Seconda Relazione Della Commissione Institiuta Dal Ministro Della Difesa Sull' Incidenza di Neoplasie Maligne tra I Militari impiegati in Bosnia 28 Maggio 2001 Rome: Ministry of Defence

Ivanov E P, Tolochko G V, Shuvaeva L P, Ivanov V E, Iaroshevich R F, Becker S, Nekolla E, Kellerer A M, (1998), 'Infant leukaemia in Belarus after the Chernobyl accident.' *Radiat. Environ. Biophys*. 37:1, 53-55.

Iwasaki T, Nishizawa K, Murata M, (1995) 'Leukaemia and lymphoma mortality in the vicinity of nuclear power stations in Japan, 1973-1987', *J. Radiol. Protect.;* 15: 271-288.

Jeffreys A J, Dubrova Y E, Nesterov V N, Krouchinsky N G, Ostapenko V A, Newmann R, (1996) 'Human Minisatellite Mutation Rate after Chernobyl', Nature, 380 , 683-6.

Jeffreys AJ and Neumann R (1997) Somatic mutation processes at a human minisatellite. *Human Molecular Genetics* 6, 129-32; 134-6.

Johnson C J, (1984) 'Cancer incidence in an area of radioactive fallout downwind of the Nevada test site' Journal of the Americal Medical Association, 251: 230-6.

Junge C E, (1963) Air Chemistry and Radioactivity (New York: Academic Press).

Judson HF (2004) The great betrayal: fraud in science. New York: Harcourt

Kadhim MA, Macdonald DA, Goodhead DT, Lorimore SA, Marsden SJ and Wright EG (1992) Transmission of chromosomal instability after plutonium alpha-particle irradiation. *Nature* 355, 738-740.

Kadhim MA, Marsden SJ, Goodhead DT, Malcolmson AM, Folkard M, Prise KM and Michael BD (2001) Long-Term Genomic Instability in Human Lymphocytes Induced by Single- Particle Irradiation. *Radiation Research* 155, 122-126.

Kassis AI, Howell RW, Sastry KSR and Adelstein SJ (1988) Positional effects in Auger decays in mammalian cells in culture. P 1-14 In Baverstock KF and Charlton DE 'DNA damage by Auger Emitters' London: Taylor and Francis

Kato H, Brown CC et al (1882) Leukemia among Atomic Bomb Survivors. *Radiation Research* 91 243

Kelly M, Assinder D J, Aston S R, (1985) 'Plutonium in intertidal coastal and estuarine sediments in the northern Irish sea', *Estuarine, Coastal and Shelf Science*, 20: 761-771.

Kershaw P J, Denoon D C, Woodhead D S, (1999) 'Observations on the redistribution of Plutonium and Americium in the Irish sea sediments 1978 to 1966, concentrations and inventories.' *J. Environmental Radioactivity* 44 (1999) 191-221.

King H and Locke FB (1980a) American white protestant clergy as a low risk population for mortality research *JNCI* 65 1115-1124

King H and Locke FB (1980b) Cancer mortality among Chinese in the United States. *JNCI* 65 1141-1148

Kinlen L (2001) Infection, childhood leukaemia and the Seascale cluster. *Radiol Prot Bull;* 226: 9-18.

Kinlen L J, (1988), 'Evidence for an Infective Cause of Childhood Leukaemia: Comparison of a Scottish New Town with Nuclear Reprocessing Sites in Britain', *Lancet*, ii: 1123-7.

Kinlen L J, (1995a) 'Epidemiological evidence for an infective basis in childhood leukaemia', *Br. J. Cancer;* 71: l-5.

Kinlen L J, Dickson M, Stiller C A, (1995b) 'Childhood leukaemia and non-Hodgkin's lymphoma near large rural construction sites, with a comparison with Sellafield nuclear site', *British Medical Journal* 310:763-768.

Kinlen L J, O'Brien F, Clarke K, Balkwill A, Matthews F, (1993) 'Rural population mixing and childhood leukaemia: effects of the North Sea oil industry in Scotland, including the area near Dounreay nuclear site', *British Medical Journal* 306:743-748.

Kiuru A, Auvinen A, Luokkamaki M, Makkonen K, Veidebaum T, Tekkel M, Rahu M, Hakulinen T, Servomaa K, Rytomaa T and Mustonen R (2003) Hereditary minisatellite mutations among the offspring of Estonian Chernobyl cleanup workers. *Radiat. Res.* 159:651-655.

Kmet J (1970) The role of migrant populations in studies of selected cancer. *J. Chronic Diseases.* 23 304-324

Knox E G, Gilman E, (1992) 'Leukaemia clusters in Great Britain. 2. Geographical concentrations', *J. Epidemiol. Community Health;* 46:573

Knudsen AG (1971) Proc Nat Acad Sci USA 68:820-823,

Kochupillai N, Verma I C, Grewal M, S, Ramalingaswami V, (1976) 'Down's Syndrome and Related Abnormalities in an Area or High Background Radiation in Coastal Kerala', Nature, 262: 60-1.

Kodaira M, Satoh C, Hiyama K and Toyama K. (1995) Lack of effects of atomic bomb radiation on genetic instability of tandem repetitive elements in human germ cells. *Am. J. Hum. Genet.* 57:1275-1283.

Koehnlein W, Nussbaum R H, (eds.) (2001) Die Wirkung niedriger Strahlendosen im Kindes und Jugendalter in der Medizin, Umwelt und Technik, am Arbeitzplatz (Bremen: Gesellschaft fur Strahlenschutz).

Koppe JG, Bartonova A, Bolte G, Bistrup ML, Busby C, Butter M et al (2006) Exposure to multiple environmental agents and their effects. *Acta Paediatrica* in print

Kovalchuk O, Dubrova YE, Arkhipov A, Hohn B and Kovalchuk I (2000) Wheat mutation rate after Chernobyl. Nature 407, 583-4.

Kovalchuk O, Kovalchuk I, Arkhipov A, Hohn B and Dubrova Y E (2003) Extremely complex pattern of microsatellite mutation in the germline of wheat exposed to the post-Chernobyl radioactive contamination. *Mutation Research* 525, 93-10.

Kuhn T S, (1962) The Structure of Scientific Revolutions (Chicago: University Press).

Lanier AP *et al* (1980) Cancer in Alaskan Indians, Eskimos and Aleuts. *JNCI* 65 1157-1159

Latour B, (1987) Science in Action, (Cambridge, Mass.: Harvard University Press).

Latour B (1999) *Pandora's Hope. Essays on the Reality of Science Studies.* Cambridge, MA: Harvard

Law G, Roman E, (1997) 'Leukaemia near La Hague nuclear plant. Study design is questionable. *British Medical Journal*; 314:1553.

Lea D E, (1956) The Action of Radiation on Living Cells (Cambridge: University Press).

Leblond C P, (1981) 'The Life History of Cells in Renewing Systems', American Journal of Anatomy, 160: 114-58.

Leggett RW, Bouville A and Eckerman KF (1998) Reliability of the ICRP's systemic biokinetic models. Radiat. Prot. Dosim. 79, 335-342.

Lehnert BE, Valdez, YE and Stewart CC (1986) Translocation of particles to the tracheobronchial lymph nodes after lung deposition: Kinetics and particle-cell relationships. *Exp. Lung Res.*, 10, 245-266.

Leon D A, (1988) Longitudinal Study: social distribution of cancer. OPCS Series LS No 3 (London: HMSO).

Lichtenstein P, Holm N V, Verkasalo P K, Iliadou A, Kaprio J, Koskenvuo M, Pukkala E, Skytthe A, and Hemminki K, (2000) 'Environmental and heritable factors in the causation of cancer.' *New England Journal of Medicine* 343 (2) 78-85.

Linke P, Clarkin KC and Wahl GM (1997) P 53 Mediates permanent arrest over multiple cell cycles in response to γ-irradiation. *Cancer Research* 57: 1171-1179.

Little J B, (1979) 'Quantitative Studies of Radiation Transformation with the A31-11 Mouse BALB/3T3 Cell Line', *Cancer Research,* 39: 1474-80.

Little J B, (2002) 'Genomic instability and radiation.' Proceedings of 4th International Conference on the health effects of low-level radiation. (London: British Nuclear Energy Society).

Little JB (1998) Radiation-induced genomic instability. *Int Journal of Radiation Biology* 74, 663-671.

Little JB (1999) Induction of genetic instability by ionizing radiation. *C R Acad Sci III,* 322(2-3): p. 127-34.

Little JB (2003) Genomic instability and radiation *J. Radiol. Prot.* 23 pp173–181.

Little JB, Azzam EI, de Toledo SM and Nagasawa H (2002) Bystander effects: intercellular transmission of radiation damage signals. *Radiat Prot Dosimetry* 99, 159-162.

Lloyd F (1999) Leukaemia Occurrence near Coastal Features. Report Submitted in Partial Fulfilment for the Degree of Bachelor of Science in Clinical Sciences. Division of Clinical Sciences, School of Medicine, University of Leeds.

Lloyd F, Gilman EA, Law GR and Cartwright RA (2002) Leukaemia incidence near coastal features. *J Public Health Med,* 24 :255-60.

Lloyd RD, Taylor GN, Angus W et al (1993) Bone cancer occurrence among beagles given 239Pu as young adults. Health Phys. 64, 45-51.

Locke FB and King H (1980) Cancer mortality risk among Japanese in the United Sattres. *JNCI* 65 1149-1156

Lopez-Abente G, Aragones N, Pollan M, Ruiz M, Gandarillas A, (1999) 'Leukaemia, lymphomas, and myeloma mortality in the vicinity of nuclear power plants and nuclear fuel facilities in Spain', Cancer Epidemiol. Biomarkers Prev.; 8: 925-34.

Lord B I, (1999) 'Transgenerational susceptibility to leukaemia induction resulting from preconception, paternal irradiation', *Int.J. Radiat. Biol.* ;75:801-10.

Lord B I, Jiang Tien-Nan, Hendry J H, (1994) 'Alpha particles are extremely damaging to developing haemopoiesis compared with gamma irradiation'. *Radiation Research* 137,380-84.

Lorimore SA, and Wright EG (2003) Radiation-induced genomic instability and bystander effects: related inflammatory-type responses to radiation-induced stress and injury? A review. *International Journal of Radiation Biology* 79, 15-25.

Loutit JF, Marley WG and Russell RS (1960) The hazards to man from nuclear and allied radiation MRC: CMMND 1125

Luning K G, Frolen H, Nelson A, Roennbaeck C, (1963a) 'Genetic Effects of Strontium-90 injected into male mice.' *Nature*, 197:304-5.

Luning K G, Scheer J, Schmidt M, Ziggel, H, (1992) 'Low Level Radiation: Early Infant Mortality in West Germany before and after Chernobyl', *Lancet*, 1081-3.

MacDonald A, (1997) A Twenty-Year Survey of a Rural General Practice in Ireland, House of Commons Library. Westminster.

Machta L, List R J, (1959) 'Analysis of Stratospheric Strontium-90 Measurement', Journal of Geophysical Research, 64: 1267.

Maclean A, (1993) The Elimination of Morality: Reflections on Utilitarianism and Bioethics (London: Routledge).

MAFF reports, various authors (1962-96), Radioactivity in Coastal and Surface Waters of the British Isles (Fisheries Research Laboratory, (now CEFAS): Lowestoft).

Malko M V, (1998) 'Chernobyl accident: the crisis of the international radiation community' in Imanaka T: Research activities about the radiological consequences of the Chernobyl NPS accident and social activities to assist the sufferers of the accident. (Kyoto University: Research Reactor Institute).

Mangano J, (2000) 'Improvements in local infant health after nuclear power reactor closing', *Environ. Epidemiol. & Toxicol.*, 2, (1) 32 - 36.

Mangano J, (1996) 'Chernobyl and hypothyroidism', *Lancet,* Vol. 347, 1482 -1483.

Mangano J, (1997) 'Childhood leukaemia in the US may have risen due to fallout from Chernobyl', *British Medical Journal,* 314: 1200.

Mangano JJ (1997) Childhood leukaemia in US may have risen due to fallout from Chernobyl. Brit Med J, 314, 1200.

Marr J W, (1973) 'Some trends in food consumption in Great Britain 1955-71.' Health Trends 5: 37-9.

Martland H S, (1929) 'Occupational Poisoning in Manufacture of Luminous Watch Dials', *Journal of the American Medical Association,* 92/6: 466-73.

May CA, Tamaki K, Neumann R, Wilson G, Zagars G, Pollack A, Dubrova YE, Jeffreys AJ and Meistrich ML (2000) Minisatellite mutation frequency in human sperm following radiotherapy. *Mutat. Res.* 453:67-75.

Mazia D, (1954) 'Untitled', Proceedings of the National Academy of Sciences, 40: 521.

McInroy J F, Kathren R I, Voelz G L, Swint M J, (1991) 'US TransUranium Registry report on the 239Pu distribution in a human body.' Health Physics 60(3) 307-333.

McKay W A, Garland J A, Livesley D, Halliwell C M, Walker M I, (1988) The transfer of radionuclides from sea to air to land in sea spray at Cumbria, UK, Report AEA-EE-0516, (Harwell: AEA).

McMillan T J, Cassoni A M, Edwards S, Holmes A, Peacock J H, (1990) 'The relationship of DNA double strand break induction to radiosensitivity in human tumour cell lines.' *Int.J.Rad.Biol.* 58(3) 427-438.

MCR (2003) Medical Research Councils review into research into Gulf War Veterans Illnesses (London: MRC)

Medical Research Council (1957), Hazards to Man of Nuclear and Allied Radiations, Cmnd. 1225 (London: HMSO).

Medvedev Z, (1990) The Legacy of Chernobyl (Oxford: Blackwell).

Michaelis J, (1998) 'Recent epidemiological studies on ionising radiation and childhood cancer in Germany', Int. J. Radiat. Biol.;73:377-81.

Michaelis J, Kaletsch U, Burkart W and Grosche B, (1997) 'Infant leukaemia after the Chernobyl Accident' Nature 387, 246.

Midgley M, (1983) 'Duties Concerning Islands', in R. Elliot and A. Gare (eds.), Environmental Philosophy; reprinted in R. Elliot (ed.), Environmental Ethics (Oxford: University Press).

Midgley (1985) Evolution as a Religion London: Routledge

Midgley M (2002) Science and Poetry. London: Routledge

Milbourne G M, Ellis F B, Russell R S, (1959) 'The Absorption of Radioactive Strontium by Plants under Field Conditions in the United Kingdom', Journal of Nuclear Energy Reactor Science, 10: 115.

Mill J S, (1879) A system of Logic (London: Longmans Green).

Miller AC, Brooks K, Stewart M, Anderson B, Shi Lin, McLain D and Page N (2003) Genomic Instability in human osteoblast cells after exposure to depleted uranium: delayed lethality and micronuclei formation. *J. Env. Radioact.* 64 247-259

Miller R C, Hall E J, Rossi H H, (1979) 'Oncogenic transformation in Cultured Mouse embro Cells with Split Doses of X-Rays', *Proceedings of the National Academy of Science,* 76: 5755-8.

Miller R C, Hall E J, (1978) 'X-Ray Dose Fractionation and Oncogenic Transformations in Culture Mouse Embryo Cells', *Nature*, 272: 58-60.

Miller R C, Randers-Pehrson G, Geard C R, Hall E J, Brenner D J, (1999) 'The oncogenic transforming potential of the passage of single alpha particles through mammalian cell nuclei.' *Proc. Natl. Acad. Sci.* USA 96: 19-22.

Miller RC, Geard CR, Geard MJ and Hall EJ (1992) Cell-cycle-dependent radiation-induced oncogenic transformation of C3H 10T1/2 cells. *Radiat. Res.* 130: 129-33.

Morgan WF (2003a) Non-targeted and Delayed Effects of Exposure to Ionizing Radiation: I. Radiation-Induced Genomic Instability and Bystander Effects In Vitro. *Radiation Research* 159, 567-580.

Morgan WF (2003b) Non-targeted and Delayed Effects of Exposure to Ionizing Radiation: II. Radiation-Induced Genomic Instability and Bystander Effects In Vivo, Clastogenic Factors and Transgenerational Effects. Radiation Research 159, 581-596.

Morris J (1993) Retinoblastoma: a possible link with radiation. *J Med Genet.* 30; 440-2

Mothersill C and Seymour C (2001) Radiation-induced bystander effects: past history and future directions. *Radiation Research* 155, 759-767.

Muirhead CR, Bingham D, Haylock RGE, O'Hagan JA, Goodill AA, Berridge GLC, English MA, Hunter N and Kendall GM (2003) Mortality and Cancer incidence 1952-98 in UK particlpants of the UK atmospheric nuclear weapons tests and experinmmental programmes. NRPB W27 Chilton: NRPB

Muller H J, (1928) 'The Effects of X-Radiation on Genes and Chromosomes', *Science*, 67:82.

Muller H J, (1950) 'Our Load of Mutations', *American Journal of Human Genetics*, 2: 111-76.

Nakanishi M, Tanaka K, Shintani T, Takahashi T and Kamada N (1999) Chromosomal instability in acute myelocytic leukaemia and myelodysplastic syndrome patients among atomic bomb survivors. J. *Radiat. Res.* (Tokyo) 40: 159-167.

Nakanishi M, Tanaka K, Takahashi T, Kyo T, Dohy H, Fujiwara M and Kamada N (2001) Microsatellite instability in acute myelocytic leukaemia developed from A-bomb survivors. *Int. J. Radiat. Biol.* 77: 687-694.

National Cancer Registry Ireland (1998), Cancer in Ireland 1995 (Cork: National Cancer Registry Board).

National Research Council (NRC) (1980) Committee on the Biological Effects of Ionizing Radiation The effects on Populations of Exposure to Low Levels of Ionizing Radiation. BEIR III. National Academy Press, Washington DC.

National Research Council (NRC) (1999) Committee on Health Risks of Exposure to Radon. Health Effects of Exposure to Radon, BEIR VI. National Academy Press, Washington DC.

Neel J V, Schull W J, (1956) 'Studies on the potential effects of the atom bombs' *Acta Genet.* 6: 183-196.

Neilsen PE, Hiort C, Soennischen SO , *et al* (1992) DNA binding and photocleavage by Uranyl VI salts. *J.Am.Chem.Soc.* 114 4967-75

Nesbitt M N, (1971) 'X-Chromosome Inactivation Mosaicism in the Mouse', Developments in Biology, 26: 252-63.

Nesterenko V B, (1998) Chernobyl Accident. The Radiation Protection of the Population (Minsk: Republic of Belarus Institute of Radiation Safety, 'Belrad').

Nikolopopou –Stamati P, Hens L, Howard CV and Van Larebeke N (2004) Cancer as an Environmental Disease. Dordrecht: Kluwer

Nilov V I, (1974) 'Effect of Sr-90 and Y-90 on the Chromosome Apparatus of Ctenopharyngodon Embryos', doc. no. Viniti 2922-74 (British Library).

Nishiwaki Y, Yamashita H, Honda Y, Kimara Y, Fujimori H, (1972) 'Effects of Radioactive Fallout on the Pregnant Woman and Fetus', *International Journal of Environmental Studies,* 2: 277-89.

NRPB (National Radiological Protection Board), (1972-94) Environmental Radioactivity Surveillance Programme (London: HMSO).

NRPB R276 (1995) Risk of leukaemia and other cancers in Seascale from all sources of radiation Simmonds JR et al. (Chilton :National Radiological Protection Board)

NRPB, (1984) The risks of leukaemia and other cancers in Seascale from radiation exposure. NRPB R-171 (Chilton: NRPB).

NRPB, (1986) The risks of leukaemia and other cancers in Seascale from radiation exposure: Addendum to R171. (Chilton: NRPB).

NRPB, (1987) Interim Guidance on the Implications of Recent Revisions of Risk Estimates and the ICRP 1987 Como Statement, NRPB GS-9 (London: HMSO).

NRPB, (1988) The risks of childhood leukaemia near nuclear establishments NRPB R-215 (Chilton: NRPB).

NRPB, (1995a) Risks of leukaemia and other cancers in Seascale from all sources of ionising radiation NRPB R-276 (Chilton: NRPB).

NRPB, (1995b) Risk of radiation induced cancer at low dose and low dose rate for radiation protection purposes. Documents of the NRPB 6/1 (Chilton: NRPB).

Nussbaum R H, (1998) 'The linear, no-threshold dose effect relation: is it relevant to radiation protection regulation?' *Medical Physics* 25 (3) March.

Nussbaum, R. and Koehnlein, W. (1994), 'Inconsistencies and open questions regarding low-dose health effects of ionising radiation', Environmental Health Perspectives, 102(8), 656.

O'Donnell, Mitchell PI, Priest ND, Strange L, Fox A, Henshaw DL, Long SC (1997) Variations in the concentration of plutonium, strontium-90 and total alpha-emitters in human teeth collected within the British Isles. Sci Total Environ; 201: 235-243.

Oberdörster G (1988) Lung clearance of inhaled insoluble and soluble particles. *J. Aerosol Med.,* 1, 289-330.

Occasional Paper 2002/3 (Aberystwyth: Green Audit)

Oftedal P, (1991) 'Biological Low Dose Radiation Effects', *Mutation Research,* 258: 191-205.

Okeanov N N, Yakimovich A V, (1999) 'Incidence of malignant neoplasms in population of Gomel Region following the Chernobyl Accident', *Int. Journ. Rad. Med.*, 1, (1), 49 –54.

Omar RZ, Barber JA, Smith PG (1999) Cancer mortality and morbidity among plutonium workers at the Sellafield plant of British Nuclear Fuels. *Br J Cancer;* 79: 1288-1301.

OPCS, (1974) Cancer Statistics Registrations 1979, Series MB1, No. 4 (London: HMSO).

OPCS, (1981) Cancer Statistics: Incidence, Survival, Mortality in England and Wales. Studies on medical and population subjects No 43. (London: HMSO).

OPCS, (1983) Trends in Cancer Mortality, ser. DN1 no. 11, ed. C. Osmond, M. J. Gardner, E. D. Acheson, and A. M. Adelstein (London: HMSO).

OPCS, (1991) Cumulative Post Neonatal Mortality OPCS Monitor ser. DH3/1

OPCS, (Office of Population Censuses and Surveys) (1971-97) Birth Statistics, ser. FM1 nos.1 to 26 (London: HMSO).

Pampfer S and Streffer C (1989) Increased chromosome aberration levels in cells from mouse fetuses after zygote X-irradiation. International *Journal of Radiation Biology* 55, 85-92.

Papineau D, (1996) The Philosophy of Science (Oxford: University Press).

Parker L, Pearce M S, Dickinson H O, Aitken M, and Craft A W, (1999), 'Stillbirths among offspring of male radiation workers at Sellafield nuclear reprocessing plant' *The Lancet* 354 1407-1414.

Parkin D M, et al.., (1996) 'Childhood leukaemia in Europe after Chernobyl: 5 year follow up', British Journal of Cancer, 73: 1006-1012.

Parkin D M, Whelan S L, Ferlay J, Raymond L, Young J, (eds.) (1997) Cancer Incidence in Five Continents. Vol. VII. (Lyon: ARC Scientific Publications No.143).

Parkin DM, Clayton D, Black RJ, Masuyer E, Friedl HP, Ivanov E, Sinnaeve J, Tzvetansky CG, Geryk E, Storm HH, Rahu M, Pukkala E, Bernard JL, Carli PM, L'Huilluier MC, Menegoz F, Schaffer P, Schraub S, Kaatsch P, Michaelis J, Apjok E, Schuler D, Crosignani P, Magnani C, Bennett BG, et al. (1996) Childhood leukaemia in Europe after Chernobyl: 5 year follow-up. *Br J Cancer* 73 1006-1012.

Pazzaglia S, Saran A, Pariset L, Rebessi S, Di Major V, Coppola M and Covelli V. (1996) Sensitivity of C3H 10T1/2 cells to radiation-induced killing and neoplastic transformation as a function of cell cycle. I*nt. J. Radiat. Biol.* 69: 57-65,

Permanent People's Tribunal / International Medical Commission on Chernobyl, (1996) Chernobyl: Permanent People's Tribunal Session on Environmental, Health and Human Rights Implications. Vienna, Austria 12-15 April 1996 (Rome: Permanent People's Tribunal / Toronto: IMCC).

Petkau A, (1980) 'Radiation carcinogenesis from a membrane perspective' *Acta physiological Scandinaviaca* suppl.492, 81-90.

Petrakis NL (1971) Some preliminary observations on the influence of genetic admixture on cancer incidence in American negroes. *Int. J. Cancer. 7 256-258*

Petridou E, Trichopoulos D, Dessypris N, Flytzani V, Haidas S, Kalmanti M, Koliouskas D, Kosmidis H, Piperolou F, Tzortzatou F, (1996) 'Infant Leukaemia after in utero exposure to radiation from Chernobyl', *Nature*, 382:25, 352.

Phillips R L, (1975) 'The role of lifestyle and dietary habits in risk of cancer among Seventh Day Adventists', *Cancer Research,* 35:3513-22.

Pierce D A, Preston D L, (2000) 'Radiation-related cancer risks at low doses among atomic bomb survivors', Radiat. Res., 154, 178-186.

Pitkayanen G B, (1978) 'Effect of Chronic Irradiation of a Pike *Esox lucius* on its Reproductive Function', *Tr. Inst. Ekol. Rast. Zhorotn. Ural. Narch.* Tsentr. (Soviet Academy of Sciences), 114: 74.

Playford K, Lewis G N J, Carpenter R C, (1992) Radioactive Fallout in Air and Rain: Results to the End of 1990, Atomic Energy Authority Report no. EE-0362; DOE/RAS/92.015 (London: HMSO).

Pobel D, Viel J-F (1997) Case-control study of leukaemia among young people near La Hague nuclear reprocessing plant: the environmental hypothesis revisited. *BMJ;* 314: 101-106.

Pohl-Ruling J, Fischer P, Pohl E, (1979) 'The Dose-Effect Relationship of Chromosome Aberrations to and Irradiation in a Population Subjected to an Increased Burden of Natural Radioactivity', *Radiation Research,* 80:61-81.

Popper K R, (1962) The logic of scientific discovery (London: Hutchinson).
Popper K R, (1963) Conjectures and Refutations (London: Routledge).
Popplewell D S, (1986) 'Plutonium in Autopsy Tissues in Great Britain' Radiological Protection Bulletin No 74 (Chilton: NRPB).
Popplewell D S, Ham G J, Dodd N J, Shuttler S D, (1988) 'Plutonium and Cs-137 in autopsy tissues in Great Britain' *Sci. Tot. Environment* 70 321-34.
Popplewell DS, Ham GJ, Johnson TE and Barry SF (1985) Plutonium in autopsy tissues in Great Britain. *Health Phys.* 49, 304-309.
Popplewell DS, Ham GJ, McCarthy W, Morgan M (1989) Isotopic composition of plutonium in human tissue samples determined by mass spectrometry. *Radiat Protect Dosim;* 26: 313-316.
Powell C (1908) *The Pathology of Cancer,* Manchester, cited by Steffanson.
Preston DL, Shimizu Y, Pierce DA, Suyama A and Mabuchi K (2003) Studies of mortality of atomic bomb survivors. Report 13: Solid cancer and non-cancer disease mortality: 1950-1997. *Radiat. Res.,*160, 381-407.
Preston-Price WA (1939) *Report of an interview with Dr Joseph Herman Romig: Nutrition and Physical Degeneration.* London and New York. Cited by Steffanson.
Priest N D, O'Donnell R G, Mitchell P I, Strange L, Fox A, Henshaw D L, Long S C, (1997) 'Variations in the concentration of Plutonium, Strontium-90 and total alpha emitters in human teeth collected within the British Isles', *Science of the Total Environment*, 201, 235-243.
Prosser SL, McCarthy W and Lands C (1994) The plutonium content of human fetal tissue and implications for fetal dose. *Radiat. Prot. Dosim.* 55, 49-55.
Purnell SJ, Allen JE, Oyedepo C and Henshaw DL (1999) Fetal dosimetry from natural alpha particle emitters. *Radiat Res* 152, S133-6.
Radiological Protection Institute of Ireland (1996), Radioactivity Monitoring of the Irish Marine Environment, 1993-1995 (Dublin: RPII).
Radiological Protection Institute of Ireland, RPII (1995), Environmental Radioactivity Surveillance Programme 1990-1993 (Dublin: RPII).
Rawls J, (1971) A Theory of Justice (Cambridge, Mass.: Harvard University Press).
Redpath J L, Sun C, (1990) 'Sensitivity of a Human Hybrid Cell Line (HeLa x skin fibroblast) to Radiation Induced Neoplastic Transformation in G2, M, and mid-G1 phases of the cell cycle', Radiation Research, 121 206-11.
RERF (Radiation Effects Research Foundation) (1971), Studies of the Mortality of A-Bomb Survivors, iv. Mortality and Radiaton Dose 1950-66, ed. G. W. Beebe, H. Kato, and C. E. Land, RERF TR-11-70; repr. in Radiation Research, 48: 613-49.
RERF, (1972) Studies on the Mortality of A-Bomb Survivors, v. Radiaton Dose and Mortality, 1950-1970, ed. S. Jablon and H. Kato, RERF TR-10-71; repr. in Radiation Research, 50: 649-98.
RERF, (1978) Studies of the Mortality of A-Bomb Survivors, vi. Mortality and Radiation Dose 1950-1974, ed. G. W. Beebe, H. Kato, and C. E. Land, RERF, TR-1-77; repr. in Radiation Research, 75: 138-201.

RERF, (1982), Studies of the Mortality of A-Bomb Survivors, vii. Mortality 1950-78, pt I: Cancer Mortality, ed. H. Kato and W. J. Schull, RERF, TR-12-80; repr. in Radiation Research, 90: 395-432.

RERF, (1987) Cancer Mortality among A-Bomb Survivors in Hiroshima and Nagasaki, 1950-1982, ed. D. L. Preston, H. Kato, K. J. Kopecky, and S. Fujita, Lifespan Study Report no. 10, pt I: Cancer Mortality, RERF Technical Report, TR-1-86; repr in Hiroshima Radiation Research, 111: 151-78.

Richardson D, Wing S, (1999) 'Radiation and Mortality of Workers at Oak Ridge National Laboratory: Positive Association for Doses Received at Older Ages', *Environ. Health Perspect.,* vol. 107. 8.

Robbins J H, Kramer K H, Lutzer M A, (1974) 'Xeroderma Pigmentosum: An Inherited Disease with Sun Sensitivity, Multiple Cutaneous Neoplasms and Abnormal DNA Repair', Annals of International Medicine, 80: 221-48.

Robinson M, (1989) Mother Country (Boston, Mass.: Faber).

Robison L L, (1992) 'Down's syndrome and leukaemia', *Leukaemia;* 6:5-7.

Robison L L, Buckiey J D, Bunin G, (1995) 'Assessment of environmental and genetic factors in the etiology of childhood cancers: the Children's Cancer Group epidemiology program', *Environ. Health Perspect.* 103:11 1-116.

Roht C, H, Selwyn B J, Holguin A H, Christiansen B L, (1982) Principles of Epidemiology (New York: Academic Press).

Roman E, Doyle P, Maconochie N, Davies G, Smith PG, Beral V (1999) Cancer in children of nuclear industry employees: report on children aged under 25 years from nuclear industry family study. *BMJ* 318 1443-1450.

Roman E, Watson A, Beral V, Buckle S, Bull D, Ryder H, Barton C, (1993) 'Case control study of leukaemia and non-Hodgkin lymphoma among children aged 0-4 years in West Berkshire and North Hampshire Health Districts' *British Medical Journal*, 306, 615-21.

Ron E, Lubin JH, Shore RE, Mabuchi K, Modan B, Pottern LM, et al. (1995) Thyroid cancer after exposure to external radiation: a pooled analysis of seven studies. *Radiat Res;* 141: 259-277.

Ron E, Preston D L, Kishikawa M, et al.., (1998) Skin tumor risk among atomic-bomb survivors in Japan. *Cancer Causes and Control,* 9, 393-401.

Rooney C, Beral V, Maconochie N, Fraser P, Davies G, (1993) 'Case Control Study of Prostatic Cancer in Employees of the United Kingdom Atomic Energy Authority', *British Medical Journal*, 307, 1391-7.

Ross J A, Davies S M, Potter J D, Robison L L, (1994) 'Epidemiology of childhood leukaemia, with a focus on infants', *Epidemiol. Rev.* 116:243-272.

Routley R, Routley V, (1979) 'Against the Inevitability of Human Chauvinism', repr. In R. Elliot (ed.), Environmental Ethics (Oxford: University Press, 1995).

Royal Commission on Environmental Pollution (1976), Sixth Report: Nuclear Power and the Environment, Cmnd. 6618 (London: HMSO).

Royal Society Working Group on the Health Hazards of Depleted Uranium Munitions (2001) The Health Hazards of Depleted Uranium Munitions, Part I. The Royal Society, London.

Royal Society Working Group on the Health Hazards of Depleted Uranium Munitions (2002) The Health Hazards of Depleted Uranium Munitions, Part II. The Royal Society, London.

Ruden C (2001) Interpretations of primary carcinogenicity data in 29 trichloroethylene risk assessments. *Toxicology* 169 209-225

Ruden C (2002) The use of mechanistic data in the handling of scientific uncertainty in carcinogen risk assessments. The trichloroethylene example. *Regul. Toxicol. Pharmacol,* 35 80-94

Ruden C (2003) Science and Transscience in carcinogen risk assessment. The European Union regulkatory process for trichloroethylene. *J.Toxicol. Envir. Health B Crit Rev.* 6 257-77.

Russell Jones R, (1989) 'Infective Cause of Childhood Leukaemia', *Lancet,* i: 94.

Russell W L, 'Repair Mechanisms in Radiation Mutation Induction in the Mouse', Brookhaven Symposium on Biology, 20: 179-89.

Rytomaa T, (1987) 'Low Dose Radiation and Cancer', Proceedings of Nordic Cancer Union Symposium Oslo 9th Dec 1987.

Rytomaa T, Lang S, Kosma V M, Servomaa K, Ruuskanen J, (1993) 'Tumour induction in mouse epidermal cells irradiated by hot particles', International Journal of Radiation Biology 63(3) 375- .

Sachev G A, (1955) 'A Comparative Analysis of Radiation Lethality in Mammals', Journal of the National Cancer Institute, 15: 1125-44.

Sagoff M, (1988) 'Can Environmentalists be Liberals?', from The Economy of the Earth; repr. In R. Elliot (ed.), Environmental Ethics (Oxford: University Press, 1995).

SAHSU (2001) The Small Area Health Statistics Unit (SAHSU) Rapid Enquiry Facility (RIF) study on Bradwell, North Essex and Ward Analysis 1995-99. March 2001, Witham: North Essex Health Authority.

SAHSU (2002) SAHSU RIF report on Bradwell North Essex: Ward Analysis 1995-99 S821 Witham: North Essex Health Authority.

Sanders CL, Lauhala KE and McDonald KE (1993) Lifespan studies in rats exposed to 239PuO2 aerosols. III Survival and lung tumours. Int. J. Radiat.Biol. 64, 417-430.

Sastry KSR (1992) Biological effects of the Auger emitter 125I: a review. Report No1 of AAPM Nuclear Medicine Task Group No 6. Med. Phys. 19, 1361-1370.

Sastry KSR, Howell RW, Rao DV, Mylayarapu VB, Kassis AI, Adelstein SJ, Wright HA, Hamm RN and Turner JR (1988) Dosimetry of SAuger emitters: physical and phenomenological approaches. In BaverstockKF and Charlton DE 'DNA damage by Auger Emitters' London: Taylor and Francis

Satoh C, Takahashi N, Asakawa J, Kodaira M, Kuick R, Hanash SM and Neel JV (1996) Genetic analysis of children of atomic bomb survivors. Environ. Health Perspect. 104 Suppl 3: 511-519.

Savchenko V K, (1995) The Ecology of the Chernobyl Catastrophe: Scientific Outlines of an International Programme of Collaborative Research (Paris: UNESCO).

Shevchenko VA and Snigiryova GP (1996) Cytogenic effects of the action of ionizing radiation on human populations. In E.B Burlakova ed: *Consequences of the*

Chernobyl Catastrophe for human Health. Moscow: Centre for Russian Environmental Policy.

Schlesselman J, (1982) Case Control Studies (Oxford: University Press) p200.

Schmitz-Feuerhake I, Schroder H, Dannheim B, et al.., (1993) 'Leukaemia near water nuclear reactor', The Lancet 342: 1484.

Schmitz-Feuerhake (1983) Dose revision for A-Bomb survivors and the question of fallout contribution. *Health Physiscs* 44 (6) 693-695

Schroder H, Heimers A, Frenzel Beyme R, Schott A and Hoffmann W (2003) 'Chromosome aberration analysis in peripheral lymphocytes of Gulf War and Balkan War veterans.' Rad. Prot.Dosim. 103(3) 211-219

Schweitzer A (1957) Preface to *Cancer: nature, cause and cure* by A. Berglas, Pasteur Institute, Paris.

Scott Cato M, Busby C, Bramhall R, (2000) I don't know much about Science: Political Decision Making in Scientific and Technical Areas (Aberystwyth: Green Audit).

Segi M, Kurihara M, Matsuyama T, (1965) Cancer Mortality in Japan, 1899-1962 (Sendai, Japan: Tohoku University School of Medicine).

Setsuda T, Iwahashi Y, Nishmura K, Inagaki Y, (1962) 'Myolegous leukaemia and anemia occurs in descendants of albino rats administered Sr90' Acta Schol. Med. U. Kyoto 38(3) 242.

Seymour CB and Mothersill C (2000) Relative contribution of bystander and targeted cell killing to the low- dose region of the radiation dose-response curve. Radiation Research 153, 508-511.

Sharp L, Black R J, Harkness E F, McKinney P A, (1996) 'Incidence of childhood leukaemia and non-Hodgkin's lymphoma in the vicinity of nuclear sites in Scotland, 1968-93', *Occup. Environ. Med.;* 53: 823-831.

Shaw W H, (1999) Contemporary Ethics: Taking Account of Utilitarianism (Oxford: Blackwell).

Sheehan P M E, Hilary I B, (1983) 'An Unusual Cluster of Down's Syndrome, Born to Past Students of an Irish Boarding School', British Medical Journal, 287 (12 Nov.).

Sherwood R J, Clayton R F, (1961) Failure of the effluent pipe line at Sutton Courtenay on 1st August 1961 - Health Physics aspects, Report- AERE M930 (Harwell: United Kingdom Atomic Energy Authority).

Sinclair W K, Morton R A, (1966) 'X-ray Sensitivity during the Cell Generation Cycle of Cultured Chinese Hamster Cells', *Radiation Research,* 29: 450-74.

Smirnova E I, Lyaginska A M, (1969) 'Heart Development of Sr-90 Injured Rats', in Y. I. Moskalev and Y. I. Izd (eds.), *Radioaktiv Izotopy Organizs* (Moscow: Medizina), 348.

Snow J (1855) On the mode of communication of cholera. 2nd ed, London. (Reprinted 1936, New York).

Sonnenschein C and Soto AM, (1999) *The Society of Cells: Cancer Control and Proliferation.* (Oxford: Bios)

Stather I W, Wrixon A D, Simmonds J R, (1984) The risks of leukaemia and other cancers in Seascale from radiation exposure, NRPB-R177, (London: HMSO).

Stather JW, Clarke RH, Duncan KP (1988) The Risk of Childhood Leukaemia Near Nuclear Establishments NRPB-R215. National Radiological Protection Board, Chilton.

Steffenson V (1960) Cancer: disease of civilization? An anthropological and Historical Study. Hill and Wang: New York

Steiner M, Burkart W, Grosche B, Kaletsch U and Michaelis J (1998) Trends in infant leukaemia in West Germany in relation to in utero exposure due to the Chernobyl accident. Radiat Environ Biophys, 37, 87-93.

Sternglass E J, (1971) 'Environmental Radiation and Human Health', in Proceedings of the Sixth Berkeley Symposium on Mathematical Statistics and Probability, ed. J. Neyman (Berkeley, Calif.: University of California Press).

Sternglass E J, (1981) Secret Fallout (New York: McGraw Hill).

Sternglass E J, Gould J M, (1993) 'Breast cancer: evidence for a relation to fission products in the diet', International Journal of Health Services, 23(4), 783-804.

Sternglass EJ (1969) Has nuclear testing caused infant deaths? New Scientist 43 178-181.

Stevens W, Thomas D C, Lyon JL, Till JE, Kerber RA, Simon SL, et al (1990) Leukemia in Utah and radioactive fallout from the Nevada test site. A case-control study. JAMA, 264, 585-91.

Steward JA and John G (2001) An ecological investigation of the incidence of cancer in Welsh children for the period 1985-1994 in relation to residence near the coastline. *J R Statist Soc* A 164, 29-43.

Steward JA, Adams-Jones D, Beer H and John G (1999) Results of a preliminary study to test the Irish Sea proximity hypothesis of Busby et al. Welsh Cancer Intelligence and Surveillance Unit, Cardiff. March 1999.

Steward JA ,White Ceri, Wade R (2006) Childhood leukemia, brain tumours and retinoblastoma near the Menai Straits, North Wales, 2000-2003. A response to the Green Audit Report, Nuclear pollution, childhood leukemia, retinoblastoma and brain tumours in Gwynedd and Anglesey wards near the Menai Straits, North Wales 2000-2003 by Busby C et al. Cardiff: Wales Cancer Intelligence and Surveillance Unit.

Stewart A M, (1982) 'Delayed Effects of A-Bomb Radiation: A Review of Recent Mortality Rates and Risk Estimates for Five-Year Survivors', *Journal of Epidemiology and Community Health*, 26/2: 80-6.

Stewart A M, (2000) 'A bomb survivors: factors that may lead to a re-assessment of the radiation hazard', *Intern. J. Epidemiol.* vol. 29, 4 , 4.

Stewart A M, Hewitt D, (1965) 'Leukaemia Incidence in Children in Relation to Radiation Exposure in Early Life', in M. Ebert and A. Howard (eds.), Current Topics in Radiation Research, i (Amsterdam: North Holland).

Stewart A M, Webb J W, Giles B D, Hewitt D, (1956), 'Malignant Disease in Childhood and Diagnostic Irradiation in Utero', *Lancet*, ii 447.

Stewart A M, Webb J, Hewitt D, (1958) 'A Survey of Childhood Malignancies', *British Medical Journal*, i 1495.

Stewart, AM and Kneale GW (2000) A-bomb survivors: factors that may lead to a re-assessment of the radiation hazard. *Int J Epidemiol,* 29, 708-14.

Stokke T, Oftedal P, Pappas A, (1968) 'Effects of Small Doses of Radioactive Strontium on the Rat Bone Marrow', Acta Radiologica, 7: 321-9.
Stone R A, (1988) ' Investigations of environmental excess around putative sources: statistical problems and a proposed test.' *Statistics in Medicine* 7, 649-60.
Strathern M (1992) *After Nature.* Cambridge: University Press
Stsazhko V A, Tsyb A F, Tronko N D, Souchevitch G, Baverstock K F, (1996) 'Childhood cancer since the accident at Chernobyl', *British Medical Journal,* 310:801.
Sumner D, Weldon T, Watson W, (1991) Radiation Risks (Glasgow: Tarragon).
Sutcliffe C, (1987) The Dangers of Low Level Radiation, (Aldershot: Avebury).
Sutherland B M, Gange R W, Freeman S R, Sutherland J C, (1989) 'DNA damage and repair in skin in situ' in Castellani, A. (ed.), DNA damage and repair, (New York: Plenum).
Suzuki F, Hoshi H, Horikawa M, (1979) 'Repair of Radiation Induced Lethal and Mutational Damage in Chinese Hamster Cells in Vitro', Japanese Journal of Genetics, 54: 109-19.
Takagi N, (1974) 'Differentiation of X-Chromosomes in Early Female Mouse Embryos', Experimental Cell Research, 86: 127-35.
Talamini R, et al.., (1984) 'Social factors, diet and breast cancer in a northern Italian population.' Brit. J. Cancer 49: 723-9.
Tamplin A R, Cochran T B, (1974) Radiation standards for hot particles. A report on the inadequacy of existing radiation protection standards related to internal exposure of man to insoluble particles of Plutonium and other alpha emitting hot particles. (Washington DC: National Resources Defense Council).
Tanchou S (1843) Memoir of the frequency of cancer: an address to the Academy of Sciences. Cited by Steffanson.
Taylor PJ (1981) The Windscale Fire October 1957. Research Report RR-7. Oxford: Political Ecology Research Group
Taylor L S, (1971) 'Radiation Protection Standards', CRC Critical Reviews in Environmental Control, 81-124 (Boca Raton, Fla.: CRC Press).
Terasima T, Tolmach L J, (1961) 'Changes in X-ray Sensitivity of HeLa Cells during the Division Cycle', *Nature,* 190: 1210-11.
Terzaghi M, Little J B, (1976) 'X-Radiation Induced Transformation in a C3H Mouse Embryo Derived Cell Line', *Cancer Research,* 36: 1367-74.
Tominaga S, Kato I, (1992) 'Diet, nutrition and cancer in Japan' Nutrition and Health 8: 125-132.
Tondel M, Carlsson G, Hardell L, Eriksson M, Jakobsson S, Flodin U, Skoldestig A, Axelson O (1996) Incidence of neoplasms in ages 0-19 y in parts of Sweden with high 137Cs fallout after the Chernobyl accident. *Health Phys;* 71: 947-50.
Travis A (1999) Scientists take flak over food scares. *Guardian* 8th June 1999
U. K. Childhood Cancer Study Investigators, (2000) 'The United Kingdom Childhood Cancer Study: objectives, materials and methods', *Br. J. Cancer;* 82: 1073-102.
UNEP (2001) 'Depleted Uranium in Kosovo. Post Conflict Environmental Assessment. Geneva: UNEP (These UNEP environmental reports are available in a

modified form on the internet. The Annex tables which are no longer available, are available from Green Audit.)

UNSCEAR (1988) United Nations Scientific Committee on the Effects of Atomic Radiation. Sources, Effects and Risks of Ionizing Radiation. UNSCEAR 1988 Report to the General Assembly, with annexes. United Nations, New York.

UNSCEAR (1994) United Nations Scientific Committee on the Effects of Atomic Radiation. Sources and Effects of Ionizing Radiation. UNSCEAR 1994 Report to the General Assembly, with Scientific Annexes. United Nations, New York.

UNSCEAR (2000) United Nations Scientific Committee on the Effects of Atomic Radiation. Sources and Effects of Ionizing Radiation 2000. UN General Assembly, with Scientific Annexes. United Nations New York.

Urquhart JD, Black RJ, Muirhead MJ, Sharp L, Maxwell M, Eden OB, Adams Jones D (1991) Case-control study of leukaemia and non-Hodgkin's lymphoma in children in Caithness near the Dounreay nuclear installation. BMJ; 302: 687-692.

Van den Hazel P, Zuurbier M, Babisch W, Bartonova A, Bistrup M-L, Bolte G, Busby C, Butter M et al. (2006) Today's epidemics in children: Possible relations to environmental pollution and suggested preventive measures. Acta Paediatrica 95 Suppl 453 18-25

Van den Hazel P, Zuurbier M, Bistrup M L, Busby C, Fucic A, Koppe JG et al (2006) Policy and science in children's health and environment: Recommendations from the PINCHE project. Acta Paediatrica 95 Suppl. 453 114-119

Vicker M, (1993) 'Radiosensitivity Mechanisms at Low Doses: Inflammatory Responses to microGray Radiation Levels in Human Blood', *Intrnl. Perspectives in Public Health* 94, 9.

Viel J-F, Poubel D, Carre A, (1995) ' Incidence of leukaemia in young people and the La Hague nuclear waste reprocessing plant: a sensitivity analysis.' *Statistics in Medicine*, 14, 2459-2472.

Viel J-F, (1998) La santé publique atomisée. Radioactivité et leucémies : les lessons de La Hague, (France, Paris: Ed. La Découverte).

Viel J-F, Poubel D, (1997) 'Case control study of leukaemia among Young People near La Hague Nuclear Reprocessing Plant: The Environmental Hypothesis Revisited', *British Medical Journal,* 14, 101-6.

Vogelstein B and Kinzler KW, The multistep nature of cancer, *Trends Genet.* 1993 9 138-141

Wanatabe S (1974) Cancer and leukemia developing among atom bomb survivors Handbuch der allgemeinen pathologie VI (5) p 461 Berlin: Springer

Ward JF, Limoli CL, Calabro-Jones P, Evans JW (1988) Radiation vs. chemical damage to DNA. Anticarcinogenesis and radiation protection. Eds OF Nygaard, M Simic and F Cerutti. New York: Plenum.

Wakeford R (2002) Infant leukaemia in Wales after the Chernobyl accident. *Energy and Environment;* 13: 294-297.

Wakeford R and Little MP (2003) Risk coefficients for childhood cancer after intrauterine irradiation: a review. *Int. J. Radiat. Biol.* 79, 293-309.

Wales Cancer Registry (1994) Cancer Incidence in Wales 1982-88 Cardiff: Welsh Office

Wallace B, Dobzhansky T, (1960) Radiation, Genes, and Man (London: Methuen).
Washburn J (2005) University Inc. The Corporate Corruption of Higher Education. New York: Basic Books
Watson GE, Lorimore SA, Clutton SM, Kadhim MA and Wright EG (1997) Genetic factors influencing alpha-particle-induced chromosomal instability. *International J of Radiation Biology* 71, 497-503.
Watson GE, Lorimore SA, Macdonald DA and Wright EG (2000) Chromosomal instability in unirradiated cells induced in vivo by a bystander effect of ionizing radiation *Cancer Research* 60. 5608-5611.
Watson WS, Sumner DJ (1996) The measurement of radioactivity in people living near the Dounreay nuclear establishment, Caithness, Scotland. *Int J Radiat Biol;* 70: 117-130.
Weimels J L, Cazzaniga G, Daniotti M, Eden O B, Addison G M, Masera G, Saha V, Biondi A, Greaves M F, (1999) 'Prenatal origin of acute lymphoblastic leukaemia in children.' The Lancet 354, 1499-1503.
Weinberg H S, Korol A B, Kiezhner V M, Avavivi A, Fahima T, Nevo E, Shapiro S, Rennert G, Piatak O, Stepanova E I, Skarskaja E, (2001) 'Very high mutation rate in offspring of Chernobyl accident liquidators.' *Proc. Roy. Soc. London D,* 266: 1001-1005.
Weish P, Gruber E, (1986) Radioactivitat und Umwelt, (Stuttgart: Gustav Fischer).
Welsh Office (1994b) Investigation of the Incidence of Cancer near Trawsfynydd and Wylfa Nuclear Installations: Report A-EMJ-28, (Cardiff: Welsh Office).
Welsh Office, (1994) Cancer Registration in Wales 1984-88, Welsh Health Common Services Health Authority (Cardiff: Welsh Office).
Whyte R K, (1992) 'First Day Neonatal Mortality since 1935: A Re-examination of the Cross Hypothesis', *British Medical Journal*, 304: 343-6.
Wilkins B T, Paul M, Nisbet A F, (1996) Speciation and foodchain availability of Plutonium accidentally released from nuclear weapons. NRPB R-281 (Chilton: NRPB).
Willett W C, (1992) 'Dietary fat and fibre in relation to breast cancer', Journal of the Americal Medical Association 268: 2037-44.
Williams Dai (2003) see website www.eoslifework.co.uk
Woodward M (1999) Epidemiology. Study Design and Data Analysis. London: Chapman and Hall
Wright E G, Marsden S J, Lorimore S A, Goodhead D T, Macdonald D A, Khadim M A, (1994) 'Alpha Emitters Inducing Lesions in Stem Cells that can Result in Transmission of Chromosome Instability to their Progeny', *Nature,* 335, 6362.
Xue LY, Butler NJ, Makrigiorgos GM, Adelstein SJ and Kassis AI (2002) Bystander effect produced by radio-labeled tumor cells in vivo. *Proc Natl Acad Sci USA* 99, 13765
Yablokov A V, (1974) Variability of Mammals, (Washington , New Delhi: Amerind Publ.).
Yaroshinskaya A (1994) Chernobyl, the forbidden truth Oxford: John Carpenter

Appendix A

Details of the Areas of residence employed in the studies of cancer in Wales 1974-89.

1. Table of Areas of Residence

AOR	AOR
71AA Buckley UD	74JG Llangefni UD
71AC Connahs Qay UD	74 JJ Menai Bridge UD
71AL Hawarden RD Part	74JL Aethwy RD
71CA Abergele UD	74JN Twrcelyn RD
71CC Colwyn Bay MB	74JP Valley RD
71CL Aled RD Part	76AA Brecknock MB
71CN Hiraethog	76AC Builth Wells UD
71EA Flint MB	76AE Hay UD
71EC Holywell UD	76AG Llanwrtyd Wells
71EE Mold UD	76AL Brecknock RD
71EL Holywell RD Part	76AN Builth RD
71EN Holywell RD Part	76AP Crickhowell
71GA Denbigh MB	76AR Hay RD
71GC LLangollen UD	76AY Ystradgynlais RD
71GE Ruthin MB	76CA Llanfyllyn MB
71GL Ceiriog RD	76CB Llanidloes
71GN Edeyrnion RD	76CC Machynlleth UD
71GP Ruthin RD Part	76CD Montgomery MB
71GR Ruthin RD Part	76CE Newtown and
71JA Prestatyn UD	76CF Newtown and
71JC Rhyl UD	76CG Welshpool MB
71JL St Asaph RD	76CL Forden RD
71LL Hawarden RD Part	76CN Llanfyllyn RD
72AC Newcastle Emlyn	76CP Machynlleth RD
72AN Newcastle Emlyn	76CR Newtown and
72CA Aberaeron UD	76 EA Knighton UD
72CC Aberystwyth MB	76EC Llandrindod Wells
72CE Cardigan MB	76EE Presteigne UD
72CG Lampeter MB	76EL Colwyn RD
72CJ NewQuay UD	76EN Knighton RD
72CL Aberaeron RD	76EP New Radnor RD
72CN Aberystwyth RD	76ER Painscastle RD

72CP Teifiside RD	76ET Rhayader RD
72CR Tregaron RD	
72JA Fishguard AND	
74AA Betws y Coed UD	
74AC Conway MB	
74AE Llandudno UD	
74AG Llanfairfechan UD	
74AJ Llanrwst UD	
74AK Penmaenmawr UD	
74AP Nant Conwy RD	
74CA Bangor MB	
74CC Bethesda UD	
74CE Caernarfon MB	
74CL Gwyrfai RD Part	
74CN Ogwen RD	
74 EA Criccieth UD	
74EC Portmadog UD	
74EE Pwlleli MB	
74EL Gwyrfai RD Part	
74EN Lleyn RD	
74GA Bala UD	
74GC Barmouth UD	
74GE Dolgellau UD	
74GG Ffestiniog UD	
74GJ Towyn UD	
74GL Deudreath RD	
74GN Dolgellau RD	
74GP Penllyn RD	
74JA Amlwych UD	
74JC Beaumaris MB	
74JE Holyhead UD	

2. Map of AORs employed in the Wales Cancer Registry studies described in Chapter 5 and 6. Not all of the AORs shown were employed for all the studies. For the main analyses the areas classified as industrial were excluded.

Fig. A1 Map of Areas of Residence used in this report and also in the *First Annual Report*

3. Composition of aggregate groups for AORs by distance from the sea

Table A2 Composition of aggregate groups of Areas of Residence used for analysis of cancer rates by distance bands from sea.

Seadist <0.8 GROUP
71JA PRESTATYN U.D.
71JC RHYL U.D.
72CA ABERAERON U.D.
72CJ NEW QUAY U.D.
72JA FISHGUARD AND
74AC CONWAY M.B.
74AE LLANDUDNO U.D.
74CA BANGOR M.B.
74CE CAERNARVON M.B.
74EA CRICCIETH U.D.
74EC PORTHMADOG U.D.
74EE PWLLHELI M.B.
74GC BARMOUTH U.D.
74JA AMLWCH U.D.
74JC BEAUMARIS M.B.
74JE HOLYHEAD U.D.
74JJ MENAI BRIDGE U.D.

Seadist >0.9 and <2 GROUP
71AC CONNAH'S QUAY U.D.
71CA ABERGELE U.D.
71CC COLWYN BAY M.B.
71EA FLINT M.B.
71EC HOLYWELL U.D.
72CC ABERYSTWYTH M.B.
72CE CARDIGAN M.B.
74AG LLANFAIRFECHAN U.D.
74AK PENMAENMAWR U.D.
74GE DOLGELLAU U.D.
74GJ TYWYN U.D.
74GN DOLGELLAU R.D.
74JL AETHWY R.D.

Seadist >2.1 and < 5 GROUP
AREA1
71EL HOLYWELL R.D.(PART)
71JL ST.ASAPH R.D.
74CC BETHESDA U.D.
74CL GWYRFAI R.D.(PART)
74CN OGWEN R.D.
74EL GWYRFAI R.D.(PART)
74EN LLEYN R.D.
74GL DEUDRAETH R.D.
74JN TWRCELYN R.D.
74JP VALLEY R.D.

Seadist >5.1 and < 11 GROUP
71AA BUCKLEY U.D.
71AL HAWARDEN R.D.(PART)
71CL ALED R.D.(PART)
71EE MOLD U.D.
72AN NEWCASTLE EMLYN
72CL ABERAERON R.D.
72CN ABERYSTWYTH R.D.
72CP TEIFISIDE R.D.
74JG LLANGEFNI U.D.

Seadist >11.1 and <20 GROUP
71EN HOLYWELL R.D.(PART)
71GA DENBIGH M.B.
71GP RUTHIN R.D.(PART)
71LL HAWARDEN R.D.(PART)
72CG LAMPETER M.B.
72CR TREGARON R.D.
74AA BETWS-Y-COED U.D.
74AJ LLANWRST U.D.
74AP NANT CONWAY R.D.
74GG FFESTINIOG U.D.
76CC MACHYNLLETH U.D.
76CP MACHYNLLETH R.D.

Seadist >21 and < 40 GROUP
71CN HIRAETHOG
71GC LLANGOLLEN U.D.
71GE RUTHIN M.B.
71GR RUTHIN R.D.(PART)
72AC NEWCASTLE EMLYN
74GA BALA U.D.
74GP PENLLYN R.D.
76AG LLANWRTYD WELLS
76AN BUILTH R.D.
76CB LLANIDLOES M.B.
76CR NEWTOWN AND
76ET RHAYADER R.D.

Seadist >41 GROUP
71GL CEIRIOG R.D.
71GN EDEYRNION R.D.
76AA BRECKNOCK M.B.
76AC BUILTH WELLS U.D.
76AE HAY U.D.
76AL BRECKNOCK R.D.
76AP CRICKHOWELL
76AR HAY R.D.
76AY YSTRADGYNLAIS R.D.
76CA LLANFYLLIN M.B.
76CD MONTGOMERY M.B.
76CE NEWTOWN AND
76CF NEWTOWN AND
76CG WELSHPOOL M.B.
76CL FORDEN R.D.
76CN LLANFYLLIN R.D.
76EA KNIGHTON U.D.
76EC LLANDRINDOD WELLS
76EE PRESTEIGNE U.D.
76EL COLWYN R.D.
76EN KNIGHTON R.D.
76EP NEW RADNOR R.D.
76ER PAINSCASTLE R.D.

4. Wales Cancer Registry first dataset. A2218. Sample page

Request 2218: Number of Registrations for Malignant Neoplasms
Period 1974 - 1989
Source: Cancer active
Processed by Susan Frost, 01222 502300
Extracted 25 MAY 95

YEAR: 87 1987

	0-4		5-9		10-14		15-19		20-24		25-29		30-34		
	Male	Female	Male	Female	Male	Female	Male	Female	Male	Female	Male	Female	Male	Female	Ma
Borough															
DIAG															
173															
All leukaemias															
All malignancies															
71AA BUCKLEY U.D.															
DIAG															
145															
151															
153															
155															
162															
173															
174															
175															
180															
182															
183															
184															
185															
186													1		
188															
189															
197															
199															
202															
208															
All leukaemias															
All malignancies													1		
71AC CONNAH'S QUAY U.D.															
DIAG															
141															
153															
154															
157															
162															
170															
173															
174															
183															
185															
191															
202															
205															

Figure B1. Page 2 of Year 1987 of text file of WCR1, A2218
Note cancer of testis in male aged 30-34 also included in 'all malignancy'. Note also the 'all leukemias' category whose cases wer missing from WCR2, A2283

5. Wales Cancer Registry second data set A2883. Sample page.

```
Preceding task required 98.52 seconds CPU time:  162.00 seconds elapsed.

There are 8,383,032 bytes of memory available.
The largest contiguous area has 8,383,032 bytes.

                         Request a2883 Cancer Registrations by year
                                   Wales Cancer Registry
                                           Clwyd
                          By area of Residence, year site sex and age
                      Processed by Hugh Warren Tel x 2363 Date:12 JUN 96

YEAR:  74
```

	AGE													
	5-9	10-14	15-19	20-24	25-29	30-34	35-39	40-44	45-49	50-54	55-59	60-64	65-69	70-74
AOR 7199														
DIAG lung														
SEX 2	0	0	0	0	0	0	0	0	1	0	0	0	0	0
SEX 2	0	0	0	0	0	0	0	0	1	0	0	0	0	0
all cancers														
SEX 2	0	0	0	0	0	0	0	0	1	0	0	0	0	0
71AA														
DIAG stomach														
SEX 1	0	0	0	0	0	0	0	0	0	0	0	1	0	0
SEX 2	0	0	0	0	0	0	0	0	0	0	0	1	0	0
colon														

Figure B3. Page 2 of CLWYD text file WCR2. A2883

6. Second sample page of A2883 which refers to the same data as the A2218 file

ovary														
SEX 2	0	0	0	0	0	0	0	1	0	0	1	0	0	0
prostate														
SEX 1	0	0	0	0	0	0	0	0	1	0	0	0	0	1
bladder														
SEX 1	0	0	0	0	0	0	0	0	0	0	1	0	0	0
2	0	0	0	0	0	0	0	0	0	0	0	1	0	0
all other														
SEX 1	0	0	0	0	0	1	0	1	0	0	0	1	0	1
2	0	0	0	0	0	0	0	0	0	0	1	0	1	0
SEX 1	0	0	0	0	0	1	0	1	3	0	3	1	0	3
2	0	0	0	0	0	0	0	1	1	0	5	5	2	5
all leukaemia														
SEX 2	0	0	0	0	0	0	0	0	0	0	0	0	0	0
all cancers														
SEX 1	0	0	0	0	0	1	0	1	3	0	3	1	0	3
2	0	0	0	0	0	0	0	1	1	0	5	5	2	5
71AC														

Request a2883 Cancer Registrations by year
Wales Cancer Registry
Clwyd

Figure B5. Page 880 of CLWYD text file WCR2, A2883, relates to 1987, 71AA BUCKLEY

Appendix B

The Strontium Wombles

I sung this to a banjo accompaniment whilst standing on the table in the Trawsfynydd Visitor Centre way back in 1992, and it has remained a favourite with the anti-nuclear movement since it was written by Richard Bramhall. The tune is used by permission of Mike Batt the composer and was written for the Wombles of Wimbledon Common TV series.

After Chernobyl we finally hear
All kinds of cancer went up the next year;
"Hard to interpret" said OPCS
Can't understand it? Well here is a guess.
Low level isotopes from the Ukraine
Drifted to Wales on the wind and the rain;
Rainfall is higher in Bangor than Kent
Cancer in Wales is up 30%.

We're breathing Strontium,
Locking it onto the structure of cellular DNA,
And each beta decay,
In an occasional,
Rather mutational
Way
Kills
Us

Even New Labour can see what it means -
Radioisotopes alter our genes;
Ghosts of dead babies will give them no rest
'Til the dosimetry's been reassessed.
Wombling strombling Bangor to Kent
Telling the truth of the Second Event;
Telling a tragedy all in two scenes, how
Solit'ry atoms are changing our genes.

We're breathing Strontium,
Locking it onto the structure of cellular DNA,
And each beta decay,

Wolves of Water

In an occasional,
Rather mutational
Way
Kills
Us

Nuclear 'stablishment, castle of lies,
Children are dying in front of your eyes,
Born with no limbs, with two heads, or no brain,
Born to a life of incurable pain.
Nuclear subsidy victims will pay,
while You take a pension and tiptoe away;
Don't reassure us 'cause we always knew
Yours was a story too slick to be true.

We're breathing Strontium,
Locking it onto the structure of cellular DNA,
And each beta decay,
In an occasional,
Rather mutational
Way
Kills
Us

Nobody's hiding these nuclear crooks,
Government stooges aren't cooking the books;
Only the mothers are guilty of crimes,
Bearing their children in nuclear times.
Radioisotopes float around free
Up in the atmosphere, under the sea;
So much disease is genetic'lly linked,
Strontium Wombles could soon be extinct.

Richard Bramhall 1993
Revised 2006

CURRICULUM VITAE

PERSONAL DETAILS

Name: Dr Christopher Busby
Email: christo@greenaudit.org, christo@liverpool.ac.uk
Date/Place of Birth: 01/09/45, Paignton Devon UK
Nationality: British

FURTHER/HIGHER EDUCATION

BSc, PhD, C.Chem, MRSC
Qualifications: 1969 University of London First Class Honours Special Degree in Chemistry
1970-71 SRC research studentship for PhD Physical Chemistry (nmr spectroscopy), Queen Mary College, London
1974 Elected Member of Royal Society of Chemistry
1974 Chartered Chemist
1981 PhD Chemical Physics (Raman spectroscopy/electrochemistry) University of Kent, Canterbury
Learned Societies: Elected: Royal Society of Chemistry; Member: International Society for Environmental Epidemiology
UK Government Committees: Member: (Department of Health and DEFRA) CERRIE Committee Examining Radiation Risk from Internal Emitters (www.cerrie.org); Member: Ministry of Defence DUOB Depleted Uranium Oversight Board (www.duob.org)
Other Committees: Scientific Secretary: European Committee on Radiation Risk (www.euradcom.org)

EMPLOYMENT

1969 – 1974 Research physical chemist, Wellcome Foundation, Beckenham
1975 - 1978 Self employed (inshore fisherman, yacht deliveries, ultrasound surveys, general boat person).
1979 – 1981 PhD student University of Kent
1981- 1982 SERC Research Fellow University of Kent
1983- 1992 Self employed scientific consultant and science writer
1992- present Science Director, Green Audit, commissioned to research the health effects of ionizing radiation and funded by a number of charities and independent bodies.
1995 Funded by the Joseph Rowntree Charitable Trust to write and produce 'Wings of Death- The health effects of low level radiation.'

1997-2000 Directed research at Green Audit Funded by Irish State to research health effects of Sellafield
1997 Appointed UK Representative of European Committee on Radiation Risk (ECRR)
2001 Appointed Scientific Secretary of ECRR and commissioned to prepare the report ECRR 2003- The Health effects of low doses of Ionizing Radiation (Published 2003)
2001 Appointed to UK Government Committee Evaluating Radiation Risk from Internal Emitters (CERRIE)
2001 Appointed to the UK Ministry of Defence Oversight Committee on Depleted Uranium (DUOB)
2002 Funded by the Joseph Rowntree Charitable Trust to write a new book on the epidemiological evidence of health consequences of exposure to ionizing radiation: 'Wolves of Water'
2003 Appointed Honorary Fellow, University of Liverpool, Faculty of Medicine, Department of Human Anatomy and Cell Biology
1992- present: Science Director, Green Audit
2003 Funded by Joseph Rowntree Charitable Trust to write Book Wolves of Water
2004-2006 Leader of Science Policy for(EU) Policy Information Network for Child Health and Environment PINCHE based in Arnhem, The Netherlands

Editorial boards (Current):

European Journal of Biology and Bioelectromagnetics

RESEARCH INTERESTS.

Chris Busby spent seven years at the Wellcome Foundation, where he conducted research into the physical chemistry and pharmacology of molecular drug receptor interactions. He subsequently moved to the University of Kent at Canterbury where he studied Laser Raman Spectro-electrochemistry in collaboration with Shell Research and later as SRC Research Fellow, a project which resulted in a PhD in Chemical Physics. He developed and published theoretical and experimental details of silver and gold electrodes with surface array properties which enable acquisition of laser Raman spectra of adsorbed molecules in dilute solution.

In the late 1980s he became interested in the mechanisms of low dose internal irradiation and developed the Second Event Theory, which distinguishes between the hazards of external and internal radiation exposure. In 1995 he was funded by the Joseph Rowntree Charitable Trust to develop his arguments and write ‘Wings of Death: Nuclear Pollution and Human Health’, an account of the results of his research into radiation and cancer and also into cancer increases in Wales, which he argued were a result of global weapons fallout exposure. In 1997 he became the UK representative of the European Committee on Radiation Risk. His analysis of the increases in childhood leukaemia in Wales and Scotland following Chernobyl was recently published in the journals Energy and Environment and the International Journal of Radiation Medicine.

From 1997-2000 he was funded by the Irish Government to carry out research into cancer incidence and proximity to the coast. In June 2000 he was invited to present evidence to the Royal Society committee on Depleted Uranium and health, and shortly after this was invited to Iraq to measure DU in the country and relate exposure to health effects which followed the Gulf War. In 2001 he was asked to visit Kosovo to investigate the dispersion of DU using field monitoring equipment. He discovered DU in many areas from analytical measurements made on samples he collected (paid for by the BBC) he showed that there was atmospheric resuspension of DU particles. His work and expertise in the field of environmental health and radioactivity has been recognised by his appointment to CERRIE a Government committee reporting on the effects of low level radiation on health. Following his evidence to the Royal Society on the effects of Depleted Uranium, he was appointed to the UK Ministry of Defence committee on Depleted Uranium in 2001. He was invited to address the US Congressional Committee on Veterans Affairs of the Health effects of Depleted Uranium in 2002. He is presently also the Scientific Secretary of the European Committee on Radiation Risk and was commissioned to organise the preparation of the new risk model on radiation exposure and to organise the publication of ECRR 2003: The Health Effects of Exposure to low Doses of Ionizing Radiation, published in January 2003 and now translated into and published in French, Russian, Japanese and Spanish. In 2004, he (jointly with two other colleagues) published the *Minority Report of the CERRIE committee* (Sosuimi Press). In 2006 he produced and jointly edited with Prof.Alexey Yablokov of the Russian Academy of Sciences *ECRR2006 Chernobyl 20 Years On*.

RESEARCH EXPERIENCE

Dr Busby's early research was in the Physical Chemistry aspects of molecular pharmacology at the Wellcome Research Labs. This involved the use of spectroscopic and thermodynamic methods for examining cell drug interactions at the molecular level. For a while he began a research degree in NMR on molecular conformational changes on protonation but left to return to Wellcome and resume his drug interaction research. From there he moved to developing descriptions of intercellular and intracellular communication mechanisms, a subject which he is still engaged in researching in the laboratory. Later he moved to examining molecular behaviour at charged interfaces and developed Surface Raman spectroelectrochemical methods as a Science Research Council Fellow at the University of Kent.

Between 1992 and 2004 Dr Busby was engaged in research in three areas associated with ionising radiation and health and also was funded for a year (1997) by the *Foundation for Children with Leukemia* to research the interaction between non ionising radiation and ionising radiation. His research in the area of ionising radiation has been split between the development of theoretical descriptions of radiation action on living cells and the epidemiology of cancer and leukaemia in small areas. After 1994 he conducted survey epidemiology of Wales and England and was the first to point out (in a letter to the British Medical Journal) that increases in cancer in Wales might be related to weapons fallout. Later he examined childhood leukaemia mortality near the Harwell and Aldermaston nuclear sites and suggested that the excess risk might be related inhalation of radioactive particles. These results were also carried in a research letter in the BMJ which attracted considerable criticism. His description of the mode of radiation action from sequential emitters (his Second Event Theory was developed originally in 1987 and has attracted a great deal of interest and also criticism. Between 1997 and 2000 he was funded by the Irish State to carry out epidemiological studies of cancer rates and distance from the Irish Sea using data from Wales Cancer Registry and through a collaboration with the Irish National Cancer Registry. Following this he and his team in Green Audit developed novel small area questionnaire epidemiological methods and applied them to a number of areas in different studies which included Carlingford Ireland, Burnham on Sea in Somerset and Plymouth Devon. In addition he carried out cancer mortality small area studies in Somerset and later in Essex. He extended these to wards in Scotland in 2002. At present he is supervising a PhD student at the University of Liverpool in the Faculty of Medicine in an epidemiological study of cancer mortality in Scotland with regard to proximity to putative sources of cancer risk. In all the small area studies he carried out it was possible to show a significant effect of living near radioactively contaminated intertidal sediment. The papers and reports were all published by Green Audit and most have been presented by invitation at learned conferences in Europe including through invitations by the Nuclear Industry itself.

In addition to this, in 1998 Busby set up a radiation measurement laboratory and equipped it with portable alpha beta and gamma measuring systems including a portable gamma spectrometer made in Dresden which uses a 2" NaI detector. He used these to show the presence of Depleted Uranium in Southern Iraq in 2000 when he was invited by the Al Jazeera TV channel to visit the country as a consultant and examine the link between leukaemia in children and levels of Depleted Uranium. In 2001 he visited Kosovo with Nippon TV and was the first to show that DU was present in dust in towns in Western Kosovo and through isotope measurements funded by the BBC was able to report to the Royal Society in 2001 and the EU Parliament in Strasbourg that DU became resuspended in dry weather and was rained out, and that it remained in the environment for a considerable time. This subsequently led to UNEP deploying atmospheric particle measuring equipment in areas where DU had been used. More recently Dr Busby has been developing laboratory methods for measuring radiation conversion and amplification by high atomic number micron diameter metal and metal oxide particles (Uranium, Gold). It is his recent contention that such particles amplify background radiation effectiveness by photoelectron conversion.

In 2005 he was invited by various organisations in New Zealand to give evidence on the health effects of Depleted Uranium. In 2005 and 2006 he worked with Prof Alexey Yablokov on the ECRR2006 report on Chernobyl which was published on the 20th anniversary of the accident. Most recently he has conducted a study of the health of people living in the vicinity of the Trawsfynydd Nuclear plant in Wales for HTV and also a study of the veterans of the Porton Down human experiments in the 50s. His study will be used in the Court action that is being brought by the veterans against the MoD.

In 2006 he was consulted by the government Committee on Radioactive Waste Management CoRWM on the health effects of exposure to nuclear waste

INVITATIONS TO SPEAK.

Year	Place, Subject etc.
1995	House of Commons. Symposium on Low Dose Radiation
1995	Jersey, Channel Islands: International conference on nuclear shipments; Health effects of low dose radiation
1995	Oxford Town Hall: Low dose radiation effects
1995	Drogheda, Ireland: Sellafield effects
1997	Strasbourg EU Parliament: Euratom Directive
1997	Brussels, EU Parliament STOA workshop on criticisms of ICRP risk models
1997	Kingston Ontario: World Conference on Breast Cancer: paper on cohort effects and weapons fallout
1998	Muenster, Germany, International Conference on Radiation: Second Event effects
1998	Manchester Town Hall, Ethics and Euratom
1999	Copenhagen: Danish parliament: Euratom Directive and low dose effects
1999	Carlingford, Ireland: Sellafield effects
2000	Kos Island: ASPIS (EC) meeting on 'Is cancer an environmental effect'; low dose radiation and cancer
2000	London: Royal Society: low dose effects and Depleted Uranium
2001	Strasbourg: Green Group; Health effects of Depleted Uranium
2001	Bergen: International Sellafield conference, Sellafield effects on health
2001	Oslo: Nobel Institute: Health effects of low dose radiation and DU

2001	London: Royal Society: Health effects of Depleted Uranium (again)
2001	Kiev: WHO conference on Chernobyl: paper on infant leukaemia
2001	Prague: *Res Publica* International Conference on Depleted Uranium
2001	Strasbourg: EU Parliament, with UNEP; Health effects of Depleted Uranium
2002	Bergen: Conference on Sellafield
2002	Helsinki: Health effects of low dose radiation
2002	London : US Congressional Committee on National Security: Gulf war syndrome and Depleted Uranium
2002	London Greenpeace: Small area statistics and radiation effects
2002	Chilton: Health effects of radioactive waste
2002	Oxford, British Nuclear Energy Society: Effects of low doses of radiation
2002	Royal Society of Physicians: Small area health statistics and radiation
2003	Birmingham: Non ionising radiation. Chaired
2003	Liverpool University: Depleted Uranium and Health
2003	Oxford University: Helath Effects of Radiation from Internal Emitters
2003	Munich: Whistleblowers
2003	Copenhagen: Radiation and the foetus
2003	Hamburg: Depleted Uranium
2004	Berlin: Low level radiation
2004	London: PINCHE, child health and environment
2004	London, Westminster: Children with leukaemia
2004	Chicago: Radiation studies
2005	New Zealand Royal Society, Wellington
2005	New Zealand, Auckland University
2005	Chicago: Small area epidemiology by citizen groups
2005	Salzburg, Austria. PLAGE; International Nuclear Law and Human Rights
2005	Stockholm, Swedish Parliament; Low Dose Radiation and Depleted Uranium
2006	ECRR, Berlin, Health effects of the Chernobyl Accident
2006	Hiroshima Japan, Depleted Uranium

Including the above, Chris Busby has given invited presentations at meetings in Strasbourg (5), Brussels (2), Jersey, Alderney, Copenhagen (2), Bergen (2), Oslo

(2), Vienna, Helsinki, Muenster, Kiev, Hartford Ct, Kingston, Ontario, Baghdad, Pristina (Kosovo), Manchester (4) Oxford, Newbury (2), Cardiff (3), London (6), Prague, Dublin (2), Carlingford, Drogheda, Harlech, Bangor, Llandrindod Wells, Hastings, Weston Super Mare, Burnham on Sea (2), Bridgwater, Reading, Ulverston, Liverpool, Plymouth, Brighton, Kingston and Aberystwyth (5).

PUBLICATIONS

See reference section of Wolves for the radiation and the epidemiological papers

Books and articles

Busby, C. C. (1996*a*), ' in Bramhall, R. (ed.), *The Health Effects of Low Level Radiation: Proceedings of a Symposium held at the House of Commons, 24 April 1996* (Aberystwyth: Green Audit).

Busby, C. C. (1998), 'Enhanced mutagenicity from internal sequentially decaying beta emitters from second event effects.' In 'Die Wirkung niedriger Strahlendosen- im kindes-und Jugendalter, in der Medizin, Umwelt ind technik, am Arbeitsplatz'. Proceedings of International Congress of the German Society for Radiation Protection. Eds: Koehnlein W and Nussbaum R. Muenster, 28 March 1998 (Bremen: Gesellschaft fur Strahlenschutz)

Busby C.C and Scott Cato M (1999) 'A Planetary Impact index' in Molly Scott Cato and Miriam Kennett eds. *Green Economics- beyond supply and demand to meeting peoples needs.* Aberystwyth: Green Audit, Numerous articles for 'The Ecologist' on low dose radiation effects have been translated into many languages and reprinted.

EXPERT WITNESS

Since 1997 Chris Busby has been engaged as an expert witness in several cases that relate to the effects of radioactive pollution on health, in several refugee appeals (Kosovo) based on Depleted Uranium risks, several trials of activists accused of criminal damage at weapons establishment and one at the House of Commons (evidence on Depleted Uranium and other radioactive substances), one MoD pension appeals tribunal for the widow of a A Bomb test veteran and once in the Connecticut State Court for an appeal against licensing releases of radioactivity from the Millstone reactor on Long Island Sound. He is currently acting or has recently acted as expert witness on two cases in the UK involving the health effects of internal irradiation from Depleted Uranium. One of these is in the Royal Courts of Justice and also in three cases in the USA. Two of these (against Exxon) have recently been won. The third, a landmark case involving childhood cancer near a nuclear plant in Florida is currently being appealed. He was also commissioned as an expert witness on the effects of Uranium weapons in the recent criminal damage case of Pritchard and Olditch and the USAF bombers at Fairford which they disabled at the time of the second Gulf War.